Music and Rhythm

Peter Petersen

Music and Rhythm
Fundamentals – History – Analysis

Bibliographic Information published by the Deutsche Nationalbibliothek
The Deutsche Nationalbibliothek lists this publication in the Deutsche Nationalbibliografie; detailed bibliographic data is available in the internet at http://dnb.d-nb.de.

Revised and expanded version of the original German edition
„Musik und Rhythmus. Grundlagen – Geschichte – Analyse"
published by Schott Music GmbH & Co. KG, Mainz/Mayence, 2010.

Translated by Ernest Bernhardt-Kabisch.

The cover illustration shows a section of Beethoven's Sonata
op. 13, 3rd mov., with rhythmic profiles from Ex. 3-126 on p. 272.

Library of Congress Cataloging-in-Publication Data

Petersen, Peter.
 [Musik und Rhythmus. English]
 Music and rhythm : fundamentals, history, analysis / Peter Petersen. — Revised and expanded version of the original German edition.
   pages cm
 Includes index.
 ISBN 978-3-631-64393-8
 1. Musical meter and rhythm. 2. Bach, Johann Sebastian, 1685-1750—Criticism and interpretation. I. Title.
ML437.P4713 2013
781.2'24—dc23

2013024307

ISBN 978-3-631-64393-8 (Print)
E-ISBN 978-3-653-03491-2 (E-Book)
DOI 10.3726/978-3-653-03491-2

© Peter Lang GmbH
Internationaler Verlag der Wissenschaften
Frankfurt am Main 2013
All rights reserved.
PL Academic Research is an Imprint of Peter Lang GmbH.

Peter Lang – Frankfurt am Main · Bern · Bruxelles · New York ·
Oxford · Warszawa · Wien

All parts of this publication are protected by copyright. Any utilisation outside the strict limits of the copyright law, without the permission of the publisher, is forbidden and liable to prosecution. This applies in particular to reproductions, translations, microfilming, and storage and processing in electronic retrieval systems.

www.peterlang.de

CONTENTS

Introduction 7

Part One: Theory of Components 17

Rhythms and Components 19
    Definition of Terms 19
    Rhythm-building Components 20
    • Sound 20
    • Pitch 22
    • Diastematy 25
    • Articulation 31
    • Dynamics 33
    • Timbre 39
    • Harmony 45
    • Texture 49
    • Phrase 52
    • Prosody 59
Rhythmic Weight 64
    Preface 64
    Weight of Components Durations 65
    Accumulation of Rhythmic Weights 73
    Rhythmic and Metric Weight 77
Aspects of Rhythm 81
    Rhythmic Proportions 81
    • Composition vs. Notation 81
    • Augmentation and Diminution 82
    • Partial Augmentation and Diminution 84
    Rhythmic Iso-, Hetero- and Symmetry 88
    • Isometry 88
    • Heterometry 93
    • Symmetry 97
    Rhythmic Characters 101
    • Upbeat 101
    • Syncope 111
    • Hemiola 117

Part Two: Rhythm in the Music of J. S. Bach 127

Introduction 129
48 Fugue Themes of the Well-Tempered Clavier 134
    Preliminary Remarks 134
    Part 1 135
    Part 2 143
    Summary 149
Two 6/4 and two 9/8 Pieces from the
    Well-Tempered Clavier 151
    Prelude C♯ Minor (6/4) 151
    Fugue F♯ Minor (6/4) 154
    Prelude A Minor (9/8) 156
    Fugue A Major (9/8) 158
    Summary 160
Chromatic Fantasia 161
From the Brandenburg Concertos 164
    Concerto I (F Major) 164
    Concerto II (F Major) 168
    Concerto III (G Major) 170
    Concerto IV (G Major) 172
    Concerto V (D Major) 174
    Concerto VI (B♭ Major) 177
The »Eilt!–Wohin?«-Aria with Chorus 180
The Chorale »Es ist genug« 183

Part Three: Theories of Rhythm 187

Preface 189
1612 Praetorius • Terpsichore 191
1650 Kircher • Musurgia universalis 194
1678 Printz • Satyrical Composer 196
1739 Mattheson • The Complete Capellmeister 198
1749 Hartung • Musicus theoretico-practicus 202
1752 Riepel • On Time Signatures 202
1773 Scheibe • On Musical Composition 203
1779 Kirnberger • Correct Musical Setting 204
1789 Türk • Piano School 207
1789 Koch • Instructions for Composition 208
1821 Momigny • Theory of Music 212
1832 Weber • Rhythm and Meter 216
1880 Westphal • Musical Rhythmics 217
1884 Lussy • The Musical Rhythm 218
1884 Riemann • Musical Metrics and Rhythmics 220
1917 Wiehmayer • Rhythmics and Metrics 225
1944 Messiaen • Rhythm 227
1951 Blacher • Variable Meters 232
1955 Keller • Phrasing and Articulation 233
1957 LaRue • Harmonic Rhythm 234
1958 Hławiczka • Rhythm and Meter 236
1959 Neumann • »Zeitgestalt« 238
1960 Cooper & Meyer • Rhythmic Structure
1963 Stockhausen • Unity of Musical Time 241
1967 Benary • Rhythm and Meter 245
1967 Dahlhaus • What is Musical Rhythm? 248
1967 Erpf • Form and Structure in Music 254
1968 Pierce • Rhythm in Tonal Music 255
1976 Berry • Structural Functions in Music 258
1976 Yeston • Stratification of Musical Rhythm 261
1986 Lester • The Rhythms of Tonal Music 266
1988 Kramer • The Time of Music 269
1989 Rothstein • Phrase Rhythm in Tonal Music 273
1995 Epstein • Shaping Time 275
1997 Agmon • Musical Durations 276
1997 Hasty • Meter as Rhythm 278
1999 Schachter • Rhythm à la Schenker 281
1999 Krebs • Metrical Dissonance 285
2001 Lerdahl • Tonal Pitch Space 289
2002 Swain • Harmonic Rhythm 292
2004 London • Hearing in Time 297

Appendix 301

Music Examples (continuing) 302
Music Examples (by composers) 309
Index of Names 311

Introduction

To think anew about the subject of »Music and Rhythm« may seem superfluous to many people. The ability to feel one's way into songs, dances, marches, or symphonies, swing along with them and, as it were, ›join in‹ on their movement, is a basic experience of every musician and every listener. Once we have ›gotten‹ the beat, we get a feeling of security enabling us to experience the varied event of a piece of music with pleasure. To sense the beat means for many to ›know‹ the rhythm.

This simplistic view of the matter has long since been controverted. Rhythm, understood as the alternation of long and short tones, was regarded as something multiform and unpredictable, unfolding over the foundation of constant metrical relations. Besides beat accents there are accordingly rhythmic accents that frequently modify the regular alternation of »heavy« and »light«. But these latter accents, which can be produced by a variety of compositional means, were regarded as accessory, whereas rhythm as such was thought to result simply from a sequence of sound durations.

I believe, however, that even this view of rhythm and accent is not altogether satisfactory, because it rests on a too narrow conception of rhythm and, by interpreting accents as extraneous events, fails to integrate them sufficiently into the temporal structure. A comprehensive theory of the temporal relations in a musical composition is overdue, one that is ready to recognize all sound signals as producing durations and consequently also rhythm. We must question the convention of regarding only tonal sequences as rhythm-building while excluding other sound signals like changes in pitch, direction of intervals, volume, or tone color (timbre).

Among the great achievements of European music history is the development of a system of signs that makes it possible to note down the gradations of different temporal distances in ever more refined form (𝅗𝅥, o, ♩, ♪, ♫, ♬, ♩., ♩.., 𝅘𝅥... etc.). These signs stand for individual tones that follow each other contiguously. Musical sequences, however, regularly include also other, secondary durations, e.g., ♩ between dynamic accents (> → >). These intervals, too, can be represented by note values. They are therefore clearly also rhythms. Primary and derivative rhythms can thus be related to each other and then analyzed as rhythmic textures.

It is high time, then, to free the concept of »duration« from its linkage to the individual tone, to expand it to include durations between other sound phenomena (»components«), and thereby to bring into our purview an entire cosmos of additional rhythms (»components rhythms«) that has until now remained occluded by accent analyses. The rhythm/accent relation is replaced by the »components theory« of a new rhythm/rhythm relation. In this way all of a composition's temporal relations are taken into account and comprehended more adequately than before. Accents and even meters are now subordinated to the central concept of »rhythm« and thus are newly evaluated.

***

Hypothesis I: COMPONENTS RHYTHMS
Musical rhythms are dependent on sounds or sound formations and their components (properties). The durations between beginnings and beginnings, or beginnings and ends of sounds, shapes, or components constitute rhythms. Since sounds and sound formations are generally determined by more than one component, it follows that even monophonic melodies have more than one rhythm. The rhythms derived from components are called components rhythms.

***

By means of durational values, sound sequences can be structured rhythmically and coordinated with each other, as they determine the intervals of contiguous tones or notes. There are, however, also temporal intervals between *non*-contiguous tonal phenomena, e.g., the appearance of a new pitch after note repetitions, the recurrence of a melodic phrase, the modification or retention of certain tone colors, degrees of loudness, harmonies, etc. Although temporal intervals thus defined by components are not noted separately, their measure is determinable.

The question, now, is whether and why it makes sense to pay any attention to durations that are not actually noted down. The answer is simple: the components-derived durations are determining parts of the music's temporal structure. Such derivative durations depend quite as much on sound phenomena as noted-down durations do on contiguous tones. Both cases involve rhythms. What that means can be shown by a simple example (Ex. 0-1).

Ex. 0-1

Traditionally one would say of these three variants of a single tonal configuration that a, b, and c have the same rhythm with different melodies. That is true, yet insufficient. The description fits as long as one regards only the noted durations as rhythms, that is to say, only the component »Sound« is considered. If by listening to the melodies in the variants b and c one takes the component »Pitch« into consideration as well, it becomes apparent that there are additional durations and hence additional rhythms. Though not noted down, they are intended by the composer and thus relevant to the temporal structure (Ex. 0-2).

Ex. 0-2

Since in variant a the pitch does not change, no rhythm other than the noted one obtains. In variant b, the melody-forming and repeated pitches C4 E4 G4 E4 F4 D4 B3 G3 follow contiguously in quarter note rhythms, and one hears this rhythm of the pitches (♩ ♩ ♩ ♩ etc.) simultaneously with the rhythm of the notes (♪ ♪ ♪ ♪ ♪ ♪ ♪ etc.) retained from variant a. In variant c, the sequence of pitches is slightly altered, inasmuch as the change from C4 to E4 and from F4 to D4 is delayed by one eighth. The result is a modified pitch rhythm (♩. ♪ ♩ ♩ etc.).

Ex. 0-3

As simple as the example I have constructed is, two additional components are of rhythmic consequence in these melodies: »Phrase« and »Diastematy« (Ex. 0-3). The noted rhythm of twice six eighths plus one quarter note causes two phrases to emerge that here have the same duration (o o). This rhythm of phrases, too, is heard simultaneously with the rhythms of tones and pitches, while the up and down of the melodies, i. e., their diastematy, exhibits a not entirely uniform alternation of the crest and keel tones (the top and bottom tones of directional change) that structures the time and generates its own component rhythm (♩ ♩ ♩ ♩. ♩.). The three melodies are thus by no means rhythmically identical: four separate components go into the ma-

king of rhythms and produce a texture of rhythms endowing each melodic variant with an individual character of its own.

A look at the original of one of the melodic variants, the second movement of Joseph Haydn's Symphony in G No. 94, confirms that real rhythmic changes can be produced by individual components, while other components are kept constant (Ex. 0-4)

Ex. 0-4

Haydn, Sinfonia in G No. 94, 2nd mov.

In the theme of the variations movement (m. 1), the components »Articulation« and »Dynamics« are added to those already cited. The rhythm of the notes articulated explicitly (*staccato* and *tenuto*) concurs with the basis rhythm of the component »Sound«, because every note has an articulatory mark. The constant volume mark (*p*) is (here) rhythmically irrelevant (but see m. 33, not included in Ex. 0-4).

M. 75 works with the basis component »Sound«, the rhythm of the tone entries changes (♪ ♪ ♪ ♪ etc.), but pitch, phrasal, and diastematic rhythms remain constant, and the articulatory rhythm in turn adapts itself to the entry rhythm.

The situation is similar at m. 107 in that the component »Sound« causes all the tone entries to appear equalized (16 ♪) and the quarter note caesuras are omitted. Here, too, the rhythms of the pitches and of the crest and keel notes remain in force, while articulatory rhythm does not apply and the dynamic situation (everything is *ff*) is rhythmically insignificant.

***

Hypothesis II: RHYTHMIC WEIGHT
Components rhythms can be isolated in analysis, but in reality they happen simultaneously and interpenetrate each other. Together they constitute the rhythm of a monophonic or a polyphonic composition. If rhythmic durations change, and if different rhythms coincide at certain points, rhythmic weighting results. The distribution of the rhythmic weights within the temporal continuum is subject to the composer's calculation.

***

Components theory and analysis serve the purpose of exploring the rich rhythmic events ›between the notes.‹ In an analysis based on components, rhythms are determined independently of the laws and limits of mensuration. In the process, differences in the weighting of specific moments in the course of musical events present themselves. This becomes apparent when one relates different component rhythms to each other and discovers that some of these rhythms coincide at certain points. The more components occur simultaneously, the more strongly the attention of listeners and performers is focused on the moment in question.

For this phenomenon of accumulated component durations resp. rhythms I have coined the term »rhythmic weight«, analogous to the concept of »metric weight.« Rhythmic weight is owing to a) the length and shortness of durations and b) the accumulation of several component durations resp. rhythms and their relative weights. That long durations are to be accorded more weight than short ones is a generally recognized axiom in rhythm theory; hitherto ignored has been the fact that rhythmic weight is increased by the coincidence of multiple component rhythms.

Rhythmic weights must not be misconstrued as accentuation, let alone dynamic amplification. If a specific volume is called for, that constitutes an independent component, whose impulses enter into the rhythmic weight but are not identical with it. As an analogy we may use the concept of mass in physics, one of whose properties it is to attract other masses. Large rhythmic weights are therefore points of attraction for the attention of listeners and players, whether they are loud or low. As we, in listening, register the interplay of the components, the moments at which several of them are simultaneously active send forth special signals that draw our attention and make them, so to speak, ›weightier‹ than others.

In the tone entries (»Sound«), the durations are ascertained on the basis of the note values. The smallest value is the sixteenth, all larger values are weighted according to its multiple by adding notes above the basis note (columns of notes).

The component rhythm »Pitch« largely coincides with that of the tone entries. An exception occurs in the repeated notes. Here two notes each are combined and the values of the repeated notes are added to the pitch holder. The result in the chain of 16ths in m. 3 and 4 is a doubly weighted syncopated rhythm of the pitches. The durations of the not repeated pitches (mm. 1-2 and 5-7), on the other hand, are singly weighted.

In the component »Diastematy«, rhythms are produced by crest and keel notes. For reasons of method I include all such turning points, regardless of whether they are approached and relinquished by leaps or merely by steps, whether they are emphatic or merely incidental in nature. Crest notes (stems pointing up) lead to rhythms in quarter notes (beginning of phrases), as do the preceding keel notes (stems pointing down).

The only »Articulations« in this example are the legato slurs, resulting in very simple rhythms composed of quarter notes and eighths. The legatos support the meter, or rather, in this example, the dominating binary motion. Interestingly, the articulation eighths in m. 3 and 4 are complementary to the syncopated eighths of the pitch rhythm.

The component »Phrase« exhibits an unusual feature: the first phrase of the eight-bar repeat period is divided into 3+5 ♩, the consequent into 4+4 ♩. The reason for this modi-

Ex. 0-5   Haydn, Sinfonia in G No. 94, 2nd mov., mm. 115-122, Vl. 1

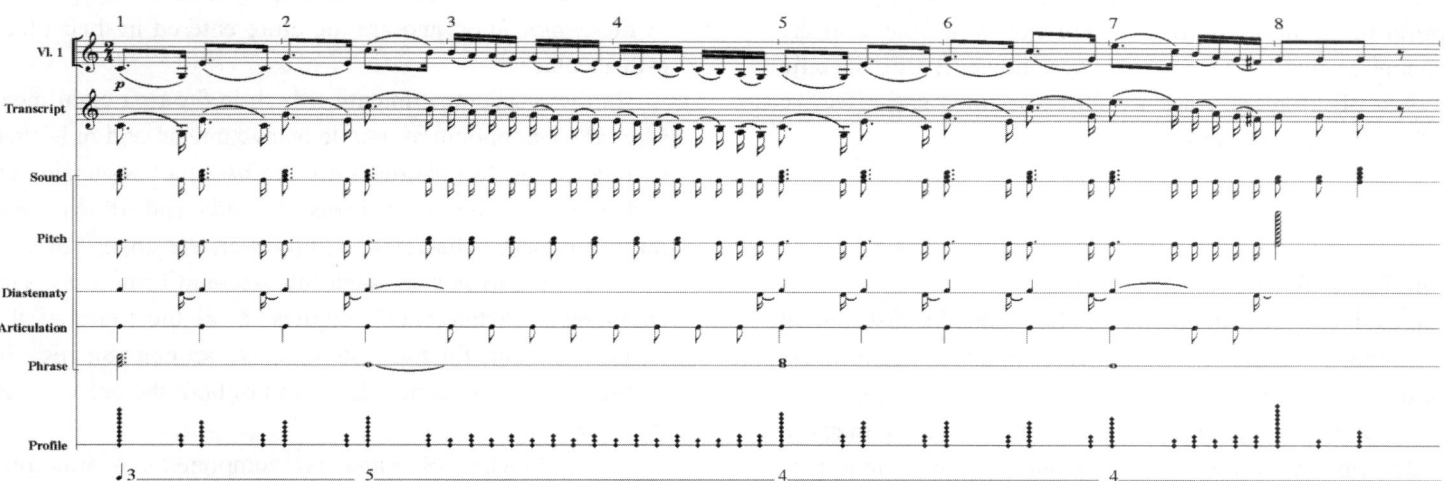

A further passage from the Haydn movement maybe adduced (Ex. 0-5) to exemplify the phenomenon of rhythmic weight and to consider the latter's impact on the overall compositional structure. In the fourth variation (mm. 115-122), the violins play a free variant of the theme, during which not only the note values but above all the melodic contour and therefore also the rhythm and the internal structure of the period are modified in comparison with the thematic melody. If beneath this melody and its rhythmic »transcript« one inscribes all of the component rhythms, the resulting schema will be that of a »rhythm score«.

fication is to be sought in the differently positioned top notes (C5 in m. 2 vs. E5 in m. 7). I have differentiated the weight of the (partial) phrases according to their validity's duration (simple, double, triple).

The line »Profile« sums up all of the component durations resp. rhythms. The more components are active at any point in sequence – that is to say, contribute a rhythmic impulse – the higher will be the rhombus towers. They symbolize the rhythmic weight that obtains at these points.

The most conspicuous detail in this rhythmic profile is the new start of the melody in m. 5. By itself this does not signify much, as one can recognize the beginning of the consequent also directly from the voice as Haydn has written it down. Even so, the comparison of the first and second phrase reveals some significant differences, the most important of which has manifested itself already under the component »Phrase«, namely the divergence in the structures of first and second phrase.

We can see from the rhythmic »Profile« that the rhythm of the tone entries (♩. ♪) is supported by several components so that it stands out markedly as the main rhythm, weighted six- to eightfold. The following chains of sixteenths seem as a result to be overshadowed by this power center and dwindle into (nearly) contourless downward movements, until the second phrase repeats the opening. Since the descending melody initially sets in after the fourth quarter note, i.e., in the middle of the second bar, whereas the second time round it does so only in the fifth quarter note, i.e., following upon the downbeat of m. 7, the rhythmic »Profile« illustrates the uneven length of the partial phrases, which is already predetermined by the position of the top notes. Hereby it is significant that only low weight values obtain in the beginnings of m. 3 and 4, so that the gravitational centers of the measures are obscured, wheras in the second phrase all the beginnings of the measures are strongly weighted rhythmically, so that the accentual order of the 2/4 beat is clearly manifested.

It should be recalled that the above analysis deals only with the main voice. The other voices are not taken into account, so that additional important components, such as »Harmony« (including suspension dissonances and cadence patterns), »Timbre« (including octave registers) and »Texture« (e.g., theme entries) are left aside. These components would bring the total profile more closely in line with the schema of the 2/4 time. Even then, however, the specific rhythm of the main voice would be retained and effective within the total structure.

**

Hypothesis III: Rhythm and Meter
Composing with sounds and rhythms and the distribution of rhythmic weights can be aimed at making regular alternations of durations and weights audible and thereby approximating, or corresponding to, the notion of metrical models (modus, tempus, meter). Isometry – the crucial characteristic of metric orders – is realized by rhythmic means. Kinds of meter are thus not merely set in advance but are objects of compositional arrangement.

**

I have so far left out meter and bar lines. To get to the bottom of the rhythmic conditions of a piece of music, it is advisable to disregard the meter for the nonce. In Haydn's time, as is generally known, a concept of beat had established itself that distinguished between »duple« and »triple« times, and between »good« and »bad« beats. Hand in hand with that went a system of notation that inscribed rhythms in accordance with the measure – as in the tie across a bar line, or the drawing of beams only within the limits of the measure and the time positions. Both the idea of an evenly pulsating alternation of heavy and light beats and the notational forms dictated by the meter are apt to distract both eye and ear from the actual rhythmic conditions. To put it more succinctly: whoever reads or plays only by the meter misses the temporal structure actually composed. No good musician does that. Consciously or unconsciously, he also hears the unwritten rhythms, as well as the fine gradations between rhythmic weights, and gives expression to them.

To illustrate the relation of rhythmic and metric weights, we will once more take a close look at a section of the Haydn movement cited earlier. We will thereby also be able to introduce an important additional component, which generally obtains only in compositions of more than one part: »Harmony«. The section in question is that of the first sixteen measures of the movement (Ex. 0-6). The top accolade reproduces, in compact form, the orchestral passage with every detail (analytical particello). For the rhythm analysis, I distinguish here betwen »Principal part«, »Accompaniment«, and »Setting« (second, third, and fourth accolades). The systems containing the component rhythms are found within the accolades. The bottom line depicts the rhythmic »Profile« along with the schema of the 2/4 time. Let us explicate this rhythm score.

The rhythm of the »Principal part« has already been delineated: it can be simply taken over at this point, except that the components »Dynamics« and »Phrase« are neglected here, as the respective results apply to the entire passage of the composition and are therefore entered in their place (4th accolade).

In the »Accompaniment«, which in the first eight measures is monophonic in double octave unison and only then exfoliates into full chords, only the bass part is considered with regard to the components »Sound« and »Pitch.« For the component »Diastematy«, however, the upper voice of the chorded part is also taken into account (mm. 5-8). The component »Articulation« applies to all the tones of the accompaniment, for the rests here are articulation rests in that they serve to shorten the sound of both the octaves and the chords.

In the bracket »Setting«, the components »Harmony«, »Timbre«, »Dynamics«, and »Phrase« all apply and are therefore taken into consideration. The rhythm of the »Harmony« (changing harmonic function) is identical in both phrases but should be weighted differently in the first eight measures than in the second. While there are only two parts (principal voice and bass line), a weight value of 2 can be assigned to each change in harmony, a value of 4 as soon as the full chords set in. The two authentic cadences in the dominant (mm. 8 and 16) are entered with the value 2 (a cadence in the tonic, which does not yet occur here, would have the value 3).

Ex. 0-6 Haydn, Sinfonia in G No. 94, 2nd mov., mm. 1-16

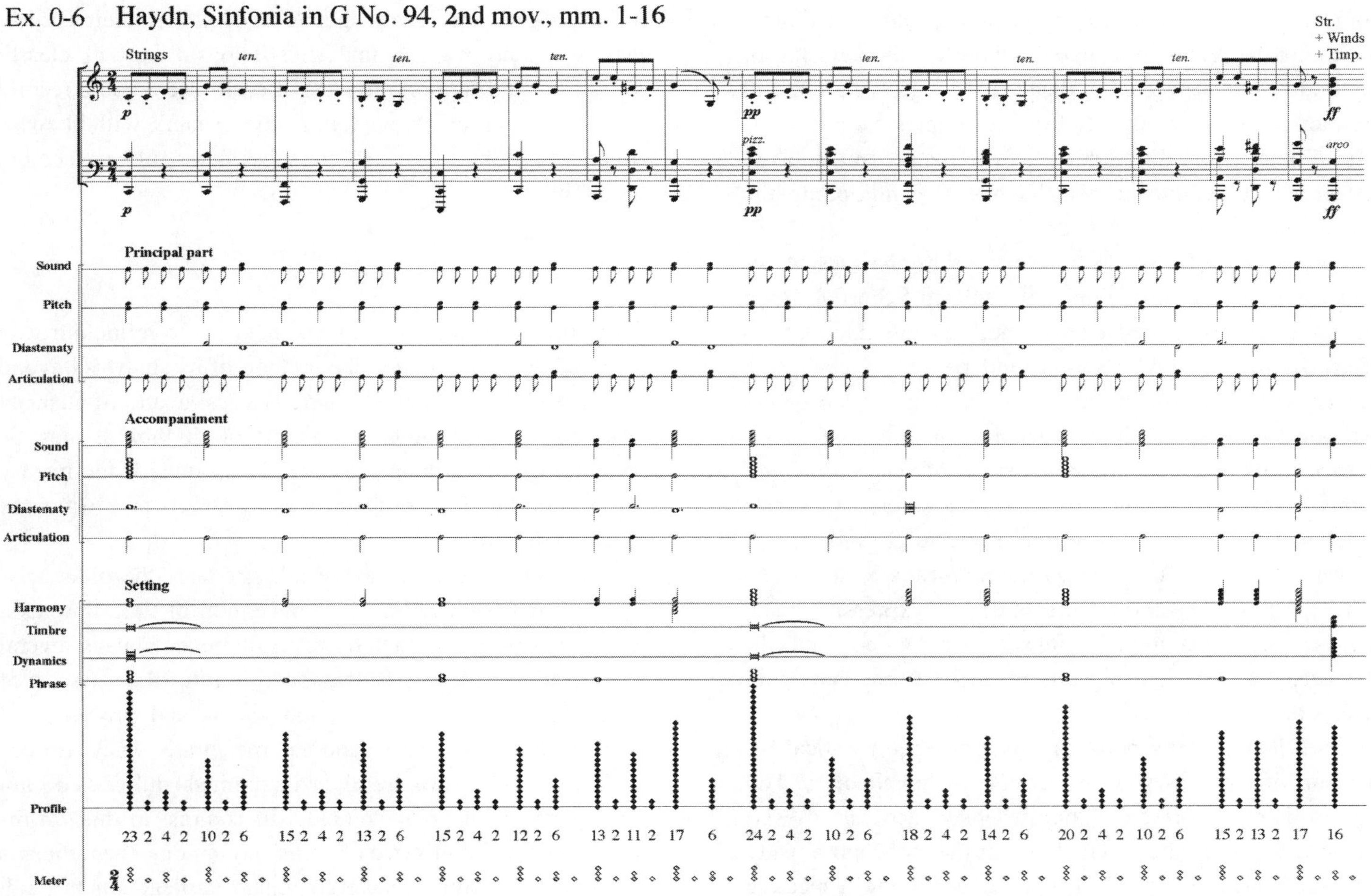

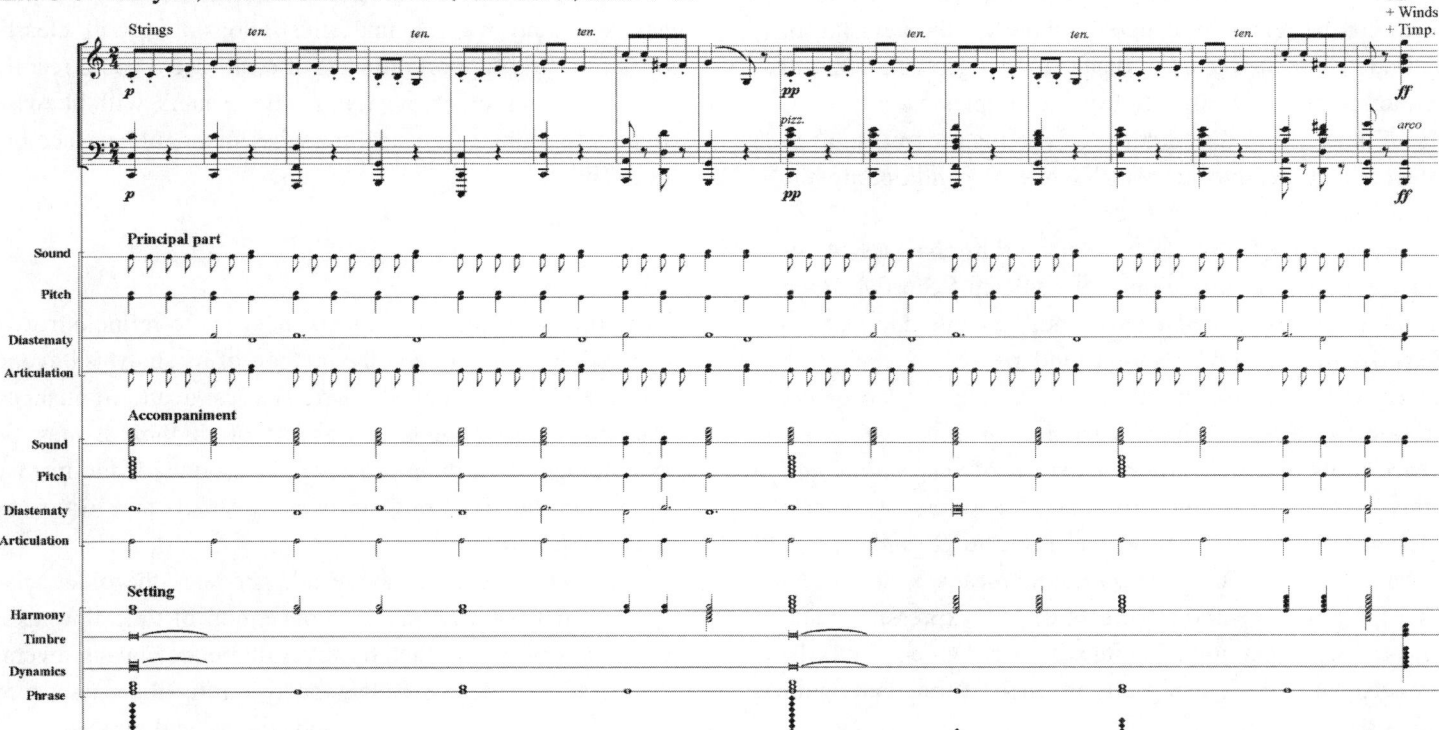

The »Timbre« changes twice, in m. 9 (*pizz.*) and in m. 16 (arco; winds and tympani); the changes are accompanied by changes in volume (»Dynamics«, *p – pp – ff*). Depending upon their length, the »Phrases« are weighted with 1, 2, or 3 points.

As is to be expected from this theme, all of the component rhythms have very simple structures. Thus it comes as no surprise that the rhythmic »Profile«, in which these rhythms are totaled, also displays a large degree of regularity. The comprehensive rhythmic profile clearly mirrors the prescribed 2/4 time, though the rhythms of the individual components do not always do so. A comparison of the rhythmic with the metric profile (»Meter«) reveals that in the rhythmic profile the second position in the measure is always weighted more lightly than the first, and that the eighths located between the beats have even lower values – which corresponds to the 2/4 time. The rhythm thus brings the graded accent meter to the fore, and that without the weights of heavy and light beats of the meter being figured in.

The purely rhythmically generated 2/4 time, however, appears in a living, that is, variable form, as the heavy and semi-heavy positions slightly differ from each other. It is conceivable that compositions of a greater complexity than this Haydn movement exhibit the metric structure, too, may be subject to greater fluctuations than the time signature would lead us to expect. The method of components analysis enables us to describe such degrees of rhythmic-metric weights with some objectivity. By this method we can also document well-known phenomena such as hemiola and hypermeasures, as well as demonstrate latent time changes and heterometric structures in the course of a composition. Meter is recognized as part of rhythm, as an object of compositional creation and not merely a norm or convention.

***

This book will substantiate and apply the components theory I have developed. In Part One I will explain in detail what components rhythms are and what relevance they have had in the course of music history. Starting with the basis component »Sound«, the most important and most widely present components will be exemplified: »Pitch«, »Diastematy«, »Articulation« (also »Ornament«), »Dynamics«, »Timbre« (including degrees of brightness), »Harmony« (as well as cadences and dissonances), »Texture« (e.g., distances between entries of voices), »Phrase«, and »Prosody« (syllabic weight, verse meter). The second Section of Part One will elucidate the concept of »Rhythmic Weight« through an analysis of the Allegretto movement of Beethoven's Seventh Symphony. The rhythm of its three themes will be precisely differentiated, and in turn again correlated, by means of components analysis. The result will be the realization that while Beethoven wrote this processional march in 2/4 time, he in fact composed it in varying meters. Part One concludes with a third section, entitled »Rhythm Aspects«, dealing with several specific problem areas of musical rhythm, such as »Augmentation« and »Diminution«, as well as »Isometry«, »Heterometry«, and »Symmetry«. Under the rubric »Rhythmic Characters«, we will also bring up some historically established phenomena such as »Upbeat«, »Syncope«, and »Hemiola«, which can be regarded as paradigmatic for the devising of rhythmic characters (e.g., in dances). This section, too, will be interspersed with (mostly brief) examples from the history of music from the Middle Ages to the present, so as to reflect the respective historical contexts conditioning the components.

In Part Two I want to present rhythm analyses of selected examples from the music of Johann Sebastian Bach for discussion. Here analysis will thus be applied to a group of works of a unified personal and period style. A side benefit will of course be yet another demonstration of the exceptional variety of Bach's music – in this case in reference to its rhythm. The juxtaposition of very simple and highly complex rhythmic processes, regardless of generic differences, in Bach's music may serve to remind us that rhythm, like every other compositional means, is at the service of a work's central idea, of a certain expressive need, of a musical dramaturgy. Complexity is not an end in itself, no matter how much, especially in Bach, it time and again evokes our wonder.

Part Three of the book, finally, presents a critical inspection of older as well as current rhythm theories. The purpose is not to present a comprehensive account of existing theories of rhythm, something for the most part already done by others. Rather, I wish to examine the respective texts solely from two aspects: whether theory and analysis are adequate to the locus of the composition in its own time, and, whether components rhythms and rhythmic weight – even if under other names – are reflected in theory construction and analysis. With respect to the first question, one can't avoid the sobering assessment that the music theory of a given era hardly ever attains the spiritual level of the contemporary masterworks. As for the second question, no simple anwer is possible. Reflections on what musical rhythm is and how to describe it have increased enormously during the last fifty years and – especially in the Anglo-American world – have frequently attained a degree of differentiation that makes once famous approaches from the 19th and early 20th centuries appear obsolete (e.g., Hugo Riemann).

What I call »component« others address under the terms »accent«, »factor«, »element«, »parameter« or similar. Examination of these writings will show, however, that accents etc., when included in rhythm analyses, have mostly ranked only as accidental to rhythm, whereas they actually have rhythm-creating import once they are recognized as musical components. Components analysis opens up an avenue that makes it possible in principle to consider each and all sound phenomena occurring in a composition under the concept of rhythm.

This discussion complex in Part Three, reserved for the end, will also disencumber the exposition of my theory in the earlier parts. There I largely dispense with any discussion of already existing analyses of the examples selected, while this is now the very subject. Concerning the examples, personal knowledge of the repertoire and – admittedly – subjective preferences dictate and restrict their choice. My sole aim was to find illustrations that will clearly document and support the facts of each case. I could readily cite numerous other examples, and readers will likewise frequently think of musical passages that could replace the ones chosen.

***

The purpose of the components theory is to refine our way of looking at rhythm and the method of its analysis beyond the level hitherto attained. There is a real dearth of nuanced musical analyses under the aspect of rhythm. It may be symptomatic that there are several accounts of the history of rhythm theories,[1] but hardly any attempts at a history of musical rhythm.

One characteristic, above all, pervades the older analyses of musical rhythm: the conception of time flow as a unilinear process. In fact, however, there are always several events taking place simultaneously during the passage of time. In music these are sound events and processes of change that can overlap and interpenetrate. They are coordinated, to be sure, but their beginnings and ends do not by any means have to coincide. In contrast to this, an inclination can be observed to this day among theoreticians of musical rhythm to make imaginary vertical cuts through a score as a way of getting at the secret of its organization. If such cuts are often already problematic in formations of medium and extended length, that is even more the case in analyses of forms of shorter extent, in other words, of rhythmic processes.

Several reasons may account for this narrow view of rhythm. To begin with, there is the tradition of classical prosody, which until the 18th century dictated the description of rhythms and meters and hampered the development of a specifically musical method of rhythmic analysis. A spoken verse is unilinear, so that it may seem adequate to divide it into stresses and unstresses and metrical feet. For the rhythmic content of single melodies, let alone compositions in many parts, however, this analytic instrumentarium is quite deficient and incommensurate. It cannot do justice to the multiplicity of rhythmic components and to the structural wealth of a developed musical art generally.

A second reason may have to do with the way European music is written. Notation became necessary for singing and playing as soon as oral tradition no longer sufficed or the composer-as-author appeared, who wished to be heard here and there in his absence. But notation is practice-oriented and not adapted for the content of a composition.

---

[1] Wilhelm Seidel, *Über Rhythmustheorien der Neuzeit* (Bern / München, 1975); *Geschichte der Musiktheorie*, ed. Frieder Zaminer and Thomas Ertelt [since 1992] by commission of the Institut für Musikforschung Preussischer Kulturbesitz, Berlin, 15 vols. (Darmstadt 1984 ff.). *The Cambridge History of Western Music Theory*, ed. Thomas Christensen, 3rd print. (Cambridge University Press, 2006).

To slightly oversimplify, it indicates which tones a musician is to pluck and how long to hold them. Since one can identify short and long notes directly from the various voices, such durational sequences were, and still are, regarded as *the* rhythm of melodies and polyphonic compositions. Rhythms that depend on other components than sound entries are not noted down as such and thus were overlooked by theoreticians. Yet there cannot be any doubt that they are part of the composition. I know of no theoretician of the 16th to the 19th century who asked about these *un*noted rhythms, while many have written about the notation of rhythms of tonal duration, rules of mensuration, types of measures, and stresses.

A third reason for the relative disregard of components rhythms has to do with the fact that, with the development of polyphony, rules of mensuration had to be established to coordinate the voices and to regulate their chords with exactitude. Thus the notion of a grid extending vertically through the texture of voices became paramount, which established itself early on in the *conductus* (in contrast to *motet*) notation. But this system dictated by performance practice was apt to distract from the actual, aesthetically intended processes. The motet notation, with its independent fields of voices, is really the more adequate form of representation when it comes to musical, and hence also rhythmic, meaning.

Metering brought about the practice of beating or treading time. The metronome, invented in the early 19th century, further mechanized this practice. The habits that musicians display in this connection may play a role as an additional reason for the tendency to interpret musical sequences metrically more than rhythmically. Even outside of lay performances, where the principal concern often is not to ›get out of step,‹ the oppressive influence of a conductor's beating of time on the playing and hearing of a piece of ensemble music is not to be underestimated. At the same time I want to put in a good word here for the often maligned guild of orchestra leaders. Good conductors have such a large and differentiated repertoire of movements and gestures that they can embody and express countless rhythmic events and processes contained in a composition besides the beaten time. Thus they can not only prevent the listening by meter but can effectively implement the complex rhythmic life that is in music.

***

The components theory was developed with reference to the pulse-determined, polyphonic, scripted music of the European sphere. Whether this approach can also serve the analysis of the music of other cultures or genres will have to be decided by the respective cognoscenti.

Pulse here refers to isometric sequences of smallest durations by which larger durations can be measured and brought into relation to each other. On the basis of the isometric pulse both heterometric and isometric (occasionally even symmetric) rhythms can be formed. If there is no metric pulse, the components remain effective but there is no standard to determine the durations and their relations to each other. Generally excluded are *senza misura* passages such as cadenzas or free-flowing fantasies, as well as miniphenomena like trills and tremoli – not to mention certain avant-garde compositions that are presented in spatial notation. Not that such free tone sequences have no rhythm, but such rhythms would have to be described differently.

Excluded from consideration here is also the subject of musical interpretation, which in our age of analog and digital music recordings could well be the object of analysis and actually also is. Everyone can observe that individual interpreters of one and the same piece not only choose different tempi but also shape the inner rhythmic structure of a composition more or less freely. Such deviations from the noted rhythmic values are principally measurable and determinable. But the masses of accumulating data quickly become unmanageable, since obviously not only different interpreters would produce different data, but even one and the same interpreter certain divergences would be observable from recital to recital. This diversity is part and parcel of the artistic substance of every good musical performance; it constitutes the vitality and the fascination of individual interpretations. But the expense of such an investigation would be immense, quite apart from a number of methodical issues that would first have to be clarified. I therefore dispense with interpretations of individual musicians. My hope is that the rhythmic analyses and rhythmographic procedures will prove stimulating for music performers and will further refine their playing and approximate it to the intention of the composer.

***

Taking up a casual remark of György Ligeti's, I start out from a very simple, formal concept of rhythm. Ligeti once defined musical rhythm as follows:[2]

»Rhythm« signifies any temporal sequence of tones, sounds, sound formations, whereas »meter« refers to a more or less regular structuring of the temporal process. Thus a Gregorian chant has rhythm but no meter. »Rhythm« (and generally »rhythmics«) is present in any kind of music; not just the »pulsating« rhythm (i.e., the one subordinated to, and unfolding within, meter) is rhythm.

If one were to derive a formal definition from this, one might say: the term »Musical Rhythm« refers to sequences of durations that are derived from shaped sound events. But I don't assign much importance to this or similar definitions. They simply provide an operational basis, on which rhythmic events in concrete compositions, whether simple or complex, can be described.

---

[2] Letter of György Ligeti from April 18, 1974, to the student Kai Jacobs, who wrote to him on the occasion of a rhythm-lecture at the Institute of Musicology at the University of Hamburg.

The methodic frame of this study is a phenomenological one. My point of departure is the music itself, not the thinking about music, let alone the musical tools-of-the-trade books, which are legion. Since music is an artifact, not a natural product, the methodical procedure is at the same time oriented towards the aesthetics of production. Although the analyst is initially a recipient, the perspective he adopts should be that of the composer.

Composing can be understood as a form of artistic work requiring continual decision-making. The choice of sounds or sound formations is one category of decisions, the consideration as to when this sound or sound formation should enter, be modified, or recur, is the other. Components are among the *what* alternatives, durations among the *when* alternatives. *What* and *when* questions thus determine every rhythm analysis, and the distincton between these two kinds of interrogation is essential.

To regard the duration of a tone or sound as one of its properties is to overlook this categorical differentiation, which already Aristoxenos conceptualized as the »rhythmicized« and the »rhythmicizing«. In the referential frame of space and time, sounds and sound shapes belong to the spatial, durations and rhythms to the temporal dimenson. If durations, therefore, can be neither components nor properties of sounds or sound formations, but, on the contrary, condition these in their succession and mutual interpenetration in the temporal continuum, they cannot be said to be tied to individual noted tones. The concept of »duration« is free vis-à-vis the entirety of the sound event, it can be used to describe any rhythm, including durations, between any components whatever, between directly contiguous tones or sounds, between crest and/or keeltones, between sharp and soft modes of attack, between shades of loudness or different volume areas, between instrumental and vocal timbres and their grades of brightness, between harmonic functions, between suspensions and other dissonances or altogether free tone clusters, between homophonic and polyphonic passages, along with any conceivable types of texture, between entries of phrases and themes, etc.

Thus construed, musical rhythm corresponds to musical form. It is no more than a convention to analyze large units, such as arias or symphonic movements, under the rubric of form, and small units like motifs and phrases under the aspect of their rhythm. Both cases involve the formation of sounding material with more or less free use of any and all components available in a given period. To accept this does not mean to posit the terms rhythm and form as synonymous. The difference in temporal dimension as regards rhythm and form remains meaningful and, not least, also psychologically relevant. But to raise rhythm analysis to the rank of formal analysis may lead to our approaching rhythmic structures from the same multiplicity of angles long since customary in the description of musical forms.

Besides, it should not be forgotten that rhythm constitutes only one aspect of music. The point of departure for any musical event is sounds and sound shapes. They have a meaning of their own, and each has a specific character. A tone, a sound, a chord, produced by the human voice or by an instrument, is an event that impresses us and which we remember and recognize. An aesthetic effect proceeds from sounds before any temporal order comes into play. Even when sounds and sound shapes are part of a rhythmic structure, they retain their own quality and efficacy. Though all components of a tone or sound composition are rhythmically relevant, the rhythm cannot by itself represent the entire composition.

***

I have been occupied with matters of rhythm for more than thirty years. In a series of essays[3], I have developed

---

[3] »Die ›dichterisch-musikalische Periode.‹ Ein verkannter Begriff Richard Wagners« [»The ›poetic-musical period‹. A neglected concept of Richard Wagner«], in *Zur Musikgeschichte des 19. Jahrhunderts* (Hamburg, 1977), 105-123; »Brahms und Dvořák« [»Brahms and Dvořák«], in *Johannes Brahms. Symposion Brahms und seine Zeit*, Hamburg 1983 (Laaber, 1984) 125-146; »Rhythmische Komplexität in der Musik J. S. Bachs« [»Rhythmic Complexity in the Music of J. S. Bach«], in *Studien zur Systematischen Musikwissenschaft* (Laaber, 1986) 223-246; »Rhythmik und Metrik in Bartóks Sonate für zwei Klaviere und Schlagzeug und die Kritik des jungen Stockhausen an Bartók« [»Rhythm and Meter in Bartók's Sonata for Two Pianos and Percussion and the Critical Comments of the Young Stockhausen on Bartók«], in *Musiktheorie*, 9 (1994) 39-48; »Rhythmische Komplexität in der Instrumentalmusik von Brahms« [»Rhythmic Complexity in the Instrumental Music of Brahms«], in *Johannes Brahms. Quellen - Text - Rezeption - Interpretation* (München, 1999), 143-158; »Die Rhythmuspartitur. Über eine neue Methode zur rhythmisch-metrischen Analyse pulsgebundener Musik« [»The Rhythm Score. On a New Method of Rhythmic-Metric Analysis of Pulse-Determined Music«], in *50 Jahre Musikwissenschaftliches Institut in Hamburg* (Frankfurt / M., 1999), 83-110; »György Ligetis *Zehn Stücke für Bläserquintett* (1968)« [György Ligeti's Ten Pieces for Wind Quintet], together with Albrecht Schneider, in: *Musiktheorie* 18 (2003), 195-222; »Der komponierte Tanzschritt. Rhythmusanalyse gemäß der Komponententheorie und ihre Relevanz für die Körpergestik im Tanz« [»The Composed Dance Step. Rhyhmic Analysis After the Components Theory and its Relevance for Gestural Movements in Dance«], in *Die Beziehung von Musik und Choreographie im Ballett* (Berlin, 2007), 35-55; »Nochmals zum Tanz-Quodlibet im ersten Akt-Finale des *Don Giovanni*« [»The Dance Quodlibet in the First-Act Finale of *Don Giovanni* once more«], in *AfMw* 65 (2008), 1-30; »»*Jede* zeitliche Folge von Tönen, Klängen, musikalischen Gestalten‹ hat Rhythmus. Über die Rhythmik in Ligetis Cembalostück *Continuum*« [»»Rhythm Signifies Any Temporal Sequence of Tones, Sounds, Sound Formations‹. On Rhythm in Ligeti's Piece for Harpsichord *Continuum*«], published on internet page http:// www. saitenspiel.org; »Zur Rhythmik in den Messen Josquins (und Bauldeweyns). Isometrische Phrasenwiederholungen und ihr Verhältnis zur mensuralen Ordnung« [»On Rhythm in the Masses of Josquin (and Bauldeweyn). Isometric Repetitions of Phrases and their Relation to Mensural Dispositions«], in *Musikkulturgeschichte heute* (Frankfurt / M., 2009), 9-29; »Primäre und sekundäre Dauern in der Musik. Über einige Grundzüge der ›Komponententheorie‹ [»Primary and Secondary Durations in Music. On some Outlines of the ›Components The-

hypotheses and substantiated concepts that can now hopefully stand up to critical discussion. It would be desirable for such a discussion to get underway so that an as yet unduly neglected area of music theory can begin to take its proper place in scholarly discourse.

---

ory«»], in *ZGMTH* 8/3 (2011), online: http://www.gmth.de/zeitschrift/artikel/667.aspx/

Part One: Theory of Components

Rhythms and Components

Definition of Terms

Sounds are the stuff of which musical structures are made. Like other objects of perception, they are subject to the categories of space and time. Because they are experienced as fleeting and intangible, we easily overlook the fact that sounds are material objects. Yet one only needs to think of membranes or other vibrating bodies that condense and compress and rarefy air and leave their traces as sensations of pressure to realize the bodily and therefore spatial nature of sounds.

This actually banal signification of sounds as »things« is important to our inquiry concerning rhythm and music insofar as it helps distinguishing the spatial character of the phenomenon of sound from its manifestation in the temporal continuum. Leibniz's graphic saying that there was »coexistences« and »successions« in all things[4] means in our context that sounds and rhythms are subject to different modes of perception. About sounds we ask »what,« about rhythms we ask »when.«

»What« questions provide access to the entire universe of the audible in music: sound and tone as simple events; harmonies, chords, tone sequences as complex formations. Every individual sound incident and every sound event can be described in terms of its specific features. Individual tones are determined by their pitch (frequency), color (sound spectrum), degree of lightness (octave position), loudness (dynamic), form (articulation), etc. Chords are distinguished according to their pitch content, interval structure, octave level, type of inversion, function, etc. Melodic figures may be determined by pitch content and tonal systems, diastematic course, rhythm and meter, extent and tempo, semantic (thematic, figural) substance, etc. All of this is potentiated by the number of voices and/or performers. From the point of view of the composer, single tones and sound formations with all their characteristics constitute »components.« Components are the materials with which the composer works.

»When« questions address the temporal order of musical configurations. When does a sound or one of its components appear? When does it stop, or change, or is overlapped? And what durations elapse between these points of time?

Durations are dependent on sound phenomena but, owing to a categorical difference between space and time, are not really part of them. It is therefore questionable to count the duration of a tone as one of its properties.[5] The concept of duration is needed for the determination of all temporal relations, whether these are measured in regard to individual tones/sounds or to their components, or with reference to composite sound formations of whatever extent.

Like the concept of »duration« that of »rhythm« belongs to the complex of »When« questions. Rhythms in music can appear only in dependence on sound; visual rhythms observable in the bodily movements of performers or conductors are ignored, as are special instances of rhythmic visualizations on the theater.[6] A piece of music is said to »have« a rhythm, not to »be« one. Even though it is customary in common parlance to refer to a knocking signal as a rhythm, strictly speaking one should say that the series of knocking sounds »follows« a certain rhythm rather than that it »is« one.

The simplest definition of »rhythm« is »a rhythm consists of successive durations.« Since there are durations of different dimensions – in music they reach from tones of different frequencies all the way to the span of entire compositions – classes of durations have to be limited to a medium measure so as to hit the temporal window typical for rhythm between perception of pitch (micro-durations) and perception of form (macro-durations). This medium-sized measure has always been derived from the human body, e.g., from steps or breathing. The borders between the perception of pitch, rhythm and form are fluid.

By relating the concepts »component«, »duration« and »rhythm« to each other, one attains an enlarged perception of what is »rhythmic« in music. The exclusive attention to the written values of tones or sounds will have to be given up so that both eye and ear are freed for the reception of rhythmic phenomena not directly derivable from the notation. If in a sequence of eighths played by string instruments every other note is to be played pizzicato, a rhythm of quarter notes results that is no less real than the basic rhythm of eighths. Such »components rhythms« are both numerous and independent of the basic rhythm of the notes. They point to the »coexistences« in Leibniz's »space«. We hear and experience them simultaneously. Applied to the time continuum, these rhythms form a fluid

---

[4] Leibniz to Clarke: »As for my Own Opinion, I have said more than once, that I hold *Space* to be something *merely relative*, as *Time* is; that I hold it to be an *Order of Coexistences*, as *Time* is an *Order of Successions*.« In *A Collection of PAPERS, Which passed between the late Learned Mr. LEIBNITZ, AND Dr. CLARKE, In the Years 1715 and 1716. Relating to the PRINCIPLES OF Natural Philosophy and Religion.* [...] *By Samuel Clarke, D. D. Rector of St. Jame's Westminster.* [...] LONDON [...] MDCCXVII. Internet-Edition: http://books.google.de/, p. 56.

[5] It is true that nothing exists without duration and that therefore no tone/sound can appear without duration either. But as soon as we talk about time intervals, that is, about rhythm, a concept of »duration« takes hold that means more than helping sound phenomena to come into being. Duration is what enables the succession of sound material to be ordered and shaped. Thus conceived, durations cannot themselves be »properties.«

[6] In the pub scene in Alban Berg's opera *Wozzeck*, there is a moment where the music stops but the dancers are to continue dancing »in the tempo of a landler« (II:iv, m. 599).

texture that is responsible for a great deal of the vividness of music. As the simple example of the Haydn theme in the introduction has shown – and the analyses of the 48 fugue themes from the *Well-tempered Clavier* will confirm again and again – even monophonic melodies have a characteristic »rhythmic texture« and not merely a »rhythm.«

Rhythm-building Components

Sound

The component »Sound« is the basic component for any music within our frame of reference. It simply means that a sound disrupts silence. In occidental music, this usually occurs through the onset of tones, often accompanied by syllables of words, but also through percussive sounds. The term »sound« is to signal that this prime phenomenon of all musical events does not yet involve distinctions between pitches, as determined by physics, or any other forms of sound. Solely the fact that a sound appears and that a sequence of such sounds generates rhythm is at issue.

Ex. 1-001   Beethoven, 5th Symphony, 3rd mov. mm. 324 ff.

In example 1-001, the note of C sounds in constant repetition on the timpani, whereby, in the frame of a fast 3/4-time, the rhythm starts as a ternary one, which after twelve measures fades into an amorphous repetition of quarter notes.

The component rhythm »Sound« thus does not have the same notation as what appears in the timpani part. The quarter pauses are omitted and are added to the value of the note actually sounded. The durations are thus measured according to the temporal intervals between the tonal entries – what in the Anglo-American world is generally referred to as »inter-onset interval« (IOI).[7]

The measuring of durations according to temporal intervals between the onset of tones makes sense for several reasons. For one thing, the pauses here as almost always are articulation pauses that determine the form of the tone rather than its rhythmic value. Such pauses correspond to staccato and other abbreviation signs. Beethoven demonstrates this himself by making the thematic melody of the third movement of his Fifth Symphony appear in several articulatory variants (Ex. 1-002).

---

[7]   Justin London, *Hearing in Time. Psychological Aspects of Musical Meter* (Oxford: Univ. Press, 2004), 4. See also Eytan Agmon, »Musical Durations as Mathematical Intervals: Some Implications for the Theory and Analysis of Rhythm«, in *Music Analysis*, 16:1 (1997), 45-75.

Ex. 1-002   Beethoven, 5th Symphony, 3rd mov.

Initially he requires legato and tenuto playing for his theme, in the da capo part legato and staccato playing, the latter indicated by means of quarter pauses. The component rhythm »Sound« is identical in both variants, while their articulatory rhythm differs.

The fact that we tend to measure the rhythm of sounds/notes by their onset intervals rather than by the absolute value of each sound probably has to do with the general predominance of beginnings over ends. That something begins is generally more meaningful than that something ceases. This principle of measuring durations initially between entry and entry rather than beginning and end also applies to the treatment of other components. Thus phrases, too, are for the time being measured only by their beginning, as followed by the beginning of a new phrase. There is no danger that in this way endings of phrases or other formal parts are altogether lost in the rhythmic structure, as the endings come into play by means of other components, e.g., by cadences.

Ex. 1-003

Berg, *Wozzeck*, II/2, m. 310, Corno

There are, however, cases where, for special effects, tones are firmly fixed also in their actual durations and not merely relative to the entry distances from subsequent tones. Alban Berg, all the way round a music-theoretically highly reflective composer, provides some pertinent examples. Thus in *Wozzeck* (Ex. 1-003) we encounter a passage where a simple rhythm (♩♩♩♩𝅝) is highly differentiated by means of durational and rest values so that a series of increasing pause durations (?, 2, 4, 6, 15 ♪)[8] is complementary to a series of decreasing sound durations (8, 6, 4, 2, 1 ♪). Since the notes are marked by tenuto-staccato signs so that their form of articulation is already predetermined, the rests must have yet another function besides that of shortening the tones.[9]

---

[8]   The caesura mark (,) after the first tone represents as an irrational value, the expected sixteenth rest (which I have indicated by a ?).

[9]   The purpose of this strange rhythmicization is to be found in the dramatic context. Captain and Doctor, who in Act II, sc. ii encounter Wozzeck in the street, have their fun with their subordinate by hinting that Marie is cheating on him with the Drum Major. The note A is the final note of the Captain theme, thus marking the attitude of the Captain in this dia-

Ex. 1-004
Berg, *Lulu* I/3, m. 833 (Strings)

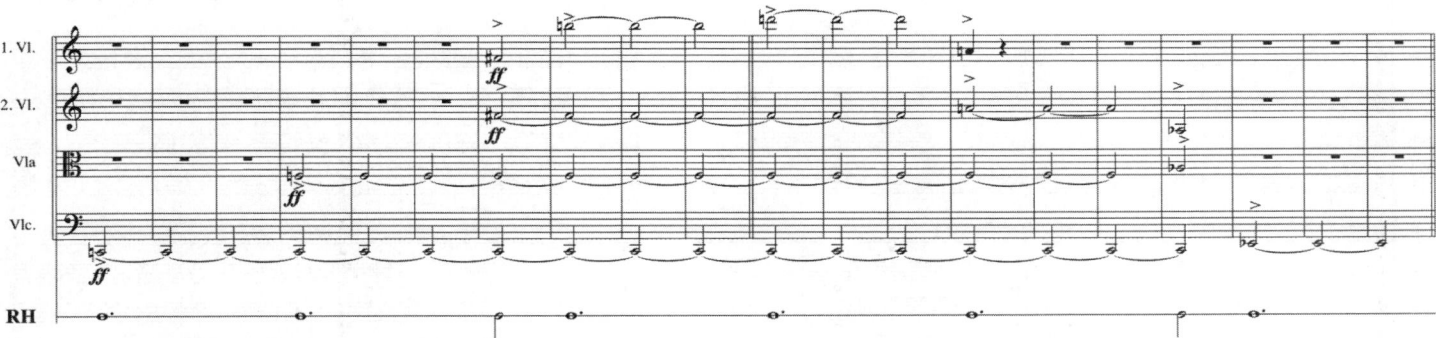

Berg's operas furnish additional exemplary instances for the problem of entering and ending notes and the formation of rhythms by these means. In Act I, sc. iii of *Lulu*, whose second part is significantly headed by the formal term »Monoritmica,« one hears – at the climax, which is also the turning point of the retrograde process of acceleration (at m. 843) – the »leitrhythm« ♩. ♩. ♪ ♩. in multiple augmentation, at first by means of newly entering notes, which in each case are held, and then by means of stopping notes, whereby the chord just built-up is dismantled again in precise rhythmic control (Ex. 1-004).[10]

No less subtle is a passage in Berg's *Wozzeck*, famous not for its intricate rhythmic structure but rather for its dramatic effect: the brief transitional music between the murder and the following tavern scene, which is shaped as a two-fold crescendo on the note of B. The first crescendo is followed by a solo on the big drum, whose strokes are timed to the rhythm that underlies the entire following scene as its »leitrhythm«. The second crescendo is followed *attacca* by the music of the tavern scene, whose »out-of-tune pianino« presents again the »leitrhythm«, this time furnished by an accompaniment that has the character of a »Schnellpolka«.

Ex. 1-005 depicts the first crescendo plus drum solo. Berg here created a classic example and at the same time a borderline case of the matter of the entry rhythm, one prompted, of course, by the internal dramatic events. Fixated on a single absolute pitch – even bass tuba and double basses are held to the B3 – the winds enter one after the other, in the measure of the (here augmented) »leitrhythm«. The strings imitate it a mere quarter note later, in such a way that a rhythmic stretto canon results. At the same time, Berg does his best to make this small contrapuntal trick *in*audible, as each newly added instrument is supposed to begin *pppp* and go immediately into a crescendo, so that the following entry is covered up.

The second crescendo (*pppp→fff*), too, can be regarded as a borderline case of musical rhythm and meter. It demonstrates, again in five alla-breve measures, a quasi-rhythmic passage, as all the instruments hold their tone during the crescendo or else play it in tremolo. There are therefore no markers to provide any clues how to structure this stretch of time rhythmically. To be sure, the two five-bar crescendos last barely eight seconds each, so that they approximate a long-held fermata (which is actually called for at the end of each five-bar passage). The subterranean rhythm of the first crescendo remains nevertheless both spectacular and mysterious – no doubt a reflection of the internal psychic processes of the characters acting on stage.[11]

Apart from such borderline cases, the handling of the component »Sound« in a rhythmic analysis is fairly simple, as this is the only case where the durations can be taken directly from the notation – though meter-related notational forms such as slurs have to be translated into simple durations and the pauses (in the case of articulation pauses) may have to be added to the value of a note.

---

bolical situation. The latter has just mentioned the Drum Major in a highly suggestive manner and now withdraws into himself – virtually disappears from the sound event – waiting for the effect his words will have on Wozzeck. See my analysis of this scene in *Alban Berg: Wozzeck. Eine semantische Analyse unter Einbeziehung der Skizzen und Dokumente aus dem Nachlaß Bergs* (Munich, 1985), 218-221.

[10] The fact that in this process the four notes of the main rhythm (RH), which throughout the opera is used as a symbol of death, are combined with the four notes of the so-called »Earth Spirit fourths« signifying the »Lulu principle,« illuminates the semantic intensification in this spot. The Painter has cut his throat because of Lulu, his corpse is discovered at exactly the moment when the main rhythm enters again and Lulu's ascending fourths (C-F-F♯-B) give way to their descent (D-A-A♭-E♭). At this point the music semantically indicates Lulu as the Painter's nemesis.

[11] As I have shown elsewhere (cf. note 9, pp. 142-145), the »leitrhythm« forms a sememe meaning »Wozzeck, the murderer,« inasmuch as it appears only after the deed, which Wozzeck is immediately afterwards charged with (in the tavern scene). At the same time it dawns on him that what he has done in a paranoid fit will mark him as a murderer in the public eye of the state. It is these processes in Wozzeck's subconscious that Berg seems to have intended to express with the implantation of the »murder rhythm« into the crescendo.

Ex. 1-005 Berg, *Wozzeck* III/2:3, m. 109

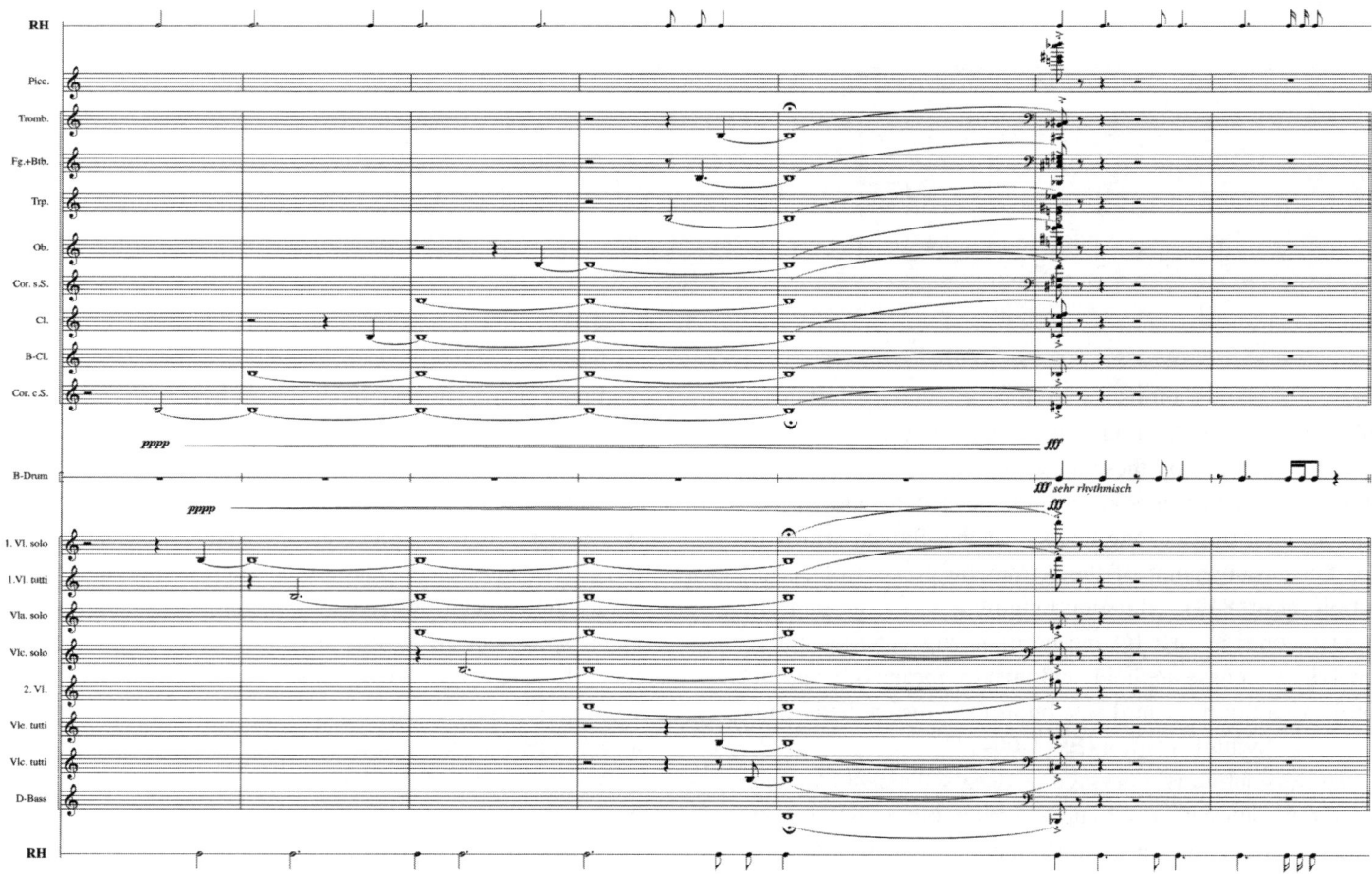

In music history, both simple, developed and highly complex rhythmic concepts have been rendered by means of the basic component »Sound«: from the *organa* to the *ars subtilior*, all the way to the serial music of the mid-20th century. The following chapters will show what role other components, which were added, or else refined, in the course of history, played in rhythmic shaping.

Pitch

That the component »Pitch« must be distinguished from the component »Sound« with regard to its rhythm-generating import can most easily be demonstrated on melodies that contain tone repetitions.

Ex. 1-006 Beethoven, 1st Symphony, 3rd mov., Beginning

The Scherzo (»Menuetto«) of Beethoven's First Symphony (Ex. 1-006) presents a case, in which the component rhythms »Sound« and »Pitch« are nearly identical. Only in the third and the seventh measure they diverge: there, because of some tone repetitions, longer values emerge at the points of pitch change. As a result, the iambic rhythm (♩♩ ♩♩♩♩) continues in one of the components in the third measure, while it changes to dactyls in the other (♩ ♩ ♩). Both rhythms are relevant: one hears them simultaneously.

This method of rhythmic enrichment is very old but has not hitherto been included systematically in rhythmic analysis. Here is an example from the Middle Ages (Ex. 1-007). This

This dramatic, almost catastrophic-seeming start, with which the first instrumental recitative, later sung to the words »O Freunde, nicht diese Töne!« begins, derives its

Ex. 1-007 *Lamento di Tristano* (13th century), triple and duple variants (cut-out)

dance song in Dorian mode,[12] transmitted in mensural notation, shows but one deviation between the component rhythms »Sound« and »Pitch« in the principal, ternary form, but in the even-measured after-dance (»Rota«) includes numerous tone repetitions, which in the chain of eighths notes in the second half inject a syncopated sequence of quarter notes that furnishes a rhythmic stimulation to this cadential melody.

force from the massive wind sound combined with a fourfold octave unisono of the main voice in *marcato* articulation and a harmony sharpened by dissonances. Add to that the syncopated rhythm, which is not actually notated but unfolds its effect from the tone repetitions. These repetitions, which maintain the pitch and even entire chords, lead to quarter notes within the eighths attacks. From a comparison with the voices of the horns one can tell that

Ex. 1-008 Beethoven, 9th Symphony, Finale, Beginning

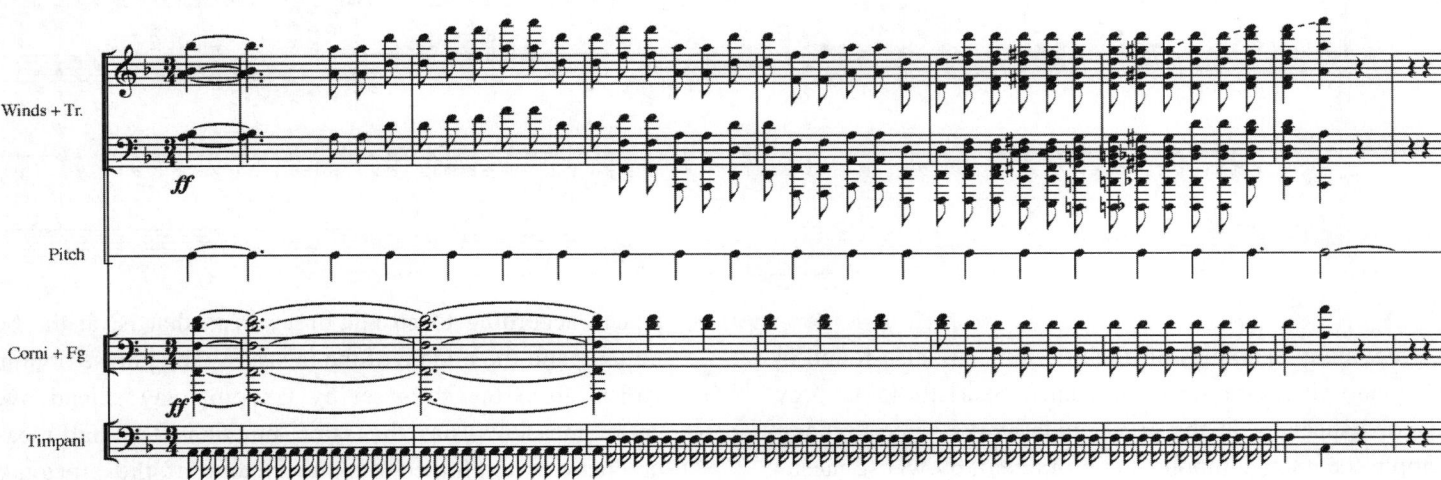

Music history is full of melodies of this type, which are also known as chains of sighs or suspensions or else successive sound anticipations. How immense an expressive potential can be gained from that is shown by the beginning of the Finale of Beethoven's Ninth Symphony (Ex. 1-008).

these pitch quarter notes are complementary to the repetitions of D-F and in that sense syncopated. From m. 5 on, the horns, too, play only eighths so that the syncopations are stripped of their metric opposite. That Beethoven has applied not only tonal, dynamic, articulatory, melodic[13] and harmonic[14] but also subtle rhythmic means

[12] See Marius Schneider, »Klagelieder des Volkes in der Kunstmusik der italienischen Ars nova,« *AmI* 33 (1961), pp. 162-168.

[13] The principal voice is built mainly from the steps of the D minor triad and describes a wave form, which at the end frays

can also be seen from the fact that the change of the timpani from A2 to D3 occurs on the second sixteenth of the 3/4 measure, that is, on the lightest possible part of the beat.

The component »Pitch« takes effect most frequently in tone repetitions. But there are also cases of an indirect melodic movement that produce a rhythm of their own. Indirect melodic trains like these are known as »core melodies« or as outer and inner voices in cases of inherent polyphony. The phenomenon is most frequently recognizable in sequences and figurations.

Ex. 1-009   Vivaldi, *La Primavera*, m. 47

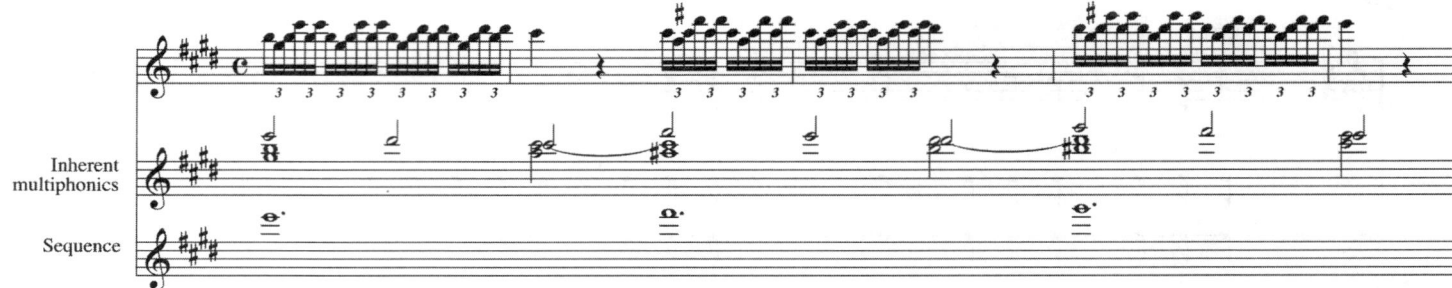

In the violin part of Antonio Vivaldi's Concerto op. 8, no.1 – to cite an arbitrarily chosen example (Ex. 1-009) – figure play and sequence technique can be described conjointly. The upper part (E-D♯-C♯ etc.) of the *arpeggio*-chords forms a rhythm of ♩, the stepwise progression of the sequence (E—F♯—G♯) proceeds in 𝅝.

bizarre rhythmic worlds are constructed despite often uniformly fast basic values (e.g., pervasive ♪).

In Chopin's Etude op. 25, no. 12, for example, the wave-like arpeggios in both hands consist from beginning to end entirely of sixteenth and are at the same time interspersed with tone repetitions, which, since never more than two sixteenths are repeated, enrich the rhythm with eighths (Ex. 1-010). As one can see in the respective line in the example, these eighths values stand »aslant« to the beat, so that durations of three or else five sixteenths elapse between the recurring pitch eighths. At the same time, the harmonically quite simple piece is carried by inner parts that, owing to the arpeggio structure, are realized simultaneously in several octave registers. If one telescopes these inherent parts into a single octave, the result is a quiet rhythm of wholes, which unfolds over a pedal point of twelve measures (four of them are included in the example). Chopin also sets dynamic accents (>), which are

Ex. 1-010   Chopin, *Etudes* Op. 25 No. 12 (schema)

A great many examples of pitch rhythms are also found in the piano literature from Domenico Scarlatti to György Ligeti. Especially in the great etude works since Frédéric Chopin the pitch component is prominent, by whose means

placed according to an alla-breve beat, that is, at the beginning and the middle of the measure. The phrase rhythm, which, from the slurs set by Chopin, may extend over entire measures, has the same function. The half-measuredness is reinforced by the contour of the arpeggios. However, the rhythms derived from pitch (tone repetitions and inner parts) are not superseded by these additional component rhythms but are superadded and intensify the rhythmic complexity of the piece.[15]

out in countermotion. It is worth noting that the initial melodic interval B♭—a returns at the end in the basses.

[14] The initial four-three chord of VI[7] is followed by a kind of Phrygian cadence to the dominant, in which the recitative sets in (Ex. 1-008a):

[15] I might add that in mm. 15f. (and elsewhere) partially ternary sequences occur, which are produced by a different distribution of the repetition: ♪♪♪ ♪♪ ♪♪ ♪♪♪ ♪♪ ♪♪ ♪ . Eytan Agmon (cf. footnote 7) gets the same results, though he divides not by tone repetitions but by ternary micro-phrases (66ff.).

Ex. 1-011   Brahms, String Quartet A-Minor, 4th mov., mm. 13-23 (extract)

A last example may be cited from the String Quartet in A minor by Johannes Brahms. The Finale is written in a fast 3/4 time, which is pervaded by hemiolas and time and again »attacked« by binary rhythms (frequently at points of harmonic changes). In its first repetition, in which the main voice is heard in the viola, the twelve-bar main subject of the movement, subdivided into 3+3+2+4 measures, displays an unexpected counter-rhythm in the first violins, which is brought about by the tone repetitions (Ex. 1-011). The pitch rhythm thus generated in violin I, which has to play a typical accompaniment figure composed almost entirely of strung-out triadic notes (in A minor, G major, D minor), has a fully contrapuntal quality. The duration of these pitches is determined by repeated eighths: 3+3+3+3+ 6+6+6+6+4+4+4+3+1+2+3+1+2+3+1+1+1+1+1+1 ♪. Initially, the three-eighths sequences in the violin stand against the ♩ (♩. ♪) of the viola, and both rhythms stand in hemiolic relation to the effective 3/4 beat (2 ♩. : 3 ♩, 2 ♩. : 3 ♩). The three-eighths units in the violin relate to the corresponding groupings in the main part, where they are underlined by the drawing of the beams, noticeable especially in the concluding measures.

Diastematy

The component »Diastematy« refers to the up and down of melodic lines. There are no melodic lines without contours and therefore no melodies without diastematic rhythms. Whether striking or inconspicuous, they always co-determine the rhythm of a linear form. For every change in interval direction has the character of an event, and it is events that articulate the temporal continuum.

A passage from the Larghetto of Beethoven's Second Symphony furnishes a prime example (Ex. 1-012). The passage consists almost entirely of sixteenths. From the middle of m. 68, chains of thirds in contrary motion structure the time lapse and by means of crest and keel notes (upper and lower directional changes) introduce rhythms not otherwise noted. These diastematic rhythms consist of quarter notes (4 ♪ = ♪ ♪. = ♩). Clearly hemiolic in structure (three ♩ spread over two 3/8 measures), they keep the eight measures rhythmically ambiguous. By means of a crescendo from *p* to *ff* and further intensifications such as octave transpositions and accumulations and additional instruments (not represented in the example) Beethoven directs the hemiolically ordered chains of sixteenths toward the destination chord in the tonic of A major (m. 73), from which then the transition to the subsidiary theme takes its departure.

Numerous passages in older music work analogously. The effect of diastematic rhythms is observable especially in sequences. An example from the *Virgin's Vespers* by Claudio Monteverdi (Ex. 1-13) shows the crest and keel tones both in the ternary version (*tuae...*) and in the immediately following binary one (*genuite*) in simple isometry and, as in the Beethoven passage, in contrary motion. Thus the rhythm of the component »Sound« (♪♪♪♪ and ♪♪♪♪ respectively) is overlaid by that of the component »Diastematy«) (♩. ♩. and ♩ ♩).

Ex. 1-012 Beethoven, 2nd Symphony, 2nd mov. mm. 66-73 (schematic)

Ex. 1-013
Monteverdi, *Vesperae beatae Mariae Virginis*, Psalm 109

Ex. 1-014 Bach, Prelude BWV 926 (selections)

Diastematic rhythms are objectively given. Whether they are always intended by the composer, so that the crest and keel notes are deliberately included in the rhythmic shaping, is another matter. In the case of J. S. Bach's Little Preludium in D minor, however, cogent reasons for the setting of the crest notes can be adduced. The piece (Ex.1-014) is largely based on broken triads. The latter having both a harmonic and a melodic effect, the two functions initiate different rhythms. The harmonic rhythm is very sedate, while that of the component »Sound« is fast (mostly ♪ in the right hand). To these rhythmic results the durations of the crest and keel notes have to be added, i.e., the »diastematic« rhythms. I have confined myself to the crest notes in the analysis of these three brief segments because they make the facts of the case sufficiently clear. As one can see especially in the beamless transcription, the downward-moving triads have their highest note at first on the »off-beat«, the second or fifth eighth of the measures. In the last bars, on the other hand, they fall into the first or fourth eighth, thus marking the *One* or the middle of the measure. The intervals between the crest notes constitute three eighths, so that the diastematic rhythm is ♩. ♩. ♩. ♩., both at the start of the piece, in the middle and also in the epilogue. I regard the fact that the composer sometimes offsets the triadic motif in the beat and sometimes makes it coincide with it as a clear indication that the component »Diastematy« was purposefully included by him for the enrichment of the rhythmics. The offset position of the crest notes in fact explains in part the appeal of this generally very modest prelude. One should also mention that the diastematic rhythm in the last four measures displays a hemiolic structure (3:2) in relation to the meter. Hemiolic conditions also have their effect at the beginning, though the sequences of ♩. there are offset in the 3/4 beat.

This line of argumentation can also be applied to an example from the 16th century (Ex. 1-015) – two successive passages from the four-part *Missa »Da pacem«* by Noël Bauldeweyn (formerly ascribed to Josquin de Prez). The tenor voice derives from the Credo, its first section starts with »confiteor«, its second with »et expecto«. For both sections the measure is prolatio perfecta and tempus imperfectum, which corresponds to 3/4 in the transcription.

Ex. 1-015   Bauldeweyn (ex Josquin), *Missa »Da pacem«*, Credo

The first section is relatively free in its diastematic rhythm, whereas the second constitutes a complex, strictly developed sequence. The segments of the sequence consist of three falling thirds that are offset downward by seconds. The repetition of the sequence is likewise stepped downward by seconds, so that an overriding structural voice of D-C-B♭-A results. After four segments, there follows a repetition, which, however, is abbreviated and cadenced off early.

The chains of thirds have a diastematic quality that is quite audible. The rhythm resulting from it could be a very simple one if all of the notes in the thirds had the same value, e.g., quarter notes (semibreves), which would result in the rhythm ♩ ♩ ♩ . Instead, however, Bauldeweyn starts every segment of the sequence with a half-note (brevis), resulting in a diastematic rhythm becoming top-heavy (♩. ♩ ♩). If one observes only the crest notes (which is advisable, as the keel notes would yield only an exact copy of the crest-tone rhythm), a diastematic rhythm of 3+2+2 ♩ emerges, from which follows a rhythm of the sequence segments of 7+7+7+7 ♩, etc.

In the preceding section »Confiteor,« one looks in vain for a similarly constructive rhythm. Here, too, there are two phases, where after nine mensural units the beginning is repeated and concluded in a shortened form. The rhythm of the crest notes is at first free (6+4+3+4+4+3 ♩) but in the consequent is well adjusted to the prolatio perfecta (9+6+6+6 ♩).

It will be agreed that the melodic contour in the sequence passage is rhythmically relevant. Without the rhythmic articulation by phrases of seven, which is multiplied by the imitative four-part setting,[16] this elaborated concluding passage would lose its individual character. It follows from this that the component »Diastematy« must on principle be a regular aspect of any rhythm analysis. Its inclusion must not be restricted to striking or somehow spectacular instances.[17]

In all of the examples hitherto cited, the components involved were more or less attuned to each other, that is, they largely coincided. If the components are linked heterometrically, the result can be complicated rhythmic conditions. A passage from Beethoven's Fifth Symphony presents a good example of this: the celebrated transition from the third to the fourth movement. The basis of this most mysterious passage (apart from the timpani solo already

Ex. 1-016
Beethoven, 5th Symphony, 3rd mov.
motivic separation

cited) is a motif that is split off from the main theme (Ex. 1-016). It consists of three notes with a clear rhythmic-metric shape (the quarter notes are on the light, the halves on the heavy beat) and a succinct contour (a falling second followed by a likewise falling large interval). During the splitting-off process, Beethoven preserves the metrical situation in the measure by means of two quarter-note rests. At m. 350, however, he brings the three-note motif without rests in constant repetition, keeping the iambic rhythm ♩♩ ♩ ♩ ♩♩ etc. Some of the notes thereby acquire the value of a half-note instead of the original quarter value and vice versa. Since the diastamatics of the motif remains the same, the modified values of the motif tones impact the durations of the repetition units, resulting in durational sequences with crest notes of four or five quarter notes (ex. 1-017). The unusual rhythmic structure of the transitional melody is probably one of the reasons for the subtle tension of the entire passage, a tension which then discharges in the exulting triumphal march in C major, with which the Finale commences.[18]

The diastematic rhythms are less striking in runs, arpeggios, coloraturas, etc. in short, virtuoso figures, which pervade the music of the centuries. Even mechanical finger exercises, which exist for all instruments, are rhythmically structured by their diastematic contour, yet without it acquiring any aesthetic function.[19]

---

[16] In the four-part setting the tenor is followed by two voices linked by thirds 1 ♩ later, another 2 ♩ later. All of the voices share the same melody and rhythm.

[17] See my essay »Zur Rhythmik in den Messen Josquins (und Bauldeweyns). Isometrische Phrasenwiederholungen und ihr Verhältnis zur mensuralen Ordnung«, in *Musikkulturgeschichte heute. Historische Musikwissenschaft an der Universität Hamburg*, ed. F. Geiger (Hamburger Jahrbuch für Musikwissenschaft, 26) (Frankfurt/M.: Lang, 2009), 9-29.

[18] Closely analogous is the shape of a passage in the »Scherzando vivace« of Beethoven's E♭ major string quartet op. 127. The metrically fitted main motif is, from m. 36 b on, repeated in close succession, resulting in a diastematic rhythm of 5+7+5+7+5+7 ♪ etc.

[19] In my essay »Rhythmische Komplexität in der Instrumentalmusik von Johannes Brahms« (in *Johannes Brahms. Quellen – Text – Rezeption – Interpretation*, ed. F. Krummacher / M. Struck (Munich, 1999), 143-158) I also attended to Brahms's *51 Übungen* for piano.

Ex. 1-017   Beethoven, 5th Symphony, 3rd mov., mm. 350ff.

Where such virtuoso passages are integrated into ambitious works, however, a closer look at the intricate rhythmic work by means of the component »Diastematy« is worth the effort. As an exemplary instance of many such passages, we may cite a spot in Brahms's Second Piano Concerto. In its first movement in B♭ major, which has the form of a concerto sonata movement, the large formal sections, orchestra exposition, development, recapitulation and coda, are each introduced by the same horn cantilena with which, unaccompanied, the entire work commences. Brahms has given special attention to the return of the theme at the start of the recapitulation (m. 260 with upbeat). Similarly to the first movement of Felix Mendelssohn's Violin Concerto, he has the soloist prepare for, and accompany, the main subject by means of figure work. It is this passage we want to look at.

Ex. 1-018
Brahms, 2nd Piano Concerto, 1st mov., mm. 260-261, Piano

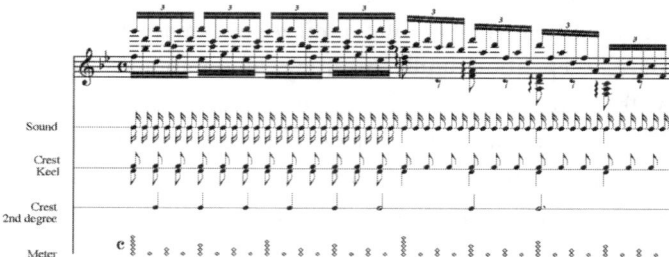

Ex. 1-018 reproduces the passages in the piano underneath which the horn plays the theme. We hear **pp** and *dolce* chords in various resolutions, as the 4/4 time is resolved into sixteenth sextuplets. While the second measure of the example has the units linked by the beams into groups of six to coinciding with the beats of the meter, the first measure displays binary groupings resulting from crest and keel tones. Thus the chains of sixteenths in the right hand are structured by eighths (stems pointing up) because of their constant directional reversals. These eighths relate like triplets to the eighths of the 4/4 meter.

The situation is analogous in the left hand, as here the keel notes (stems pointing down) form the triplet-like eighths rhythm, which, as already in the basic component »Sound«, merges into simple quarter notes in the second measure. What is interesting here is that the upper voice formed by the crest notes in the right hand (B♭6-C7-B♭6-C7 etc.) has a, quite audible, contour of its own, whose crest notes – as it were a second-tier diastematic – each combine two triplet eighths, or else four sextuplet sixteenths, into quarter notes. These quarter notes, too, have a ratio of 3:2 to the quarter notes of the meter.

The onset of the recapitulation is preceded by four measures in which the figuration already starts. It sets in with an F6 and slowly climbs up to a C7. This ascent is accompanied by a harmonic movement that begins with a secondary dominant A major and reaches the tonic of B♭ major via the F-major seventh chord. In Ex. 1-019, this harmonic path is indicated together with the associated steps. The component »Harmony« thus included is relevant also for the results of the diastematic rhythm analysis. For if one telescopes both hands into a single octave, it becomes apparent that the seconds in the (indirect) upper voice (e.g., in m. 256 the notes F6-E6-F6-E6 etc.) always have a function as a suspension. The suspension notes are, moreover, reinforced by their character as crest notes. Besides, the harmonic rhythm creates durations of its own, which do not always coincide with the crest tone changes. For example, the darkening from A major to A minor begins, in my view, already with the last triplet eighth of m. 256, although the C5 sounds only on the *One* of the following measure.

Altogether one can say that the interaction of components – crest notes of the first and second degree, harmonic changes plus suspensions – produces a highly filigree-like rhythmic texture that seems to suspend the metric order. At work is a process of effacing the temporal markers, whose function is to make unpredictable the point at which the main subject returns. That its onset is anticipated by a quarter note (before m. 260) and this early, extended note (the B♭ in the horn) is already harmonized with the tonic is one of the exceptional subtleties of Brahms's rhythm and his compositional art generally.

In the 20th century, too, the component »Diastematy« is often used for the building of rhythms. A good example is furnished by György Ligeti in his piece *Continuum*. This virtuosic character piece for two-manual harpsichord rests on a single durational value of strokes, written in eighth notes under an endless beam. Their length depends on the tempo. Ligeti notes: »The correct tempo is attained if the piece (minus the concluding pause) lasts less than four minutes.« That amounts to more than 816 ♪ per minute.

Ex. 1-019   mm. 256-261, Piano (both hands) and entrance of Horn (Recapitulation)

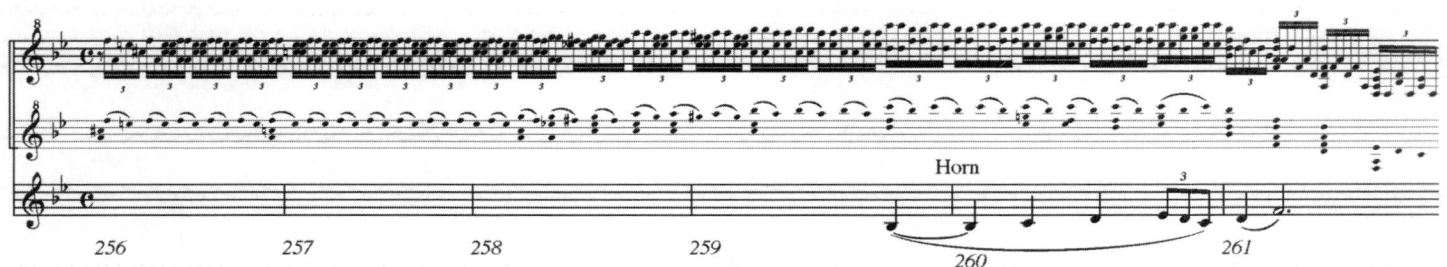

Rhythms in *Continuum* result almost entirely from the contours that are produced by the contra-rotating scale play, which makes for micro-phrases of up to five ♪ duration, which, moreover, are offset in the two hands (ex. 1-020). A notation in a simplified form, i.e., without stems and without accidentals, shows the rhythmic figure play of the two hands. Since the hands move on two different manuals, the pitches actually played can be identical without any mutual hindrance (e.g., at the beginning: r. hand: B♭4-G4, l. hand: G4-B♭4). When tone figures interact in this way, melodic contours are obscured. What is clearly visible in Ex. 1-020 is not at all audible. Only when the figurations drift apart upwards and downwards are the diastematic rhythms noticeable. Thus the 8-♪ figures, which from the fifth accolade are slightly staggered, emerge in fact as a phase with an isometric rhythm. Other formations, e.g., the proportions 4:5, 5:5, 5:4, 5:5, 4:5, 3:5, 3:4, 3:3, 2:3 and 2:2 may be registered as rhythmic iridescence or as rhythmic arrest (2:2).

The component »Diastematy« is nevertheless the most important means of temporal articulation in this otherwise monochronic piece. To the performer, the diastematic rhythms will become far more apparent in the movement of the hands and fingers than they do to the listener. One can speak downright of a haptic rhythmics here that does not fully reveal itself in the listening event. That additional rhythms, not cited here, come to the fore in the process of the superimposition of pitch levels I have shown in detail else where.[20]

---

[20] Peter Petersen, »›Jede zeitliche Folge von Tönen, Klängen musikalischen Gestalten‹ hat Rhythmus. Über die Rhythmik in Ligetis Cembalostück *Continuum*,« internet publication at http://www.saitenspiel.org (2009).

Ex. 1-020   Ligeti, *Continuum* (Diastematics)

Articulation

The component »Articulation« comprises those tone forms that are based on irrational values (save notes with articulation rests). Notes marked legato, tenuto or staccato can be classified as long, medium or short, but the notation does not signal anything more precise. However, the intervals between notes such qualified are measurable, so that, as with the component »Sound«, it is the temporal

Ex. 1-021 Beethoven, 4th Symphony, 3rd mov., Beginning

gaps that are again relevant rather than the actual durations. The beginning of the third movement of Beethoven's Fourth Symphony provides a prime example (Ex. 1-021). Here the shortened notes are followed by eighth or quarter rests or else furnished with a staccato point. The unabridged notes are linked by legato slurs, whereby the starting points of the slurs add up to a rhythm of their own. The slurs spanning two or more bars could also be regarded as phrasing slurs; in the present instance, however, they are bound to be articulation slurs owing to the fast tempo. The articulation reinforces the rhythm produced by the melodic contour, that is, a binary subdivision in the framework of a very fast 3/4 time. This dance-like beginning with its alternation of thrice two and twice three units of quarter notes reminds me of the Czech folk dance Furiant.

To exemplify articulation rhythms in *slow* movements we may take Beethoven's *Pastoral* Symphony (Ex. 1-022). The *Andante* makes use of legato slurs, pizzicatos, articulation rests and grace-notes. The principal feature of the melody-carrying voice in the first violins (Ex. 1-023) are the long rests between the briefly sounding notes. Brevity of sound, however, does not necessarily mean brevity of effectiveness. Since the seemingly isolated notes of the main voice certainly add up to a coherent melody – one comprising seven measures and, besides, consisting of long notes without rests from the fifth measure on (not included in the example) – the short notes can be taken only as effectively *long* up to the next note. The fact that they are to be played as relatively short (quasi tenuto) is the specific ›event‹. The durations between these ›tenuto notes‹ result in an articulation rhythm that is not identical with the component rhythm »Sound.«

The remaining component rhythms of the main voice also diverge from the rhythms of the tone entries (»Sound«). Thus the tone repetitions (»Pitch«) produce slight modifications of the basic rhythm. Another articulation rhythm, one resulting from the legato slurs (»Legato«), likewise has a certain life of its own, while the mordent-like grace-notes that have to be added to the first beat of measure 3, as a singular event reinforce other rhythms.

Ex. 1-022 Beethoven, 6th Symphony, 2nd mov., Beginning

Ex. 1-023

At the beginning, the merely dabbed-in melody notes of the first violins are reinforced by the horns (see ex. 1-022), which hold the violins' B♭4 for the whole measure, though they diverge from m. 3 on. The rhythm of the horns, in turn, is matched by that of the pizzicati in the double basses, which have a durational validity of whole measures.

The accompaniment, too, is carefully articulated and thus rhythmically independent (see the extract of the 2nd violins in Ex. 1-023). The sound entries have constant ♪ (»Sound«). This uniform pulsation is matched by the persistently repeated down-beat-iambic »Pitch« rhythm (| ♪♩ ♪♩ ♪♩ ♪♩ |). Not quite as smooth in its effect is the rhythm of the »Legato« articulation (| ♩♩ ♩ ♩ ♪ |). Evidently these diverging component rhythms in the accompaniment correspond to the unpredictability of the fluid element (»Szene am Bach«).

Ex. 1-024 Bartholomeus de Bononia, *Vince con lena* (segment)

Articulation marks as compositionally relevant components emerged only in the 18th century. A special exception, however, are the pauses in hoquetus passages in the Middle Ages. They seem to have served the purpose of securing a brief execution of notes. The hoquetus (as a compositional technique) is based on the complementary alternation of short individual notes or note groups in diverse voices. Ex. 1-024 shows a hoqueting passage from a motet of Bartholomeus de Bononia, in which the eighth rests (minima) in the treble and countertenor practically take on the function of staccato points.[21]

---

[21] Facsimile and transcription in Willi Apel, *The Notation of Polyphonic Music. 900-1600*, (Cambridge MA, [4]1953), 143 and appendix No. 20.

From the early 18th century on, there are, for example in Arcangelo Corelli, legato slurs (Ex. 1-025) and trills (Ex. 1-026) with articulative function. In the »Pastoral« of his Christmas Concerto, the legato bows support the 12/8 meter, while in the »Allemande« of his op. 6, no. 9, trills emphasize the middle of the 4/4 measures.

Ex. 1-025
Corelli, *Pastorale* from Concerto op. 6 No. 8, Beginning

Ex. 1-026
Corelli, *Allemande* from Concerto op. 6 No. 9 (segment)

Gradually additional types of articulation came into being, like staccato, portato, marcato, tenuto, indicated sometimes graphically, sometimes in writing. Instrument-specific forms of play, such as pizzicato, spiccato, gettato, ricochet, downbow, upbow etc. became compositionally and therefore rhythmically relevant. The palette was still further enlarged in the 19th and 20th centuries, especially since the percussion instruments introduced altogether new forms of articulation. The borders to other components are blurred. Thus there would be good reason to treat the large group of decorations separately, and from time to time this will indeed happen. The component »Dynamics« likewise overlaps with »Articulation« but deserves to be presented separately, as degrees of loudness often relate to differently shaded passages and do not concern merely the form of individual tones or sounds.

Ex. 1-027 Schumann, *Davidsbündler* No. 12, Beginning

A few additional examples may serve to illustrate the enormous variety of forms of articulation; they could easily be multiplied. The beginning of one of Robert Schumann's *Davidsbündlertänze* (ex. 1-027) effects, in a characteristic manner, a polka rhythm, whose principal stresses underline the meter of the 2/4 time. This can be noticed both in the keel (l. h.) and the crest notes (r. h.) as well as in the harmonic progression. Staccati further sharpen the rhythm. Two dynamic accents (>) underscore the mid-measure. The legato slurs start in both hands on the second eighth of both the first and the third measure, thereby producing a syncopated effect. The thirty-seconds I regard as written-out appoggiaturas, which as slides to the $C\sharp5$ and $C\sharp6$ on the second beat lend a strong emphasis to these notes. The pedal, which is to be released before the middle of the measure, acts in the rhythm of double beats and reinforces the phrasal structure of the upper voice, while the bass traverses the entire four-measure passage without any mid-caesura.

Ex. 1-028 Mahler, 9th Symphony, 2nd mov., mm. 18f., Vl. 2

In the example from Gustav Mahler's Ninth Symphony (ex. 1-028), literally each and every note is freighted with articulation marks. The chorus of the second violins is here meant to simulate Alpine fiddles, which play a »leisurely landler« »ponderously« (instructions in the score). The main stresses of the first four measures gain added weight by a number of means – double tone length, legato, trills, and *sf* – which reinforce each other. All of the eighths have staccato points, but some are further qualified – by drastic double-down-bows. The affected eighths are thereby offset against the meter. In sum, the component »Articulation« here serves the creation of a rhythmic character (robust peasant landler).

Ex. 1-029 Webern, Konzert op. 24, 1st mov., Beginning

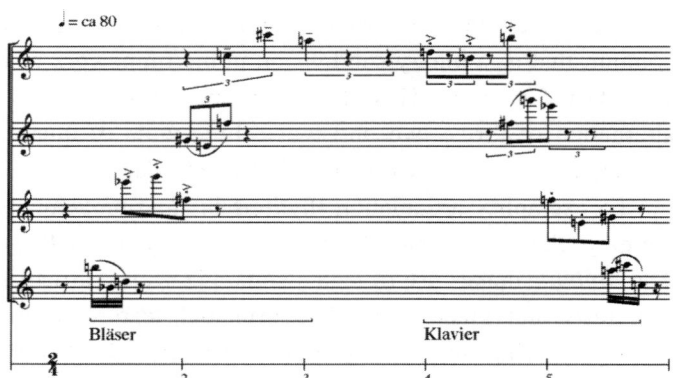

In his Concerto for Nine Instruments (ex. 1-029), Anton Webern picks up Mahler's art of differentiation. The work is composed in strict dodecaphonic technique. It starts with two runs through the series: P_{11} (winds) and RI_0 (piano). The four trichords of the series, which are also in a double inverse relation to each other (in minor seconds: –1+4/+4– 1/–4+1/ +1–4) are set off by articulatory sound markings. There are slurs (four times), staccato accents (twice), tenuto strokes and staccato points (one each). These four types of articulation, however, are coordinated with the trichords, not serially, but freely. The rhythmic expansion and contraction processes (duplet ♪ → ♪ and triplet ♪ → ♩ and back) are not brought into line with the articulation. Inasmuch, however, as the type of articulation of the telescoped trichords changes with every new onset, their distinguishableness in the musical event is ensured. The changing durations of the individual notes here virtually result in a notated rubato effect. Webern formalized the component »Articulation,« but applied it independently of the serial structure. It was only the serialism of the 1950's that produced full-scale series consisting of »tone forms« (Stockhausen).

The final example (Ex. 1-030) is designed to show that even the articulation type *vibrato* can be of a subtle rhythmic significance. Béla Bartók opens the slow movement of his Fourth String Quartet with a successively building diatonic hexachord cluster (G♯-F♯-E-C♯-B-A) in the rhythm of slow ♩. It is to be played without vibrato. Once the hexachord is complete, it is started up anew, sounding once more for the duration of a ♩. *senza vibrato*. On the following moved-up quarter note, however, the four string players start to vibrate – a new sound form is introduced, which, despite the throughout prevailing *pp* intonation, comes in as a special event and therefore can also claim to carry rhythmic weight.

Ex. 1-030   Bartók, 4th String Quartet, 3rd mov., Beginning

Dynamics

Volume is first specified in the 17th century, mainly in Italian scores. Most common were terms or their abbreviations, such as piano (*p*), or forte (*f*) for passages or notes to be played soft or loud, the latter also at times pointed as sforzato (*sf*) or forte piano (*fp*). As a graphic symbol for volume accents the sign > also came into being. During a certain phase in musical evolution the bar line could also function as a dynamic accent sign, whereby the special quality of a measure's first beat did not necessarily depend on the degree of loudness (e.g. in instruments like the harpsichord or the organ).

As a prime example of dynamically generated rhythms we may cite a passage from the first movement of Beethoven's Second Symphony (Ex. 1-031), where the difference between volume levels and volume accents can be readily demonstrated. The dominant dynamic specifications lead to a differentiation according to levels of 2+2+2+2+6+x measures, while the volume accents (predominantly *sf*) have the effect of syncopes, because they rest consistently on the weak beats and thus are equal to tie-overs. One should note that the *sf* accents coincide with harmonic accents, whose acuity results from the sustained A underneath the diminished dominant seventh chord D-F-G♯-B. The effect of the foreshortened dynamic accent rhythm is heightened by the fact that the brass and the timpani exactly duplicate the accentual sequences.

Elementary facts in musical practice may correspond to the dynamic contrasts. Thus the distribution into precentor and chorus known from medieval times (e.g., in responsorial song) is also connected to a dynamic change. Volume accents result likewise from prosodic stresses, at least

Ex. 1-031   Beethoven, 2nd Symphony, 1st mov., mm. 112-127 (segment)

Ex. 1-032   Monteverdi, *Vesperae beatae Mariae Virginis*, »Audi coelum«, mm. 23 ff.

where the language is an accentual one. Dynamic shadings may also be linked to spatial notions: what lies close sounds loud, what is distant sounds low – and vice versa.

A special case is the play with echoes in instrumental and vocal music. The following example derives from Claudio Monteverdi's *Vesperae Beatae Mariae Virginis*, which was published in 1610 (Ex. 1-032). The performer of the echo voice sings the repetitions *piano*, so that the alteration of forte and piano creates a rhythm composed of 4+4+3+3+ 3+3+x ♩ . That in turn creates a discrepancy with the tempus imperfectum of 4/2. (It should be mentioned in passing that the answering echoes in this case are linguistically inexact, in fact ›tendentious.‹ What the tenor introduces as mária (object plural of mare = sea) comes back in the echo as María – not altogether without effect, as the passing pick-up of the Virgin's name by the tenor shows.)

as dynamically emphasized staccati. They, as well as the *fz* accents, all fall on the third beat in the measure, thus emphasizing the upbeat. Haydn proceeds systematically here. At first two such accents coincide, then three and then four (1 wedge, 3 *fz*).

Mozart, in the first of his six quartets dedicated to Haydn, goes yet one step further. In the Menuet of the G major Quartet K. 387 (Ex. 1-035), dynamic specifications attain thematic status. A chromatic melodic line, well fitted into the overall 3/4 time, is given a binary structure by means of the alternation of *p* and *f*. In the main voice, introduced by the second violin and after four measures switching to the viola, an isometric sequence of ♩ is thus generated, indicated by the alternating *p* and *f* signs. Interestingly, however, the imitating voices, offset by one measure, likewise cling to the sequence *p-f-p-f*, so that each time a *f* and a *p* coincide. Here volume markings are part of the thematic substance.

Ex. 1-033   Corelli, Concerto op. 6 No. 6, Vivace, mm. 137-148

Such echo effects were frequently used in 18th century concerto practice. An example by Corelli picked at random will confirm this (Ex. 1-033). *f* and *p* here alternate in strict isometry, without an accompanying change between concertino and ripieno.

The component »Dynamics« acquired steadily increasing prominence in the 18th century, with a concomitant relevance to *rhythmic* structures and processes. The Allegretto-Scherzo of Haydn's 6th string quartet from op. 33 shows that dynamic specifications could already be an indispensable part of a composition at that time (Ex. 1-034). According to the Haydn complete edition, there are both

Ex. 1-034
Haydn, Strimg Quartet D-Major, Hob. III, 42, 3rd mov. Beginning

Ex. 1-035
Mozart, String Quartet G Major K. 387, 2nd mov., mm. 65-70

marcato and *fz* markings here. The wedges can be regarded

Ex. 1-036
Schumann, *Davidsbündler* No. 13, Beginning (extract)

Often dynamic accents support rhythms that are already pre-established on the basis of other components. Especially in compositions for instruments with short sounds like the piano, where sustained sounds are simulated by arpeggios and other techniques, these procedures are common practice. Here melody notes that are embedded in broken chords or passage figurations are given emphasis by longer note values, sometimes also by larger note heads (e.g., in Chopin's Piano Etude op. 25 no. 1). Such tones may be additionally furnished with accent markings. The situation is different in the example from Schumann's *Davidsbündler* (Ex. 1-036). Here the dynamic accents (>, *sf*) serve to interpret the basic rhythm all of the notes differently. This rhythm (♪ ♪ ♩) is accentuated now on the first, now on the third note. It is also placed now on the downbeat, now on the upbeat. The result is a kind of contrariety of voices that brings out the announced character of the piece – *wild und lustig* (wild and jolly).

In the 20th century, dynamics matured into a self-evident core component. Differentiation continually increased, all the way to speculative attempts to arrange twelve volume levels into series and to treat them accordingly. I will limit myself to three examples from different stylistic directions.

I begin with a detail from a scene in Richard Strauss's one-act music drama *Electra* of 1909 (Ex. 1-037). A single but spectacular accent in the orchestra irrupts into an even structure – like a shock, set off by Electra. Initially alone, Electra vows to her dead father Agamemnon that the day of revenge will soon come. The great monologic scene (no. 35-64) starts with an invocation of the dead king in gloomy minor and culminates in the major-bright vision of the triumphal dance with which the opera will end. At the start and at first stares at Chrysothemis as if wakening from a dream.«

The composition would not be Richard Strauss's if the chord did not have a specific make-up marking it as a musico-dramatic semanteme. This »leitchord« thus introduced at the very beginning of the opera can be characterized as »Electra's hatred.« It is a five-note chord consisting of the notes E-B-D♭4-F4-A♭4 (cf. no. 1_6). Several components contribute to the effect of this chord: it contrasts with its environment dynamically (*pp – ff – pp*), it is pointed in its articulation (♪, + ♪>), it has a color all its own (wood – brass – wood/strings) and it is harmonically strained (D♭ major over E-B).

Admittedly this multi-accent is an isolated event, which as such does not generate a rhythm of its own. In connection with the rhythm of the entire phrase, however, the accent naturally does have a specific function – such as that of a stressed upbeat in the transition from the 6/4 to the faster 2/2 measure. The dynamic accents in the woodwinds and strings (*sfz*) two measures later are likewise sensed primarily as solitary events, which here have a syncopating effect. They emphasize the F minor triads in the following sixteenths, which appear in quick alternation with the longer B minor triads.[22]

Ex. 1-037 Strauss, *Elektra*, fig. 64 (analytical particello in C)

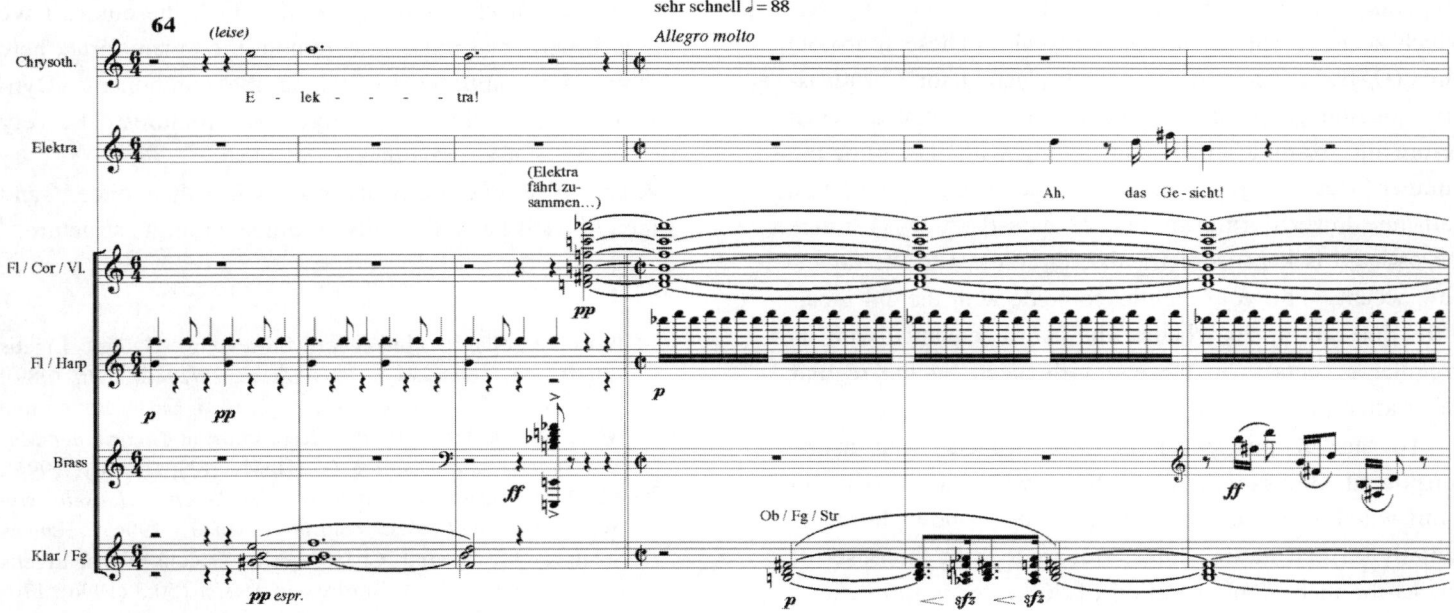

moment when the rejoicing fades, Electra's sister Chrysothemis enters (no. 64) and softly calls Electra's name. Fitted into the dance rhythm (6/4 meter) but placed on a weak beat, a brief, sharp *ff* chord is heard in the brasses. The accompanying stage direction reads: »Electra gives a

[22] Additionally, a sustained chord in the flutes, horns and violins is sounded parallel to the punctuation motif, in which B minor and F minor are both present – a bitonal constellation that was already introduced at the beginning of the opera (no. 1_{2-3}).

Ex. 1-038 Strawinsky, *Sacre du Printemps*, 3 mm. before fig. 13 (extract)

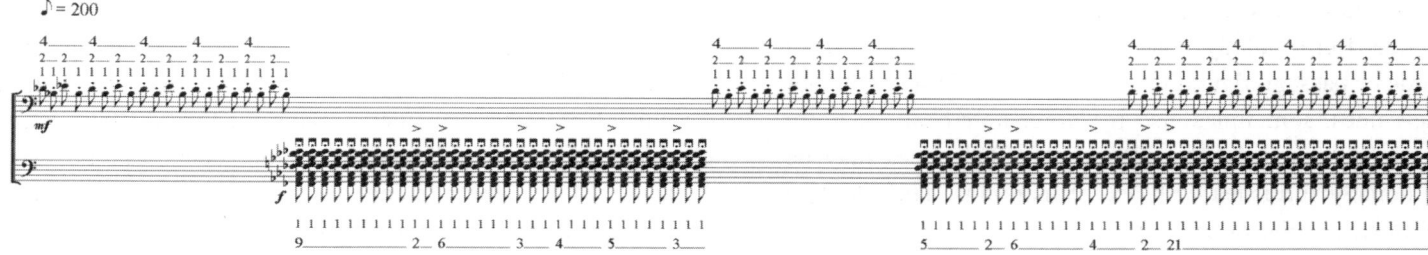

In Stravinsky's *Le Sacre du Printemps* (1913), elementary body and rhythm experiences are evoked that even today can produce an arousal in the audience. The beginning of the »Danse des Adolescentes« (Ex. 1-038) is notorious. The chords played by the strings throughout with down-bow generate an elementary force. The dark chord, which sounds dissonant despite its saturation with thirds, is repeated unchanged 32 times and, after an interruption, another forty times, always in close succession and with a hard spring, as every down-bow that starts close to the heel of the bow generates small articulation rests between the chords. It is again a matter of isolated events, as it were, of 32 and then 40 one-eight-measures. Only thanks to the dynamic accents, which are to be executed by all the strings, a rhythmic structure (9+2+6+3+4+5+3 ♪) enters into this amorphous, utterly equalized succession of pulses. Though noted in 2/4 meter, it would be a mistake to make the meter audible. The irregular succession of accents – the first chords regularly have no > but nonetheless carry the natural onset accent – is supposed to have the arbitrary effect of lightning bolts or whiplashes on the listener (or dancer).

These massive rows of impulses, to be sure, do not occur by themselves. They are surrounded by harmless preparatory and intermittent melodic pendulum figures, which seem to spread an apparent calm. These four-note units (D♭-B♭-E♭-B♭) create an ostinato lasting for 179 measures, beginning seven bars before no. 13 (that is, even before the example cited) and ending with the following number (»Jeu du rapt« no. 37), with the ostinato sounding a half-tone lower during the last 22 bars (C-A-D-A). Since the ostinato is kept isometrically, in contrast to the down-bow accents – the four eighths coincide with the 2/4 meter – the question arises whether the chord sequence with its irregular accents is in the end influenced by the regular meter after all.

To answer this question, several facts need to be considered. One should note to begin with that the ostinato motif which starts already before the down-bow chords, is actually written in sixteenths. But since with the onset of no. 13 the metronome notation of 50 switches from ♩ to ♪, the previous ♪ correspond to the present ♪ and are therefore, for the sake of clarity, also written as ♪ in Ex. 1-038. The ostinato motif thus adapted to the chordal sequence in its note values is assimilated to the chords also in its pitches: its three highest notes, E♭4, D♭4 and B♭3 are identical with the top notes of the chords. In terms of the actual sound, however, there are extreme contrasts. The melodic ostinato is relatively soft: it is played ***mf*** pizzicato by the first violins, then staccato by the English horns. Against these tender individual tones stands the drumming of the remaining fifty or so strings. On top of that, the accentuated notes are ›underlined‹ by eight horns, which likewise reproduce the seven-note sound (the F♭ is doubled) but now in the rhythm of the dynamic accents.

The suddenly irrupting power sound of the chords obliterates the preceding 2/4 pizzicato pendulum from memory. As in a film cut, a quiet rural scene abruptly changes into a wild, barbaric ritual. To be sure, the pentatonic-like pendulum (the intervals minor third, fourth and major second form a pentatonic figure) and the down-bow chords stand against each other separately only at the beginning, whereas they overlap the second time. Although the pendulum is only barely heard behind the chord strokes, its periodic measure does produce a certain effect during the remaining 21 chords, of which none is accentuated any longer, and hints at the 2/4 meter.

A final example dates from 1985, the year in which the first volume of György Ligeti's *Études pour piano* appeared. In contrast to the harpsichord piece *Continuum* discussed in the section on »Diastematy,« with which the etudes have the fast, perpetual pulse in common, the »pianoforte« here enables the composer to include the component »Dynamics« in the formation of rhythmic structures. The very first etude, »Désordre,« makes that clear.

This piece has been analyzed more than once,[23] and Ligeti himself has repeatedly commented on its structure.[24]

---

[23] Denys Bouliane, »Imaginäre Bewegung. György Ligetis ›Études pour piano,‹« in *MusikTexte*, 28/29 (March, 1989): 73-84; Hartmuth Kinzler, »György Ligeti. Entscheidung und Automatik in der 1er Étude ›Désordre,‹« in *Theorie der Musik. Analyse und Deutung* (= HJbMw 13), (Laaber, 1995), 337-372; Constantin Floros, *György Ligeti – Jenseits von Avantgarde und Postmoderne* (Vienna, 1996); Hannes Schütz, »Musik und Chaostheorie. Gedanken zu Ligetis Klavieretude Nr. 1 – Désordre,« in *Musica*, 50:3 (1996): 170-176; Richard Steinitz, *György Ligeti. Music of the Imagination* (London, 2003); Jörg Rothkamm, »Ordnung in der Unordnung. Neues zur Polyrhythmik in György Ligetis Klavieretüde Désordre,« in *Musiktheorie*, 19:1 (2004), 63-68.

[24] György Ligeti, »Études pour piano – Premier livre,« introduction in the accompanying text to the CD from Wergo (WER 60134-50) (Mainz 1987); reprinted in *György Ligeti.*

Ex. 1-039   Ligeti, *Désordre*, Beginning (schematic*)

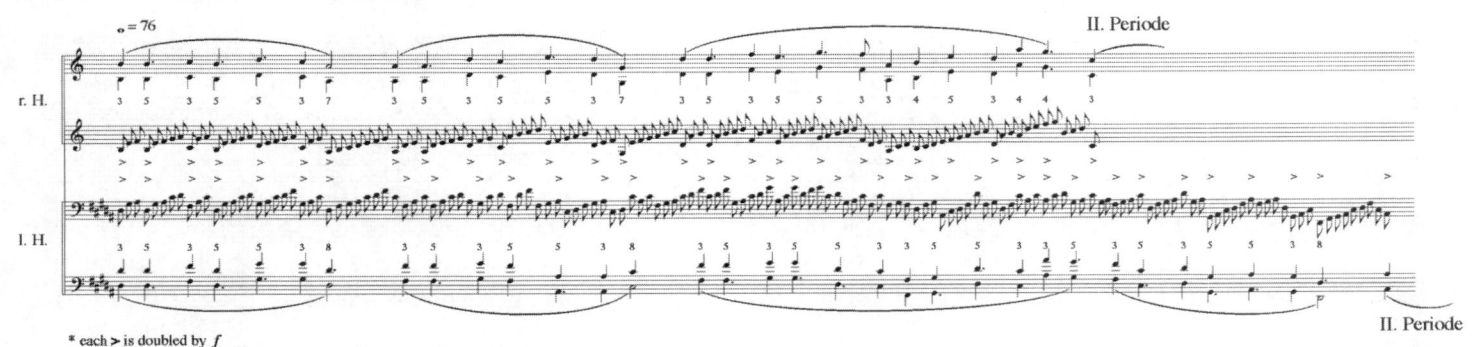

* each > is doubled by *f*

The accent sequences marked by Ligeti throughout with both > and *f* bring out two melodies that can be clearly differentiated on the ground of their modal basis (Ex. 1-039). These melodies – one tripartite, the other quadripartite – are sequenced in both hands: the tripartite upper one step-by-step upward, the quadripartite lower one in double steps downward. They are of different length and thus increasingly offset against each other.

Bouliane has noted that the rhythm of the melodies corresponds to the »aksak« wide-spread on the Balkans, in Turkey and in the Arab-speaking regions: the division of 8/8 units into 3+5, 5+3 or else 8 ♪ with reference to the intervals between the onsets of the accent tones. Since these distributions involve a heterometric proportion between a shorter and a longer value, the aksak can be effective even if the rhythms of the accent melodies are compressed, while the durational classes »short« and »long« remain recognizable, e.g., 3+5+3+4+5+2+7 ♪ in the right hand of the fourth period, or 1+3+1+2+2+1+3 ♪ in the left hand of the fourth period. As readily observable in Ex. 1-040 a and b, it is such compressions that determine the form of the etude, whose first part reduces the length of he periods (103→30 ♪ in the right hand, 144→47 ♪ in the left),[25] while the second part stretches them (a constant 144 ♪ in the right hand, 146→158 ♪ in the left).[26] Before the start of the recapitulation, that is, at the return to the original aksak meter, the composition reaches its climax, marked by top volume (*fff*) and the widest octave distance between the voices (A0-F8). Corresponding to this is the final note (C6 in both hands), preceded again by a crescendo to *fff* and more.

The highly conflicting melodies in counter-motion in the right and left hand are highlighted not only by the dynamic *f* accents but also by octave doublings – later, in the second part, also by chords of two to four notes. Strangely, even inexplicably, the durations of two notes that are combined into octaves diverge from each other. The pianist has to perform the upper note of the octave as ♩., the simultaneously struck lower one only as ♩ – and vice versa (e.g., immediately at the beginning). Quite apart from the fact that given the mad tempo of the etude (608 ♪ per minute) such a subtle difference is simply unrealizable, this difference would also be without effect in view of the briefly sounding piano tone. In his 1957 polemic against Pierre Boulez, Ligeti himself has stated that something the listener cannot hear can also not be taken as intended by the artist.[27] As it happens, the etude »Désordre« is dedicated to Pierre Boulez. A piece entitled »Disorder« is intended for the champion (at the time) of the strictest »order« in all musical processes! I cannot but suspect an ironic connotation in this and surmise that the absurdly subtle differences in the note values within the octave dyads of *Désordre* have to be understood in that way. Hartmuth Kinzler seems to be of the same opinion, since in formulating the title of his essay as »Entscheidung und Automatik in der 1er Étude ›Désordre‹« he clearly alludes to Ligeti's early reckoning with the method of serial composition.[28]

Ex. 1-040 a+b is designed to illustrate the rhythmically relevant interior structuring of the two accent melodies. At the lowest structural level (see numbers referring to ♪) the contour results in melodic elements of two, three or four notes. At the intermediate level (phrasing arcs), the recurring rhythms result in partial phrases. The entire periods, finally, comprise three and four partial phrases respectively. If one classifies the dynamic durational values into »short« and »long«, a ›self-similarity‹ between element and phrase sequences: »short« – »short« – »long« determines the structure of the partial phrases as well as that of the entire period. This is true only of the right hand, however. For the theme of the left hand, one should assume what might be called ›other-similarity.‹ I see a similarity, e.g., to the Bulgarian Dance No. 3 in Béla Bartók's piano work *Mikrokosmos*, and, beyond that generally, to the type of the quadripartite (Hungarian) peasant song.[29]

Gesammelte Schriften, ed. M. Lichtenfeld, 2 vols. (Publications of the Paul Sacher Stiftung 10) (Mainz, 2007), 290-293.

[25] The low value refers to the seventh member of the sequence (A♯), the following period in the left hand overlaps into the second part of the etude and consequently has at first very short note values but then abruptly longer ones again.

[26] The final periods are incomplete in both hands: the piece breaks off at the highest pitch and volume.

[27] György Ligeti, »Pierre Boulez. Entscheidung und Automatik in der Structure I a,« *die reihe*, 4 (Vienna 1958): 33-63. Also in *György Ligeti. Gesammelte Schriften*, ed. Monika Lichtenfeld, 2 vols. (Publications of the Paul Sacher Stiftung 10) (Mainz 2007), 1:426 f.

[28] See footnote 23.

[29] See Ex. 1-156 on p. 94.

38   Rhythms and components

Ex. 1-040a   Ligeti, *Désordre*, Sequence of the r.-h.-melody (schematic)

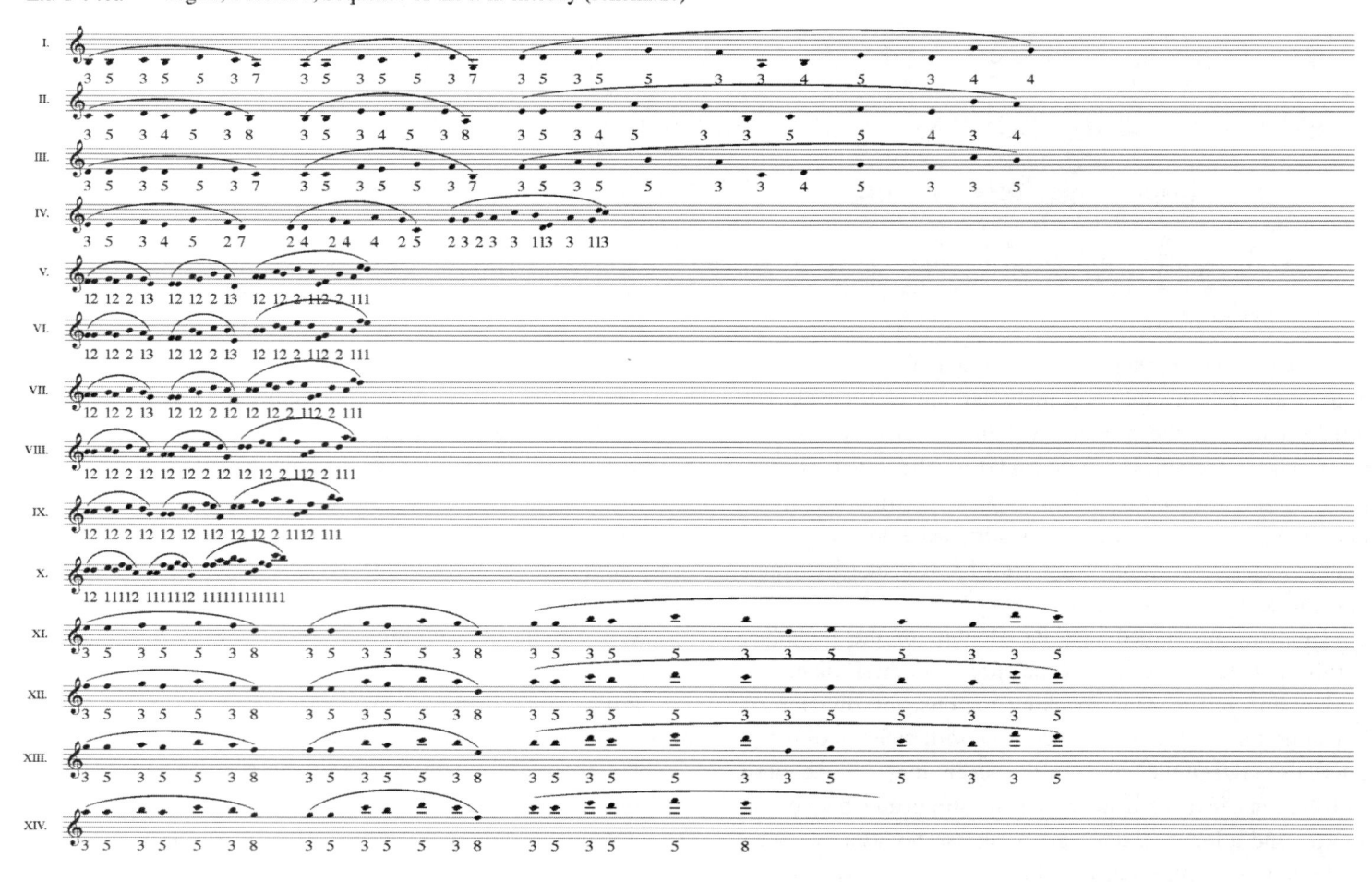

Ex. 1-040b   Ligeti, *Désordre*, Sequence of the l.-h.-melody (schematic)

Ex. 1-041   Beethoven, 3rd Symphony, 3rd mov., mm. 127-133

Timbre

In line with instrumental music's gaining its independences since the 17th century, the component »Timbre« has acquired increasing significance, for composition generally and therefore also for rhythm. Since the contrast between bright and dark is part of the color phenomenon, the octave registers should be dealt with under the aspect of »Timbre« as well. I am therefore beginning with two examples, the first of which shows the rhythmic relevance of instrumental timbres (Ex. 1-041), while the second illustrates the bright-dark contrast (Ex. 1-042).

In the Scherzo of Beethoven's ›Eroica‹ (Ex. 1-041), the alternation between winds and strings marks a uniform 6-♩ unit. The component »Timbre« is decisive here inasmuch as most of the other components are not involved. All the notes are quarter notes, which, additionally, are all staccato and marked *p*. The »Diastematy« consists of a binary melodic pendulum in contrary motion, which derives from the main theme of the movement and structures the two-bar units hemiolically. The »Harmony« supports this binary structure by a constant alternation between dominant and tonic (later also subdominant and tonic), but initially also underscores the changes in timbre by a sequence of fifth drops, though that stops after four double measures. At the end, winds and strings unite in a mixed color and thus put a stop to a sixteen-bar phrase whose rhythmic design is very simple but which demonstrates the rhythmic significance of »Timbre« exceptionally clearly. The bright/dark contrast plays a minimal role in this example, since both the winds and the strings act almost exclusively in the fifth and sixth octave.

The situation differs in the second example (Ex. 1-042): the transition to the recapitulation in the first movement of Beethoven's Fourth Symphony. This section is played by the strings alone, grounded only by a tympani roll on B♭. The slide-like sixteenth figures, which are derived from the head part of the main theme (F-G-A-B♭, or else D-E♭-F and B♭-C-D), set in the fourth octave in m. 312 and are immediately repeated echo-like in the fifth octave. Thus commences a steady alternation between low and high, which produces a separate rhythm of octave registers. This rhythm consists at first of whole notes or else double wholes (if one notes the octave pairs), then of halves (or else wholes). At m. 325 the octave registers coincide into simultaneity (forming, as it were a zero distance) whereby the octave-register rhythm, which here would have had the durational value of quarters (or else halves) merges into the reiterating slide figures. In line with the crescendo, lower octaves join in as well. Shortly before the onset of the reprise, we hear a fourfold octave unison (enlarged by thirds).

Of chief importance in this connection, however, is the fact that the beginning of the intensification process is propped mainly on a shrinking octave-register rhythm. The latter can be observed all the more clearly as the harmonics remains constant in this passage; if one considers the fourth-sixth chord over F2-F3 in m. 311, the altogether 32 measures with their elaboration of the B♭ major triad seem to have a latent dominant function, in spite of the timpani roll on B♭3.

The change in octave registers is one of the basic phenomena in music. The bright-dark contrast connected with it came much earlier into use as a time-structuring component than the written documents indicate. It must be presumed, for example, in organ music, where change in registers is one of the core properties of instrument construction – whether a simple switching between octave levels by means of 16-ft, 8-ft or 4-ft registers or as addition of specific pipe levels each with their own sound color (analogously also with other keyboard instruments). Obligatory stops, to be sure, are known only since the 17th century.

Ex. 1-042   Beethoven, 4th Symphony, 1st mov., mm. 311-333 (schematic)

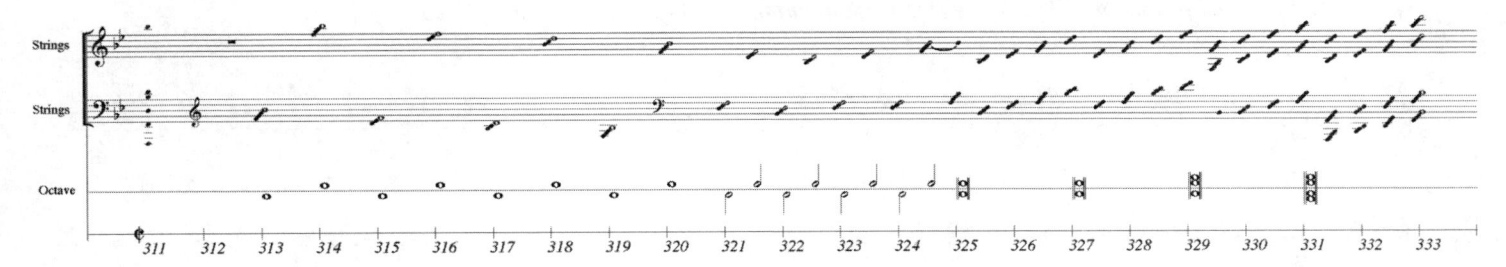

Ex. 1-043 Schütz, *Geistlich Chor=Music* No. 16, Beginning

The bright-dark contrast is no less elementary in vocal music, since the tessitura of women or boys is an octave higher than that of men. Here, too, therefore, one can presume an age-old practice of register change, e.g., in responsorial and antiphonal singing. It is manifest in the motets and masses as well as the coro-spezzati technique of the 16th and 17th century.

I cite one of many possible examples from a collection of motets by Heinrich Schütz from the year 1648 (Ex. 1-043). Here a six-part mixed chorus is divided initially into a high and a low chorus. A first line, »Ein Kind ist uns geboren« (A child is born to us), which comprises 12 ♩, is presented by the high chorus and answered by the low one. This double four-beat measure applies basically also to the second line, »Ein Sohn ist uns gegeben« (A son is given to us), which likewise consists of twice 12 ♩ – admittedly expanded by a final note, which introduces the new, now alla-breve tempo. The division into pairs of four beats, however, no longer depends on a bright-dark contrast but is due to a motivic repetition, as can be seen from the voices of tenor 1 and bass.

Schütz, to be sure, does not leave it at that simple structure. He does not wait for the end of the repetition of the first line by the low chorus, but starts the high chorus on a new line and a new motif. Thus the caesura after the eighth measure in the low chorus is covered up and the movement carried over from nearly homophone song into a polyphone motet.

The bright-dark contrast, of course, has played and continues to play a role in evolved instrumental music as well. Two examples from different genres shall illustrate this.

In the slow movement of Mozart's String Quintet in G minor, K. 516, bright-dark contrasts crop up in close succession already in the main theme. The 13-measure, internally expanded period, which corresponds to the form of the theme, consists of a four-bar head phrase and two consequents, of which the first occupies six, the second three measures (Ex. 1-044). While the first consequent remains rhythmically open, the second ends in an authentic cadence in E♭ major.

The four-eighths motif introduced in m. 5 sets the pattern for the following bright-dark play, which only at the end of each consequent issues into a homogeneous, full-sounding five-part string statement. Before that, the motif's repetitions are combined with octave shifts, three times by two octaves, the fourth time even lowered tentatively by three octaves. The passage is not least noteworthy and memorable because it begins monophonically. In m. 6, three-voiced high and low choruses then stand against each other, linked from m. 7 on by very subtle motivic deviations in the middle voices. Though the second consequent is full-voiced from the start, the octave shifts continue to be recognizable. The rhythm of bright-dark sequences consists of ♩, which coincide with the length of the four-eighths motif and its phrase marks.

Ex. 1-044 Mozart, String Quintet G Minor, 3rd mov., mm. 5-13

Ex. 1-045 Brahms, *Variations on a Theme by Robert Schumann* Op. 9, Var. No. 5, mm. 12-23

Our second example of rhythms produced by octave shifts is taken from Brahms. The Variations on a Theme of Robert Schumann op. 9, which Brahms wrote at the age of 21, have as their fifth part a very free, capriccio-like character variation, which Brahms accordingly signed »Kreisler.« Its idea is a play with octave shifts behind which the reference to the Schumann theme disappears almost entirely.

The passage excerpted in Ex. 1-045 shows the middle section of the variation, which, in line with the Schumann theme, is shaped as an a-b-a form. The notation diverges from the original in order to bring out what is actually heard: the purely piano playing notations and the key changes and bar-lines have been dissolved. In an additional line (»core melody«), I have indicated the progression of the tonal steps, disregarding the octave levels. Thus one can see, for example, that in the first measure the C♯ continues all the way through as a pitch class, while the actual tone levels (»pitches«) change every second sixteenth, in either simple or double octave leaps (C♯6 – C♯4 – C♯5). The C♯ thus appears in three degrees of brightness, whose change results in a four-eighths rhythm. From the *pianissimo leggero*, melodic pendulums consisting of thirds and larger intervals dominate, but the octave shifts continue to provide for sound shadings. After the crescendo, the recapitulation sets in *ff* and at the same time a new degree of brightness is introduced with C♯7, for the time being a culmination of the peak of the gamut.

The rhythm of this variation is, as always, determined by several components, but the octave colors in this case are preeminent. Aside from that, of course, the rhythm of the tone onsets (»Sound«), combined with paired repetitions (»Pitch«), is prominent, especially as few measures are without sixteenths. Quieter rhythms are audible in the background, as already the core voice shows: it is fitted into the prescribed 2/4 meter and several times forms double measures, though no regular periods as in the underlying Schumann theme (theme: 8+8+8 bars, variation V: 11+10+22 bars). In the end, all the components thus work together to support the »Allegro capriccioso« character intended by Brahms through rhythmical means.

Gradations of brightness and color go frequently hand in hand. This can be observed, inter alia, in the following examples, where the component »Timbre« in the narrower sense of instrumental colors is the decisive factor. As a first example, we may cite the opening of Richard Wagner's music drama *Tristan und Isolde*. The harmony of this epochal work has been rightly praised, as the ambiguity of the »Tristan chord« and the circling about the tonic of A minor in the Prelude constitute a decisive step toward the »crisis of Romantic harmony« (Ernst Kurth). What has been noted less to date is that the rhythmic-metric conditions, too, herald a new degree of freedom and that the instrumentation plays a part in that.

The first period of the orchestral Prelude, comprising 17 measures (Ex. 1-046), is based inter alia on the contrast in timbre between strings and wind instruments. Initially, the »Death motif« is given to the celli, the »Yearning motif« to the woodwinds. The places where strings and winds briefly overlap significantly introduce the »Tristan chord.« The change in timbre produces a kind of hyperrhythm, which divides the initial four-bar unit into 1 + 3 measures. At the eighth measure, where the cello – sooner than expected – recites an expanded variant of the »Death motif,« the regularity of the beginning disintegrates. The string cantilena is now played solo for a measure and a half, until the winds add their two-bar variant of the »Death motif,« now enriched in color by a French horn. The following echo play (or interplay of calls) shows the »Yearning motif« or its components in a different light and color: two bars of woodwinds in exact octave transposition, one bar of violins with »yearning« second (E♯-F♯) at a lower level, one measure of flute, oboe and clarinet at a high pitch, and finally two bars of the »Yearning motif« with full, mixed orchestral sound, whereby the strings (first and second violins) carry the main voice (an exchange in color and semantic function).

The rhythm resulting from the change in timbre coincides with the rhythm of the phrases, which can well be described in terms of the bar form: 4 measures of stollen, 3,5 measures of stollen, 9,5 measures of abgesang. That does not yet include the phenomenon of up- or downbeats so important for rhythm and meter. Strictly speaking, the celli occupy seven eighths before the winds set in downbeat in m. 2 – the third »Death motif« takes even ten eighths. That suggests that the cello cantilenas have altogether an upbeat function, so that only the second measure provides the first real metrical emphasis. The timbre rhythm cert-

Ex. 1-046   Wagner, *Tristan und Isolde*, Beginning

Ex. 1-047   Bruckner, 4th Symphony, 3rd mov., mm. 93-112

ainly says as much, as the durational values of the wind color are considerably longer than those of the string colors. The relation of monophony to polyphony, too, plays a important role. If the first entrance of the winds, therefore, marks a virtual first measure, the result would be the strikingly simple metrical form of 4 + 4 + 8 measures for the *Tristan*'s opening period.

Bruckner is known for the colorfulness of his orchestral sound. His instrumentation technique has with some justice been related to the register technique of the organ: an instrument, as we know, that Bruckner was a master of.

A section in the Scherzo of his Fourth Symphony will support this idea (Ex. 1-047). Here Bruckner works quasi with three registers, woodwinds, brasses and strings. The woodwinds function like a 4-ft stop in relation to the strings, which play in 8-ft, while the brasses are motivically independent. Only at the end of the passage – the beginning of the middle period of the main Scherzo part – the registers blend together. If one traces the entrances of the three different orchestral groups, one comes up with an extremely simple rhythm of eight double measures followed by two final double measures of mixed registers. Since the woodwinds are dependent on the strings as their echo voices, the result is two four-bar units in mm. 97-100 and 105-108. And since m. 101 comprises a harmonic sequence, an eight-bar unit likewise appears as a hypermeasure.

In the context of this chapter we must not overlook Arnold Schoenberg's orchestra piece entitled »Farben« (Colors), the central movement of the Five Pieces for Orchestra op. 16 (1909), which belong to Schoenberg's pre-dodecaphonic phase. With regard to »timbre«, the present description of the work takes off from Schoenberg's own statements in the score, where he says with regard to the beginning of the piece: »The change of chords should be so gentle that there is no emphasis at all on the entering instruments and the change is noticeable solely from the changing color.«

The analytical particello I have constructed of the first eleven measures of »Farben« (Ex. 1-048) is designed in such a way that the rhythmic process produced by the sound color within an almost static sound becomes clearly recognizable. Three levels have to be distinguished with regard to the rhythm of this opening phrase: the four-part

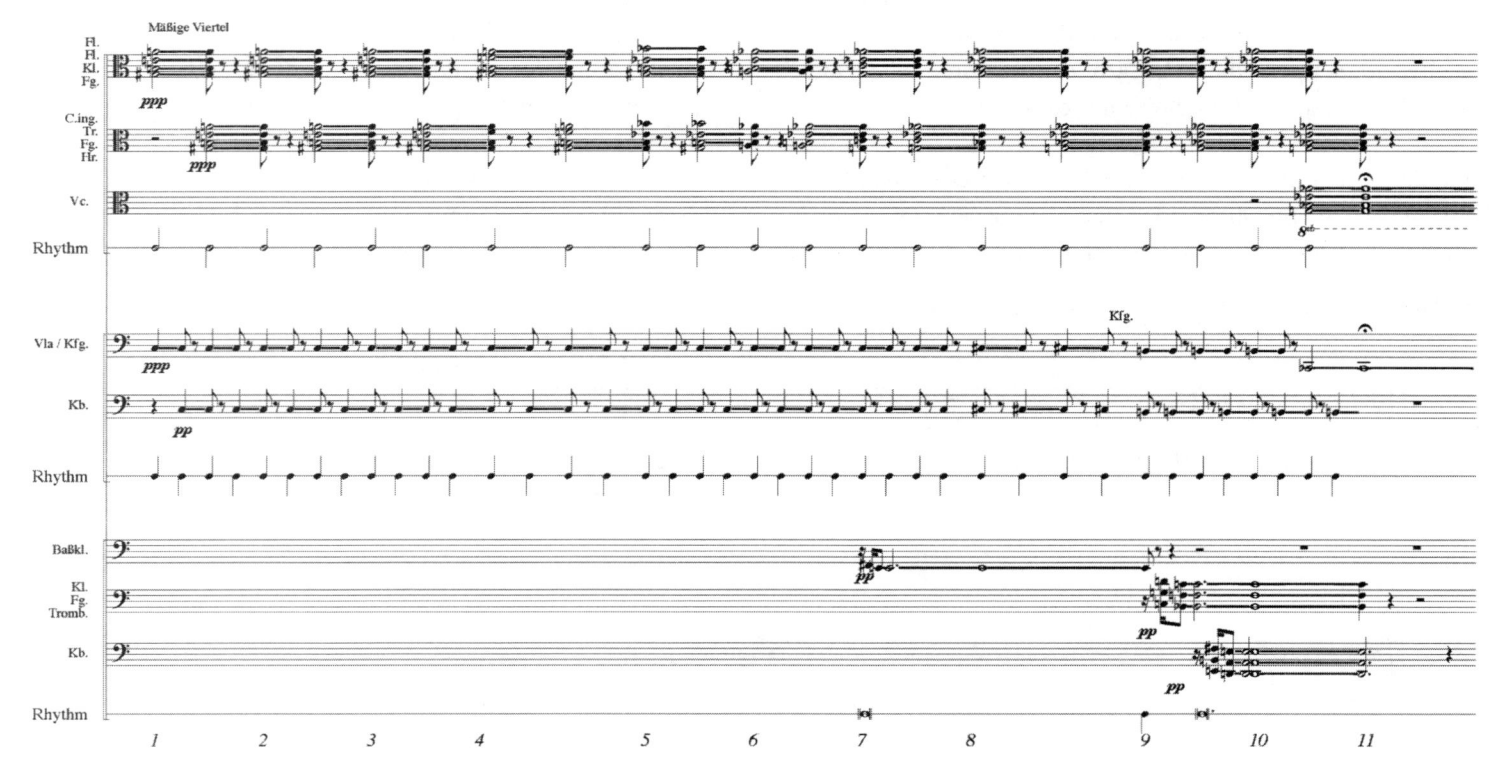

Ex. 1-048   Schoenberg, *Five Pieces for Orchester* op. 16, No. 3: »Farben«, Beginning

chord sequence in two groups of wind instruments (1st accolade); the voice of the viola (contrabassoon after m. 8) and double bass (2nd accolade); and the intonation of a whole-tone motif in three additional instrumental groups (3rd accolade).

The two wind quartets that, offset by a half, realize the four-part chord sequence differ little, though still audibly. Especially the two upper voices diverge in sound, owing to their different spectra of overtones: two flutes in the first chord, English horn and trumpet in the second. Since the two chords, overlapping by a ♪, are throughout identical in pitches, interval structure and octave position – even after they change at m. 4 – nuances of color are indeed the only phenomena producing any rhythmic division of the sustained chords. That rhythm consists exclusively of ♩. Only the final chord – because of the addition of four solo cellos, which play the chord an octave lower, complemented by a C♭ in the contrabassoon – has a longer duration signaled by a fermata.

The voice of viola and double bass, reproduced in the second accolade, is constructed analogously to the wind phrase, though diminished by half a durational value. Again two barely distinguishable sound colors succeed each other, which realize the always identical pitches (14 times C4, twice C♯4, four times B3) and produce an isometric rhythm consisting entirely of ♩. Where the range of the viola is exceeded, the contrabassoon takes over the voice (down to the B3 that, an octave lower, as a C♭2, grounds the final chord of the winds). Technically, though, the voice of viola and contrabassoon is part of the chords of the winds and also of the melodic fabric within them (in minor seconds: +1–2).

By means of the pulses of ♩ (winds) and ♩ (strings) a kind of meter is made audible, though it appears no stronger than the weak breathing of a living organism or the barely perceptible motion of a still water level. By comparison with that, the events at the third level are downright hectic. The entrance of the bass clarinet with the notes F♯2-E2 (3rd accolade) is preceded by a likewise descending whole tone step A3-G3 in the horn (1st accolade). The immediately following rhythm of sixteenths and tied eighths, which two bars later is repeated twice, now with a mixture-like tripled major-second drop, clearly dominates the rhythm derivable from the newly added sound colors. In sum, this orchestral piece of Schoenberg's, which has a fascination far exceeding the mere rhythmic factors, yet offers an example for the subtle dealings with the component »Timbre,« whose rhythms are nonetheless real and aesthetically effective.

I take a final example from the cycle entitled *Antifone* by Hans Werner Henze, which was completed and premiered in 1960. The orchestra here consists of 12 musicians but comprises over fifty instruments. Most of these instruments are assembled in four percussion groups, which in a semi-circle from right to left include the entire percussive sound palette from the low tamtam (4,1) to the very high triangle (1,1). Four tuned bright bell-sticks, which are in the four »batteries,« provide a bridge to the pedal timpani, while the latter are linked in turn to the four chromatic percussion instruments marimbaphone, vibraphone, celesta and piano, which are located in front of the semicircle like an inner ring. Four additional groups represent the class of held notes: a quartet of flutes in different registers, a saxophone quartet, a quartet of two trumpets and two trombones and finally eleven solo strings, which are also apt to join together in quartets, e.g., four violins for the high register or two violas and two celli for the low one.

	B	T	A	S
Tamtam				
	4,1	4,2	3,1	3,2
Cymbals (hanging)				
	4,3	3,3	1,1	1,2
Cow bell				
		2,3		
Crotales				
			1,3	
Triangel				
	1,4	1,3	1,2	1,1
Great drum				
	4,4			
Tomtom				
	3,1	3,2	2,4	2,5
Military drum				
		3,4		
Tambourine				
		3,5	2,6	

Immediately at the start of the first movement, one can hear how in a single crescendo gesture an acoustic curtain is opened from the right (ex. 1-049), which at the end of this part closes from the left in the same way. A total of 22 percussion instruments are involved at this point, each of which is struck only once, resulting in a chain of 22 durations results – a rhythm of sound colors. An arrangement by skin and metal instruments creates a specific sound palette (see table). The two aspects of »timbre,« color spectrum and brightness, are thus demonstrable here as well. The degrees of brightness are indicated by Henze with the terms bass (B), tenor (T), alto (A) and soprano (S). Added to that is a specification of the modes of attack by the use of different sticks or mallets: felt, leather and metal. The rhythm resulting from this opening sound color curtain (5+3+1+5+1+1+6+3+2+6+2+4+0,5+0,5+5+4+1+3+2+0,5+ 3,5+x ♪) is thus established like a theme and used repeatedly throughout the work.

Ex. 1-049, Henze, *Antifone*, Beginning

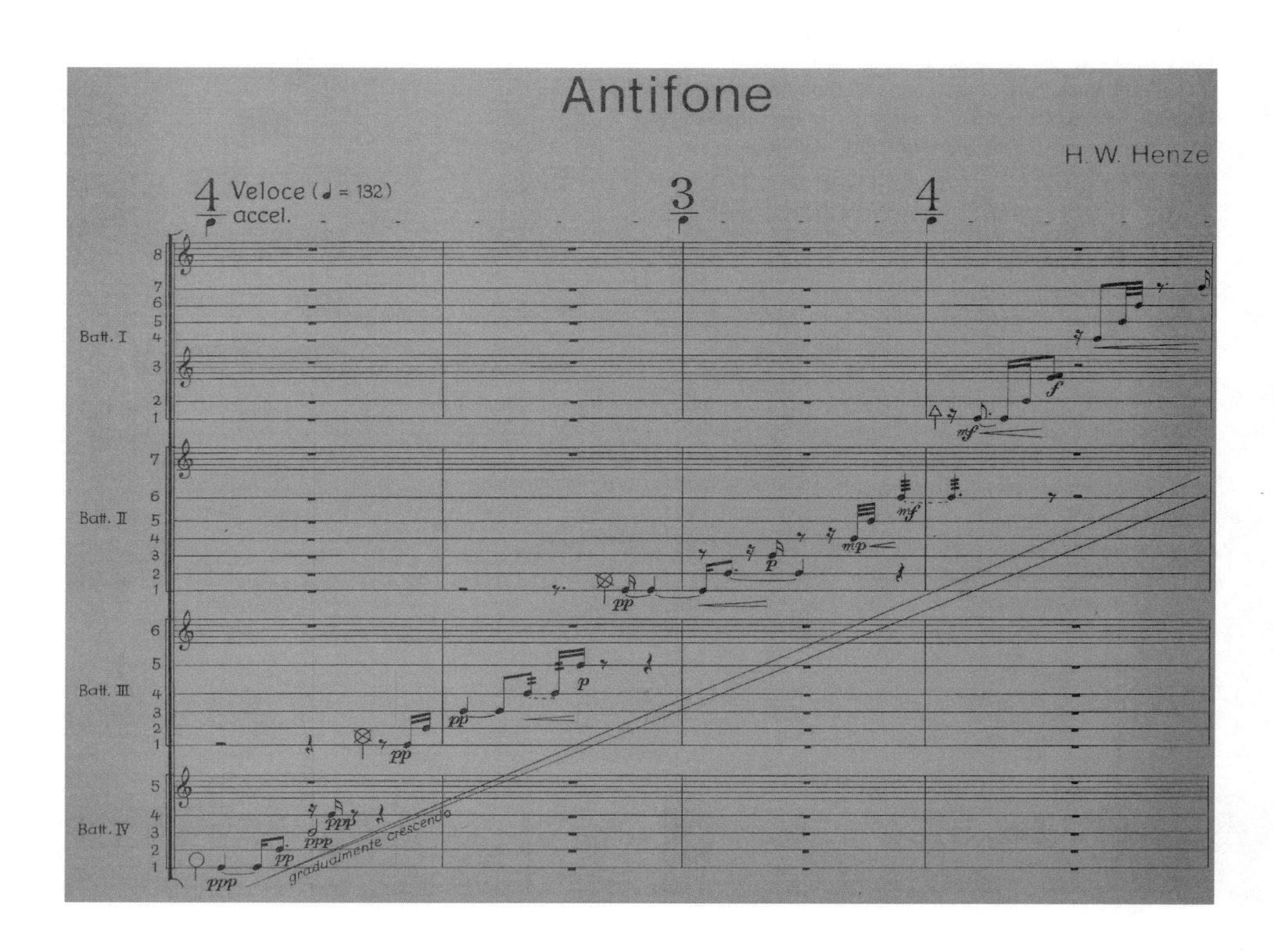

Ex. 1-050   Beethoven, 7th Symphony, 2nd mov., Beginning

Harmony

In his 1957 essay »Harmonic Rhythms in the Beethoven Symphonies,« Jan LaRue has drawn attention to Harmony as a component.[30] He noted that the changing of harmonic functions occurs at varying speeds and showed on numerous examples that Beethoven pursueded a strategy of materially shaping both phrases and entire periods or movements by means of these harmonic rhythms.

Taking off from LaRue's observations, I want to differentiate the aspect of harmony as a rhythms-building component further. Besides changes in harmonic function in relation to music of major-minor tonality, I want to consider also cadences and so-called non-chord tones (e.g., suspensions). We also need to ask if and how the harmony component is to be included in extended tonalities and atonal music.

As a first example, I take the beginning of the second movement of Beethoven's Seventh Symphony (Ex. 1-050), which LaRue did not analyze. The rhythm in this theme, as far as it is derived from the changes in harmonic function, is altogether more sedate than would be expected from the ceremoniously striding, constantly repeated rhythm produced by the strings. But one notices that the durations of the harmonic change become shorter and more irregular toward the end of the phrase.

Interestingly, the onset of the low strings, that is, the beginning of the actual theme, occurs, in harmonic terms, without impulse, for the wind chord preceding it as a kind of »curtain« (Hugo Riemann) already presents the A minor tonic, with which the theme commences. The fact that the first bar of the theme (m. 3) appears like the weaker half of a 4/4 or 2/2 measure is due not only to the prepositioned tonic (with a fifth in the bass) but also to the generally double-measured duration of the major harmonies. What contributes particularly to this is the dominant suspension six-four chord (m. 8) with its modulation to C major, which has to be taken together with the following measure.

This double-measure structure is slightly disrupted once: at the change from A major to A minor in m. 14. Here the harmonic rhythm brings a kind of syncopation to the fore, which is generated by the anticipation of the tonic chord before the measure. Both of the authentic cadences at the end of the two periods of the 16-bar theme – the repetition of the second phrase is not considered here – underline the regularity of the rhythm in this altogether rather unconflicted theme.

Numerous examples of the power of harmonic rhythm can be found in Mozart. In the Finale of the ›Jupiter‹ Symphony K. 551, which over large stretches is composed in fugato form, a sequence starts shortly after the beginning of the development section whose parts comprise of durations of seven or ten half-notes. These proportions, unusual for Mozart, derive their full effect partly from harmonic processes.

Ex. 1-051
Mozart, Symphony K. 551, 4th mov., m. 19ff.

The thematic basis of this sequence passage is an idea from the transitional portion of the exposition (Ex. 1-051). The later sequence begins with this short phrase in m. 172, whose position is defined through an upbeat in alla breve tempo. The entry, in turn, occurs on the second beat, though the latter has the effect of a down-beat, like a premature tonic, here in A minor. This A minor is prepared for by a regular cadence (Ex. 1-052), a preparation that is actually conceived in eight measures, of which at the end two entire measures would be reserved for the dominant.

Ex. 1-052   Mozart, Symphony K. 551, 4th mov., mm. 166-172

Instead, the A minor tonic disrupts prematurely the quiet flow of time, forcefully supported by the (subito) f and by the brasses, which play along in the initial rhythm of the transitional idea (♩. ♪♩). Given such massive means, one is inclined to take the phrase originally introduced with an

---

[30] Jan LaRue, »Harmonic Rhythms in the Beethoven Symphonies,« *The Music Review*, 18 (1957), 8-20. See my discussion of LaRue's essay in part 3 of this book.

Ex. 1-053

Mozart, Symphony K. 551, 4th mov., mm. 172-207

vs. quarter notes motion). A special role is played by the brass, which have been setting a strong signal ever since the beginning of the sequence (m. 172). They provide considerable disorientation in the ten-halves segments, because they sometimes support the beginning of a phrase (mm. 186, 196), at other times come in only for the second half (mm. 192, 202). Thus Mozart keeps the listeners from settling on the admittedly skewed (sevens and tens) but nevertheless isometric phrasal durations, as well as from ›forgetting‹ that they are in the middle of a development, which is meant to unfold in an unpredictable way.

In all multi-part music, the component »Harmony« is of great importance – as exemplified in the following by four additional cases from the 16th, 19th and 20th centuries.

In 1596, the composer Gesualdo di Venosa, famous for his effusive, always affect-laden harmonies, published a fourth volume of five-part madrigals. I quote the beginning of the Madrigal »Invan dunque, o crudele« (Ex. 1-054). The first line (»In vain, then, of cruel one«) is set polyphonically, the second one (»you want that my pain hide from your pride«) homophonically. With the direct address (»Vuoi«), the initially hesitant gesture suddenly becomes massive and fierce. The harmonic rhythm corresponds to that. While in the initial measures, which are filled with three and two halves (breves), it moves with the beats of the meter, it becomes wild and syncopated in the homophone passage – fully in accord with the emotional content of the text.

upbeat as a full measure, while Mozart subsequently does everything to reinforce that doubt. The transitional idea (which incidentally is always immediately imitated three times in half-note intervals) enters altogether eight times, and each time the entry is in the tonic (Ex. 1-053). In the seven half-note phrases with which the sequence begins this can be recognized, among other things, from the descending tetrachords (e.g., B♭-A-G-F).

In the schematic representation in Ex. 1-053, the short hooks in the staves do not mark bars but halves (♩). Thus one can readily count that the durations of the sequence segments consist of four times seven and three times ten ♩. The last segment is enlarged. It weaves a slightly polyphonic period in the winds, which, as before on the ten-halves phrases, quote the main theme of the movement (C-D-F-E♭), up to a length of 17 ♩; underneath this texture of voices cadencing in the dominant of E minor, the transitional idea is now heard again in the original up-beat position.

The phrases of seven and ten halves are marked off not exclusively by the harmonic component, but the latter nevertheless dominates. The minor/major sequence of fifths (A/A^7 – D/D^7 – G/G^7 – C/C^7 – F – C – G – D), downward at first and then upward, structures the time flow more than clearly. The entries of the sequence segments are reinforced by the components »Texture« (the incipient canon), »Timbre« (strings/ winds alternation) and »Sound« (eights

Franz Liszt's great Sonata in B minor appeared in 1854. The one-movement work of 760 measures is written in a double function form with integrated developments and variations. The original sonata pattern becomes audible i.a. in the second theme in (regular) D major, which is hymnic in character (»Grandioso«).

This theme, which forms a modulating repetitive period of 16 measures, is interesting also in terms of its harmonic rhythm (Ex. 1-055). The first phrase, which, after a Neapolitan turn (E♭ major) followed by the dominant (A major), progresses unexpectedly into the double dominant (E major) via chromatic modulation (m. 113), forms a very simple harmonic rhythm. All harmonic changes occur on the *One*, while at the end the dotted whole notes are divided into wholes and halves.

The consequent, by contrast, has a very complicated harmonic rhythm: it takes over both the harmony and the rhythm of the head of the theme, then ›hijacks‹ a split-off

Ex. 1-054   Gesualdo, *Madrigali* 4th book, »Invan dunque«, Beginning

Ex. 1-055   Liszt, Sonata, »Grandioso«-Theme, mm. 105-120 (schematic)

motif onto neighboring degrees (the A♭ major is an enharmonically altered III of E major with a raised third), and halts finally in a half-close in B minor (diminished seventh-ninth chord over A♯). The principle here is to pull the new harmonies along with the melody notes out in front of the metric stresses, in the quarter notes as well as the eighths. Thus, for example, the C♯ major of m. 114/115 has a value of twelve eighths (C♯ and D♭ major are here identical), which, however, are metrically by three eighths off the meter, which likewise extends over twelve eighths. In addition, values of fives and sevens are generated in this way.

However, rhythmic complexity is not Liszt's main concern here. Rather, the point of the procedure seems to be to give an added weight to the rhythm of the melody notes by reinforcing change in pitch by way of harmonic change. This, however, is precisely what is not wanted in the first phrase. Here the thematic melody unfolds as in a single move, borne up by throughout repeated chords in eighths (not visible in the Ex.). The melody on the basis of a 3/2 meter is as it were freely flowing, while in the second phrase it seems carefully articulated, even carved up. That goes hand in hand with the performance indication »poco calando« at the beginning of the second phrase, as well as with the *p diminuendo* of the theme's conclusion.

In 1910, the first volume of Claude Debussy's Préludes pour Piano appeared. No. 10 of the twelve character pieces, each of which has a title at the end in square brackets, is the Prélude »La Cathédrale engloutie« (The Sunken Cathedral). This calm, predominantly soft piece, which spans nearly the entire octave spectrum of the pianoforte, is based on a harmony determined less by individual sounds than by the tonal stock occurring in expanses of sound. The changes in the tonal stock over low-lying hollow fifths leave a trace that can be grasped as an large-scale harmonic rhythm.

The tone systems used are pentatonic, hexatonic and heptatonic. At three points, transpositions enter (in 4 ♯-steps and 2 ♭-steps respectively). While the melodies, which are mostly reinforced by octaves, are rhythmicized in quarter notes and halves, the accompaniment contributing also eighths and triplet eighths and occasional sixteenths, the harmonic rhythm progresses very slowly. A first, tonally uniform section is comprised of two measures of ♮-pentatonic over G, two measures of ♮-heptatonic over F and two measures ♮-pentatonic over E. The following section of seven measures with the hexatonic scale of E-G♯-A♯-B-C♯-D♯ adds a new harmonic highlight to the piece, whose duration can be experienced as a large rhythmic one. Then follows an interior recapitulation with two measures of ♮-hexatonic, followed by twice three measures of sound expanse of a special coloration: B-pentatonic with B-C♯-D♯-F♯-G♯ and E♭-hexatonic with E♭-F-G-B♭-C-D. These two groups of three measures, too, can be clearly differentiated as long durations because of their approximation to the major mode. At the end of our segment, there is a second inner recapitulation, where, however, all seven steps of the ♮-scale can be heard over the empty fifth G-D.

Ex. 1-057   (mm. 28-32)

These six measures, for the first time played *f*, not only refer back to the beginning but at the same time introduce an exceptional theme, which might symbolize a remembrance of the »cathedral« (which somewhat later is heard once more – now sunken – in *pp* »come un echo«). This theme, composed in strict parallel motion, is interesting in our context because it offers an example of a melody-dependent »unfree« harmony (Ex. 1-057). This should be regarded more as a ›multiplied unison‹ than a change of

Ex. 1-056   Debussy, »…La Cathédrale engloutie« from *Préludes* 1er livre, mm. 1-28 (sets of tones)

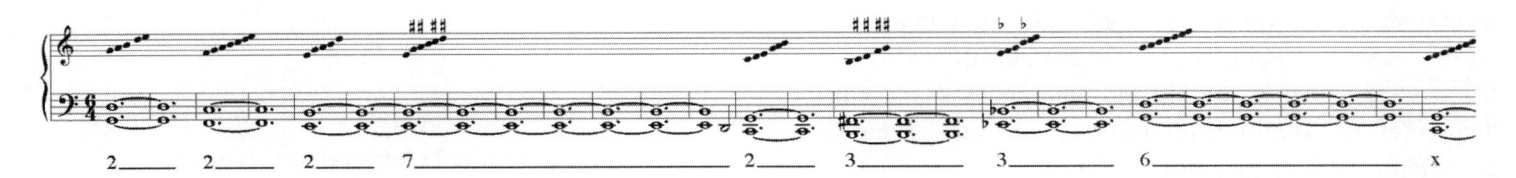

chords. More harmonic in nature is the ♮-heptatonic, which also determines the preceding section pan-tonally (a kind of ›white-keys harmony‹).

The concept of harmony has changed since the abandonment of the major-minor tonality as tonal frame of reference in favor of other, free or differently bound tone and interval constellations, as is already obvious in the music of Debussy. Basically, however, the phenomenon of simultaneous sounding notes in the processes of music remains; only the inner intervallic structure of resulting chords, and of simultaneous sounds generally, has become more differentiated – a music-historical development A. Schoenberg called the »emancipation of dissonance.«

Ex. 1-058 Ligeti, 2nd String Quartet, 2nd mov., Beginning

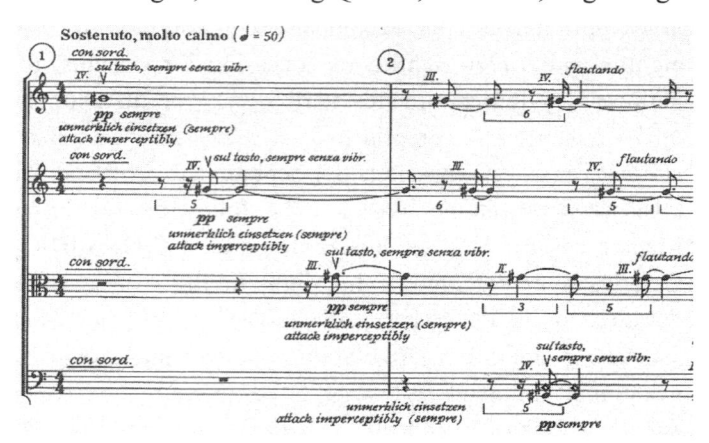

With a final example, the start of the second movement of György Ligeti's Second String Quartet of 1968, I am deliberately approaching to the limits of my analytic method. As Ex. 1-058 shows, the degree of differentiation in composition has grown considerably. Timbre, dynamics and disposition of durations are aimed at obliterating the borders between sound and non-sound (as well as between pitch and timbre). Every part is marked »enter imperceptibly.« At the same time, the entry points are prescribed exactly, according to the slow quarter notes divided into three, four, five and six values. Thus, e.g., the second violin has to join the already sounding $G_\#4$ on the fourth quintuplet sixteenth of the first measure's second quarter note, but it should not be »perceptible.« This, initially ›monotonous,‹ apparently wholly unmarked sound event confined to the pitch of $G_\#4$ has an enormous fascination. Evidently an irrational temporal perception is induced here by rational means. Durations are noted but are no longer rationally apprehensible. To try to determine »rhythm« here would be to miss the point.

Even so there are noticeable modifications over longer stretches, which do after all make certain durations delimitable and comparable with each other. Thus the first segment of the movement reaches a marked closure in a three-octave chord ($F_\#4/F_\#5/F_\#6/F_\#7$), which suddenly stands out like a clear signal in the hitherto amorphous sound continuum (cf. Ex. 1-059). Until then there are only pitches in the middle octave, specifically eleven quarter-tones between $G_\natural$ und $B_\natural$. The $F_\#4$ in m. 12 is thus the twelfth note that follows after the $G_\natural$.

In Ex. 1-059 I provided a separate line for each of the occurring pitches. Notes on adjacent lines are thus a quartertone apart, two lines apart represent half-tones, four lines whole tones. The diagram thus shows that, all four strings playing, the note $G_\#4$ is heard initially for some time (ca. 20 sec.), then an A4 joins in, while in mm. 6-8 most of the remaining quartertones are introduced. Since none of the four instruments uses double stops, trills or other tremolos, so that never more than four pitches can be played simultaneously, the twelve-tone field of quartertones spread out here constitutes an imaginary tonal space.

Around m. 10, however, a real chord, which was not expected in this form, is heard for several seconds: the diatonic tri-chord G-A-B, which suddenly appears freely and pure, unhampered by any micro-intervals. It has the effect of a consonance such as a major triad in an atonal context could not unfold it more powerfully. The trichord of seconds thus constitutes a striking harmonic phenomenon, which notably structures the temporal continuum. Its starting and stopping points can be indicated precisely – from the ninth sixteenth of m. 9 to the ninth eighth in m. 10 – yet no one can put this phase in relation to the time hitherto passed.

Ligeti believed that »any temporal sequence of tones, sounds, musical shapes« had a rhythm, no matter whether bound to regular pulses or not.[31] From this maxim one should not depart. Even so, the example forces us to concede that as yet no adequate mode of description exists for such free-flowing (albeit exactly noted) rhythmic processes like in the beginning of the 2nd movement of Ligeti's 2nd string quartet.

---

[31] See the quotation in the Introduction above, p. 13.

Ex. 1-059   Ligeti, 2nd String Quartet, 2nd mov., mm. 1-12 (pitches, schematic)

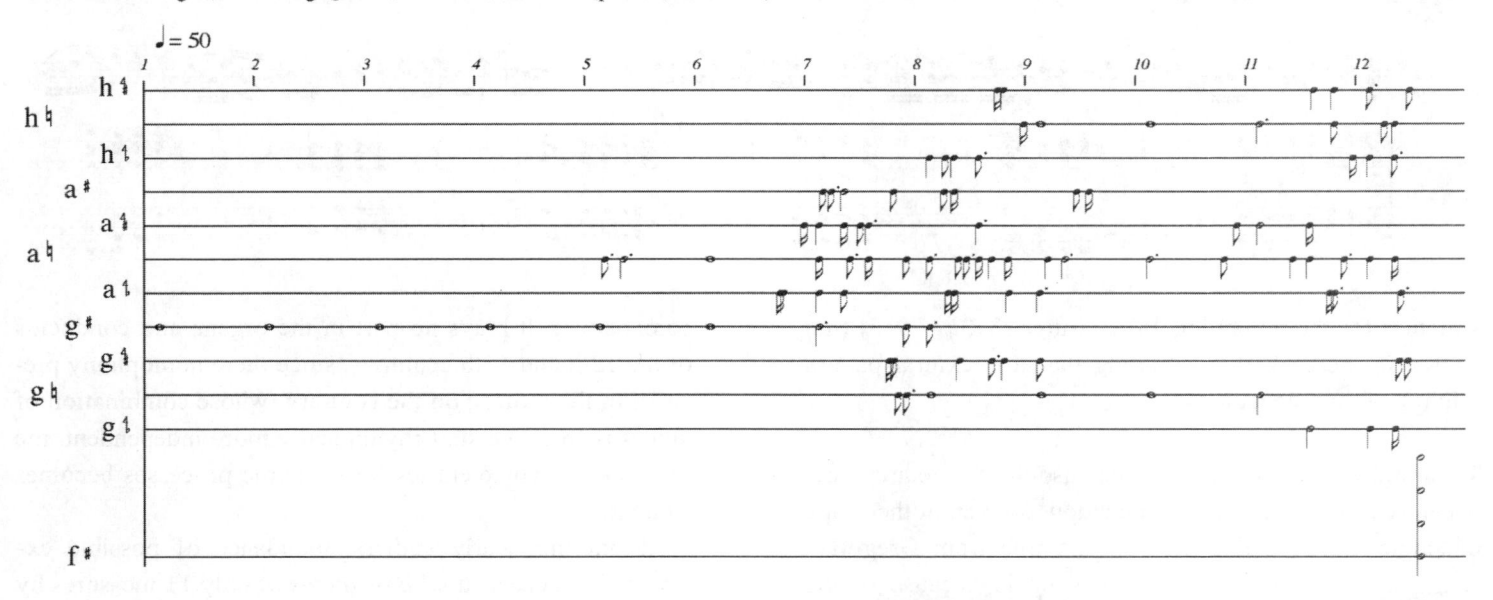

Texture

The component »Texture« refers to the structure of compositions, that is, the interweaving of voices, their loose or firm, polyphonic or homophonic setting, etc. Now it could be said that every sound phenomenon contained in a score is also a component and condition of its texture. If the texture aspect is to be suitable for the analysis of rhythmic processes, it should be limited to phenomena involving either a substantial event – e.g., the onset of a theme – or a general change of compositional structure – e.g., changes from solo to tutti or vice versa.

Both instances are observable in our example from the first movement of Beethoven's Eighth Symphony (Ex. 1-060). What is shown is the beginning of the development section in a transcription that presents the substantial content of the first 24 measures (3/4) with its real pitches and tonal durations. The most noticeable change in texture is surely the twofold irruption of the *ff*, each time after eight preceding measures. The wide-span chords are played by the winds, the first time with the addition of the timpani. At the same time the chords are pervaded by trembling string figurations, which in the basses at first are hemiolic in rhythm (4+4+4 ♪). The preceding *p* phrases consist of an interrupted pedal point (C) as well as tied tones (both in the strings). Thematic happenings, that is, textural changes in the second meaning of the term, take place in a separat layer: the head motif of the movement's principal theme is sequenced upward over two octaves by four woodwinds (bass., clar., ob. and fl.), without leaving the harmony (the D^7 of C major or else the foreshortened $D^{79♭}$ of B♭ major). If the play with the head motif produces a rhythm of ♩. ♩. ♩. ♩. , the part is also static like the other blocks of 4 measures. If one divides the first four measures in each case in two halves (as makes sense because of the belatedly entering held tones or chords), the result is a textural rhythm of twice $2+2+4^{=1+1+1+1}+4$ measures. That rhythm is very simple. It marks a situation at the beginning of a section whose stirring and conflict-laden events are still to come (e.g., the syncopated accents starting at m. 168).

Even simpler than the Beethoven example are often the textural changes in solo concertos. That is true in any case of the slow movement of Antonio Vivaldi's third Concerto of the cycle *L'estro armonico*, published in 1712 (ex. 1-061). Here the structure of the composition changes in every measure from many parts to solo part, from ♩ to ♪ values, from staccato to legato and back. The resulting textural rhythm thus consists of a sequence of dotted halves and double measures respectively. The double measures are, moreover, confirmed by the durations of the harmonies, whereby the penultimate dominant, the $F_♯^7$ chord lasts only three ♩. Vivaldi thereby introduces an irregular phrase

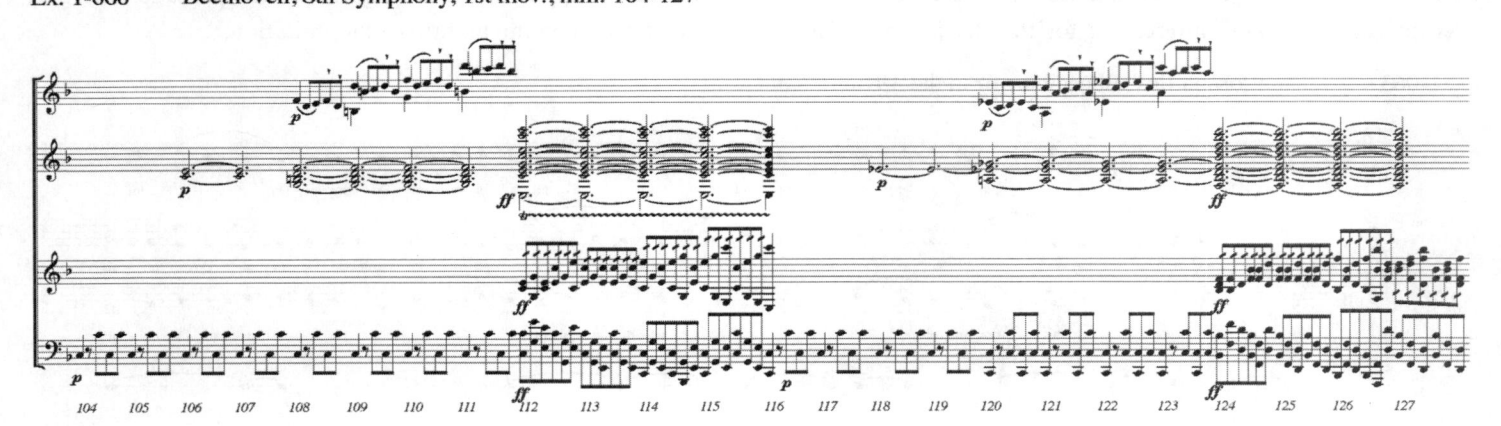

Ex. 1-060   Beethoven, 8th Symphony, 1st mov., mm. 104-127

Ex. 1-061   Vivaldi, Concerto G Major, op. 3 No. 3, 2nd mov., Beginning

structure for the remaining 18 measures (3+3+4+5+3) (not shown in the ex.), thus avoiding that the textural pattern might be felt to be tedious.

Textural features are observable also in the relation between several voices in a composition, or even in the shape of single voices. I add here an example from Gregorian chant, although it is only partly suitable because of the undefined durations. The *Allelujah* from the *Christmas Mass* (Ex. 1-062) exhibits a repeated alternation between syllabic and melismatic song, which certainly can be called a textural change. Admittedly, the resulting rhythm cannot be exactly measured.

Ex. 1-062   *Allelujah*, Christmas Mass

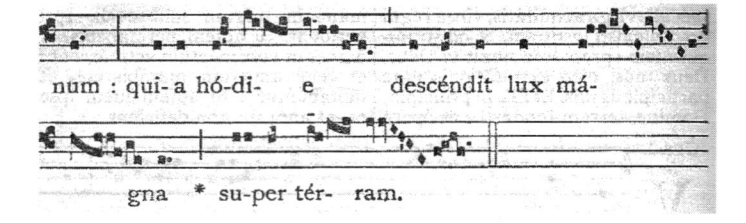

With the emergence of polyphony, the durations of the notes had to be fixed so as be able to coordinate the voices, regulate the chords exactly and order simultaneity and successiveness of the voices. From then on the question at what point another voice enters and how it relates to voices entering earlier became interesting for the rhythmics of a composition. It plays no part in the organa and conductus of the 12th and 13th centuries, since there homophony prevails. In the motets, on the contrary, whose combination of voices is from the start rhythmically more independent, the relevance of voice entries for rhythmic processes becomes evident.

From the nearly endless abundance of possible examples I choose a small *Benedictus* of only 11 measures by Johann Joseph Fux (Ex. 1-063). The three-part vocal composition written in strict canon of the lower fourth and octave lets the Comes enter one ♩ later, the second Ductus two ♩ after that. Since the second line of the melody (repeating the text of the first) starts in syncopated form and the third begins with an upbeat, the result is theme entry rhythms that are pushed out of equilibrium, though the distance between the voice entries remains constant from beginning to end. It follows, however, that one cannot speak of metric hierarchy here. The prescribed 4/4 dissolve de facto into the basic beat of a ♩.

The principle of the thematic and motivic entries had a continued effect later on in the technique of obligato accompaniment, which, with the appearance, in 1781, of Joseph Haydn's String Quartets op. 33, established the school of Viennese Classicism. A typical example occurs right away in the first of the six quartets (Hob. III:37). I select a section from the second movement, which, as a »Scherzo,« takes the place of the Minuet (Ex. 1-064).

The middle section shows in its first ten measures an imitational play with a motif split off from the theme. The entries of this five-note, upbeat motif come measure after measure and wander through all four instruments. The first interval is almost always descending; only the first violin has some rising initial seconds (with stems upward in the Ex.), thus suggesting a pseudo-inversion. The motif is twice doubled by thirds, giving additional emphasis to the entries. It appears that the rhythm of the passage is largely determined by the texture of the imitation.

Ex. 1-063   Johann Joseph Fux, Benedictus from the *Missa di San Carlo*

Ex. 1-064
Haydn, String Quartet Hob. III, 37, 2nd mov., mm. 13-21

We know that in the technique of the fugue the themes can appear in stretto. The shortening of the entry intervals connected with that are also a rhythmic phenomenon. The same technique, however, occurs also outside of fugues or canons. An example is found in Brahms's Sextet for Strings op. 36. Its slow movement (Poco Adagio) has the form of a theme and variations. In the third variation, the tempo accelerates (Piú animato) and the character of the music changes. An octave leap motif is introduced, whose

Ex. 1-065 Brahms, String Sextet op. 36, 3rd mov., 3rd variation (extract)

upbeat consists of a dotted repetition furnished with an articulatory rest. This octave leap is illustrated in Ex. 1-065, with all other figurations, which consist of ♪ triplets, left out. One can see that the motif is taken through all six instruments and that the entry intervals get shorter: first 𝅗𝅥, then increasingly 𝅘𝅥. The last measure presents false entries of the motif in the second viola and the second cello, where only the upbeats (which since the third measure can also be on the strong beat) remain. A sequence of fourths is connected with the motif entries: B – E – A – D and a hint of G (first cello) and C (first viola), whose rhythm goes in wholes and at the end is also diminished. The sequence of fourths, incidentally, maintains the connection to the subject of the variation, as that begins with two melodious fourths in the main voice.

Ever since Beethoven's Fifth Symphony, rhythms, too, can be themes, that is, a sequence of durations can bear meaning without being connected to any melos.[32] Alban Berg was the first to use such a »leitrhythm« in an opera (*Wozzeck*). This rhythm, already introduced in the chapter on the component »Sound,« is elevated, in scene III:iii, to the theme of an »invention«. In the process, variants in proportion and above all strettos occur. The latter are dramatically motivated, since in that scene Wozzeck, who is suspected of murder, finds himself in considerable straits and in the end flees from the tavern.

In Ex. 1-066, the entries of the rhythms are consecutively written (which differ from the recurrence in the score). The degree of rhythmic augmentation corresponds to its exposition in the big drum, immediately before the tavern scene (m. 114; cf. above p. 22) The measure here remains constant throughout the scene-change music between tavern and pond scene:

𝅘𝅥 𝅘𝅥 𝅘𝅥𝅮 𝅘𝅥 𝅘𝅥𝅮𝅘𝅥𝅮𝅘𝅥𝅮

By contrast, the entry distances between the thematic rhythms change, which, as can be seen, are in each case linked to other tone sequences. From the beginning of this »stretta,«[33] the rhythm appears in stretto. But the latter is even more compressed, so that the following rhythm of entry intervals comes about:

(♪): 2+2+4+6 ‖ :+2+3+2+1+1: ‖

The distance between the onsets of non-stretto rhythms would be 16 ♪. Such a distance actually occurs in the scene (mm. 122-129). The rhythm appears also, however, in various diminutions and augmentations throughout the scene, including free ones, where the proportions are not completely maintained.

The stretto structure may not be exactly graspable without studying the score; it has above all a symbolic function, in that it gives expression by purely musical means to the distressing situation in which the paranoid hero finds himself. The overall features of the texture, however – the condensing weave of voices and continuous acceleration, which resembles a whirlpool – will no doubt be picked up by the audience.

---

[32] Cf. Constantin Floros, »Leitrhythmen,« in *Gustav Mahler II: Mahler und die Symphonik des 19. Jahrhunderts in neuer Deutung. Zur Grundlegung einer zeitgemäßen musikalischen Exegetik* (Wiesbaden, 1977), 267-282, 411-418.

[33] Hans-Ulrich Fuß was the first one to apply the term »Stretta« to this scene. See Hans-Ulrich Fuß, *Musikalisch-dramatische Prozesse in den Opern Alban Bergs* (Hamburg, 1991), 95-100.

Ex. 1-066   Berg, *Wozzeck* III:iii-iv, mm. 211-218 (extract)

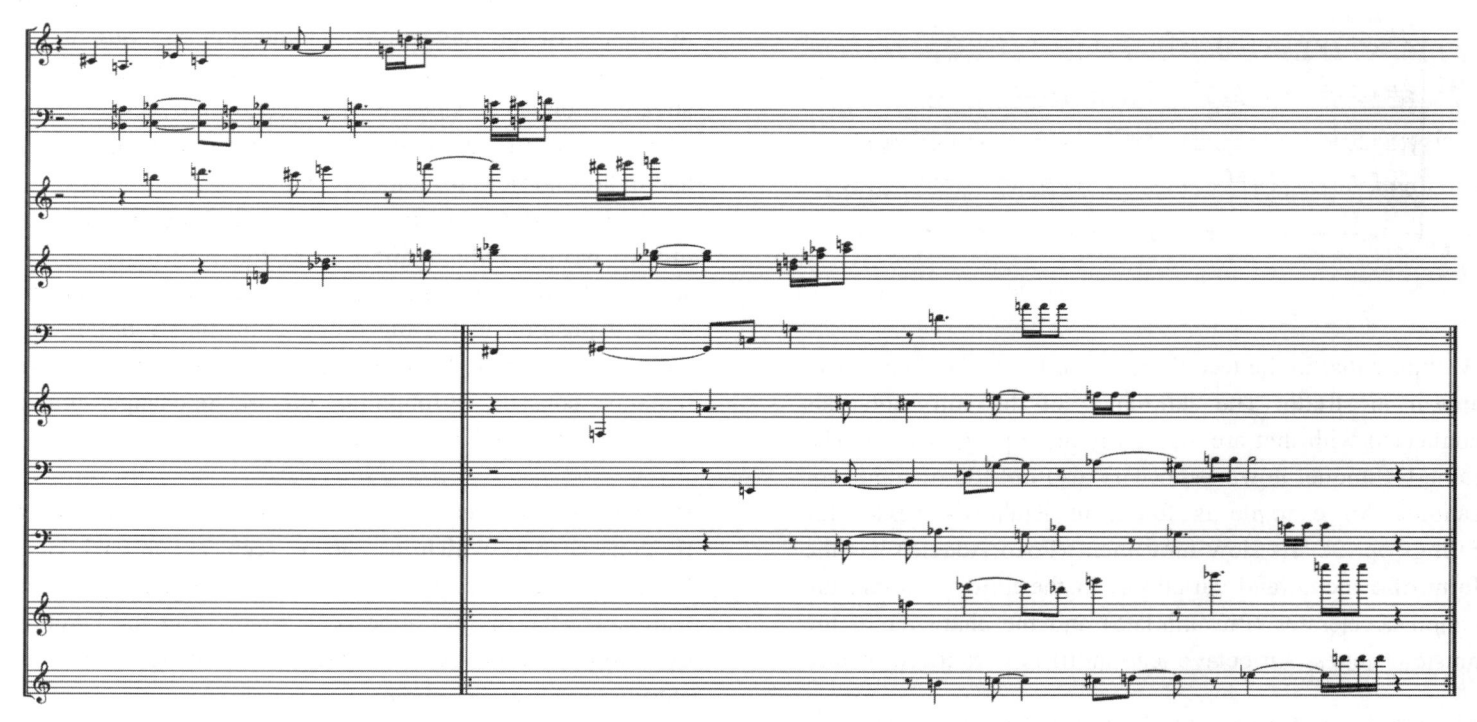

Phrase

The components »Phrase« and »Texture« are frequently used together, but they are not identical. A textural change can take place within the course of a phrase, and conversely phrases may end or begin while the texture remains constant.

The term phrase is grammatical in origin. In music it mostly refers to monophonic units of varying length, which are composed of shorter elements. Later, the term was also used for sections of a polyphonic composition.

Our example from Beethoven's Sixth Symphony shows the main theme of the final movement in six variants, whose changing phrase marks were set by Beethoven himself (Ex. 1-067). The main theme is preceded by two times four measures of soloist wind instruments, in which the character of the pastoral-sounding theme is loosely prepared for and the F major tonic is successively installed. The following main statement consists of a three-fold presentation of the theme, first in *pp*, then in crescendo from *p* up to *ff* with tutti instrumentation (mm. 9, 17, 25). The same construction obtains in the recapitulation, which presents the theme thrice in diminution, again heralded by the winds (mm. 117, 125, 133).

The six appearances of the main theme were all phrased differently by Beethoven. That means also that the rhythmics of the theme changes on the basis of the component »Phrase,« while the rhythm of the component »Sound,« in the exposition and the recapitulation versions respectively, remains the same.

To understand the procedure Beethoven applies here, we have to introduce a seventh, so to speak analytic, variant, that of the theme in its naked form, i.e., the mere melody with its inner motivic structure (ex. 1-068). Reproduced here is the part of the clarinet in mm. 25ff., which goes hand in hand with the violas and celli, but which instead of the ongoing rhythm has a blunt, downbeat closure. This makes clear the model of a regular repetition period, whose schema is as follows: a first phrase of 1+1+2

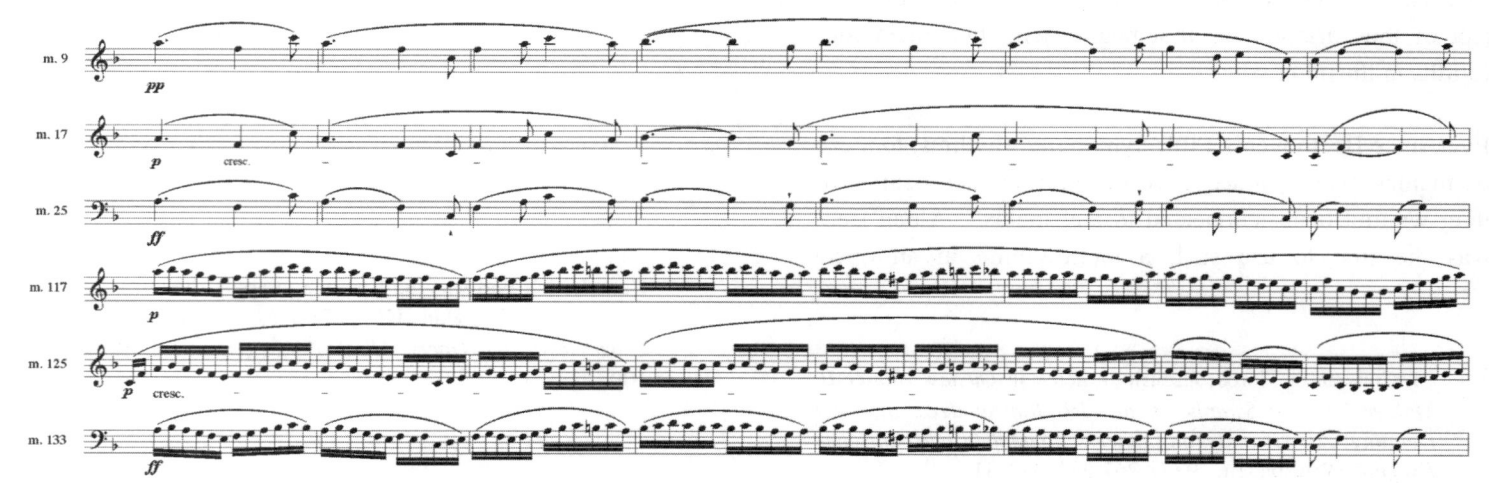

Ex. 1-067   Beethoven, 6th Symphony, 5th mov., Variants of the Main Theme

measures with half-close on the subdominant, and a second phrase of 1+1+2 measures with whole close on the tonic (in letter ciphering: a a b a' a' b').

Ex. 1-068

If we now look at the phrasing, which Beethoven indicated by means of slurs, and which the players are to execute, we will notice differences in the rhythm of the motivic phrases. In the version of m. 9, for example, the half close caesura is deliberately covered over in that the arc begins already on the last note of the antecendent and extends to the end of the fifth measure. In the second variant (m. 17), the phrase mark links the second and third measure, while in the consequent it spans even the full measures, so that again the caesuras dictated by the form of the phrases are occluded. The first *ff* variant shows a predominant coincidence with the inner structure of the period, because in it a new mark starts with every measure – only the fourth measure is not included under the slur, so that there is no phrasal two-bar unit.

The oddest phrasing occurs in the diminution variant in m. 125. Here phrase marks twice cover the entire three measures, followed by two half-measures and a complete one. This rhythmicization into 3+3+0,5+0,5+1 measures has no longer anything in common with the rhythm of the period structure of 1+1+2+1+1+2 measures. This is, moreover, the only variant that is fronted by an upbeat to be played also within the arc. Such values that are included under the phrase mark ahead of the first beat occur also in other variants, for example in mm. 14/15 and 20/21, whereby the eighths are turned into stressed upbeats. In the bass version of the theme (m. 25), on the other hand, which also begins downbeat, the upbeat quality of the last eights in the second, fourth and sixth measure is given emphasis by staccato accents.

Beethoven's handling of phrasing must be called disparate. Since we can exclude error and arbitrariness, we can conclude that he wanted to add an element of unpredictability to the very simple motivic structure by repeatedly including counter-structures by means of the phrasing marks. Since both procedures belong to the area of the component »Phrase,« we thus have here two contrary phrasal rhythms. If one includes the free handling of the upbeats, the result is already a considerable degree of complexity in regard to just this one component.

An analogous case can be observed in the main theme of the first movement of Mozart's Symphony in E♭ Major. Here, too, the form is that of a repetitive period, albeit one structured more richly and having a wider span (first phrase 14 mm., second phrase 16 mm.). Our example (Ex. 1-069) shows only the beginnings of either part, like in the Beethoven example, first in the exposition and then in the recapitulation. Here, too, the phrasing marks provided by

Ex. 1-069   Mozart, Symphony E♭ Major K. 543, 1st mov.

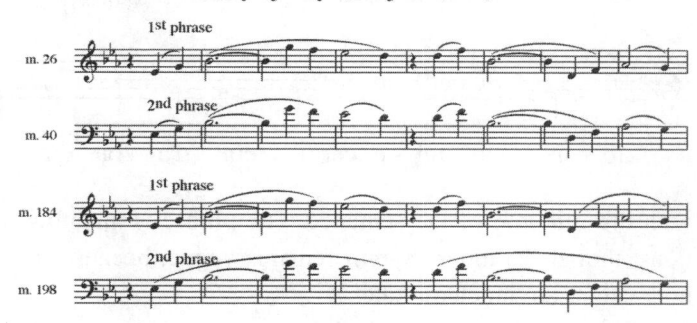

Mozart diverge. While the eight-measure partial phrase, which, except for the octave change, is the same each time and simply divides into 4+4 measures, the phrasing marks divide the passages into 1+3+1+2+1 (m. 26), 1+2+1+1+2+1 (m. 40), 1+2+1+1+1+2 (m. 184) and 4+4 (m. 198). Only the last presentation of the theme thus results in a coincidence of the durations of phrase marking and motivic partial phrase.

The case is not always as clear as it is in these examples by Beethoven and Mozart. One reason for this is that the graphic symbol of the arc can indicate different meanings. Ties prolong the duration of a note, slurs belong to the group of articulation marks and mean that the notes should be played contiguously (legato) without any break, while phrase marks say something about the import of phrases and partial phrases: they indicate to the performer what should be presented as belonging together. Thus one can also discuss in the examples from Beethoven and Mozart whether in a given instance the slur is not meant to signal a legato rather than a phrasing. The two first quarter notes of the Mozart theme, for example, are certainly to be played legato, and the same is true of the last measure of the bass variant of the Beethoven theme (m. 32). On the other hand, it is impossible that the basses in the fourth presentation of the Mozart symphony's main theme (m. 198) should be executed in a single stroke of the bow extending over four measures. It is up to the musicians here to decide how to go about getting four measures to be experienced as a unity.

Phrase marks are a relatively recent articulatory device. Much older is the phrasing by means of melodic structure. In the oldest vocal music, the duration of textual unit and melodic phrase was identical, as, e.g., at the beginning of the *Canticum Beatae Mariae Virginis* in tonus I (Ex. 1-070):

Here singing is simply an elevated form of speaking. Stylized by coordinating the words with a certain tone system (authentic Dorian) and largely rendered syllabically, the melody of the song traces an arc that could similarly constitute the speech melody and whose finalis D coincides

Ex. 1-071   Machaut, *Motet No. 20*, Tenor

Je ne sui mi-e cer - teins d'a-voir a-mi - e,   mais je sui loy-aus_ a-mis.

with the full stop of the sentence. The phrase is unambiguous, though its inner rhythm remains vague, because the note values are indeterminate.

With the invention of the mensurational notation, phrase durations became measurable, so that the unity of spoken and musical sentences could be rationally determined in rhythmic terms as well. A good example of this is the tenor part of the three-part, non-isorhythmically organized motet »Trop plus est bele...« (Triplum) / »Biaute paree de valour...« (Motetus) / »Je ne suis mie certeins...« (Tenor) by Guillaume de Machaut. (Ex. 1-071)[34] Two wave-like phrases shape this basis voice, which is rhythmicized exclusively in breves and semi-breves. The first phrase (a) comprises seven measures accommodating twelve syllables, while the second phrase (b) contains four measures with seven syllables. The entire piece is structured by these phrases, whereby it can be assumed that the text is underlaid in the same way each time: a-b-a-a-a-b-a-b. That the upper voices Triplum and Motetus are adjusted to the rhythm of the Tenor is proved by the community of several components, as will be shown later in the chapter on iso- and heterometry.

NB 1-072   Machaut, *Motet No. 1*, Color

Ex. 1-073   Machaut, Motet No. 1, Talea

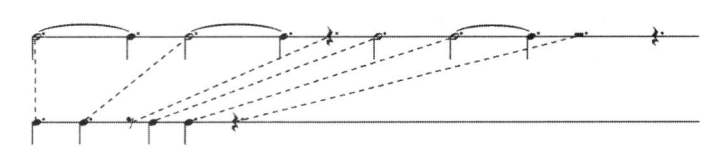

In contrast to this simple phrase construction, Machaut's iso-rhythmic motets (among others) are highly artificial in structure. Melos and rhythms diverge. Likewise based on the principle of repetition, the melodic sequences (Colores) are repeated according to a measure *differing* from that of the rhythms (Taleae).

In the Tenor of the Machaut motet »Quant en moy...« / »Amour et biuaute...« / »Amara valde,«[35] the Color consists of 30 notes (Ex. 1-072). The Talea, which occurs in a basic form and in a diminished version (divisor of 3), have an unvaried rhythm (Ex. 1-073).

The Tenor, looking at the motet as a whole (Ex. 1-074), consists of two iterations of the Color and of altogether twelve Taleae, whereby the second Color and the second six Taleae begin with the diminution. If one were also to consider the Triplum and the Motetus, whose iso-rhythm is less stringent but nevertheless noticeably related to the structure of the Tenor,[36] the result would be further subdivisions in periods. The phrasing of this motet shows, in any case, three dimensions: Color, Period and Talea.

The separate handling of the components »Pitch,« »Diastematy« and »Sound« (entry intervals) generates also additional rhythms, which admittedly are not intended by the composer but are nonetheless present. They result from the contour of the Color: their crest notes fall on diverse positions of the Taleae, so that irregular durations obtain between the latter (7+14+10+5+12 +9+10 𝅗𝅥. and 𝅘𝅥. respectively).

In the 19th century, the phrasing by means of slurs reached full flowering. Of course there always were and are also unmarked phrases and mixed forms, in which motivic phrase structure was only occasionally marked by slurs. The overlapping of phrases, when a new phrase commen-

Ex. 1-074   Machaut, Motet No. 1, Tenor *

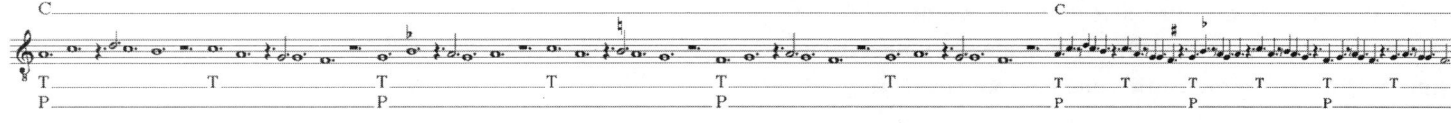

* C = Color; T = Talea; P = Period

---

[34] In the Machaut edition of Friedrich Ludwig (vol. 3), the motet bears the number 20. P. 70 in the volume has a reference to the non-isorhythmic construction of the motet, as well as to the origin of the Tenor in a secular rondeau.

[35] Machaut Edition Motet no. 1, vo. 33, 2-5; see ibid. Friedrich Ludwig's structural analysis and evidence of the liturgical origin of the Tenor.

[36] See also the account and analysis of the motet by Georg Reichert, »Das Verhältnis zwischen musikalischer und textlicher Struktur in den Motetten Machauts,« *AfMw*, 13 (1956): 197-216.

ced already on the last note of the preceding one, as happens both in unison or homophone and in polyphone compositions, may confront the analyst with problems of delimitation. In any case the rhythm is determined by the entry of the phrase more than its end. The impulse emitted by a newly beginning phrase in a sense covers up the end of the previous one. The situation is similar to that of the entry of notes or sounds, as here, too, the intervals between the entries range ahead of their actual duration (see the chapter on the component »Sound«).

A number of examples from the 19th and 20th centuries will further demonstrate the rhythmic relevance of phrasing. A piano piece from Robert Schumann's *Album for Youth* is of downright didactic clarity. In its second part, »For Adults,« there is the »Winter Time II,« whose open-

Ex. 1-075   Schumann, *Winterszeit II*, op. 68 No. 39

ing is shown in Ex. 1-075. The eight-measure repetition period (half-close on I in third position, full-close on V in octave position) is divided by two phrasing slurs covering the entire first and the entire second phrase in the lower

downbeat-phrased closing measures stand out somewhat, especially since they are supported by modestly swelling dynamics.

The ternary subdivision of the unison passage, on the contrary, which can be read off from the crest notes (G3-A_b3-B_b3-C4), belongs to the unmarked phrasing. It generates a rhythm of three-eighths units (♩. ♩. ♩. ♩.), which makes the rhythm of the piece appear a little more complex than the first impression would suggest.

In 1835, Schumann, whose praise of Chopin's piano music is well known, put together an survey entitled »Shorter and Rhapsodic Pieces for the Pianoforte.« In it he made special mention of Chopin's G minor Nocturne op. 15 No. 3, whose closeness to Schubert, forward-looking nature and seriousness he liked.[37] One can assume that in a detailed discussion he would also have adverted to the unusual phrase construction of the piece.

The composition begins like a lento waltz and ends in a »religioso« tone (Ex. 1-076). A first, in itself further subdivided part (mm. 1-88) has a heterometric phrase structure, a second one (mm. 89-152) is arranged in strict isometry. The main voice of part I a and I b tends to upbeat, while the religioso part usually enters on the downbeat. Ex. 1-076 shows the phrase structure along the motivic-thematic content (in measures):[38]

Ex. 1-076   Chopin, Nocturne op. 15 No. 3 (main part)

voice. When the number of parts increases, additional slurs are drawn in the upper voice, which in each case mark the cadencing measures. Since the upbeats in mm. 1 and 5 are ranged under the following phrase slur, the contrasting

[37] Robert Schumann, *Gesammelte Schriften über Musik und Musiker*, 3rd ed., 2 vols. (Leipzig 1875), 1: 335.

[38] Cf. the similar view in Hugo Leichtentritt, *Analyse der Chopin'schen Klavierwerke* (Leipzig, 1922), 1: 15f.

I a 7 (1+2+4) + 5 (2+3)
     7 (1+2+4) + 5 (2+3)
     7 (1+2+4) + 5 (2+3)
     7 (1+2+4) + 7 (2+5)
I b 8 (4+4)
     8 (4+4)
     2+ 4 (1+1+1+1) + 4 (1+1+1+1) + 2 (hemiol.) + 6 (2+2+2) + 4
II a 8 (4+4) + 8 (2+2+4)
     8 (4+4) + 8 (2+2+4)
II b 16 (4+4+8)
     16 (4+4+8)

The phrase slurs drawn by Chopin largely coincide with this division, except that they are not always the borders of the measures but repeatedly include the upbeats under the slur. The phrases' beginnings and ends are also ambivalent, as the first measures in the sections I a and I b are quasi isolated, while the last merge into the first following measures, as is partly even marked by slurs (58→59, 66→67).

Striking and clearly central to the idea of the piece is the contrast between the first and second part. In line with the expression marks »languido« and »religioso,« the beginning consists of dissolving phrases, while the end is marked by its clear divisions into two, four and eight measures. The divergent character of the second part is all the clearer as one expects to hear the languishing theme of the beginning again, for the section I b has all the earmarks of a development-like middle part of a dance in A-B-A form: modulations, abridgment of phrases down to single measures or hemiolas (mm. 77/78), intensification and recapitulation. But instead of the expected recapitulation, a new theme in F major enters, which with its *semplice* intonation feels as if coming from another world.

In 1854, Franz Liszt wrote his *Faust Symphony*. It begins with a wide-flung phrase of eleven measures (Ex. 1-077). A single (imaginary) arc spans this theme, although the latter's internal structure is richly subdivided into motif and phrase repetitions.

Tie together six phrase marks separate units of different lengths: from three eighths (mm. 7 and 8) to three-and-a-half 4/4 measures. The smallest slurs mark an isolated motif, while the longest spans the core phrase of the theme (mm. 2-5), which begins in the strings and is concluded by the oboe. Since the first note of the movement, the A♭, to be played *ff* with following decrescendo, should be regarded as an isolated upbeat, the four following augmented triads (which, as we know, include all tones of the chromatic scala) are strongly exposed, also because of the sudden *p* intonation. Liszt pulls the first three triads under a single slur, so as then to start into the actual main phrase in the third and fourth measure.

All the eighths upbeats are put under phrase marks, and the timbre changes several times within a single slur, without the phrase being disrupted thereby. It is also interesting that the beams here are evidently put in the service of the phrasing. In any case, the three-eighths, especially in mm. 5 and 7, suggest that. The crescendo marks, too, support the course of the phrases (as already in the Schumann piece). The rhythm of the phrases (entries) may not seem to be very impressive, but it does play a role in the community of all the components.

Similarly wide-flung phrasal units can also be found in Brahms (Ex. 1-078). Thus the 16-measure subsidiary theme of the first movement of the String Quartet in A minor, whose contour describes a single wave-like rise and fall, is divided by phrase marks, which comprise four alla-breve measures at their longest, two quarter notes at their shortest.

Ex. 1-077 Liszt, *Eine Faust-Sinfonie*, Beginning, main part

Ex. 1-078 Brahms, String Quartet A Minor, 1st mov., Violins, mm. 46-61

Ex. 1-079 Brahms, String Quartet A Minor, 4th mov., mm. 108-115

Other than with such a largely periodic theme, Brahms elsewhere employs phrasing to bring confusion into the even measure of a composition. A good example can be found in the finale of the same A minor Quartet. I am thinking of a transition passage of this movement, which is written in sonata rondo form (Ex. 1-79). Brahms here seemingly cancels the 3/4 meter. Minimal phrases of 4, 3 and 5 ♪ duration follow each other contiguously, so that by the end of the eight measures probably no one is any longer ›in time.‹ It remains to note that Brahms marks the mini-phrases here not only by slurs but also by beams. Several times, in fact, the beams are drawn across the bar lines.[39]

With the appearance of heterometric meters in central Europe's art music of the 20th century – well-known forerunners are e.g., the Larghetto of Chopin's Piano Sonata op. 4 (1827/28) or the waltz of Tchaikovsky's ›Pathetique‹ (1893), both of which are in 5/4 meter – phrasing was used also to underscore the uneven beats.

Ex. 1-080   Ravel, Piano Trio, Beginning

This can be studied in the main theme of Maurice Ravel's Piano Trio (Ex. 1-080). In the right hand of the piano part, one finds an unusual beaming: 3 + 2 ♪, followed by a Lombardic rhythm of ♪ and ♩. There is thus an uneven division of the 8/8 meter. Since the sequence of 3+2+3 is stereotypically repeated, what emerges here is an actual meter (Aksak). The slurs (in the right hand) can be regarded as both articulation and phrase marks. They always occupy the same position in the measure – second to sixth ♪ – and thus contribute to the stabilization of the Aksak.

The left hand shows a different ›reading‹ of the 8/8 meter. Even without bars, the part of the left hand would be taken for a regular West European 4/4 measure. The overhanging bass notes always fall on the *One*, and the quarter notes and eighths conduct to it. The four-measure phrase of the theme thus divides into four single measures, whereas their internal structure is in a right/left-hand tension – a clear case of polymetry, which is recognizable not least through the phrasing.

The composer Béla Bartók, who, as we know, was also an ethnologist, picked up the idea of heterometric meters and further developed it, e.g., in the »Six Dances in Bulgarian Rhythms« at the end of his *Mikrokosmos*. But even outside the dance idiom, Bartók picked up the heterometric internal structuring of measures. A good example is presented by the *Music for String Instruments, Percussion and Celesta* from 1936.

Its first movement is constructed as a diversified circular fugue, whose thematic entries traverse the complete circle of fifths twice. The chromatically melodized fugue theme is quoted in the Finale, now transformed to indicate an apotheosis, as well as transposed into the diatonic (Lydian and Mixolydian) (Ex. 1-081).

The extent of the individual measures, whose internal structure changes, varies (five to twelve ♪). Again the drawing of the beams (the microphrasing, if you will) provides initial hints. Moreover, Bartók introduces dotted subsidiary barlines, which remove the last doubt about the heterometric nature of the meters. Here is the internal structure of the respective theme measures in the first and fourth movement:

1. Satz	3+3+2 ♪	4. Satz	3+3+2 ♪
	3+3+3+3 ♪		3+3 ♪
	3+3+2 ♪		3+2 ♪
	4+3 ♪		3+3+2 ♪
			4+3 ♪

No less important are the phrase marks, which remain independent of the metrical conditions and are wholly oriented on the course of the melody. I have entered the sequence of durations of the phrase marks in eighths values below the parts: it shows a remarkable irregularity. That goes together with the shaping of the upbeats, which contain one or two ♪ in the first movement, but also three ♪ in the fourth one. Generally, the phrase rhythm is more vital in the diatonic version than in the chromatic one. In the

Ex. 1-081   Bartók, *Music for String Instruments, Percussion and Celesta*, Fugue theme 1st and 4th mov.

---

[39] A parallel instance occurs in the very same first movement of this quartet, from which the side theme just discussed derives. A sequence of ternary phrases here crosses the alla breve meter, and again this happens in a formally unstable section, this time in the development section of the sonata movement (mm. 162ff.).

three-eighths upbeats in the fourth movement the phrasing even affects the melodic structure, in that in mm. 206 and 207 the last note, in each case, of the melodic line (D in m. 206, E in m. 207) is tied to the following line.

My last example I take from the Sinfonie No. 10 by Hans Werner Henze, which was completed in 2000. Henze, who is known for his productive engagement with the traditions of European music, regards the thinking in musical phrases and sentences, which ultimately derive from language and vocal music, by no means as passé. He even knows how to convincingly revitalize the gesture of the »grand tone,« which characterizes the symphonic music from Beethoven to Mahler.

Our example is taken from the fourth movement, which is entitled »Ein Traum« (A Dream). It includes a passage headed by the general expression mark »gran canto« (Ex. 1-082). The complex sound event can be divided into three strands, which are furnished with figurative and percussive actions (not included in the example). A characteristic of the three strands is the linking together of two or four voices in free parallels (changing intervals). At the end of the seven-measure phrase, the three sound strands merge together into a standing but internally mobile sound ($_1$89-90). Each sound strand is individually phrased. The higher strings commence with several short gestures of two or three impulses, followed by an upswing of six impulses under a slur. The winds stay with small phrases but are distinguished altogether by a rise in pitch from the small to the three-line octave. The low strings are phrased similarly to the higher ones, but having shorter note values also produce smaller phrases.

All the way round, this »gran canto« can be experienced as a multi-faceted fabric of sound, whose rhythm has the effect of unpredictability not least because of the partial phrases being offset against each other. But by directing the sound strands toward a focal point – the third eighth of m. 88 – the gesture of a grand song is created.

Ex. 1-082   Henze, 10th Symphony, 4th mov., mm. 84-90 (extract)

Prosody

Entire treatises have been written about the subject of music and language. Here we will deal only with language as a rhythmically relevant component. Sung words and sentences in vocal music, after all, have a rhythm of their own, which relates in a certain way to the component rhythms of the musical setting. The proportions of stress and length of syllables – depending on whether the language concerned is accentual or quantifying – are for the most part analogous to the dynamic accents or relative note values of the music. In addition to such prosodic givens of natural languages, versification and strophic form, in the case of composed poetry, may also be rhythmically significant.

Ex. 1-083   Beethoven, 9th Symphony, Finale, mm. 216-248

Both forms of language – prose and verse – occur in the Finale of Beethoven's Ninth Symphony. The entry of the vocal part in m. 216 (Ex. 1-083) may serve as a prime example of the component »Prosody.« The cantata-like movement is preceded by an instrumental introduction, which in the low strings, among others, imitates the gesture of vocal recitative. After some recapitulating quotations from the opening movement, the Scherzo and the Adagio, the »Freude« melody – likewise purely instrumental – is introduced and developed. Then the Presto of the Finale starts anew, and a baritone lifts his voice.

In emphatic prose, the singer turns to the ensemble and the audience like a master of ceremonies and invites them to take part in a celebration of joy. »...nicht diese Töne« refers back to the catastrophic beginning of the Finale in a D minor exacerbated by both chord structure and rhythm (cf. Ex. 1-008 in the chapter on »Pitch«), while the »angenehmere« and »freudenvollere« (more pleasing and joyful) herald the immediately following setting of Schiller's »Ode to Joy,« which, the unusual expression mark tells us right away, is to be recited »angenehm« (pleasingly). (Del Mar Edition).

I have added a rhythm line to the voice part, which contains the components »Prosody« and »Verse.« The stressed syllables are throughout signalized by single or double x's. In the prose lines one can see that the stressed syllables are highlighted either by relatively long notes or by crest notes or both. It is worth noting that the two words that have five syllables but only one stress – »angenehmere« and »freudenvollere« – have exact correspondences in the music, that is to say, the four light syllables in each case are weighted neither by stretched nor by high notes – only on the second syllable of »freudenvollere« there is a weak crest-note accent.

With the onset of the ode, the simple rhythmic pattern of the cross-rhymed tetrameters is added, here schematized with – . – . – . – . Fitted into the 4/4 beat, the meter of verse and music are fully congruent. Later, the same verse form is made to coincide also with 6/8 meter (from m. 378), the 3/2 meter (from m. 595), the 6/4 meter (from m. 655), the 2/2 meter (from m. 763) and the 3/4 meter (at m. 916), whereby stress and unstress taken together sometimes fill a whole, sometimes only half a measure.

More interesting, however, than the unions of verse and musical meter are the divergences of actual syllabic from the metric stress. Contrary to the basic verse meter, the distribution of stressed syllables (including monosyllabic words) is not subjected to a rigid schema. The line »Tochter aus Elysium« (daughter of Elysium) has four metric accents but only two stressed syllables. And in the line »Himmlische, dein Heiligtum« (celestial one, thy sanctuary), there is a notable weight shift of a metrical stress (on -sche) onto the next, metrically unstressed syllable (dein), which carries the rhetorical stress.

If one now looks at the verse rhythm in relation to the rhythmics of the melody, one finds that, despite some points of contact, the melody neglects the rhythmic variants of the verse in the detail. That is the problem – though perhaps also the appeal – of all strophic songs, whose melodies are as a rule rigid vis-à-vis the varying contents and rhythmic forms of individual stanzas: the rhythm of a melody frequently takes precedence over that of the verse. Thus the contour of the *Freude* melody does not agree to the same extent as the following consciously bad constructed variant (Ex. 1-084).

Ex. 1-084   (Construct)

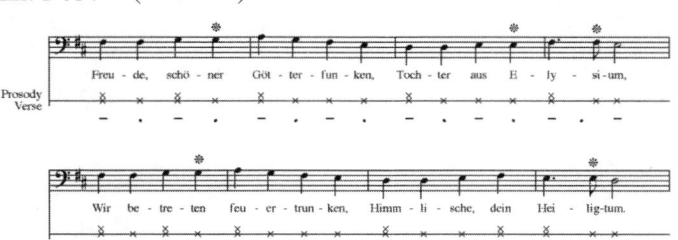

The altered notes are marked with an asterisk (*). The changes are not to durational values but only to the points at which the pitch, that is, the component »Pitch,« changes. In comparison with the original, the pitch changes in the constructed variant happen more regularly and to that extent metrically more adequately: ♩ ♩ ♩♩♩♩ ♩ ♩ ♩ . In the original, there is a slightly syncopated and hence invigorating pitch rhythm. Incidentally, Beethoven has the instrumental version of the *Freude* melody begin with a ♩, i.e., pulls the two F♯'s into one, thereby making pitch rhythm and note entry congruent (cf. mm. 92, 94, 96, 98, 100 etc.).

In sum one can say about the rhythm of the singing voice in the Finale of Beethoven's *Ninth* that the prose recitatives meticulously convert the stress relations of the text, while the sung melody retains a measure of independence vis-à-vis the meter and rhythm of the verse. Here it was evidently more important to Beethoven to invigorate the purely musical melody by means of divergent component rhythms (Ex. 1-083) than to choose a textually completely ›correct‹ but rather tedious solution.

Richard Wagner attached the label »patriarchal« to Beethoven's *Freude* melody and thought it had sprung from an »absolutely musical impulse« and was only »as it were spread over« the poet's verse. Knowing well that Beethoven had deliberately sought the simplicity of a folksong or -dance at this point in the Ninth Symphony, Wagner strove for a new form of vocal melody for all future music, namely a »melody growing on the verse from the poetic intention« (R. Wagner, GS, vol. IV, 149-151).

Ex. 1-085

Wagner, *Siegfried* III:i, mm. 291-306 (Erda)

In Wagner's music dramas, there are in fact such novel vocal melodies, which represent a hitherto unknown organic unity of word and tone. An example from *Siegfried* shows that rhythm, too, is involved (Ex. 1-085). These eight dimeters of alliterative verse are a little masterpiece of a freely rhythmicized vocal melody determined solely by the prosody and by the construction and content of the text. All of the stresses (two x) are in keeping with the components »Sound« (♩.,♩,♩.,○) or »Diastematy« (crest notes). The first four verses, which Wagner preformed poetically into long lines with chiastic structure (Trotz / Trotz; That / That; lehren / strafen; zünden / zürnen) are shaped analogously in rhythm (eighths upbeats, distribution of the large intervals, and syncopated entries) and parallel in length (phrase rhythm: four times 6 ♩).

The fifth to the eighth verses continue to have two stresses each and therefore would not seem to require any changes; but they contain crucial contents: Erda reproaches Wotan not only with contradictory actions but with breaking the law. Wagner therefore combined these four lines into a unity already as poet by continuing the chiasmus across lines (fifth and seventh line: Recht / Recht; sixth and eighth line: Eid / Meineid), and thereby achieves a climactic emphasis on the word »Meineid« (false oath, perjury). The semantic content in connection with the growing psychic arousal of the singing figure produced in Wagner the conception of enlarged phrase rhythms: (the last four verses have durations of 8, 10, 8, and 11 ♩, counting the final pauses in).

Hand in hand with that goes the enlargement of the interval leaps and the tonal durations, as well as the successive rise of the crest notes (1st verse: G♯4, 8th verse: A♭5). If we think of the durations between the crest notes as rhythms, we get the following sequence (in ♩): 3-7-2-3-7-8-9-11-8. No less bizarre is the pitch rhythm, which, owing to several tone repetitions (including C♯4-D♭4), fully counts among the relevant components (♪): 2-4-3-3- /4-8- /2-3-1-3-3- /4-8- /1,5-0,5-6-2-6- /1,5-0,5-6-2-4-6- /4-2-10- /6-8-8.

That there is a steady succession of 4/4 measures behind these divergent component rhythms is altogether lost track of.[40] What Wagner stipulated theoretically in 1871, that is, the overcoming of the »quadrature of conventional musical period construction« (R. Wagner, GS, vol. IX, 149), he frequently actually implemented in his music dramas.

---

[40] If one includes the orchestral melodies, the beat naturally becomes more noticeable. See my essay: »Die dichterisch-musikalische Periode. Ein verkannter Begriff Richard Wagners,« in *Zur Musikgeschichte des 19. Jahrhunderts*, HJbMw, vol. 2 (Hamburg 1977), 105-123.

Ex. 1-086   Strauss, *Elektra*, before fig. 37

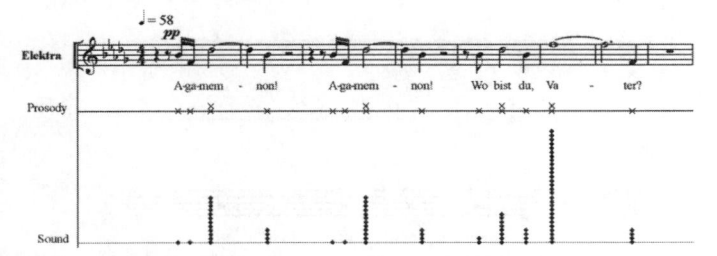

German (like English) is an accentuating language. As a rule, therefore, in German-language vocal music, stress-bearing syllables are underscored by means of musical components. »Underscore,« however, does not necessarily mean »amplify,« as evident in the example from Richard Strauss' *Electra* (Ex. 1-086). Electra's invoking of Agamemnon is in *pp* for altogether eight measures. Nevertheless, her singing has an enormous intensity, which results not least from the rhythm of the vocal part. There is a broad spectrum of note values: from 1 ♪ to 7 ♩ (= 28 ♪) per syllable. The extreme durations are on the stressed syllables, which are thereby given great weight. A captivating pianissimo tension develops. The outlines of the Agamemnon motif copy the speech melody exactly: this is a text-generated motif. Since the crest notes initially occur on the weak beats, a rhythmic suction is created toward the princess's last word, placed on the downbeat: »Vater.« To him, to the avenging of her father's death, Electra feels obligated.

Another interesting, though entirely different example of a rhythmic-melodic motif generated from a proper name occurs in Alban Berg's opera *Wozzeck* (Ex. 1-087). The name of the protagonist is normally pronounced with the stress on the first syllable: Wózzeck. Only the doctor indulges the quirk of accentuating the name of his ›protégé‹ on the second syllable: Wozzéck. Whenever the doctor addresses Wozzeck, he uses a rising minor third, whose high note carries a dynamic accent; sometimes, also, both syllables are stressed. In the orchestral accompaniment, this linguistic-vocal oddity, which appears at the very start of the scene, turns into a kind of leitmotif. As the example shows, the motif appears eight times, in high and/or low position, at the end of the scene, in various instruments and in irregular intervals – the first time conjointly with the Doctor's arbitrary intonation of the name »Wozzeck.« The idea behind this may be that the hated pronunciation of his name keeps ringing in the tormented Wozzeck's ears, as he is forced to subject himself to the Doctor as a guinea pig.

Modernist works at times deliberately contravene the natural prosody of texts. Unlike the example from *Wozzeck*, where the deviation has a natural explanation, the contraventions in Bernd Alois Zimmermann's opera *Die Soldaten* (The Soldiers) are very differently motivated (cf. Ex. 1-088). In a dialogue between the Countess and Marie, the elevated diction of the former is linked to a riven melos and an unpredictable rhythm interspersed with diverse subdivisions (1:2, 1:3, 1:5) and irrational values (♪), to which the bourgeois Marie tries to adapt herself. There are constant discrepancies between stressed syllables and high or long notes, as a comparison between light and heavy syllables (represented by single or double x) makes clear.

Ex. 1-087   Berg, *Wozzeck*, I:iv, »Wozzéck«-Motive

Ex. 1-088   Zimmermann, *Die Soldaten*, III/5, after fig. **e**

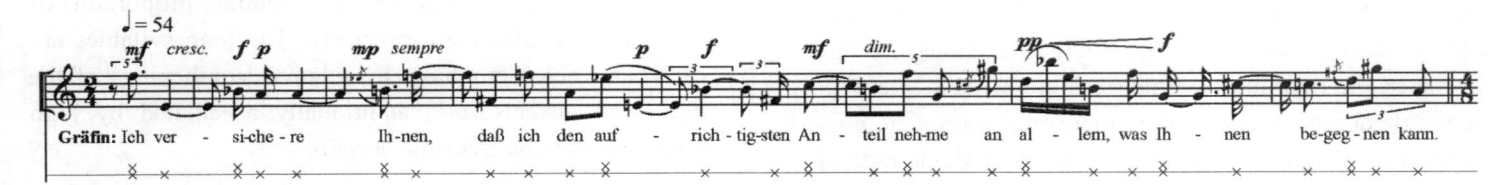

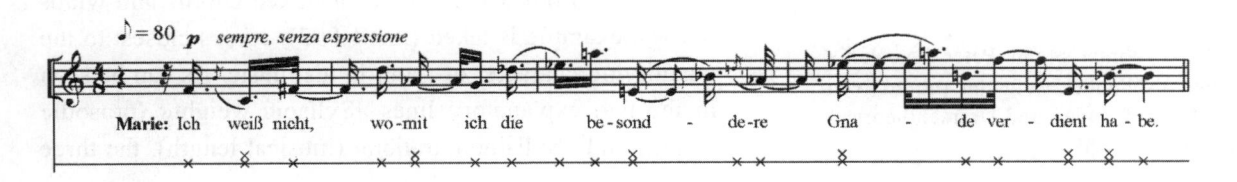

The strangeness produced by these vocal parts is probably intended by the composer. Perhaps Zimmermann wanted to emphasize the fact that the sung text derives from a past period. Jakob Michael Reinhold Lenz wrote the play in 1776. In line with the idea of a literary opera as a timely genre of the 20th century, the discrepancy between a modern musical language and a text nearly 200 years old was to be noticeable to the senses at all times.[41]

The distinction between accentuated and quantifying linguistic families plays a larger role in poetry than in vocal music. If one conceives the linguistic accent as a loudness stress and the relative length of a syllables as a lengthening stress, then both forms coincide in music in the concept of rhythmic weight, which is attainable by reinforced sound as well as by a larger note value.

The most important quantifying language for us is Latin, from which several Romance languages derive. We will therefore consider a number of exemplary settings of Latin texts. I select specifically the line »Hosanna in excelsis« from the Sanctus of the Ordinarium missae. It contains two long syllables (san and cel), the remaining five being short.

Ex. 1-089
Monteverdi, *Messa a 4 Voci da Cappella*, Sanctus (Osanna)

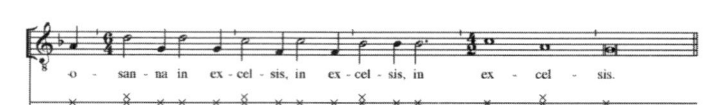

We begin with an example from Claudio Monteverdi's posthumous Messa a 4 Voci da Cappella (Ex. 1-089). It presents two different rhythmicizations of the line: the long syllable san is given emphasis once by a crest note, the other time by a long note. In both cases, though, the greater emphasis is on the words »in excelsis.« The long syllable cel is first linked to a very long melisma, the second time to lengthened notes and crest notes. In the process, however, short notes, too, at times obtain an »undue« rhythmic weight (in and ex).

Bach's B Minor Mass likewise presents an accentuating reading of the Latin (Ex. 1-90). Within the frame of a fast 3/8 meter, the rhythmic accents (crest notes) coincide with the metric accents (downbeats). Interesting here is the elision of two syllables with open vowels into a single note in

[41] For details, see Hans-Gerd Winter's and Peter Petersen's essay, »Das Musiktheater als Sonderzweig der produktiven Rezeption von J. M. R. Lenz' Dramen und Dramentheorie,« in *Lenz-Jb.* (St. Ingbert 1991), 1: 9-58.

Ex. 1-090   Bach, ›*Missa*‹ *B Minor*, Osanna

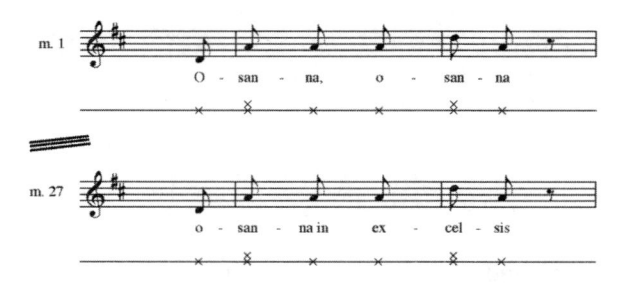

»osanna in excelsis.« The result is a perfect rhythmicization of the Latin line, as only the two long syllables are weighted, while the short ones remain light.

Ex. 1-091
Mozart, Missa K. 317, Sanctus (Hosanna)

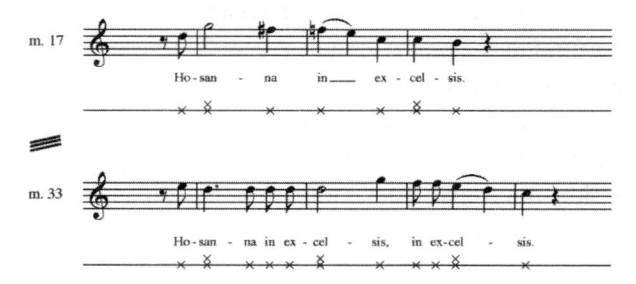

A ternary meter for the Latin words is likewise chosen in Mozart's ›Coronation Mass‹ (Ex. 1-091), albeit in larger proportions than in Bach. Again rhythm is largely accentual thanks to the heavy beats of the meter: downbeats and long syllables coincide; only mm. 34-35 deviate. The syllable -sis there is clearly stressed by the leaping crest note G5, though the effect is lessened somewhat by the hemiolic harmony at this point, causing the long syllable –cel in the next measure to fall on a six-four chord suspension with a relatively strong position.

Ex. 1-092
Bruckner, *Missa F Minor* (Hosanna)

Bruckner, in his F Minor Mass (Ex. 1-092), uses the same meter as Mozart, but renders the durational proportions of the Latin syllables more precisely. The long syllables are each time given emphasis by relative lengthenings of the note, and »excelsis« is additionally articulated by high notes and even by dynamic accents.

Stravinsky, from whose Mass for mixed chorus and winds our last example is taken (Ex. 1-093), comes closest to the quantifying character of Latin in his music. As can be seen in the two explanatory lines »Syllabic weight« (prosodic length) and »Syllabic duration« (musical length), the three

Ex. 1-093   Stravinsky, *Mass*, Sanctus (Hosanna), Discanti

syllables of the word »hosanna« are sometimes emphasized, sometimes not. Thereby the composer approximates the pure, flat syllabic rhythm of the Latin. The word »excelsis,« by contrast, is regularly accentuated on the second syllable by means of crest notes, while the short last syllable is stretched by means of long notes (caesural lengthening).

After this survey of five »Hosanna« passages from different eras, I want to add one example of prosodic marking in instrumental music. Arnold Schoenberg, among others, occasionally used the accent signs of spoken language as an aid in articulating instrumental music. In those cases he puts the marks for accented (/) and unaccented (u) syllables directly above the note of a voice, so as to prompt the performer to recite the melodic motif like a spoken word – whereby the normal musical accent and articulation signs may well be employed simultaneously.

In the scene »The Golden Calf and the Altar« in the opera *Moses and Aaron* (II:iii), Schoenberg makes liberal use of this method (Ex. 1-094). In the section, in which the cattle is slaughtered and chunks of meat are thrown to the crowd, several instruments play dance-like melodies of a heterometric cut over an isometric ground characterized by ostinati. Beams, durations, melodic contours and prosodic accent signs mark a wild, irregular rhythm, which well expresses the increasingly orgiastic behavior of the dancers. Trombone and piccolo flute engage in an almost strict canon. The fact that the staccato points are not always set in the same way may be due to careless writing. But that the flute initially sounds an extra ♪ (F6) is surely intentional as a way of representing the ruling chaos. At the beginning of the phrases, in any case, the two prosodic accents (/) occur thus once in immediate succession (tromb.), once not (picc.). It is also noteworthy that the prosodic accents do not always agree with the rhythmic units as determined by the beams. The lengths of the phrases, moreover, are independent of the measure of the 2/2 time. I might add that the prosodic signs in this scene occasionally also occur over the vocal parts. In these cases they serve to assert a »correct« pronunciation against the metric beat (e.g., mm. 718ff., 810).

Ex. 1-094   Schoenberg, *Moses and Aaron* II:iii, mm. 380-384 (extract)

Rhythmic Weight
(The Allegretto of Beethoven's Seventh Symphony)

Preface

Musical rhythms are founded on tone events that stand like segmentation marks in the temporal continuum. This is true regardless, initially, of how important or unimportant the sound events are. If one then also considers the rank of these sounds and their components, one discovers that they mark the temporal flow more or less distinctly. Elementary contrasts like long and short, high and low, loud and soft, dense and loose, dark and light furnish an inexhaustible wealth of possibilities for creating gradations among the sound events and thus differentiating between important and less important rhythmic points of demarcation.

Irrespective of whether one assumes that music originates from body movements (dance, strike gestures) or from voice intonations (song, vocal signals), or from both, graded weights always play a role in the structured bodily or vocal actions. The dancer puts down a foot and ›lifts‹ the body over it, or he relieves the foot and ›lowers‹ the body again, in other words, shifts his own weight. Already the ancient Greeks transferred such body experiences to linguistic description, coining the concepts of »thesis« (i.e. setting) for long (accented) and arsis (i.e. raising) for short (unaccented) syllables.[42] The singer or speaker, on the other hand, narrows the vocal cords and increases bodily tension in other ways to produce higher tones. These tones that stand out from a flat recitation have come to be called accent (from Latin accentus [accantus] after Gk. prosodia = add-to song, ›high tone‹).

Such elementary facts tell us no more and no less than that, apart from »durations,« »weights« also determine musical rhythm. As already explained in the introduction, the concept »rhythmic weight« denotes not sound volume but degree of value. Something can be heavy without being loud. At issue is the control of the player's or listener's perception. A sound phenomenon that persists for a time, or the coming together of several sound phenomena, will call special attention to itself. Metaphorically speaking, rhythmic weights have a gravitational attraction that increase with the mass of the sound event. A soft but long-held or repeated note develops a mass that derives from its duration, not its volume. The same goes essentially for the durations or else the rhythmic values of the other components or sound shapes, e.g., pitch durations in note repetitions, durations of harmonic functions or gradated phrase or semi-phrase durations.

The question is then how rhythmic weights are to be measured. What is unproblematic for the horizontal line, because pulses enable the measuring of durations in any components category, requires special reflections for the vertical level. The following sections will seek to formalize as much as possible the determination of the weight of a component and its contingent rhythmic duration. In addition, attention will be directed to a largely ignored phenomenon: the »accumulation« of rhythmic weights. Since, as already discussed, every tone or sound sequence contains multiple rhythms (component rhythms), the coincidence of such rhythms results in an accumulation. Imagine that over the course of a melody a note is at once extended, elevated, increased in volume and articulated in a special way, and that there is also a harmonic change, a new timbre is added and a new phrase begins: in such a case, the tone will have to be accorded an increased component-rhythmic weight. This diversely qualified note is obviously among the ›important,‹ that is, the heavily ›weighted,‹ demarcation points in the temporal continuum and therefore will send out a strong signal to attract the attention of player and listener.

Concepts borrowed from prosody cannot but fail to account for this phenomenon of rhythmic accumulation with its innumerable shades. Terms like arsis, thesis, accent or stress denote situations that are much too coarse-grained to correspond to the degrees of rhythmic differentiation in music.

The application of the word »weight« to musical situations has hitherto referred mainly to matters of meter and beat. One speaks of strong and weak or of heava and light beats, as I have done myself and will continue to do. Components theory with its inherent aspect of rhythmic accumulation, however, permits a more exact gauging of what is felt to be heavy or light. In addition, it opens an entirely new perspective on musical metric. For a comparison of the (accumulated) rhythmic weights with the (historically given) metric ones reveals similar structures. In most cases, the analytically ascertained rhythmic weights even duplicates the weight relations of the prescribed meter. That means that, say, a 2/4 time and its metric hierarchy can be determined just from the rhythmics without the weight schema of the meter having to be included. Analysis thus catches up with everyday listeners' experience: we recognize the meter without knowing the time signature (cf. also the analysis of the Haydn Allegretto theme in the Introduction, pp. 10 f. above).

The decisive difference between my method and conventional metrical analysis consists in that the rhythmically determined measures are modified from one bar to the next. They may resemble each other without being identical. It can be shown that in aesthetically significant music hardly one measure is like another, even though they may all be oriented according to the same model – for example, the schema of a 2/4 time. It becomes clear again that the ana-

---

[42] The terms thesis and arsis are no longer used in prosody because in Greek antiquity, when dance, language and music were a unity, a reversal of meaning and hence some confusion occurred. »Thesis« originally signified the heavy, »arsis« the light syllable; in late antiquity, however, the opposite was the case. See the article »Hebung« in *Reallexikon der deutschen Literaturwissenschaft*, ed. Harald Fricke, 3 vols. (Berlin/New York: Gruyter, 2007).

lysis according to components theory is phenomenologically oriented. The sound event is the starting point of every investigation. To put it differently: the road to rhythm runs through what is composed and only indirectly through what is notated. Notation serves the execution of music: an analyst should not regard it as a body of laws to be followed "to the letter."

In order to facilitate the reader's understanding of the argument in the following sub-chapters (Weight of components and durations – Accumulation of rhythmic weights – Rhythmic and metric weight), all of my examples will this time be taken from a single piece: the Allegretto of Beethoven's Seventh Symphony. This procession-like movement in A minor combines elements of the march (with twofold Maggiore part), the variation form (theme and six variations) and the sonata form (fugato development section); the Coda is also the final variation. Two identical wind chords in the A minor tonic (in an oddly unstable second inversion) provide a frame that seems to invite an endless repetition of the movement from the start – a symbol of suspended time.

The movement has a time signature of 2/4 and is relatively limited in terms of the note values used. The longest values rarely exceed dotted half notes (except for a few pedal points in the middle voices), the shortest values are sixteenths; in between there are duplet and triplet eighths, which, like the half notes, frequently seem prolonged by rests.

For the three chief themes I use freely invented names in order to remain as concrete as possible and to intimate their musical characters. The main sections have a ›Procession‹ theme with its ›Wanderer rhythm‹ (♩ ♪♪♩ ♩) and a ›Cantabile‹ theme developed from a harmonic inner voice. Both of the themes in these Marcia parts are set forth by the strings. Their form is in keeping with a repetition period with a half close in the parallel key and a perfect cadence in the tonic, with the second phrase being repeated, so that a length of 24 bars is attained (| 8 |: 8 :|). The two A major sections have a different, altogether independent ›Trio‹ theme, whose main voice is in the winds. In spite of its pastoral, self-contained character, it is formally open, as it modulates to C major at the end, followed by a transition (8+7+6+8+8) to the fourth variation of the A minor complex.

In what follows I shall transcribe the original score notation, omitting beams, bar lines and ligatures. This will also make graphically clearer that all weight specifications, represented in the form of noteheads set one upon the other, are purely (components-) rhythmic in nature.

One may question the need to analyze a symphonic movement that immediately discloses itself to the listener in so thoroughgoing a manner, as will be done in the following sections. But my goal is a refinement of musical perception, specifically here, of course, in regard to rhythmic relations. I want to understand how the special motivic character of a melody or a multi-voiced and multi-layered setting comes about. How does it happen that a theme that, at first glance, simply repeats the same rhythm – ♩ ♪♪♩ ♩ – does not bore us? I am convinced that this is owing to those other simultaneously registered rhythms and rhythmic weights produced in the setting by the components other than the duration of the notes. Their weight exceeds not infrequently that of the basic component »Sound.« Our perception of rhythmic relations is shaped by the totality of all the component rhythms and their respective gradations of weight. These latter are the subject of the following sections.

Weight of Components Durations

Sound

We will begin with the basic component »Sound,« whose rhythms do not have to be determined because they can be read directly in the notes. A simple procedure for determining the rhythmic weight presents itself: the multiplication of a durational value by the smallest occurring value.

The situation is very simple in the ›Procession‹ theme (Ex. 1-095). The smallest value is an eighth note (♪ = 1). The quarter notes are therefore doubly weighted (♩ = 2), the halves, originally written as quarter notes with quarter rests, have the fourfold weight (♩ = 4). The three quarter rests are part of the Articulation, which will be described later along with other articulatory forms.

In regard to the component rhythm »Sound« and its rhythmic weights, thus, a division into 4/4 units emerges as the result of recurring patterns – the ›Wanderer‹ rhythm. The half notes at the end of the phrases mark the threefold recurrence of 16/4 units. The time signature of 2/4 fits smoothly into this pattern, though it is not shown here in its own form.

Ex. 1-095   mm. 3-26, Procession Theme (»Sound«)

Ex. 1-096   mm. 27-50, Cantabile Theme (»Sound«)

The ›Cantabile‹ theme is rhythmically livelier than the ›Procession‹ theme, to which it appears as a new counter-voice. Here the smallest value is the sixteenth, whereby the grace-note sixteenths are disregarded as irrational durations, to be included later under the component »Articulation/Ornament.« The component »Sound« exhibits a shape of the theme that strongly differs from the rhythmics of the ›Procession‹ theme – a contrast significantly reinforced, as we shall see, by the remaining component rhythms. The emphatic nature of the ›Cantabile‹ theme is due, among other things, to the juxtaposition of notes with simple and eight-fold weighting. In other ways, too, the durational weights produce a lively billowing in relatively narrow spaces. Noteworthy is also the fact that in the ›Cantabile‹ theme the heaviest weights appear at the beginning, whereas in the ›Procession‹ theme they mark the end of the phrases. In consequence, the double measures here seem downbeat, while in the simultaneously sounded ›Procession‹ theme the first 2/4 bar is weighted like an upbeat to the macro-measure. A melody shaped in this manner can be easily distinguished from the surrounding sound, even if, as an inner voice in *p*, it is potentially covered up.

Ex. 1-097   mm. 101-116, Trio Theme (»Sound«)

The ›Trio‹ theme (Ex. 1-097) has a rhythm that differs from that of both of the Marcia sections, just as its difference in mode – it is written in A major rather than in A minor – gives it a character all its own. As in the ›Procession‹ theme, the smallest value is the eighth, used along with a majority of quarter notes and some half-notes. The wide melodic span of this theme appears rhythmically in the numerous sequences of quarter notes with a low weight value, which appear to connect the theme's quadruple-weighted ›pylons.‹

The principal earmark of the theme is its syncopations (♩), which in the original appear as tied quarter notes (see the small notes at the head of Ex. 1-097). In addition it should be noted that as long as one considers only the rhythmic weights of the basic component »Sound,« the time signature of 2/4 does not stand out, neither in this nor in the other two themes.

The fourth variation is followed by a fugato (mm. 183-213), whose subject is built from the ›Procession‹ theme. Since it is furnished with a counter-subject consisting of regular ♪, which sets in right at the beginning, the proportions of the fugue theme shift: The ♩ now have the value of 4, the ♪ that of 2 and the ♪ that of 1 (Ex. 1-098). Apart from that, the rhythm, also with respect to the durational weights, is quite similar to that of the ›Procession‹ theme; only the runs of the counter-subject (stems pointing downward) contribute a different kind of movement.

Ex. 1-098   mm. 183-187, Fugue Theme (»Sound«)

Rhythmic Intensification

In going through the variations, one notices an overriding rhythmic intensification, which Beethoven has taken over from the tradition of the variation cycle: an introduction of successively smaller note values. Whereas the first three sections of the movement consist throughout of duplets, predominantly of ♩ and ♪, triplets of eighths appear at the first dynamic climax in m. 75, which is also the onset of the third variation (cf. Ex. 1-099). These triplets, occurring at first only in the accompaniment of the low strings, are in ›conflict‹ with the duplet values of the ›Procession‹ and ›Cantabile‹ themes. To determine a smallest value, which our method would normally call for, makes little sense here, especially since there are occasional ♪ along with the predominant ♪ in the ›Cantabile‹ theme. Arithmetically, of course, it would be possible to determine the distance between a duplet ♪ and a triplet ♪, i.e. the smallest distance: the quarter note would have to be divided into twelfths, so that the first notes of the ›Cantabile‹ theme (♩♩) would have to be thought of as amounting to 24/12 each. That would require a tower of 24 note heads! In order to obviate that, one does better to analyze settings that are clearly thought of as consisting of various rhythmic layers as what they are: relatively independent, in this case interconnected binary and ternary sequences. The construction of a common denominator would obscure, rather than clarify, the rhythmic actuality. In the present case, one would also have

Ex. 1-099   mm. 75-78

to consider yet altogether different weight gradations, such as the relation between principal voices and accompaniment, as well as the massive instrumentation of one of the four levels, here above all the ›Procession‹ theme as played by the winds in four octaves (see the analysis below, p. 76).

Of greater importance for the musical course and thus also for the overriding rhythmic process is the fact that by introducing the eighths triplets at the end of the first Marcia part, Beethoven is preparing the motion mode of the Trio. What Ex. 1-097 does not yet show, nevertheless plays a considerable role in the overall rhythm of the Trio: the clarinet is accompanied in the violins by chords broken into triplet eighths (see also Ex. 1-103 below). As the theme is spun out, these triplets also spread to the main voices (from m. 117). Altogether the eighths triplets dominate even the two A major Trios, in spite of the ostinato pounding of the duplet ›Wanderer‹ rhythm in the string basses (mm. 102-142).

Ex. 1-100   mm. 150.153

With the start of the fourth variation, which drops back into *p* (after the first Trio), we first hear sixteenths figurations, which thus continue the diminution of the note values. But since anything that has happened in Beethoven's music rarely remains without consequences, we now hear triplets also in the high-pitched voice of the ›Cantabile‹ theme (Ex. 1-100), where before they have appeared only in the accompaniment. The melody of the ›Cantabile‹ theme, basically conceived in duplets, thus ›reacts‹ to the preceding events, in which triplets played a growing role.

The already mentioned fugato, which follows presently, contains no triplets, and neither does the heavily abbreviated fifth variation. Then the (likewise abbreviated) Trio is repeated, followed by a Coda (Variation VI), once again wholly in duplets.

Pitch

Let us now turn to rhythmic weighting with regard to the component »Pitch.« As we will remember, this component is operating in all note repetitions, but also in secondary melodies, which can occur as inner lines or else as outer edges.

Since the ›Procession‹ theme is rich in tone repetitions, one can easily see that, besides the rhythm of tonal entries, there is also a rhythm of pitch movement, which naturally is slower. The longer a pitch is held, however, the greater its rhythmic weight. It would not make sense to determine the weight of pitches exactly like that of short or long notes, that is, by the multiplication of a smallest occurring value. Instead one can proceed by assigning every change in pitch the weight value 1. If thus in a sequence of tones a new pitch appears at every entry, only the value 1 is added each time to the values of the note entry rhythm. If, on the other hand, there are note repetitions so that the pitches have a longer validity than the entering notes, the weight values of the repeated notes are added to the respective pitch. This is represented in Ex. 1-101.

As repeatedly emphasized, the towers of notes do not represent increases in volume but the value weight of a component and its duration. The pitch E3 is initially held for 19 ♪, thus drawing the listener's attention over this relatively extended time span. This duration develops its rhythmic effect coincidentally with the durations of the ›Wanderer‹ rhythm. The weight values of the repetition rhythm after the first note introducing a new pitch are added to the weight of the pitch. At the beginning of the example, thus, these amount to 1+1+2+2+2+1+1+2+2+2+1 (=17) units of weight, for a total value of 18.

In the ›Cantabile‹ theme (Ex 1-102), the note repetitions attain an increased rhythmic significance, as they considerably reinforce the lively character of the theme. Repeatedly, here, pitches are anticipated, thus providing emphatic ›upbeats.‹ This is the case with typical grace-notes like appoggiaturas (e.g. right at the beginning B-B in the rhythm of ♪ ♪), as well as with longer durations. On the other hand, there are also passages in which the pitch changes with every note entry so that the pitch rhythm is identical with that of the notes (weight value 1).

Ex. 1-101   mm. 3-26, Procession Theme (»Sound« and »Pitch«)

Ex. 1-102 mm. 27-50, Cantabile Theme (»Sound« and »Pitch«)

Ex. 1-103 mm. 101-116, Trio Theme with Accompaniment

The ›Trio‹ theme (Ex. 1-103) contains relatively few note repetitions. They simply continue what is already laid out in the basic rhythm of the component »Sound«: the merging of two ♩ into one ♩. On the other hand, this theme, in its figurative accompanying voice in the violins, offers a good example of the subcomponent of a secondary part. For the triplet figures of the violins, consisting mostly of broken triads, duplicate, in their upper notes (stems pointing upward) the melody of the clarinet, albeit in a rhythm that does not always coincide with that of the main voice. The divergence subsists, on the one hand, between the triplet string eighths and the duplet values of the clarinet voice, and, on the other, between syncopations (a) and the extended dottings (b), which the inherent upper voice produces on the basis of the triplet eighths. This rhythmic soft focusing contributes much to the tender character of the theme.

Articulation – Diastematy – Dynamics

On the level of the individual voices, the components »Articulation« (including ornaments), »Diastematy« and »Dynamics« play a lesser role in this movement. The corresponding rhythms should therefore not be additionally weighted. The rhythmic life initiated by these components is nevertheless of some importance for the total character of the themes as well as the other passages of the movement. I shall illustrate the relations based on the example of the ›Cantabile‹ theme (Ex. 1-104).

This time the main voice of the ›Cantabile‹ theme is given in Beethoven's original notation, including not only the dynamic and articulatory marks but also the original beams and bar lines (suggestions only). The staccato wedges, the slide figures and the articulatory rest (all below the line) likewise fall on the primary or secondary beats of the 2/4 meter.

If we recall the riven weight conditions of the components »Sound« and »Pitch,« it becomes clear that the component »Articulation« brings back a measure of calm into this theme. The rhythm of the component »Diastematy« is ambivalent in this respect, while that of »Dynamics« can be slighted altogether (there is only a single diminution of the volume – the *pp* at the repetition of the consequent; it is therefore appropriate to doubly weight of the *p* at the beginning)

Phrase

Regarding the component »Phrase,« it is generally requisite to gauge the weight of each phrase according to its length. As already shown in the section about this component, one must distinguish between a) phrases determined according to their motivic-thematic content, and b) those that are linked by the composer by means of slurs. Both variants are found in this movement.

Thus the ›Procession‹ theme is clearly subdivided by rhythmic and motivic turns, as well as rests/caesuras, while there are no phrasing slurs. In Ex. 1-105, the partial and complete phrases are graded by weight. Together, the three groups of eight bars constitute the largest unit and are thus weighted by the value of 3 (at the beginning). Each individual eight-bar unit receives the value 2, the partial phrases constructed from the ›Wanderer‹ rhythm a 1. The simplicity of this phrase structure seems appropriate given the processional character of the movement.

Ex. 1-104 mm. 27-50, Cantabile Theme (»Articulation«, »Diastematy« and »Dynamics«)

Ex. 1-105   mm. 3-26, Procession Theme (»Phrase«)

[musical notation: viola part with phrase analysis]

Ex. 1-106   mm. 27-50, Cantabile Theme (»Phrase«)

[musical notation: viola part with phrase analysis]

Ex. 1-107   mm.101-116, Trio Theme with Accompaniment (»Phrase«)

[musical notation: clarinet and violin I parts with phrase analysis]

The ›Cantabile‹ theme is phrased quite similarly to the ›Procession‹ theme, which is hardly surprising, as both melodies are connected contrapuntally. But the partial phrases are often longer, because the ›Wanderer‹ rhythm, while underlaid beneath the ›Cantabile‹ theme, does not determine it (Ex. 1-106). The slurs here I take to be articulation marks rather than phrasing ones.

Phrasing slurs occur mainly in the ›Trio‹ theme, being fully differentiated according to primary and secondary voices. I confine myself in Ex. 1-107 to the melody-bearing clarinet, along with the accompanying voice of the violins. The phrases in the clarinet voice result initially from the slurs drawn by Beethoven, while in the continuation of the theme, motifs and thematic imitations determine the phrase structure. In the accompanying voice of the violins, only the phrasing slurs are decisive; the distribution of weights is a matter of interpretation. One notices immediately that the violins phrase more minutely than the clarinet. The weighting roughly accords with that. Thus the longest phrase in the clarinet part (12 ♪) has the greatest weight value, while the triplet figure comprising a quarter note has the smallest. Despite the relatively diminutive phrasing in the violins, the beginnings of their phrases are pretty exactly coordinated with those of the clarinet. Only at the start of the elaboration they are complementary to each other, specifically where the clarinet enters anew with the note A5, whereas the violins counter with two-bar slurs already begun earlier.

Timbre

The component »Timbre,« which, as explained above, comprises the two aspects instrumental color and light-dark shading (octave registers), is of predominantly formal, not rhythmical, significance in this movement. Changes in timbre of sufficient brevity that they can come under the rubric of rhythm do, nevertheless, occur occasionally, as,
e.g., at the beginning, when the opening chord in the winds is, after two bars, replaced by the strings, whereby a contrast in both instrumental color and light-dark shading is produced (oboe: E5, viola: E3).

Quite striking, because rhythmically and metrically slightly disorienting, is the transition from the Trio to the Marcia. Here the last three quarters before the entry of the fourth variation are strongly accentuated and isolated by ascending octaves (E4-E5-E6), so that for a moment the illusion of a ternary meter is evoked (Ex. 1-108).

Ex. 1-108   mm. 144-149, »Timbre«

[musical notation with Timbre analysis]

A really outstanding example of timbre rhythm occurs in the Coda of the movement. This is the formal part in which the ›Procession‹ theme is varied for the last time, with timbre change (instrumental colors and octave register) being the principal means of modification (Ex. 1-109). As a comparison with the original theme melody will show, the tonal steps of the melody are kept the same, albeit with changes in the octave register after every second measure, that is, in the measure of the ›Wanderer‹ rhythm – changes in instrumental color going hand in hand with the changes in octave register.

The example reproduces only the melody tones; in reality they are, as in the original theme, harmonized by three or four voices. But whereas in the original form the voice carrying the melody is always the upper voice, the main voice here, owing to the changes in position, can be upper as well as middle or lower voice.

Ex. 1-109   Procession Theme + Coda Variant (»Timbre«)

In the last six bars, the final tetrachord is split off and there is a brief imitational play in stretto. Disorienting – deliberately on Beethoven's part – is the last entry of the ›Wanderer‹ rhythm on the weak beat of the 2/4 meter in the first violins, with the result that the notes $F_\sharp5$-$G_\sharp5$-$A5$ coincide with the A minor tonic chord of the winds, which, entering on the $F_\sharp5$, concludes the movement. Its *f* intonation spreads also to the first violins, so that the technical irregularity cannot under any circumstances be missed.

The timbre rhythm that structures the last variation of the ›Procession‹ theme – i.e., the Coda variation – is less spectacular than the method of varying the theme. Since the timbre changes at progressively shorter intervals at the end (because of the upwardly transposed octaves), a heavier weighting of the longer timbre-rhythm durations suggests itself. I therefore assigned the value of 3 for the whole notes, the value 2 for the halves and the value 1 for the quarter notes. Since the entire Coda, except for the final forte, is to be played *pp*, the weights cannot signify levels of volume but only the varying durations of the respective timbres.

Harmony

We now come to the important »Harmony« component. In the chapter about this component, the ›Procession‹ theme has already been adduced (see Ex. 1-050). Neither the changes in harmonic function nor the suspensions and cadences were assigned increased weight there. Given the present context of the rhythmic *weight* of components, this will now have to be modified. For it would be inadequate to value sound events that, in a setting of many parts, regularly combine several voices – and that includes harmonic progressions – exactly like, say, a staccato point of the component »Articulation.« In a major-minor triadic harmony, it therefore seems appropriate to me to assign a fourfold value to every change in harmonic function. Cadences and suspensions are to be differentiated on a case by case basis.

In the examples 1-110 and 1-111, the harmonic rhythm of the A minor themes (›Procession‹ and ›Cantabile‹ themes combined) is juxtaposed with the A major (›Trio‹) theme. From the harmony extracts one can tell what function changes happen at what intervals. It turns out that the harmonic rhythm of the Marcia themes is much more differ-

Ex. 1-110   Procession- and Cantabile Theme (»Harmony«)

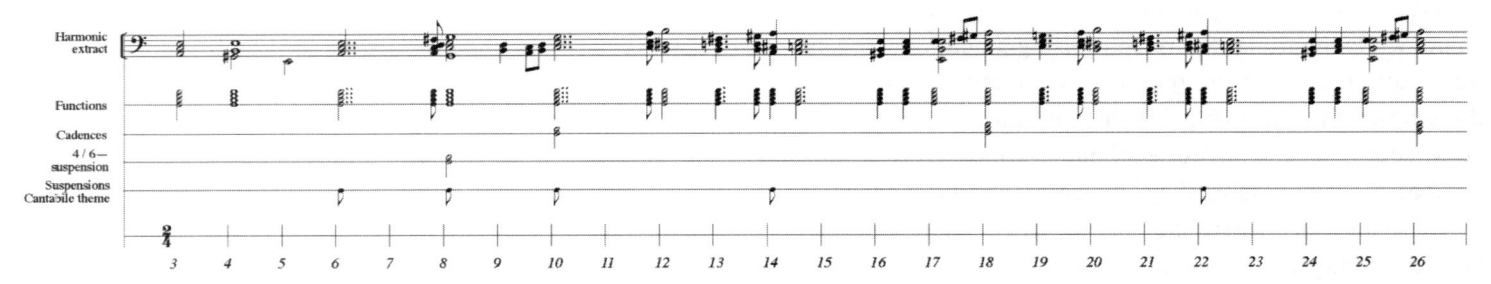

Ex. 1-111   mm. 101-116, Trio Theme (»Harmony«)

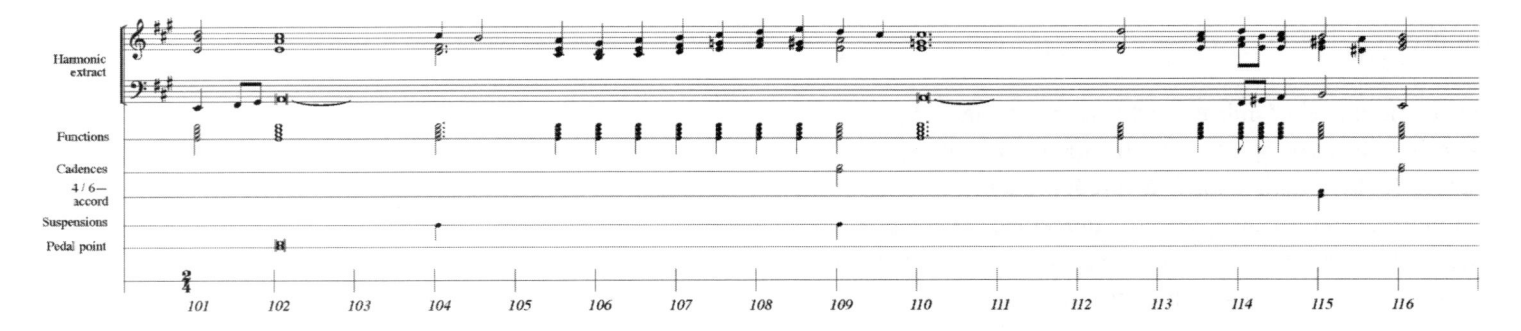

entiated than that of the Trio theme. The characteristic major-minor-changes in the ›Procession‹ theme (mm. 12/13, 14/15, 20/21, 22/23), which is reinforced by the melodic-chromatic steps of the ›Cantabile‹ theme, twice produce a quasi-syncopated turn of the harmonic rhythm, caused by he anticipation of the A minor sound before the bar line.

The A major theme, too, has a ›harmonic syncopation,‹ which here, however, coincides with, and supports, the syncopation of the melody. In the second part of the theme, the dominant seventh chord on A is held for five quarters, until the subdominant in D major is reached (mm. 110-112) and extends beyond the bar line. The pedal point on A, which subtends all of the theme's first, and more than half of its second, phrase, also corresponds to the plain character of the ›Trio‹ theme. Pedal points as special harmonic events, which always exist in tension with the main harmonic happening, have to find expression within the total rhythmic structure, though it is probably impossible to set up a generally valid rule for measuring their rhythmic weight. In the present case I have oriented myself according to the phrase structure and have assigned a value of 2 to the pedal point, because it almost completely grounds both halves of the theme's period.

A more systematic procedure is possible in weighting the cadences. In the 18th and 19th century, three types of cadence occur regularly: the perfect cadence on the tonic, the perfect cadence on a neighboring degree, and the half-close on the fifth degree. These three cadences can be sensibly distinguished from one another by the weight values 3, 2 and 1, though one should in each case scrutinize the contexts in which such primary and secondary cadences occur and distribute the weights differently if appropriate. One such case occurs in the Trio theme, where the tonic at the end of the first phrase ›deserves,‹ not the value 3, but only one of 2, because neither a bass clause (fourth or fifth step) nor the basic position of the tonic triad is given and, on top of everything, the C♯ third is retarded by a fourth's suspension (m. 109). We have here a hybrid form: a half-close in the tonic.

The harmonic rhythm of the Marcia and Trio themes have in common that they tend more toward double-measure formations than toward the prescribed 2/4 meter. In addition, the durations of the harmonic changes and especially the position of the dominant six-four chord suspensions point to the likelihood that the first 2/4 measure of each phrase was regarded as an upbeat to double-measure units by Beethoven. The harmony of the ›Procession‹ and ›Cantabile‹ theme has the duration of the initial tonic (2 ♩) being followed by harmonic durations that are all approximately twice as long (mostly 3 or 4 ♩). The case is similar in the ›Trio‹ theme, whose upbeat character became clear already from the anticipatory syncopation in the main voice (Ex. 1-107). Correspondingly, the harmonic rhythm of the first measure has a dominant (2 ♩) followed immediately by a tonic of twice that length (4 ♩).

Suspensions, which in major-minor (and in part already in modal) music are always connected with dissonances and thus belong among the harmonic special events, can generally be given a weight value of 1 and thus be included in the total rhythmic structure. In the ›Procession‹ theme, there are no suspensions besides the six-four chord referred to earlier. The ›Cantabile‹ theme, on the other hand, introduces altogether five melodic suspensions, which as major seconds, tritones or fourths are dissonant in relation to the triads and thereby set harmonic accents. In the ›Trio‹ theme, there are only two suspensions (besides the second inversion chord in the double dominant), of which the first (the major seventh of $C_♯5$ over D4 in m. 104) gives strong emphasis to the second double measure with its turn toward the subdominant, whereas the second (m. 109) only slightly retards the tonic at the end of the first phrase. All of the suspensions occur – quite properly – on heavy metrical stresses and thus contribute to the formation of isometric structures.

Texture

It remains to discuss the component »Texture,« which has rhythmic effects especially in the development-like fugato (mm. 183-213) (Ex. 1-112). The theme comprising eight ♩ maintains a quadruple meter in the exposition of the four theme entries. A little later there follows a stretto section with foreshortened and fragmented themes and progressively smaller intervals between entries.

To weight the durations resulting from the entry intervals (texture rhythms), I take ♩ = 1 for the smallest intervals, and a multiple of that for the larger ones. The long durations at the beginning are thus balanced by the many shorter ones toward the end.

The category »Texture« may also be said to include the difference between main setting and accompaniment. How ever differentiated in form such accompanying voices (obbligato accompaniment) may be, they must be distinguished according to their weight from the main happening to do full justice to the rhythmic character of a given setting. How Beethoven proceeds in the individual variations of the movement can only be suggested here.

Ex. 1-112   mm. 183-213, Fugato (extract)

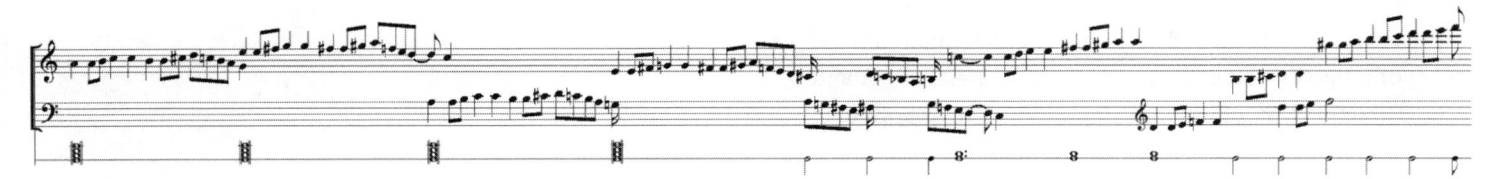

Ex. 1-113 mm. 27-30

To take one example, the first variation (mm. 27-50) is shaped as a transparent three-voiced setting, in which the ›Procession‹ and the ›Cantabile‹ theme sound in their original rhythm, while the bass strings play an ostinato rhythmic counterpoint to it, consisting of a two-bar melodic-rhythmic model that is repeated twelve times (Ex. 1-113). The model has an upbeat consisting of two eighths, which refer to the second measure of the ›Procession‹ theme, and which are followed by an extended syncopation,

which clearly marks a double measure ($4^{2+2}/4$). This seems to confirm what became recognizable already in the harmonic rhythm of the Marcia themes, namely that the first measure forms a kind of upbeat for the following double measure.

Ex. 1-114 mm. 51-54

The situation is again different in the accompaniment of the second variation (mm. 51-74). Here a one-bar rhythmic-melodic model is repeated 24 times (Ex. 1-114). If one looks at the accompanying setting by itself, the abstract pattern of the 2/4 meter practically obtrudes itself. Nowhere else in the movement does the time signature have such a well-fitting rhythmic counterpart. Regarding macro-measures and upbeats, however, this example provides no further insights. Because of the isolation of the measures, the double measures written in the main themes are neither confirmed nor negated.

Accompanying rhythms may not be ignored, but they must be set in proper proportion to the rhythmics of the main event. There can be no firm rules for that: the only criterion must be the specific givens of the individual case. In general, one can say that a complete analysis of the entire composition has to precede the rhythm analysis. In the process one can also determine, among other things, which components of a setting represent the main event and are thus intended as of special importance. In accordance with such gradations of import, the rhythmic weights can then also be assigned to the respective areas.

Accumulation of Rhythmic Weights

Having, in the preceding section, discussed the subject of rhythmic weight in regard to individual components, I want now to consider the combined weights of component rhythms. This can be demonstrated both in single-voiced melodies, whose component rhythms, of course, have different weight relations, and in settings with multi-part structure. In both cases, we are concerned with the phenomenon of weight accumulation.

The bringing together of individual component rhythms, as well as of voices with individually shaped rhythms, can yield unexpected insights to the analyst. What seemed dominant to him may turn out to be overshadowed by other phenomena, and vice versa. I will therefore in each case present the accumulation of rhythmic weights step by step, beginning with the three main themes of the movement.

›Procession‹ Theme

To begin with the ›Procession‹ theme, in a first step the weights of the component rhythms »Sound« and »Pitch« are accumulated (Ex. 1-115). As will be remembered from the previous section, the numerous note repetitions in this theme result in very long pitch durations, which in turn produce correspondingly high weight peaks (towers of notes).

As is to be expected, the overly long durations of the component »Pitch« are in the foreground of the rhythmic profile: the persistently held notes E or else G captivate a good part of our attention. Our curiosity grows: when will the voice carrying the melody finally move on from its original scale degree? At the same time, the ›Wanderer‹ rhythm pulses steadily ›inside‹ this held pitch level and likewise claims our attention. Then, in the second and third eight-bar unit, we notice an increasing differentiation in the distribution of rhythmic weights, because here the pitches do not remain quite as long and their weights approximate the durational weights of the entries.

In a second step, I add the light-weight component rhythms »Diastematy« (single), »Articulation« (single) »Dynamics« (single and double) and »Phrase« (single, double and triple) to the others (Ex. 1-116). A comparison of the weight profiles of Ex. 1-115 and Ex. 1-116 yields few differences, but the weight level as a whole is, of course, higher. Since every note in this theme has an articulation mark – I take Beethoven's marking »*ten.*« (tenuto) to mean that *every* first quarter note of the ›Wanderer‹ motif is to be held – all the weights are raised by a notch. In the component »Phrase,« the ›Wanderer‹ rhythm, which consists of partial phrases of four quarter notes each, comes through particularly strongly, especially as a keel note coincides repeatedly with the first note of the ›Wanderer‹ rhythm. The profile of the third eight-bar phrase in Ex. 1-116, for example, is clearly distinct from that in Ex. 1-115, because at its beginning a longish partial phrase enters anew, the ›Wanderer‹ rhythm commences, a keel note is sounded and a change in dynamic level is indicated. Thus, for a while, there is a profile similar to that of a 2/4 meter.

In a third step, the weights of the component »Harmony« (including the six-four chords and the imperfect and perfect cadences) are added (Ex. 1-117). The change of harmonic functions (cf. Ex. 1-050 in the section about »Harmony« in the preceding chapter) brings about a considerable animation of the musical happening. Thus the

Ex. 1-115   Procession Theme (»Sound«+»Pitch«)

Ex. 1-116   Procession Theme (»Sound«+»Pitch«+»Diastem.«+»Articul.«+»Dynamics«+»Phrase«)

Ex. 1-117   Procession Theme (»Sound«+»Pitch«+»Diastem.«+»Articul.«+»Dyn.«+»Phrase«+»Harmony«)

beginning of the theme, which, rhythmically speaking, was, until now, fairly lacking in contour, acquires more structure through the alternation of tonic and dominant. Above all, however, the harmonic changes on the last eighth in several measures (fifth measure of the first group of eight bars, third measure of the second and third eight-bar segment) have the effect that the last thesis of the dactylic ›Wanderer‹ rhythm (– . .) attains added weight – though that is canceled out again in the final cadences, where the notes of the melody are harmonized as transitions.

On the other hand, the now complete weight profile of the ›Procession‹ theme shows that a phenomenon like that of harmonic syncopation (cf. p. 71) may be eclipsed by the weights of other component rhythms. Since at the points in question (*) the repeated note A is accompanied by a change from A major to A minor, and the A minor continues in the following measure, we are dealing with a harmonic anticipatory syncopation – though the high value of the following pitch E (10 ♪) lessens the effect of this harmonic syncopated rhythm.

All in all, the weight profile of the ›Procession‹ theme reveals a rhythmic subtlety that helps us realize why the basic rhythm indicated by the mere notes does *not* sound monotonous. A statement that »the« rhythm of the ›Procession‹ theme is limited to the three-fold repetition of a certain sequence of quarter and eighth notes:

would in any case miss the complexity – which is essentially rhythmic in nature – of the seemingly simple theme.

›Cantabile‹ Theme

Let us now look at the ›Cantabile‹ theme, considering it likewise as a monophonic, even though harmonized, melody, since it is introduced, as shown above, as a more turbulent counter-voice to the ›Procession‹ theme.

If one compounds the rhythmic values of the components »Sound« and »Pitch,« the result is a relatively diverse structure (Ex. 1-118). The most conspicuous melodic-rhythmic features of the ›Cantabile‹ theme are the long-held starting notes of the three eight-bar settings, each time with descending minor second (C4–B3 and E4–D♯4), contrasted by the following small note values and the slide-accented dotted quarter notes. The numerous (9) pitch anticipations (*) likewise contribute to the passionate character of this theme and result in small, but sometimes also large, weight increases. In each case, they are placed in the metric shadow (♪ before ♩, ♪ before ♩, ♩ before ♩).

Owing to the heavily weighted pitch durations, the ›Cantabile‹ theme differs substantially from the ›Procession‹ theme. In the latter, the long pitches always coincide with the beat, whereas here they are upbeat. How Beethoven counteracts this crosswise relation by means of other component rhythms can be seen if the present profile is complemented by the components »Diastematics,« »Articulation,« »Dynamics« and »Phrase.« (Ex. 1-119). Since nearly all of the articulation marks lie, or start, on metrically heavy beats, the component »Articulation« by itself already produces weights that even out the extreme pitch weights. The same goes for the phrase beginnings, none of which are upbeat.

This trend is further reinforced if we now take into account also the weights of the harmonic rhythm, especially the five melodic suspensions and the second inversion chord suspension in the temporary modulation to C major (Ex. 1-120).

Ex. 1-118 Cantabile Theme (»Sound«+»Pitch«)

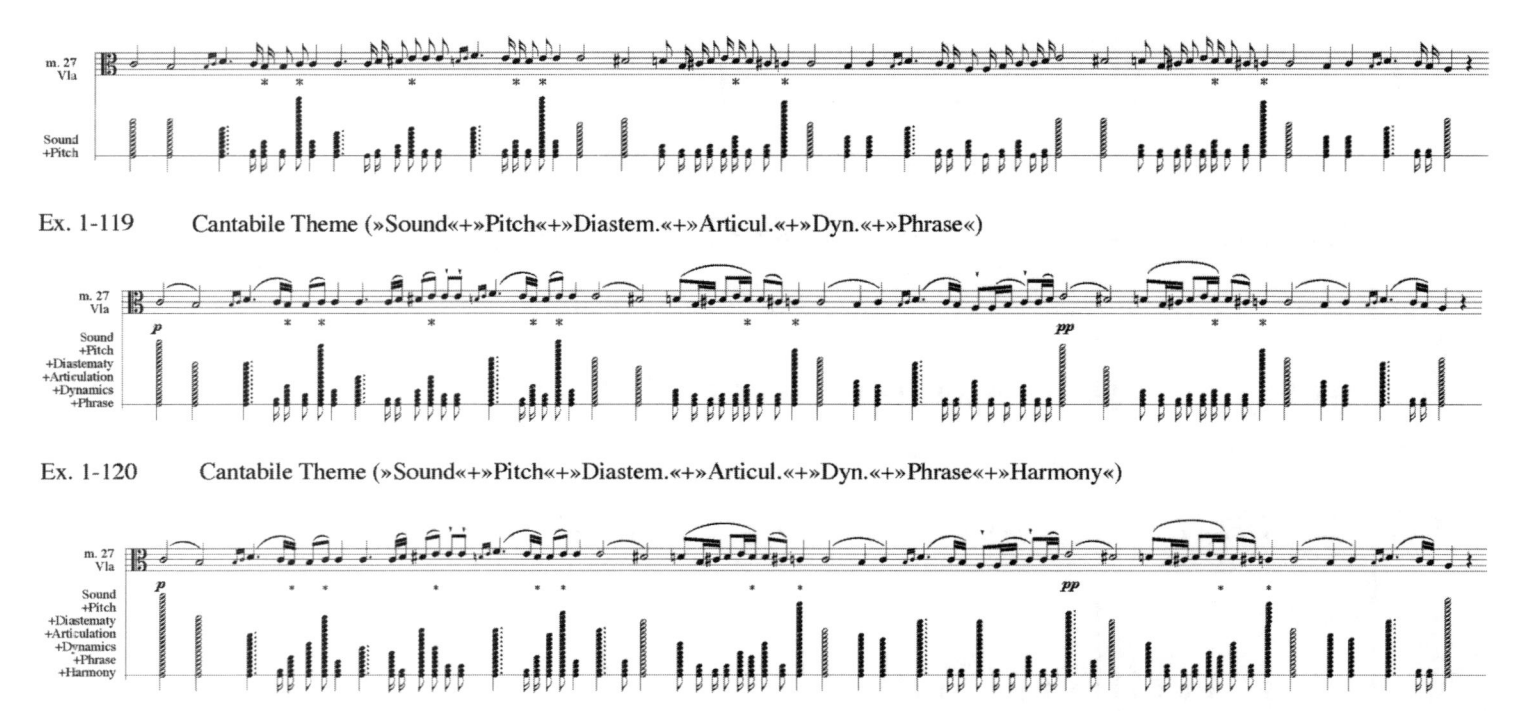

Ex. 1-119 Cantabile Theme (»Sound«+»Pitch«+»Diastem.«+»Articul.«+»Dyn.«+»Phrase«)

Ex. 1-120 Cantabile Theme (»Sound«+»Pitch«+»Diastem.«+»Articul.«+»Dyn.«+»Phrase«+»Harmony«)

Since the harmonic changes and the suspensions do not coincide with the anticipating pitches – except for the A major / A minor switch – the weights increase before or after the long pitches and result in a certain equilibrium. The repeatedly cited major / minor switch under the notes C♯-C♮ is of special interest here because the weight under the C♮ grows by four degrees owing to the anticipated A minor tonic and thus considerably exceeds the heavy beat under the following ♩ C♮. In fully considering all seven components, we thus do, after all, get that syncopated effect in the transition from major to minor.

The rhythmic profile thus essentially confirms what is revealed in listening to or playing the two main themes: a ceremonious, throughout striding first theme and an emotional, quasi-sung second one. This contrast in expression, produced by the contrapuntal linking of the two themes, finds its fully nuanced reflection down to the smallest detail in the rhythmic profiles, which in Ex. 1-121 are now directly juxtaposed.

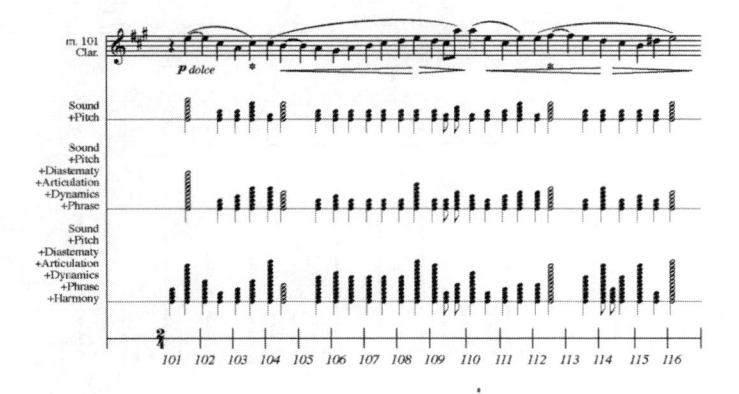

commences already on the *One* of the measure – which is taken into account in the rhythmic profile. The second detail concerns the dynamics. The only markings are the ***p*** at the beginning and the crescendo and decrescendo forks. The latter are generally useless for rhythmic analysis, because, like glissandi, accelerandi and ritardandi, they signal continuous processes. In the present case, however, the swelling marks are set so precisely that quite specific notes constitute dynamic turning-points: E5 in the second phrase and D5 in the fourth. In my gauging, 3 points are added to the rhythmic profile for the ***mf***.

The distribution of rhythmic weights in the ›Trio‹ theme yields overall a fairly calm picture. This is owing above all to the predominance of ♩ values, which in the second phrase are combined with constant harmonic changes. The larger weights, however, permit the syncopations to come to the fore, which were identified as a characteristic of this theme already in the preceding chapter (pp. 66).

In looking at details, the echeloned accumulation shows

Ex. 1-121   Rhythmic Profiles of First and Second Theme

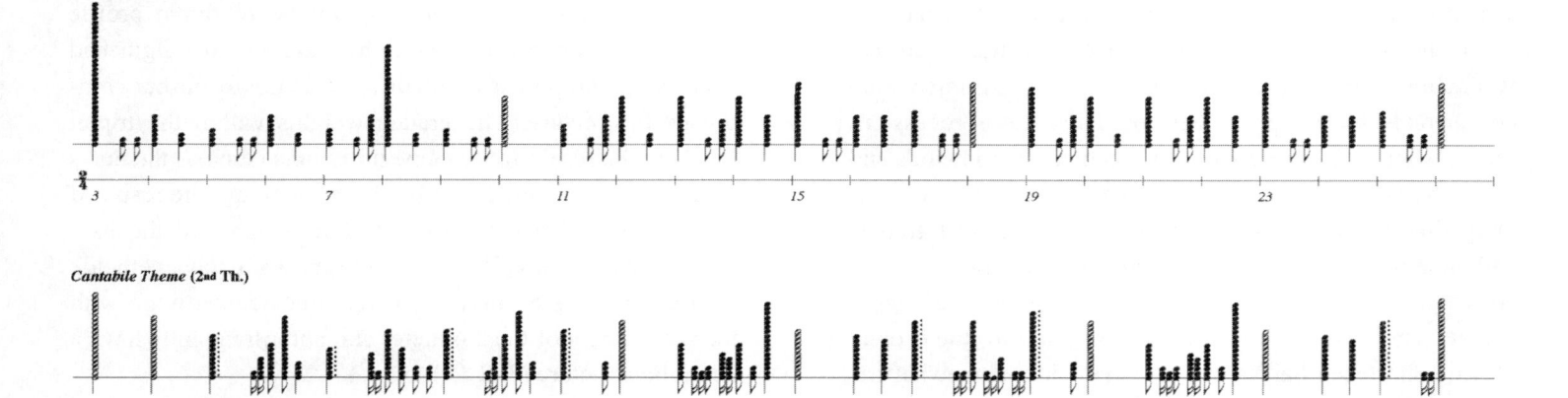

Procession Theme (1st Th.)

Cantabile Theme (2nd Th.)

›Trio‹ Theme

Considering the contrasting nature of the ›Trio‹ theme, its rhythmic weight profile is bound to differ markedly from those of the ›Procession‹ and ›Cantabile‹ themes. To speed things up, I am bracketing the three accumulative steps together in Ex. 1-122. Two details to begin with: the melody of the clarinet starts only on the second quarter note of m. 101, while the corresponding harmony (the V^7 of A major)

Ex. 1-122   mm. 101-116, Trio Theme

clearly how a rhythmic phenomenon is modified by added components. Take as an example the transition from the first to the second phrase: if one looks solely at the component rhythms of tone entries and pitches, one comes up with three syncopations – two that are tied over and one that is repeated. The pitch weight under the first, not tied-over, note C♯5 (*) corresponds to the durational weights under the first tied-over note E5 and the likewise bound-over note B4 soon thereafter, which are assigned the weights 6 and 5 respectively. Three rhythmically weighted notes – E5=6, C♯5=5 and B4=5 – are thus positioned on a light beat, which by itself at first produces a syncopated effect.

In the second step of the accumulation, this effect is to some extent revoked again, because the C♯5 after the * has the same weight as the one preceding it. If, in the third step of the accumulation one adds the harmony along with the seventh suspension here (C♯5 before B4), the syncopation disappears. The weight value of the second C♯5 exceeds its environment, including even the first note.

A counterexample occurs in the last phrase with its tied-over F♯6 (*). Here Beethoven delays the harmonic change normally to be expected under the preceding E5 (suspension of E5 before F♯5 failing to appear) and puts the weight of the new harmonic function (subdominant D major) onto the already syncopated F♯5. Of all the syncopations occurring in the ›Trio‹ theme, this one therefore has the strongest impact.

This conspectus of all the rhythmic weights may explain somewhat how the wonderfully hovering character of this ›Trio‹ theme could come about. It has already been mentioned that the timelessly pastoral mood is due also to the widely spanned phrasing units and the long-continued pedal point on the tonic.

Tutti Passage

In a final example in this section (Ex. 1-123), the rhythmic weights are to be determined in the context of a complete score. The passage to be considered is the first 16 measures of the fourth variation (mm. 75-90). As evident from my analytic particello, in which pitches are always written as sounding and all directions concern matters of content, the tutti variation consists mostly of a combination of the two main themes, the ›Procession‹ theme (winds) and the ›Cantabile‹ theme (violins). A massive instrumentation corresponds to the prescribed *ff*. Thus the ›Procession‹ theme is intoned in parallel in four octaves, woodwinds and horns having already been threaded in earlier. What is altogether new in this section is the appearance of trumpets and timpani. They are strictly coupled, the two clarions consistently sounding the two timpani notes in a higher octave. Besides this they have a rhythm of their own, playing shortened halves in a somewhat irregular order.

From a rhythmic point of view, the eighths triplet in the low strings are again noteworthy (cf. p. 66 f., above). The triplet movement in the basses, together with the duplet eighths in the violins laging behind and the ›drums and trumpets‹ pair, provides the accompaniment of the wholly fore-grounded main themes.

It is the job of the interpreter(s) to bring the weights of the accompanying apparatus and of the thematic main event into adequate relation. There is always more than one ›correct‹ solution. In the present case, I choose a ratio of 1:2 between accompaniment and principal voices in determining the rhythmic weights.

In drawing up the total rhythmic profile, I proceeded as follows: the smallest occurring note value is ♪ with the weight value of 1. Its multiples determine the weights of all the component rhythms in the two main themes, as already demonstrated in the discussion of the themes. In the ›Procession‹ theme, ♪ is the smallest value, but owing to the ♪-relation, the weights have to be doubled in this context. For the accompanying voices, I choose ♪ = 1, in order, as I said, to take a proper ranking into account – I do not differentiate between the weights of straight ♪ and triplets. Though the triplets do show up in the rhythmic profile (underneath the profile line), they are not distinguished from the predominant ›normal‹ ♪, so as not to further complicate the picture. The graded weights within the triplet level are the result of component rhythms (such as the notes of the celli being ›octaved‹ by the basses), not the result of a separate yardstick for triplets. The weights of the bass triplets, incidentally, do not by any means always coincide with the dictates of the main voices but frequently go with the second beat of the 2/4 meter and not infrequently have a hemiolic structure (3x2 ♪³ : 2x3 ♪³).

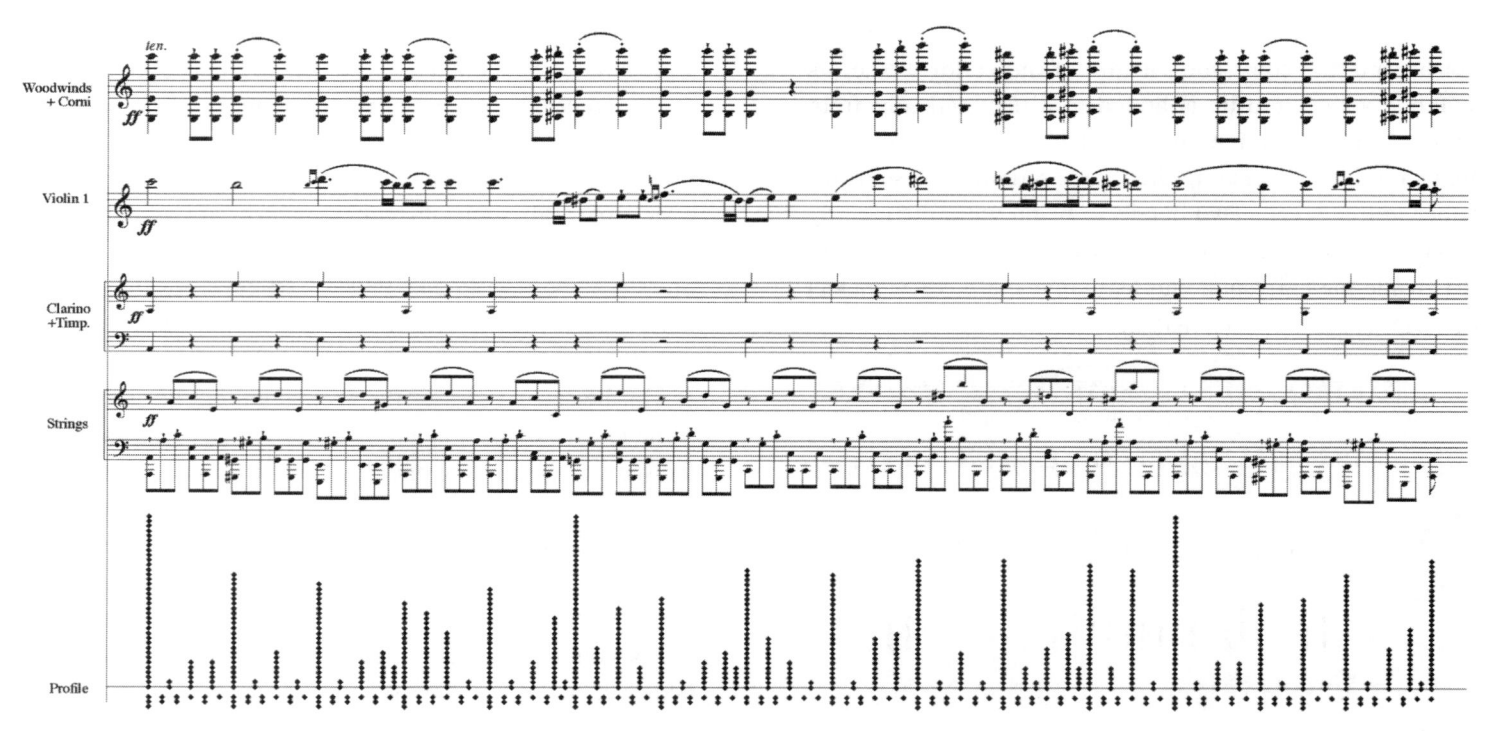

Ex. 1-123   mm. 75-90

I should point out that the top values in Ex. 1-123 have been clipped at mark 36 so as not to exceed the scope of the total image too much. Thus the column of rhombuses at the beginning actually has the value of 82, the point at which the six-four chord suspension on G enters is valued with 47 points, and the beginning of the last partial phrase actually weighs 42 units. One can take that into account in studying the rhythmic profile, but it hardly changes the actual conditions.

If one looks at the rhythmic weight profile as related to the total tone setting, remembering, at the same time, the profiles of the single-voiced theme melodies, one will realize that in this tutti variation Beethoven has repressed the rhythmically complex inner life of the themes in favor of simpler structures. The tall and medium weight columns essentially reveal a rhythm composed of the basic durations of the two main voices.

I think it is worth noting, however, that this massive, heavy tonal time structure is based on an insecure, because triplet, foundation. As we recall, the triplet eighths notes crop up for the first time at this point, that is, at the beginning of the fourth variation. They ground an otherwise stable setting, which is the result of a double intensification process: from low to high and from soft to loud. This process extending in a straight line over 3x24 bars culminates in a climactic passage that could not be exceeded any further if one were going by some simple conceptual model like ›per aspera ad astra‹ or ›from far to near.‹ Beethoven, however, says, at the moment of greatest brightness and closest proximity: ›the last word has not yet been spoken.‹ His vocabulary for this is eighths triplets, which intimate future events in this movement.

Rhythmic and Metric Weight

The terms rhythm and meter are related as the general to the specific. ›Musical rhythm‹ means the totality of temporal relations within a tonal event: simple and complex as well as rational and irrational durational sequences. Meter, on the other hand, is confined to rational structures. In this study, as set forth in the introduction, I concentrate on rhythms that are measurable to the extent that they are based on a uniform pulse. Even so, I do not first and foremost ask about meter but about rhythm. I want to fathom the multiformity of rhythmic temporal relations in metrically pulsing music. Metric patterns and hierarchies (e.g. time signatures) will come into view as merely one result of the rhythmic analysis.

The fact that metric temporal relations were initially understood to mean relations of length is connected with the proportional notation developed in central Europe. Thus the six rhythmic modes in force in early polyphone writing are to be understood as purely proportional or quantifying, that is, in modern transcription as (I) ♩ ♩ ♩ ♩; (II) ♩ ♩ ♩ ♩ ; (III) ♩. ♩ ♩ ; (IV) ♩ ♩ ♩. ; (V) ♩. ♩. ; (VI) ♩ ♩ ♩ ♩ ♩ ♩. In the course of musical history, metric models gradually formed that, in addition to longitudinal proportions, also included weight relations, e.g., ♩ ♩ ♩ ♩ . Thus the modern mensuration developed, to which Heinrich Besseler has given the name »Akzentstufentakt"[43] – graduated accent mensuration.

If one accepts the thesis that, besides durational relations, weight relations also play a role in musical rhythmics, one will perhaps also accept the extension that ›meter‹ is a special case of ›rhythm.‹ Durations and weights can be both metrical and rhythmic in nature, and the earmark of regularity specific to meter can be produced also by rhythmic means. But since rhythm as the more general concept can refer to both isometric and heterometric structures, metric, always periodically organized, time patterns come under the rhythmic temporal orders.

This realization impelled me to approach the question of meter and mensuration anew. The point of departure for the analyst is not the form of metric notation with the usual global specifications of meter and time signature, but rather the sound shape imagined by the composer in a composition, which, though not always discernible in the notation, must nevertheless be realized by the musician. To put it tersely: how much or how little meter is actually in a composition? By determining the *rhythmic* durational and weight relations, I can compare them with the *metrical* patterns. From the vantage point of the composer, this should mean that while taking the time signatures into account, he constantly modifies them in the process of composing. Meter is not simply prescribed once and for all, but is an object of musical shaping. The contrast of rhythm and meter thus dissolves in an expanded concept of rhythm.

---

[43] Heinrich Besseler, *Das musikalische Hören der Neuzeit* (Berlin, 1959), 29.

Ex. 1-124   mm. 3-26, Procession Theme, Rhythmic and Metric Weights

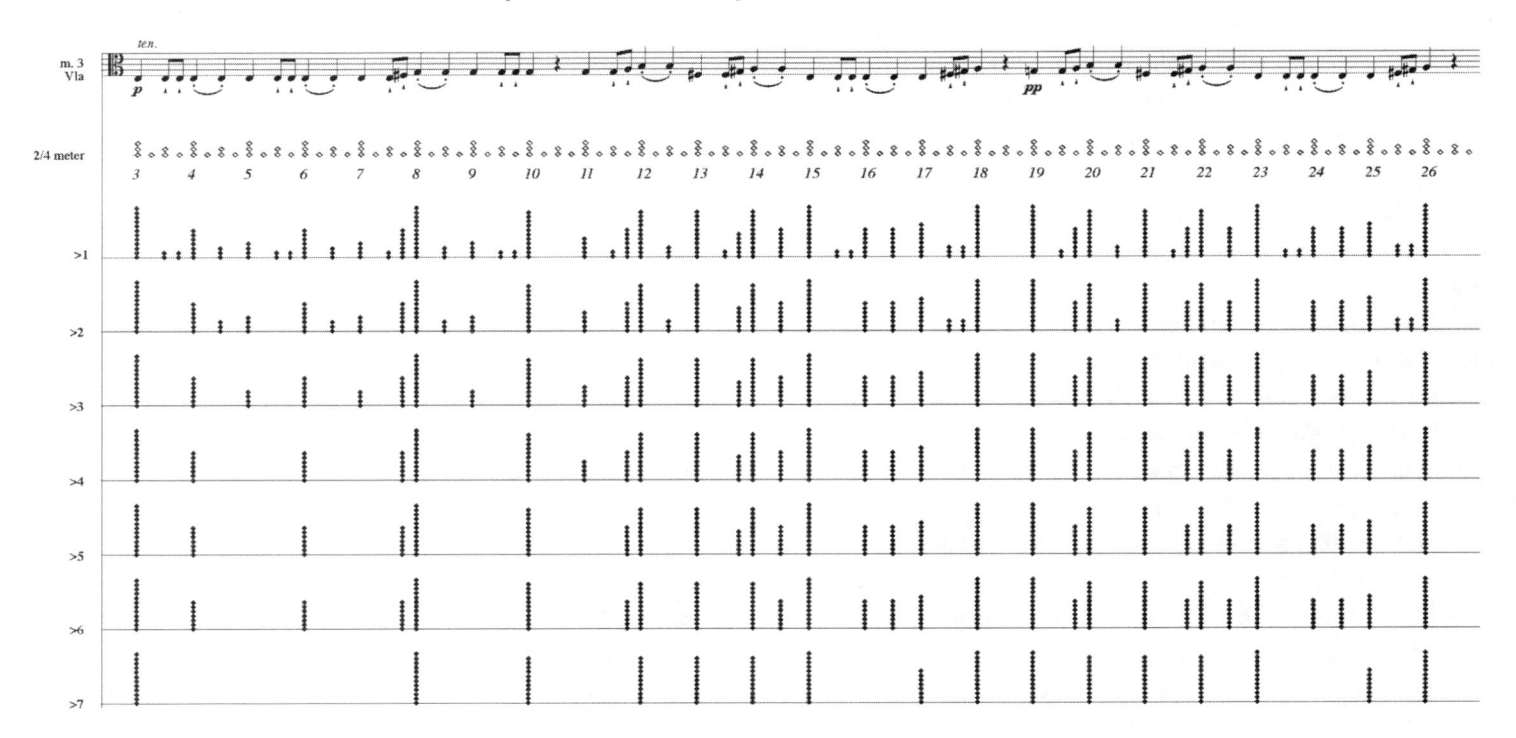

Let us take another look at the rhythmic weight profiles established in the preceding section for the three themes and the tutti passage in the Allegretto movement of Beethoven's Seventh Symphony. Ex. 1-124 depicts the ›Procession‹ theme. Added is the schematic representation of the weight relations of a 2/4 meter in Beethoven's time, that is, with a heavy *One* (3), a lighter *Two* (2) and the even lighter weak beats (1).

I have thinned out the rhythmic profile step by step by rendering the lower weights invisible. At >2 the weights of two are left off, at >3 those of three as well, etc. In the end, only the tallest weight towers remain standing, clipped at 12 for greater perspicuity.

If one compares the seven profile representations with the schema of the 2/4 meter, one can draw some conclusions as to the latter's components-rhythmic elaboration, of course only with regard to this specific theme. All large weights clearly coincide with the *One* of the 2/4 meter. On the other hand, it is to be noted that there are first beats that are rhythmically weak. Thus the *Ones* of the third, fifth and seventh measure disappear from view already at level >4.

Here precipitates out as well what can also be actually heard, namely, that in the first phrase of the ›Procession‹ theme there is a tendency towards double measures, whereby the first measure moves into an upbeat position. These double measures do not continue subsequently, though. Diverse components see to an irregular distribution of weights, so that there is no clear grouping of measures.

An additional interesting observation is the relatively high weights occurring on certain ›light‹ eighths notes, specifically in those five harmonic changes on the fourth eighth of the 2/4 meter, which, in combination with the components »Sound«, »Pitch« and »Articulation" (staccato wedges), achieve the value 6 (see mm. 7, 11, 13, 19 and 21). The rhythm thereby generated (♩. ♪) is still efficacious up to level >5.

The ›Wanderer‹ rhythm can be traced ›only‹ on the lowest level (>1). That does not mean, of course, that it is negligible. It simply serves to show that the rhythmically produced 2/4 meter has a noticeable drop on the second beat, especially when it is filled by two ♪. Very generally, it can be said from looking at the profile gradations that the rhythmics of this theme underscores the unity and structure of the 2/4 meter. The fact that no overriding groups of measures are generated in the (repeated) consequent of the period may explain why Beethoven chose the smallest possible binary measure (2/4).

In the ›Cantabile‹ theme (Ex. 1-125), the 2/4 meter and its accentual grades play a completely different role than they do in the ›Procession‹ theme. To the extent that it even sounds through the rhythmic profile – its second beat remains for the most part rhythmically unoccupied – it is more than once emphatically missed, owing to the very heavy weights on light or very light beats of the measure. I am referring to the long pitch durations already discussed in detail, which appear repeatedly in anticipatory manner. Up to the highest level of 7, these towers of rhombuses hold their own even with the heavy and semi-heavy part of the measure. A special weight falls again on the A major / minor change (mm. 38_2 and 46_2), whereby the otherwise whole-measure course is enlivened by a macro-syncopation.

The ›Trio‹ theme (Ex. 1-126) is marked by a pervasive hovering character and by several syncopes. If one looks at the highest level (>7) in the again gradated profile field by itself, one can see that three of the ten heavy weights fall onto the weak beat of the 2/4 meter. Since the *One* that follows in each case has a rhythmically low weight – insofar as it has any rhythmic profile at all – the result is a syncopated effect. That the syncope in m. 104_2 (B–B), has

Ex. 1-125   mm. 27-50, Cantabile Theme, Rhythmic and Metric Weights

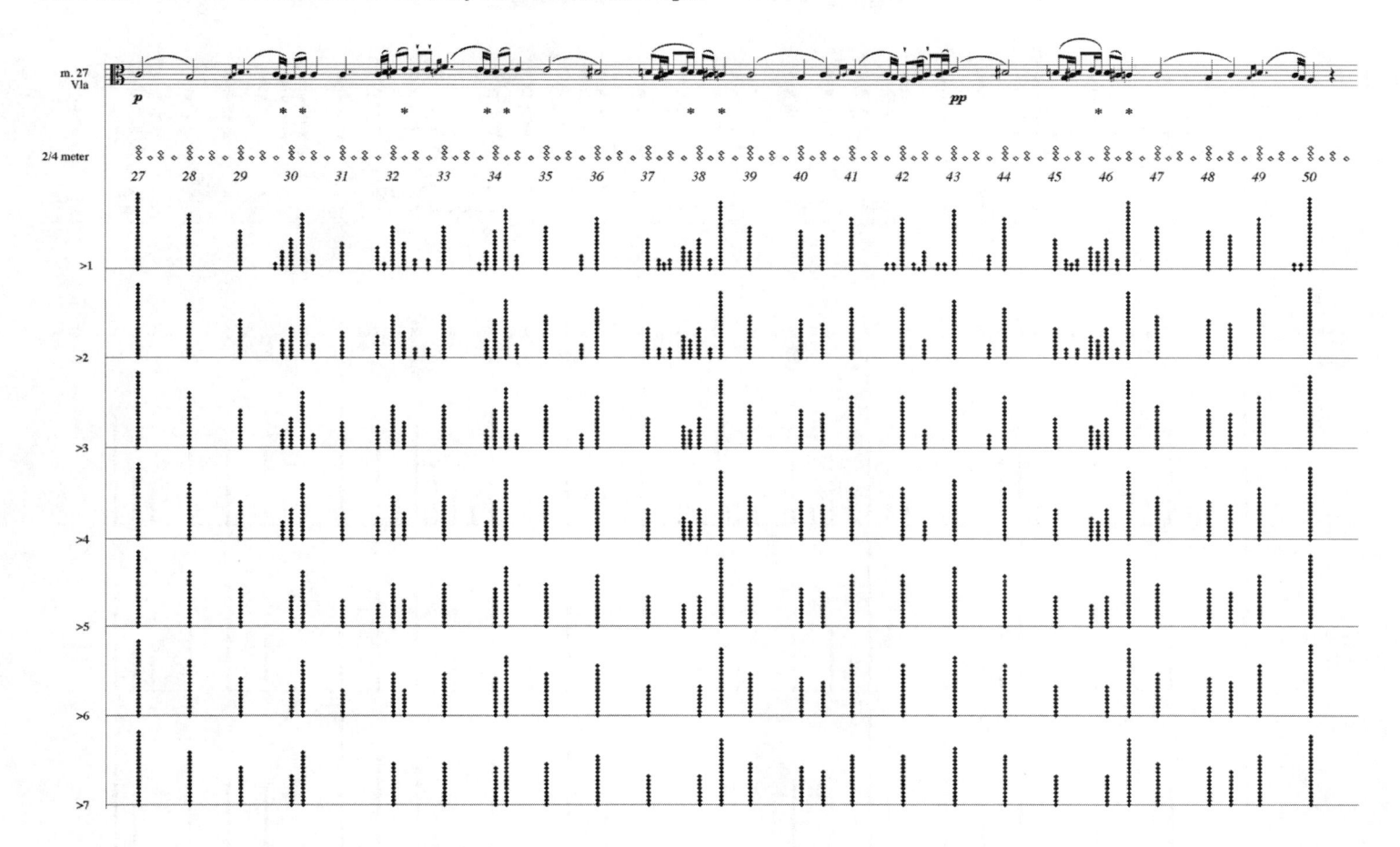

a lower rhythmic weight value – from level 5 on it no longer appears – is owing to the fact that besides the lengthening of the note there is here neither a harmonic change nor any other components-rhythmic event.

Altogether, the ›Trio‹ theme seems to have little metric profile. Only at the end, in the course of the cadence in E major, a 4/4 meter pattern emerges fairly clearly, noticeable especially on level 2 but also on the higher levels. Looked at in this way, the preceding syncopation on F♯5 (m. 112$_2$) is a typical 4/4 meter syncopation that extends over the middle of the measure.

We should also take another look at the tutti passages already analyzed in the chapter on accumulation (Ex. 1-123), using again the method of gradated profile representation (Ex. 1-127). In order to be able to display at least three grades of the weight-reasing on one page, I have reduced the analytic particello (see p. 76, above) to the two thematic voices.

Here we find full confirmation of what was ascertained already in describing the accumulations: this variation aims at a simple, metrically succinct rhyhm. Even at the highest level (>10), every *One* beat receives a high weighting. On the lowest level (>2), on the other hand, the accent order of

Ex. 1-126   mm. 101-116, Trio Theme, Rhythmic and Metric Weights

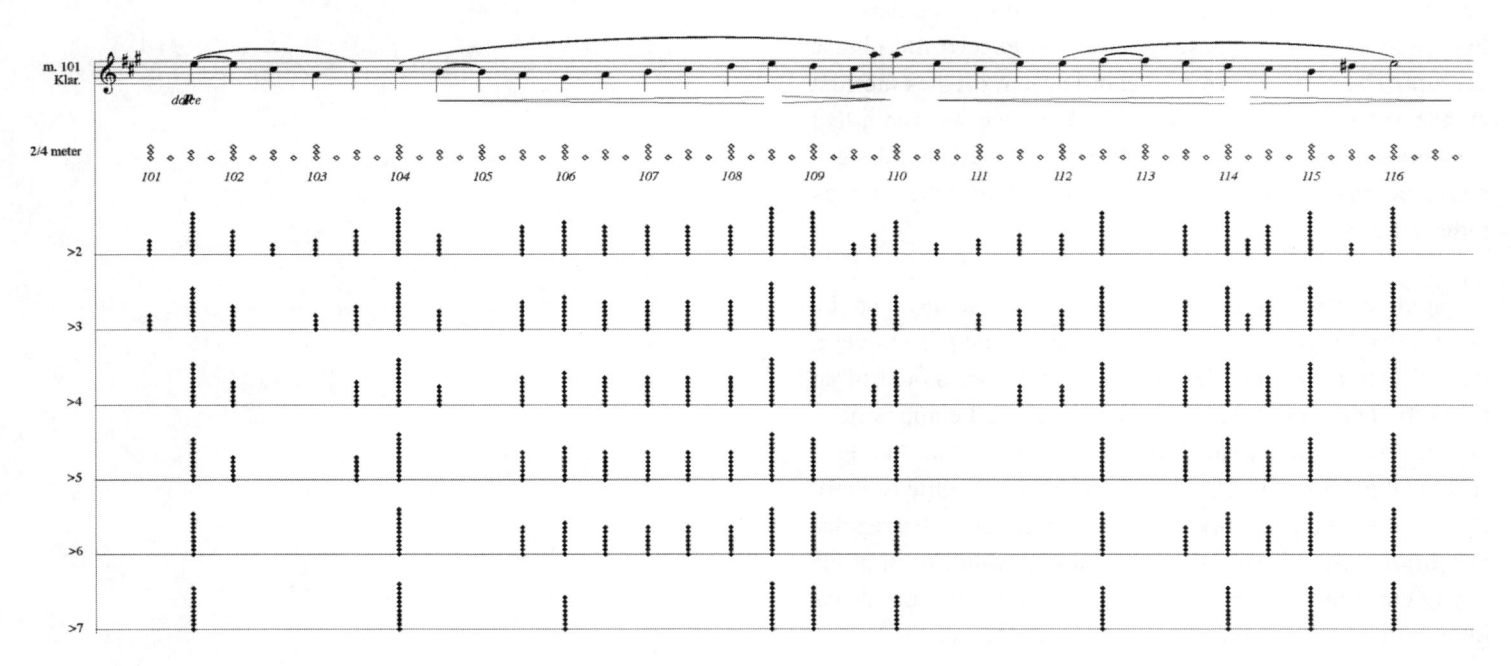

Ex. 1-127   mm. 75-90, Extract of the Main Parts, Rhythmic and Metric Weights

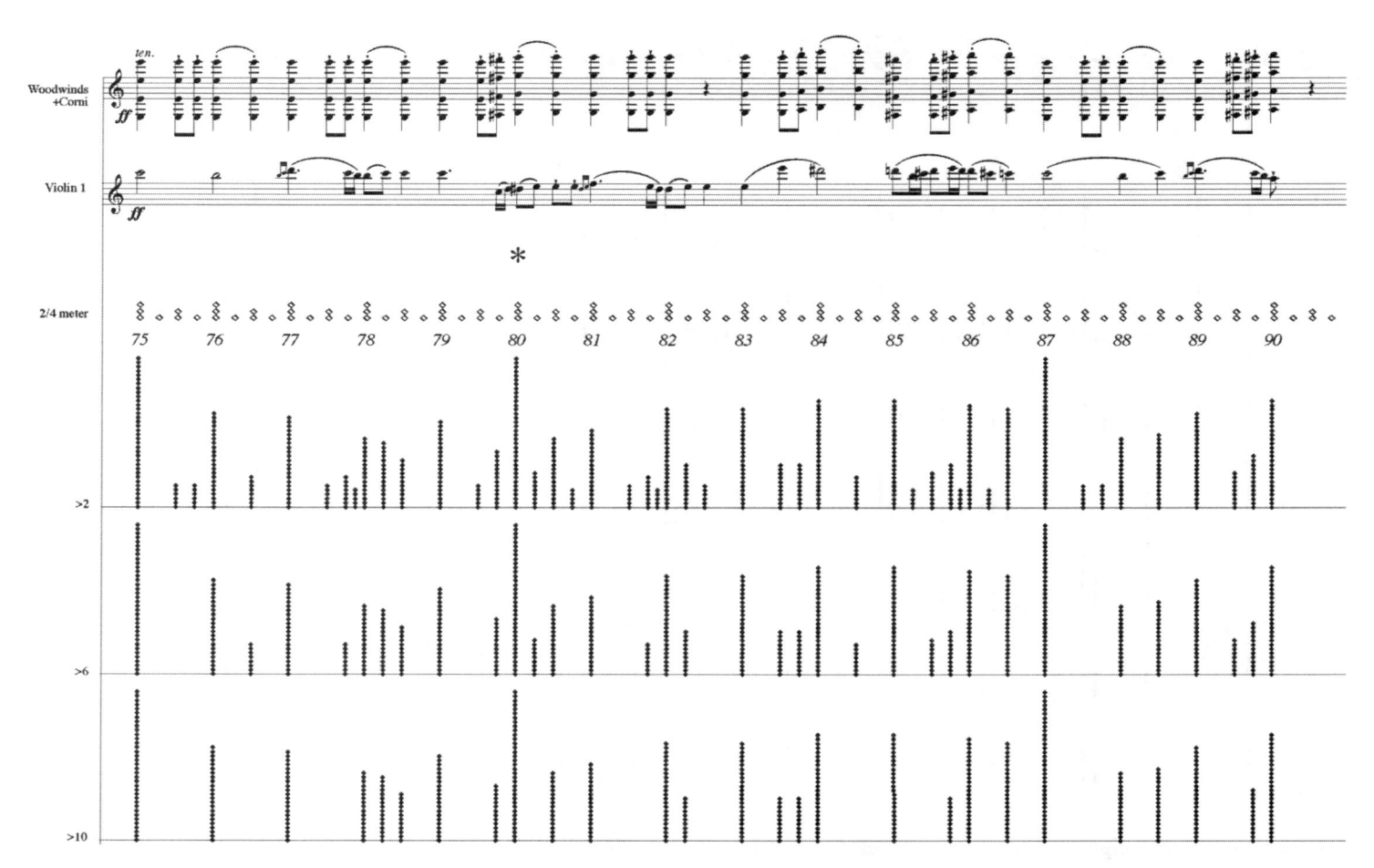

the 2/4 meter comes to the fore repeatedly. On the other hand, the emphatic ›missteps‹ of the ›Cantabile‹ theme, which on level >2 can clearly still be found to be active, are regularly drowned out by the massively accruing components in the accompanying apparatus of basses, timpani and trumpets.

One irregularity (besides the eighths triplets in the basses not considered here) persists, however: the super-weight on the dominant six-four chord used as a transition to the tonic parallel (*, m. 80). This tower of rhombuses with the value 47 (not graphically realized here) has its counterpart only in the first and the fourth to the last measure. Although the period consists quite regularly of two eight-bar halves, these top weights exceed the phrase caesura. The second inversion chord accent divides the first eight-bar group into 5+3 measures. Here we see again that Beethoven rightly chose the 2/4 meter as the general signature, because in view of a free joining of phrases it is indispensable.

To sum up: the metric quality of a tone setting can be ascertained by analyzing the rhythmics. In the present case, the 2/4 meter functions less as a law than as a model of an isometric temporal ordering, which is realized compositionally in countless variants. In the process, other models, such as the 4/4 or the 2/2 meter, will be discernible as well. Even more frequent, however, are formations of irregular bar groupings. The overall character of a calm, even striding is confirmed, to be sure, but the reality of sound has little to do with the simple schema of a 2/4 meter.

The much-discussed relationship between rhythmics and metrics, which, depending on the respective point in music history as well as on the mental, psychic and ideological disposition of the individual music theoretician, will be perceived sometimes as a contrast and sometimes as a hierarchy, loses much of its explosive force if one sets out in principle from an infinite diversity of rhythmic shapings and regards temporal regularity as a prominent special instance of musical rhythm.

Aspects of Rhythm

Rhythmic Proportions

Composition vs. Notation

The invention of (Western) musical notation was based on the principle of division. By means of note shape, sequence and coloration and after the introduction of mensuration marks, it became gradually possible to indicate the relative duration of tones with precision and thus to coordinate the individual voices with on-the-dot exactness. The function of the notational script was fulfilled when the performers implemented the directions given correctly. The larger function, however, of providing, by means of notation, an image of what actual happens in the music, was only partly realized and to this day exists only to a limited degree. Individually notated voices and tablatures in the Middle Ages are proof of this as much as the representation of tone durations across the bar line or the group formation by means of beams within the confines of a measure in modern times.

One must therefore make a basic distinction between proportional specifications that serve merely to specify the durational value of a note and proportions arising from actually composed rhythm. Often, rhythmic relations correspond to the proportion of the prescribed mensuration, but just as often they do not. In the following small melodic segment from the Credo of Noël de Bauldeweyn's *Missa »Da pacem«* (Ex. 1-128), the mensuration tempus perfectum cum prolatione imperfecta and the rhythm of the melody converge. That one brevis comprises three semibreves, for example, can be seen from the first measure of the tenor voice. Besides, the longer note values correspond repeatedly to the position of the brevises at the beginning of the mensurations. And the crest and keel notes are fitted into the frame of the measure.

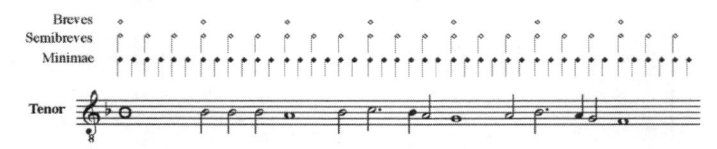

Toward the end of the Credo, the setting is dominated by two double phrases, of which the first (Confiteor) is convergent with, the second (et expecto) divergent from the measure (Ex. 1-129). The consecutive sections »Confiteor unum baptisma in remissionem peccatorum« and »Et expecto resurrectionem mortuorum. Et vitam venturi Saeculi. Amen« are both in tempus perfectum cum prolatione imperfecta (here reproduced as 3/4 meter). The rhythmic profiles established with regard to the components »Sound,« »Pitch,« »Diastematy« and »Phrase« exhibit marked peaks. At the same time, the proportions revealed in the rhythm of the »Confiteor« section resemble those of the mensural order (see Ex. 1-128), while the section »et expecto« exhibits divergent septuple proportions.

The differences come out most clearly if one looks at the structuring of the two sections by the component »Phrase.« In the »Confiteor« section the partial phrases display a rhythm of 6+6+9+6+6+6+12 ♩. All the values are divisible by three, and the proportions are correspondingly simple. In the »et expecto« section, on the other hand, the phrase rhythm is 7+7+7+7+7+7+12 ♩. The value 7 predominating here is incompatible with the ternary mensuration. The proportions 3:7, 6:7 or 9:7 resulting from the embedding of the septuple rhythm in the tempus perfectum are highly complex. The ratio of the two long phrases in the

Ex. 1-129   Bauldeweyn, *Missa »Da pacem«*, Credo, Tenor (Altus)

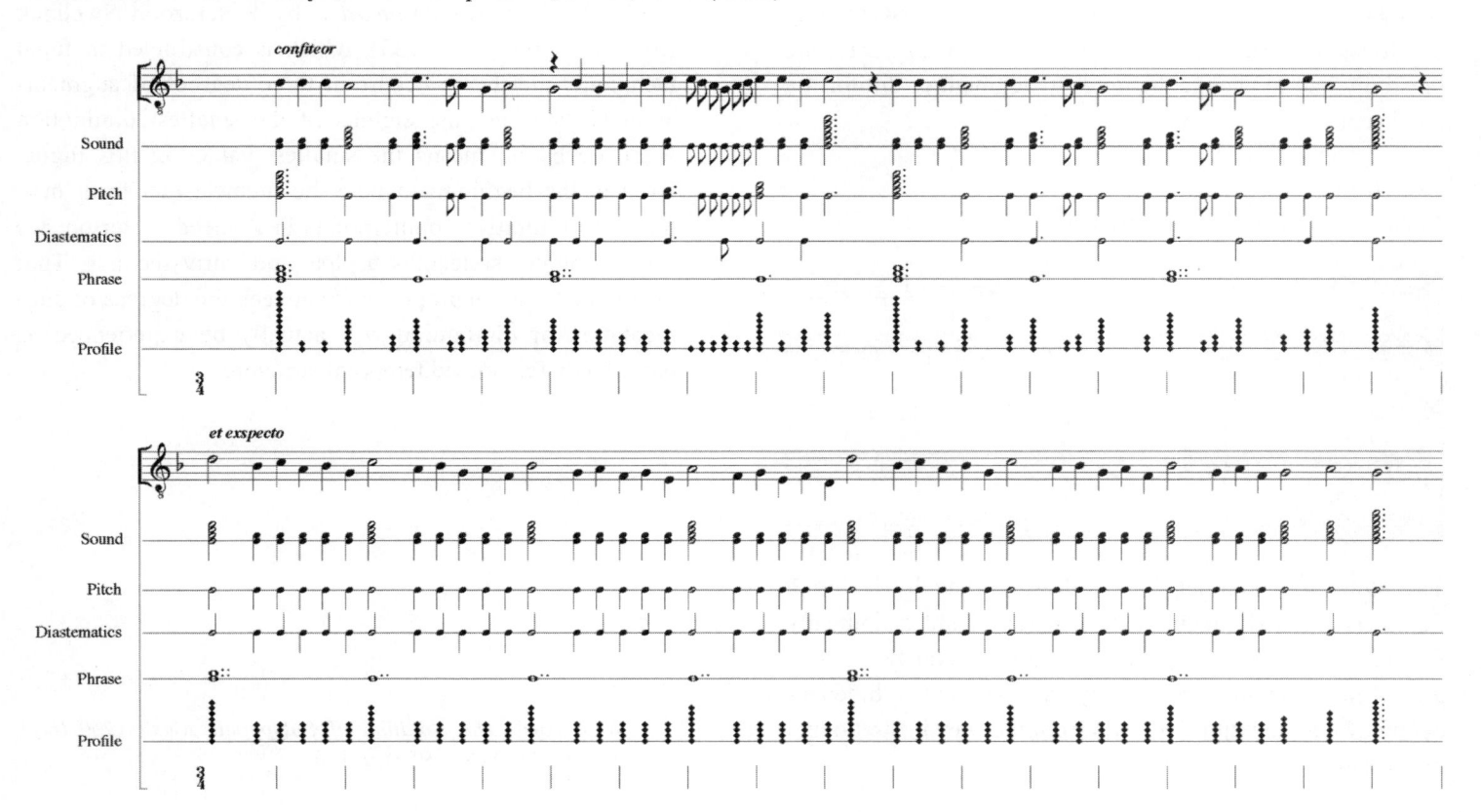

Ex. 1-130   Bauldeweyn, *Missa »Da pacem«*, Credo, …et exspecto…

»et expecto« section is nearly irrational. The sequence consisting of descending thirds starts anew after every four times seven ♩, without, however, being regularly concluded. Thus the first phrase of 28 ♩ is followed by a second phrase of 26 ♩, yielding a proportion of 14:13.

The rhythmic complexity of the »et expecto« section doubles once one includes the four-part setting (Ex. 1-130). The descending sequence of thirds initiated by the tenor voice is canonically imitated by the rhythmically coupled soprano and bass voices at an interval of one quarter note and by the alto after two quarter notes. Although that does not alter the lopsided proportions between rhythmic and mensural order, the units of seven quarter notes gain in internal tension.

Bauldeweyn does not carry the repetition of the first sequence of four times seven ♩ to its conclusion but introduces a premature cadence leading to the final G of the G Dorian setting and restoring the coincidence of rhythm and mensuration. The harmonic-modal cadence is thus in the end accompanied by a rhythmic-metrical one.

Augmentation and Diminution

The rhythmic procedures of augmentation and diminution are likewise accommodated by the system of proportional notation. In the white mensural notation, all imperfect divisions – and below the semibrevises there was always only the division imperfecta – are in the ratio of 1:2 or 2:1. One thus only had to change the notes to augment or diminish a tonal sequence.

Ex. 1-131
Schütz, Motette No. 11 (1648) (extract)

The motet »So fahr ich hin zu Jesu Christ« by Heinrich Schütz (Ex. 1-131) begins with a textually and melodically formed motif that is presented simultaneously in two grades of augmentation, namely in ♩ and in ♩. Independently of that, the motif appears from the start in stretto and in inversion.

Such procedures of rhythmic variation were used even before Schütz. Willi Apel refers to clausulae from the time of Perotinus in which a liturgical tenor recurs in halved or doubled values.[44] To this day, augmentation and diminution are part of the regular repertory of rhythmic organization. To be excluded are pseudo-augmentations and diminutions, when note values are changed simultaneously with a change in tempo: here the case is simply one of an agogical trans-notation, which can be regarded as analogous to enharmonic changes. A plain example of this occurs in Stravinsky's *Sacre du Printemps* (Ex. 1-132).

Ex. 1-132   Stravinsky, *Sacre du Printemps*, near fig. 13 / 14

Actually sounded cases, on the other hand, are those where rhythmic tonal sequences or entire settings present different grades of augmentation within an unvaried tempo. From the nearly infinite abundance of possible examples, I cite two from different eras. They are among the arithmetically simple instances, in which an assumed value 1 is multiplied and all the notes of a tonal structure are subjected to this proportion.

In the *Fantasia chromatica* by Pieterszoon Swelinck from ca. 1600 (Ex. 1-133), which is constructed in fugal technique, the theme occurs in three degrees of augmentation (1:2:4). Yet the eighths of the smallest diminution form are by no means the smallest values in this fugue. Even at the beginning, where the theme is set forth in ♩, there are figurative counterpoints in ♪ speed. Later on, we also encounter sixteenths triplets and thirty-seconds. That guarantees that the proportions between the degrees of augmentation or diminution will actually be experienced as part of a differentiated temporal structure.

---

[44] Willi Apel, *The Notation of Polyphonic Music. 900-1600*, (Cambridge MA, 41953), p. 145.

Ex. 1-133   Sweelinck, *Fantasia Chromatica* (extract)

The second example dates from the second half of the 20th century. In Bernd Alois Zimmermann's opera *Die Soldaten* (The Soldiers) – undoubtedly his magnum opus – the liturgical melody of the »Dies irae« from the medieval Requiem Mass is cited at the end of the Prelude prior to Act I. 36 players of the string section (1st and 2nd violins and violas) recite the first lines of this sequence in 36 augmentations. Here is the beginning of the Gregorian original from the 12th or 13th century (Ex. 1-134).

Zimmermann's fantasia on this melody is multi-leveled. At the beginning, after fig. L, three levels, which are defined by long, medium and short durations of the notes, can be distinguished. Ex. 1-135 exhibits an excerpt of eight voices in long note values. Each of the eight Second Violins intones the beginning of the »Dies irae« melody in the high harmonics (*flageolet*) register (written as sounding in the example), each in long note values but each in his own degree of transposition and augmentation. Zimmermann's method here can be readily seen in the eighth of the Second Violins. In this part, the transposition degree corresponds to the original D Dorian in a higher octave, and the unity measure of the notes customary in Gregorian chant, too, is preserved: every note has the value of 4 ♪ or 1 ♩, although displaced anticipatorily by a triplet ♪ in 2/4 meter.

All remaining voices play the Dorian melody on degrees that lie 1, 2, 3, 4, 5, 6 or 7 half-tones above the original final D. They all have their unified durational value, partly in crooked proportions, as, e.g., in the third of the Second Violins with its duration of 24 ♪-septuplets per note, partly in simpler ratios, as in violin 6, with its 5 ♩ per note. Entries occur at different points in the measure – only once does the entry coincide with the downbeat *One* (violin 2 of the Second Violins, 7 ♪ value).

This gradually rising texture of voices, sounding ethereal because of the relatively long not values and the high octave register, is juxtaposed immediately after the first entry by fast and articulatorily vivid sound figures that also cite the »Dies irae« melody (Ex. 1-136). The top line shows the (already depicted) long-tone voice entering first (Vl. 4 of 2nd Vls.). The rest of the score is presented only in excerpt: in reality there are 24 additional string voices divided between the violins (32nds) and the violas (triplet 16ths), some of them with fast figures, others with medium durations, and again others with the already described long notes.

Ex. 1-135   Zimmermann, *Die Soldaten*, Preludio, fig. L 5 ff. (extract)

Ex. 1-136 Zimmermann, *Die Soldaten*, Preludio, fig. L 5 ff. (extract)

The First Violins (the 5th, 4th and 7th in the example) each by itself reel off the first two phrases of the »Dies irae« melody (»Dies irae, dies illa« and »Solvet saeclum in favilla«) at top speed, while the violas simultaneously cite the third phrase (»Teste David cum Sibylla«) quasi as continuation and only slightly slower. Each voice is carefully articulated by legato arcs and staccato dots and thus given individual rhythms. The voices, moreover, follow each other in closest possible canonic succession, with beams shifted chromatically transposition degrees.

The ratio between violins and violas, in this excerpt, is 4:3. Other proportions are in part so complicated that they border on the irrational. Overall, in the 26 2/4 measures of the »Dies irae« section the 32nd note is the smallest occurring value, referred to the individual note of the Gregorian melody (e.g., the first syllable »Di«). The longest value is a forty-fold one (5 ♩). In between lie 34 proportional degrees, which have denominators of 2, 3, 5 and 7. Their common denominator is 420. To obtain the ratio between the note A5 held by the fourth of the Second Violins and the first note C of the 7th viola, one would have to express it in 420ths and then get a result of 4032:315, in terms of 420ths.[45]

The meaning of this highly complex »Dies irae« fantasia probably resides solely in the area of the symbolic: the structures cannot be grasped by mere listening. Guided (and impelled) by a spherical conception of time, in which a subject regards all times and tempos as gathered about him at every moment, B. A. Zimmermann conceives the passage as a symbol for the chaos of the human condition, from which there is no escape.

Partial Augmentation and Diminution

The examples by Schütz, Sweelinck and Zimmermann have in common that rhythmic augmentation and diminution are tied to specific melodic motifs (shapes) and are also equally valid for all the notes of the motif. But there are also numerous instances in which only isolated notes of a motif are augmented or diminished. That opens up a large expanse of rhythmic variations.

This procedure of partial proportional changes, too, is provided for in mensural notation and thus in our modern musical script. This becomes clear from a look at the four basic mensurations of the white mensural notation (Ex. 1-137). Following Willi Apel,[46] abbreviations are used for the basic mensurations: 2, 2 for the tempus imperfectum cum prolatione imperfecta $_C$, 3, 2 for the tempus perfectum cum prolatione imperfecta $_O$, 2, 3 for the tempus imperfectum cum prolatione perfecta $_C$ and 3, 3 for the tempus perfectum cum prolatione perfecta $_O$. A comparison of the note values of the four mensurations will show that the minima (M) in all of them have the same proportional value. In the semibreves (S) and the breves (B), on the other hand, there are augmentations, though not equally for all mensurational forms. In changes both from 2, 2 to 3, 2 and from 2, 3 to 3, 3, the breves are augmented in the ratio of 2:3, but they remain the same in a change from 3, 2 to 2, 3. Analogously, the semibreves twice remain the same (2, 2 to 3, 2 and 2, 3 to 3, 3) and are augmented once (3, 2 to 2, 3).

Ex. 1-137 Mensural notation, the four basic mensurations

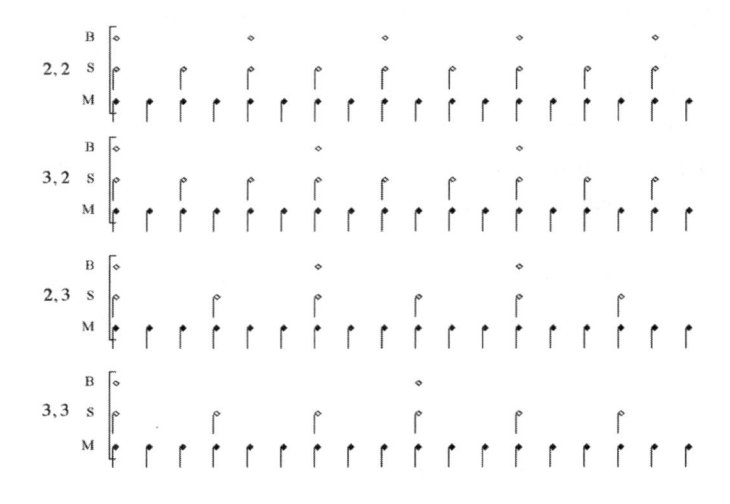

---

[45] See the complete list of proportional degrees in Peter Petersen and Hans-Gerd Winter, »Lenz-Opern. Das Musiktheater als Sonderzweig der produktiven Rezeption von J. M. R. Lenz' Dramen und Dramentheorie,« *Lenz-Jahrbuch*, 1 (St. Ingbert, 1991), 9-58.

[46] Willi Apel, *The Notation of Polyphonic Music. 900-1600*, (Cambridge MA, 41953), 97.

Ex. 1-138 Ockeghem, *Missa Prolationum*, Kyrie I, Parts and Harmonies

In the Kyrie I of the renowned *Missa Prolationum* by Johannes Ockeghem, the four basic proportions are initially distributed between the four voices (Ex. 138). Two voices each (soprano / countertenor, tenor / bass), moreover, are bound canonically to each other and thus produce a proportional canon. From the first four notes in the upper canon, which describe a broken F major triad, one can register a ratio of 2:3 in reference to the brevises (𝅗𝅥, 𝅗𝅥.), but already the semi-brevis rest immediately following is not augmented but maintains the ratio of 1:1. The phenomenon of partial augmentation is even more obvious in the lower canon: the melody here is initially based on the durations 𝅗𝅥., 𝅗𝅥. and 𝅗𝅥.., which (transcribed on a scale of 1:4) corresponds to 3 ♪, 6 ♪ and 9 ♪. Since the semibrevises here all have the same duration (♩.), the result is a distinct rhythm for each of the two canons, which is not the case with an augmentation by means of simple multipliers.

Dragan Plamenac's edition of Johannes Ockeghem, Collected Works, vol. 2, no. 10, contains a reproduction of the Kyrie I (Plate 2). From it one can see that the canons are each noted only once, albeit with different mensural specifications (Ex. 1-139). In the upper canon, C and O stand for the mensurations 2, 2 and 3, 2; in the lower one, ⊙ and ₵ stand for 3, 3 and 2, 3, respectively. The blackening of the notes in the lower voices points toward a change in mensuration; no such change is apparent in the upper voices.

Ex. 1-139

These relations are reflected in Plamenac's transcription insofar as in the tenor and bass, mensural changes are signaled by a hook, whereas there is none in the soprano and countertenor. But how is the change in the tenor from 3, 2 to 2, 3 and that of the basses from 3, 3 to 2, 3 to be explained, since the mensuration 2, 3 is not at all indicated in the respective voices? One will have to presume that the change of the lower canon into the mensuration of the countertenor in the upper voices is only one of several conceivable solutions, albeit a sensible one. But if such freedom is given, might one not also presume (as Plamenac does not) a mensural change for the soprano, i.e., from 2, 2 to 2, 3? For only in that case do the voices following each other in the canon in identical rhythms and melodies (ex. 1-138) also progress in the same mensural measure (see * in the soprano). My own solution thus is that from the last mensural change on (see * in the bass), all four voices follow a unified measure corresponding to the modern 3/4 meter.

In the Ex. 1-138, in which the note text of the Kyrie I is reproduced completely, I have added a harmony extract of this four-part setting. It will show that a standing F major sound with the duration of two mensural units of the scale 3, 3 (18 ♪) is realized. In what follows, the sounds change in the manner of a modern harmonics, that is, triads on the neighboring degrees III (A), V (C) II (G) and IV (B♭) are formed. The harmonic rhythms resulting from the changes are largely congruent with the mensural conditions, as the solution proposed above shows. At the end, incidentally, there is a typically plagal turn (B♭ major / F major) in a twofold half-note / whole-note rhythm. Although there is no hemiolic notation at this point in the original, this overarching harmonic rhythm nevertheless seems to suggest a hemiolic turn.

Beyond mensural and metric relations, the partial augmentation exists above all as a means of rhythmic variation of motifs or melodic figures. Examples for this are legion. I shall confine myself to a famous case from the 19th century: the Second Symphony of Johannes Brahms. Its first movement, based on a double theme, commences in the basses with a melodic motif that fulfils the function of a motto, as it occurs in all four movements. This four-note motif, consisting of a changing note phrase with a swerve at the end is augmented or else diminished both completely and partially. Particularly exciting is its recurrence at the beginning of the recapitulation (Ex 1-140).

86   Aspects of Rhythm

Ex. 1-140   Brahms, 2nd Symphony 1st mov.

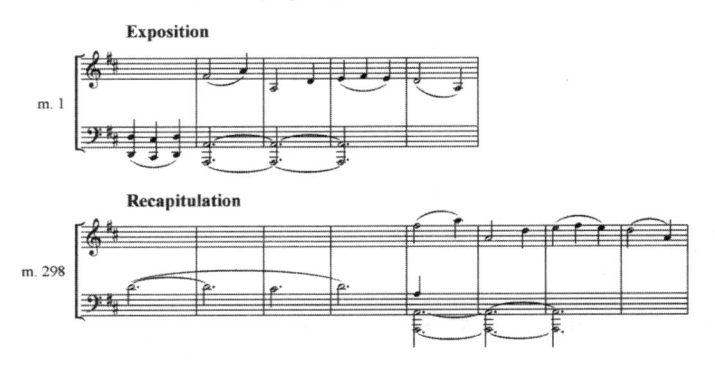

Exposition

m. 1

Recapitulation

m. 298

Ex. 1-141   Brahms, 2nd Symphony 1st mov., Beginning (Bass Theme)

being recognized as the real beginning of the (thematic) recapitulation, whereas generally m. 302 is viewed as such.

In Ex. 1-141, the complete extent of the bass theme (as one part of the double theme) is represented – including the 23 measures, here omitted, that prolong the dominant. The entire thematic complex constitutes the first group (43 bars) of the first movement, which is composed in sonata form. What is obvious is, to begin with, the elaboration of the motto-like four-note motif and its melodic variants (interval changes, partial inversion). Secondly, the example exhibits two augmentation and diminution variants: the first, complete (A-G♯-A-D) two bars before the cadence, the second, partial (A5-G♯5-A5-F♯5) at the beginning of the cadence. Brahms here initiates a process that will pervade the entire

The quarter notes D-C♯-D are augmented at the ratio of 1:3, whereby the first note appears magnified once again by a ratio of 1:2. The head note of the bass theme, specifically, thus stands in a ratio of 1:6 to the corresponding initial note in m. 1.

Ex. 1-142   Brahms, 2nd Symphony, 1st mov., Motive Augmentations / Diminutions

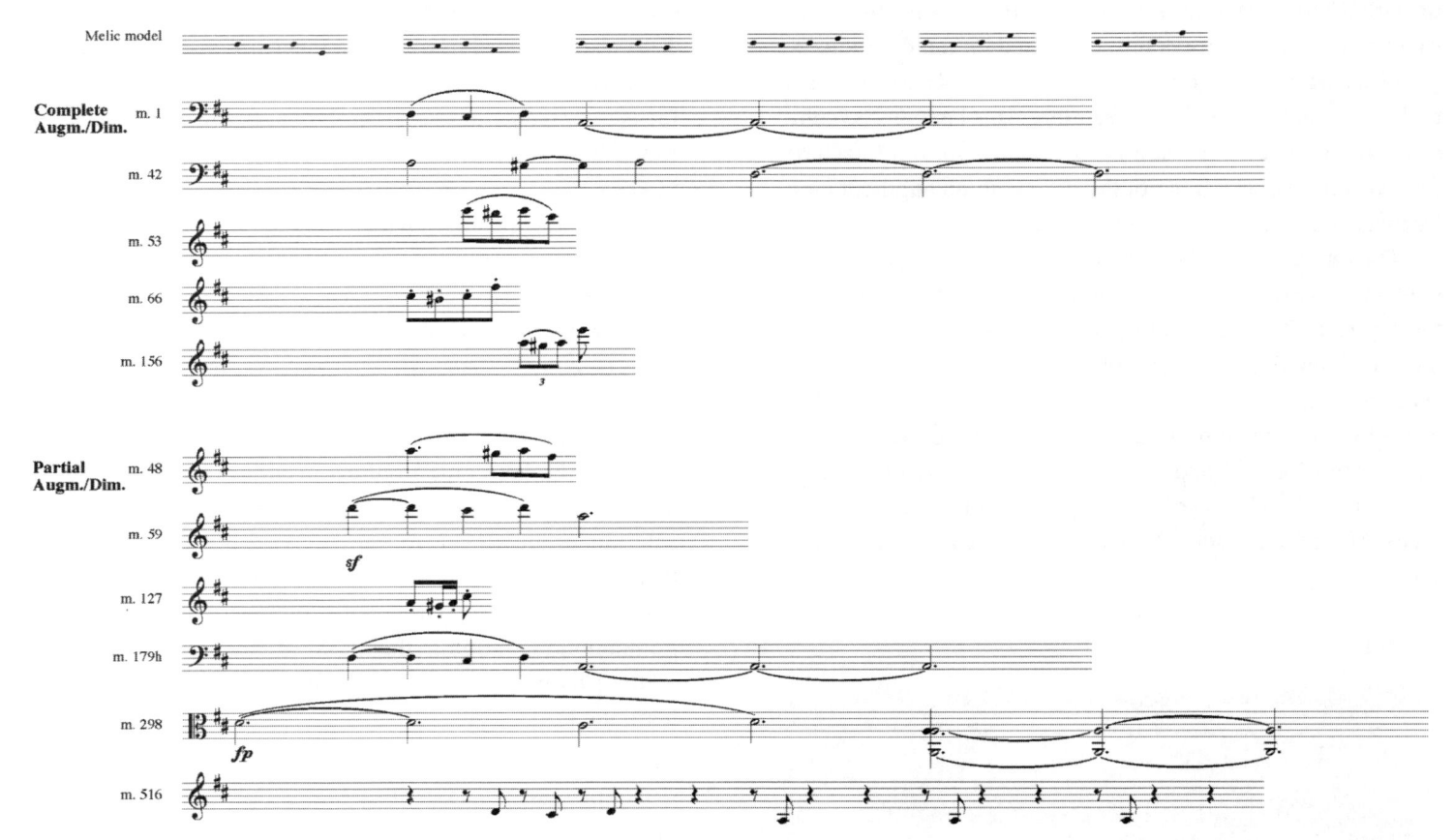

Melic model

Complete Augm./Dim.   m. 1
m. 42
m. 53
m. 66
m. 156

Partial Augm./Dim.   m. 48
m. 59
m. 127
m. 179h
m. 298
m. 516

Ernst Toch has pointed out this augmentational variant[47], Reinhold Brinkmann[48] was not quite willing to agree; but there are solid arguments in support of Toch's view. These arguments incidentally also result in m. 298

movement and beyond that even the other movements. In variant after variant, the four-note motif is transformed by complete or partial augmentations or diminutions. Since these procedures are virtually omnipresent in this symphony, the aforementioned ›great‹ recapitulation variant (Ex. 1-140) duly attains the status of an ideal climax.

The augmentation and diminution variants of the first movement collected in Ex. 1-142 are arranged by »complete« and »partial« cases. In the complete instances, all note values (except for the final note) are equal, in the

---

[47] Ernst Toch, *The Shaping Forces in Music. An Inquiry into Harmony Melody Counterpoint Form* (New York, 1948), 175 ff.

[48] Reinhold Brinkmann, *Die zweite Sinfonie von Johannes Brahms*. Musikkonzepte 70 (Munich, 1990), 65.

partial ones some notes are extended. In the Coda variant (m. 516), whose notes are played pizzicato, we have a compositionally realized ritardando, whose third note is three times as long as the first two – and this together with a metric shift by one ♪. The top line indicates the melodic variants of the four-note motif, which are set off by the size of the concluding intervallic leap. That is important insofar as only in this way the motivic identity of some of the rhythmic variants can be proved.

As for the controversial augmentation variant at the beginning of the recapitulation in m. 298, the table of variants fully demonstrates the genesis of this biggest of all the rhythmic enlargements: in m. 59, the ♩ of the original four-note motif are still preserved – only the value of the first note is doubled, whereby the *sf* on the anticipated note is designed to create the appearance of a new ›metric‹ One. The rhythmic and harmonic structure of the preceding measures contributes to this effect. At the recapitulation point, the partial augmentation variant thus given prominence is now fully augmented in the exact ratio of 1:3.

Ex. 1-143

Brahms, 2nd Symphony, 3rd mov., Motive Variants

Let us now look at the ›fate‹ of the four-note motif in the third movement, *Allegretto grazioso*, a dance-like movement with two contrasting Trios (Ex. 1-143). The motif is again present throughout the movement, in the three Allegretto parts in 3/4 meter, as well as in the first Trio in a quick 2/4 meter and the second one in a quick 3/8 time. In the example, the variants are coordinated with the three formal parts. In each case, an excerpt of the respective main voice and, immediately beneath it (in small print), the melody's pitch rhythm are shown. One can tell that Brahms here composed ›in line with components theory,‹ in that he individualized the tonal entries, on the one hand, and the pitch changes, on the other. This is especially clear in the somewhat elegiac-sounding main theme, since the four-note motif, after all, stands out only when one heeds the pitch changes and ignores the three impulses on the B (including the brief appoggiatura). The thereupon recognisable inversion of the four-note motif (B-C-B-E) is trochaic in rhythm (♩ ♩ ♩) and returns in the same way in the final (3/8) variant – diminished at the ratio of 2:1.

The additional variants, which sometimes sound in the recto and sometimes in the inverso form of the motif, have diverse rhythms, which are linked both to the component »Pitch« and component »Sound.« Thrillingly modern is the equalization of the rhythm in the first variant of the Presto I. Here the sheer notes of the main theme are regularly counted out and transformed into a plain ♪-rhythm; even the brief appoggiaturas are taken into account. This is clear proof that Brahms thought about the component »Pitch« in the abstract, that is, without connecting it to a tone duration. The appoggiaturas have, besides, an accentuating function and thus reinforce the dynamic accents set by Brahms. In view of that, the various presto variants – including the analogous 3/8 variant in Presto II – are not entirely profile-less ♪-rhythms, after all.

As for the proportions, the variants correspond to the complete as well as to the partial type. The second variant in Presto I divides the original values (♪) at the ratio of 2:1, whereby, because of the rapid tempo, a much more extreme relation has to be assumed (ca. 8:1). The pitch rhythm of the third variant in the first Trio, inherent in the dotted rhythm, corresponds exactly to the values of the original motif from the first movement, albeit only if one regards the faster tempo. In the variant of the Presto II, iambic and trochaic rhythms take turns, connected partly with the recto and partly with the inverso form.

Variants of the four-note motif also occur in the second (slow) and fourth (fast) movement, but these will not be set forth here in detail. In the *Adagio non troppo*, the allusions are more covert (mm. 55 ff. horns & trombones; mm. 10-11 flute; mm.45 ff. violas & 2nd violins; mm. 55 ff. basses; m. 90 basses); in the *Allegro con spirito*, they are open at the beginning of the main theme (m. 1) and repeatedly hidden (m. 26 violins; mm. 51 ff. violins; m. 66 violas & 2nd violins; m. 138 upper voice,[49] mm. 206 ff. flute & violins; m. 216 violins). The principle of rhythmic variation by means of complete or partial augmentation or diminution will have been sufficiently documented by the examples given.

---

[49] Only Reinhold Brinkmann (footnote 48, 106) has hitherto pointed out this inverted variant with its accentuated top notes C♯-D-C♯-F♯.

Rhythmic Iso-, Hetero- and Symmetry

The Greek derivatives »iso-«, »hetero-« and »symmetry« refer to units of measurement (metron) with which objects are determined as equal (iso-) or unequal (hetero-) in length or else as fitting together (sym-). Isometry includes symmetry but not necessarily heterometry. In rhythmic contexts, iso- and heterometric sequences can be continued indefinitely, whereas symmetric ones are always limited to two comparable instances: image and mirror image or rhythm moving forward and in reverse.

If one combines three heterometric elements (♪, ♩, ♩.) into a single unit and subjects that to a permutational procedure, the result is numerous isometric variants (a, b, c, d, e) but only one symmetric repetition (f). All of the rhythms have the overall measure of 6 ♪, and are thus isometric. The variant f is additionally qualified by the mirroring feature and is therefore the only one that is symmetric.

	I	II	III
a	♩. ♩ ♪	♩ ♪ ♩.	♪ ♩ ♩
b	♩. ♩ ♪	♩ ♩. ♪	♩ ♪ ♩.
c	♩. ♩ ♪	♪ ♩. ♩	♩ ♩. ♪
d	♩. ♩ ♪	♩. ♪ ♩	♪ ♩. ♩
e	♩. ♩ ♪	♩ ♪ ♩.	♩ ♪ ♩
f	♩. ♩ ♪	♪ ♩ ♩.	

In common music-theoretical parlance, this circumstance is mostly ignored: all even rhythmic or metric phenomena are called symmetric. This distinction is an important one, however, for enabling one to both conceptualize the special and problematic case of retrograde (symmetric) rhythms and to differentiate in the description of isometric structures.

Isometric relations in one dimension do not exclude heterometric relations in another. In the schema above, the note values are heterometric, that is, uneven in length, but the rhythms of three impulses are isometric, that is, of the same length. The pervasive pulse of ♪ (least common denominator), too, is isometric, as are some possible time signatures (e.g., 3/8, 6/8 or 3/4).

Another term for »isometric« is »periodic.« The Greek word means something like circular course. If I walk around something for a second time, I notice that the way round is equally long each time, i.e., isometric. The concept is applicable to all areas of perception and therefore occurs in many technical terminologies. In acoustics, for example, the waves produced by instruments may be periodic and thus result in distinct pitches. And the annual return of the Bayreuth Festival is no less periodic than the centenaries of its founder's birth. Because of the wide, not discipline-specific use of the concept of periodicity, I prefer the term »isometry« as being more appropriate to the language of music theory. The term »isorhythm« is an established one for denoting specific features of many 14th and 15th century motets, whose ordering principle dictates the repeated use of a fixed, identical rhythm (talea), not necessarily simultaneously with a repeated sequence of pitches (color). The duration of the talea is iso*metric*, the recurring sequence of short and long notes within the talea is iso*rhythmic*.

The terminological pair isometry / heterometry also enables us to deal with the widespread concept of heterometric meters, commonly called »asymmetric meters.« These meters, or rhythmic patterns, whose earmark is the regular recurrence of sequences of unequal duration (e.g., 2+3, 3+2, 3+4, 4+3, 3+2+2, 2+2+3, 2+3+3, 3+2+3, 3+3+2), can be precisely described as a mixture of isometric and heterometric phenomena. To denote them as asymmetric would be to repeat the error cited above regarding unequal durations as being asymmetric per se and equal ones being automatically symmetric. In reality, such meters or rhythms are internally heterometric in organization, but isometric in their sequence.

Isometry

It would be pointless to cite examples of isometric tonal sequences if they referred only to mensurations or modern meters, inasmuch as they are simply among the main features of polyphonic music of the last 800 years of European cultural history. But if one frees oneself of the dictate and limitations of conventional notation – to this day, e.g., there are no established graphs for values of five or seven – and performance practice – a conductor's signals, for example, can be quite cramping – isometric relations appear within the complex world of components rhythms that leave the mensural and metric orders far behind. They may correlate with, supersede, and sometimes even abolish them.

Let us look to begin with at a composition of the 14th century: Guillaume de Machaut's Motet No. 20, *Trop plus es bele / Biaute paree de valour / Je ne suis mie*. Though not iso*rhythmically* constructed, it largely follows an iso*metric* course (Ex. 144). The example shows the beginning of the first iteration of the tenor refrain. I have added the rhythmic profile of the several voices (based on the components »Sound,« »Pitch,« »Diastematy«) and the mensurational schema (3, 3).

It is not surprising that the tenor, which traverses exclusively brevises and semi-brevises, has an isometric order (3, 6, 9 ♪) (cf. Ex. 1-071, above p. 54). The case is less unambiguous in the upper voices. Here, too, to be sure, all the note values that are greater than 2 ♪ coincide with the mensural times, but pitch anticipations and the change in direction of the melodic steps (crest and keel notes) lead not infrequently to rhythmic weights that lie *next to* the ›beats.‹

Ex. 1-144

Guillaume de Machaut, Motet No. 20: *Trop plus est bele / Biaute paree de valour / Je ne suis mie* (Beginning)

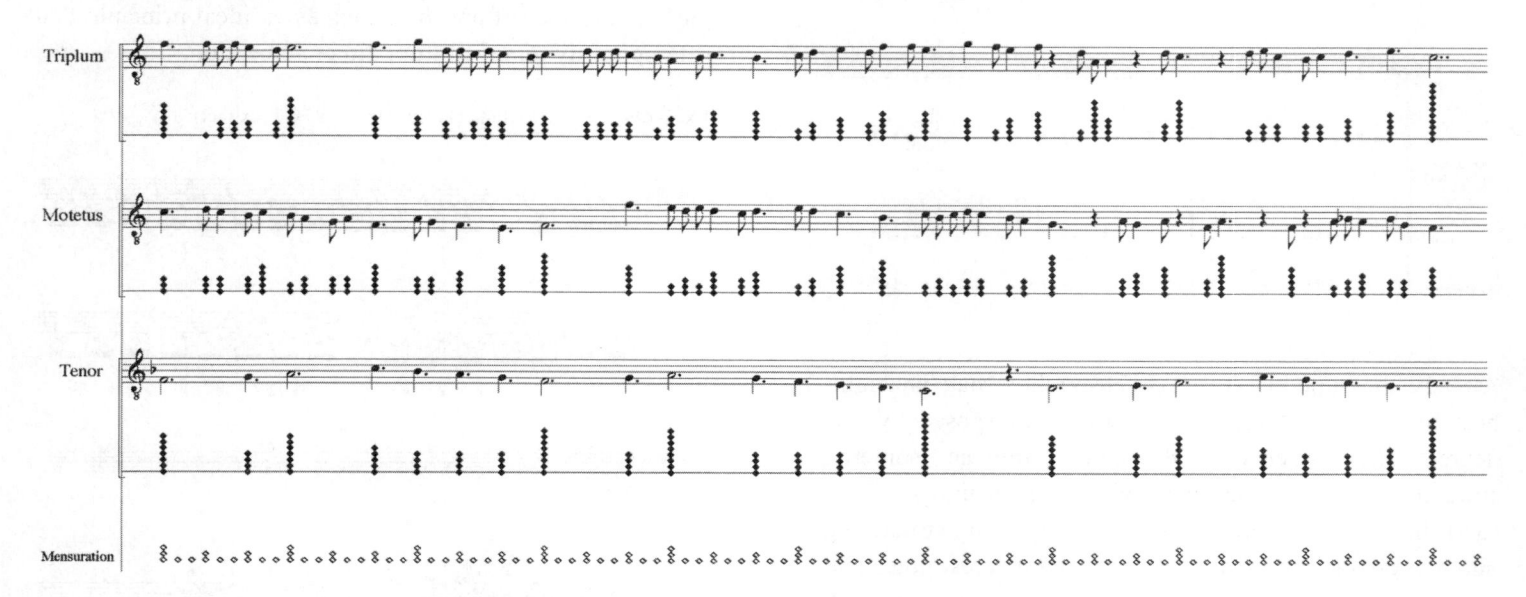

Yet if one accumulates the rhythmic profiles of the three voices into a synoptic profile of the setting, a picture emerges that is largely isometric (Ex. 1-145). On the lower levels of the total rhythmic profile (up to 6 weight units), the complex time structure of the three-part setting is reflected in quite subtle differentiation. But by isolating the weights that are >6 the pervasive isometric structure of the composition is made quite clear: distances are mostly of ♩., sometimes of ♩, once of 1 ♪. Of interest are also the largest rhythmic weights (>12), as they hint at a further mensuration (modus), which is not indicated in the notation (there are no longas). Some sections of the tenor are rhythmically articulated as though we were dealing with the division of a perfect longa into three imperfect breves (Ex. 1-146, see also the duration values of 18 in Ex. 1-145).

Ex. 1-146

Along with the predominant coincidence of mensural structure and the distribution of rhyhmic weights in Machaut's motet, there are examples to demonstrate a superimposition of rhythmic and mensural isometry together with a discrepant measure. In the previous section (Rhythmic Proportions), I discussed a case of sevenths rhythm as illustrated by an excerpt from Bauldeweyn's *Missa »Da pacem«* (Ex. 1-129). An interesting counterpart to that is found in the Gloria of the *Missa »De Beata Virgine«* by Josquin Deprez, where eight-beat rhythms supersede a six-beat mensuration.

Ex. 1-145   Guillaume de Machaut, Motet No. 20, Total Rhythmic Profile (>0, >6, >12)

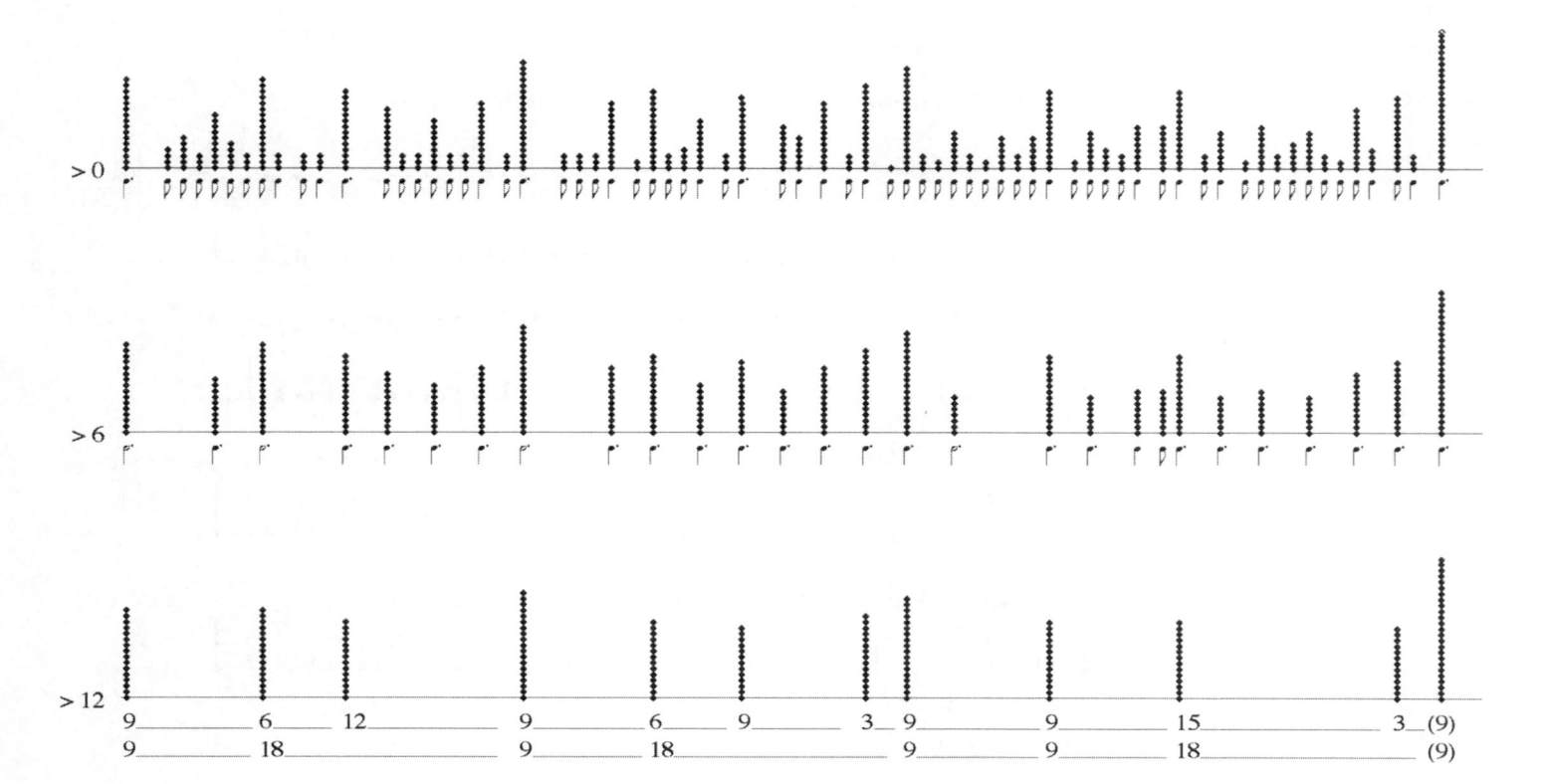

Ex. 1-147

Josquin, *Missa »De Beata Virgine«*, Gloria, Superius, mm. 242-246

Already the superius (Ex. 1-147) exhibits that: an eight-beat link of a melodic chain is twice transposed by one degree. The sequence of 8 ♩-units forms an isometric structure that is not congruent with the mensural structure (6 ♩). In addition, there is an interior rhythmic structuring into ♩, produced by tonal duration weights, crest notes and mini-phrases. This isometric rhythm, too, is at odds with the ›beats‹ of the mensuration (compare the rhythmic and the mensural profile).

If one listens to the four-voice »Amen« in its full length and shape (1-148), the enormous rhythmic complexity of the entire structure becomes apparent. At the beginning, there is the paired exchange between soprano and alto and tenor and bass in the exact measure of a 6/4 meter (2, 3). After five bars, the sequence is threaded in, soprano and bass making the beginning on the second semi-brevis of the sixth measure (F5: ♩ / D4: ♩). From here on, the phrases built by the links of the sequence have the unchanged measure of 8 ♩: they are isometric. The imitating voices also enact the 8-♩-measure, but staggered by 1 ♩. At the same time, their rhythm profiles reveal a different internal articulation: while 2+2+2+2 ♩ fill the 8-♩-frame in the soprano, it is 3+3+2 ♩ in the lower voices – a clear case of heterometry.

At the end, the four voices fit themselves back into the measure of the tempus imperfectum cum prolatione perfecta. That mensural order is by no means annulled during the sequence based rhythmically on eight beats, but is pushed into the off and functions as an ideal principle that is temporarily removed from direct perception.

Ex. 1-149 Bach, Prelude D Minor from WTC I (extract)

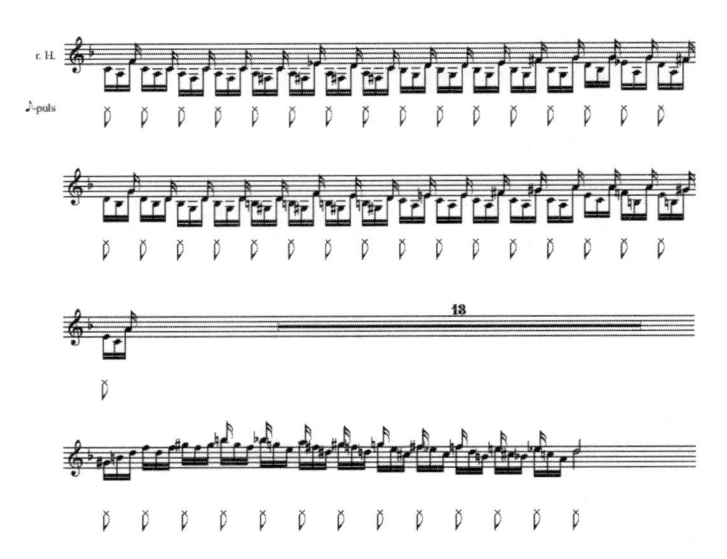

There are many examples of rhythmic isometry that are not congruent with the prescribed metric conditions and yet are immediately audible. A familiar instance is the Preludium in D minor from the first part of Bach's *Well-Tempered Clavier* (Ex. 1-149). The piece moves from beginning to end in sixteenths triplets, marked by eighths in the bass. The figures in the right hand all have the same shape: descending triads, placed in such a way that their first note – the crest note – is positioned before the eighths in the bass. These crest notes occur at intervals of three triplet ♪, and thus form their own isometric rhythm (♪. ♪. ♪. ♪. etc.). Since the sequence of crest notes is used to create the melody (see the upward-stemmed notes in the Ex.), their rhythm, set off against the eighths of the bass voice, is clearly audible.

Ex. 1-148 Josquin, *Missa »De Beata Virgine«*, Gloria, »Amen« (Sequence extract and rhythmic profiles of parts)

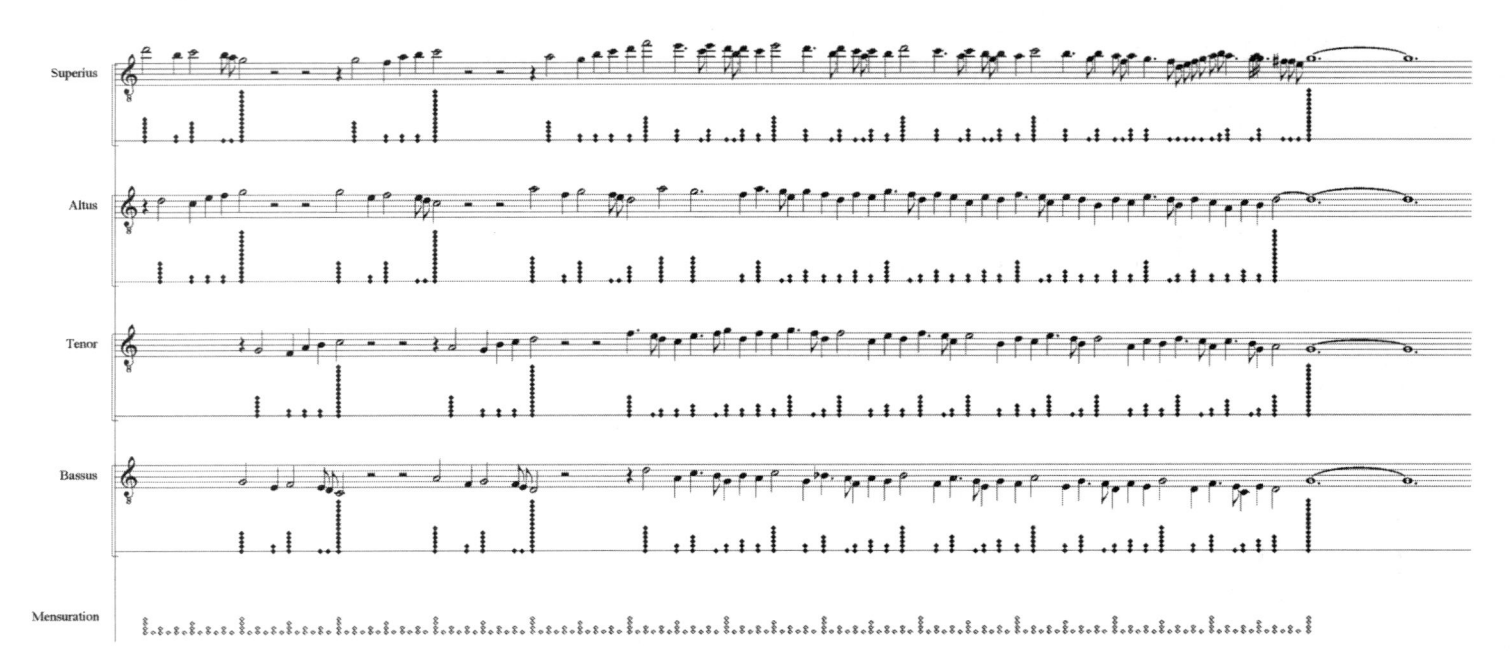

At the end of the (etude-like) piece, the position of the triads in the measure is altered: the crest notes now coincide with the eighths of the meter (which are no longer played by the left hand). The chromatic descent from B5 via B♭5 to D5 thus appears on the beat at the end, while during the entire preceding piece it was off the beat. I have described an analogous case already in the chapter about the component »Diastematy« (Ex. 1-014).

A fascinating example of the problem of rhythmic isometry in changing constellations is found in Beethoven's last string quartet in F major op. 135. Its second movement is a Scherzo marked »Vivace« and written in a fast 3/4 time (Ex. 1-150). I have reproduced the beginning of the quartet in three different forms: in the original notation, in a transcription and finally as a schematic model. The latter shows the melody-carrying (trochaic) low voice with the accompaniment above it in undisguised rhythms. In the transcription, articulatory rests and ligatures are dissolved and dynamic marks, bar lines, etc. omitted.

From the model-like excerpt, one can readily make out the isometry of the dance-derived form, as all the sections comprise exactly eight bars: a first period, its varied repetition, a middle section with a suggested temporary harmonic modulation, and the recapitulation of the first period (only the first two bars visible in the Ex.). The schema of the form seems as if on display. The fact that the middle portion, usually an arena for modulations and passing modulations, shrinks into monophony, sounding only the alien notes E♭2/E♭3/E♭4 and E2/E3/E4, may, however, be regarded as an indication that Beethoven here wanted to make the convention itself his subject, that he was reflecting compositionally, so to speak, about the relation between subjectively lived shape and objectively ossified schema.

A further indication for such a conjecture is the rhythm of the accompanying voices, whose only task is actually to put a harmonic dress on the main voice played by the cello. The simple tonic-dominant changes can be read in the model line. But this unassuming setting is worked in such a way that its temporal structure seems distorted. This emerges with particular clarity from the transcription. The harmony notes C4 and A4 in the violins really belong on the *One*. Their wrong location – before or else behind the bar line – is, moreover, established, for both voices sound in isometric ♩., as would be the case in an undistorted harmonic setting.

There are isometric processes also in the eight-bar middle portion, which again is made clear in the transcription by dispensing with the rests. From the second E♭ on, six ♩ sound in monophonic directness, then three ♩., combined with the returning *p* in all parts. Since the first E♭ also has the value of a ♩., one can describe these eight transitional measures as a mixture of iso- and heterometric values.

There is probably a particular idea connected to this dissociation of the tone setting. One might have assumed that the composer just wanted to be witty here, as he certainly is in other contexts. But the movement does not sound humorous. If one also looks beyond to the Trio of this movement with its nearly unending ostinati and the ›scandalously‹ difficult part of the first violin, one could think more easily of a symbolic torture by the increasingly mechanized conditions of working life than of a convivial joke. Beethoven's intervention in a composition's conventionally ordered temporal structure by dislocating the voices rhythmically should more likely be seen as the precipitation of a crisis other than compositional in nature.

Ex. 1-150   Beethoven, String Quartet op. 135, 2nd mov., mm. 1-34

Alban Berg used Beethoven's invention of rhythmically deconstructing an intact setting for his own dramatic purposes. In his opera *Wozzeck*, there is a theme that expresses in sound the personality of the title figure when he is not immediately beset by psychic or social conditions. This theme is introduced in the scene in which Wozzeck comes ›home‹ to Marie and the child (II:i). In the following scene (I:ii), in which he meets his tormentors, the Doctor and the Captain, the theme has at first a well-ordered form (Ex. 1-151). Shortly thereafter, when he has been tipped off that Marie might be unfaithful to him, he ›sounds‹ inwardly stressed (Ex. 152).

Ex. 1-151   Berg, *Wozzeck* II:ii, mm. 273-274 (trombones)

Ex. 1-152   Berg, *Wozzeck* II:ii, mm. 313-317 (trombones)

What originally was quietly placed one above the other is later on dislocated. Although the individual voices preserve their largely isometric gait, in the building up of the multi-voiced and successively transposed setting the lower voices are delayed by one triplet ♪ each. Thus the foundations go out of plumb, and the building threatens to collapse. It seems likely that the setting should be seen as analogous to Wozzeck's frame of mind. When he first encounters his two superiors, he is still in good shape, but after they have maliciously plunged him into doubt, his inner being threatens to rupture. Wozzeck, being »white as chalk«: »What do you mean by that, Herr Doctor, and you Captain, Sir?!"

Pure or predominant isometry is generally a mark of ›occidental‹ musical art. It goes without saying that it is customary also in popular music. Depending on the era of music history, and also on the musical genre, isometric temporal orders have been in use. The distance between the Notre Dame Organum and Steve Reich or Philip Glass is smaller than the historical distance would suggest. Among musical genres, toccatas and etudes are particularly ›susceptible‹ to isometric courses, as are, of course, all forms that allude to work, marching and dance music.

Heterometry

The difference between isometrics and heterometrics is in the final analysis, one of degree, not of category. In the following, I will cite two waltzes by Tchaikovsky, one written and composed in 3/4 time, the other in 5/4 time, to make clear how close these metric types can be.

To begin with the A major »Valse« from Tchaikovsky's Fifth Symphony in E minor (Ex. 1-153), I present only the main voice, which is played by the strings. Pertinent to it are the components »Sound,« »Diastematy,« »Articulation« (inclusive >) and »Phrase« (weighted according to length), with the component »Harmony« (including suspensions) added.

typical of the genre, though in genuine danced waltzes they do not lead to such skewed proportions as in this example, whose first phrase has a duration of eleven measures.

Now to compare the D major waltz from Tchaikovsky's Sixth Symphony in B minor (Ex. 1-154). Again only the main voice, played in this case by the celli, is represented. The components, too, are the same as in the waltz from the *Fifth*, the harmonic rhythm included. A peculiarity here are the eighths triplets, which I interpret as embellishments (mordent or inverted mordent) and therefore not as melodically/rhythmically relevant. They are so, however, in terms of the component »Articulation,« through which they do enter into the rhythm score.

Ex. 1-153   Tchaikovsky, 5th Symphony, 3rd mov., Beginning

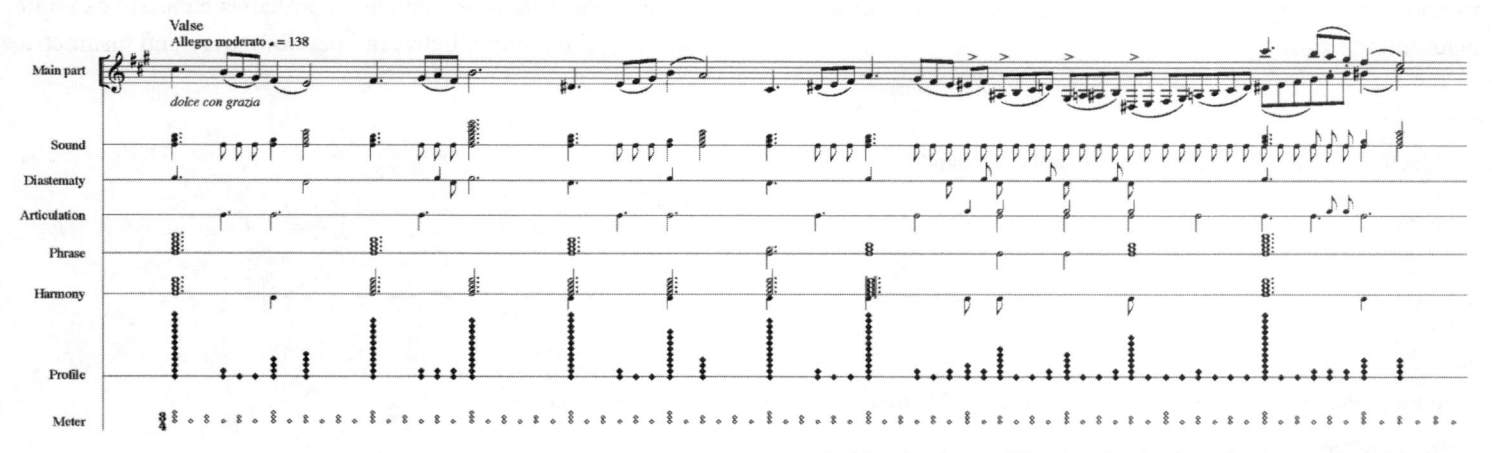

The largest weights in the resultant rhythmic profile indicate the isometric structure of the theme, which from the third bar on coincides exactly with the meter. At the beginning, there is the hovering effect so characteristic of many waltzes, which results from the fact that in the second measure the second beat is emphasized, while the first is withdrawn because of the change in harmony failing to occur. Similar in effect are the hemiolic formations following upon the isometrically stabile measures 3-8, which go hand in hand with the outer expansion of this section, to be regarded as the first phrase of a period. With some finesse, the composer introduces these hemiolic 4-♪-rhythms in the middle of the measure, as can easily be seen by comparing the meter line. Components involved are those of »Articulation,« »Dynamics« and in part also »Phrase« (drawing of beams). The hemiolas, too, are

The rhythmic profile clearly depicts the heterometric movement of the theme, without the 5/4 time signature with its metric weights having to be considered. The steady division into 2+3 ♩ by means of legato arcs is more or less supported by the other components. The second, longer part of the measures is given now a light stress, now a heavy one, an alternation that creates the impression of double measures. The rhythmic weights, at any rate, do not by any means suggest that the first beats are always the most ›stressed‹ ones; rather, this 5/4 waltz, too, exhibits that hovering so typical of the waltz. To bring this out even more clearly, one would have to include also the accompanying settings of these two unalike twins, which here, however, are treated only in sketch form. The similarities are patent: pizzicato basses and delayed chords in steady (isometric) regularity, as is ›proper‹ for waltzes.

Ex. 1-154   Tchaikovsky, 6th Symphony, 2nd mov., Beginning

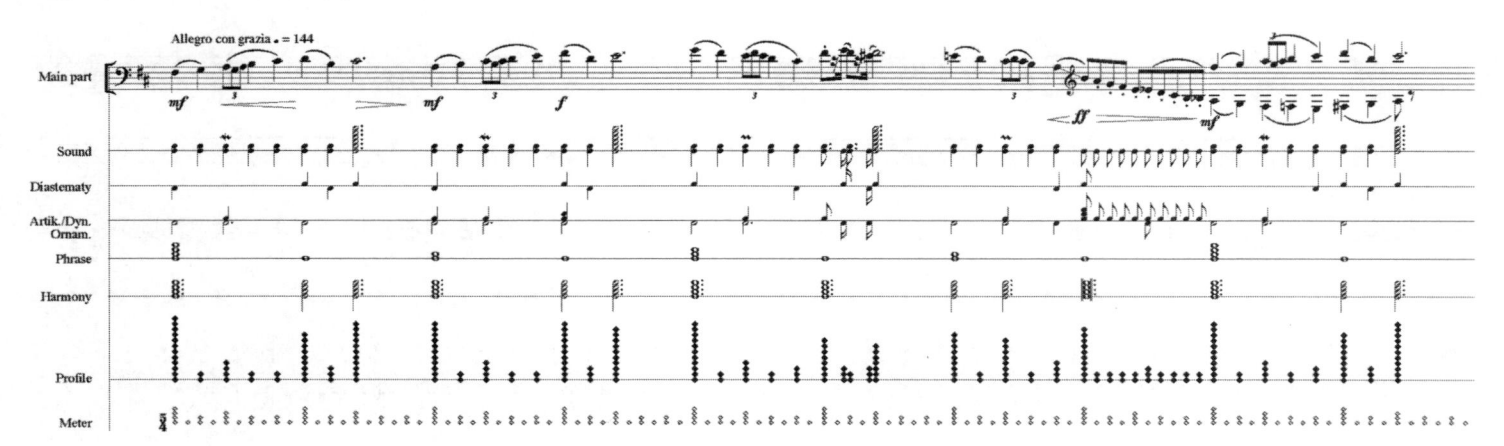

Ex. 1-155

There remains the question of the provenance of the rather unusual 5/4 meter. The practice of heterometric folk dances in the East European region is a possible source. On the other hand, the tradition of partial diminution or augmentation is to be considered as well. In Ex. 1-155, I have juxtaposed the two themes each with a proportional variant to show how easy it is to switch between isometric and heterometric forms.

phrases of the two themes, the nearly identical structure is apparent from the sequence of short and long times:

Ligeti s l s l l s l -
Bartók s l s l l s s l

Both pieces are also linked to the idiom of East European peasant music in terms of the tone system (Ligeti: D♯ La-Pentatonic, Bartók: A Plagal Dorian) and form (four-part song form). Even though the compositions exhibit a high degree of stylization, the folkloristic background of the heterometric rhythm, which here picks up the Aksak, is surely present.

The first movement of Béla Bartók's Sonata for Two Pianos and Percussion can be regarded as a classic example of an alternation between heterometric and isometric

Ex. 1-156

Ligeti, *Désordre*, Beginning, Theme in the left hand

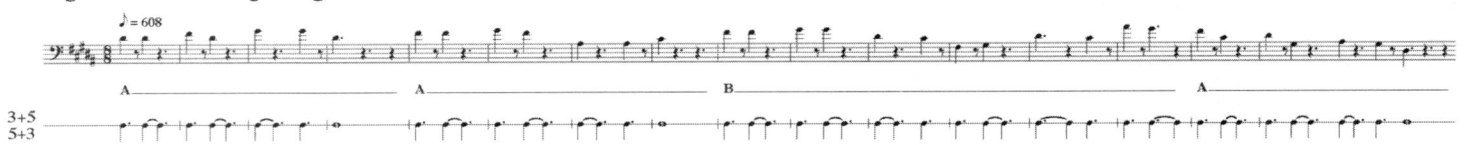

Bartók, *Bulgarian Dance No. 3* (Mikrokosmos 150), mm. 58 ff., Theme in the right hand

In the case of the two Hungarians Ligeti and Bartók, the folkloristic origin of certain heterometric themes is beyond question. This is immediately evident if one compares one of the themes (left hand) from Ligeti's etude *Désordre*, which I discussed above (p. 36 ff.), next to one of the »Bulgarian Dances« in Bartók's *Microcosmos* (Ex 1-156).

Both pieces have a fast pulse (Ligeti: ♪ = 608, Bartók: ♪ = 400). Ligeti groups 8/8 units heterometrically into 3+5 and 5+3 ♪, Bartók 5/8 units into 2+3 and 3+2 ♪. The measures are thus unevenly divided into a shorter (s) and a longer (l) part, or vice versa. If one compares the first

rhythm. The movement is throughout written in a fast 9/8 meter (only exceptions: mm. 4 and 6: 6/8 and m. 133: 3/4, only timpani). The 9/8 meter, however, is interpreted differently by purely rhythmic means: heterometrically in the main and secondary theme, isometrically in the theme of the final group, and both heterometrically and isometrically in the introductory theme.

I commence with the main theme of the movement, which is in sonata form (Ex. 1-157). After an introduction of 31 measures, which moves from darkness to light, from soft to loud and from slow to fast, there follows the very wild Allegro theme, based on a ping-pong play of timpani

Ex. 1-157   Bartók, Sonata for Two Pianos and Percussion, 1st mov., First Theme (mm. 32ff.), extract

and pianos. Four times the pianos, playing *ff* in four octaves, answer a pendulum of eighths of the timpani, whose binary ♪-structure with prepositioned 𝄽 is transformed into repeated ♩. If the pianos thus basically repeat the rhythm of the timpani, they play the ♩-sequences *without* the prepositioned 𝄽, so that the result is ♩ against ♩ at an interval of one ♪.

If one looks at the parts separately, their heterometric structure becomes apparent, although Bartók notates the timpani isometrically, the pianos heterometrically. A few measures earlier, the Piano I, too, is written in isometric

Ex. 1-158

form, which is really inadequate to the theme (Ex. 1-158). The reason may be that Bartók did not want to saddle the performers of the 1930s with a genuine aksak, because ›classically‹ trained musicians simply could not handle such rhythms. What he had in mind, however, was rhythms like 2+2+2+3 ♪, or, if one includes the rest on *One*, 1+2+2+2+2 ♪. In the timpani part of the main theme, an augmented reading of 4+4+4+6 ♪ is also possible, since in the transition from the second to the third measure, there is a real duration of 4 ♪, which thus could also be the meter of the first two measures.

never lost sight of, since a contra D regularly, i.e., isometrically, marks the beginning of every measure. Interestingly, the heterometric rhythm of the main subject lives on in the right-hand voice of Piano II. Fitted, in terms of the notes, into the rhythm of the secondary theme, the delayed eighths on D seven times put the durational sequence of 2+2+2+3 ♪ into effect (rest counted in).

The theme of the concluding group differs in character from both of the preceding ones: it is light and quick like a Gigue, due, not least, to the ›normal‹ execution of the 9/8 meter (Ex. 1-160). The iambically articulated main voice proceeds isometrically from beginning to end, which does not exclude tied-over notes, frequently hemiolic in effect – even consistently so in the accompaniment. The interplay of accompanying chordal setting and dance-like ›swinging‹ melody, in any case, yields a pervasive pulse of 3 ♪ per 9/8 measure. As the theme continues, all of the voices merge into the small-scale gigue rhythm, whereby the pedal drums mark the complete meter by ascending and descending glissandi at the end (from m. 133 on).

The introductory theme, consisting of a sequence of nine notes from the chromatic scale (A-G♯-G-F♯-F-E-D♯-D-C♯), does not have a character of its own. Like a melodic model, it can take on the most varied forms, and can also crop up as a ferment in the three main themes of the movement (Ex.

Ex. 1-159 Bartók, Sonata for Two Pianos and Percussion, 1st mov., Second Theme (mm. 87ff., recte: 84ff.), extract

The secondary theme, which, with its *p dolce* intonation, gentle line (initially in a tritone-grounded G♯ minor) and more sedate tempo (♪ = 132), is of a contrasting character, produces a new hetermometric variant of the 9/8 meter (Ex. 1-159). Its structure can be gathered from the drawing of the beams in the left hand of Piano II: the beams comprise mostly 4+2+3 ♪, in the second bar there is one variant of 2+3+4 ♪, and at the end there is the isometric form of 6+3 ♪, into which even the regular rhythm of ♩. ♩. ♩. inserts itself in Piano I.

The principal voice in Piano I, furnished as major sixth chords with brief appoggiaturas before every note of the melody, initially sets forth the measures of the pounding piano basses in non-repeated notes (4+2+3). The elegiac expression of the theme is intensified by the heterometric rhythm, so that the movement seems plodding and dragging as if on tired feet. The unity of the 9/8 meter, to be sure, is

1-161). At its introduction – in complete form first in mm. 4 f. in Piano I – the theme is in an even ♪ rhythm. In the course of the introduction, and later also in the Allegro exposition, it is repeatedly enlarged by partial augmentation, so that it expands to a length of twelve ♪ (Ex. 162).

Ex. 1-161

The pitch model with its internal structuring by minor ascending or descending seconds maintains rhythmic relations to the main theme of the movement, as the sequence of the seconds amounts to the heterometric rhythm 2+2+3+3 ♪, which is quite similar to that of the main theme (2+2+2+3 ♪) (Ex. 1-163).

Ex. 1-160 Bartók, Sonata for Two Pianos and Percussion, 1st mov., Third Theme (m. 105), extract

Ex. 1-162

Whereas the commonality in substance between introductory and main theme is thus a rhythmic one, the relations to the secondary theme are melodic in nature. The last four notes of the introductory theme (E-G-D-C♯) are identical in intervals with that of the secondary theme (A-C-G-F♯).

Ex. 1-163

In the development section, finally, there also appears a purely isometric variant of the introductory theme formed on the basis of octave accentuations, whose mode of movement is approximated to that of the theme of the final group (Ex. 1-164).

Ex. 1-164

Hetero- and isometric patterns are always clearly distinguishable when certain subdivisions of the measures are regularly repeated for a while. The large main theme complexes in this movement are a case in point. But even in such processes of metrically unified order, there is always also the ›normal‹ rhythmic elaboration, which means that rhythmic variants are formed, rhythmic imitations are carried out and metric shifts are introduced. An instructive instance of this can be observed in the transition to the recapitulation (Ex. 1-165).

The sequence passage of ten 9/8 measures reenacts the introduction preceding the Allegro once more. Based on a clear tone systematic concept – the chromatic circle (C2-C♯2-D2-D♯2 . . . B♭6-B6-C7) is realized together with the circle of fourths (C2-F2-B♭2-E♭3-G♯3-C♯4-F♯4-B4-E5-A5-D6-G6-C7) – the two pianos play the rhythm of the main subject in mutual imitation (with occasional changes in rhythm). The rhythm 2+2+2+1+1 with ♪ before or after the notes. The variants are 2+2+1+ 2+1 and 2+2+1+1+1, at the end also once 2+2+2+2+2 on Piano II. The imitating entries overlap and are conducted increasingly in stretto. The result is a freely floating, goal-directed rhythmic formation, in which the heterometrically defined main theme rhythm is heard in constant repetition and increasing condensation, without a referral back to the 9/8 units of the measures being possible.

Ex. 1-165 Bartók, Sonata for Two Pianos and Percussion, 1st mov., Transition and Reprise (schematic)

Symmetry

Contrary to all the isometry and heterometry, the first movement of Bartók's Sonata for Two Pianos and Percussion contains only one example of rhythmic symmetry. As much as Bartók loved mirror reflections along a horizontal axis, he was skeptical of all crablike inversions, that is, mirroring with a vertical axis. The example is typical of Bartók in its combination of rhythmic with diastematic symmetry (Ex. 1-166).

Ex. 1-166   Bartók, Sonata for Two Pianos and Percussion, 1st mov.

The pitches follow contrary, wedge-shaped courses in chromatic steps (upward: D-E♭-E-F-F♯-F𝑥-G♯ ; downward: D-C♯-C-B-A♯-A-G♯), and the 13 durational values coordinated with the pitches are retrograde, that is, symmetrically arranged: 1 5 1 2 1 2 1 2 1 2 1 5 1 ♪.

Rhythmic symmetry, viewed phenomenologically, is rather a problematic structure, since the temporal symmetry cannot be recognized by ear. It realizes itself solely in the idea and is thus the result of a mental effort. It is easy to write down a rhythm in retrograde form, e.g., ♩ ♩. ♩ ♪ ♪ ♩ ♩ ; and it is not hard to imagine such a formation as a symmetric unity of 4+3+2+1+2+3+4 ♪. But once the rhythm is implemented in sound, i.e., actually realized in the temporal continuum, the laws of listening take over: we perceive a growing and shrinking density of events, but not the reversal of time. Yet the dream of arresting time, even reversing it, is one that humanity has dreamed in every age. Perhaps that is the reason why composers, too, try again and again to reverse time in music.

A few prominent examples may suffice to document this special case of rhythmic construction of time. One of the earliest cases occurs in a rondeau by Guillaume de Machaut (Ex. 1-167). The piece begins with the words »My end is my beginning.« This cyclic conception of time presented in the text is implemented musically by the composer in the form of a retrograde repetition, preserving all of the pitches and durations, of a section twenty ›measures‹ in length. One can, for example, tell directly from the voice of the countertenor that the end equals the beginning (C-G-C). Tenor and Cantus exchange their voices, but that does not change the retrogression of the entire setting. The singer of the Tenor voice, to be sure – as also that of the Cantus – is robbed of the experience of ›his‹ beginning and ›his‹ end being actually identical: he might at best notice (and with him the listener) that ›his‹ end equals the beginning of the neighboring voice.

Another example is taken from Josquin's *Missa »L' Homme armé sexti toni«* (Ex. 1-168). In the Agnus Dei of this ›Cantus Firmus Mass‹, tenor and bass both recite the song »L'Homme armé« in long notes in such a way that the (›ideal‹) listener can experience how the melody of the one voice is simultaneously sung backwards by the other. From the midpoint on, the three-part canon, whose first and third phrase are identical (ABA), is sung by the tenor in forward motion, interspersed by rests and in a specific rhythmic and melodic version, while the bass simultaneously recites the voice of the tenor with all of its peculiarities in retrograde form. In the middle of the piece, there is a moment when the B phrase ends in the tenor, only to be immediately repeated in reverse form. There may be a chance for the listener here to actually notice the symmetric construction. What matters more, however, is that the original beginning of the melody, which will have been familiar to contemporary listeners, is sung by the tenor at the end of the Agnus (and thus of the entire mass). Thus this hall-of-mirrors game is dissolved, as it were, at the end.

Ex. 1–167   Machaut, *Rondeau* »Ma fin est mon commencement«, Beginning

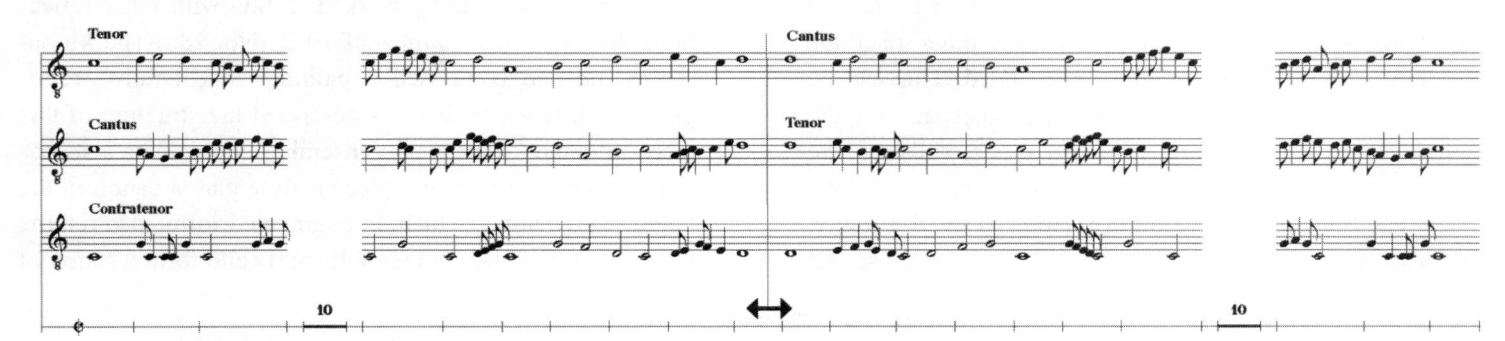

Ex. 1-168   Josquin, *Missa L'homme armé sexti toni*, Agnus III, c. f. simultaneously retrograde

Ex. 1-169   J. S. Bach, »The Musical Offering«, No. 1 of Ten Canons

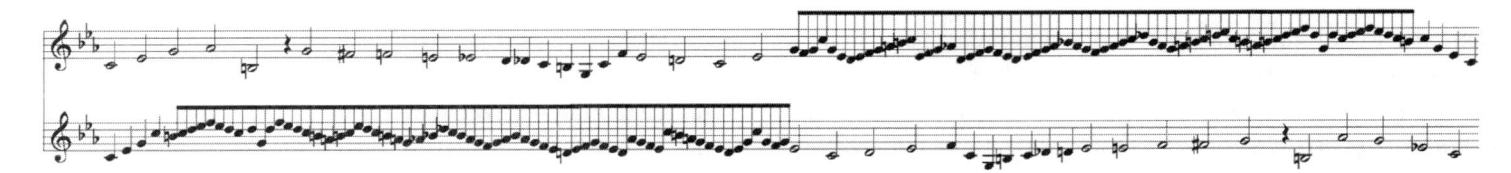

J. S. Bach, who can be regarded as the great consummator of the contrapuntal thinking handed down from the Middle Ages, has contributed an example of rhythmic symmetry in his *Musical Offering* (Ex. 1-169). The two-part canon is noted with only a single voice in the original, which is furnished with clef and key signature at both the beginning and the end – to indicate that the melody can also be played in reverse. Since the retrograde voice occupies the same range as the progressing one, the piece can be played only on two instrument or on two manuals. In my transcription, the mirror axis appears more clearly than could be confirmed by a listener. This is because, except for the first and last measure, where 𝅗𝅥 and 𝅘𝅥 reign, 𝅘𝅥𝅮 are pervasive and run across the structural caesura in the center of the canon.

Ex. 1-170

It remains to note that the rhythmic symmetry in this example (as principally in every retrograde tone sequence) partly disappears as soon as components other than the duration of the individual notes are included. This can be demonstrated on the chain of eighths notes around the symmetric axis (Ex. 170). Here I have established the rhythm of the component »Diastematy« (crest and keel notes) and marked its position in relation to the 4/4 meter. The sequence of durational values between the crest and keel notes (3 2 1 2 2 3 𝅘𝅥𝅮) is asymmetrical immediately before and after the symmetric axis (broken line), owing, in this case, to the repetition of the note G4. More important, and more relevant for listening, however, is the fact that the notes that are sounded in the upbeat position on the ›way there‹ fall onto the downbeats on the ›way back‹ (e.g., the crest notes G4, A♭4 and C5 at the beginning and the end of the extract). This makes clear again that the rhythmic mirror symmetry always has an element of the illusory about it.

Interest in the reversal of temporal processes revived in the 20th century, after having dwindled in the Classic-Romantic era (exceptions by, e.g., Haydn, Mozart and Brahms prove the rule). In explaining the »method of composition with twelve interrelated notes« developed by him, Arnold Schoenberg wrote that a unified space could be created in the imagination of the artist, in which up and down, forward and backward no longer play a role:

Just as our mind always recognizes, for instance, a knife, a bottle or a watch, regardless of its position, and can reproduce it in the imagination in every possible position, even so a musical creator's / mind can operate subconsciously with a row of tones, regardless of their direction, regardless of the way in which a mirror might show the mutual relations, which remain a given quantity.[50]

Even before his formulation of the twelve-tone technique, Schoenberg occasionally worked in line with these reflections. In his *Pierrot lunaire* of 1912 (No. 18, »The Moonspot«), he had composed a palindrome (literally »retrogression«). Horst Weber has described the structure of this piece in detail.[51] The 6 part ensemble implements a seven-voice setting: clarinet and piccolo flute play a canon in the upper twelve notes, which, in augmented form, also returns in two voices of the piano. Violin and cello form a canon of

Ex. 1-171   Schoenberg, *Pierrot lunaire*, No. 18 »Der Mondfleck«, mm. 8-12 (extract in C)

[50] Arnold Schoenberg, »Composition with Twelve Tones«, in A. Schoenberg, *Style and Idea* (New York, 1950), 102-143; pp. 113 f.

[51] Horst Weber, »Kalkül und Sinnbild. Eine Kurzgeschichte des Kanons,« *Musikforschung*, 46:4 (1993), 355-370; on the »Moonspot,« see ibid., 364-370.

their own at an interval of one octave. The speech/ singing voice goes its own ways, being concerned with the imitation of the »speech melody« (Schoenberg) and the correct implementation of the prosodic givens.

Except for some deviations and added chords, the canon on the piano is melodically and rhythmically identical with that of the winds and augmented at the ratio of 1:2, thus taking twice the time of clarinet and piccolo (19 vs. 9.5 bars). Schoenberg has the wind part being played twice, though in retrogression the second time. Violin and cello insert themselves into this palindromic figure with their canon. The result is thus a rhythmic symmetry: the vertical mirror axis is exactly in the center of m. 10 (Ex. 1-171).

Overall one can say that the symmetry aspect overshadows the counterpoint. This can be gathered from the sequence of the intervals between the entries of the canon voices, which, in the case of the clarinet and piccolo, take turns being in the lead, shrink from 4 ♪ to 2 ♪ (m. 8) to 1 ♪ (m. 9) and enlarge again correspondingly in the retrograde part (beginning not shown in the example). The compression of the entry intervals is, with some liberties, repeated on the piano at twice the scale (8, 4, 2 ♪); the extension, of course, is not.

Two additional details require separate mentioning. In the canon of the strings, there is a repeated exchange of voice in mm. 8-12, which leads to an ostinato repetition structure. Thus the figures played by the violin in m. 8, which already fill that measure symmetrically, are played four times in a row. The accompanying counter-voice in mm. 9, 10 and 11 ($C\#7$-$C\#7$-B6 etc.) occurs three times in a row. The altogether five measures are thus symmetrically formed in several ways: each measure of each voice is symmetric, the voice change of violin and cello is symmetric, and the five measures taken together are symmetrically divided in the exact center of m. 10. The thus long anticipated turning-point – and this is the second important detail – is given tonal emphasis by the fact that with the two ♪ framing the mirror axis, $A2$–$A\flat 7$, the largest ambit of the entire composition is sounded out at one time.

It must not be forgotten that the palindrome is operative only in four of the seven voices. The augmentation canon on the piano is only forward-moving, as is the speaking voice. The latter even dispenses with intoning the identically repeated lines »Einen weißen Fleck des hellen Mondes« (A white spot from the bright moon) (mm. 10, 19) in the same way: the speaking voice is musically free and seems to provide a commentary on the sound event of the instruments. The essence of the text – a fleck of light on the back that annoys the Pierrot – probably suggested the symmetric construction to Schoenberg. As it is impossible to look at one's own back, so it is finally vain to reverse a rhythm, except in the head of the composer or the listener.

When Arnold Schoenberg turned fifty, his pupil and friend Alban Berg wrote a Chamber Concerto for Piano and Violin with Thirteen Winds, which besides containing numerous semantic allusions to the constellation Schoenberg, Webern and Berg, was to demonstrate the newly learned virtuoso mastery of the twelve-tone technique.

The slow central movement is designed as a palindrome: 100 measures go forward, to be instantly repeated in retrograde fashion. In the Ex. 1-172, the moment of the ›time-turning point‹ is reproduced in the form of the original score. Berg seems to celebrate the center of the movement like a magic zone by having the piano, which in this movement is otherwise silent, play a $C\#1$ twelve times like the strokes of a bell – six times before the mirror axis and six times after, and in the symmetric rhythms of 5 2 2 2 2 2 2 2 2 2 2 5 ♪³. One can see from the image of the score, which was printed under Berg's own supervision, with what meticulous care the composer saw to it that the smallest detail, even the agogic markings, would subserve the optic-acoustic concept of a perfect symmetry.

Pierre Boulez called the passage, not without some irony, a »sort of esoteric ›midnight.‹«[52] And Berg observed self-ironically in his open dedicatory letter that, thanks to his obsession with details, his »reputation as a mathematician will grow in proportion as that of the composer will fall with the square of the distance from the former."[53]

Less esoteric than symbolic in function is Berg's large-scale palindrome in the film music of his opera *Lulu* – a scene-change music accompanying sequences of a film intended to show scenes of Lulu's capture and liberation. Exactly at the center of this entr'acte, the music seems to halt momentarily before immediately embarking on the ›way back.‹ In the Ex. 1-178, I have limited myself to an extract of the main voices at the beginning, the turning-point and the end.

Set around the mirror axis is one of Lulu's personal leitmotifs, the so-called »Erdgeistquarten« (Earth Spirit fourths) (C4-F4-$F\#4$-B4 and D4-A3-$A\flat 3$-$E\flat 3$). This interval constellation is symmetric in the diastematic sense, as is the melodic contour of the two motif quotations. In using the rhythm of triplet eighths, Berg actually accepts a slight blurring. In order to maintain the rhythmic complementarity of the two ›Earth Spirit‹ voices, the upper voice is symmetric (1 1 1 <u>4</u> 1 1 1), the lower one asymmetric (1 2 1 6 2 1 1). All the other voices are symmetrically written backwards.

---

[52] Pierre Boulez [Introductory text to Alban Berg's *Chamber Concerto*], in Alban Berg, Kammerkonzert für Klavier und Geige mit dreizehn Bläsern, Philharmonia Paritur No. 423 (Vienna/London: Universal Edition, n.d).

[53] Alban Berg, [Open letter to Arnold Schoenberg in dedication of the Chamber Concerto on Schoenberg's 50th birthday], in Alban Berg, *Glaube, Hoffnung und Liebe. Schriften zur Musik*, ed. F. Schneider (Leipzig: Reclam, 1981), 228-235.

Ex. 1-172   Berg, Chamber Concerto
2nd mov., mm. 117-124 (Philharmonia, U.E.)

The turning-point is again rendered mysterious, in that the music is hushed to *ppp* and becomes »ganz langsam« (very slow). Additionally, another leitmotif of the opera is heard in an ethereal height, played by the piano and the celesta: the »ringing motif,« which always announces catastrophic turning-points in the action. For all its brevity (1+1 triplet eighths), this arpeggio motif, too, is symmetric.

One can surmise that with this peripety, and the entire retrogressive orchestral setting in the middle of the opera, Alban Berg wanted to express his view that the successful liberation of Lulu also initiates the decline of her career. Behind it is the notion that retrograde time signifies the same as extinction of history.

Ex. 1-173   Berg, *Lulu* II:i-ii, mm. 658-716 (extract)

Rhythmic Characters

To the extent that rhythm has a part in forming *musical* characters, one can also speak of *rhythmic* characters. The term is to refer to the core of the traits constituting the typical formation as which any character manifests itself. Because of the proximity of rhythm and bodily movement, rhythmic characters are found with particular frequency and prominence in dance, marching and work music, regardless of the extent to which the customary musical genres may have been artificially sublimated and stylized. If the analysis is as meticulous as the method and tools of rhythmic component analysis allow, one will be able to differentiate precisely between the rhythmic characters of different dances – among dances in triple meter, for example, between courtly minuet, sedate landler, danza tedesca, Viennese waltz, French valse, Czech furiant and Polish mazurka. The same goes for the group of civilian and military marches and all other forms of individual or collective bodily movements.

To present a full catalogue of rhythmic characters would be both futile and senseless within the framework of this study. If I limit myself to three basic characters, upbeat, syncope and hemiola, the analytic procedure will become clear enough to be readily applicable to additional cases.

Upbeat

Every musician knows the phenomenon of the unstressed upbeat, but also the practice of, in fact, emphasizing upbeats for pointed effects. Both cases presuppose that the metric structure of a composition is based on the schema of heavy beginnings in a measure and light in-between beats, and that, generally speaking, the feeling for accentual degrees in meter has already been developed, as has been the case since the 16th century. In line with the questions that components theory endeavors to answer, the issue regarding the phenomenon of the upbeat cannot be what emphasis a *musician* gives to a particular upbeat, but what weights the *composer* has placed on the notes before and after the bar line. As shown in detail in the section on rhythmic weights, the subtlest weight gradations can be obtained by way of manipulating the components and the rhythms resulting from them. On that basis, for example, the metric structure of a composition can manifest itself purely rhythmically, thus also making it possible to distinguish between heavy and light upbeats.

In the case of ›stressed‹ heavy upbeats, there are similarities to the phenomenon of syncopation. As the latter derives its effect from a heavy mensural or metric weight being to all appearances rhythmically shifted, as when, for example, a note tied over a bar line produces a durational weight prepositioned to the *One*, while the heavy beat itself is lightened, so the heavy upbeat means that its rhythmic weight exceeds that of the downbeat *One*. Since the entire components arsenal can be used for suchlike effects, it is clear that upbeats can be shaped not only by tonal durations but also by other means.

A special constellation is present in vocal music, because the text by itself already exhibits syllabic weights that depend on the verse meter and/or the weight and meaning of individual words and syllables, whether in formal or in free verse.

Light and Heavy Upbeats

The weights of the upbeats generally differ from case to case and can easily switch from light to heavy or vice versa within a single musical phrase. As a prime example for heavy and light upbeats I choose the beginning of the Minuet in Beethoven's Eighth Symphony (Ex. 1-174), in which the mature master, combining several minuet models, once more reflects on the old-fashioned predecessor of the scherzo.

Ex. 1-174   Beethoven, 8th Symphony, 3rd mov., Beginning

Of the three upbeats (marked with arrows), the first two are heavy, the third light. Bar one and two are like a curtain, seeming, with their naïve, landler-like pendulums of fourths and thirds, to merely set out the 3/4 meter. At the same time they do not make it fully clear whether this ›minuet‹ begins with an upbeat or a downbeat. This is owing to the fact that the tonic is in effect from the beginning and remains so for more than two measures. In addition, the change to the third of F major – A4 in the upper voice – takes place on the third beat of the first measure, combined with a first F major chord in root position upon the entry of timpani and trumpets. As a result the intrinsically weak beat all but attains the quality of a strong *One*. Since all of the quarter positions are furnished with *sf* accents, mm. 1 and 2 sound like a conductor's clumsy preliminary downbeat-counting: One, Two, Three | One, Two Three. The result is that the upbeat at m. 3 with which the thematic melody begins (A5) – and which now is really recognizable as a light upbeat – conveys the feeling of being supernumerary or belated in coming.

The cantilena in the violins, of which this upbeat is a part, brings on the first harmonic change, so that the weight relations at this point are unambiguous: light → heavy, while the weights at m. 1 and 2 are heavy → heavy. The component »Phrase« (here in reference to the slurs in the notation) indicates a beginning rhythm of ♩ | ♩ ♩ | ♩, which, taken by itself, still suggests a relatively light upbeat. The same is true of the first two dynamic signs *f* | *sf*, the second of which signifies somewhat more weight than the first. All of the components taken together, among them especially »Timbre,« »Texture« and »Harmony,« all of which produce changes on the *Three* of m. 1, contribute to making the upbeat heavy. The third upbeat, now to be played piano, is in any case light by comparison. I might mention that in the course of the movement Beethoven time and again plays humorously with surprising weight shifts.

m. 2 to m. 3, on the other hand, includes an upbeat, whose rhythmic weight is somewhat greater than that of the following *One*. It can therefore be called a heavy upbeat, whereas the upbeat at the beginning of the melody is light (see also the arrow marks). The relations are even more distinct in the duple version (in 2/4 meter). Here the first upbeat is clearly recognizable as light, whereas the second is as heavily weighted as the *One* in m. 1. This is owing to the repetition of the note D4, which occasions a weight shift to before the start of the measure. If the two notes were tied over, one could speak of a genuine syncopation. The same goes for the second part of the melody, whose numerous note repetitions (as shown above) in the »Pitch« line lead to a sequence of syncopated ♩ (G-F-E-D). One can see from this 13th-century example that play with changes between light and heavy upbeats has existed from early on. The phenomenon in the medieval dance tune does not

Ex. 1-175   *Lamento di Tristano* (13th cent.), ternary and binary variants (»chiusso«-version)

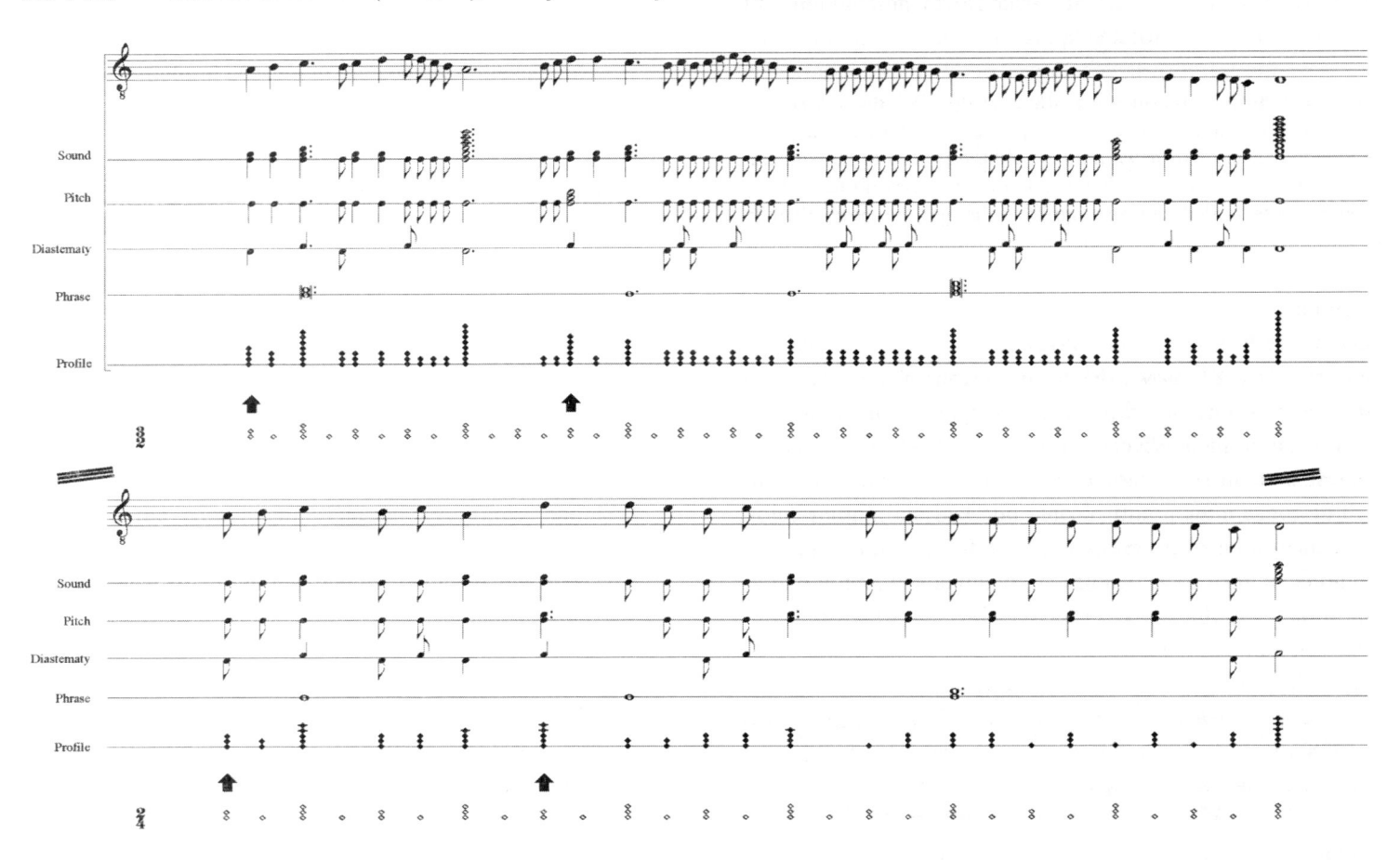

The instrumental dance piece *Lamento di Tristano* already cited in the section on the component »Pitch« (p. 23, above) likewise has light along with heavy upbeats (Ex. 1-175). The dance exists in a duple and a triple meter version, indicated here by the time signatures 3/2 and 2/4. Shown in each case is the beginning period of the concluding repeat version (»chiusso«). The rhythm scores comprise four components: »Sound,« »Pitch,« »Diastematy« and »Phrase.« The result is a set of rhythmic profiles that depict the rhythmic weight distributions in a differentiated manner.

In the triple-measure version, the weight peaks largely coincide with the metric weights, as a comparison with the schema of the 3/2 meter will show. The transition from

principally differ from that in Beethoven's minuet. The same goes for vocal music, differentiated only according to the degree of textual dictates and to the stage in the development of accent-degree meter.

To demonstrate the combination of prosodic and musical accents, I refer to one of the most prominent examples in music history, the lied »Gute Nacht,« which opens Franz Schubert's *Winterreise*. In the six-bar prelude, several strong upbeats can be found, which, as is natural, are formed exclusively by purely musical components (Ex. 1-176). In this piano setting, nearly all the upbeats are accentuated. This is caused by several components that, partly

Ex. 1-176 Schubert, *Winterreise*, No. 1, Prelude

Ex. 1-177 Schubert, *Winterreise*, No. 1

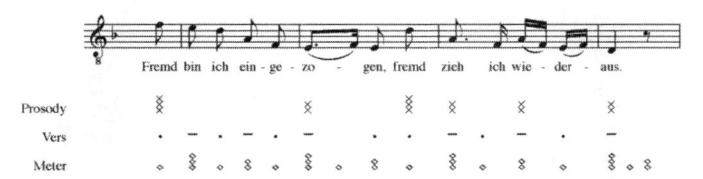

individually and partly also in concert, produce more or less strong weights on the fourth eighth of the 2/4 meter. The first upbeat is given prominence by the peak note F5. Added to that is the phrase mark, which includes the note before the bar line. Of special interest is the function of the second note, the dissonant E5, which falls on the *One* and therefore would have to be interpreted as a ›stressed‹ passing note. Because of the shift of the rhythmic weight to the note F5 before the bar line, however, the harmonic function of the E5 is changed: it becomes an ›unstressed‹ passing note from F5 to D5, which is all the more conspicuous because of the standing D minor tonic.

The second upbeat is weighted a good deal more strongly than the first. It is accentuated by two dynamic marks (*fp* and >), a dissonant chord provides additional weight, and the phrasing again begins before the bar line. A corresponding situation obtains in the third and fourth upbeat. Here, moreover, crest note accents are added, and yet another component (»Timbre«) is deployed through the octaval doubling of the melody.

The melody of the piano anticipates the singing voice (Ex. 1-177). A close look at the latter makes clear that its accentual condition provided the impulse for the piano prelude's having nothing but strong upbeats. The upbeat accent connected with the word »fremd« (strange), spreads, as it were, throughout the entire composition. The condition of being a »stranger« thus becomes a decisive musical-lyrical semanteme.

What the poet Wilhelm Müller set forth textually, Schubert transmutes congenially into music. By choosing the word »Fremd« as the opening word, the simple meter of

the iambic trimeter is thrown off balance, with the same effect as the heavy upbeats in Schubert's setting, in the first »fremd« upbeat as much as in the second. The fact that over the course of the lied prosodically weak upbeats occasionally collide with musically strong *Ones* is one of the compromises to be accepted in a strophic song like this first one: they are of little consequence compared with the aesthetic gain the song obtains from the semantically grounded, nearly omnipresent emphatic upbeats.

At times, upbeats can acquire so much weight that they are taken for an actual, as it were, »false,« downbeat. Johannes Brahms' Second Symphony contains in mov. I a striking example of this, namely at the point where, after a brief intermezzo (mm. 44-58), the transitional passage with the initial use of the motto idea D-C♯-D-A sets in (Ex. 1-178).

The ›upbeat‹ in question is again marked by an arrow. The way to it involves a process of condensation evident from the foreshortening of the phrases in the two main voices. The melody in the violins, which commences already eight bars before the excerpt in our example, is now foreshortened (from m. 54). The phrasing arcs span 8, 4 and 2 ♪ in the upper voices and 6, 4, 2 ♪ in the imitating basses. If one goes not only by the phrasing slurs but also by the phrase contents, the leading upper voice reveals an even more rigorous stringency: 8+6+4+4+2+2 ♪. At the end, both main voices unite in a seven-note plunge of descending thirds (B-G-E-C♯-A-F♯-D), whose destination is the D major tonic. That point is reached on the third beat of the 3/4 meter (m. 58) and is weighted dynamically, texturally, thematically and by timbre. In addition, the motto motif

Ex. 1-178 Brahms, 2nd Symphony, 1st mov., mm. 54-60 (analytical particello)

entering here sounds in partial augmentation, in that the first note (D) has twice its original value.[54]

Ex. 1-179

If one writes the main voice in purely rhythmic notation, i.e., without beams or slurs, it becomes clear that Brahms did everything here to create the illusion of an early ›false‹ One (Ex. 1-179). The precondition for it is the dissolution of the 3/4 meter's isometry, so that the listener is relieved, as it were, to regain solid ground under his feet upon reaching the destination point. The deception, to be sure, becomes patent immediately afterwards, for the 4-♩-measure of the changing note D-C♯-D in the motto motif by no means determines the further course, as the secondary theme follows shortly afterwards, which is cradled as securely in the ternary meter as one could wish for the most blissful of idylls.

The remaining voices, represented in smaller print in Ex. 1-178, participate in the dissolving of the metrical structure, mainly by means of chains of syncopations throwing off the three-step. Important, likewise, is the trumpet voice, which is confined to the (octave-doubled) fourth A-D-A-D-A but places it in such a way that, after an A held for 8 long ♩, the first D falls on the ›false‹ One, that is, on the strong upbeat. Hand in hand with that goes the four-measures-long dominant seventh chord, whose resolution likewise occurs on the third beat of m. 58.

I will conclude this section on light and heavy upbeats with two examples taken from works by Richard Strauss and Gustav Mahler. In both cases, the principle of weight increase is taken to the extreme, once in order to give expression to an extravagant euphoria (light→heavy), the other time to dramatize the frustration of a longing (heavy→light).

The Strauss example occurs in the recognition scene of Electra. Orestes has returned incognito to the court of his mother Clytemnestra to avenge the murder of his father. He finds his sister miserably enslaved. Only after a number of clues enable Electra recognize her brother.

The upbeat (see arrow in Ex. 1-180) is performed a cappella by Electra, who sings her brother's name »crying out.« The first syllable of the name is short and low, the second long and high. The exclamation, not unusual as such, derives its special energy from its preparation and its aftermath. With his singing in chromatically rising seconds (»The dogs in the yard recognize me, and my sister doesn't?«), Orestes leads directly into Electra's entry. The voices of the orchestra duplicate the chromatic upward steps, only celli, basset horn and bass trumpet (D♯-D-D♭) counteract in (likewise chromatic) descent. The volume is increased from p via f to ff. At the same time, the harmony stretches into a complicated cadence ending in a double-dominant diminished seventh chord on B, so that the interval C5-A5 on which Electra sings her brother's name, like dominant and tonic, brings the resolution of the harmonic tension.

But it is only the entry of the orchestra tutti, which occurs while Electra is still holding her tone, that makes this upbeat so immensely noteworthy. Although the expected tonic F is heard in basses and timpani, the chord intoned above them is of the most acute inner tension and

Ex. 1-180   Strauss, *Elektra*, near fig. 144a (analytical particello)

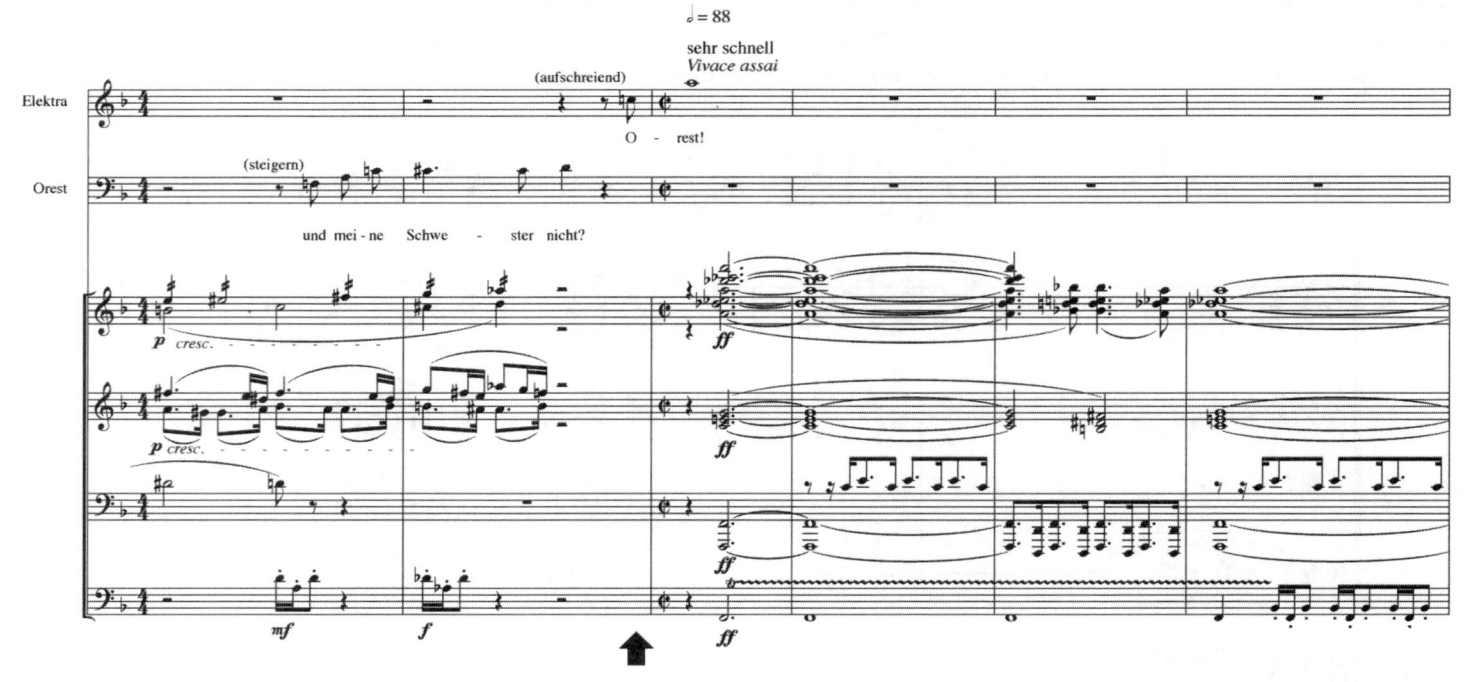

[54] For details, see my analysis in the chapter on »Proportions,« p. 86ff., above.

tonal power: one could say, it is stronger than strong. Simultaneously with the F in the depth, we hear the bassoons and trombones playing a C major chord in the middle register, and, in the top register, a trenchant sound of winds over several octaves, whose notes D♭ and E♭ are dissonant in relation to C major, while the top note A seeks consonance with the bass note F. Two bars later, this dissonance is rendered even more extreme in the chords in the middle and upper parts that are set in chromatic countermotion, so that a triad B-D♯-F♯ in the trombones is in friction both with the chord D-E-B♭ in the wind instruments and with the F-D pendulum of thirds in the basses.

The upbeat which Electra sings on the name O-rest expresses above all the fulfillment of her hopes and desires. This is suggested also by the shift to a faster tempo and the rewriting of the 4/4 meter into an alla breve one. At the same time, however, the massive instrumentation of the orchestra, which seems to prolong Electra's outcry, also expresses the psychic destructions and contortions that make it impossible for her to feel pure happiness about the regained brother. Thus the simple upbeat is magnified by musical as well as dramatic-psychological means into a monstrous act that coincides with the climax and peripety in the action of the opera.

Although the two pieces have nothing to do with each other, the example by Gustav Mahler is laid out like a deliberate negation of the Strauss passage. The measures containing a heavy upbeat followed by a *One* in *p* subito occurs in the D♭ major Adagio of Mahler's Ninth Symphony, which ends with this slow movement (Ex. 1-181).

Three expressively played *fff* measures prepare the reentry of a section of the main group. The intensification to this point includes diverse components, of which a »molto crescendo,« together with a widening of the ambit, are the most conspicuous means. One can regard the entire third measure of the example as a mighty upbeat gesture, whereby the ♩-impulses especially in the violins are emphasized by four *sf* marks, two-eighths ties and a kind of staircase of sevenths. The eight-step descent of seconds furnished with accents on nearly every note in the violas and cellos appears also in the violins, albeit in upwardly transposed octaves, whereupon the last seconds drop B-A prior to the entry of the ***pp*** one occurs in four parallel octaves.

The harmony, which progresses at first in ♩ and then in ♪, likewise produces a rhythmically cumulative effect. The destination of the harmonic progression is the tonic D♭ major at the point of the reentry of the »old tempo« (m. 4 of the Ex.). The last chord prior to the D♭ is an augmented six-five chord of the lowered VI (B♭♭ = A), which is not immediately recognized, neither as such, nor, therefore in its double dominant function. Mahler writes C♯ major before the bar line, D♭ major after it, whereby the G before the change actually belongs to the D♭-major nexus (Ex. 1-182). The upbeat successively charged with tension in three measures leads unexpectedly into a very soft thematic phrase played by few instruments, which stands for the renunciation or negation of a promise.

Ex. 1-182

To prevent any misunderstanding, one should note that this Adagio also contains examples in which a magnified expectation is followed by an unrestricted fulfillment (cf., e.g., the parallel passage in mm. 23/24 and the transition to the recapitulation in mm. 125/126). The moment of renunciation represented by this example can thus not be generalized, any more than the affirmative fulfillment expressed by the »Orest« passage.

Ex. 1-181   Mahler, *9th Symphony*, Adagio mm. 70-74 (analytical particello)

Long Upbeats

One of the earmarks of an upbeat is normally its light weight. The examples cited in the last section should be regarded as (frequent) exceptions to the rule. If upbeats are prolonged in their rhythmic duration, it does not necessarily mean that they become heavy thereby. A lovely, charming example of this occurs in the introduction to the Finale of Beethoven's First Symphony (Ex. 1-183).

Ex. 1-183
Beethoven, 1st Sympony, 4th mov., Introduction

Ex. 1-184   Beethoven, 1st Symphony, 4th mov., mm. 238 ff. (extract)

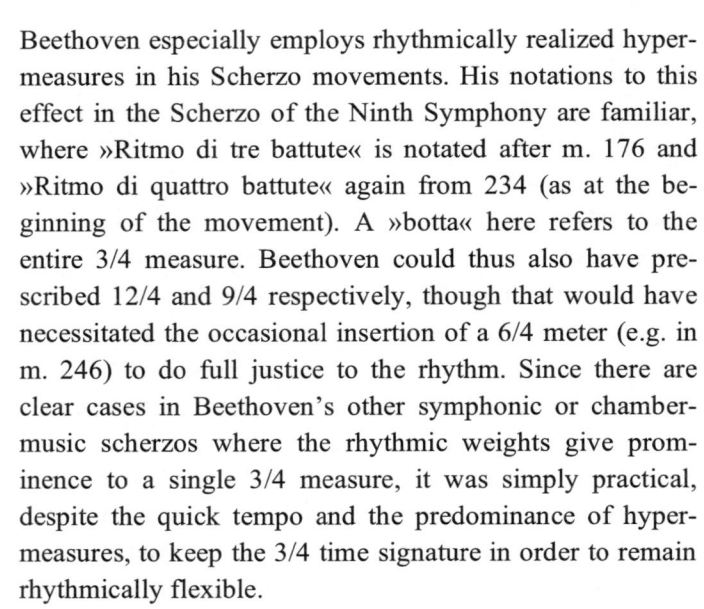

The slow introduction consists of the successive build-up of a C major scale from the fifth degree. Hand in hand with the extension of the ladder rungs from three to eight notes goes the expansion of the upbeats, which finally, – at the sudden entry of the Allegro tempo – amounts to an upbeat duration of an entire measure. This can also be regarded as an indication that this Finale, which is written in 2/4 time, is really thought of in terms of double measures. If one were to ascertain all of the rhythmic weights of this movement, the result would clearly be an uninterrupted isometric sequence of four ♩ throughout the entire piece – the rhythmic realization, so to speak, of a quaternary meter. At the resumption of the rondo-like theme shortly before the Coda, Beethoven increases this expansion process once more considerably, so that altogether six measures appear like a single subdivided upbeat (Ex. 1-184).

Beethoven especially employs rhythmically realized hyper-measures in his Scherzo movements. His notations to this effect in the Scherzo of the Ninth Symphony are familiar, where »Ritmo di tre battute« is notated after m. 176 and »Ritmo di quattro battute« again from 234 (as at the beginning of the movement). A »botta« here refers to the entire 3/4 measure. Beethoven could thus also have prescribed 12/4 and 9/4 respectively, though that would have necessitated the occasional insertion of a 6/4 meter (e.g. in m. 246) to do full justice to the rhythm. Since there are clear cases in Beethoven's other symphonic or chamber-music scherzos where the rhythmic weights give prominence to a single 3/4 measure, it was simply practical, despite the quick tempo and the predominance of hyper-measures, to keep the 3/4 time signature in order to remain rhythmically flexible.

The Trio in the First Symphony – in contrast to the main part of the ›Menuetto‹ – runs its course in undisturbed isometry of twelve and sometimes six ♩. As its beginning shows (Ex. 1-185), its upbeats occur in different contexts, whose duration extends from 1 to 9 ♩. At the very beginning, the winds (upper system) play a short quarter-note upbeat, while generally trochaic (feminine) endings are to be presumed (♩ ♩ | ♩ ♩). The runs of eighths in the strings (lower system), on the other hand, form longer upbeats that repeatedly exceed the compass of a single 3/4 measure.

If one takes the 12/4 meter as the metric unit, in line primarily with the harmonic rhythm, the upbeat arabesques of the violins enter on the second beat of the theoretical 12/4 measure and lead over in the course of three beats to the beginning of the second phrase. If, therefore, that A minor phrase in the winds no longer has an upbeat of its own, it is because the long upbeat of the violins now conducts to the new hyper-measure *One*.

Ex. 1-185   Beethoven, 1st Symphony, 3rd mov., Trio, Beginning (extract)

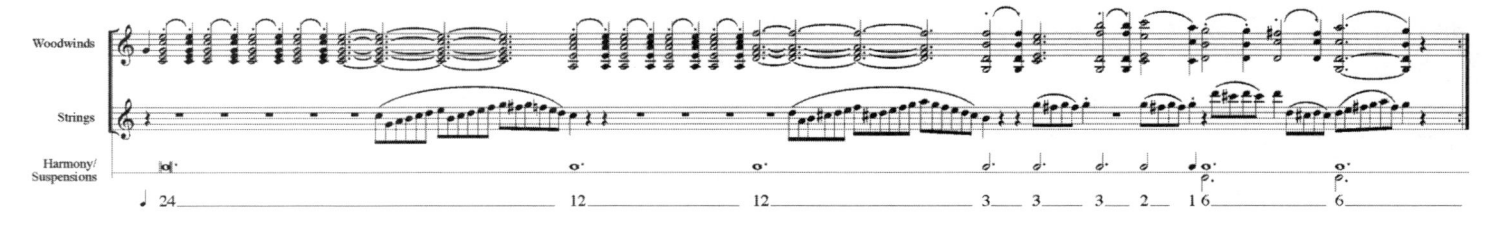

Ex. 1-186   Weill, *Mahagonny*, No. 18, fig. 15 (extract)

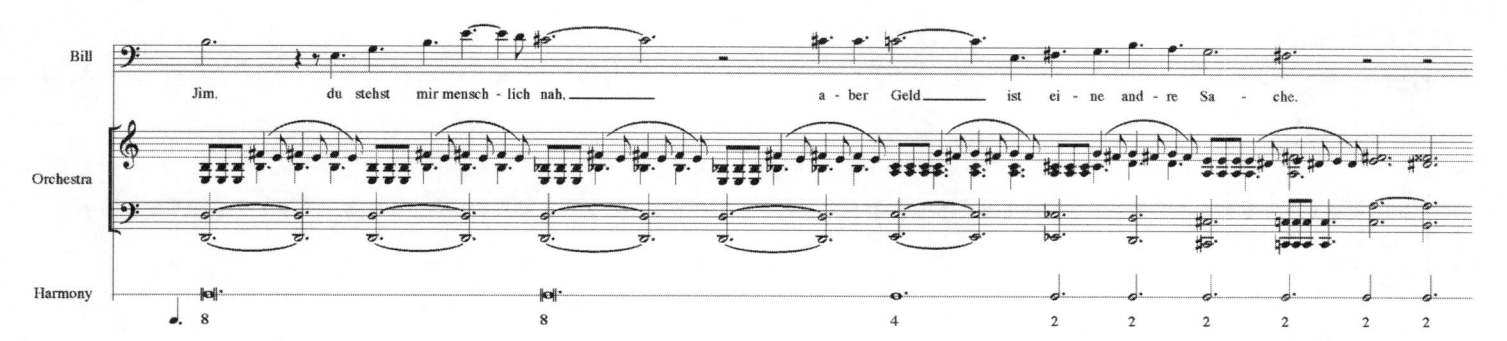

In the last third of the Trio's A section, the phrases become reduced in size, and the harmonic rhythms speed up. The rhythmically produced hyper-meter could now be a 6/4 one, certainly not a 3/4 one, as the suspensions toward the end indicate. The motif of alternating notes in the violins occurs twice on and twice off the beat of the large-scale measure, so that here somewhat longer upbeats are once more suggested.

The fact that note repetitions in the first two 12/4-meter phrases shape the rhythm in such a way that a trochaically lively hyper-measure is followed by one that is kept static suggests perhaps a conception in the manner of light→heavy (4+4 measures). But one could also hear or read it the other way round, as the rhythmic conditions here are not unequivocal. In general, one should take care not to overuse the concept of the long upbeat – as, I think, is the case in Cooper & Meyer, who enlarged and applied certain metrical feet – for the most part iambs and trochees – to the scale of entire symphonic movements.[55]

Long upbeats occur also in vocal music, where the language then acquires a particular accentuation. By countless examples I choose one by Kurt Weill, whose rhythm is oriented on the ballroom dances of the 1920's and 1930's and thus frequently derives its zest from the combination of small-scale rhythms in the accompaniment with large-scale rhythms in the singing voice. Ex. 1-186 is an excerpt from Weill's opera *The Rise and Fall of the City of Mahagonny*. We are in the middle of the trial of Jim Mahoney, which takes place as a public spectacle. Jimmy begs his friend Bill for 100 dollars, which might save him from hanging, but Bill replies: »Jim, du stehst mir menschlich nah, aber Geld ist eine andre Sache« (Jim, you are humanly close to me, but money is another matter).

Melody and accompaniment here seem to follow different tempi, although both are written in 6/8 meter. The small-scale ostinato accompaniment forms double measures, while the singing part, supported initially by the harmonic movement, proceeds in hyper-measures of four 6/8-bars each. Here, therefore, there are also the long upbeats, as a result of which altogether no more than four syllables have a downbeat accent: »Jim,« »nah,« »Geld,« and »Sache.« The words »du stehst mir menschlich« and »ist eine andre,« on the other hand, are intended as upbeats, whose melodies describe simple curvatures and thus underline the upbeat units. In the orchestra accompaniment there are no upbeats at all. Its motifs stand for the indifferent milling of the crowd in the courtroom.

A special group of long upbeats is the cadenzas of instrumental concertos to the extent that a transition or return to a theme is connected with them. Such passages are generally executed »senza misura« or under a fermata. One such passage occurs in the Second Piano Concerto in A major of Franz Liszt (ex. 1-187). It is found at the end of the first introductory part, where it leads to a repeated, bombastic presentation of the theme, now already in D minor, the key of the second part of the Adagio introduction. Embedded into a cadence of Neapolitan character ($B_\flat$-$G_\sharp$-A), a chromatic scale (in second inversion chord mixture) plunges from D7 down to A0, that is, over virtually the entire keyboard. This wild, pathos-laden gesture is to be taken as a single upbeat, heralding – not unlike the theatrical entrance of a play's protagonist – the introductory theme as though it were an entire orchestra.

Ex. 1-187   Liszt, Piano Concerto A Major, m. 64 (simplificated)

---

[55] Grosvenor W. Cooper and Leonard B. Meyer, *The Rhythmic Structure of Music* (Chicago, London, 1960), 203.

Ex. 1-188   Beethoven, 6th Symphony, 3rd mov., mm. 87 ff.

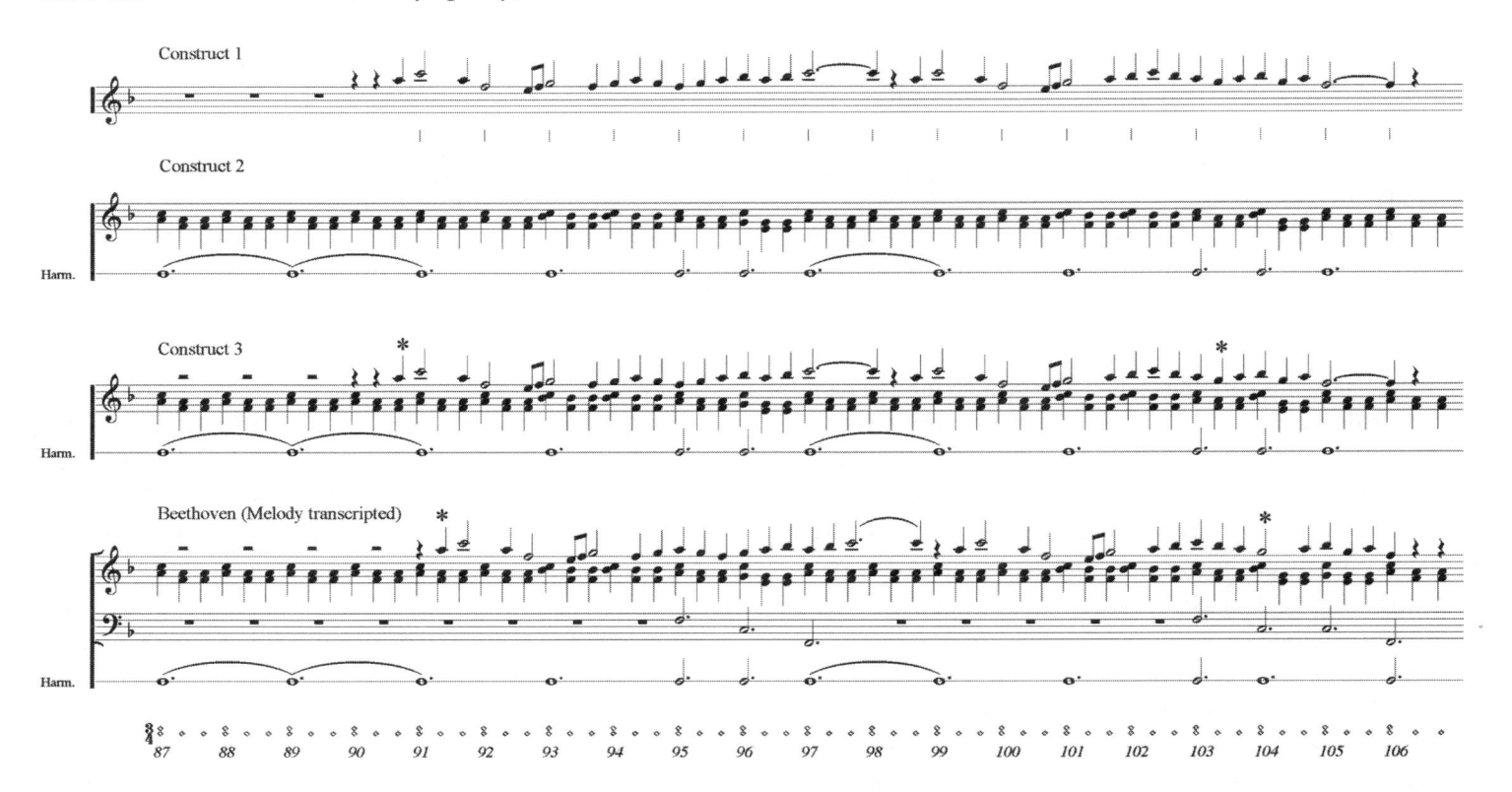

Shifted and Ambiguous Up- and Downbeats

Upbeats occurring at the beginning of a piece are for the most part readily identifiable as such. Within movements or periods, one can not always decide whether a note before the bar line is meant as an upbeat or as the ending of the preceding rhythm, as, e.g., in the case of the so-called ›feminine‹ endings. The case is altogether confusing if a melody or an entire setting undergoes a metric shift. A famous instance of this sort occurs in the third movement of Beethoven's Sixth Symphony, where one player seems to enter late, thus obfuscating the upbeats (Ex. 1-188).

The case in question is the beginning of the first Trio of a Scherzo with two Trios in doubled course.[56] Following the simple pattern of melody and accompaniment, a melody springs up in the oboe in m. 91 that consists entirely of syncopations (Ex. 1-189). The latter, however, are merely the result of a metric shift whereby sounding ♩ are written as ♩♩, tied together.

Ex. 1-189

If the melody is written purely rhythmically, that is, without ties, its dance-like simple, iambic-upbeat structure becomes patent. With the aid of three constructs (the first, second and third accolade in Ex. 1-188), one can now demonstrate that the joke at this point is precisely that the oboist seems to ›sleep through‹ his entry and thus comes in late by two ♩ – as has been recognized ever since Schindler.[57] In construct I, the melody has been set ›correctly‹ in 3/4 meter, thereby clearly revealing its simple, periodic structure of two times eight bars. Construct II depicts the accompaniment of the violins, exactly – with the exception of a deviation in the last measure – as Beethoven wrote it down. This accompaniment exhibits a rhythm that unfolds mostly in double measures and is based exclusively on the alternation of tonic and dominant. This rudimentary harmonic setting rises in part over a pedal point F, whereby in those instances the dominant manifests itself solely by the B♭/C second standing for a dominant seventh chord. In construct III, melody and accompaniment have been put together. Here one can see that the metrically regular melody coincides exactly with the changes in harmony. Looked at rhythmically, the harmonic and the phrasal rhythm confirm each other in this version.

In Beethoven's actual setting (bottom accolade), the melody enters two ♩ late (see *). What is at first baffling is that in this position, too, the melody fits correctly into the harmonic setting – as confirmed also by the first bass figure of the bassoon. At the second bassoon figure at the end of the phrase, however, the ›oboist's dilemma‹ of having ›slept through‹ his proper entry now also comes to the fore:

[56] The overall course of the movement is as follows: Scherzo I – Trio I – Trio II – Scherzo II – Trio I – Trio II – Scherzo III (attacca sequel of the »Storm« movement).

[57] Anton Schindler, *Biographie von Ludwig van Beethoven*, 4th ed. by Eberhardt Klemm (Leipzig: Reclam 1988), 186.

he is unable to properly cadence off with his belated melody. He therefore adds the prolongation of a single note, the G5 in the third from the last measure (see *), so that then the last notes of the melody (B♭-G-A-F) are as exactly on beat as the original melody was – albeit now one whole measure late. The bassoon, too, adapts to this stretching by playing the dominant C twice, as do the violins in their harmonic accompaniment. Numerically, the ›faulty‹ version is thus again correct (two times eight bars), though in terms of musical content the ›mistake‹ remains, because the second phrase of the period is too long by one measure.

In terms of the subject ›upbeat,‹ the following question now arises: does the upbeat character of the melody persist even when the meter has been displaced, or does the shift cause it to be perceived predominantly as now being syncopated? If one goes by the composer's intention, who here wanted to depict a comical situation among village musicians, the displaced variant of the melody, as Beethoven composed it, would have to be played with the same upbeat gesture as the metrically ›correct‹ version, or the joke would be spoiled. It boils down, I suppose, to the presumption that there are upbeats here, each time, to the third beat of the 3/4 meter. But this goes only for the melody. For the accompanying pattern has no upbeats at all: rather, the violins stereotypically emphasize the *One* of every measure by means of crest notes.

Ex. 1-190
Schumann, *Kinderszenen*, »Träumerei«

The problem of the apparent dislocation of a beat by rhythmic means exists also in a famous piano piece by Robert Schumann – though in an altogether different expressive context than that of Beethoven's *Sixth*. I am referring to the seventh of the *Children's Scenes* for piano, which bears the title »Träumerei.« The piece, which is designed in song form (|: A :| B A |), consists entirely of four-bar phrases, of which the first and last two are merged into periods – modulating to the dominant at the beginning, concluding in the tonic at the end. All of the four-bar sections are in a certain respect alike in design: an upswing of eight ♪, followed by a subsidence of equal length. In Ex. 1-190, I have isolated the six upswings and arranged them one underneath the other for comparison. In the second measure of each period, there is always an emphasis (the last note or chord of each line) that suggests the dislocation of the strong beat, with consequent changes in the upbeat situation.

All phrases begin with an ascending fourth on an upbeat and a downbeat additionally weighted by a low bass note. Even when the upbeats are shortened from ♩ to ♪, as happens twice (mm. 9 and 13) or reduced to a short gracenote (m. 17), there is never any doubt about the beginning of the phrase being an upbeat, something that is evident even when, as in the Ex., no bar lines have been drawn. (cf. also the schema of the 4/4 accent-degree meter in the bottom system).

The culminations of the six phrases are all different, despite their unchanging position on the second beat of the 4/4 meter. In all cases, the end notes are underlaid with chords of relatively long duration but having (mostly) different functions: in m. 2, a subdominant sound in B♭, in m. 6, a first inversion secondary dominant chord over C♯, in m. 10, a secondary dominant ninth chord on D, in m. 14, the same chord on A, in m. 17 (recapitulation), the same chord as in m.2, and in m. 22, a double-dominant seventh ninth chord on G. This last one has the most notes, namely seven; the analogous chord in m. 6 (with the melody note A5), has six notes, the others have no more than five or four.

Together with the melodic crest notes of the phrases, the chords appear as heavy as otherwise only a measure's downbeat *Ones* are. This is all the more the case as the actual *Ones* of all six of the ›second‹ measures are nearly void of any rhythmic weight: the melodic eighths movement upward is always in a straight line and thus does not mark the *One* of the measure (though the two eighths on the *One* are sometimes phrased or articulated in separation); and the harmony of the preceding measure is tied over, so that the harmonic duration is lengthened to five ♩. In the opening and recapitulation phrase, Schumann even writes crescendo forks into the second beat, which further underscores their quality as shifted first beats.

A rhythmic peculiarity that is thus also relevant to the question about the upbeats is the anticipations of the summit tones by a ♪ note. Such anticipations by means of note repetition always have the character of upbeats, especially if the repeated note is substantially longer than the anticipatory one. One could thus say that in all six instances, the impression of a strong ♪ upbeat to the second beat is created. This is especially true of mm. 10 and 14, where harmonic changes in a ♪-tempo occur together with the repeated notes. It is moreover possible to regard the melody's five eights ascending in a straight line as a long upbeat – albeit again with reference to a false *One* on the second beat.

Now it would surely be beside the mark to assume that in this quiet, calm recital piece Schumann wanted to hint at latent metric changes by rhythmic means, such as unwritten 5/4 measures at the beginning of all six phrases. What is rather more likely is that the massive rhythmic weight shifts serve emphatic gestures, which exacerbate the tendency already present in the piece to emphasize the second beat (see already the postpositional chord in m. 1). What we hear are evidently emotional outbursts becoming sound, which get more and more turbulent in the course of the piece, up to the last climax in m. 22 – the only one, incidentally, that has a fermata on the melody note. Here we seem to hear Faust's »Then to the moment I shall say: / Ah, linger yet, thou art so fair!« (*Faust* II:v.).

For a last example of the problem of ambivalent upbeats, we may turn to a finely woven setting for strings by Hans Werner Henze: the beginning of the »Agnus Dei« of his (instrumental) *Requiem*. This piece for seven string instruments and piano commences with seven bars for strings alone, with the piano answering. It is these seven measures that concern us here (Ex. 1-191).

I have converted the multi-part string setting into an analytical particello. Here, other than in the score, voices that belong together in terms of their content are combined in a single system. The meters used by Henze predominantly serve practical performance purposes. In two places, however, the composer utilizes the prospect of a strong *One* as a dynamic destination point: the fifth measure (3/4) is the peak of a crescendo, from *pp* to *p* / *mp*, as is the beginning of the seventh measure (5/4), where *ff* is reached in the upper voices, *f* in the middle voices and *mf* in the cello.

The longer first part of the phrase contains virtually nothing but sustained and repeated chords, which, thanks to their duplet or triplet subdivision, seem slightly distanced from one another – like differently tinted color bands. The second, shorter phrase section, on the other hand, is kept linear in the outer voices. Here there is a passage where one can assume that the gesture of upbeats has been intended. After the cellos have held two triads and let them die away (A♭2/C3/A3 and G2/C♯3/A3 in mm. 4 and 5), the first cello for one stroke of the bow hints at a cantilena, which, beginning on the second eighth and softly growing in volume (m. 6) leads via the notes D4-C♯4-D4 to an E♭4 (♪ 𝄾) provided with articulatory emphasis. This melodic turn sounds like a typical (long) upbeat, even though the crescendo still continues.

The voices of the two violins, too, contain some marks of the upbeat. The first violin enters – very lightly – after a 𝄾 and climbs over diatonic steps (G♯4-A♯4-C♯5-D♯5) in a strong crescendo to a *ff* climax. This church-mode-colored cantilena, too, can be regarded as a single long upbeat, especially since here the goal note coincides with the *One* of the 5/4 measure. Neither of these putative upbeats need have been consciously intended as such. Altogether, Henze's rhythm is so multi-faceted and pervaded by so many ultra-fine ups and downs that upbeat gestures may indeed occur but not always clearly and notably.

Such ambivalent upbeats can be found in any music. To estimate them precisely, and to describe them as more or less clearly defined, can be an objective of rhythm analysis according to components theory.

Ex. 1-191   Henze, *Requiem*, »Agnus Dei«, Beginning

Syncope

Modern syncopes generally convey an impression of increased vitality in both listeners and players. Always related to graduated accent meter, syncopes play with the shifting of rhythmic weights to a point before or after a measure's strong beats. Syncopes thus involve the same effect as the accented upbeats discussed in the previous section. But unlike strong upbeats, syncopations hardly occur at the beginning of rhythms or phrases but almost always in an inner position, i.e., over the course of a rhythmic process.

Syncopation, however, is older than the graduated accent meter. The Greek word simply means a striking together. Since the 14th century, it was used in its Latin form »sincopa« in the context of the notation of tonal durations, where it referred to deviations from the normal (perfect or imperfect) modus of dividing breveses and semibreves. Such departures led to divergences of note durations and mensuration, that is, in terms of modern notation, to ties. These, however, did not function as weight shifts but were part of the altogether highly complex rhythmic structure of polyphonic vocal music in the Middle Ages, whose characteristic, to begin with, was the systematically staggered short and long notes of the individual voices.

Syncope as a modern rhythmic character was widespread particularly in the 17th through the 19th centuries. In the 20th century it lost importance as the graduated accent meter was replaced by free forms of rhythmic organization. In musical practice outside of the higher art music, of course, accentual syncopation continued and continues to be in use, playing a prominent role especially in dance and all forms of music that emphasizes the body or accompanies work, as well as in certain styles of jazz.

As a prime example of various kinds of syncopes, we may adduce a section from the Finale of Beethoven's Fifth Symphony, namely the extension of the first main theme, which leads into the transition group. The excerpt chosen (Ex. 1-192) is written homophonically. The main voice, which here is always also the upper voice, played by woodwinds and violins (1st system in each case), exhibits a drop from E6 to C4, with upper and lower octave formations multiply the unison voice in the last measures.

Generally noteworthy, with regard to rhythm, is the abbreviation of phrases from eight over four down to two ♩. Hand in hand with that goes the thinning out of the orchestration, noticed at first (starting with m. 18) from the diminished rhythmic activity of the lower voices (2nd to 5th system) and then (m. 22 and onward) from the unisono.

The most conspicuous syncopation occurs right away in m. 14, where the main voice and the entire accompaniment place a ♩ on the second beat of the 4/4 meter. Since in the preceding measure the basses have already played ♩ in metrically ›correct‹ positions, the effect of the syncopated ♩ here is all the stronger. These two measures (along with the upbeat) are immediately repeated twice, with the strong and

Ex. 1-192   Beethoven, 5th Symphony, 4th mov., mm. 13-26

semi-strong beats (*One* and *Three*) being additionally weigh

ted by (dissonant) suspensions – except for those syncopated measures where only the *One* has a suspension. The third, more strongly varied pair of measures is rhythmically the tightest, inasmuch as the dotting of the upbeat – expressively heightened by an articulatory rest in the main voice and now also in most of the lower voices – applies to all beats, so that there are no longer simple pairs of eighths.

Along with the shortening of the phrase durations from m. 18 onwards, the syncopes and other rhythms, too, are reduced. The main voice at first retains the syncopated ♩, with the basses supporting the entry of the syncopated note on the *Two* with their iambic rhythms. All of the middle voices, on the other hand, with their note and harmony changes, lapse into the measure of the meter in mm. 18 and 19, thus disrupting the syncopation of the main voice. To be noted are the suspensions in the principal voice (♪ A5), which now emphasize the fourth beat, instead of the first and third one as before. Since these ♪, which obtain additional weight from their position as crest notes and from the legato slurs above the runs of 16ths, are retained for several measures and basically do not change their position in the measure, they form (together with the half-notes) a syncopated rhythm within themselves, which spans four measures. Here, too, the basses support the syncopes of the main voice with their iambic rhythm.

The middle voices in mm. 20 and 21 have their own syncopated structure, though reduced to the scale of ♪ and ♪. In the violins and violas playing quasi tremolo (4th system, stems up), the fourfold change from G major to C major is played in syncopated rhythm of ♪ ♩., while the octave-playing winds in the 2nd and 3rd system perform this dominant-tonic alternation always after 3 ♪, thus picking up the anticipatory rhythm of the main voice at the beginning of the example.

In the syncopes referred to, the components »Sound,« »Pitch« (repetitions), »Harmony« (changing function, suspensions), »Diastematy« (crest notes), and »Articulation« (slurs) are involved. In the last measures, the components »Dynamics« and »Texture« are added, while »Harmony« and »Sound« drop out.

The unison sequence that leads in several waves down to the tonic of C major consists exclusively of ♪. Since every second and sixth eighth is weighted by several components, they stand out in the regularly pounding pulse of eighths: they are louder (*sf*), higher (crest notes) and longer (legato) than the surrounding eighths. To be added is the successive entry of the woodwinds, which likewise occurs always on the second and sixth eighth. At the end, there is, moreover, the expansion of the unison from one and two to three octaves, which also falls systematically on the weak eighths. The syncopated quality of the eighths accentuated by legato is further supported by the fact that this form of articulation appears elsewhere in the Finale in even, rather than syncopated position (Ex. 1-193).[58]

Ex. 1-193

Syncopation in the music of the Middle Ages was structured similarly to its modern counterpart, but had an entirely different effect, as an example that Willi Apel has described will demonstrate.[59] The case in question is an Italian motet from ca. 1400. Ex. 1-194 gives the beginning of the discantus in the original script, Ex. 1-195 as transcribed in modern notation.

Ex. 1-194   »Benche partito«, Discantus, Beginning

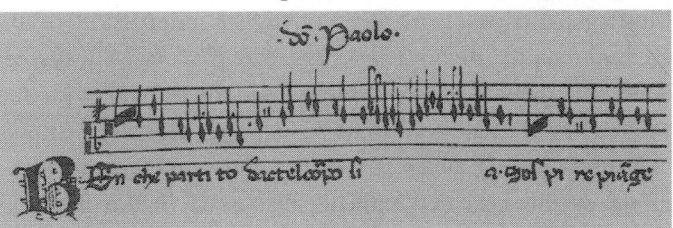

Ex. 1-195   »Benche partito«, Discantus, Beginning

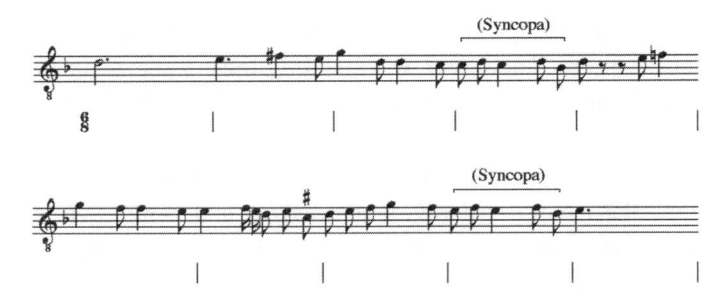

The decisive signal of a syncopated notation comes from dividing points. At the first syncopated passage (see the brackets in my transcription), there are four dots in the original. As Apel explains:

The first of these dots is a normal *punctus divisionis*, since it occurs exactly in the middle of a (6/8) measure. The second is a *punctus divisionis* in irregular position or, in other words, a *punctus syncopationis*; it prohibits the alteration of the third *M* [Minima] and, at the same time, indicates imperfection *a.p.a.* [a parte ante] for the subsequent *S* [Semibrevis]. The other two dots would not seem to be absolutely necessary. They are added merely for the sake of clarity, the third obviating alteration for the subsequent *M* and the fourth indicating return to the normal beat (*punctus divisionis*).[60]

What this adds up to are two syncopated measures, in which an imperfect *S* enters on the 3rd eighth and is held beyond the middle of the measure. In terms of notational practice, this *S* with following *M* functions like an insertion of a perfectly divided *B* (brevis), whereby the first two eighths, together with the last, likewise add up to a perfect divided *B*. The rhythmic result is simpler than the form of the notation. It still took some time to develop a sign system that would indicate the durational value of every note without any ambiguity.

In the subsequent centuries, certain expressive patterns became associated with the rhythmic character »syncope.« Since syncopes by definition seek to inject a disequilibrium into a fixed (isometric) order, they were well suited for representing extra-musical human experiences like corporeal or psychic fluctuations: playfully in dance, emphatically in song.

---

[58]   The passage at m. 363 occurs in the Presto-Stretta of the Finale, where the tempo is accelerated to more than double speed. In the autograph, Beethoven notes in alla breve, but indicates the metronome number for the whole note:

[59]   Willi Apel, *The Notation of Polyphonic Music. 900-1600*, (Cambridge MA, 41953), pp. 398-400 and appendix No. 54.

[60]   Ibid., 398.

Ex. 1-196   J. S. Bach, *St. Matthew Passion*, No. 39, Aria »Erbarme dich«, Beginning, Solo violin

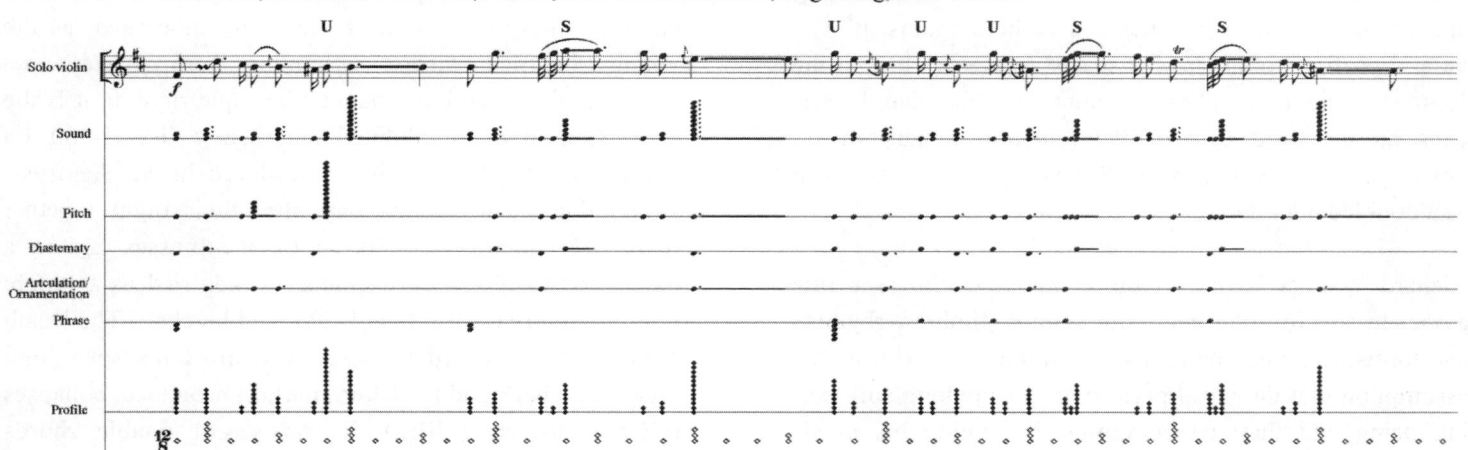

In Bach's *St. Matthew Passion*, there is the heart-rending aria »Erbarme dich, mein Gott« for alto and obligato violin with strings and organ continuo. It follows directly upon Peters' denial and takes up from the gospel narrative about Peter's remorseful despondency: »And he went out and wept bitterly« – »Have mercy, oh my God, for the sake of my tears.« (in the New Bach Edition it is the No. 39)

The long, affect-laden piece is in B minor in 12/8 time. Orchestra and basso continuo provide a calm, metrically secure ground by means of a harmonic rhythm mostly in whole or half measures and an almost uninterrupted pulse of eighths of the plucked basses. From this, the two solo voices – one vokal, the other instrumental – stand out like actors in a pastoral scene. The contrast is produced above all by rhythmic means: if the orchestral strings almost never drop below the measure of ♪, the soloists, especially the solo violin, move in figures all the way down to ♫. An essential role is also played by syncopes.

Confining myself to a rhythmic analysis of the first four measures of the solo violin (Ex. 1-196), I have transcribed the latter by dissolving beams, omitting bar lines and replacing tie slurs by tie beams. Besides, only those components that are involved in this one voice, thus neither the harmonic rhythm nor the rhythmic data of the orchestra, are included. The rhythmic profile, too, thus tells us something only about the violin theme.

The smallest note values occurring are the ♫. But since these are present only sporadically at the beginning, I have chosen the ♪ as the smallest value, in order not to let the rhythmic weights (notes columns) tower too high. Besides, I had to decide whether the numerous grace-notes should enter into the analysis as the irrational values as which they are written or as the rational values as which they sound. If one chose the latter, one would find many more syncopations than if they are considered only under the component »Articulation« (including embellishments) (cf. Ex. 1-197). Both procedures are possible. I have decided to go by Bach's notation, in which the main note determines the durational value of the tone.

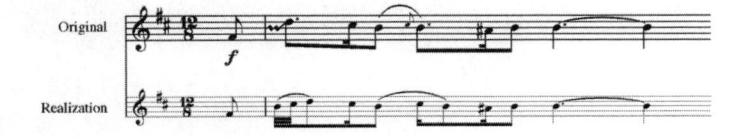

In Ex. 1-196, letters have been entered above the violin voice: U stands for »Upbeat« (strong), S for »Syncope.« Here one can clearly see the kinship between these two cases of shifted weight. The syncopes consist mostly of anticipatory tones, where a note that is expected on the strong part of the measure is moved up and lengthened accordingly. In all three instances, the syncopated notes are reinforced by crest-note accents.

Ex. 1-198

One can easily visualize, and make audible, the powerful impact of these syncopations if one constructs variants in which the course of the melody has been smoothed out (Ex. 1-198). Construct 1 still has a simple syncope, construct 2 just an un-syncopated course of eights. By juxtaposing smallest durational values (the 32nds F$_\sharp$5 and G5) with relatively long ones (A5 is 10 ♪ in length!), in connection with a weight shift from a strong to a weak beat, Bach generates rhythmically riven tonal movements that can express the psychic turmoil of the ›protagonist.‹ The situation is similar with respect to the strong upbeats (Ex. 1-196). The first of the four stressed upbeats derives its weight from the anticipation of the pitch B4, the others from the coincidence of crest notes and phrasal beginnings.

In now looking at the profile I have established for the violin part, one can see that syncopes (S) actually do appear as heavy weights before the beats of the measures: the upbeats (U) are always relatively strongly weighted, without, however, exceeding the weights of the metric beats (except for the anticipated B4 at the transition from *Six* to *Seven* in m. 1).

Taken by itself, the rhythmic profile of the violin part does not reveal the meter of the time signature of 12/8, as one can verify by comparing the metric schema in the lowest system. The same goes for the vocal part. The pic-

Ex. 1-197

ture would be entirely different if the rhythm of the strings and basso continuo were included or held against it. The latter's profile would show a steady isometric flow in the form of whole, half and quarter notes. The fact that the aria ends on the third beat of the four-fold ternary meter, however, indicates that the 12/8 meter could also be taken as a doubled 6/8 one.

Richard Wagner is one of the composers who as a rule associate specific concepts with sounds, timbres, rhythms and forms. His ideas about musical drama proceed from the assumption that the vocal performer is a thinking and feeling being and that the composer, in writing his music dramas, likewise has to bring thinking and feeling to bear. Even the smallest tonal and rhythmic motions may be significant.

This can be readily observed in those »leitmotifs« that undergo alterations in the course of a work or a dramatic

Ex. 1-199

situation, i.e., form variants having their rationale in the inner or outer action of the drama. A suitable example is a group of Siegfried motifs in the *Ring of the Nibelung*, specifically the »Horn,« »Hero« and »Death« motifs. They are selected for this chapter, because they contain syncopations that undergo changes. Moreover, they are all three developed out of the same melodic nucleus (Ex. 1-199).

The Horn motif first appears together with Siegfried's first entrance (*Siegfried* I:i). It is scenically motivated, as the young Siegfried carries a hunting horn. Always set monophonically and in a dance-like triple rhythm, it is the expression of an uninhibited nature boy (Ex. 1-200 1st accolade). The Hero motif is introduced in the Siegfried-Brünnhilde scene on the day after their night together (*Götterdämmerung* I:i). Played by the brasses and in a moderated tempo, it corresponds to Siegfried as a knight »in full armor« (score) (Ex. 1-200, 2nd bracket). The Death motif first occurs after Hagen has thrust his spear into Siegfried's back and the latter, mortally wounded, collapses (*Götterdämmerung* III:ii). It consists of double chords without pitch variation, separated by relatively long rests (Ex. 1-200, 3rd bracket). In what follows, I intend to show how the thus generated and internally tense syncopated rhythm derives from the Hero motif and thus is also connected with the Horn call.

The motif variants follow the melodic model represented in Ex 1-199. It has a wave-like progression with intervallic leaps at the beginning and end. In the rhythmic shaping of the Horn motif (1st bracket), the high note leapt up to at the beginning (C5) appears stretched, which gives it added weight. Embedded into a downbeat 6/8 meter, this doubly accentuated note is identifiable as a syncope. The rhythm of the first four notes of the Horn motif thus reads (represented numerically) 2+3+1+2 ♪.

Ex. 1-200   Wagner, *Der Ring des Nibelungen*, Siegfried Motives (changing syncopations)

In the Hero motif at the beginning of *Götterdämmerung*, the syncopated note – it is no longer C5 but B♭4 because of the new context E♭ major – is lengthened and the entire motif transformed into a 4/4 meter (2nd accolade).[61] The syncopated rhythm of the first four notes produced by the stretching of the B♭ is now 2+5+1+4 ♪.

The Death motif and two further variants of the Hero motif first sound in Act III of *Götterdämmerung*. The variant of the Death motif I have selected (*Gött.* III, m. 928) opens the funeral march that accompanies Siegfried's body being borne from the scene of the murder to the Hall of the Gibichungs. Again we are initially dealing with a syncopation, though one nearly unrecognizable as such (3rd accolade). For the two very short double chords are identically articulated and therefore seem both downbeat, although in reality the second chordal pair stands in an upbeat position. Even so, one experiences a slight insecurity after the gaping pause between the strokes, as if the second double impulse was coming a little too soon. To my mind it is as though a mourner overwhelmed by grief were stumbling at his second step, because his strength no longer suffices to lift the foot sufficiently. We encounter such a type of movement regularly in symphonic funeral marches, where drum rolls or slide figures nearly always precede the downbeat *One*. In addition, the syncopated rhythm of the first four notes of the death motif now exhibit a further stretching of the second note: 1+6+1+4 ♪.

After the Death motif we still encounter two additional variants of the Hero motif. The rhythm of the first one (m. 969) is shaped after that of the Death motif (4th accolade): the rhythm is nearly identical, namely 1+6+1+5 ♪. The second variant, following a few bars later (m. 973), stretches the syncopated note once more (5th accolade): the rhythm is now 2+7+1+2 ♪. Since Siegfried is no longer alive at this point – at the moment of his death the Death motif sounded once more very softly on the note C♯ in the timpani (at m. 915) – the last two variant distortions convey probably the memories of the men carrying the body of their hero.[62]

In summing up, one can say that (1) the syncope pertains to Siegfried's character; that (2) the mutual dependencies of the Siegfried motifs are not only melodic but also rhythmic in nature; and that (3) a process of stretching of the tone that is weighted by the syncopation (partial augmentation) is to be noted, at whose end stands an alto-

Ex. 1-201

gether overextended version of the original motif (see the listing in Ex. 1-201).

We should not fail to mention that with the Hero motif, additional syncopes are introduced at the end of the phrase. Like the rhythm, harmony and instrumentation, they serve to convey the change in Siegfried's character. His identity is preserved in the tonal sequence at the base of all the variants, but his nature has changed as a result of his love for Brünnhilde. Wagner was conscious of this – it corresponds to his concept of »poetic intention« (»dichterische Absicht«), which he develops systematically and theoretically in *Opera and Drama*. His compositional tools for representing the mature heroic character are in the present case essentially rhythmic in nature.

A final example of syncopation in the dance idiom will be drawn from the 20th century, where, as stated, syncopation becomes less frequent because in a freed rhythm it loses its basis. Béla Bartók constitutes an exception here, like other composers who let themselves be inspired by folk music or other forms of body-oriented popular music.

His 1923 *Dance Suite* for orchestra has for the second of its five movements a fast dance of Hungarian character, which gets its folkloristic coloration mainly from the use of the minor third. At the beginning of the Allegro molto (Ex. 1-202), this minor third (D♭4-B♭3) is part of a modally modified B♭ minor. In the horns, it is used for establishing a 2/4 meter. The strings, at first supporting, from the third measure pick up the falling third in diminution and repeat it six times in ♪. Since the horns place a rhythmic weight on the third's first note (D♭), it adheres to this pitch like an inherent quality. The falling ♪-thirds in the strings, however, start on weak beats (2nd or 4th eighth), which results in a syncopated effect, one that is underlined by the articulation of the paired eighths by means of slurs. Added to that are durational syncopations in the basses, which go together with the crest notes of the minor thirds figures. The result in mm. 3 to 6 is a whole series of free-floating syncopations without any instrument marking any strong beat.

In the second part of the phrase, which commences with glissando thirds in trombones and violins (B♭-G), the middle strings play the syncopes that were allocated to the

---

[61] My representation in Ex. 1-200 departs from the original to the extent that there the theme appears in augmented form. But since the subsequent variants of the Hero motif are noted in diminution, I chose the smaller division also here in *Gött.* I, mm. 354 f. for readier comparability.

[62] After Hagen's deed, they had exclaimed in total bewilderment: »Hagen, was tust du?« – »Hagen, what are you doing« – using the simplest form of the syncopated rhythm, one not appearing elsewhere: 1+2+1+2(+2) ♪.

Ex. 1-202   Bartók, *Dance Suite*, 2nd mov., Beginning (analytical particello)

basses earlier, but now juxtaposed by sharp chordal strokes in piano, bassoon, harp and basses. Here the minor thirds no longer play a role: the syncopated rhythm is realized – now in *ff* – at fixed pitches.

The rhythm at the beginning of the second movement is overall rather simple, but of vital power – not unlike the famous *Allegro barbaro* for piano, which Bartók wrote in 1911. Things get much more complex as the movement unfolds, inasmuch as, above all, the components »Phrase« (three-, five- and seven-eighths units) and »Dynamics« (accents, building of dynamic degrees) come into play. Several of the phrase rhythms also lead to changing time signatures.

Hemiola

The hemiola as a rhythmic character resembles a temporary change in meter: a double ternary measure (𝅗𝅥. 𝅗𝅥.) changes into a triple binary one (𝅗𝅥𝅗𝅥𝅗𝅥), something describable also as a change from a 6/4 to a 3/2 meter (or, differently proportioned, 6/8 to 3/4). Unlike syncopation, the hemiola thus primarily involves not a shift of weight within a constant metric order, but a change in the structure of the beats: from 1 2 3 4 5 6 in the normal double ternary meter, to 1 2 3 4 5 6 in the hemiolic, triple binary meter. In compositional practice, to be sure, syncopated and hemiolic formations are often closer than theory will have it. If the middle of a six-beat measure is occupied by a sound component, the bi-ternary meter (6/4) remains ›alive‹ even with a hemiolic structure, so that two different accentual schemata overlap here, with the result that syncopated effects can materialize.

The hemiolic principle is most easily grasped in terms of the proportions 3:2 and 2:3. 3:2 equals 1,5, which is precisely the meaning of the Greek word *hemiolios* (one-and-a-half). The characteristic of this proportion is that the division does not result in a whole number. Viewed in this way, hemiolas are also »conflict rhythms« – Hugo Riemann's term for those rhythmic structures in which, e.g., three- and four-beat, four- and five-beat (etc.) combinations are executed simultaneously. The newer literature therefore also speaks of »generalized« hemiola. I will here, however, limit myself to the basic form of the hemiola, defined by the proportion 3:2 or 2:3. Of course the issue will not just be one of time signatures, as hemiolas also occur in other rhythmic layers of a tonal setting, e.g., in voices that are organized for a longer period of time in ternary or triplet rhythms.

From the perspective of the components theory, it has to be said that hemiolic rhythms do not by any means have to be based solely on the duration of individual notes or sounds, but that in principle any component can form hemiolic conditions.

I take some prime examples from the first movement of Beethoven's Third Symphony, which bears the time signature 3/4. In Ex. 1-203, which contains a transitional section within the concluding group of the exposition, hemiolas are generated by the components »Diastematy,« »Texture,« and »Harmony.« The four-part setting consist exclusively of ♪, which are also all articulated alike (staccato wedges). The 𝅗𝅥-measure typical for hemiola in a 3/4 meter occurs immediately at the beginning of the passage, produced by the entry of the cellos and basses, which imitate the violins, after 4 ♪. Together with the joining in of the lower voices, a characteristic four-note chord (E♭-G-A-C) also appears, to be regarded as the inversion of a seventh chord over A and thus as the quasi-dominant of B♭ major, the key of the concluding group. This chord, now, is sounded in isometric regularity on every fourth eighth, thus prolonging the 𝅗𝅥-measure of the beginning. Additionally, crest and keel notes of both voice lines form a rhythm of 𝅗𝅥 and 𝅘𝅥 that are in turn fitted into the hemiolic structure. Since there are no voices in this passage that mark the prescribed 3/4 meter, we are dealing here with a purely hemiolic formation without »conflict« potential – a temporary metric change, if you will.

Ex. 1-203 Beethoven, 3rd Symphony, 1st mov., mm. 103-109

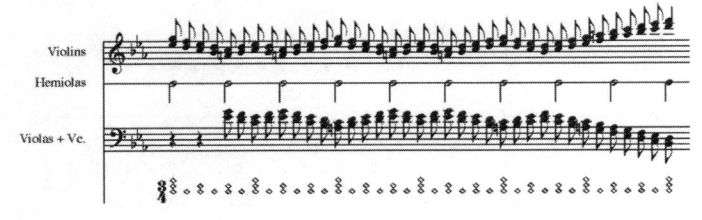

Ex. 1-204 Beethoven, 3rd Symphony, 1st mov., mm. 338-345

At a later point in the movement (the last part of the development section), the situation is different (Ex. 1-204). Here the regular 3/4 meter actually contrasts with simultaneously realized hemiolas. In the winds, the head of the main theme is heard in a stretto imitation, whose durational rhythms (𝅘𝅥 𝅘𝅥), entry intervals (𝅗𝅥.) and phrasing slurs (mostly over two bars) are within the meter. In »conflict« with that is the rhythm of the string basses, which, because of its zig-zag movement, is throughout binary in form. Regardless of whether one goes by the held base note B♭, or by the upward-leaping triads, there is in any case a hemiolic sequence of all 𝅗𝅥 (or double-𝅗𝅥).

The component »Dynamics,« too, can lead to hemiolic duration sequences, mostly in combination with other components. In the concluding group of the exposition, a two-voiced transition runs into a series of chordal strokes (Ex. 1-205). Both the (partly canonic) chain of eighths at the beginning and the chords at the end, acutely articulated by rests, are marked *sf* at 𝅗𝅥-intervals. In the eighths runs (with repeated ♪ in the octaved upper voice), crest and keel notes coincide with the *sf*, while the rhythm of the tonal entries consists entirely of ♪. The chords are at first in ternary rhythm (mm. 123-127), whereby the position of the articulatory rests on *One* (cf. the meter schema in the bottom system) produce a syncopated weight shift to the weak *Three*, further reinforced by the constantly recurring harmonic V:I relation (e.g., D⁷-g). At the end (mm. 128-131), an unchanging dominant chord (C⁷) is repeated six times *sf* at distances of 𝅗𝅥. The rhythm of 𝅗𝅥 thus produced can be regarded as a syncopated hemiola: hemiolic because of the binary structure, syncopated because of the positioning on weak beats (the first on *Two*, the last on *Three*).

Ex. 1-205   Beethoven, 3rd Symphony, 1st mov., Strings, mm. 118-132 (simplificated)

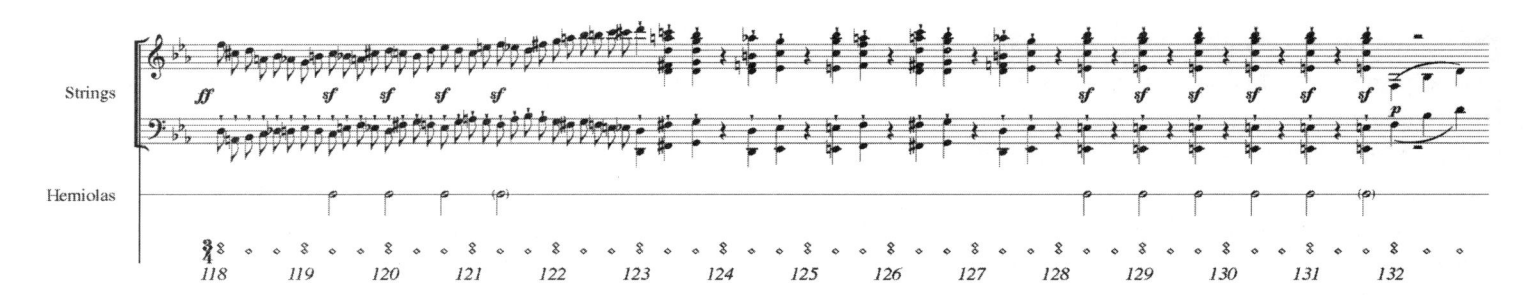

The play with hemiolas and syncopations commences already in the first group of the exposition. In a continuation passage still within the main period, Beethoven produces hemiolic effects by means of the components »Sound,« »Diastematy,« and »Dynamics« (Ex. 1-206). The setting permits a subdivision into main voice (1st violins) and supporting orchestra tutti (small print). The main voice begins with an upbeat and initially resembles the rhythm of the first theme. With the appearance of the *sf* at intervals of 2 ♩, the evenness of the 3/4 meter is upset. This promptly recurs in a reinforced manner, where a rhythm of six ♩ de-

changes, too, contribute materially to the hemiolic or syncopated rhythm. Thus while the seconds chord over A♭ enters on the *One*, the sixths chord on G does so on the *Two*. The subsequent chords have the value of ♩ and merge, in the same beat as the violins, in the already mentioned shifted trochees.

The longest and most exciting hemiolas, which have the effect of aggressive syncopations, appear at the climax of the development (and of the entire movement) (Ex. 1-207). Already 18 bars earlier, a catastrophic happening starts to build up: beginning with the double dominant of E

Ex. 1-206   Beethoven, 3rd Symphony, 1st mov., mm. 23-37

termines the sequence of dynamic accents and crest notes, until the latter are expanded into metrically shifted trochaic rhythms (♩ ♩) and return to the tonic via an ascending series of eighth notes. The tutti setting supports the rhythm of the main voice by underlaying the hemiolic melodic movement, created by leaping intervals on the base note of B♭4, with held chords and thus adding tonal duration as a third component in the formation of ♩-rhythms. The harmonic

minor (A♯-C♯-E-G) – here the example comes in – a 19-bar Neapolitan cadence is executed, only to give place, quite unexpectedly, to a new, lyrical theme. For the hemiolic-syncopated chords it matters considerably that the Neapolitan sixth chord of E minor (A-C-F) features here with an exacerbating fifth (E), thus lending additional pithiness to the hemiolic rhythm.

Ex. 1-207   Beethoven, 3rd Symphony, 1st mov., mm. 266-284

The rhythm of 𝅗𝅥 typical for hemiolas (given a ternary metrical background) is brought about again by the components »Dynamics« (*sf* in 𝅗𝅥), »Diastematy« (crest notes in 𝅗𝅥) and »Sound« (chords in 𝅗𝅥). If one reads the main voice by itself, one gets a sequence of twelve 𝅗𝅥 following each other and another three 𝅗𝅥 at the end. The syncopated effect, which disrupts the purely hemiolic order, is produced by certain isolated bass notes, which repeatedly intrude into the 𝅗𝅥-hemiolas in such a way that they emphasize the metric *One* (in the excerpt of the Ex., they are A♯1, A1, G1 and A1). These low, voluminous single notes have all the more weight as the chordal tutti setting there each time calls for quarter rests; only at the entry of the Neapolitan six-five chord, the winds (secondary voice) also enter on *One*. Thus it comes about that the hemiolas are always tied back to the meter again and seem dislocated like syncopes. While this does not change the 3:2 structure, it combines it with the character of accentual syncopation. The tension finally discharges in a rhythmically amorphous repetition of 𝅗𝅥-chords in the low strings – a passage that may remind faintly of Stravinsky's *Rite of Spring* (cf. Ex. 1-38 above, p. 36).

Ex. 1-208 Hemiola by colored notes

Hemiolas have existed ever since the 15th century. Since the durational value of the individual note is not absolutely fixed in mensural notation, but has to be inferred from the context, a mark was needed to represent a plurality of sequent note values that were smaller by a third than the regular one. The solution was to color these notes while maintaining their external form. Brevises remained brevises, but the reddened or blackened ones counted as two-beat (imperfect), regardless of what went before or came after. The uncolored brevises, on the other hand, could in some cases be perfect, in others imperfect; the latter had to be compensated by the note values that followed. Thus it became possible to represent the ratio of 3:2 between perfecta and imperfecta in the actual tone setting and to write hemiolas as well as triplets (cp. Ex. 1-208).

Hemiolic turns of phrases spread rapidly in all genres of vocal and instrumental music. Since most of them occurred at the end of phrases, that is, immediately before the cadence, one can assume that they originally served as composed ritardandos. In the examples I have selected from the 17th and 18th century, in any case, non-retarding cadence formations can easily be construed as well.

In the anthem »O Sing unto the Lord« written by Henry Purcell in 1688, a »symphony« of the string orchestra and six introductory measures of the bass solo (»O sing … a new song!«) are followed by a Halleluja for chorus and orchestra, whose second part is homophonic and nearly dance-like in character (Ex. 1-209). The four-part chorus plus basso continuo enters into a game of exchange with the three-voiced string chorus (1st and 2nd violins and violas), in which the upper voice of the smaller group imitates the lower voice of the larger one. If one looks at or listens to the choruses separately, it appears that both ensembles have a tendency toward hemiolic rhythm. The word »Halleluja« is introduced by an upbeat (2 𝅗𝅥) and its four syllables are distributed over two pitches. Together with the following half-rests, there is a continuous beat of three wholes, which engages in a hemiolic relation of 2:3 with the meter (twice 3/2). But since the echoing chorus of the strings enters after three halves and thus shifts the hemiolic sequence to the odd beats, there is at first no clear hemiolic overall impression. Only at the end, where the low chorus falls in metrically with the high chorus, the hemiola, in line with the final cadence, emerges plainly in all the voices. Here it is noteworthy that the strings, which from the fourth measure on had taken the lead in the antiphonal game (B♭5-A5-B♭5-F5), find their latent hemiolic form now fully confirmed, as the cadencing hemiola dove-tails seamlessly with the preceding hemiolas of the strings. For comparison, a non-›retarding,‹ that is, non-hemiolic variant of the cadence would look like this (Ex. 1-210):

Ex. 1-210

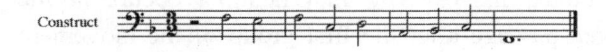

Ex. 1-209   Purcell, *Anthem »O Sing unto the Lord«*, first Halleluja (Beginning)

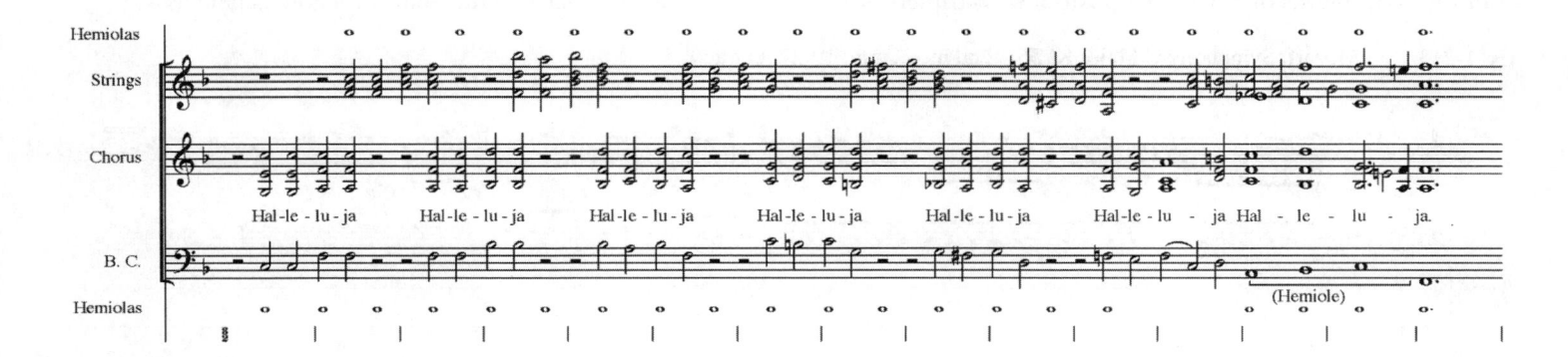

Ex. 1-211   Handel, Allegro from *Sonata for Recorder and B.c.* C Major, HWV 365 (Beginning)

The music of George Frederic Handel and his contemporaries likewise offers numerous cases of hemiolic phrases – here, too, mostly in the context of harmonic cadences. The example, chosen at random, is from a sonata for recorder and basso continuo, which Handel composed prior to 1726 (Ex. 1-211). The dance-like movement is in 3/8 meter and in ternary form (||: A :||: B A :||). The first part, reproduced in the Ex., has two phrases of 8 measures, one with half close, the other with full close. The latter is brought on by a two-bar hemiola. Here, too, I have constructed a non-hemiolic, smoothly proceeding variant for comparison (Ex. 1-212).

Ex. 1-212

In the later 18th century, the hemiola emancipated itself from the function as cadence-supporting end signal but remained a frequently used rhythmic character. In the slow movement of Mozart's ›Jupiter‹ Symphony (K. 551), which has a time signature of 3/4 and is constructed in accordance with the classic sonata form, 28 of the 101 measures are hemiolic in rhythm, only two of them being in final position. The F major movement is headed »Andante Cantabile.« Its rhythm is highly differentiated: the scale of note values extends from 32nds through triplet 16ths all the way to dotted halves. The first hemiola occurs in the transitional passage after the first group of the movement (Ex. 1-213). My nine-bar excerpt is limited to a skeleton setting of main voice and bass. To convey an impression of the rhythmic restlessness of the setting, I show the first two measures ›in enlargement‹ (Ex, 1-214). Chains of syncopes and micro-hemiolic formations enliven the tonal event. Owing to the post-positioned syncopations – always one ♪ behind the bass-♪ – the units for the beats seem to switch from ♩ to ♪. In the second bar, post-positioned ♪-triplets are added in the first violins, which stand in the ratio of 3:2 to the now staccatoed and likewise post-positioned duplet ♪. For the rhythmic fine-tuning, the suspension notes in the violins ($C_\sharp 4$) are also significant, as they take the accentual quality of the beginning of the measure into the now post-positioned triplets. Owing to the whole-measure harmonic changes, the 3/4 meter remains initially unchallenged, but the rhythm as a whole nonetheless conveys the impression of aural opacity and fosters a premonition that other, even more startling irruptions might follow.

In the hemiolic passage beginning after four ›normal‹ measures (Ex. 1-213, m. 23), the double measures are divided into thirds from the start – strongly marked by *f-p*. By means of the joint effect of the components »Phrase,« »Dynamics« and »Harmony,« Mozart, almost in the symphonic manner of Beethoven, carves out ♩ units, the last one of which, entering on the third beat, is prolonged so as to lead back to the regular meter.

Ex. 1-214   mm. 19-20, Strings

The rhythm of the low middle voices in the strings (not shown in the Ex.) is one of triple ♪, which also measure out the change from *f* to *p*. The wind instruments playing in octaves (also not shown) provide for an overall phrasing by contributing an upper voice in ♩ and ♩ , whose chromatic upward movement (C-D♭-D-E♭-E-F-F♯-[G]) strives toward the dominant of C major, the key of the second group of the movement. In this voice the *f* and *p* marks are likewise set in the rhythm of hemiolas, regardless of whether a key change takes place in the voice or a note is held as ♩ .

Ex. 1-213   Mozart, Symphony C Major K. 551, 2nd mov., mm. 19-27 (extract)

Ex. 1-215

Hemiolic 3-bar-phrases by Mozart (K. 550) and Brahms (op. 51/2)

Ex. 1-216

Mozart, Symphony G Minor K. 550, Menuetto, mm. 28-36

Perhaps the most famous hemiolic passage in Mozart's œuvre – if one ignores the dance Finale of Act I of *Don Giovanni*, where a country dance in 2/4 and a *teitsch* (German dance) in 3/8 meter are forced upon a minuet in 3/4[63] – occurs at the beginning of the minuet of his great Symphony in G minor. Mozart's idea of stretching a first minuet measure hemiolically so as to turn one measure into two and thereby achieving triple-bar phrases was picked up by Brahms in the Finale of his Quartet in A minor op 51 No. 2. Here are the two beginnings in juxtaposition (Ex. 1-215). Mozart quickly abandons the triple-bar phrases but returns to it in the middle part of the minuet. In the recapitulation, a maximum of complexity is reached, in that the hemiolic theme is played in a stretto at the distance of 3 ♩ and hemiolic phrases are thereby heard in a staggered relation in two voices (Ex. 1-216).

By contrast, Brahms, in his A minor string quartet, adheres longer to the triple-bar measure, occasionally with reversed order of the measures. An interesting procedure of his is that of going through additional permutations of dividing the measures while developing the theme, that is, of further pursuing the »hemiolic« principle (Ex. 1.-217). Already the repetition of the main theme, presented initially by the first violin and now (m. 13) played by the viola two octaves lower, generates a counter-voice that lets figures come to the fore first of three eighths, then of six eighths and finally of four eighths. This occurs via the component »Pitch« combined with note repetitions (cf. also Ex. 1-011). In the stretto Coda of the movement, finally, we discover also the non-hemiolic variant of the theme I had cited at first as a construct (Ex. 1-215). What is interesting at this point (Ex. 1-218), is that the dotted quarters conductive to the formation of hemiolas are at first equalized into sequences of eighths, within which then, however, new hemiolas form themselves by means of phrase repetition. Since these mini-phrases (D–E–F–E and D♯–E–F♯–E) each consist of four ♪, the result is the typical hemiolic rhythm in ♩. Moreover, the theme originally exhibits three-eighths upbeats and endings, so that the mini-hemiolic 2:3 ratio, too, pervades the setting (cf. the previous Examples).

Ex. 1-217 Brahms, String Quartet A Minor op. 51/2, 4th mov., mm. 13-21 (extract)

Ex. 1-218 Brahms, String Quartet A Minor op. 51/2, 4th mov., mm. 334-342 (extract)

---

[63] Peter Petersen, »Nochmals zum Tanz-Quodlibet im ersten Akt-Finale des *Don Giovanni*,« *AfMw*, 65:1 (2008):30.

Ex. 1-219   Brahms, 2nd Piano Concerto, 3rd mov., mm. 92-96 (Analytical particello)

Hemiolas are probably found in works by all 19th-century composers. Especially dance-like settings in ternary meters (e.g., landlers, waltzes, furianti, round dances, »Zwiefache«, scherzi) are full of them. Johannes Brahms is perhaps the composer who dealt most extensively and subtly with this age-old rhythmic character. I will therefore cite one other, especially beautiful as well as instructive, passage from one of his works. I am speaking of the conclusion to the slow movement of the Second Piano Concerto – the third of its four movements. Its key is B♭ major, the time signature is 6/4, and the form corresponds to that of a simple song with a development-like middle section.

The segment reproduced in Ex. 1-219 corresponds to the conclusion of the exposition, whose theme of 24 measures is presented by the cello with orchestral accompaniment, and which now in the recapitulation, starting at m. 78, recurs with participation from the piano. The main voice is in the solo cello, which recites the last notes of the theme (D4-G3-C4) in sedate hemiolas (♩ ♩ ♩) and thus at the end displays the same rhythmic disposition that was decisive already at he beginning of the theme (♩. ♪ ♩. ♪ ♩. ♩ ♩ ≈ ♩ ♩ ♩). Strings and piano, which are linked rhythmically, likewise produce hemiolas – shifted by 1 ♩.

Ex. 1-220   mm. 92-94 (extract)

In order to better visualize the hemiolic structure, it is advisable to look at the strings and the solo cello separately (Ex. 1-220). The displacement can be readily seen in the descending ♩-sequence (C-B-B♭-A). But even before that, the chords have the duration of ♩: they are merely articulated differently by rests. Thus the solo cello presents the hemiola that is ›normal‹ for the 6/4 meter, i.e, beginning on the *One*, while the strings play a delayed hemiola, beginning on the *Two*. This displacement also affects the harmonic rhythm, as the respective harmonies always enter one ♩ too early (see the construct in Ex. 1-221). The fundamental bass notes of the harmonic sequence are D-G-C-F-D-G-C-F. Their reiterated sequence of fourths underlies the independence of these two 6/4 measures, as does the voice of the solo cello. If, on the other hand, one observes the going of the bass voice with the semi-chromatic progression E♭-F-F♯-G in the middle of the two-bar phrase, a perspective opens onto a hemiolic formation of the next-larger dimension. For the *One* of the second measure is blurred, rather than accentuated by the basses, so that from this aspect – but *only* from it – a mega-hemiola of three whole notes suggests itself. It is weakly developed and also does not contradict the ♩ hemiolas, but it does seem to me to have been considered as a possibility by Brahms.

Ex. 1-221   mm. 92-93 (Harmony)

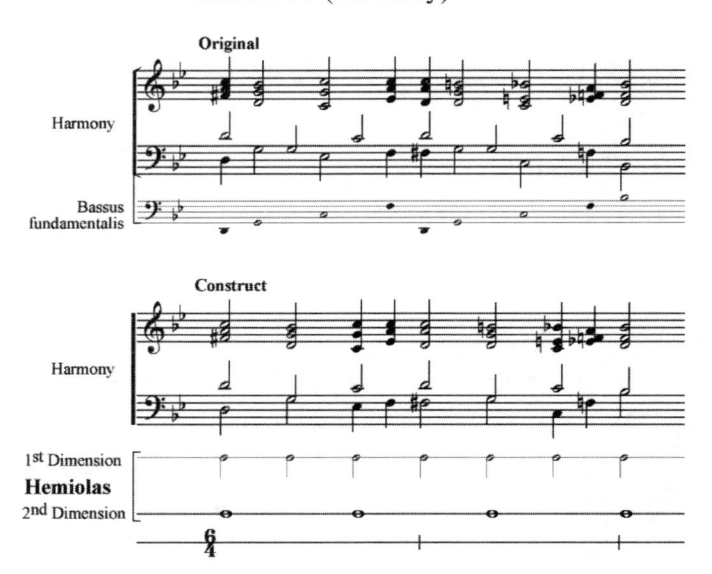

Ex. 1-222   mm. 92-95 (extract)

The piano setting, finally, indicates a tendency toward diminution – contrary to the rhythm of the orchestra setting. As Ex. 1-222 shows, the individual quarter notes are treated in »conflict rhythm.« The right and left hand form a relation of 3:2 in mm. 92 and 93. The bass notes of the left hand duplicate the voice of the string basses and thus also the hemiolic rhythm post-positioned in relation to the voice of the solo cello. The various dimensions of the 3:2 ratio are thus united in the piano part. At the end of the passage, from m. 94, yet another dimension is added. Here the piano switches from triplet to duplet ♪ in both hands. At the same time, the large-interval unison melody forms mini-phrases of three ♪, whose second interval is mostly a seventh. Two of these three-eighths phrases fill half a 6/4 measure, that is, three ♩, while the third phrase augments the last two notes, thereby filling the second half of the measure, this time in the normal ♩-rhythm. From the point of view of the metric quarters, there is here thus a relation of 3:2 (♩. : ♩), which in the actual sound is confirmed by the succession of the first and second half of the measure.

The beam-linking into groups of three eighths in Ex. 1-222 is mine: Brahms groups into units of six eighths. However, I derived the grouping into units of three eights from another passage in the movement – in the development section, where the analogous phrase appears in the right hand in ternary beaming (Ex. 1-223) – so that it has Brahms' legitimation, after all.

Ex. 1-223   m. 41, Piano

Summing up, one can say that in this hemiolic passage, which, incidentally, retards and embellishes the end of a theme in the ›tried and true way,‹ the most diverse dimensions of hemiolic rhythms come together in the narrowest space: 3♪³ : 2 ♪; 3 ♪ : 2 ♩; 3 ♩ : 2 ♩. ; 3 𝅝 : 2 𝅗𝅥., plus displacements and distortions (mm. 94f.). Such a plethora of rhythmic elaborations must be unusual even for Brahms.

In the 20th century, 3:2 hemiolas appear wherever a dance idiom is picked up or cited – unfractured in Richard Strauss (*Arabella*), estranged in representatives of modernity or the avant-garde.

In the program music of Alban Berg's Violin Concerto, the landler or waltz idiom serves to characterize the person whose life and early death the work commemorates: Manon Gropius, the young woman from Berg's closest circle of friends, who was stricken by polio and died at the age of eighteen. The dedication in the score – »In commemoration of an angel« – refers to Manon.

Ex. 1-224
Berg, Violin Concerto, 1st Part, 2nd mov., Beginning

The four-movement work has a bright first part and a funereal second one. In part one, Manon is portrayed with a fast landler, which derives its delicate verve not least from its hemiolic rhythmics (Ex. 1-224). The structure of the 6/8 meter emerges in the plucked basses (keel notes and heavy beats), while the clarinets playfully (»scherzando«) counter with a hemiolic theme in a homophonic two-voice setting. The articulation provides for minor syncopated effects (legato beginning on weak beat) or a skipping kind of movement (staccato, portato-staccato). In terms of the original landler rhythm, the theme is fully adequate, only the harmony is out of place by its queer combination of thirds. Somewhat later in the same movement, Berg installs a likewise landler-like original Carinthian tune in G♭ major into his twelve-tone structure. It is intoned by a horn and accompanied by the harp with defamiliarizing minor and major triads (Ex. 1-225, top accolade). Perfectly fitted into the 6/8 meter, this theme, too, stands for Manon.

Ex. 1-225 Berg, Violin Concerto, Deduction of the Main rhythm (RH) from the Carinthian folk song

In accordance with the program of the concerto – which Berg did not formulate explicitly, but which can be found in its main outline in the score and in sketches – Part Two of the work imagines the suffering and death of Manon, as well as the grief of those who loved her. This is immediately graspable in the transition to the Coda of the fourth movement. Here the Carinthian tune is played once more – now enriched by a (genre-typical) thirds yodler in the solo violin – which then leads immediately into a variation of the funeral chorale »Es ist genug! So nimm, Herr, meinen Geist« (It is enough! My spirit take, o Lord) by J. S. Bach.

In the third movement, which opens the second part, Berg reenacts the process of the young woman's paralysis leading to the catastrophe of her death by means of sound symbolism. In doing so, the composer also applies rhythmic means, which, because of their proximity to bodily motor activity, are naturally suited to such a creative intention. What the musicologist soberly identifies as rhythmic variation, in this case signifies a body movement distorted by disease and pain: the hemiola as an expression of paralysis.

In the lower accolades of Ex. 1-225, I have collated the rhythms newly introduced in the third movement (see also the bottom system) with the landler rhythm from the Carinthian tune (second measure). The original rhythm, with its initial dotting and serene swinging-out in the second half of the 6/8 measure, has four impulses (♩. ♪♪ ♩.). These retain the main rhythm presented by the horns in m. 23 of the second movement. We can also see and hear that the initial dotting, which suggests the image of a skip, has likewise been kept. The third impulse, which is dynamically accentuated (*fp*), while in the folk tune it is very lightly weighted, now gets hung up instead of flowing smoothly into the strong beat. The tie to the next beat and the one after that gives the hemiolic note an excessive length that seems as unmotivated as the hindrance of a step by muscle failure. Although the fourth impulse still follows, it seems to require a special effort (crescendo fork), which discharges in the renewed, reinforced accent (*sfz* plus >) on the tenth sixteenth of the measure. The secondary rhythm of twice three ♪ (♪. ♪.) in the bassoons, taken by itself, is in a (mini-)hemiolic relation to the beats of the 6/8 meter and thus under a similar tension.

My interpretive suggestion that Alban Berg in this particular instance developed the distorted hemiolic rhythm from the image of a dancer being defeated by paralysis is confirmed by an annotation in Alban Berg's sketches that Constantin Floros discovered and communicated.[64] Underneath the very brief side rhythm, Berg jotted the following ›performance direction:‹

Stöhnen immer nach [moaning always after]

Later in the third movement (II m. 125), the listener is confronted with the catastrophic version of these hemiolic rhythms, which, if one accepts the associational background sketched above, can indeed produce a powerful emotional shock in the listener during a performance. Marked by Berg explicitly as »HÖHEPUNKT« (climax) in the score, both primary and secondary rhythm here resound in *fff*. The rhythm is played by the entire orchestra with repeating, intensely dissonant chords. That Berg wanted to represent the death of the protagonist here becomes ap-

---

[64] Constantin Floros, *Alban Berg. Musik als Autobiographie* (Wiesbaden, 1993), 350.

parent in the subsequent measures (Ex. 1-226). Here one is made to feel how strength is draining from the rhythm, that is, from the body: the rhythm gets shorter and shorter, the sound continuously weaker and the timbre ever darker. With the last note, the Adagio sets in – »Es ist genug!"

Ex. 1-226   The 'Dying' of RH

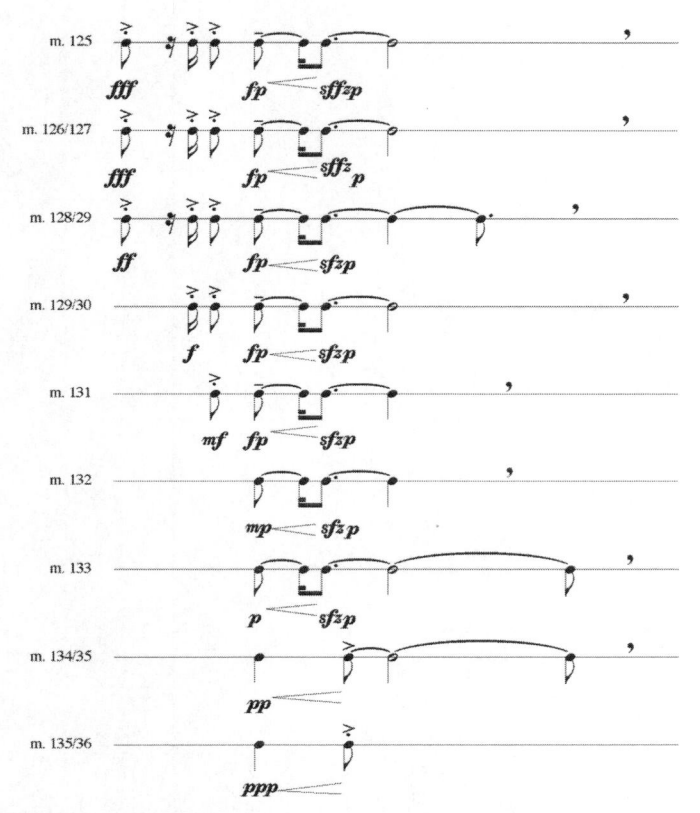

I select a final example from Hans Werner Henze's *Tristan Preludes* for piano, sound tapes and orchestra of 1973, which, like Berg's Violin Concerto, is a programmatic work. Toward the end of the concerto, the composer lets the soloist play for a brief moment in the waltz mode, whereby hemiolas play a characterizing part.

The sixth movement commences with an extended »Prelude« of the solo piano. This piano piece is *senza misura* and mostly notated on four staves. The notes consist of black dots without stems, so that their duration can only be guessed. If bar lines, time signatures and distinct rhythmic values do occur, a mode of reminiscence is thereby signalized, as if the music-making subject recalled times past. Included in this area is the genre mark »valse.«

The first (and longest) waltz quotation (Ex. 1-228) has the time signature 3/4 and the addition »valse (rapida).« The setting corresponds to the conventional model of melody and accompaniment. An upper voice repeats in stereotypical manner four times the rhythm ♪| ♩ ♩. (Ex. 1-227), with articulating rests, legato and staccato marks making for the typical waltz mode. The lower voice, throughout in ♪, has a contour in which the low notes fall on the *One* and occasionally also mark the midst of the measure. The ternary keel notes thus produced exhibit a ratio of 2:3 to the ♩ of the meter and are thus hemiolic. The soloist has the task of, in a flash, erecting the genre character of the waltz within the free-flowing prelude (whose beginning bears the

Ex. 1-227

performance mark »silenzioso, fluido, meditativo«), only to quickly relinquish it again. All of the later allusions to the waltzes are shorter than the example cited here, the shortest one comprising only three ♩.

The quiet, contemplative piano prelude is preceded by an orchestral setting, to whose noisy, shrill climax Henze assigned the connotation »scream of death.«[65] Like Berg's Violin Concerto, Henze's *Tristan* is pervaded by an imagined event, at whose end stand death and grieving. The point where Berg quotes from the Bach chorale is paralleled by a literary quotation in Henze's work: a child's voice, recorded on sound tape, cites some lines from the Tristan epic of Thomas of Britanny: »She takes him in her arms […] and of sorrow for her lover dies thus at his side.«

The allusions to the hemiolic waltz idiom are fitted into the surreal events around Tristan and Isolde. They constitute memory traces referring back to a life before death. The work's title »Tristan« suggests an idea-driven music that circles about the subject of »love« and musically reflects the course of musical and cultural history. The main focus of these reflections is on the 19th century with its divergent attitudes, which Henze epitomizes in the figures of Wagner, Brahms and Chopin. The waltz quotations may well refer to Chopin's music in particular, which the preludes and the orchestral movements echo time and again.

Ex. 1-228   Henze, *Tristan*, 6th mov. »Epilogue«, Score p. 150, 4th Bracket

[65] Hans Werner Henze, *Music and Politics. Collected Writings, 1953-1981*, (London, 1982), 227.

Part Two: Rhythm in the Music of J. S. Bach

Introduction

A comprehensive study of the rhythm of Bach's music is still outstanding. At the same time, probably no one has any doubt that rhythm is an essential aspect of Bach's personal style. Musicians and music historians have always sensed and praised the rhythmic vitality and complexity of Bach's compositions. They did so mostly under the impression of the polyphonic texture of voices with its perfect balance of horizontal flow and vertical anchorage.

The fact that a man like Igor Stravinsky, who has enlarged the rhythmic means of expression like no other composer, saw above all a rhythmist in Bach should suffice to prompt a more intensive investigation of this side of Bach's music. In 1924, Stravinsky went on record saying that »the works of Johann Sebastian Bach, whom I regard as the imperishable ideal of us all, consist entirely of rhythmics and architectonics.«[1] Hans Werner Henze shows himself to be equally fascinated by the rhythmic qualities in Bach's music. In a lecture on »Johann Sebastian Bach and the Music of our Time,« he said in 1983:

Let us imagine a multi-part setting of Bach's vocal and instrumental music performed solely with percussion instruments without fixed pitches: we would hear only the contrapuntally counteracting rhythms, no harmony, no melody. But the energies, the elasticity, the pulsating effect, the altogether worked-out and thought-through quality of such a structure is what would appear surprisingly and spectacularly to our ears and eyes in all its psychic power.[2]

It remains a task for musicology to render such picturesque descriptions in theoretical terms. Older attempts to apprehend the rhythm in Bach's music analytically and conceptually have not always been satisfactory.

Rudolf Westphal, who in the 19th century presented an *Allgemeine Theorie der musikalischen Rhythmik,* »with special regard to Bach's fugues,« was stymied by his dogmatic attempt to apply classical prosody to Bach-type polyphonic settings.[3]

Altogether different in their approach but in their own way no less one-sided were the studies of Hugo Riemann, who, in 1890, analyzed all of the preludes and fugues of the *Well-Tempered Clavier* and, in 1894, *The Art of the Fugue*.[4] Already committed to supposedly irrefutable laws of musical rhythm and meter – his *Musikalische Dynamik und Agogik*, claiming a radical »revision of the doctrine of musical metrics and rhythmics,« had appeared in 1884 – Riemann projected thoroughly subjective notions, shaped by the music of the 19th century, onto the music of Bach. His interventions in the Bachian musical scripts are hard to take today, as he not only meddled with the drawing of note beams (to make supposed upbeats visible) but did not shy away from altering bar lines and measure counts, not to mention adding articulation and phrasing marks as well as expression and tempo notations of his own.[5]

Ernst Kurth's much-cited book *Grundlagen des linearen Kontrapunkts* of 1922, which bears the subtitle »On Bach's melodic polyphony,«[6] while allowing one to infer very rich and differentiated listening experiences on the part of the author, is limited to an approach derived from music psychology more than music theory. Afraid to lose sight of the holistic effect of music, Kurth basically rejects analytical thinking. In the chapter on the »Rhythm of the Bachian line,« we thus nowhere hear anything about rhythm proper, but instead much about »kinetic energy« (»Bewegungsenergie«), »basic excitation« (»Grunderregung«) or »weight and accent sensation« (»Schwere- und Akzentuierungsempfinden«).[7] Kurth maintains explicitly that »the power of the lines in Bach« resides »not so much in *rhythmic* as in *melodic* animation.«[8] But since all melodies have their own specific inherent rhythm, sheer logic forbids playing one off against the other.[9]

After 1945, Bach scholarship temporarily turned to philological more than to analytical questions. The memorial year of 1950 produced the *Thematisch-systematisches Ver-*

---

[1] Igor Stravinsky, interview in *Le Matin*, Antwerp, on Januray 10, 1924; quoted (and retranslated) from Igor and Vera Stravinsky, *Ein Fotoalbum 1921 bis 1971. Texte aus Interviews mit Stravinsky 1912-1963*, ed. Rita MacCaffrey et al, transl. Hans-Horst Henschen (Herrschin, 1982), 14.

[2] Hans Werner Henze, »Johann Sebastian Bach und die Musik unserer Zeit,« in *Reden anläßlich der Verleihung des Bach-Preises 1983 an Hans Werner Henze*, Publication of the Authority for Culture of the Free and Hanseatic City of Hamburg (Hamburg, 1983), 27-36; pp. 31f.

[3] Rudolf Westphal, *Allgemeine Theorie der musikalischen Rhythmik seit J. S. Bach, auf Grundlage der antiken und unter Bezugnahme auf ihren historischen Anschluss an die mittelalterliche, mit besonderer Berücksichtigung von Bach's Fugen und Beethovens Sonaten*, (Leipzig 1880, Reprint Wiesbaden, 1968). See also the Westphal chapter in Part Three of this study.

[4] Hugo Riemann, *Katechismus der Fugen-Komposition. (Analyse von J. S. Bachs »Wohltemperiertem Klavier« und »Kunst der Fuge«)*, 2nd ed. (1906 et seq.) (1st ed. 1890 et seq.).

[5] Cf. also the Riemann chapter in Part 3 of this study. To cite only one example: Riemann rewrites the theme of the A major Fugue of WC I from the original 9/8 measure into an alternating sequence of 6/8 and 3/8 measures, counting these separately (two measures thus turn into four), arbitrarily dissolves note beams, introduces legato arcs, and titles the whole »Poco lento, con molto espressivo« (ibid., pt. 1, p. 131).

[6] Ernst Kurth, *Grundlagen des linearen Kontrapunkts. Bachs melodische Polyphonie* (Berlin, 1922).

[7] Ibid., 188.

[8] Ibid., 189, emphasis is Kurth's.

[9] See also my commentary on Kurth's Bach interpretation in my essay »Rhythmic Complexity in the Music of J. S. Bach,« *Studien zur Systematischen Musikwissenschaft* (HJbMw vol. 9) (Laaber, 1986), 223-346; esp., pp. 236ff.

zeichnis der musikalischen Werke von Johann Sebastian Bach (BWV) and provided the impulse for the gigantic project of a *Neue Ausgabe sämtlicher Werke*. To the extent that there was any subsequent interest at all for so specialized a question as that concerning the rhythm and meter of Bach's music, the focus was mostly on the time signatures used by Bach,[10] later also on performance practice and tempi.[11]

The Proceedings *Bach in Leipzig – Bach und Leipzig* from the Bach year 2000 included an essay by Wilhelm Seidel on the ›French Suite‹ BWV 813, entitled »Wie rhythmisch ist Bachs Musik?«[12] Seidel answers his question by arguing that the music loses rhythmic quality in proportion as the evenness of the phrases or settings is diminished. Seidel does not mean this in a pejorative sense, as the lost rhythmic quality is replaced in the event by a formal quality or conciseness.[13] The essay shows once again that Seidel is not willing to accept the now generally held view according to which irregular durations, too, can be regarded as rhythmical.[14]

A very instructive essay by Peter Breslauer appeared in 2001 in the *Journal for Music Theory* on »Diminutional Rhythm and Melodic Structure,«[15] whose first part deals with Bach. The term »diminution« is used by Breslauer in its secondary meaning, that is, as division of a melodic line into smaller values, rather than as reducing note values into halves or thirds. The examples Breslauer cites correspond terminologically to the »pitch rhythm« in components theory (note repetitions and inherent multi-voicedness), »diastematic rhythm« (melodic contour) and »articulation rhythm« (e.g., phrasing marks, slurs). The author calls the corresponding secondary rhythms »durational patterns,« which he writes as »effective« rhythms above the melodic lines, rather than regarding them as accents.[16] Breslauer is able to show that Bach works with these component rhythms as though they were ›normal‹ sequences of tonal durations. That can be seen in the examples he cites as »syncopation of durational patterns,« among them those »diminutional forms,« in the second part of the fourth movement of Bach's Violin Sonata in C minor BWV 1017, that result in rhythms of 3 ♪ against 2 ♪, the sixteenths not being triplets.[17]

The most extensive study to date of the rhythm in Bach's music is by Mauro Botelho, whose doctoral dissertation, *Rhythm, Meter, and Phrase: Temporal Structures in Johann Sebastian Bach's Concertos*, was accepted in 1993 at the University of Michigan.[18] Nearly 600 pages strong, the dissertation analyses the opening movements of the Concerto for Harpsichord and Orchestra in D minor BWV 1052, the Violin Concerto in E major BWV 1042 and the Brandenburg Concerto No. 3 in G major BWV 1048.

Botelho is particularly interested in metric ambiguities, which he sees as realized by rhythmic means,[19] and he tracks down virtually every signal that Bach's settings yield and that has any kind of parsing effect. These may be motif or phrase delimitations or repetitions, changes of register in individual voices, texture modifications like voice entries in

---

[10] E. g., Edna Kilgore, »Time Signatures of the Welltempered Clavier: Their Place in Notational History,« *Bach: The Quarterly of the Riemenschneider Bach Institute*, 4:2 (April 2, 1973), 3-16; Owen Jander, »Symmetry in the Goldberg Variations,« *MQ*, 75:4 (1991), 188-193; Don O. Franklin, »Das Verhältnis zwischen Taktart und Kompositionstechnik im Wohltemperierten Klavier I,« in *Das Wohltemperierte Klavier I. Tradition, Entstehung, Funktion, Analyse. Ulrich Siegele zum 70. Geburtstag*, ed. S. Rampe (Munich: Katzbichler, 2002), 147-160; Hermann Gottschewski, »Takt und Metrik in Bachs Fugen,« in *Bach-Interpretationen. Eine Zürcher Ringvorlesung zum Bach-Jahr* 2000, ed. H. J. Hinrichsen / D. Sackmann (Frankfurt a. M. et al., 2003), 81-120.

[11] E. g., Robert Donington, *The Interpretaion of Early Music* (London: Faber, 1963); Nikolaus Harnoncourt, *Musik als Klangrede. Wege zu einem Musikverständnis. Essays und Vorträge* (Vienna / Salzburg, 1982); N. Harnoncourt, *Der musikalische Dialog. Gedanken zu Monteverdi, Bach und Mozart* (Munich / Kassel et al., 1987); Klaus Miehling, *Das Tempo in der Musik von Barock und Vorklassik. Die Antwort der Quellen auf ein umstrittenes Thema*, revised and enlarged ed. (Wilhelmshaven: Noetzel, 2003) (earlier eds. 1993 and 1999); Ido Abravaya, *On Bach's Rhythm and Tempo* (Kassel: Bärenreiter, 2006).

[12] Wilhelm Seidel, »Wie rhythmisch ist Bachs Musik? Erwägungen über die Französische Suite in c-Moll BWV 813,« in *Bach in Leipzig – Bach und Leipzig*, Proceedings Leipzig, 2000, ed. Ulrich Leisinger, (Hildesheim et al., 2002), 219-233.

[13] Ibid., 222f.

[14] See the beginning of the essay: »Rhythm today means anything that has somehow to do with time and temporality. I do not ask my question about Bach's music in terms of this baggy concept, which says everything and therefore says nothing«. See also my remarks about Seidel's definition of rhythm in my essay »Die ›Rhythmuspartitur.‹ Über eine neue Methode zur rhythmisch-metrischen Analyse pulsgebundener Musik,« in *50 Jahre Musikwissenschaftliches Institut in Hamburg. Bestandsaufnahme – aktuelle Forschung – Ausblick*

(HJbMw 16), ed. P. Petersen / H. Rösing (Frankfurt a. M.: Lang, 1999), 83-110.

[15] Peter Breslauer, »Diminutional Rhythm and Melodic Structure,« *Journal of Music Theory*, 32:1 (2001), 144-177.

[16] Ibid., 2ff.

[17] Ibid., 6-9. The five relevant passages are in mm. 59f., 73f., 85f., 98f. and 104f.

[18] Mauro Botelho, *Rhythm, Meter, and Phrase: Temporal Structures in Johann Sebastian Bach's Concertos*, Ph.D. diss., U. of Michigan, 1993. The dissertation can be ordered at http://disexpress.umi.com/dxweb as a copy or a PDF file.

[19] Cf. also Botelho's essay »Meter and the Play of Ambiguity in the Third Brandenburg Concerto,« *In theory only*, 11:4 (1990), 1-35, which was largely incorporated into the dissertation. Justin London's riposte, entitled »Metric Ambiguity (?) in Bach's Brandenburg Concerto No. 3,« *In theory only*, 11:7-8 (1991), 21-53, is also discussed in the dissertation.

Introduction

the polyphonic weave, or partially homophonic sections, harmonic shifts, etc.

Following music theoreticians like Lerdahl and Jackendoff, Kramer and Rothstein,[20] Botelho sticks to a narrow conception of rhythm, which takes off from the written note values. The temporal distances between other phenomena of the tone setting are included under the aspect of »grouping,« but are not included like rhythms in the analysis. Thus Botelho operates with two marks that are to convey the results of the rhythmic analysis: square brackets for units of duration and dots for metric weights. Below is the example for Botelho's analysis of the beginning of the Third Brandenburg Concerto, one, to be sure, he follows up later with several alternative analyses, depending on the particular question he asks (Ex. 2-001; in Botelho ex. 4.3).[21]

Ex. 2-001 (Botelho)

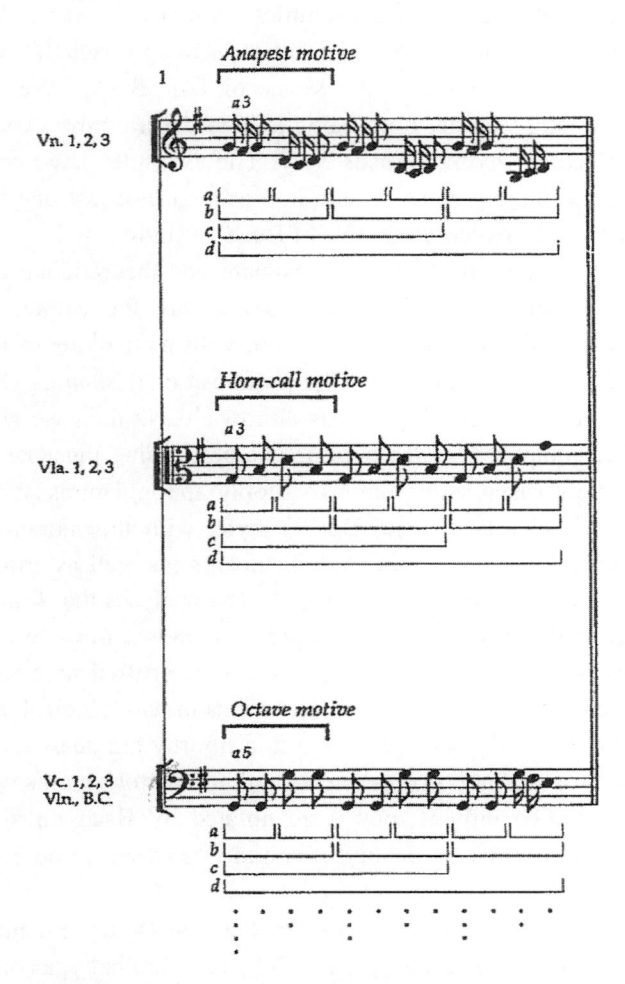

The aim of this representation, in which the beams are dissolved and bar lines and time signatures are omitted, is to demonstrate a metrical ambiguity in the smallest rhythmic dimension (♪). In the original score, the »anapest motive« appears in an upbeat position, but because of the shape of the bass voice (»octave motive«) and the viola voice (»horn call motive«), the first eighth receives so much weight that the anapest motive, too, appears as if accented in reverse, that is, | ♪ ♪ ♪ instead of ♪ ♪ | ♪. Botelho describes in detail[22] how, because of the note repetitions, the change in octave register and the repetition of the motive, temporal units of quarter-notes, half-notes, whole notes and dotted whole notes are created (brackets a, b, c, d). The case is said to be similar in the violas and violins. The last note of the example is written without a stem in each voice to signal that with these notes the metrical shifts come to an end. As the subsequent bars show, metric and rhythmic weights coincide again from the middle of m. 2. The last »boundaries« should therefore really have been open on the right, or else have been prolonged by 1 ♪, though Botelho does not raise that as a problem.

Beneath the cello part, Botelho has placed columns of dots that hang down four, three, two or one steps deep like stalactites, at distances of ♪. He evidently meant them as graphemes to signal degrees of metric accents and referring to the whole setting, but he is silent as to the criteria for assigning 1, 2, 3 or 4 dots to a given point in time. In the example given, the points in the accent schema might suggest a 3/2 time, something Botelho, in the subsequent analyses, in fact takes to be the ›composed‹ meter at the beginning of the ritornello theme – with a restituted eighth upbeat in the end (cf. his examples 4-5, 4-6, 4-9, etc.). One discovers later on, however, that by no means every 3/2 unit in this movement has four points on the (fictional) *One*, and that the other metric ›levels‹ are not weighted according to the same schema, either.

By using this system of signs, Botelho evidently wants to express a part of the felt, as well as substantiated, ambiguity between metric and rhythmic events. In the »Introduction« to his treatise, he rejects the notion that »meter (including hypermeter)« functions like a »clockwork,« ticking, as it were, alongside or behind the music.[23] »I will argue,« he announces, »that meter and hypermeter in Bach are supple and malleable, and indeed carefully manipulated by the composer, becoming an important compositional resource.«[24]

---

[20] Botelho reemphasizes these names at the end of his dissertation (342f.). See also my discussion of these authors in Part 3 of this study.

[21] Ibid., 511.

[22] Ibid., 259ff.

[23] Ibid., 2.

[24] Ibid., 3.

Ex. 2-002   Bach, 3rd Brandenburg Concerto, 1st mov., Beginning

I fully agree with this statement but think that such a »composed« meter can be represented more objectively and adequately than by the means Botelho employs. If one applies the principles of the components theory presented and elucidated in the first part of this book, as well as the analytic instrument of the »rhythm score,« to Botelho's example (Ex. 2-002), the result will be a »rhythmic profile« very similar to Botelho's schema. The longest of Botelho's ›stalactites‹ (4 points) agree with the highest of my ›stalagmites‹ (the towers of rhombuses in the »rhythmic profile« line). Even so, there is one fundamental difference: in my case, what is at issue are *rhythmic* weights, which are derived directly by accumulation from the component rhythms of the three voices plus the harmonic rhythm, while Botelho's *metric* weights are the results of an interpretive estimation.

If in Ex. 2-002 one compares the rhythmic profile with the profile of the 2/2 meter, one can clearly see that the rhythmic weights are moved up by 1 ♪ in front of the start of the measures, in other words, that Bach has composed pronounced upbeats. Botelho wants to show exactly that. But by leaving the royal road of rhythmic analysis to stray into the area of metric interpretation, he brings about a semblance of the very unambiguousness he actually wants to disprove (see the identical brackets in all three voices in Ex. 2-001). In the rhythm score, by contrast (Ex. 2-002), the individual component rhythms are preserved in their differentiation. Besides, the process of returning from a ›shifted‹ time back to the coincidence of rhythm and meter (m. 2) can be followed exactly in the rhythmic profile (see the rhythm of the largest weight peaks of 4+4+5+4 ♪). Here the harmonic rhythm plays a major role, which, after having been stationary for 11 ♪, suddenly, with the temporary modulation to the dominant, shows activity in the tempo of individual ♪.

In summing up, I want to stress that Mauro Botelho's analyses make for fruitful reading and that I can agree with them to a large degree. For example there can be no doubt about the ambiguous oscillation between 3/2 and 2/2 units in the first movement of the Third Brandenburg Concerto – an ambiguity Botelho also traces in the D minor Harpsichord Concerto. However, in order to be able to demonstrate the fundamental variability of metrical orders as the result of compositional decisions, the time-dividing phenomena have to be placed under the master rubric of rhythm, so that the classification of »rhythmic grouping,« »tonal grouping,« meter and hypermeter used by Botelho[25] and others can be dispensed with. They are all subsumed under the description of music as a texture of components rhythms and the resultant rhythmic weights.

The analyses of selected examples from Bach's works that follow are to be understood as attempts to approach the vast subject of »Rhythm in the Music of J. S. Bach.« We are still a long way off from being able to describe the variety of Bachian rhythm exhaustively. The examples have been selected largely so as to take into account not just one but diverse genres representative of Bach's Œuvre.

A special problem both musicians and theoreticians are confronted with in J. S. Bach's case are the embellishments, which are often written out with meticulous exactitude and are thus objects of compositional shaping, but also are often missing – as is almost always the case with other composers of the period. The performing musician is in many cases called upon to supply appoggiaturas, trills, etc. in accordance with Bach's style, with the numerous instances of written-out embellishments (as well as articulating marks) serving as models.[26] The analyses that follow had to dispense with such supplementations, however, as they would entail a departure from the certified note text, which would be attended by enormous methodological difficulties. I will therefore proceed in my rhythm analyses in such a way that embellishments and articulatory marks will be included only if they were notated by Bach himself, fully aware that the reality of sound was meant to be even richer.

In a first section, I want to analyze the 48 fugue themes of the *Well-Tempered Clavier* (WTC) rhythmically, as one-voice structures, in a kind of ›serial investigation,‹ according to consistent rigorous criteria, in order to determine whether the themes follow essentially isometric or heterometric models.

---

[25] Ibid., 2.

[26] Already Albert Schweitzer expressly referred to this whole area of ›correct‹ supplementation and practical execution, at a time when Bach criticism was not yet at today's level of sophistication. Cf. Albert Schweitzer, *J. S. Bach*, 1st ed. (French) (Paris, 1905), 2nd ed. (German) (Leipzig, 1908), 10th ed. (Wiesbaden, 1979).

Introduction

This is followed by two comparative analyses – also from the *Well-Tempered Clavier* – each juxtaposing two preludes and fugues with the same time signature (6/4 and 9/8). Here we will see how little the mere time signature tells us about the greatly contrasting rhythmic character the compared pieces actually possess.

The rhythmic analysis of a group of measures from Bach's *Chromatic Fantasy* will touch on the genre of the piano fantasy. From those fast runs and arpeggios, which Bach notated strictly in the meter, we will be able to perceive how, in the area of micro-rhythmic processes, the composer lets simple and complex time structures merge into each other and thus is able to steer the perception of listeners and players in terms of games of raveling and unraveling. The fantasy and improvisation character is thus reflected also in the pulse-bound rhythm.

Bach's orchestral works are represented by the six Brandenburg Concertos. In going through the movements, we will ask about the rhythmic characters but also about the means employed to create variants through rhythm. This relatively unified corpus of compositions is well suited for showing how Bach time and again offers very simple forms of motion along with highly complex rhythmic textures – an aesthetic balancing strategy applied also in other works of his (as well as that of other composers).

An analysis of a number from Bach's *St. John Passion* will serve to include also the component »Language.« The bass aria with chorus »Eilt! – Wohin?« is exceptional within the *Passion*. Bach here evokes an imaginary scene centered on Golgotha and charged with wild emotions of the participants. This is reflected, in the rhythmics of the vocal and instrumental parts, in emphatic syncopations of the vocal solo and in five-eighths phrases in the orchestral and choral parts, all in a rapid 3/8 meter.

I conclude with a rhythmic analysis of a four-part chorale (»Es ist genug« from the Cantata *O Ewigkeit, du Donnerwort* BWV 60). This simple case is to demonstrate once more the effectiveness of the method of components-rhythmic analysis. We will see that identical melodic lines that Bach starts differently result in a different rhythm. The image of the rhythmic profile of this chorale will also show that meter means almost nothing, while prosody and verse order are the all-determining categories.

48 Fugue Themes of the *Well-Tempered Clavier*

Preliminary Remarks

The body of 48 fugal themes from the *Well-Tempered Clavier* (WTC) provides an ideal opportunity for testing the method of a rhythmic analysis of one-voice settings according to the components theory. The number of components in this body is clearly limited, since considerations of texture (of the polyphonic setting) are inapplicable, as is the component »Harmony.« Although one-part subjects have a harmonic content as well, that is interpretable in different ways and is, in fact, implemented differently by Bach in the course of a given fugue. It therefore makes sense to omit harmonic phenomena like the change of functions, the creation of suspensions and the aspect of cadences. In line with the reduction in the number of components, the results of the analysis are correspondingly limited in range. They are nevertheless instructive, as the rhythmic ambivalence the subjects, taken by themselves, often display is in keeping with the listener's impression. Time and again it can be shown that the themes, presented in isolation, do not reveal their meter and that the listener is from case to case even deliberately put on the wrong track. This initial rhythmic-metric openness is a part of the compositional strategy. The subsequent smoothing-out, to be sure, or rhythmic evening in the contrapuntal structure, is something we will note, though without going into analytic detail.

The main components in the fugue themes are »Sound,« »Pitch,« and »Diastematy.« As shown in Part One of this book, the durations between notes are measured according to distances between entries, which are then weighted according to a multiplication of the smallest occurring note value: the larger the entry distance, the heavier its rhythmic weight. As a rule, the small values in written-out embellishments like (trill) terminations or slides are disregarded, as it would be disproportionate to project these minimal values for each and every occurring duration.

In most of the 48 themes, the pitch changes are identical with the entries. But since there are some themes that include note repetitions, the pitch rhythm has to be entered in every case into a rhythm system of its own. And since note repetitions produce a longer durational value of the given pitch, corresponding weightings result here as well. The aspect of »Pitch« also includes those occasionally occurring inherent melodic traits that exhibit an additional effect as upper or inner voices and therefore make their way into the rhythm scores.

Closely linked to the component »Pitch« is that of »Diastematy,« which is sometimes singly responsible for the structuration of a theme, notably in subjects consisting entirely of eighths or sixteenths. Only crest notes will be included in the rhythms score in this investigation, in order to keep the 48 analyses comparable and to avoid having upper and lower changes in direction (crest and keel notes) neutralize each other.

Besides the components »Sound,« »Pitch« and »Diastematy,« the less influential ones of »Articulation« and »Phrase« will also be noted. The component »Articulation« will include the occasionally occurring staccato wedges and legato slurs. Not infrequently, there will also be articulating rests corresponding to a written-out staccato accent. Embellishment, too, will be included in the articulatory system. Phrasings will generally have to be inferred, as phrasing slurs were not yet in use in Bach's time. A phrase can be derived from repetitions within the melodic theme lines. Here there is considerable room for interpretation, which will be justified from case to case.

The rhythmic »profiles« resulting from the accumulation of component weights serve above all for a comparison of rhythmic with metric weights; the accent schema of the respective time signature is therefore registered underneath the profile. Otherwise the fabric resulting from the individual component rhythms is frequently more instructive than the rhythmic profile.

The representation of the 48 analyses follows a uniform pattern. First there is the »rhythm score,« whose design is always the same: Bach's original notation is followed by a transcription, after which the six rhythm staves are listed (1 line without clef), and finally the time schema of the graduated accent meter. In the transcription, time signature, possible initial rest (being inaudible) and all beams and ties written only for the better information of the players have been omitted. Besides, the stems are all pointed downward so as to give greater prominence to the crest notes and the overall contour of the themes.

The commentaries begin with a general characterization of the respective fugal theme[27] and discuss the con- or diverging component rhythms. The analyses conclude with a look at the position of the theme within the rhythmic structure of the entire multi-part polyphonic composition.

---

[27] I restrict myself to analyzing one theme per fugue: in the case of double or triple fugues, subsequent themes are thus not considered.

Part 1

Ex. 2-003   WTC I Fugue C Major

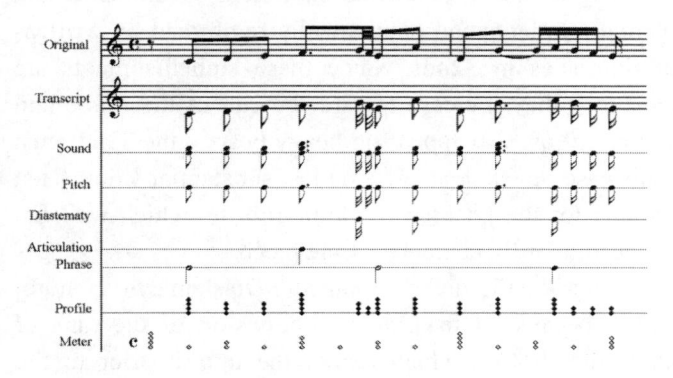

The basic idea of the first C major theme is a tetrachord, used in ascending and descending direction, and in changing augmentation grades, for creating the melody, and resulting in an arch-like, self-contained and rhythmically uncomplicated structure. Only the syncope in the second bar, whose value (♩.) is known from he first bar, introduces a slight tension into the rhythmic makeup. The smallest value is basically the sixteenth; the occasional 32nds function rather as terminations, that is as mere flourishes, and thus not as basis values. The entry in the system »Articulation« (third beat) is to be understood in the same way. The partial phrases of the theme result, at the beginning and the end, from the tetrachord model and, in the middle, from the sequence of ascending fourths. The three crest notes seem as if set freely and arbitrarily.

The rhythmic profile reveals little regularity, so that the 4/4 meter is in no way recognizable from the rhythmic analysis. This changes with the entry of the comes, which, owing to complementary rhythms and above all to suspension formations quickly makes binary structures visible. Owing to the extension of the theme over one-and-a-half bars, the 4/4 meter does not stand out anywhere, major rhythmic weights occurring frequently at intervals of *two* quarter notes. So it is not surprising that the fugue ends on the third, rather than the first, beat of the measure.

Ex. 2-004   WTC I Fugue C Minor

In the C minor fugue of WTC I, too, the subject is structured by a tetrachord, though this time not in the form of a melodic sequence but as an inner voice: the notes A♭ – G – F – E♭ by themselves form a rhythm of halves, which marks the generally falling tendency of the theme and makes for a subdued rhythmic character. Animation and inner tension are again provided by a syncope in the second bar. The inner voice in this case seems structurally so significant to me that the four notes have been inserted into the pitch system with double value (notes below the line). The partial phrases of the theme form themselves after the recurring anapestic rhythm together with the alternating note C-B♮-C. They are two, two and four quarter notes long and stand in firm relation to the stressed notes of the inner voice. Several crest notes, however, intrude into this isometric structure, as does the heavily weighted syncope at the end of the theme.

The rhythmic profile is not very telling in this instance. The relatively simple rhythmic conditions of the theme are more clearly evident in the rhythm systems »Sound,« »Pitch« and »Diastematy« than in the »Profile.« Here the parallel processes of the tonal entries and tonal durations, as well as of the contouring of the melody, can be traced separately and observed in their interdependence. This mixture of joint and contrary action gets lost in the representational mode of the overall profile.

Ex. 2-005   WTC I Fugue C♯ Major

The C♯ major theme of WTC I has a somewhat dance-like character, derived mainly from the upward-leaping and, in the second bar, syncopated crest notes. The unity of the subject is achieved by an inner voice, which descends from the fifth as a prolonged starting-point, traversing a complete pentachord (G♯–F♯–E♯–D♯–C♯). As already in the C minor fugue, this inherent progress has to be included in the rhythm score (notes below the line).

The component rhythms and weights again tell us more about the rhythm of the theme than does the total profile. Thus in the second bar, where the sixth leaps start, one can easily see how the melodic core notes and the off-beat crest notes balance out. What manifests itself as a pendulum motion between the component rhythms is lost in the evenness of the profile values resulting from the addition of the rhythmic weights. Neither does the profile tell us anything about the metrical situation: the 4/4 meter is in no way reflected. In the subsequent course of the fugue, half-measures come to the fore, corresponding to which the fugue ends, not on the *One*, but on the *Three* of the last bar.

Ex. 2-006   WTC I Fugue C♯ Minor

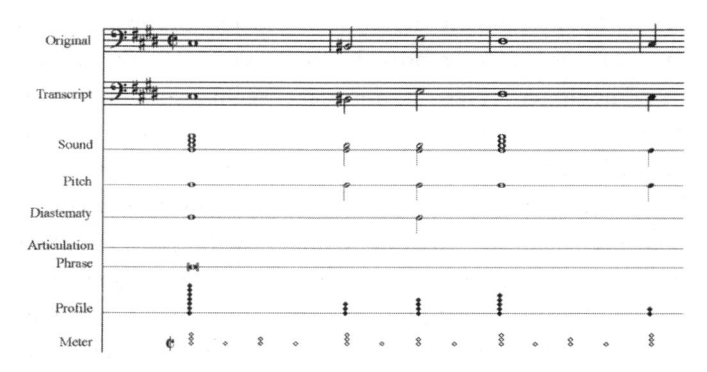

The archaically sounding subject of the C♯ minor fugue, written in alla breve measure, derives its intensity almost exclusively from the interval of the diminished fourth (B♯2-E3), which points toward tension-laden harmonic motions, though these do not as yet obtain the one-voice theme itself.[28] The smallest note value of this fugue is the eighth. However, since eighths do not appear in the theme, the quarter note serves as the smallest value for this theme's rhythm diagram. (The counterpoint introduced in m. 35, which can also be regarded as an independent second theme that determines the middle part of the fugue, consists almost exclusively of eighths, which are sequenced in whole measures.)

The components, as well as the rhythm profile, display a division of the theme by double measures. The remainder of the fugue does not confirm this, however. Already the entry of the comes occurs in the 4th measure, i.e., in the middle of the second double measure expected from the dux. Add to this that in later entries the theme frequently appears with a shortened first note, i.e., in a metrically light position. Taken together, the rhythms of the individual voices, as well as the components »Harmony« and »Texture« pertinent to the polyphonic setting, confirm the alla breve time signature.

Ex. 2-007   WTC I Fugue D Major

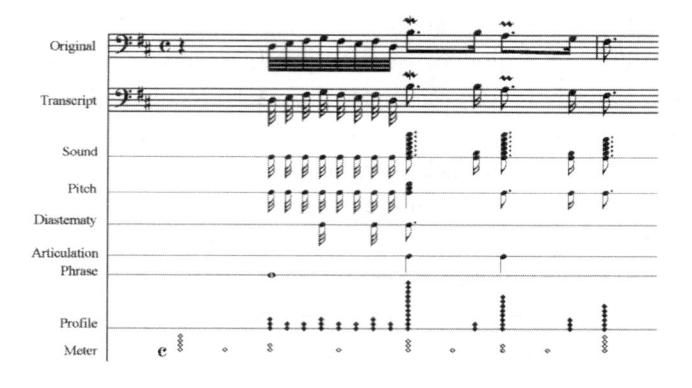

---

[28] One may note incidentally the accord in the fourth to the last measure of the fugue, in which the melodic interval of the diminished fourth in its complementary form as augmented fifth (A3-E♯4) is part of a dissonant five-tone-sound (C♯2-A3-E♯4-G♯4-C♯5) which, in retarding function, introduces the plagal cadence toward the D major conclusion.

The D major fugue makes its appearance in the form of a French overture. The rhythm ♪. ♪ pervades the piece from beginning to end, prominently supported by mordents and inverted mordents and emphatically reinforced by written-out flourishes in 32nds. Since these embellishments are thematic – they increase toward the end of the fugue and from m. 10 on also appear on heavy beats – the 32nd must in this case be taken as the smallest substantial value. That accounts for the fissured rhythmic profile, which well fits the courtly, lordly character of the piece.

As for detail, the component »Diastematy« is noteworthy, because it leads to a subdivision of the runs of 32nds into 3+3+2, which render the upbeat prior to the dotted rhythm dynamic; this would not be the case with a simple slide figure (e.g., traversing the octave D3 to D4 via a scale). The rhythmically generated metric weights prefer the middle of the measure already in the theme, something that prevails in the course of the fugue. However, imitational condensation then foregrounds the individual quarter-note positions. Only in the five-bar epilogue, which reinforces the already reached tonic with an expanded cadence, does the profile of the 4/4 time signature emerge clearly. The fugue ends downbeat on the *One*.

Ex. 2-008   WTC I Fugue D Minor

The sixth fugue of Part I is the first one to introduce a ternary rhythm, as shown also by the time signature 3/4. The particularly pithy rhythm of the subject is fed by the fact that relatively long note values (♩) appear at the end, which the shorter ones (♪, ♫) seem to lead up to. What emerges is a subdivision, stereotypical for the entire D minor fugue, of the measures with a special weighting of the second beat. The component rhythms, as well as the rhythmic profile, suggest that all nine of the notes that precede the B♭4, which is given prominence by its articulation and crest position, can be taken like an extended upbeat, one that then, however, precisely does not lead to a *One*, but instead to a *Two* beat.

The rhythm staff »Articulation« unites three different forms that, given enough space, could also be noted on individual systems: legato slur, staccato accent and trill. On them depends also the phrasing with its new beginning in m. 2, which might be worth discussing; one could perceive the theme also as an undivided unity.

I might additionally draw attention to the inversion of the theme, which, first hinted as in m. 12, in m. 14 appears thematically in the middle voice, in a stretto leading back to the recto form (not shown in the Ex.). In a complete rhythmic analysis of this fugue, it would be desirable to pay attention to the keel notes, since Bach repeatedly hints at, and thus at the equality, of the upper and lower turning-points (crest and keel notes) (see also the last two bars of the fugue).

Ex. 2-009   WTC I Fugue E♭ Major

The cheerful E♭ major theme from Part One of WTC shows a clear partition into a downbeat first and an upbeat second section. The first phrase is rhythmically more turbulent than the second one. The subdivision, by the crest notes, of the first eight sixteenths, for example, is slightly heterometric (♪. ♪ ♪. ♪), while the corresponding 16th figures in the second phrase are regular in their flow. The scale-like step progression in the second phrase (E♭-D-C-B♭-A♭-G) in a simple rhythm of ♪ ♪ ♩ ♩ ♩ ♪ (downward-stemmed in the »Pitch« line) also plays a role. I interpret the eighth rest in the first measure as an articulating one and therefore take account of the B♭ ⁊ on the Articulation staff.

The rhythm of this fugue is generally more small-scale than the beats of the 4/4 meter would lead one to expect. Time and again there are harmonic progressions in a quarter-note and also an eighth rhythm. The 4/4 meter nowhere develops in the sense of a hierarchical accented meter: the tendency is nearly toward a 2/4 meter. The piece ends on the *Three*, though bass and descant in the last measure already enter on the *One* and have a fermata. As a result, the middle voices (the three-part fugue adds a fourth part at the end) have the effect of a termination and a soft finish.

Ex. 2-010   WTC I Fugue D♯ Minor

The D♯ minor fugue of WTC I is one of Bach's much-admired master fugues. The peculiarities begin already with the rhythmic shaping of the subject, which – as is clear even from a look at the transcription – is evidently supposed to leave the listener in the dark about the subsequently recognizable, actual metric situation. The second note downright obtrudes itself as a false *One*, especially since it is followed by eighths that – together with the dotted quarter note – generate a possible, quasi shifted 4/4 meter. In the three-part setting, too, the 4/4 meter remains unrealized, as the halves, and even the quarter notes, assert themselves as dominant units. This is owing to the frequent harmonic changes and the theme's entries in the middle of the measure, as well as to the *stretti* at an interval of one quarter note. The fugue ends on the third beat.

The smallest note of the theme itself is the eighth; after m. 5 16ths appear, which (in contrast to the lone 32nd in m. 11) are rhythmically substantive and would have to be regarded as basis value in a complete analysis of the fugue but are excluded here.

My perception that the subject divides into two phrases of unequal length is based on the twofold appearance of the rhythm ♩ ♩. in connection with an upward-leaping interval. The rhythmic profile points to a binary or quaternary structure from the second note on and to a ternary formation at the end: it thus confirms the rhythmically free form of the theme. Regrettably we cannot dwell on the inversions, augmentations and variations of the theme in the subsequent exposition sections. Altogether the rhythm of this fugue is highly complex, corresponding to the formal complexity of the overall piece.

Ex. 2-011   WTC I Fugue E Major

The E major theme of WTC I, while rhythmically rather simple, is very striking in form. The graphic gesture of the entry – an upbeat to the third beat – carries multiple weights: by the stretched note, the ascending second, the F♯ crest note and an articulatory rest. The following drive of 16ths evinces virtually no irregularities and in any case does not really run counter to the accentual conditions of the 4/4 meter. Since the subsequent entries of the subject are at times shifted by half a measure (by a fourth in the penultimate measure), the signature time asserts itself only weakly. Even so, the fugue ends on an authentic cadence on the *One*.

Ex. 2-012   WTC I Fugue E Minor

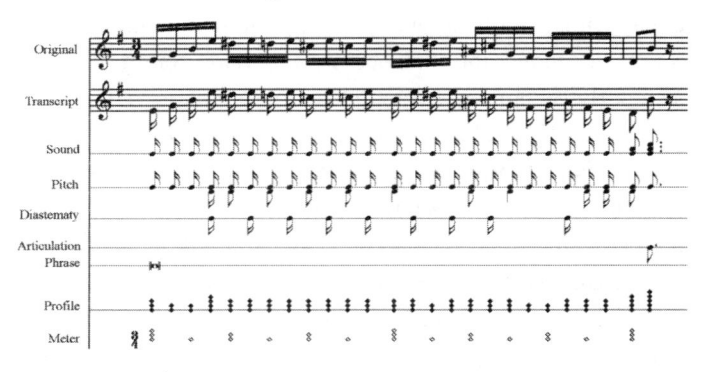

The quasi concertant, almost etude-like theme of the E minor fugue has, except for the concluding notes, only 16ths as its written values. Rhythmic differentiation results from the component »Pitch,« which indicates an inherent melody of E-D♯-D-C♯-C-B-A♯-G-F♯-E-D audible. Corresponding to the rhythm of this falling, partly chromatic progress are the crest notes, which provide a counterbalance as slightly off-beat, typically pianistic pendulum notes. Hence all the triple-weight 16ths in the opening phase of the rhythm profile. In the second part of the theme, certain irregularities do appear, though they hardly disturb the loosely flowing temporal stream.

The theme comprises two 3/4 measures plus a following *One* beat. The subsequent entries of the theme, however, are always on the *One*, i.e., they overlap with the final note of the theme. The double-bar character set by the theme dominates also in other parts of the fugue, though not throughout. Thus the 3/4 unit eventually comes to the fore as the basic measure, providing the optimistic, playful tenor of the piece as a whole.

Ex. 2-013   WTC I Fugue F Major

The F major fugue is the first in WTC I that is written in 3/8 measure. This dance-like beat manifests itself already in the way the rhythm of the theme is differentiated by components. Right at the beginning, crest tones or long notes fall twice on the *One*, suggesting whole measures as the mode of the piece's motion. This is confirmed by the later theme entries, which also repeatedly form two-bar units, e.g. during *stretti* or hemiolas, without the 3/8 measure mutating into an overall 6/8 one.

The principal earmark of the F minor fugue is the chromatic character of the theme's melody. In terms of rhythm, the theme yields little. Judging from the subject, one would not expect that from m. 4 on, 16ths determine the rhythmic events (not shown in the Ex.). The quarter notes of the theme, which there constitute the smallest values, run through the entire four-part polyphonic piece – almost like the cantus firmus of a chorale variation.

Ex. 2-014   WTC I Fugue F Minor

Even so, there are already in the exposition of the theme subtle rhythmic differences that are produced by individual components. Of major importance is the extended chromatic sequence from D♭4 to G3, which is interrupted once (in the second measure). Along with the simple changes in pitch in isometric quarter rhythm, the rhythm of this chromatic core line must thus also be included in the rhythm score; the distance between B3 and B♭3, viewed thus, is enlarged up to three quarter notes and is weighted accordingly (as is the last note G3). In this way we can explain the listener's sense that the subject is rhythmically speaking not as single-minded as the sequence of quarter notes would lead one to expect.

Ex. 2-015   WTC I Fugue F♯ Major

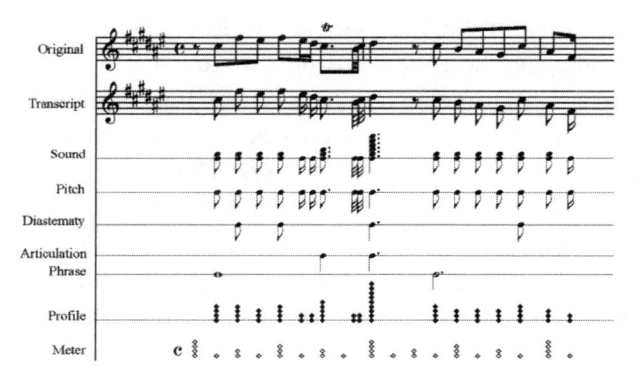

The F♯ major theme of WTC I consists of two phrases of unequal length: ten and six eighths. The more energy-laden phrase stands at the beginning and is followed by a kind of melodic cadence. The rhythmic situation reinforces this reading. As in an extended upturn, the rhythmic weights are accumulated so as to culminate on the last note of the first phrase. That note, a D♯5, is the longest (the ⸴ included), is a crest tone and one with articulating accentuation (again from a ⸴). Since the weighty caesura note simultaneously falls on the *One* of the second measure, we get from the beginning a clear indication of the 4/4 graduated accent meter. Six of the altogether eight thematic entries are positioned exactly like the first, so that in this instance one can actually speak of a ›composed‹ 4/4 meter. The fugue thence ends downbeat on a *One*.

Apart from that, the rhythmic life of the fugue is enriched above all by the fine-grained counterpoints (with note repetitions within groups of four sixteenths), which, however, can not be described in detail here. The playing with the head motif, which lets one forget the weak presence of the actual theme in this fugue, more or less confirms the initial mode of motion.

Ex. 2-016 WTC I Fugue F♯ Minor

The F♯ minor fugue of WTC I is one of the most rhythmically exciting fugues of the entire series, even though the basic tempo must be regarded as stately. The subject strikingly combines a melodic intensification with a rhythmic condensation. This is most clearly evident in the three progressively shortened climactic notes of the melody's spiraling up in trichords and tetrachords: A = 8 ♪, B = 4 ♪, C♯ = 3 ♪. The distances between these climactic notes, too, get progressively shorter, the five quarters value between the A and the B being particularly enigmatic to the listener who seeks to grasp the structure of the theme. Each of the climactic notes of the three-step ascent is also a crest note, so that the weights coming to rest on these points in time are quite heavy. A comparison of the rather heterometric structure of the melody with the schema of the 6/4 time signature reveals a substantial divergence. If the F♯ minor theme is played by itself, its 6/4 meter is practically undetectable to all being not already familiar with the fugue, even to a musically trained ear.

In a later part of this chapter on Bach, I will present a rhythmic analysis of the four-voice piece in its entirety down to the end of the exposition and compare it with the corresponding section of the C♯ minor Prelude of WTC I. The analysis will show that in the fugue the rhythmic license and complexity initiated by the subject continues after the entry of the counterpoints and including the harmonic component, whereas the theme in the prelude produces isometric structures from beginning to end.

Like the subject of the F major fugue, the G major theme embodies a terpsichorean triple, this time noted as 6/8 meter. The 16ths are taken as the smallest value; the occasional isolated 32nds are to be regarded as turns, slides or terminations and thus are excluded as basis values. The

Ex. 2-017 WTC I Fugue G Major

long notes and partial phrases of the theme mark an isometric-ternary rhythm, the crest notes lie mostly on the second and fifth eighth of the measures but are again isometric by themselves (except for the B of the second bar which is on *One*). The rhythmic profile thus closely matches the accentual schema of the 6/8 meter. Characteristic, however, are the heavy weights in the second and third measure, which are off the metric accents and provide for a certain dance-like verve.

The fugue later repeatedly exhibits inversions of the theme, which, however, do not change the rhythmic situation, provided one replaces the crest-note component by the keel-tone one in the inversions. Scale runs and complementary rhythmic interplays between the voices often occupy entire bars, and even the harmonic rhythm not infrequently acknowledges the dotted half-note as durational value. One can thus say in this case that the 6/8 meter appears as unitary, whereas elsewhere it frequently divides into two 3/8 times.

Ex. 2-018 WTC I Fugue G Minor

The G minor theme exhibits a considerable parallelism of its partial phrases, demonstrable, e.g., in the long notes at the phrase ends (F♯-G and B♭-G respectively). Since the smallest value of the theme (as of the entire fugue) is the 16th, these concluding notes accordingly acquire a heavy weight, while the preceding notes seem like upbeats. The position of the heavy-weight tones is the same in both instances: the ♩ falls on the *Three*, the ♩ ♪ on the *Four*. One can see already here that in a rhythmic respect the 4/4 time signature is to be regarded as a twofold 2/4 measure, as the conclusion of the fugue on the third beat also suggests. Even assuming a 2/4 meter, however, the most heavily accented notes characteristically fall on a light beat. This stress extending beyond the bar line endows the theme with its special rhythmic tension.

With the entry of the coes, and throughout the course of the four-part fugue, counter-forces come into play, which produce a certain evening-out of the rhythmic energy. The comes, which responds tonally to the dux, enters even before the theme has come to its end: on the sixth eighth of the second bar, which serves to counteract the overly obvious parallelism of the theme's phrases. The theme entries continue to alternate arbitrarily between the second and the sixth eighth of the measures. The harmonic cadences then do their part in keeping the first and third beat equivalent and thus interchangeable.

The component »Articulation« does not apply in this instance in my view. There are no markings of Bach's to this effect, and the eighth rest appears meant to prolong rather than to accentuate. The parallel design of first and second phrase of this altogether quite short theme also supports this, as the initial rest corresponds exactly to the rest at the beginning of the responding phrase: the rests are, so to say, part of the phrases.

Ex. 2-019   WTC I Fugue A♭ Major

From the broken triads of the very short and simple A♭ major theme of WTC I we can anticipate a strongly harmonically determined fugue setting. Rhythmically, the sequence, consisting exclusively of eighths, is differentiated only by its crest notes. On the other hand, the A♭ major triad's being stretched across four eighths suggests a downbeat beginning. The situation is quickly clarified, however, by the comes's entering, tonally dove-tailed, exactly one bar later. Yet the 4/4 meter is never completely stabilized, as the last entry of the theme in the descant at the conclusion of the fugue shows. Here the first two eighths are in an upbeat position; as a result the piece ends, two measures later, with an authentic cadence in A♭ major on the third beat. In the compositional, that is, specifically, the rhythmic implementation, the 4/4 time signature thus reveals itself once again as a doubled 2/4 meter.

That the G♯ minor subject of WTC I modulates from the I to the V can be clearly ascertained even from an unharmonized, single-voiced version, inasmuch as a regular perfect cadence is intimated by the bass clause (V→I) in the theme's final notes. Rhythmically, this fact is significant

Ex. 2-020   WTC I Fugue G♯ Minor

insofar as the tonic note G♯, that is, the start of the modulatory process, falls, not on the *One*, but on the *Two* of the 4/4 meter, producing a rhythmic irritation from the start, especially since this note has the longest value of the entire subject.

A further peculiarity consists in the note repetitions toward the end of the theme, which result in stretchings, and corresponding weightings, among the values for changes in pitch. If we add the entries of the partial phrases – the first consists of the meandering sequence from G♯ to G♯, the second comprises the steps up to the cadence – the upshot is so many divergences between the component rhythms that the resultant rhythmic profile does not even begin to suggest the accentual schema of the 4/4 time signature.

In the course of the fugue, however, things are thoroughly clarified. The meter, above all, clearly emerges rhythmically, thanks to the frequent (thematic) use of the bass clause, which regularly leads up to the *One* of a 4/4 measure. We thus have here an actually *composed* 4/4 meter, not just a time signature, something also borne out by the concluding downbeat sound on the first beat of the final measure.

Ex. 2-021   WTC I Fugue A Major

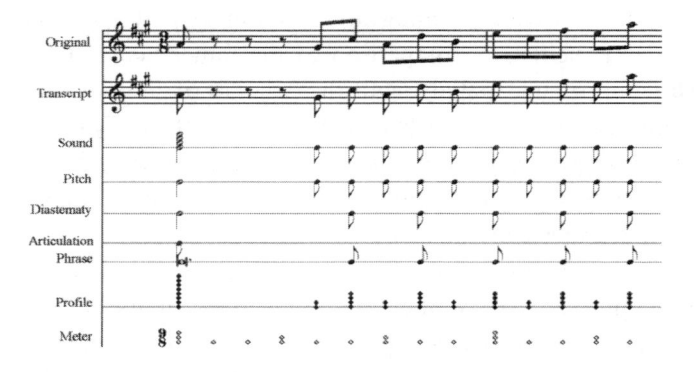

To my personal feeling, the A major fugue of the 1st part of the *Well-Tempered Clavier* is rhythmically the most exciting of the entire cycle. The reason for this is not the compound triple meter appearing here for the first time: in fact the 9/8 time, and the consequent beaming dividing the measure into groups of three eighths each, if anything hamper the analysis, since the actual complicated rhythmic situation is more concealed than made visible by the notation.

If, instead, one looks at the transcription with its flagged eighth notes and omitted bar lines, the special rhythmic problem that Bach has set himself – and which is compositionally ›debated‹ in the course of the fugue's 54 bars – can already be intuited. The ternary meter is overlaid and potentially disabled by binary melodic units. The rising fourth is a motivic element that completely dominates the theme (as it dominates the entire fugue both melodically and rhythmically). Taken as a micro-motif, its natural stress is on the second note, which accounts for the fact that in the component line »Phrase« the measure is set by these notes that are regularly leapt up to from below. They are reinforced by their status as crest notes (something that is not automatic, as the shifting of the fourths could conceivably be followed by an upward continuation). Accordingly, from the third note on, the rhythmic profile shows a binary sequence of weighted tones.

The first note has a durational value of four eighths, the rests having an articulating function. The distance between the first note (A) and the next motivic stress (C♯) is one of five eighths, a measure that does not chime in any more with the structure of the 9/8 meter than does the binary division by the motif of fourths.

As the rhythmic condition of the theme is thus apt to make the assigned meter disappear completely, one might think that with the entry of the comes on the *One* of the second measure the 9/8 meter would regain the upper hand. That this is not the case is shown by the following example (2-022). I have this time beamed the fourths, so that one can clearly see that, immediately after the entry of the comes, two motivic stresses follow each other at a distance of one eighth (A5 and F♯4).

Ex. 2-022   Dux and Comes

That continues at the third entry of the theme. Only toward the end of the exposition does Bach allow the regularity of the 9/8 time to shine through a little by inserting several ♩. on the regular beats of the meter. As the complete analysis, later on in this chapter, of the three-part setting down to the cadence on the tonic in m. 9 will confirm, the harmonic cadence is paralleled by a rhythmic drop from high-grade complexity to simpler isometric structures.

Compared with the A major fugue, the one in A minor largely returns to isometry. The subject, spanning three complete 4/4 bars, introduces a relatively large overall form with several expositions, which include thematic inversions and *stretti* as well as pseudo-entries.

The smallest value is the 16th, interspersed most frequently by eighths. The bipartite theme consists of a longer

Ex. 2-023   WTC I Fugue A Minor

first and a shorter second phrase. The first begins after the metric *One*, the second before it, so that in both cases an upbeat effect can be registered. Sequences play a role in both phrases, so that rhythmic flow is determined by a measure of uniformity. The fact that the rhythmic profile nevertheless does not clearly indicate the hierarchical meter is due to the absence, from the theme's single-voiced exposition, of the components »Harmony« and »Texture« (all of the theme entries come after the first or third beat). The fugue as such is a genuine 4/4 piece well balanced in its character.

Ex. 2-024   WTC I Fugue B♭ Major

The B♭ major fugue is somewhat reminiscent of the F major fugue, with which it shares, besides the ternary meter (3/8 there, 3/4 here), especially the cheerful, concertant character. Isometry is the rule: the four measures of the subject are subdivided into four phrases of equal length, each of them commencing on the eighth after the *One*. Variation (m. 2) and repetition (m. 4) make for double phrases. If crest notes appear off the stressed beats, they mostly do so in the same position within the respective measure, reinforcing the isometry.

The rhythmic profile reveals the regular repetitions quite clearly, though the first beats of the 3/4 meter disappear or get lost, owing to the excluded harmonic component. Harmonic functions in this fugue frequently extend over an entire measure. Suspensions all occur on the first beat. Thus a complete analysis would make the ternary meter with the heavy first beat quite plain.

Ex. 2-025   WTC I Fugue B♭ Minor

The theme of the B♭ minor fugue of WTC I is one of sublime simplicity. Bach here stakes everything on one card. An emphatic ninth leap, which in the tonal response is widened to a tenth leap, expresses a single emotion, that of lament – the minor ninth is the sister of the minor second, but one with a stronger expressive force. With regard to the fugue's overall form, too, Bach aims at a single, extensively prepared-for climax: the stretto of the theme in five parts

Ex. 2-026   Stretto m. 67

with maximal compression (Ex. 2-026).

If in this stretto all of the half-notes seem equivalent, the theme by itself displays a tendency of transcending bar lines, that is, toward the double measure (in the E major fugue of WTC II, Bach for once actually writes the alla breve meter as a 4/2 time). This is owing to the syncopation at the start of the second measure. The quarter rest effects an enchainment of the two measures, because the half-note F on the light beat (𝅗𝅥 𝄽) remains without a weighty follow-up event and thus appears prolonged. One finds these traits reflected in the rhythmic profile: commencing on a high plateau, the rhythmic weights begin to diminish only in the

Ex. 2-027   WTC I Fugue B Major

second measure, letting the subject appear as a unit.

The subject of the B major fugue is self-contained. Its first and last note is B, its ambit comprising a fourth each above and below the tonic. At the same time the division into two partial phrases is heterometric: a brief upswing is followed by a cadence-like concluding turn of twice the length of the first phrase, with a long trill on the penultimate note. The heaviest weights fall twice on the third beat of the 4/4 meter. In the instances where the theme commences on the sixth instead of the second eighth (mm. 11 and 21), the rhythmic stresses fall on the *One*. The dactyl-rhythm scale in the middle of the theme, however, provides, in any case, for a cover-up of any metric stress, be it the *One* or the *Three*. Thanks to the strong end effect of the trill – noted only once but surely meant to be executed every time in the course of the fugue – the 4/4 meter nevertheless asserts it-

Ex. 2-028   WTC I Fugue B Minor

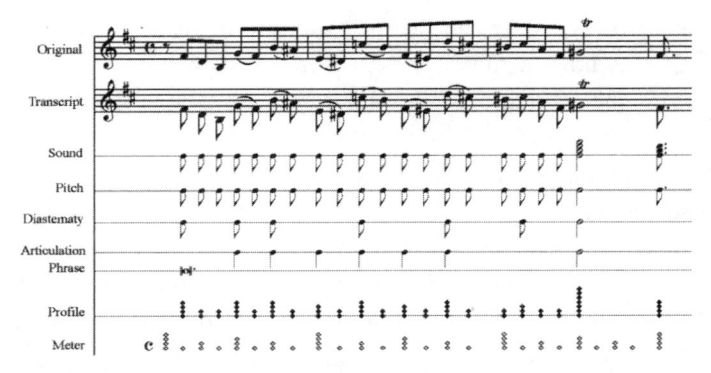

self against the turbulent rhythmic happening. As a result, the fugue ends on a downbeat B major chord.

The final fugue of the first part of the *Well-Tempered Clavier* has a strongly chromatic subject, which with its 21 notes and 12 pitch classes can be understood as a symbolic summation of the plan of the two cycles, which, after all, consists of a major-minor paired passage along the chromatic scale from C to B. The rhythmic situation is relatively simple, since apart from the half-note with the trill before the endnote, the notated durations consist entirely of eighths. However, one can read the articulating slurs as ›notations,‹ resulting in a rhythm of quarter notes. Not notated as rhythmic values but nonetheless rhythmically relevant are, moreover, the crest notes of the melodic line, which coincide only in part with the articulatory rhythm. They inject a slightly irregular rhythm of 3, 2, 4, 4, 3 and ca. 7 ♪ into the total rhythmic structure. Thus the rhythmic profile in the end exhibits some complexity after all, which the simple sequence of eighths would not have led one to anticipate.

The counterpoint to the comes introduces ♪, which run through the entire piece. Altogether, the B minor fugue exhibits a finely modeled rhythm, which gives prominence to the accentual schema of the 4/4 meter – though that is not the case in the single-voiced theme.

Part 2

Ex. 2-029   WTC II Fugue C Major

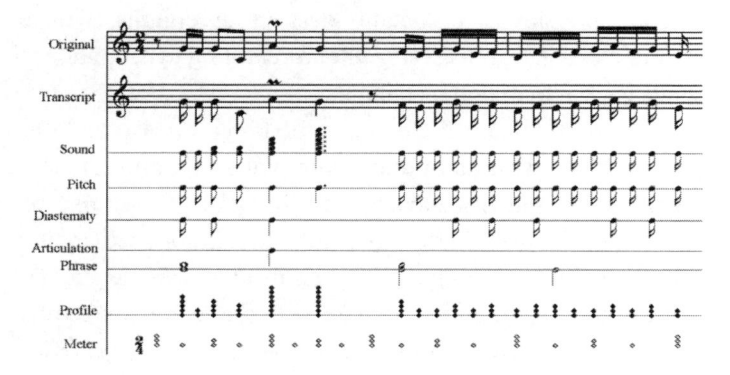

The subject of the merry C major fugue in 2/4 time that opens Part 2 of the *Well-Tempered Clavier* divides into two phrases of equal length that are separated by a rest. This parallelism, however, which is underscored also by the anapestic upbeat at the beginning of both phrases, is superimposed by a melodic contour whose climax occurs already after three eights and which from there runs downward in a figured conjunct. This climax with its inverted mordent, together with the extended next note, seems to concentrate all of the mobile energy of the theme onto itself.

This rhythmic design is apt to burst the narrow frame of the 2/4 meter. There is no discernible reason why Bach did not assign a 4/4 time signature to the piece. The fugue would end in the same way on a downbeat *One*, nor would the fact interfere that the theme entries coincide with even beats only toward the end – until m. 51 all of them come in on the off-beat. One may surmise that the sounding rhythmics finally mattered more to Bach than the notational form.

Ex. 2-030   WTC II Fugue C Minor

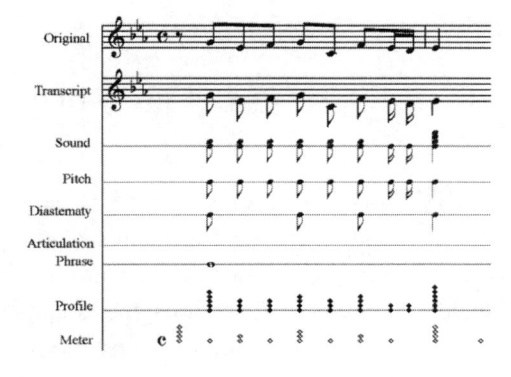

The theme of the C minor fugue of WTC II is brief, essentially one measure in length and all of a piece. Its diastematic upper limit, the G4, gains some prominence, partly because it is the first note to recur already after three eighths. This recurrence also makes for the only slight irregularity (there are three ♪ between G4 and G4) in the theme's otherwise altogether uncomplicated rhythmics.

In the subsequent course of the fugue, in which augmentations, inversions and melodic-rhythmic variations of the theme occur (together with *stretti*), the ♪ assert themselves as the basic value. The single-bar, undivided theme and its predominantly unvaried positioning in the metric scheme, confirm the 4/4 time signature also rhythmically.

Ex. 2-031   Beginning as Stretto

The C♯ major fugue of WTC II is unique in that from m. 1 on the theme is presented in stretto and inversion. When connected with the comes, a rhythmic disequilibrium characterizing the theme – the very light weight on the *One* of the second bar – is compensated.

Ex. 2-032   WTC II Fugue C♯ Major

From m. 8 on, the extremely densely composed piece, with its tentative diminutions and ›strettissimi,‹ adds 32nds, which gain increasing significance toward the end. The type of motion is small-scale, so that it is difficult to actually hear the 4/4 beat as the metrical unit. The concluding measures, however, are symptomatic, in that a dominant pedal point enters on the *One*, a tonic pedal point on the *Three*, and the final chord likewise on the *Three*.

Ex. 2-033   WTC II Fugue C♯ Minor

The subject of the C♯ minor fugue II is one of the figural themes that, while making do with a single note value, nevertheless exhibit rhythmic differentiation. Here the latter can derive solely from the melodic contour (»Diastematy«), and its effect is subtle rather than marked. Even so, the crest notes have repeatedly a binary distance from each other, which would be easily overlooked if one were to analyze according to the ternary drawing of the beams.

This minimal rhythmic oscillation, however, is perceptible only at the beginning. Later on, things get ›straightened out‹ by the counterpoints and, above all, by a second theme (m. 35) with longer values ($\downarrow$. $\downarrow$. $\downarrow$. $\downarrow$. $\downarrow$. $\downarrow$.), which are fitted smoothly into the 9/16 meter. On the other hand, a ›subsidiary theme‹ (first in m. 13, then in mm. 33, 34, 35), exhibiting small hemiolic turns on the level of the 16ths, keeps things from total calm.

Ex. 2-034   WTC II Fugue D Major

The D major fugue of WTC II is set in alla breve meter. The latter, however, is to be understood as a half-measure, as both the theme entries and the ending on the *Two* (with a fermata over the last bar rather than over the final chord) clearly prove. A three-eighths figure in an upbeat position, which dominates the subject, goes through the entire piece and produces an isometric basic structure that appears suspended only at the moment of maximal condensation (stretto at an interval of two eighths).

The initial tonal repetitions, however, make for a relatively heavy beginning, because the pitch D has a duration of three eighths, with the first note being also a crest note and the start of a phrase. Meanwhile the B is in a syncopated position with a durational real value of $\downarrow$., combining the components »Sound« and »Diastematy.« The result is a considerable internal tension of the theme in its single-voiced version, whereas the total impression conveyed by the fugue is rather one of organic and quietly flowing motion.

Ex. 2-035   WTC II Fugue D Minor

The subject of the D minor fugue of WTC II is striking in several respects. It unites contrasting types of motion within itself, and it exhibits a diatonic-chromatic contrast with regard to melody. The result is a solid double-measure form with two phrases that differ in both kind and length. A brief, rapid diatonic ascent in triplet 16ths is followed by a longer and slower chromatic descent in eighths, whose melodic cadence, however – after a retarding syncopation – leads back into diatonic channels.

The rhythmic profile exhibits the biggest peaks on light beats (D5 as crest and phrase note, G4 as long tone). The rhythmic complexity increases further over the course of the fugue, in that duplet sixteenths are introduced in the counterpoints and, above all, in a subsidiary theme (m. 7), which most of the time alternate with the triplet sixteenths but repeatedly also form conflictual rhythmics (in Riemann's sense of the term). The smallest written value of the fugue is the triplet sixteenth, but the smallest occurring temporal distance is that of a triplet 32nd.

Overall one can say that the counterpoints in this fugue are designed and distributed in such a way that the triplet theme start is linked to triplets, the chromatic sequence of eighths generally to straight sixteenths. Though this is not the case with the inversion exposition in m. 17, the contrast presented in the subject communicates itself in this way to the overall form.

As for the time signature of 4/4, the conclusion on the *Three* suggests that a double 2/4 meter should be assumed. The harmonic rhythm points here and there to even smaller-scale structures, as can be heard, for example, in the last cadential measure, where tonic, subdominant and dominant follow each other at a $\downarrow$ tempo.

Ex. 2-036   WTC II Fugue E♭ Major

The sound of the WTC's second E♭ major fugue is generally folksy, almost dance-like. This is due mainly to the design of the theme, which is purely diatonic, consists of a catchy sequence, includes snappy syncopations and is simple in its contour. Because of the omission of the harmonic component (for the reasons given), the rhythmic profile of the subject does not readily display the relative simplicity of the rhythm. In a theme of this kind, however, one inevitably hears the main harmonic movement in whole measures and thus grasps the rhythmic character from the start. This is not to say that the weights the rhythmic profile registers also on the light beats are irrelevant: they constitute the tension in relation to the isometric patterns that are not yet in effect in this representation.

Ex. 2-037 WTC II Fugue D♯ Minor

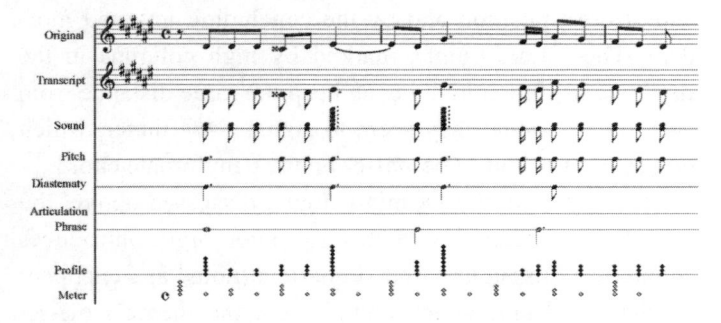

Ex. 2-040 WTC II Fugue E Minor

The subject of the D♯ minor fugue of WTC II is a model of the systematic shifting of a rhythmic formation against its metrical background. Apart from the fact that the 4/4 time signature is realized compositionally as a 2/4 meter (as suggested by the conclusion on the *Three* and the occasional entries of the theme after the middle of the measure – cf. especially the last two entries in the bass and descant), the component-dictated weights are so invariably positioned on the light beats that the theme's original form must have been a version like this constructed one:

Ex. 2-038 Construct

But since Bach sets the exposition of the theme in metrically shifted form, he evidently plans to present the theme's internal rhythmic tension belatedly, after the introduction of the counterpoints, in a structure of complementary rhythms. This indeed happens presently in mm. 3 and 4, where the rhythmic formula ♩. ♪♪ falls onto the heavy beats – exactly as in our construct – so that even and odd structures make for tension-laden contrasts.

Ex. 2-039 WTC II Fugue E Major

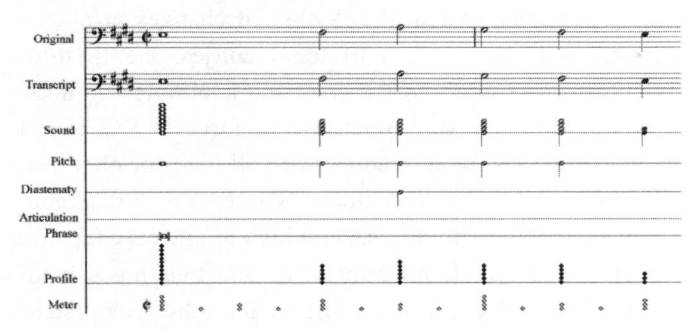

The E major fugue of WTC II is written in an enlarged alla breve (4/2), though that is not confirmed compositionally (note the conclusion on the *Three*). The theme, with its archaically long note values, as yet altogether omits the quarter notes repeatedly occurring elsewhere (e.g., in the diminished versions of the theme) and the eighths. As in the *stile antico* (Bach even uses the old brevis form ⌶ once), the six notes describe a simple arc, whose crest occurs on the fourth half of the measure as the only deviation from the otherwise quite regular progress of the melody (taken by itself, the melody suggest a division into twice three halves). The rhythm of this fugue generally has an old-fashioned imprint, whose motet-like character seems like a stylistic quotation.

To understand the subject of the E minor fugue of the *Well-Tempered Clavier*'s Part II, one ought to transcribe it in a 12/8 meter, as I have done in Example 2-040. The binary ♪♪ rhythm thereby turns into a ternary ♩ ♪ one, while the 4-16th figures can be made to appear as turns and thus ignored as substantial tonal durations. In the first measure, one thus hears, after the upbeat-like eighths, a calm rise in pitch over G and A up to B at the rhythm of halves (♩ or ♩.). The turns will be regarded as articulation events and entered as such into the rhythm score. Altogether, the rhythm is simpler in the actual sound than in the notation.

A prominent feature of this theme are the three quasi-syncopated anticipations on the long notes C4, A4 and F♯4, whose heavy rhythmic weights momentarily rob the metrical structure of its evenness. The meter clearly exhibits a four-part ternary graduated accent beat, which achieves its concluding emphasis with the final tonic sound on *One* plus expiring figure work.

Ex. 2-041 WTC II Fugue F Major

The F major fugue of WTC II has the gigue-like character that occurs, for example, also in the final movements of some of Bach's concertos. The theme already reveals this character clearly, in that several components are piled onto the beginnings of the measures, so that the 6/16 of the time signature is also prominent rhythmically. The smallest value in the theme is the sixteenth, whereas 32nds appear toward the end of the fugue, which underline the generally concertant character of the piece also in its rhythm.

The subject of the F minor fugue, too, is to be thought of as relatively fast. The static repetitions of eights at the beginning, which recur throughout the fugue like a basic character trait and are often reinforced by a second voice, are counterpointed with runs of sixteenths, which, together with frequent broken triads in the bass part, again convey an overall concertant impression. The repeated eighths pro-

Ex. 2-042   WTC II Fugue F Minor

duce an extension of the pitch and thus a heavy weighting of the beginnings of the measures. Despite its emphatic upbeats, the subject is thus embedded securely in the 2/4 meter of the time signature (see the beginning of the rhythmic profile).

Ex. 2-043   WTC II Fugue F♯ Major

The F♯ major fugue is written alla breve with an upbeat. The ♩-upbeat returns in the form of two quarter notes, which gives the whole piece something of a gavotte character. The smallest note value of ♪ is actually represented only rarely in the piece. But since the theme already includes 16ths that can *not* be regarded as embellishments (see the melodic transition in m. 2), the value should nevertheless be fully counted.

The biggest peak in the rhythmic profile is on the *One* of the first full measure, because the applicable components include, besides the long note, also »Diastematy« (crest position) and »Articulation« (♩.). The second *One* beat also has a major rhythmic weight. Thus the theme already announces an isometric structure, which accounts for the dance-like overall character of the piece.

Ex. 2-044   WTC II Fugue F♯ Minor

The F♯ minor subject of WTC II derives its very distinct shape from a hexachord (D4-C♯4-B3-A3-G♯3-F♯3) that will continue throughout the fugue as an inner line. The notes of the hexachord are heavily weighted by their lengthening and/or crest position and by the concluding inverted mordent. These time points, marked by high columns in the rhythmic profile, initially even keep the same distance from each other, so that they seem to signal a 4/4 meter, which however turns out to be ›false‹ on the penultimate chord.

Exactly as in the D♯ minor fugue discussed above, the very first counterpoint of this F♯ minor fugue introduces counterweights, in that dotted quarters (noted as ♩.) appear on the odd beats, which complement the theme's off-set dotted values on heavy beats. The fugue, whose two additional themes, incidentally – like the first one – enter on the fourth eighth of the measure, gains momentum starting with the third theme, which consists exclusively of runs of 16ths. Altogether three times the three themes are in stretto (mm. 54, 60, 66), whereby the 4/4 time signature loses its never greatly developed form, shrinking to the smaller unit of 2/4, with the piece also ending on the third beat.

Ex. 2-045   WTC II Fugue G Major

With its runs purely of sixteenths, the theme of the second G major fugue has the character of a toccata. As with other subjects that are based on a single durational value of the component »Sound,« the rhythmic vitality here is due entirely to the component »Diastematy.« Since there are no tonal repetitions, so that the rhythm of changes in pitch is identical with the rhythm of tonal entries, the rhythmic structure is due solely to the crest and keel notes. In a rare deviation from the rule otherwise in force in this investigation of the 48 fugue themes, we will here for once consider both crest *and* keel notes. These two partial components generate a rhythm each, which in one case (upward stems) consists predominantly of ♪., and thus has a hemiolic tendency (3 ♪ : 2 ♪.), while in the other case (stems pointing downward) it produces only ♪ and ♩ and thus approximates the 3/8 meter.

In the further course of this fugue, there are numerous rhythmic irritations (e.g., in the descant in mm. 16ff.) but along with them also instances of isometric smoothing-out (cf., e.g,, the trochaic ›sound feet‹ in the alto at the same point). The introduction, in the form of a cadenza, to the last subject entry is unusual. A virtuoso run of ♪ traverses the tonal space from D2 to D5 while forming a hemiola by means of the crest notes: mm. 63 and 64 are divided into 3x8 ♪, which stand in a hemiolic relation to the 2x12 ♪ of the two bars.

Ex. 2-046   WTC II Fugue G Minor

The subject of the G minor fugue of WTC II appears to suggest a shifted 3/4 meter: owing to long notes, articulating accents (obtained by ‚) and beginnings of the partial phrases (sequence portions), the largest rhythmic weight always accumulates on the second beat. These ›false‹ downbeats are ›corrected‹ only in the fourth measure, where, continuing regularly from the sequence model of third (↓) and fourth (↑), a very long pitch, as well as a new rhythmic character, are introduced by the sevenfold repetition of the C4. What commences like a sarabande, leads to a persistent knocking gesture, which later on, in the counterpoints, changes into a partly vehement motion of 16ths. Even so, in a case care for Bach the ternary meter in this fugue is formed and held by rhythmic means, including several hemiolas, in which the theme's beginning can be readily embedded. All of the subject entries, of which several appear doubled by parallels of thirds or sixths, come on the *Two*. What is presented in such striking manner in the theme basically goes for the whole piece: an internally tensed triple meter in perpetual repetition and variation.

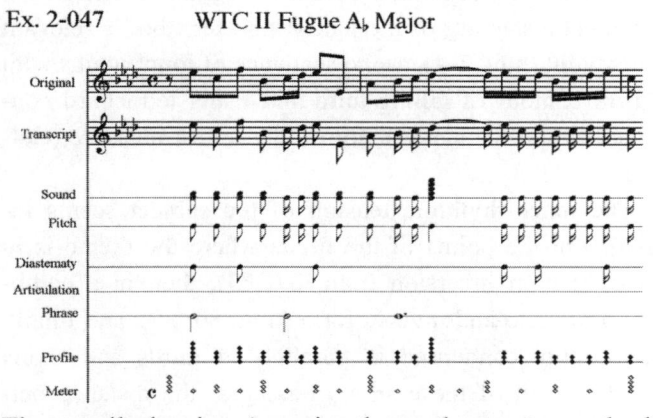

Ex. 2-047   WTC II Fugue A♭ Major

The merrily leaping A♭ major theme does not reveal what the character of the fugue as a whole will really be like. For the first counterpoint (not shown in the Example) injects a chromatic train of six descending steps, which may be perceived as an element of lament, and which in any case is in tension with the purely diatonic subject: laughter amid tears.

In a rhythmic respect, one note of the theme commands total attention: the D♭5, which enters on a light beat, has the longest value, and in addition comes just before the chains of 16ths that seem to emerge from it as if in relaxation. The note can unfold its syncopated effect because, owing to the parallelism of the partial phrases, a binary metric condition of the theme was established before. Bach evidently composed this fugue with the sense of a divided 4/4 meter, as the final tonic chord on the third beat of the time signature's 4/4 meter clearly suggests.

Ex. 2-048   WTC II Fugue G♯ Minor

The subject of the G♯ minor fugue sounds like the beginning of a character piece of nebulous mood, that is to say, not at all fugue-like. Consisting solely of eighths, its rhyhm has virtually no contours. The crest notes, the sole component that could make a mark, seem irregular and arbitrary in their distribution. Only the new start in m. 3 gives a faint sign of structure in this otherwise quite monotone sequence. To the end, one would be baffled by such a lack of decisiveness, if it were not for a second theme joining in at m. 61, which, with its stepwise chromatic progression in the form of an inverted arch, introduces a markedly different character. Since the rhythm of this second theme is quite isometric in its iambic ›sound feet,‹ even the first theme acquires some rhythmic profile when it combines with the second – somewhat as in a berçeuse (lullaby).

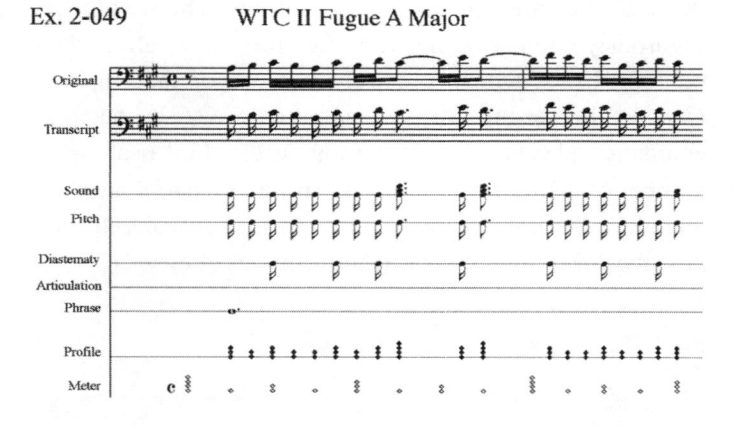

Ex. 2-049   WTC II Fugue A Major

The A major fugue of WTC II is wholly dominated by 16ths. Only in the theme are there any entry durations of ♪., made to function as syncopes by means of ties. These syncopes (C♯4 and D4) are not audible as such in the exposition of the theme, as the melodic contour rather suggests a downbeat start (Ex. 2-050).

Ex. 2-050 Construct

Contrary to the subject, the counterpoints in this fugue have almost throughout the straight form of the rhythm ♪. ♪. That first makes the rhythmically tense character of the subject perceptible, and it remains effective to the end of the fugue. The signature time of 4/4 is again composed as a 2/4 meter, as the final chord sounding on the third beat also demonstrates.

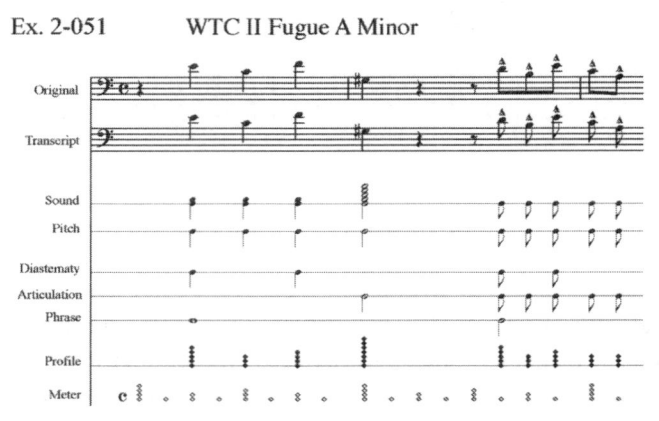

Ex. 2-051   WTC II Fugue A Minor

The A minor fugue of WTC II has a character that is only vaguely suggested by viewing the theme in isolation. From the entry of the answer, the counterpoints introduce 32nds, which together with small-scale syncopations and numerous embellishments (trills on dotted eighths) evoke the festive mood of a French overture. The majestic attitude, to be sure, is announced already in the theme with its four-note motif in quarter notes, which is promptly sequenced in diminuted form, but the rhythmic opulence is added only by the counter-voices.

The main rhythmic weight in the subject rests on the G♯, because of its length and the articulatory rests, which in this case are simultaneously also caesuras. The weights are vigorously counterbalanced by the crest notes, all of them on light beats, which, precisely because of the emphatic *One* on the second bar, can admittedly also be taken as emphatic upbeats. The piece ends on the third beat, and a number of theme entries, too, are shifted by half a measure, including the last one in the bass, so that now the 4/4 and now the 2/4 time functions as the ›composed meter.‹

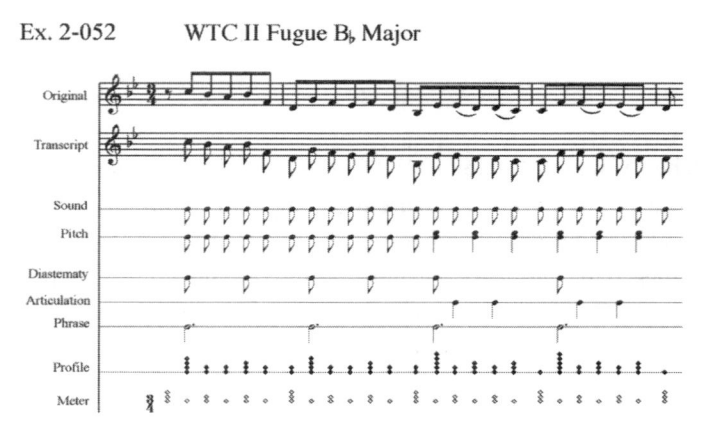

Ex. 2-052   WTC II Fugue B♭ Major

The B♭ major theme of WTC II represents again a rhythmic type whose tonal impulses are based on a single value, the ♪. Thus all the rhythmic life depends on other components, in this case on the crest notes, the note repetitions and the articulating slurs. As the rhythmic profile shows very clearly, the first two bars are like 6/8 measures in rhythm, the last two like 3/4 measures. Both forms, however, are shifted by an eighth against the 3/4 of the actual time signature. The listener is deliberately led astray, and that in a two-fold way: by the allusion to 6/8 and by the shift in the meter, so that he perceives the theme roughly as in Ex. 2-053. The tone puzzle concerning the actual metric condition of the subject is resolved only in the counterpoint to the comes in m. 7, where quarter notes appear on the regular beats.

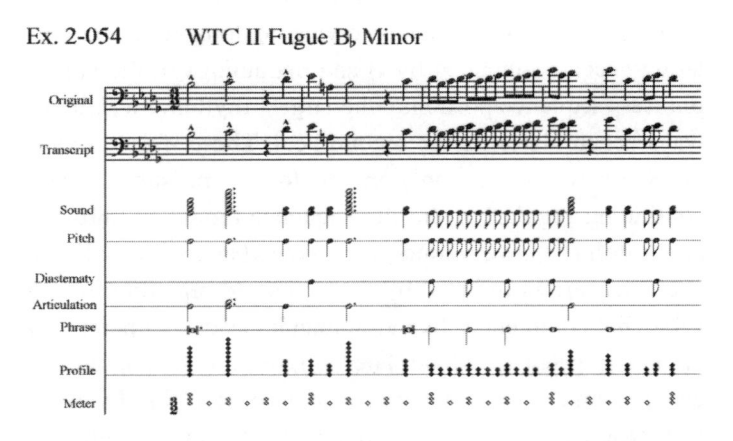

Ex. 2-053   Construct

Ex. 2-054   WTC II Fugue B♭ Minor

The B♭ minor fugue in Part II is in 3/2 time and exhibits some traits of a sarabande, evoked by the dotted half on the second beat. This syncopated accent produced by note prolongation returns in diminution in the penultimate measure (the F4 here comes on the second quarter, not on the second half note), so that the rhythm of the subject, brought to life already by the introduction of an upbeat before the third bar and its beginning chains of eighths, is further vitalized. The shaping of the partial phrases, too, is relevant at this point (mm. 3-4), as the sequence of four eighths with its firm contour of falling third and rising tetrachord continues beyond the syncopation in the fourth measure (G♭4-E♭4-F4-G♭4).

The inner rhythmic tension of the subject seems intensified at the points of the fugue where the theme is in stretto, first in inversion (mm. 67, 73), then in a combination of recto and inverso form (mm. 80, 89), and finally even doubly condensed in parallels of thirds and sixths (m. 96). In all of these stretto passages, the distance between theme entries is that of a half note, whereby the second beat, accentuated already in the theme, gains additional weight from the theme entry. In a rhythmic profile of the entire composition, the half would clearly emerge as the basic value, but with the accentual character of the saraband meter also manifesting itself as a determining motion mode of this fugue.

Ex. 2-055   WTC II Fugue B Major

The second B major theme of the *Well-Tempered Clavier* exhibits an aspiring, forward-pointing character. Clearly divided into 3+2 bars, the first phrase is based solely on halves, while the second phrase produces acceleration through quarter notes and eighths as well as a characteristic syncopation within the melodic cadence. The crest notes on the second and fourth *One* of the alla breve meter suggest taking the first two half notes as quasi an upbeat to a 4/2 meter. In fact, the entire fugue displays this metric pattern. Only once a theme entry occurs on a heavy beat of the assumed hyper-meter; the concluding chord, too, falls on an even heavy beat (m. 104), thus confirming the isometry of units of four halves throughout the entire piece.

Ex. 2-056   WTC II Fugue B Minor

The Second Part of the *Well-Tempered Clavier* ends with a fugue in a dance-like 3/8 meter. After two measures the subject runs in a rhythm that coincides largely with the accentual conditions of the meter: main rhythmic weights correspond to main metric weights. Included in the former are the notes of the melodic scaffolding G-F♯-E-D at distances of ♩. and the (indirect) lengthening of the pitch on G and F♯ (if one discounts the octave leaps), which endows these grades with a durational value of three eighths. The octave leaps are pianistic in provenance, as suggested by a later counterpoint, which exhibits similar pendulum motions in a tempo of sixteenths.

The altogether uncomplicated piece – besides *stretti* there are no special ›fugue tricks‹ here – is also unproblematic rhythmically. Trills on *Two*, hemiolas and terminating 16ths in pianistic figures enliven the rhythm within the stable 3/8 meter and endow the piece with a brisk, terpsichorean concertant tone.

Summary

The rhythmic microanalysis of the *Well-Tempered Clavier*'s 48 themes lets the individual shape of each theme stand out clearly, hopefully causing the interpreter to become sensitive to, and curious about, the complex rhythmic inner life of these mostly quite short melodies.

The guiding principle in this analytic survey has been to take the themes seriously as *single-part* formations, fully aware that they would appear in a different light, and also reveal different qualities, in their polyphonic context. The powerful components »Harmony« and »Texture,« which were excluded here, in most cases make for a greater prominence of isometric conditions even within the subject.

It may come as a surprise (and was unexpected also to me) that in spite of Harmony and Texture being ignored, most of the themes of the *Well-Tempered Clavier* evince an isometric structure – in terms of having equal temporal distances between dominant points of structural division. The subjects having this kind of structural regularity are, in Part I, those in C♯, D, e, F, F♯, f♯, G, g, A♭, a, B♭, B, in Part II, those in C, c, E♭, e, F, f, F♯, g, a, B♭, B and b. To be added are three special cases, which, although largely isometric in their structural design, are shifted in terms of their time signature, being, as it were, permanently syncopated (and thus actually also isometric). These themes are those in D♯ minor, A major and B♭ major in Part II.

The themes that are more nearly heterometric in structure, and thus also free in relation to the metric scheme, are those in d, d♯, f, f♯, g♯, A and b in Part I, and those in C♯, c♯, D, d, E, f♯, G, A♭, g♯, B♭ and b♭ in Part II. In this group of themes, whose rhythm exhibits a heightened complexity, the degree of irregularity varies greatly. Downright enigmatic appears to me the rhythmic structure of the following four themes: d♯, f♯, A in Part I, and G in Part II. In these themes, it is impossible to recognize the meter. The melodies seem to be set in a free rhythmic structure, though a definite structuration is manifest. The most bizarre one is in the first A major theme.

The rhythmic components analysis, as explained, aims not only at the sequence of durations within the individual component rhythms, but also at the rhythmic weights that result from the coincidence of components durations and can change from point to point. The sequence of these rhythmic weights stands in a changing relation to the weights of the metric scheme. In our analysis we also regularly considered this relation, in view especially of the further progress of the fugue in question. One can distinguish between the meter of the time signature and the actual composed meter. In most cases, the rhythmic weights loosely coincide with the abstract accentual schemas of the time signatures. In numerous cases, however, it can be shown that the prescribed large meters (4/4, 2/2 or 4/2) remain unrealized in the actual composition and instead are thought of as halved (»composite«): 4/4 → 2/4 (in Part I: C♯, E♭, d♯, g, A♭; in Part II: C♯, d, d♯, f♯, A♭, A and a); 4/2 →2/2 (E in Part II); and 2/2 → 2/4 (D in Part II). In two instances, the relation is reversed: the fugues in C and B in Part II expand the time signature from 2/4 to 4/4 and 2/2 to 4/2.

By way of qualifying this finding, it should be noted that in the course of a fugue, the actual, that is, compositionally realized, isometric structures can resemble the larger as well as the smaller metrical units. We must therefore assume metrical ambiguity. Since the rhythmic weights resulting from the accumulated component rhythms in any case only rarely reflect the abstract schema of a time signature exactly, but rather exhibit countless variants, it is only ›natural‹ for any given piece to also tack between simple and composite meters as the composer chooses, or better, as the living material of his composition demands.

Two 6/4 and two 9/8 Pieces from the *Well-Tempered Clavier*

The time signatures 6/4 and 9/8 occur twice each in Part I of the *Well-Tempered Clavier*. The Prelude in C♯ minor and the Fugue in F♯ minor are set in 6/4, the Prelude in A minor and the Fugue in A major in 9/8 time. Identical meters are a useful *tertium comparationis* for comparative rhythmic analyses.

The repeated use of an identical meter in a prelude and a fugue each suits in rhythmic conditions in the present case that could not be more contrary. Isometry clearly rules in the preludes, planned irregularity and a complex texture of components rhythms in the fugues. The contrary character of the formal types Prelude and Fugue, readily perceptible to the listener, is fully confirmed by the rhythm. At the same time, the ›law‹ of meter is observed also in the fugues. There are (of course) no time changes, and in both the imperfect and the perfect cadences the respective rhyhm even echoes the accentual situations of the measures; besides, both fugues end on the *One* of the final bars. But where the preludes unquestionably realize the meter rhythmically from the start, the meter at first remains hidden behind other rhythmic layers in the fugues. How much meter should there be, the composer seems to ask himself at every point of the unfolding form. Bach manipulates the rhythmic weight relations by means of the components and is thus able to adapt or not to adapt the former to the metrical weight relations. The meter is shaped, not merely obeyed.

To analyze the four pieces from beginning to end would exceed the scope of this chapter. I therefore confine myself to the opening sections up to the point where the end of the first exposition is reached (in the fugue) and a cadence provisionally rounds off the section.

The selection of components and criteria of their weighting are identical in all four analyses. In accordance with the methodical guidelines set down in the first part of this book, the rhythm of the tones (»Sound«) is raised by multiplying the smallest durational value, the pitch changes in note repetitions (»Pitch«) by the value of the repeated notes. Crest notes (»Diastematy«) are added on the Pitch line; keel notes are ignored. The (rarely occurring) articulation marks and embellishments are (from case to case) accommodated in the Pitch system as well. The phrasing is measured according to the smaller or larger signifying units (»Phrase«), the harmonic rhythms (»Harmony«) are determined by the change of functions, so that in the four-part settings (C♯ minor prelude, F♯ minor fugue) the function changes are weighted by four units, in the three-voiced ones (A minor prelude, A major fugue) by three. Harmonic accents will include suspensions and anticipations, but neither transitions nor the seventh and ninth chords, which in Bach no longer function as suspensions. Since both the preludes and the fugues are polyphonically composed and furnished with subjects, the theme entries (line »Theme«) have a structural function of their own; they are weighted according to the number of voices.

The presentations of the analytic results follow an unchanging pattern. Initially the notation is combined with the overall rhythmic profile. The rhythm score that comes next, presenting the protocol of all the component rhythms active in the three or four voices, serves as an explanatory follow-up to the overall profile. Here the voices are given in transcription with the time signatures, the bar lines and the beams being left off and the ties being dissolved.

Prelude C♯ minor (6/4)

Ex. 2-057 Bach, WTC I, Prelude C♯ Minor (with Rhythmic Profile)

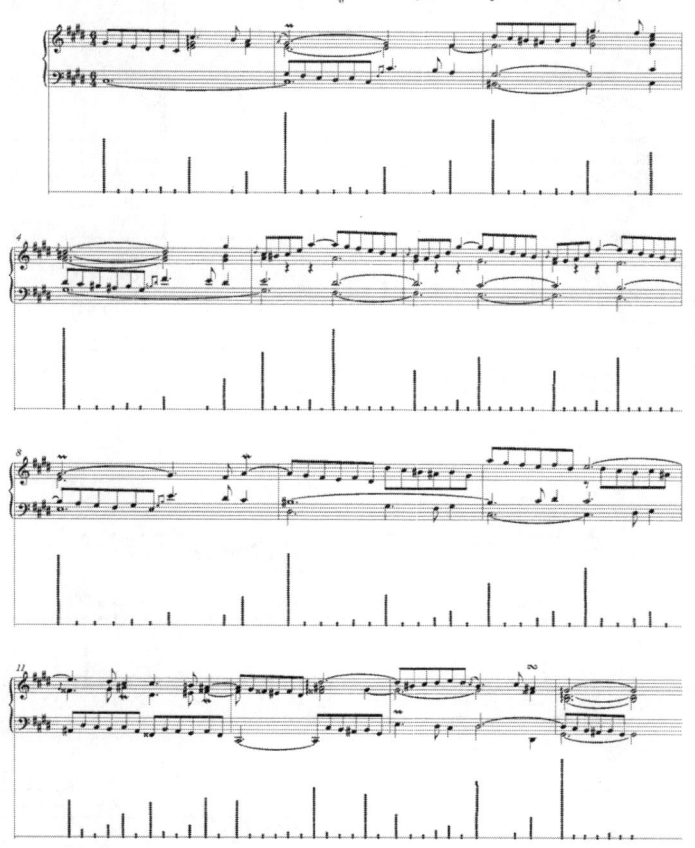

The C♯ minor prelude of WTC I (Ex. 2-057), comprises altogether 39 measures in free form. Based monothematically on a Siciliana-like melody, the piece wanders through the harmonic space of the basic key of C♯ minor in a loosely polyphonic setting. In m. 8, it reaches E major, in m. 14, G♯ minor. In m. 20, three shorter modulatory steps (G♯ minor, B major, C♯ minor) lead to F♯ minor, which, however, quickly gaining the function of the subdominant, returns via the neapolitan sixth chord (m. 24) back to C♯ minor, without as yet forming a cadence. The latter, repeatedly evaded, is saved until the final bar of the composition. The section selected here (mm. 1-14) can be seen as a kind of double exposition, in which first the descant and then the tenor (m. 8) commences with the subject.

Ex. 2-058 Bach, WTC I, Prelude C# Minor, Exposition (Rhythm Score)

The rhythmic profile clearly shows the 6/4 meter as a two-part unit, and as the principal rhythm emerges 𝅗𝅥. 𝅘𝅥 𝅘𝅥 – with the last quarter note functioning as an increasingly emphatic upbeat. It is readily observable how the thematic thickening from m. 8 on also entails a greater rhythmic density. Overall, however, the rhythmic image is a simple one and in keeping with the calmly swaying character of the piece.

Comments on the Rhythm Score

The component »Sound« in this prelude (see Ex. 2-058) results in unusually large weights on the long caesural notes (e.g., m. 2 in the descant) and on the long values of the secondary voices (extremely so in the three-part sequence of mm. 4f.). This is owing to the rule that the weight of a duration between note entries is measured according to the multiple of the smallest value (♪). Weight, of course, is not synonymous with stress but means validity. If one considers, e.g., the long-held C♯ in the bass of the first two bars, it is not essential whether this note is really audible for 12 quarters (if played, say, on the organ rather than the harpsichord or clavichord). It retains its value in any case as a pedal point, above which harmonic changes take place in the last quarters of the measures that the C♯ does not go along with. The same goes for the chain of suspensions in the same sequence, where fully three quarters are assigned to each suspension note, whose duration is also actually noticeable because of the expected resolutions.

The component »Pitch« results in a singly weighted duration sequence, which is identical with the rhythms of the entries (there are no tone repetitions, the suspensions in mm. 6 and 7 do not count here). Of importance, however, are the crest notes, which *inter alia* lead to a reinforcement of the already extended melody notes that precede the secondary stress in the middle of the measure (mm. 5-7). The Pitch system also registers the arpeggios, grace-notes and trills (each with a note point below the line). Although a number of appoggiaturas can be transformed in the execution into rational values, they are here conceived, like the trills and arpeggios, as phenomena with an irrational time structure and are to that extent rhythmically ignored. Moreover, the arpeggioed chords in mm. 1, 3 and 12, as well as all multi-part sounds inspired by the through-bass, which I have distributed over two voices, result in one or two additional values each being reckoned in for the tone entries in the alto. This does not apply to the grace-notes in the tenor (mm. 2, 4 and 8), because they are regarded as embellishments and not as chords.

Phrasings, which concern the musical meaning, are always also a matter of opinion. In the present case, however, the solutions proposed for each voice will hardly be controversial. Of importance in any event are the upbeats introduced from m. 2 on, since the prelude began on a downbeat. As significant I also regard the rhythmic anticipations of the first note of a number of *soggetti*, whereby the weight of that note is pulled *ahead* of the metric stress (descant, mm. 8 and 11; tenor, mm. 7 and 14, bass, m. 13). Incidentally, I phrase the bass voice only from the point at which it gains an independent melodic quality (from m. 9).

The harmonic rhythm in this piece is inordinately slow. Function changes fall almost always on heavy beats, which contributes to the impression of a swaying motion. In m. 2, the change to the subdominant is induced by the F♯-A-C♯ slide in the third voice, whereby G♯ and E in the upper voices turn into suspensions. I took account of short suspensions as well as of long ones, which in the sequence of mm. 5-7 occur together. Two special instances are debatable: in the bass of m. 11, I regard the D♯ and the B as freely entering suspensions on light beats.

Summing up, one can say that the C♯ minor prelude has rhythmic conditions that fully correspond to the metric conditions of the 6/4 time signature. Even without bar lines, the rhythmic profile obtained from the component rhythms clearly reflects the composite binary/ternary meter. A glance at the fine gradations, however, shows that no measure equals any other. In addition, a process can be observed within the segment of 15 bars selected here, in which the contents of the measures are filled up with rhythmic weight and occasionally heaviest beats are even surpassed by lightest ones (mm. 12-13). With the cadence to G♯ minor, the rhythm, too, finds its way back to the calm of the *siciliana* meter.

Fuga F♯ minor (6/4)

Ex. 2-059   Bach, WTC I, Fugue F♯ Minor (with Rhythmic Profile)

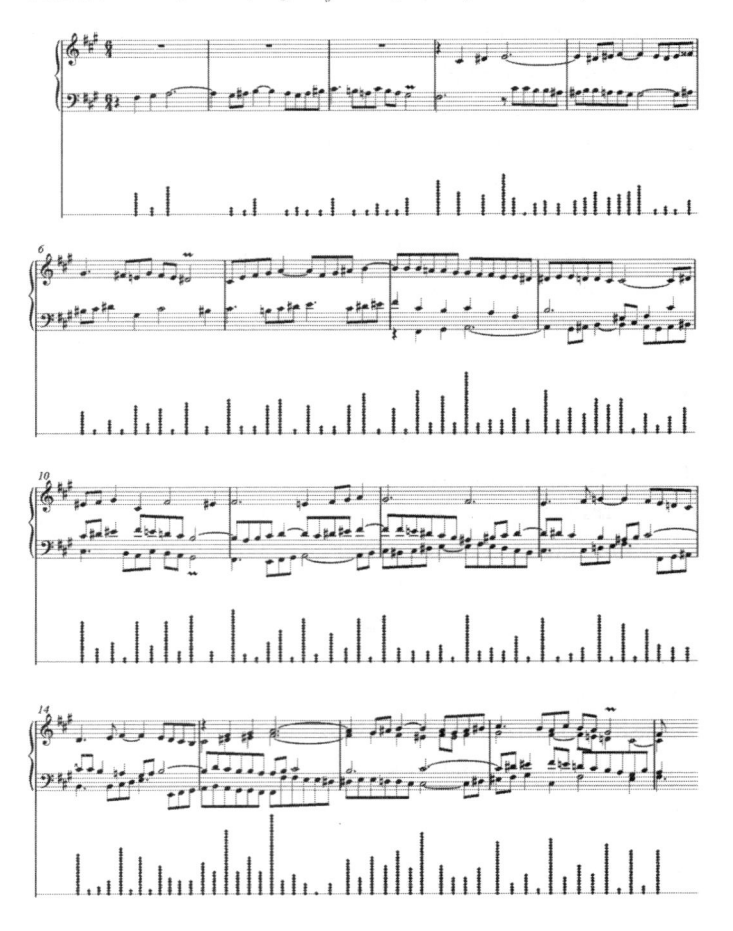

The F♯ minor fugue from Part I of the WTC (Ex. 2-059) has almost exactly the same length (40 measures) as the C♯ minor prelude. The simple structure of the fugue – three expositions, the third (m. 20) also with an inversion of the theme, and a final theme presentation in the descant – is vaulted over by an arc that has the top line rise in contiguous steps from F♯3, its first note, to the B5, the highest one, and then descend again in the same sequential manner. The piece as a whole thereby follows the same path as the theme does by itself. The segment here selected comprises the entire exposition (mm. 1-18). It is a pure F♯ minor complex, because the theme does not modulate and the fourth entry is another dux.

The rhythmic profile furnishes an inkling of the rhythmic complexity of this fugue. As already described in the analysis of the single-voice theme (p. 139 above), both the entry intervals and the positions of the rhythmic weights are organized seemingly independently of the 6/4 meter. With the counterpoint composed predominantly of eighths from m. 4 on, the weights increase even on the light and lightest beats. A glance at the beginning of the fourth accolade reveals rhythmic densities of a kind that never occur in the C♯ minor prelude. It is all but impossible to detect a 6/4 meter here.

Notes on the Rhythm Score

The component »Sound« (Ex. 2-060) in the thematic expositions of the four voices exhibits the already mentioned irregular rhythms within identical structures. Upon the entry of the chains of sigh figures constituting the counterpoint, the tonal entry rhythms of all the voices add up to a dense, nearly uninterrupted texture of eighths. The weights on the entry rhythms extend from 1 to 8. The eight value, which later on, too, is rarely exceeded (descant mm. 22-23. alto mm. 32-33, bass mm. 37-38, final chord), always falls on the third note of the theme, so that, because of the accumulation of the voices and all the components, the highest weight grades always occur here (mm. 10, 14, 21, 27).

The component »Pitch« contributes greatly to the enormous rhythmic complexity of the F♯ minor fugue. Since the first counterpoint consists of pairs of repeated eighths, the pitch changes have a rhythm of quarters that occur in syncopated positions. A doubled value accrues to the thusly prolonged pitches, so that this transversal rhythm actually shows to advantage. The crest notes provide reinforcement, underscoring the melodic-rhythmic contour of the theme (as well as of the counter-voices).

The phrasing of the parts, too, contributes to the overall impression of a composition hardly bound by meter. In the theme, the ascending (at the end also falling) triads, tetra- and pentachords are the decisive criterion for the beginning of the mostly short phrases. That the rise in m. 2 from the 10th eighth on (G♯-A♯-B♯-C♯) is thematic appears from the voices of the interludes, which time and again enact the upbeat rhythm of ♪♪♪|♩., mostly in stretto imitation. The harmonic motion is relatively lively in this fugue, certainly by comparison with the C♯ minor prelude. Taken by itself, too, the harmonic rhythm bears little similarity to the ›normal‹ accents of the 6/4 meter, excepting only the interlude in m. 13ff. and the hemiola in m. 17.

Ex. 2-061

What is most interesting is the large number of suspensions and anticipations (Ex. 2-061), as these are always notes unrelated to the chords and hence dissonant, which in the case of suspensions coincide regularly with stressed, in that of anticipations with unstressed beats. All thusly qualified notes, which fulfill the function of harmonic accents, are found, slightly set off, beneath the fourfold-weighted notes of the harmonic change system.

Ex. 2-060   Bach, WTC I, Fugue F♯ Minor, Exposition (Rhythm Score)

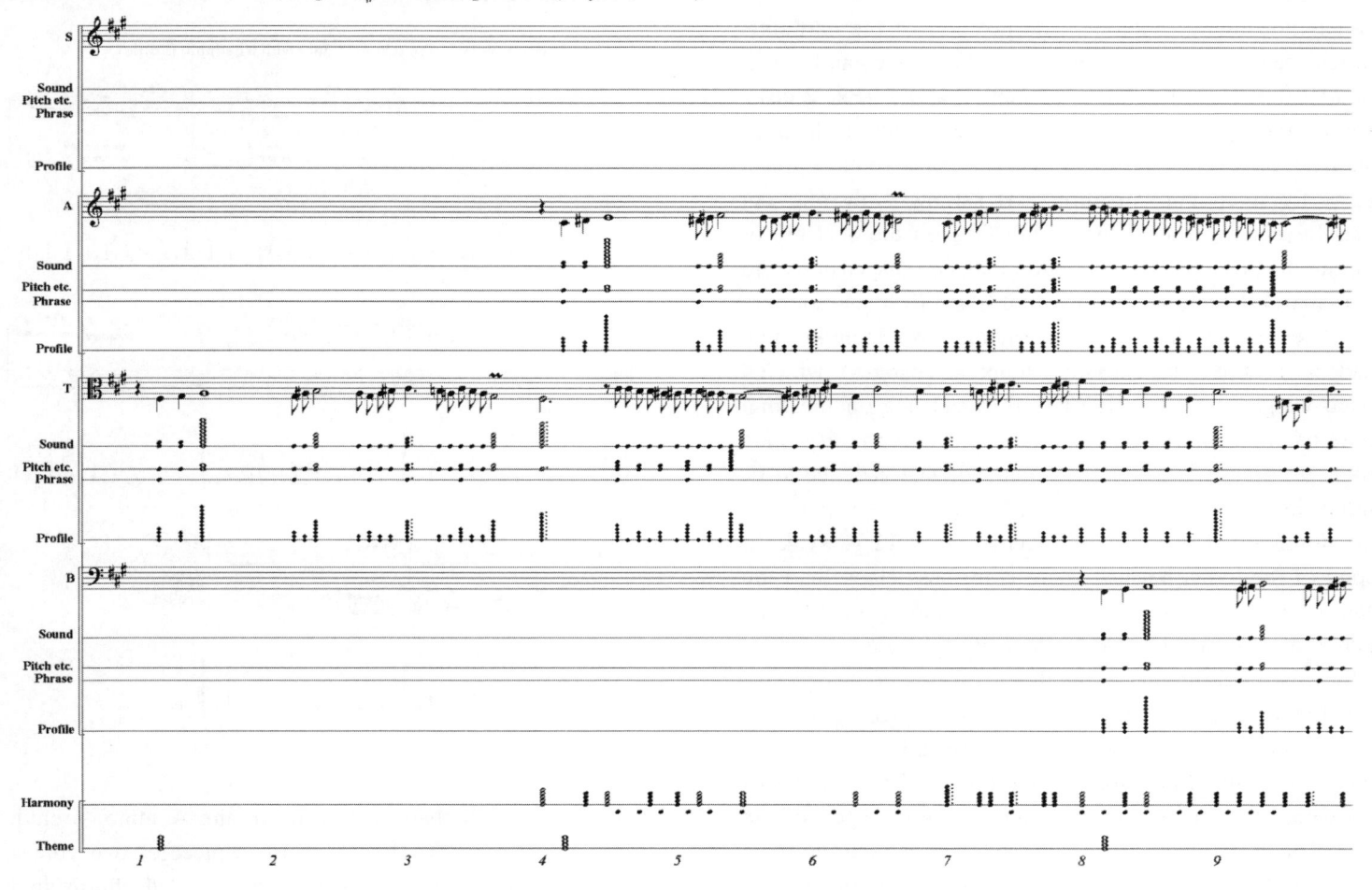

(Continuation)

The distinction between suspensions (S) and anticipations (A) is not always obvious. The position of the harmonic accent depends on it, however. The difference can be well demonstrated on the voices in mm. 8 and 9 (Ex. 2-061). Below the upper voice, which is shaped like a chain of sighs, I have entered a smoothed version of this voice, correctly fitted into the three-part setting. Now one can clearly register whether an eighth falls on the beat (S) or before the beat (A). The alteration between suspensions and anticipations occurs during the fourth and fifth quarter.

The line of the harmonic rhythm also includes five cadences (above the harmonic function changes), which I have weighted differently. The first cadence on the final note of the single-voice thematic exposition has the value of 1, because it is not yet harmonized. The cadence to C♯ minor in m. 7 has the value of 2, because it takes place on the dominant. The F♯ minor cadence in m. 11 is weak, in spite of the tonic, because there is no bass clause and the fourth suspension diminishes the concluding effect. The penultimate cadence (of our segment) coincides unexpectedly with the third note of the theme (as dux in the descant) (m. 15). But once again the bass clause is missing and the counterpoints seem to want to cover over this tonic entry; a value of 2 should therefore be appropriate. The last cadence, which concludes the exposition, is the strongest of the five. The entry of the tonic is preceded by a hemiolic measure, and the rhythmic condition quiets down in other ways as well. But there is no bass clause here either. If one compares this cadence with the final cadence of the fugue as a whole, the difference in degree will be plain at once. The cadence in m. 18 therefore gets a value of 3, whereas the conclusion in m. 40 should be accorded the top value of 4 (not seen in the example).

The F♯ minor fugue is one of the finest and most unusual compositions of the entire double cycle. Its rhythm contributes much to this, which, in spite of the stately tempo, exhibits a very rich inner life. Events occasioned by the components often crowd together to distances of mere eighths, so that even on the lightest beats the rhythmic weights occasionally pile up to as many as nine points. The 6/4 meter is at times totally lost sight of, especially in the presentations of the themes. Only toward the end of the fugue, where, in a final interlude, a whole-measure unit, derivable from the first counterpoint, is sequenced in thirds, the 6/4 time does emerge unobstructed from the rhythmic weave.

By comparison with this fugue, the previously discussed C♯ minor prelude, likewise written in 6/4 time, is rhythmically very simple. Isometry in the binary-ternary meter reigns from beginning to end, which endows the piece with a calmly swaying motion as in a siciliana or a barcarole. It is the rhythm, rather than the meter, that accounts for this difference in character.

Prelude A minor (9/8)

Ex. 2-062 Bach, WTC I, Prelude A Minor (with Rhythmic Profile)

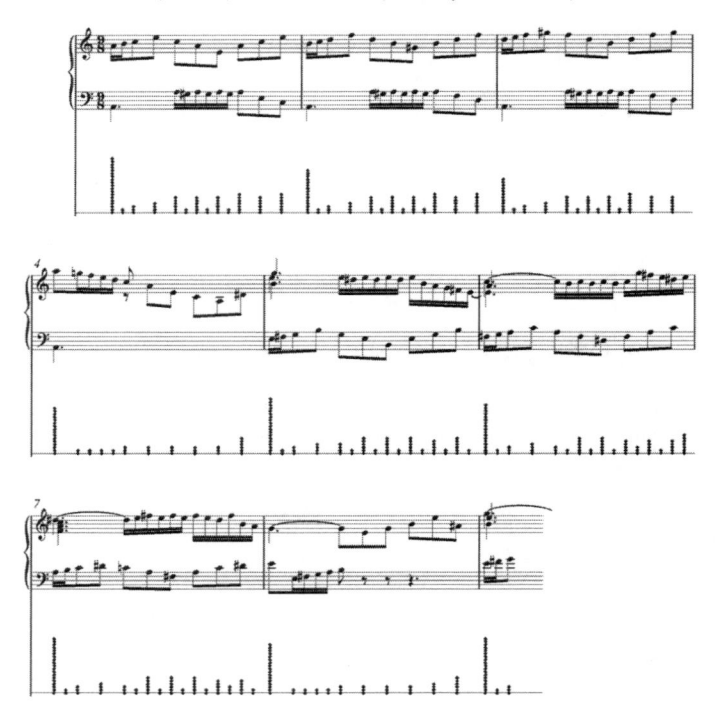

Consisting of 28 bars in 9/8 meter, the A minor prelude from Part I of WTC (Ex. 2-062) is a piece of two voices, which are sometimes augmented by isolated chords in a pianistic manner. Its design is that of a single extended cadence: four bars I, five bars V, four bars modulation to III, followed by ten bars of return to I. Since the A minor regained in m. 22 ›misses‹ the basic form of the tonic (the bass has a third), four additional bars are needed for the perfect cadence (m. 26) and another three for a (plagal) affirmation of the tonic.

Much as with the C♯ minor prelude, the segment shown in Ex. 2-062 can be regarded as the exposition with a twofold presentation of the theme: the descant commences, the bass counterpoints; after four bars, the voices are switched and slightly varied. The division into segments of four bars and the subject's filling exactly one measure make for isometry from the start. In the rhythmic profile, the accentual condition of the 9/8 meter stands out. The rhythmic weights on the first ten ♪ are as follows:

```
∴  .  .  :  .  .  :  .  .  ∴
20 3  4  6  6  6  7  6  7  18
```

The motive mode of this prelude is somewhat static, at least at the start. The (interrupted) pedal point on A in the first four measures fits in with that. Stereotypical motif repetitions and a marked underlining of the main beats add some traits of a toccata.

Ex. 2-063 Bach, WTC I, Prelude A Minor (Rhythm Score)

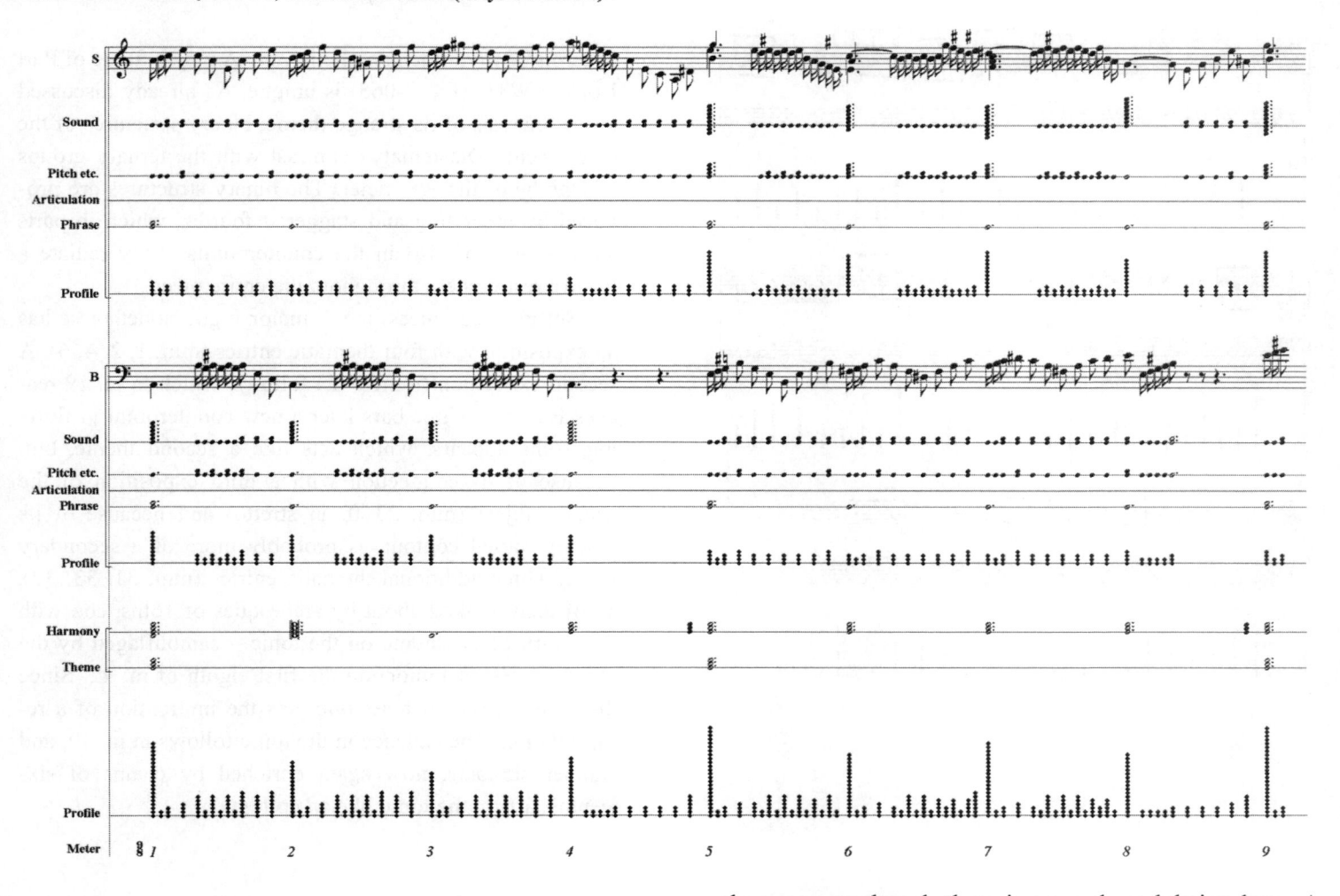

Notes on the Rhythm Score

The component »Sound« (Ex. 2-063) shapes the profile of the main rhythm of this prelude almost single-handedly, inasmuch as the weak ♪ on the *One* of the first voice are compensated by the strong entries in the second. The four chords in the descant are registered as additional entries below the line (in the second chord, the E4 is not sounded again but is tied to the preceding 16th).

The rhythm in the system »Pitch« deviates from the basic rhythm of the tonal entries only insofar as the crest notes in the first four bars produce slight accents and in the second four bars the chords are added. While the latter weight the *One* of the measure, the former fall consistently on the off-beat – except for the last bar of both semi-phrases, where they come on the *One*. Even so, the off-beat crest notes bring about a noticeable rhythmic animation in the otherwise uniform measures.

The harmonic rhythm almost exclusively marks the complete measures; these changes are weighted with the value 3. The dominantic diminished seventh chord entering in m. 2 over the pedal point counts also in the following measure. The pedal point itself is registered with the value 1, both at the beginning and in the two measures where the A is in dissonance with the harmony sounding above it. The D♯4 on the 9th ♪ of the fourth measure (and analogously the A♯4 in the eighth bar) merit the weight of a harmonic change, even though there is no real modulation here: A minor and E minor are starkly juxtaposed, only tentatively mediated by an intervening double dominant.

A very clear and simple rhythm meets us in the A minor prelude of WTC I. It is largely adapted to, or productive of, the weight distribution of the 9/8 meter. This is true also of the rest of the piece.

Ex. 2-064

The concluding phase is interesting, as here, in a last major melodic turn before the tonic is reached (mm. 23 ff.), rhythm is produced by crest notes (Ex. 2-064). Here one can observe how subtle rhythmic irritations come about through a shift in the melodic contour. In this cadence-like passage, the crest notes are regularly preceded by an upward-leaping fourth. The fourth time, however, the latter enters one ♪ later, so that the skewed value of 7 comes up.

Ex. 2-065   Bach, WTC I, Fugue A Major, Exposition (with Rhythmic Profile)

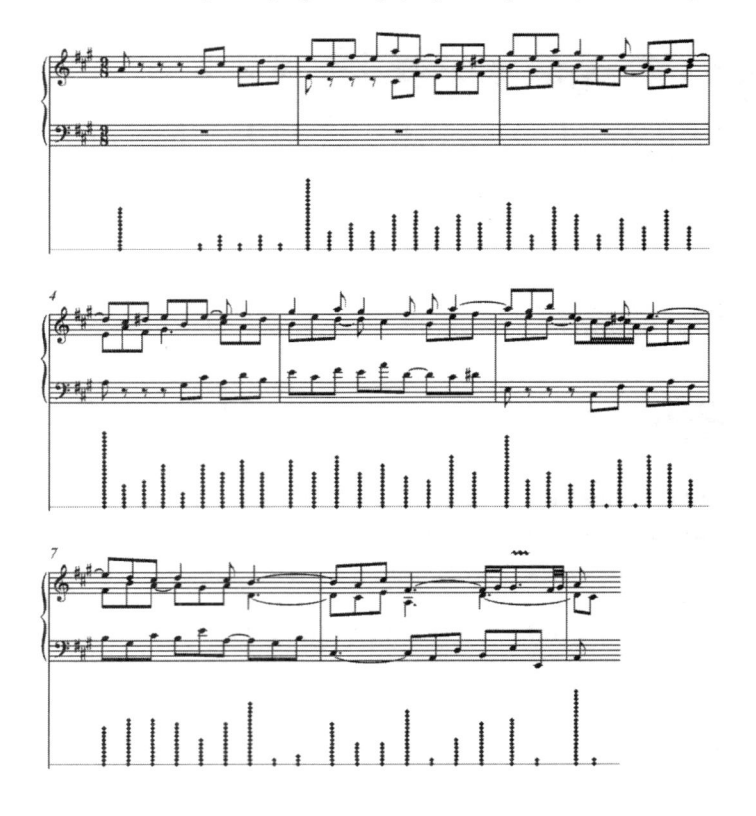

Fugue A major (9/8)

In terms of rhythmic complexity, the A major fugue of Part I of the WTC (Ex. 2-065) is unique. As already discussed in the analysis of its strange theme, binary structures of the component »Diastematy« contrast with the ternary groups of eighths of the 9/8 meter. The binary structures are produced by ascending and staggered fourths, which in parts are determinant also in the counterpoints. They radiate a bizarre restlessness throughout the entire piece.

Set in three voices, the A major fugue nonetheless has an exposition with four thematic entries (mm. 1, 2, 4, 6). A second exposition (mm. 9 ff.) follows, which in m. 19 reaches E major. Three bars later a new counterpoint in flowing 16ths appears, which acts like a second theme, but, because of its connection with a third exposition of the actual subject (mm. 23 ff. in stretto) and because of its quickly varied contour, is probably more of a secondary voice. Three additional thematic entries (mm. 31, 33, 39), all of them ranked about by arabesques of 16ths, end with the return of the theme on the tonic – camouflaged by the chord on VI (F♯ minor) on the first eighth of m. 42. Since the 16ths break off here, one gets the impression of a recapitulation. The cadence in the tonic follows in m. 49, and another six bars, now again enriched by chains of sixteenths, affirm the tonic like an epilogue.

Ex. 2-066   Bach, WTC I, Fugue A Major, Exposition (Rhythm Score)

Our example shows only the exposition of mm. 1-9. The rhythmic profile resembles a turbulent play of waves, whose crests have the distance of 1, 2 or 3 eighths. The 9/8 meter is completely hidden. Only with the cadence to the tonic, commencing in the third 3rd of m. 7, does the rhythm allow groups of 3/8 and thus the 9/8 meter to become vaguely recognizable.

Notes on the Rhythm Score

The transcription of the piano score in three voices (S, A, B), omitting the bar lines and all note beams and ties (Ex. 2-066), gives us a good picture of the free flow of the voices, which with all their rhythmic bizarreness, extend in a well-planned arc, over, respectively, eight (S) and seven (A) bars. The technique of the transcription also dictates that the trill on the penultimate note of the theme, partly written out by Bach, be reduced to its original rhythmic form.

For the component »Sound« in this segment (mm. 1-9), the ♪ is selected as the smallest value, even though the alto already announces the ♪ that emerge in such massive numbers later on. In an analysis of the entire fugue, the ♪ would have to be taken as the smallest value; the ♪ suffices for our purpose here.

The component »Pitch« simply doubles the rhythm of the tone entries, since no note repetitions occur. A weighty component, »Diastematy,« is added by the crest notes, included here on the »Pitch« system. For in both the subject and, in part, also in the counterpoints, the crest tones fall on the second note of the thematic interval of the fourth and thus give additional emphasis to their natural accent.

While the system »Articulation« shows only the head notes of the theme – staccato notes set off by rests – plus the trill in the soprano, the line »Phrasing« is replete with relevant markings. As already described, the subject is very finely structured: the head note is followed by five staggered melodic fourths. This always ascending interval has the function of a micro-phrase and thus has a structuring function. It reminds me of the »Wohin?« motif in the bass-plus-chorus aria No. 24 of the *St. John's Passion*, which we will look at more closely a little later. What is made quite clear there by the prosody of the word »wohin?« (where-to?), namely that the second note of the ascending fourth carries the stress, can be presumed as well for the theme of the A major fugue. Hence the structuration points are always on the second note of the sequenced fourth, so that this note is regularly distinguished by four components: »Sound,« »Pitch,« »Diastematy« (crest note) and »Phrase.« By comparing the rhythmic profiles of the three voices, one can see how the thus emphasized high fourth notes follow each other, often in close imitation (at distances of one ♪). That makes for heavy weights on individual eighths, regardless of whether they are located on heavy or light beats. Toward the end of our segment, larger phrases also crop up, which, in the soprano in mm. 6ff., consist of the rhythm ♪♪♪♪♪; alto and bass refer to it by free imitation in mm. 7f.

The theme always enter on the full beat – as they are triple-voiced, they are valued at 3 – and thus are the only events to support the prescribed 9/8 meter. The harmonic changes, on the other hand, are integrated into the very tight polyphonic texture and thus contribute much to the extreme rhythmic complexity of the fugue. Most of the harmonic changes take place at the pace of eighths, a few at that of quarters. Only at the start of the cadence in m. 7 do the harmonic progressions at a pace of ♩. or greater, typical for the 9/8 meter, begin to emerge.

Below the line in the system »Harmony,« I have noted the suspensions, of which there are several (m. 5 has three suspensions in a row at a rhythm of ♪). To be added are the cadences: two weak ones (m. 4 and 6) have one weight each, the strong final cadence has two.

The total profile resulting from all of the components (see Ex. 2-065) reveals the high degree of rhythmic complexity in this fugue. In addition, it makes impressively clear that the metric concept of 9/8 is quite overwhelmed by the labyrinthine tangle of the component rhythms.

The tension-laden contrasts created by the rhythms of the three voices, which are already heterometric within themselves, and of the compositional components »Harmony« and »Texture,« can, of course, not be found in the profile. The following diagram may convey some impression of that, in that there the rhythmic profiles of the three voices, as well as the rhythm of the harmonic changes and the theme entries, are set closely one beneath the other (Ex. 2-067).

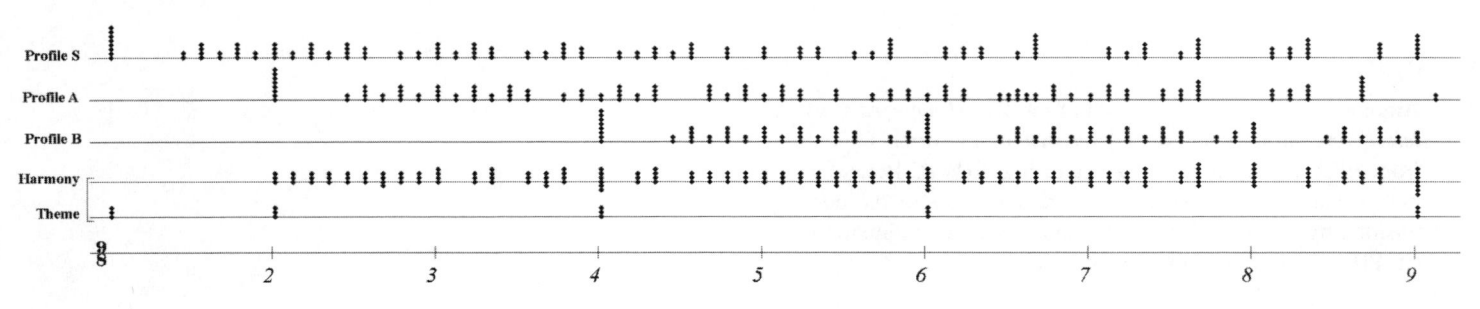

Ex. 2-067 Fugue A Major, Exposition (Rhythmic Profiles)

Summary

The comparative analyses of two 6/4 and two 9/8 pieces from Bach's *Well-Tempered Clavier* have made clear that the components »Sound,« »Pitch,« »Diastematy,« »Articulation« (plus embellishment), »Phrase,« »Harmony« (including suspensions and anticipations) and »Texture« (theme entries) shape not only the rhythmic conditions but the metrical ones as well. Whereas the time signatures in the preludes in C♯ minor and A minor appear prominently in the rhythmic profiles and produce a self-contained static character, in the fugues F♯ minor and A major they are lost in the texture of component rhythms and yield to a free, dynamic movement. These differences are manifest without the accentual relations, respectively, of the ternary-binary and ternary-ternary meters even being included. All four analyses were conducted using the same criteria, these being purely rhythmical in terms of the component theory.

The preludes and fugues compared with one another are not adjacent in the *Well-Tempered Clavier* (though they would be excellent matches): they were selected solely because of their identical time signatures as a *tertium comparationis*. Generalizations regarding the structure of preludes or fugues are not to be derived from this. As has already been shown in the analysis of the 48 fugal themes of the *Well-Tempered Clavier*, there are certainly fugues that are pronouncedly isometric – whose rhythm has, so to speak, been assimilated to a meter. Conversely, preludes could be found whose motive mode is dynamic rather than static.

The results are thus to be confined to the four cases discussed here. Nevertheless they can be generalized as having furnished proof that meters are not merely *set* but *shaped*. Rhythm leads to meter, not vice versa. The degree to which rhythmic conditions approximate metrical patterns depends on the choices of the composing subject. Composers in this way also determine the general character of the composition, which in turn depends largely on the work's rhythmic motion. In the C♯ minor prelude, the rhythm corresponds to the type of a siciliana or a barcarole, while the A minor one approximates the character of a toccata. The F♯ minor fugue conveys a brooding or melancholy mood, while the A major fugue is a bizarre presto-piece that points forward to scherzos of Haydn or Beethoven.[29]

---

[29] Among the numerous recordings of the *Well-Tempered Clavier*, I was strongly impressed by that of Friedrich Gulda's from 1972. Especially in the A major fugue (WTC I), he does not hesitate to bring out the extreme character of the composition by means of fast tempi and audacious accentuations. Cf. PHILIPS CD 446545-2 and 446548-2.

Chromatic Fantasia

Bach's famous *Chromatic Fantasia* in D minor for harpsichord, which is followed by a three-part fugue in the same key, has not to date been scrutinized for its rhythmics. Unlike his son Carl Philipp Emanuel Bach, who cancels the bar lines in his fantasias, Bach realizes the fantasia character to which the title points *within* an unvaried meter. Neither in the preluding first part of the fantasia nor in the recitative-like second one is the 4/4 meter ever abandoned as far as the notation is concerned. That is true even of the first two bars, which precede the beginning proper like the separating of a curtain. Two tonal gestures appear in two undulating scale runs that seem positively to hang in midair. They begin and end with rests on full beats (Ex. 2-068).

Ex. 2-068 Bach, *Chromatic Fantasia* mm. 1–2

Eight emphasized notes within these two waves – starting and ending notes, crest and keel tones – mark the outlines of a simple two-voiced cadence:

| D5 | E5 | | G5 | F5 |
| D4 | C#4 | | A4 | D4 |

If thereby the key of D minor (which Bach incidentally writes as D Dorian without B♭) is staked out, the runs of 32nds point forward to a series of similar virtuoso passages in the course of the fantasia. Our concern here is with these highly dynamic and rhythmically interesting scales.

The structure of the first part, extending to m. 49, is revealed among other things by the rhythmic occurrences. Triplet and duplet subdivisions alternate: mm. 3-20 triplet or sextuplet 16ths, mm. 21-26 duplet 32nds, mm. 26-30 triplet 16ths (including probably the first arpeggio passage), mm. 31-49 again duplet 32nds, which continue in the second arpeggio part and merge into duplet 16ths with corresponding arpeggios. Then follows the second part of the Fantasia, marked »Recitativo.« Its principal distinguishing feature consists of mostly short, speech-like phrases, which, much as in a *secco recitativo*, are interspersed by frequent chords. Both parts of the fantasia include fast passages, of which three exhibit a special rhythmic structure.

The passage starting in m. 17 (ex. 2-069) concludes the first triplet section of the first part. The single-voiced run is reproduced in our example initially with Bach's own original beams (in accordance with the 4/4 meter) and in two systems (treble and bass clef), and then in simplified form with note heads without stems or beams and in a single line system. The latter is made possible by the fact that, except for the final note with the mordent, only one durational value is present: the triplet 16th.

Rhythm is built solely by the melodic contour (»Diastematy«). If one considers only the crest notes as structuring points, a rhythm of the partial phrases presents itself that consists of very different durations athwart the meter, whether the latter is regarded as 4/4, or, because of the pervasive triplets, as 24/16 time.

At the start of the passage, six triplet 3 ♪ groups mark the eighths positions, which to that extent still coincide with the meter. This is followed by a group of seven ♪ (5+2) and then by two groups of twelve ♪ (10+2), so that here the first deviation from the meter occurs. The latter is presently forgotten altogether in that short, descending and upwardly sequenced scale sections with the durational values of 5, 5, 5, 5 and 6 (5+1) ♪ follow each other. The rest is again fitted into the meter in the form of triplet triads at normal eights (♪♪♪ = ♩).

Noteworthy here are above all the 5 ♪ units. Bach could have set them as quintuplets, but then we would have had a comparatively simple rhythmic structure lacking the wild, dynamic effect of these four measures.

The passage of duplets immediately following the first section of triplets (Ex. 2-070) comprises exactly six measures. The uniform durational value here is the 32nd. As the transcription into stem- and beamless notes shows clearly, this fast, single-voiced run describes a simple inverted and slightly undulating arc, which is retraced as a melodic line. The crest and keel notes of the small undulations add some rhythmic motion to the otherwise wholly uniform tonal process.[30]

Bach's drawing of the beams marks units of eight 32nds having the value of a quarter note each. The rhythmic measure, on the other hand, is determined predominantly by ternary units, as can be gathered from the frequent partial phrases with durational values from 6 to 3 ♪, occasionally also 9 to 12 ♪. To these one may add the

Ex. 2-069 Bach, *Chromatic Fantasia* mm. 17–20

---

[30] Hławiczka has already drawn attention to this passage under the aspect of a »confounding of the proportion 6 : 5.« See Karl Hławiczka, »Die rhythmische Verwechslung,« *Musikforschung*, 11 (1958), 33-49; p. 47.

Ex. 2-070   Bach, *Chromatic Fantasia* mm. 21–26

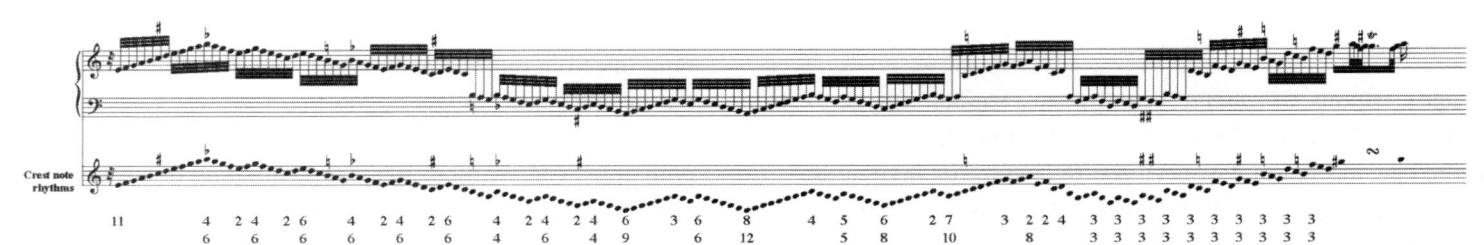

ascending initial run, whose eleven notes, together with the ♪-rest, adds up to the value of 12 ♪.

The most spectacular features, however, are the ten groups of 3 ♪, which directly precede the final upbeat trill – simplified in the transcription as a quarter plus turn mark. Here, at the latest, the listener will suspect an abandonment of the time signature, i.e., a *senza misura* episode. Bach, however, keeps to the ›law‹ of the meter, because he values the tension between the metrical time, which remains in effect quasi in the background, and the rhythmic reality actually realized by the listener. The fact that the subtlest of processes are at work here is also evident from the triplet 16ths setting in m. 26 (following the last note of our example), which exactly are *not* identical with the preceding 3 ♪ groups. But it is evidently such super-fine differences that the composer is keen about.

The uniform durational value is the ♪. The six 8 ♪ groups at the beginning thus mark the quarters of the 4/4 time. From the low D on, however, which can be thought of as a latent pedal point, the phrases are extended. In this now upward-pointing sequence, seven or eight notes of the scale are regularly traversed, with the last three notes being promptly repeated, independently of whether seven or eight degrees were heard just before. The result are the »skewed« proportions of 10:8 or 11:8 ♪. These proportions would remain the same, even if the division were based on the distances between the crest notes rather than on the number of scale tones.

How a non-analytical, albeit musically sensitive listener perceives this passage can be gleaned from a passage by the music theorist Ernst Kurth:

Ex. 2-071   Bach, *Chromatic Fantasia* mm. 63-69

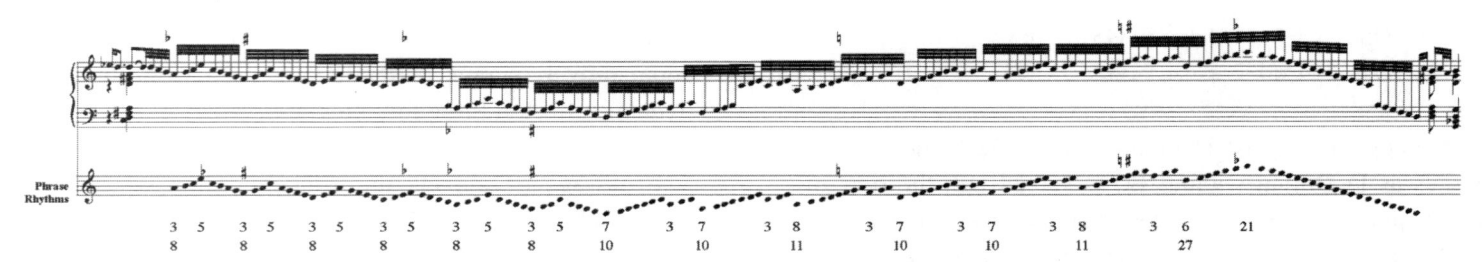

The third passage, this time from the recitative second part of the Fantasia, is particularly suited to our investigation in that here a rhythmic process that is adapted to the meter and another that deviates from it follow each other directly (Ex. 2-071).

Harmonically speaking, the five scale-filled measures contain only the step from the dominant to the tonic in G minor. The dominant is held by an imaginary fermata, and the melody-bearing upper voice finds a sensible continu-

Ex. 2-072

ation at the end (Ex. 2-072). The dominant sound, to be seen as a seventh-ninth chord, is permeated by scales that, besides steps of seconds, contain also minor thirds of the chord: F♯-A, A-C, C-E♭, and once also the augmented second E♭-F♯. These thirds also always involve crest notes, and the ascending scale segments always start on keel tones. Together they form a phrasal rhythm that is indicated in numbers beneath the (once again stem- and beamless) notes of the transcription.

Its content and its power lie in the really melodic, kinetic phenomena spontaneously issuing forth here, the enormous developing tensions of the upward-whirling impetus, which traverses a space of three octaves and whose very climax, of all things, does not fall on a rhythmically strong beat.[31]

Kurth's rather imprecise conception of rhythm is problematic, even though his analyses or descriptions of music can otherwise be read with profit even today. It is exactly not the melodic quality that renders the ascending sequence so remarkably dynamic but the rhythms of the components »Diastematy« (crest and keel tones) and »Phrase« that produce the disturbing overall impression of the passage.[32]

It should be stated again that Bach creates the impression of irrationality by rationally controlled means, or, putting it technically, that he shapes heterometric rhythms on the basis of isometric sequences of pulses and beats. The cited

---

[31] Ernst Kurth, *Grundlagen des linearen Kontrapunkts. Bachs melodische Polyphonie* (Berlin, ²1922), 13.

[32] It was again Hlawiczka (op. cit, 49) who perceived this passage altogether correctly.

examples from Bach's *Chromatic Fantasia* have furthermore made clear that isometry does not have to mean lack of tension. For if isometric sequences of divergent meter clash with one another, the result – produced, *nota bene*, by purely rhythmic means – is a conflictual metric structure. This is illustrated especially by the groups of five within sextuplet 16ths, but also by the groups of three, ten and eleven formed on the basis of 32nds in a 4/4 meter.

From the Brandenburg Concertos

Turning from Bach's hitherto discussed piano literature – restricted to the *Well-Tempered Clavier* and the *Chromatic Fantasia* (without the fugue) – to his instrumental ensemble works – likewise narrowed down to the collection of the *Six Concerts avec plusieurs instruments* called the *Brandenburg Concertos* – entails a considerable increase in structural and thus also rhythmic complexity of composition. On the other hand, the genre of the »concerto« restricts the delight in experimentation. Outbursts into extremely free, i.e., partially heterometric rhythms, such as they are observable in some fugues in the *Well-Tempered Clavier* and in several passages in the *Chromatic Fantasia*, will not be found in the *Brandenburg Concertos*. Independently of that, however, the larger number of voices (the number of instrumentalists varies from 7 to 13) naturally brings with it a proportionate growth in compositional, and, above all, polyphonic diversity, which, in turn, leaves its traces in the rhythm of the pieces.

In what follows, I want to try to address all six of the concertos and each of their movements and to make a rough determination of their rhythmic character. More probing analyses of their rhythm, to be sure, can be undertaken only at selected, especially interesting points. The textual basis, in every case, is the Köthen Version of the concertos, dated 1721 (BWV 1046-1051).

Concerto I (F major)

The generously instrumented first concerto is based above all on the sound of three oboes and three high strings (two violins, one viola). These six instruments are mostly set *colla parte*, though they also depart from, and occasionally even line up against, each other. A violin tuned a minor third higher than normal (»violino piccolo«) reinforces the first violin but also appears solistically in the second (slow) and third (fast) movements and, in the Polonaise (one of the three alternatives of the Minuet movement), has to imitate the sound of a fiddle. Two other instrumentalists contribute to the generally festive and optimistic character of the piece with the sound of two natural horns. The horns sometimes join the oboes, sometimes the strings, but now and then act like exotic birds demanding an independent existence – also, and especially, in rhythmic respects. Their *pièce de résistance* is surely the last trio (in the Menuet), which they, accompanied by three oboes playing in unison, present with a dashing folksiness. That leaves the continuo group, forcefully orchestrated with bassoon, cello, bass and harpsichord. The bass is not figured (except for one passage in the third movement) and participates in the thematic action.

Ex. 2-073 Bach, Brandenburg Concerto I, 1st mov., Beginning

The 1st movement, with its seven ritornellos F, F→C, d, C→a, g→F, F→C and F (capitals: major; minuscules: minor) and its (mostly only hinted-at) episodes, gestures toward the Italian concerto form. Its theme can best be grasped in rhythmic terms. A rhythmic-thematic cell (‚♪♪♪ | ♪) is the point of departure for two motifs that pervade the entire movement in numerous variations (Ex. 2-073).

Already in the first half-measure, which is different in the oboes and the strings, the two starting motifs are exposed (Ex. 2-074): a auxiliary note sequence in 16ths (motif a) and an ascent through the triad in eighths (motif b). Both motifs start after the *One* and end on the *Two* of the alla breve meter. That the motif b derives from the basic rhythm (‚♪♪♪ | ♪) cited above can be recognized immediately from the notes. The component »Diastematy,« however, makes clear that motif a likewise embodies this rhythm: the rhythm of the crest notes of motif a is identical with the rhythm of the entries of motif b. At the same time, of course, the 16ths' entries are dominant in motif a, while motif b is determined by the rhythm of eighths. Even so, there is a partial subterranean identity.

These two motifs keep recurring in ever new variants throughout the 84 measures of the movement. Following the cadence of the first ritornello (m. 6), variants are introduced for both motifs, which function quasi as solo episode motifs (Ex. 2-075). By injecting a progression of seconds (conjuncts) in place of, respectively, the broken triad and the changing-note pendulum, the character of the motifs is slightly altered. In motif a, the crest-tone rhythm (‚♪♪♪ | ♪) is wholly lost, while the motif b suddenly exhibits a proximity to the variant of motif a. If motif a and its variant are combined (as in m. 10), the eighths rhythm of the auxiliary note pendulum settles back into the rhythmic structure. In places like this, moreover, Bach formally demonstrates the process of variant-building (2-076).

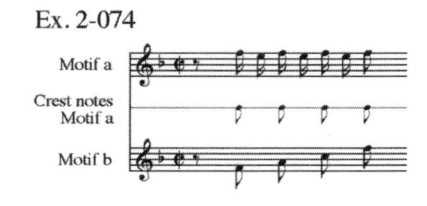

Ex. 2-074

Ex. 2-075

Ex. 2-076 m. 10
Motif a var.
Motif a

Ex. 2-077 m. 20
Motif b var.
Motif b

Ex. 2-078 m. 14
Motif a Original
Motif a Inversion

That is the case also with the analogous combination of motif b with its variant, which Bach presents to his listeners once (Ex. 2-077). The single, upturned, changing note in the variant of motif a (m. 14) evidently derives from a plan to directly juxtapose basic form and inversion at certain points (Ex. 2-078).

With respect to rhythm, this combination provides a reinforcement of the basic thematic rhythm, which is enacted markedly by the four times repeated F major tonic chord. By contrast, the basic rhythm of eights is made to disappear completely by the melodic leveling of motif a on a single tonal degree, which occurs twice in the horns (mm. 29, 32) and once – in the very last bar – in the basses.

In the last two bars of the movement, the horns play their triplet eighths once more, which already at the beginning appear strangely unwieldy in the otherwise organic combination of eighths and sixteenths. Even stranger than the triplets seem to me the sudden cutoffs on a sixteenth note that is attached to a dotted eighth (cf. mm. 2 and 3 in Ex. 2-073). Perhaps these rhythmic extravagances of the two natural horns are simply some fun Bach wanted the musicians to have – unless it is a means of distinguishing the part of the horns from what happens the *tutti* group, since, of course, they are more distinctly audible if they sound in rhythmic conflict with the other voices than if they were interwoven into the overall texture.

These capers, to be sure, do not affect the overall rhythmic character of the first movement, which is determined from beginning to end by the motivic model of the upbeat eighths and 16ths and the countless variants of motifs a and b. Though the rest on the *One* or *Two* of the alla breve meter is frequently passed over in performance, the ever renewed, goal-oriented energy directed at the heavy beats remains dominant and imprints itself upon the senses of the listeners (and players) as the basic motive mode.

The second movement is one of the great Adagios in 3/4 time that Bach was so fond of writing (Ex. 2-079). It opens a temporal field of maximal width and filigreed inner structure. The rhythmic-metric range is determined by the harmony in combination with the phrase structure. Thus the first four measures are shaped by a single harmonic function, the dominant of D minor (the double dominant on the bass note A is to be understood as a transitional chord), which is resolved into the tonic in the fifth bar. There is little difference in the next four measures, which, departing from a D minor instantly made to appear as the dominant (note the E_b6 in the solo violin in m. 5), turns to G minor. The accompaniment underscores these harmonic durations

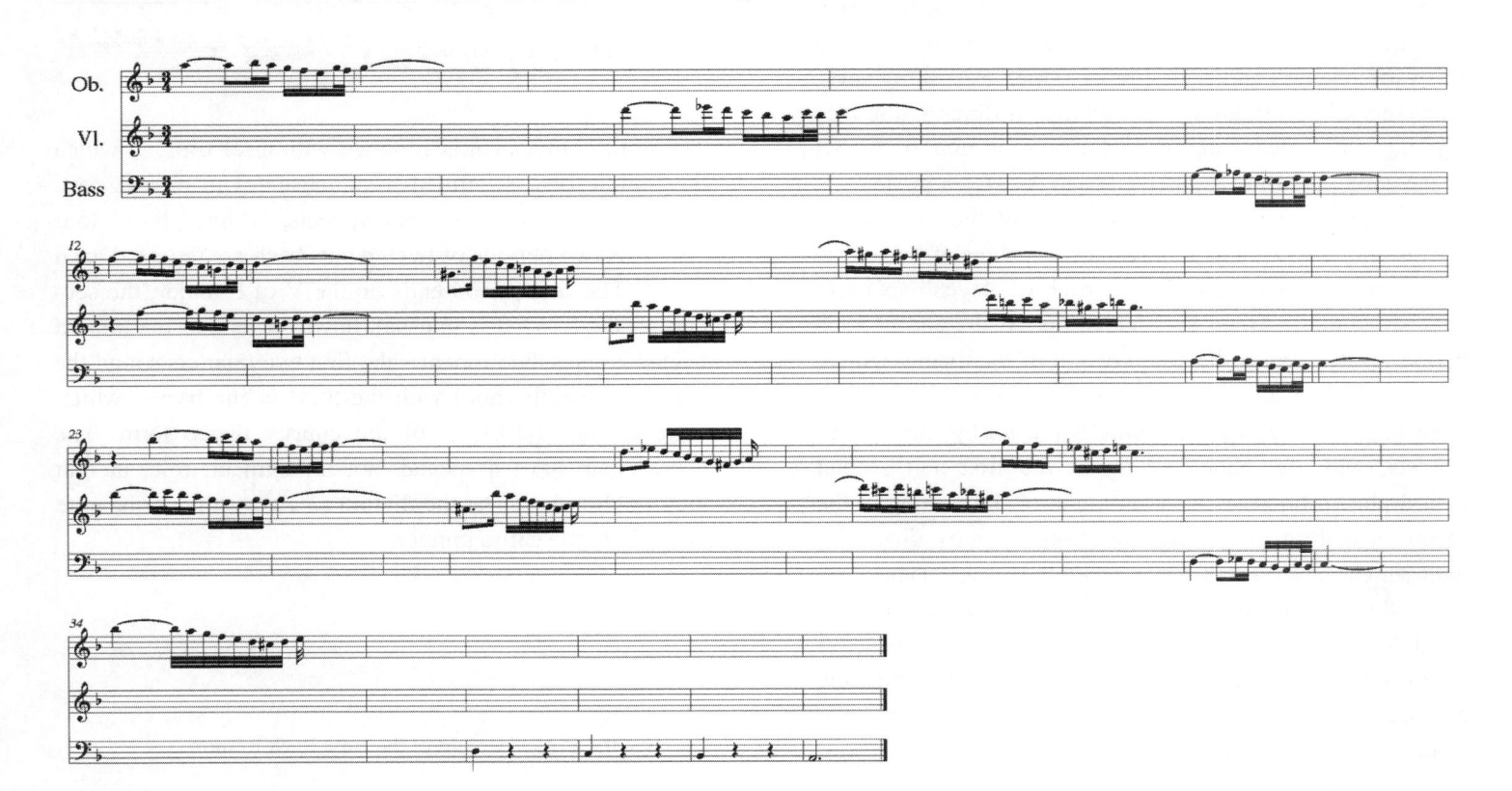

Ex. 2-079 Bach, Brandenburg Concerto I, 2nd mov., Entrances of Soggetti

(twice four bars), in that woodwinds and strings trade places in the second four measures – following their leaders in this, who also take turns: initially the 1st oboe plays a four-bar cantilena, then the solo violin repeats it a fourth higher.

The harmonic durations of four measures contrast with entry distances as small as 32nds in the ornamentally formed cantilenas (shortly before the end we even encounter two 64ths). These are written-out embellishments, but the small note values should be fully counted rhythmically, as proven by the precisely replicated durational relations in the answering phrases. Twice such arabesques stand in a completely augmentative relation to each other, whereby the 32nds, like the 16ths, are raised to the rank of full rhythmic values (Ex. 2-080).

Ex. 2-080

If one takes the tonal entries at intervals of 32nds as the smallest and the changes in harmonic function as the largest durational values, the proportion is 384:1. This (really grotesque) proportional value confirms my initial observation: this Adagio realizes a rhythmic structure that unites, by means of diverse components, extremely wide durational sequences with very narrow tonal entries.

Meanwhile we have not yet begun to consider the rhythmic microstructure, for example in the arabesques, and also in the harmonic details. We do not have the space here to do this exhaustively. The cantilenas would yield a rhythmic profile that in its strong accents would emphasize the meter, but heterometric structures in the weak ones. The harmony, besides does not at all retain the slow rhythm of the beginning; on the contrary, the distances between harmonic functions diminish to quarters and eighths, fleetingly even down to 16ths (mm. 19, 29). To be added are numerous dissonances and cross-grains, which as striking special events all contribute to the rhythmic differentiation (see e.g., the simultaneous diminished octaves in mm. 9, 20, 31, or the unprepared-for augmented triad A-F-C♯ in m. 35).

As one can tell from the overview of the main voice entries (Ex. 2-079), which is also a conspectus of forms, the movement is divided into three periods of eleven bars each, with an epilogue of six bars added on. At the end of each period always stands the bass version of the theme, which, as the epilogue shows, is a four-bar phrase abridged to three bars. Before that the theme is played by the descant soloists, with the oboe leading in the first and second period, the violin starting out in the third. Interesting in the second and third period are the changing entry distances, with which the soloists imitate each other: 1 ♩, 3 ♩ and 2 ♩. Altogether this makes for a considerable parallelism between the three periods, so that their total duration of 33 quarters each is experienced as a replete temporal unit. One can see from this analysis that the border between rhythm and form is a fluid one.

Ex. 2-081   Bach, Brandenburg Concerto I, 3rd mov., Beginning

The third movement (Ex. 2-081) resembles the first, almost as though it were its triple variant. Especially the auxiliary note motif entering in 16ths at the start of the measure in the horns is derived from the first movement (motif a). Separate from it is a second motif (motif b) sounding in the oboes and the strings, which begins on a weak beat and, similarly to the basic rhythm in the first movement, leads as an upbeat to the *Two* and the *One* of the 6/8 time. This is used in the concertino passages (which are more prominent here than in the first movement) for spinning-out processes (see. e.g., m. 30).

Deserving special attention are the hemiolas at the end of the ritornello theme – which, incidentally, is modeled quite regularly on the sequence introduction, spinning-out 1 (from m. 4), spinning-out 2 (from m. 8) and epilogue (mm. 12-17). The hemiolas are played by the *tutti* orchestra, while the horns oppose a 6/8 rhythm (♪♪♪♪♪). The hemiola-type division in ♩♩♩ (as against ♩. ♩.) is almost entirely due to the component »Phrase« (emphasized in Ex. 2-082 by the beams); only at the end, the component rhythm »Sound« (♪. ♪♪. ♪♪. ♪) is added (not included in the example).

Ex. 2-082   3rd mov., mm. 12-15, Hemiolas and Non-Hemiolas

The fourth movement is a minuet with three trios, of which the middle one is entitled »Polonaise.« The minuet part, written in 3/4 meter without upbeats, is thus played four times. Its two periods of twelve bars each are repeated each time.[33] The first period ends on the V of F major, the second on the I. What is unusual, however, is that the minuet begins in the subdominant – the first two quarters sound the F major seventh chord with the third in the bass – which suggests the stylization of the courtly dance form. The horns again have a special, not un-comical, role, in that they stubbornly repeat the rhythm ♩♪♪♪♪ on the same note throughout the entire minuet.

---

[33] See the Critical Report of the New Bach Edition.

Ex. 2-083   Bach, Brandenburg Concerto I, Menuet

mm. 1-12

mm. 13-24

The rhythmic-metric condition of the minuet, too, makes it appear likely that the type »Minuet« is here being parsed in a learned manner rather than a genuine minuet being played. This can be made clear by a juxtaposition of the two periods' main voices (Ex. 2-083). The parallelism of the two periods is patent, the first twelve bars being essentially repeated a fifth higher in the second. The contour of both periods describes a slight descent after an undulating beginning, followed by a steep ascent with a brief concluding formula.

What is decisive for the rhythmic-metric structure, however, is the point in time at which the ascent begins: m. 9 in the first period, a measure earlier in the second. The regular internal division into thrice four bars is thus underlined in the first period, whereas in the second the moved-up trill produces a division into 4+3+5 bars.

A further detail that would be reflected in a rhythmic profile of the voices concerns the crest note in the third to the last bar. Because of the leaping intervals before and after it, this C6 has much more weight than the analogous C5 in the first period. The hemiolic structure of mm. 22 and 23, latent already in the first period, is thereby clearly emphasized and the concluding effect thus enlarged.

The artificial, inordinate character of this ›minuet‹ also manifests itself in the imitation of the main voice in the bass in mm. 2f. (Ex. 2-084). In the first period, the bass part is additionally formed as a continuous melodic drop of more than two octaves (E♭4→C2). One can recognize therein a means of covering up the caesuras of the main voice that occur regularly every four bars – a further rhythmically/ metrically relevant phenomenon pointing to the composer's artful intention.[34]

Bach proceeds quite analogously in the D minor Trio for two oboes and bassoon, which closely resembles the minuet: the once again downward-directed bass part of the first part is superimposed upon the four-bar structure of the main voice. In the second part even the beginning of the recapitulation in m. 21 is covered over in this way (cf. the bass mm. 14-24).

The »Polonaise,« for strings only, is again in F major. It is a little genre piece in 3/8 time with a clear separation of melody and accompaniment. The melody, presented by the violins, consists mainly of 16ths, linked into pairs by slurs and thus adapted to the nearly pervasive rhythm of eighths of the accompanying parts. Since the basses are partly conducted like a bourdon voice, the result is a folk music-like manner that lets the melody-carrying voice sound like a fiddle. The rhythmically nearly monotone piece has, besides the uniform 16ths and eighths, only occasional dotted eighths on the second beat and, surprisingly, a four-bar insertion of minstrel-like virtuosity, in which the otherwise predominating thirds are filled up by dactylic rhythms composed of 16ths plus two 32nds.

The last recapitulation of the minuet is preceded by a Trio for two horns and three oboes playing in unison, written in 2/4 time and F major key. The piece, composed of two 16-bar repeat periods, has the simplicity of folk music, consisting solely of quarters, eighths and 16ths without any dotted notes or ties. The horn setting is playfully light and only occasionally enlivened polyphonically by brief imitations. The oboe part has the character of a bass voice (see especially the beginning of the second part), although it occupies the one-line octave and occasionally rises above the horns (mm. 23f.).

Ex. 2-084   mm. 1-12, Soprano and Bass

[34] The metric superimposition is all the more obvious the faster the minuet is played. Cf. the arguments of Klaus Miehling in his study *Das Tempo in der Musik von Barock und Vorklassik. Die Antwort der Quellen auf ein umstrittenes Thema*, improved and greatly enlarged new edition (Wilhelmshaven: Noetzel, 2003), 274.

Concerto II (F major)

With its colorful orchestration, including trumpet, recorder, oboe and violin as concertino and strings plus basso continuo as ripieno, the second Brandenburg Concerto is of a festive and cheerful mood, from which only the second of the three movements with its melancholy *affettuoso* tone deviates. The fast outer movements are in duple (2/2 and 2/4), the middle movement in triple (3/4) time. In a rhythmic-metric respect, isometry rules supreme, with no ›problematic‹ rhythmic processes going contrary to the regular metric flow. The fast movements are dance-like and spirited, while the D minor middle movement is somber and sluggish.

Ex. 2-085 Bach, Brandenburg Concerto II, 1st mov., Ritornello Theme

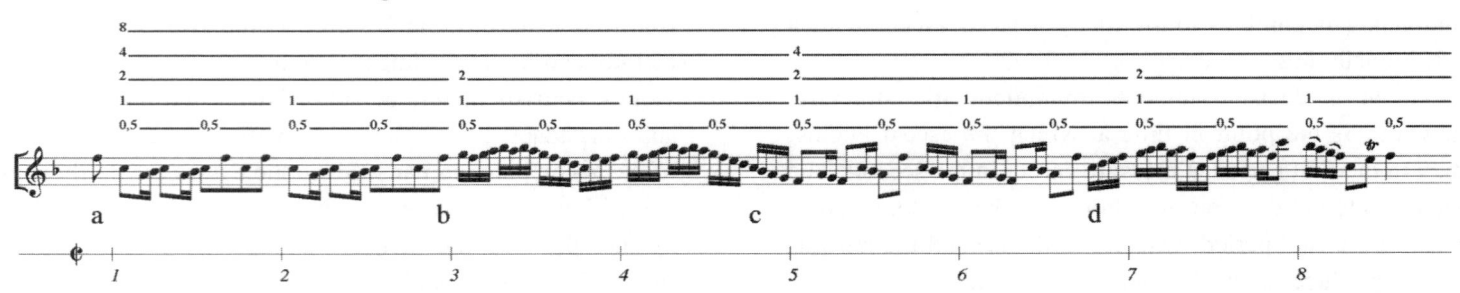

The opening movement presents a memorable ritornello theme (Ex. 2-085), whose sequence of periods seems downright mathematical: 8 : 4 : 2 : 1 : ½. The four lines of the theme (a, b, c, d), all of which exhibit internal repetitions, are, however, pervaded by processes of intensification and condensation, which orient the entire phrase toward its end. In this process, the component-shaped rhythms play a major role.

The phrase is self-contained, the C5 constitutes a center, from which things go up or down, with brashly emphasized upbeats (F5) or light fillips of 16ths (A4-B♭4). Except for the first upbeat, the phrase b consists entirely of 16ths (coming from the basses in mm. 1 and 2), which take the form of downward-pointing runs of seven and even eleven degrees and thus provide for animation. One interesting detail is the expansion of the eighth upbeat to three 16ths in the recapitulation of the beginning (m. 5 onto 5); another is the overlapping of the second long run onto the beginning of the next phrase. The expanded ambit in phrase b (B♭5-F4) is at first reduced again to the frame of an octave (F4-F5) in phrase c. This third phrase is to be seen as in parallel to the first, as confirmed both by the rhythm of the notes (♩ ♪♪) and by the return to the I of the F major. A comparison of phrases a and b also makes clear, however, that the raised crest-note 16ths in the variant (A4-C5-F5 mm. 5 and 6) effectuate a directional tendency that was lacking at first. This upward tendency continues in phrase d, which after two upswings reaches the top note of C6. That note comes as a stressed eighth immediately before the *One* of the final bar and as such reminds once more of the likewise stressed upbeat at the beginning of the theme. Phrase d corresponds with phrase b, just as phrase c and a

are related to each other. If in phrase b the runs of 16ths move downward, they now go up. To be added is the shortening of the repeated parts from four to two quarters, which produces a noticeable condensation. There is, besides, an increase in the directional change of the melodic motion and thus in the number of crest and keel tones. And the harmonic rhythm, which until now consisted of four halves, accelerates to quarters and even to eighths. The climax of the theme on the eighth ♪ of the penultimate bar has thus been long in preparation. The entire eight-bar structure is end-oriented.

This formal thinking, whose earmark is the interpenetration of static and dynamic forces, determines not only the ritornello theme but also the form of the entire movement. For each of the altogether seven major sections of the movement of 118 alla breve measures implements the structure of the ritornello, albeit with insertions and internal expansions. What remains constant is the sequence of the phrases a, b, c and d and thus the orientation toward the end just described. There are always authentic cadences at the end, which turn each and every degree of the F major scale into a tonic once (except for the VII, on which no pure triad can be erected).

m.	form (a→d) with cadences (S = Solo Idea)
(1)	a, b, c, d (F major)
(9)	S, a, S, a, S, a, S, b, c, d (C major)
(29)	S, a, b, c, d (D minor)
(40)	a, a, a, a, b, c, d (B♭ major)
(60)	S, S, S, S, a, b, c, a, b, c, d (G minor)
(84)	a, a, a, b, a, b, c, d (A minor)
(103)	a, b, c, d (F major)

The solo idea, a small, self-contained setting of two bars (first in m. 9) provides some variety but does not alter the principle of the sevenfold theme presentation. The first movement of the Second Brandenburg Concerto is thus a marvelous example of the development of a large form out of the structure of the theme presented at the outset. Once again, rhythmic-metric and formal categories prove to be kindred.

The second movement, an »Andante« in D minor, in 3/4 time, reminds of an expanded trio sonata: three solo parts (flute, oboe, violin) concertize above the basso continuo group. The contemplative serenity the movement radiates derives in part from the uniform rhythmic motion of the accompanying apparatus. The basses move from start to finish in eighths and describe broken chords; only in the cadences (A minor, C major, B♭ major, G minor, D minor) are there any quarter values for the bass clauses, and at the end even halves are adduced for a hemiolic cadence. The slow harmonic rhythm progresses almost entirely in whole measures.

Ex. 2-086
Bach, Brandenburg Concerto II, 2nd mov., Beginning

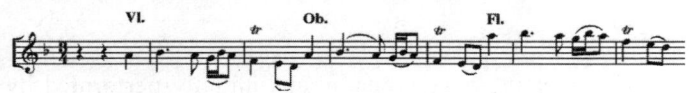

The movement commences on a downbeat, but its character is upbeat (Ex. 2-086). This is due to the two-bar *soggetto*, which the soloists execute mostly in the form of a free canon. The motif has a quarter for an upbeat and ends on the second beat of the second bar. The motif's upbeat effect would exist even if there were no bar line before the second note. Four components are accumulated in this B♭ : tone length, new pitch, crest position and harmonic change.

The length of 6 ♩ introduced by the main motif dominates the movement from beginning to end. Even when the motif is varied, its rhythmic character and its position in the measure remain constant, as do the entry intervals of 6 ♩ in the imitational setting. Even in those passages where a one-bar secondary motif occurs, which now has two upbeat quarters (mm. 34-37, 46-57), the double measures continue. The resulting impression is that of a ritualistic striding dance, in which the same sequences of steps and bodily gestures are performed unvaryingly.

Rhythmic variation is produced by the modifications of the main motif, which occasionally picks up additional 16ths and melodic suspensions. Additional rhythmic differentiation is provided by the contrapuntal voices, though these are never formed into extended arcs, let alone cantilenas. Above all, numerous harmonic suspensions and other events unrelated to the respective chord contribute to the subtler rhythmic process. The suspensions, which often occur in two parts at once, are mostly on the *One*, but are found also on the other beats and even on light eighths.

The expression »variety in unity« well summarizes the rhythmics of this movement, since the motion is unified, even constant like an ostinato, while the inner process is finely elaborated and differentiated.

Ex. 2-087
Bach, Brandenburg Concerto II, 1st and 3rd mov., Beginnings

In the third movement, the qualities of the »Andante« flip over into their opposites: from slow to fast (»Allegro assai«), from ternary to binary (2/4 time), from minor to major. The trumpet, having remained silent in the second movement, opens with the subject of a four-part fugue, whose first development also has the marks of a ritornello.

One cannot miss the reference of the third movement to the theme of the first (Ex. 2-087). A look at the component »Pitch« will reveal the springy syncopated character at the start of the 3rd movement's downbeat theme. The repetition of the C5 there contains the pitch rhythm within itself. Just such a rhythm is also realized in the counterpoint of the theme, even without tone repetitions (m. 10 and others). The trumpet had introduced such syncopated repetitions already in the thematic exposition of the *first* movement as counter-voice (see mm. 5f. there). The syncope is heard markedly for a final time in the plagal twofold cadence at the conclusion of the third movement; here the remaining instruments emphasize the strong beats of the meter with staccato chords, so that the preceding tone repetition is set off clearly.

Ex. 2-088   Bach, Brandenburg Concerto III, 1st mov., Ritornello Theme (Phrasings)

Concerto III (G major)

The third Brandenburg Concerto dispenses with winds (as does the sixth). Instead it has a differentiated string instrumentation with three violins, three violas and three cellos, as well as double bass and harpsichord as continuo group. The three instrument groups are generally combined into a single-voiced or homophonic texture, but are also apt to split into three individual voices, so that we encounter pretty much every variation between total unison (e.g., 1st movement, m. 7) and nine separate parts (1st movement, mm. 62-63). At the division points, of course, the entries of the voices have a heightened rhythmic significance; they make for isometry in the dimensions of quarter, half and whole measures.

The first movement opens with a ritornello theme (Ex. 2-088), in which the three groups each play in unison, so that, besides the thorough-bass, a three-part setting comes about, which at the end issues into a single-voiced octave unison.

The by no means regular internal division of the eight-bar theme can be most clearly discerned in a transcription without beams or bar lines. The beginnings of the phrases are at first simultaneous. The first phrase consists of 13 ♪. This ›odd‹ number is due to the piece's beginning upbeat but changing to downbeat in the second phrase. If one disregards the ♪ of the upbeat, the first phrase has a durational value of 12 ♪ (6 ♩) – a length promptly repeated by the second phrase. The dividing lines of the alla breve time signature are thus played across. The third phrase (one could also read it as the beginning of the one following) is very brief and functions as a transition. A quick cadence – after a brief temporary modulation to the double dominant – restates the tonic and thus recalls the beginning.

With the start of the fourth phrase (m. 4), the three voices begin to drift apart rhythmically. The violins play a variant of the first phrase of ten ♪, remodeled on the melodic pattern in which one degree is fixed, while micro-motifs are sequenced on the remaining degrees. For 14 ♪, the violas take over the octave pendulums initially performed by the basses, while the basses shape a 12 ♪ long phrase initially paralleling the violins but then progressing independently to the V (via the double-dominantic C♯ in m. 5₈). The descent of the violins from G4 to G3 is followed, analogously to the second phrase, by a ten ♪ long ascent from G3 to D4 and F♯4 to D5. The latter ascent is duplicated by the violas, but ›on the beat‹ rather than, as done by the violins, ›off the beat.‹

The conflict between the individualized voices intensifies at the temporary modulation to the dominant (mm. 5-6). At this point (bass: B-C♯-D), the violas with their 14 ♪ octave pendulum stay on G, even after the basses have already reached the V, while the violins, having started their ten-♪ ascent with the pentachord G-A-B-C♯-D already on the 4th quarter of m. 5, reach the V one quarter later than the basses. One can thus say that the rhythmic conflict is accompanied by an analogous harmonic one. Only in the last phrase, which commences simultaneously in the violins and the violas, while the basses join in somewhat tardily, the equilibrium between the three voices is reestablished, as is customary in epilogues that conclude ritornello themes of this sort.

Besides the component »Phrasing,« which derives from the motivic/thematic process and the harmonic movements, the components »Pitch« and »Articulation,« too, are relevant to the rhythm of the ritornello theme. Whoever listens to or plays the piece will get the sense that the upbeats at the start appear accentuated, although they bear no accents. This is because in the first and third voice the high pitches are pulled in front of the beats (the beat here, in spite of the alla breve meter, is the quarter). In the basses, this can be read directly from the notes (G | G); in the violins the repetitions (G4-G4, D4-D4, G4-G4, B3-B3, G4-G4) are covered up by auxiliary notes, but their anticipatory position is the same. Even the violas contribute to this slightly syncopated effect, because they play keel and crest notes always on light beats.

Ex. 2-089   Bach, Brandenburg Concerto III, 1st mov., Solo Theme (extract)

From the second phrase on (m. 2), the violin voice has a downbeat rhythm. This is suggested by the fixed changing-note figure D4-C#4-D4 on the *One*, which amounts to a lengthened note (♪♪♪ = ♩.), especially since it is articulatorily connected by slurs. Violas and basses stick with their (indirect) syncopations at this point.[35] In the further course of the theme, upbeats and downbeats can no longer be meaningfully distinguished. By his meshing of phrases of unequal length and other rhythmic and formal means, Bach in general sees to it that the ritornello theme does not exhibit a real main caesura. That may be the cause of the impression that the eight-bar theme is as of a single cast.

Later on in the movement, an independent solo idea is launched, derived from the tied changing note figure (Ex.2-089). It reveals that the down- and upbeat changing notes (m. 1 and m. 2) spring from the same root. Even later (m. 114), this solo idea is transferred to the basses and expanded in its ambit (D2/E♭4). The reverse anapestic rhythm (| ♪♪♪ instead of ♪♪ | ♪) is now injected alternately by violins and violas on every quarter, with the offset triads now also appearing in inverted form. This wildly and somberly sounding passage in G minor (feared by cellists because of its difficulty) forms the climax of the movement. Deviating from all other appearances of the solo theme, it comprises five bars, bringing a certain irregularity into the phrasal order of the movement.

The final ritornello theme in G major entering shortly thereafter provides some relaxation of the tension. It has been expanded by a three-bar insertion (m. 132), so as to let the alla breve meter for once appear to undisturbed advantage (ex. 2-090).

Ex. 2-090   m. 132

We must not let the downbeat counter-theme, introduced in m. 78, go unmentioned: though it looks like a new counterpoint to the main voice of the ritornello theme, it is of an altogether different mode of motion (Ex. 2-091).

Ex. 2-091   m. 78, Second Theme

This soggetto, which appears only here, has been developed from m. 1f. of the viola voice, as Mauro Botelho has shown.[36] By its length of two bars, it expands the phrase measure dictated by the ritornello theme at the beginning from six ♩ (13 or else 12 ♪) to eight ♩, a measure to which the simultaneously sounded ritornello theme immediately adapts itself. Laid out like a fugue exposition with dux, comes and dux, the section terminates in a sequence of descending fifths that consists entirely of seventh chords (D^7, G^7, C^7, $F_\#^7$, B^7, E^7) with a concluding A minor with a confirming Neapolitan cadence. The harmony changes in a rhythm of half-notes. These points of demarcation are, however, played across by a bass run, which leads downward in 29 (!) steps of ♪, evoking the illusion of a never-ending drop.

The second movement of the third Brandenburg Concerto is noted only in outline: under the heading »Adagio« and with the new time signature **C**, Bach writes two chords in halves embodying a Phrygian cadence to the dominant of E minor. The composer presumably meant to fill in this torso with a personal improvisation at the harpsichord.

Ex. 2-092
Bach, Brandenburg Concerto III, 3rd mov., Beginning

The third movement follows with a key change of a major third (B major to G major) and a quick 12/8 time, handled as a triple alla breve. Rhythmically, the movement, racing along like a perpetuum mobile in the character of a fast round dance (less of a gigue) is kept very simple. The component »Sound« is limited to the 16ths that uninterruptedly run through the 48 or 96 bars of the piece, and eighths (mostly in 3/8 units). Only just before the double bar-lines, marking repetitions at the end of both parts, do larger values occur, and only in two places are there any slide-like insertions, noted in 32nds (mm. 15, 35). All thematic entries of the predominantly canon-like texture follow each other at distances of a half-measure or multiples thereof (Ex. 2-092). The harmonic rhythm exhibits mostly intervals of ♩., whereby harmonic pendulums, e.g., between I and V as at the beginning, again conduce to half-measure units.

The movement is isometric throughout. In comparison with the first movement, which provides for rhythmic variety with subtle irregularities and a more differentiated compositional technique, the third movement can be described as a dance-like, more vital than mental, counterpart to the head movement.

---

[35] These analytic results, insofar as they concern the ritornello theme, largely coincide with the observations of Mauro Botelho (see above, pp. 131f.).

[36] Ibid., 315.

Ex. 2-093   Bach, Brandenburg Concerto IV, 1st mov., Main Theme

Concerto IV (G Major)

The fourth Brandenburg Concerto, in its Köthen version, is written for violin and two recorders, which form the concertino, and a string quartet with basso continuo as ripieno group. The three descant instruments make for a light, summery overall sound of the three movements, which in the first movement radiates an almost Alpine flair. The solo violin is notated at the top of the score and not, as in the second concerto, included in the ripieno violins group. In numerous passages it accordingly stands out brilliantly and virtuoso.

The first movement is written in 3/8 measure (ex. 2-093). If the main theme presented by the recorders still seems designed in a landler-like 6/8 meter, the further course of the movement exhibits a rhythm oriented towards eighths as the actual beat. Melodically broken triads, a fifth held for two measures, short bass notes loosely added (accompanied chordally by the ripieno and the solo violin) and harmonic changes every 3/8 measure add up to a clear weight profile; once installed, it lets the following runs of thirds and sixths and their characteristic syncopations by means of eighth rests on the *One* be felt not as disturbances but as animations of the meter.

The spinning out in the solo violin after m. 13 (Ex. 2-094) picks up the syncopation idea but reduces the reference measure and camouflages the syncopes with note

Ex. 2-094   mm. 13ff., Syncopation Theme

repetitions. This is instantly manifest if one jots the rhythm of the pitch changes beneath the violin part: entire chains of syncopated eighths become visible thereby. These grow all the more audible as more instruments participate, especially where the basses join in with the off-set 16th repetitions (not notated in the example).

These indirect eighth syncopations, formed solely by the component »Pitch,« reinforce the motion of the pulse being based on the eighths. The same happens when imitations at intervals of eighths occur, which happens at several points in the course of the movement (e.g., mm. 198ff., 235ff., 251ff.). If passages of 32nds are superadded, which, moreover, are articulated in values of two eighths, the conductor knows with certainty that Bach has composed a genuine 3/8 meter here and that he should therefore beat eighths accordingly (Ex. 2-095).

The form of the first movement is more complicated than is to be expected given the simplicity of the theme. If one takes the five hemiolic cadences as a criterion (mm. 83, G major, 157 E minor, 235 C major, 344 B minor, 427 G major), the form that emerges is again that of the Italian concerto, albeit greatly modified and enlarged. Already the ritornello theme – or more accurately, ritornello complex – has an extent of 83 bars, within which the main theme occurs three times, each time followed by diverse spin-out sections. But the cadence in G major is introduced so massively that there can be no doubt about the end of the exposition part. The strong cadential effect derives above all from the rhythm (Ex. 2-096). A double hemiola formation, which initially is further multiplied by being staggered by one eighth (see the transcription in the Ex.), leads via a sequence of falling fifths back to the tonic.

Ex. 2-095   mm. 202ff., 32nd Episode

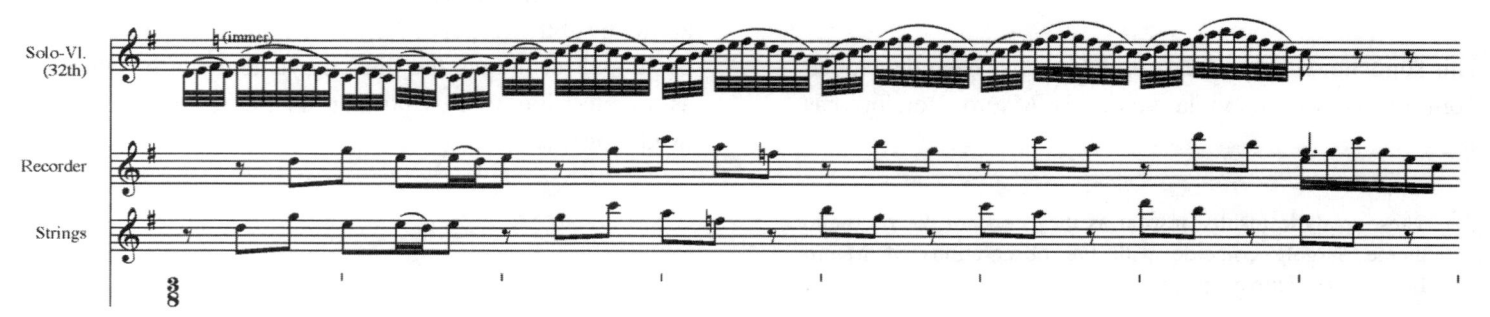

Ex. 2-096   mm. 79-83, Hemiolic Cadence

Ex. 2-097   Bach, Brandenburg Concerto IV, 2nd mov., Beginning

The second movement, with the heading »Andante,« is a luxuriantly melancholy genre picture with pastoral traits (Ex. 2-097). Thirds and sixths dominate the sound, and echo play pervades the piece from beginning to end. The echo effects are produced by thematic, dynamic, textural and coloristic means. They pertain each time to two preceding bars. This initially creates the impression that two bars are each time combined to form an imagined 6/4 measure. Later on, though, there are also constellations in which only one of two measures is answered by an echo. Thus groups of one, two, three and four bars occur next to each other, so that the only possible notation is the simple 3/4 time signature.

The movement striding along in divided quarters – most of the eighths, too, are articulated in pairs – makes use six times of the rhythmic model of the hemiola: mm. 16f., 26f., 43f., 53f., 65f. and 67ff. The most interesting of these is perhaps the last one, which introduces a Phrygian cadence as a transition to the third movement (Ex. 2-098). In

Ex. 2-098   2nd mov., Ending

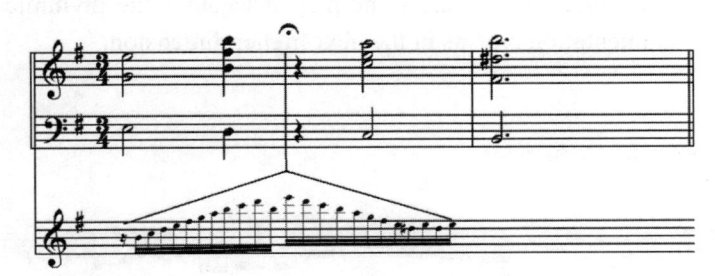

the original, Bach here notes five bars, that is, two extra ones for the cadenza-like run of the first recorder. My representation makes visible what is intended: a hemiola of three halves, occupying two 3/4 measures, is internally lengthened, arrested in its course, as it were, so as to make room for a retarding gesture of 16ths by the soloist. There are, incidentally, two additional episodes of this kind in mm. 29 and 31.

The third movement combines the form of the fugue with that of the concerto. Under the tempo marking »Presto,« 244 alla breve measures, containing eighths, quarters and halves, flow along without a hitch, animated by alternating ripieno and concertino instruments and by counterpoints in the interludes, which provide rhythmic variation by means of crest notes on the 4th and 8th eighths.

The fugal subject itself commences downbeat with an accented second beat, which, however, is immediately leveled again in favor of the binary pattern of the 2/2 meter. The respective rhythmic weights form clearly in the rhythm score of the single-voiced theme, into which the harmonic rhythm has also merged (Ex. 2-099).

Ex. 2-099

Bach, Brandenburg Concerto IV, 3rd mov., Fugue Theme

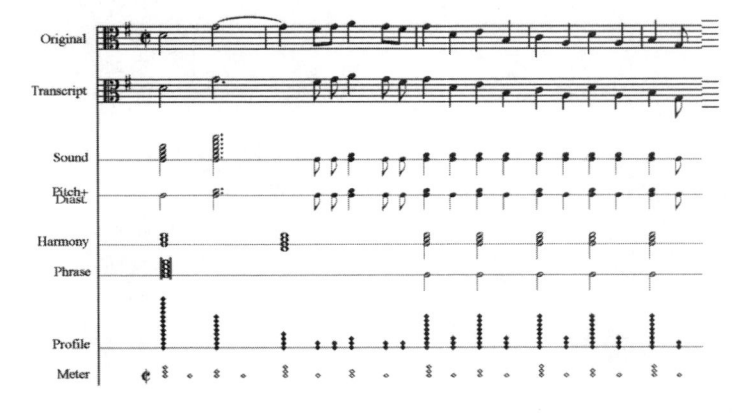

Rhythm and motivics of the theme's beginning are also used for the apotheosis-like ending of the movement (Ex. 2-100). Immediately before the subject is sounded once more in stretto and the movement is concluded thereby, Bach inserts a purely homophonic passage, whose purpose is to intensify the syncopated rhythm of the thematic melody. With the use of all the instruments and of a large number of components, all the available rhythmic weight is shifted to the second note of the theme, which, because of the repetition of the two-bar phrase, appears three times. To the tonal lengthening, known already from the theme, are now also added harmonic changes and articulating rests, the latter doubly called for by staccato dots and quarter rests. At the third time a steeply rising crest is formed by a seventh leap in both descant and bass, which makes the D6 in m. 233 the absolute climax of the entire movement.

Ex. 2-100

Compared with such discharges of rhythmic energy, an episode containing the fastest motion, but together with slow harmonic processes, seems downright calm and contemplative. The reference is to the violin solo beginning in m. 106, which over 14 measures forms a long chain of suspensions by means of 16ths bariolage technique (Ex. 2-101)

Ex. 2-101

Concerto V (D Major)

The fifth Brandenburg Concerto features flute (»flauto traverso«), violin (»violino principale«) and harpsichord (»cembalo concertato«) for soloists, while the ripieno consists of violin, viola, cello and bass, with the harpsichord as basso continuo. Since Bach himself, who usually played the viola, took over the harpsichord both concertante and for basso continuo (as is rightly surmised), the second violinist had to take over the viola part, with the result that there is no second violin in the ripieno group.

The first movement is a gigantic formation of 227 alla breve measures of extraordinary complexity. It is famous above all for the unaccompanied harpsichord cadenza inserted before the last ritornello.

The downbeat ritornello theme comprises eight bars, with the concluding tonic being reached on the *One* of the ninth bar (Ex. 2-102). The theme is divided into five phrases: a = 15 ♪, b = 16 ♪, c = 9 ♪, d = 11 ♪, e = 14 ♪. Since the second, third and fifth phrase are upbeat, this results in phrasal duration values that are odd in number. The fourth phrase (d), which echoes the second one (b) and might likewise have been two measures in length, breaks off prematurely, yielding to the epilogue e, which varies and expands the phrase c. This final phrase (like other phrases as well) is used for spin-outs in the course of the movement. One of the peculiarities of this movement is the rarity of strong cadences. Thus the sections that are based on the epilogue material of the theme always lack the concluding formula ♪. ♪ | ♪ . The cadence at the end of the ritornello theme, elaborately prepared for with in-between dominants in eighths tempo, recurs in fact only once: in the final measure of the entire movement.

The flute does not play the ritornello theme, probably because of the tone repetitions in 16ths rhythm, which are unfavorable to the flute. However, by developing one of the solo ideas directly from the theme by contracting the repetitions (flute mm. 21, 27 and elsewhere), Bach lets the flute belatedly partake of the ritornello theme after all. Besides, this form of variant forming shows that the eighths rhythm of the pitch changes is inherent in the 16ths rhythm of the tones. Since the variant in turn brings in a new component – two eighths each are to be played legato – the rhythmic augmentation repeats in the next-higher dimension:

Ex. 2-102 Bach, Brandenburg Concerto V, 1st mov., Ritornello Theme and Deductions

(original)   *(variant)*

onset: ♪
pitch: ♪ → onset: ♪
articulation: ♩

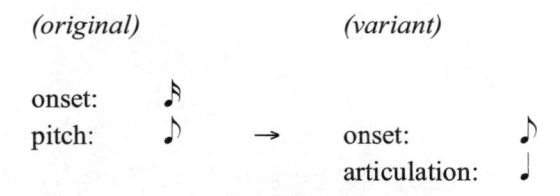

If one changes all the note repetitions back into eighth values, as I have done on the line »Transcription« (Ex. 2-102), the interrelationship between the phrases becomes clearer than it is in the original notation: a, b, c, d, e, is actually a, b, c, b', c'. Yet another instance of rhythmic finesse can be observed on this line. The phrase b contains an inner repetition of six notes in an octave shift (G-F♯-B-A-C♯-D), which, owing to the ternary structure of this phrase (3 ♪), stands in a subtle tension to the quaternary metric one.

Ex. 2-103   Solo Theme

The actual solo theme (Ex. 2-103) is introduced directly after the exposition of the ritornello theme. The major earmark is a four-note conjunct progression in eighths with a light beginning and a heavy conclusion on a primary or secondary beat. This element determines large portions of the movement: it is the cantabile response to the triadic ascent with which the ritornello theme begins.

Ex. 2-104   Solo Theme, Variants

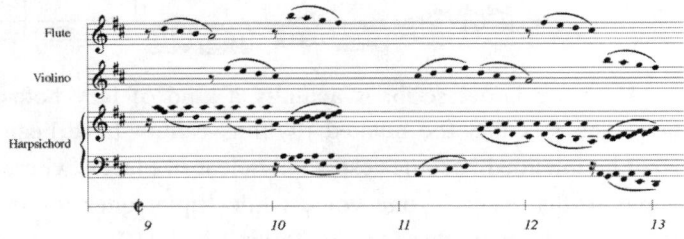

The solo subject, or motif, is introduced early on (mm. 9ff.), also in inverted form and with embellishing variants (Ex. 2-104). In the right hand of the harpsichord part there is a typically pianistic version with pendulum motions of the hand, with the tetrachord of the flute and violin voices being internally duplicated in motions of thirds and sixths, while externally the fifth terminates off-beat (sometimes the first note of the melody is preceded by a slide). Another variant occurs likewise in the harpsichord's right hand immediately afterwards, with triplet 16ths on the eighth values, which, while the melody rises, sound like a chain of mordents, but, in the opposite direction later on, like inverted mordents (e. g., m. 27). In m. 10, all three forms are right away combined. They add up to a rhythmic structure that, while containing conflict in detail, is yet calm and unified in its overall effect, because the main rhythm ♩ ♪♪♪ | ♪, which is tied to the melody, asserts itself throughout.

In the harpsichord's solo cadenza the elaboration of the solo subject is downright excessive. At the very start (mm. 154ff.), Bach reminds us once more of the exposition of the theme in m. 9. Accordingly, it also seems not improbable to me that the voice of the solo violin, which conducts to the cadenza with four notes, is meant as a doubly augmented version of the solo motif (Ex. 2-105). Conversely it may be that Bach also wanted the double diminution of the motif to appear here (Ex. 2-106).

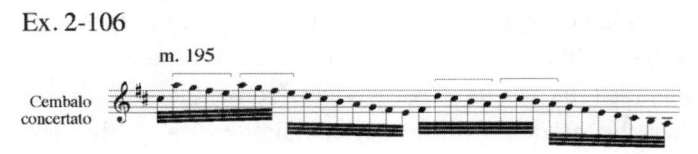

Ex. 2-105

Ex. 2-106

Within the cadenza, where the 32nds begin (m. 195), the solo motif clearly crops up several times. Somewhat later, the process merges into an enormously fast but nevertheless uniformly flowing channel, in which the bass notes stride downwards in eighths rhythm and (chromatic) seconds and the remaining tones of the arpeggiated diminished seventh chords are played off-beat by the right hand. At the pedal point on the dominant, reached in m. 201, the melodic motion in eighths comes to a stop. The ascending runs after that, which always start from the low A, are then accelerated by yet two more notches: to sextuple 32nds and to 64ths (Ex. 2-107). After this moment of greatest condensation, the rhythmic tension is successively diminished again, in that the durational values are reduced to 32nds, to triplet 16ths, to 16ths, and then, immediately before the recapitulation of the ritornello theme (m. 219), to eighths.

Ex. 2-107

Summing up we can state that the already spectacular solo cadenza of the fifth Brandenburg Concerto forms the climax of the movement also in a rhythmic respect. Its only soggetto is the tetrachordal solo motif, whose mode of motion (♩ ♪♪♪ | ♪) is lengthened, compressed and ornamented both in the horizontal (›infinite‹ conjunct progresses), and in the vertical dimension (augmentation, diminution).

Ex. 2-108

Bach, Brandenburg Concerto V, 2nd mov., Ritornello Theme and Secondary Theme

The second movement is headed »Affettuoso«; it is written in 4/4/meter and its key is B minor. A four-bar ritornello theme (Ex. 2-108, upper system), which is repeated four times (mm. 10-14 in D major [varied], 20-24 in F$_\sharp$ minor, 32-34 in G major [abridged], and 45-49 again in B minor), structures the movement in terms of the ritornello form. A side idea (Ex. 2-108, lower system), formed less stringently than the ritornello theme but containing clearly divergent motifs, provides the modulations between the ritornellos.

As to the question, which of the two melodies embodies the »Affettuoso,« the subsidiary theme has probably the greater emotional force. Rhythmically relevant in this respect are the respective first notes of the six-♪ upbeats, which – speaking in terms of components theory – strike the ear as crest notes and endow the entire upbeat group with an emphatic, gestural character. The gestures are imaginary ones of exhaustion, just as the entire phrase from m. 6 on evokes associations of the sinking down of a debilitated person. In contrast thereto, the ritornello theme develops the gesture of striding, represented rhythmically by dotted notes and a uniform basic measure of eighths, even though the falling tendency of the theme is also akin to the Affettuoso idea. After an ascent of a mere nine eighths, beginning with the F$_\sharp$5 in m. 2 – heavily weighted rhythmically by its lengthening and crest position – there follows a slow descent in three stages. Of great expressive power at the end is the wholly unexpected tenth leap upward (m. 4), which, moreover, is paralleled by the contrapuntal voice. The movement presents itself with the instrumentation of a trio sonata, the ripieno section being silent. Even so, the harpsichord changes from time to time from »accompagnement« to obbligato play with two voices, so that repeatedly a four-part polyphonic setting results. Time and again, also with fewer voices, the head of the ritornello theme is imitated in counterpoint, the preferred dimension being the half-measure. Since the dotted rhythm and the corresponding motivics are contrapuntally added also to the side theme, the main effect is that of the gesture of striding. The rhythm of the movement could well be epitomized by the modified direction ›Andante affettuoso‹; Bach, however, writes simply »Affettuoso.«

The third movement is a concertante fugue with the character of a gigue. Written in triplet 2/4 time, the piece, in both composition and execution, nevertheless realizes a pure 6/8 measure. The typical gigue rhythm (♪♩ ♪♩) appears at the start of the theme and is additionally implemented by slurs over the groups of eighths, i.e., by means of the component »Articulation.« The durational sequence ♩♪ adds up to the value ♩., which reappears in the rhythm of the counterpoint (♪₇₇). Since all of the theme entries, even in stretto, occur on the 3rd eighth of the 6/8 meter, the entire movement is ruled by a strict evenness of twice three eighths, creating the impression of a quick whirling movement.

Ex. 2-110   mm. 257ff.

Bach's original script is actually a kind of lazy notation. The fact that the notated rhythms cannot have been what he intended becomes especially clear in places, where duplet 16ths occur in one voice while triplet ones do simultaneously in another (e.g., m 259 in Ex. 2-110).

Ex. 2-111   mm. 79ff.

Ex. 2-109   Bach, Brandenburg Concerto V, 3rd mov., Beginning (transcr. from 2/4 to 6/8)

Concertino and ripieno groups are not always separated in this movement. Thus the fugal exposition, which simultaneously fulfills the function of a ritornello theme, is opened by the (at first unaccompanied) concertino, specifically the violin (dux), flute (comes), harpsichord left hand (dux) and right hand (comes). After the tutti passages, the solo or episodic theme commencing at m. 79 (Ex. 2-111) and clearly revealing its derivation from the fugue theme in the upper voice, is again supplied by the concertino.

In looking for departures of the rhythm from the otherwise pervasive gigue model, one comes, in the accompaniment of the solo part, upon a hemiolic formation that is achieved by note repetition. Though the chains of eighths (stemmed downward) are articulated as in both the fugue theme and the solo theme, the component »Pitch« nevertheless injects rhythmic weights that play across the middle of the measure. The F♯5 struck twice in mm. 79f. has a pitch duration of one quarter; being a crest note gives it additional weight. Though this hemiolic weight shift is hardly noticed, it is undeniable and is confirmed by a comparison with chains of eighths that are articulated in the same way but do not have the tone repetition.

Overall, the movement is rhythmically uncomplicated and of a uniform character. Because of the displaced upbeat of the subject and its derivations, caesuras are weakly developed. Only once is there a pronounced one: at the beginning of the da capo of the faithfully reiterated ritornello theme. Here the preceding B minor complex ends downbeat with a quarter note (m. 232). There follows a quarter rest, and then directly the continuation with a D major chord on the *One*.

Concerto VI (B♭ Major)

The sixth Brandenburg Concerto has an all-strings instrumentation and to that extent resembles the third concerto. With its two violas, two gambas, cello and basso continuo, it is rather low in timbre. Violas and cello come forward solistically, while the gambas and thorough-bass serve exclusively as accompaniment. With its three movements in the order of fast – slow – fast, the concerto corresponds to the Italian type, though the slow movement is unusual in that, ambiguous in key, it begins in E♭ major and ends in G minor with an imperfect cadence in the dominant. The link to the third movement via a major third shift from D major to B♭ major is again conventional.

The first movement is very unusual. Especially strange are the constant harmonic expanses, which are enlivened only by the regular pounding of the chords, and above which a melodic-figural life unfolds that is likewise fitted into the standing harmony. Such rhythmical ostinatos determine not only the ritornello theme but largely also the episodes. Though motivically differentiated from the ritornellos (B♭ major, F→B♭ major, C minor, G minor, E♭ major, B♭ major), they are likewise determined by the static lingering on a single harmony.

I present the ritornello (Ex. 2-112) in a transcription that puts the structure in bolder relief than does the original notation. Only the first five measures are included, though the theme comprises a total of 16 alla breve measures plus the *One* of the 17th, with which the first episode begins in an upbeat and thus in an overlap of phrases.

The two violas play in an extreme stretto canon (distance 1 ♪). The lengthened notes (♩.), which in the first viola are positioned in syncopation, appear on the (quarter) beats of the alla breve meter in the second. Within the first period of the four-and-a-half bars represented in the Example (the start of the second period a fourth lower is just barely visible), the rhythms of the voices are at first in a somewhat complementary relation, whereas in the second phrase there are only 16ths, resulting in a denser structure.

Of interest are also the inner melodic repetitions of partial phrases, as they make for irregularity. The durations of the five partial phrases (marked by brackets) measure 2, 2, 5, 6 and 4 ♪. Since this heterometric phrase structure is

Ex. 2-112 Bach, Brandenburg Concerto VI, 1st mov., Beginning (Transcript)

additionally staggered by the canon formation of the two voices, the rhythmic complexity in the second half of the first period of the ritornello theme increases considerably.

The overall structure of the 16-bar theme, too, is somewhat heterometric. The criterion of the division is the rhythm. All major phrases start with the accented anapest | ♪♪♪., but then follow either several 16ths or single upbeat iambs. Down to m. 9, all the anapests are linked by auxiliary notes, after that by melodic triads. The ritornello the-

Ex. 2-113   mm. 17ff., Episode Theme

me is thus rhythmically/metrically opaque. In contrast, the subsequent episode theme (Ex. 2-113) makes for ›clear conditions.‹ This theme, with its hint of the cantabile, is introduced in the form of a five-part canon. All of the entries are a half, the recurrences of the octave position a whole measure apart. Corresponding to the half-measures is the even melos with the central note of B♭3 or B♭4. This degree receives additional emphasis from the ascending fourth interval. Upbeat and smooth melos, however, are the opposite of the downbeat and jagged triadic melos predominant in the ritornello theme; only the pounding basso continuo remains unchanged. The entire movement lives on the contrary character of these themes; their alternating sequence also changes the rhythm from section to section.

The second movement, too, is unusual in several respects (Ex. 2-114). As previously mentioned, it lacks a uniform key – it begins in E♭ major and ends in an imperfect cadence in the dominant of G minor – and it exhibits a form that fits no schema. The subject repeats ten times, varying in length between three and six bars (mm. 1, 5, 11, 14, 20, 24, 30, 44, 48). At m. 54, an epilogue, whose last four measures form a Phrygian cadence, concludes the movement.

Ex. 2-114   Bach, Brandenburg Concerto VI, 2nd mov., Beginning

The rhythm of the thematic melody is marked by free diminution. The steady rise from the third note on (D4) has, in terms of pitch change, two wholes, of which the second consists quasi of tied ♩ (♩ on the *One* of the third bar). This ›great‹ syncopation is immediately answered by a ›small‹ syncopation consisting of tied ♩. Eights, beginning in m. 3, increase steadily later on, occasionally occurring even minimized to 16ths (first in m. 7). The process of diminution, tantamount to a condensation of the rhythm, as well as the rising of the melody make up the growing intensity of the theme. Since no inversion at all occurs, the entire movement is pervaded by ever new intensifications. All the more striking is thus the conclusion with its descending Phrygian tetrachord in the bass (G-F-E♭-D) leading to complete rest on a D major triad. The familiar major third shift from D major to B♭ major then leads to the lively, gigue-like third movement.

That leaves the rhythm of the accompanying apparatus of cello, double bass and harpsichord to be mentioned (the ripieno does not play in the second movement). As can be seen in Ex. 2-114, the bass moves in halves and whole notes, while the cello sounds a diminished variant of the bass part. This pattern remains unchanged for 39 bars, making for a calm flow below the dynamically turbulent interweaving of the two violas. Only in the epilogue does the cello go its own way by picking up the arabesque runs of eighths that supply the counterpoints of the violas and thus at long last taking some part in the soloist play after all.

The third movement is a fast gigue in 12/8 time (as in the third English Suite BWV 808). In its form it combines the overriding tripartition with the ritornello design: a B♭ major complex of 45 bars with an inner ritornello structure forms the outer parts, while two sections in minor keys of twelve (G minor) and 8 (D minor) measures occupy a contrasting middle portion. Thematic material from the eight-bar ritornello theme (Ex. 2-115), however, is used everywhere, and the individual phrases of the theme occur also in varied and diminished (in the sense of figurative reduction) form, as well as contrapuntally enriched.

The most conspicuous mark of the theme's rhythm are the syncopes produced by anticipation of a note prior to a bar line or beat. Before the syncopes begin, however, Bach lets the gigue rhythm achieve equilibrium. After an upbeat ♪, half-measure phrases follow each other, and each group

Ex. 2-115   Bach, Brandenburg Concerto VI, 3rd mov., Ritornello Theme

of three ♪ is weighted on the first note by articulation and mostly also by crest position. The bass concurrently strides along on the main positions of the 12/8 meter, and it, too, is given some articulatory emphasis by the eighth rest after each bass note. From the third measure on, the tones of the melody pop out of line and do it so excessively that new periodic sequences result between the long notes, which are always also crest notes (Ex. 2-116). This regular offbeat results in the simultaneity of two sequences of isometric durations of ♩, staggered by one ♪. The bass tones obviously retain the upper hand, since they only continue what two bars earlier had been installed by the entire rhythm of the tone setting.

Ex. 2-117   Ritornello Theme, Diminutional Variant

From m. 9 on, the ritornello theme is repeated in a variant in embellished diminution with runs of ♪ (Ex. 2-117). The outlines of the original melody are retained, even the slurred auxiliary notes (B♭4, B♭4, C5 and D5) are found in a 16ths version. The two violas, which had recited the theme melody in unison, now move apart, with the tension between syncopated eighths and downbeat runs of 16ths returning again. Later on, the cello, too takes part in this fast play.

A new rhythm is presented by the middle section starting at m. 46 (ex. 2-118). Though shaped externally like a ritornello in diminution, the sequence of ♪ here has an entirely

Ex. 2-118   mm. 46ff., Episode Theme

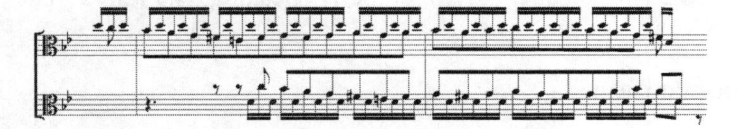

different rhythmic quality. A melodic rhythm not notated in the original is formed of ♪ in both voices, which describe melodically far-flung wave lines consisting entirely of conjuncts. The ♪ come into play by means of offbeat fifth tones in this passage, which is generally in the dominant of the G minor key signature. The offbeat notes are crest or keel tones in a formal sense, but have a different function musically: they are not part of the melody but represent a static tone that is quasi a second, unmoving voice. Crest and keel notes, on the other hand are of concern in the eighths melody, though their effect is a weak one. The ♪, of course, are part of this theme's rhythmic structure, since the component »Sound« remains in effect, even if an overriding main rhythm of eighths is introduced by an (inherent) melody-carrying voice. Though turbulent in detail, the episode theme, which does without harmonic changes, radiates a calm that is altogether missing from the ritornello theme. Nor does that change when, somewhat later, the D minor version of the episode theme emerges, this time rhythmically on the beat and with tonic/ dominant pendulums in the basses.

A recapitulation of the entire first ritornello complex concludes this wildly turbulent, impish movement, and with it the sixth Brandenburg Concerto as a whole.

The »Eilt! – Wohin?« Aria with Chorus

In Bach's *St. John's Passion*, the account of Jesus's crucifixion is immediately preceded by a dialogical bass aria with chorus (No. 48) that, wedged between recitatives, opens a dramatic scene, in which the people are urged by a believer to follow the cross-bearing savior to the place of skulls outside the city: »Haste!« »Whereto?« – »To Golgatha!« Designed in G minor and in a fast 3/8 time, the composition, comprising 191 bars, is dominated by two musical figures: a run of 16ths, coordinated with the appellative »Eilt!,« and an upbeat, upward-leaping motif embodying the interrogative »Wohin?« (Ex. 2-119).

Ex. 2-119a

Ex. 2-119b

In accordance with the agitated state of the preacher, the piece is very freely designed, both rhythmically and formally (see the table below). Outwardly, it roughly follows the form of a concerto with ritornellos on I, V, VI and again I, but the episodes do not contrast with it, but are based, like the ritornello theme itself, almost exclusively on the two contrary figures »Haste!« and »Whereto?«

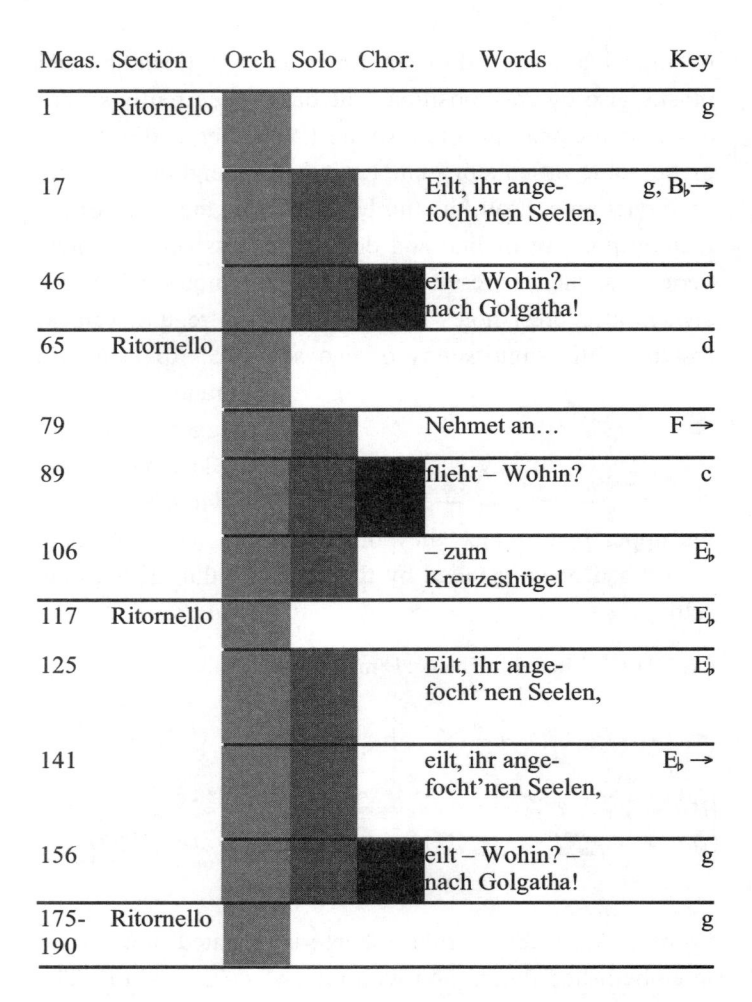

Meas.	Section	Orch	Solo	Chor.	Words	Key
1	Ritornello					g
17					Eilt, ihr ange-focht'nen Seelen,	g, B♭ →
46					eilt – Wohin? – nach Golgatha!	d
65	Ritornello					d
79					Nehmet an…	F →
89					flieht – Wohin?	c
106					– zum Kreuzeshügel	E♭
117	Ritornello					E♭
125					Eilt, ihr ange-focht'nen Seelen,	E♭
141					eilt, ihr ange-focht'nen Seelen,	E♭ →
156					eilt – Wohin? – nach Golgatha!	g
175-190	Ritornello					g

Already the ritornello theme (Ex. 2-120) exhibits rhythmic features that let the uncontrolled and unpredictable character of the entire piece emerge from the start. This can be demonstrated by a rhythm score of the main voice. The subject has a very marked contour: in the space of four bars, the melody climbs two-and-a-half octaves (G3-D6), followed by a conjunct descent occupying 13 measures (D6-C6-B♭5-A5-G5-F5-E♭5-D5-C5-B♭4-A4-G4). The descent is interrupted once by a countermotion, which, however, connects with the A5 of the overriding descent (E♭5-F♯5-G5-A5). The top note D6, we should note, falls on an unaccented beat, so that the ratio of ascent and descent of the two unequal halves, properly speaking, is 11:38 ♪. The

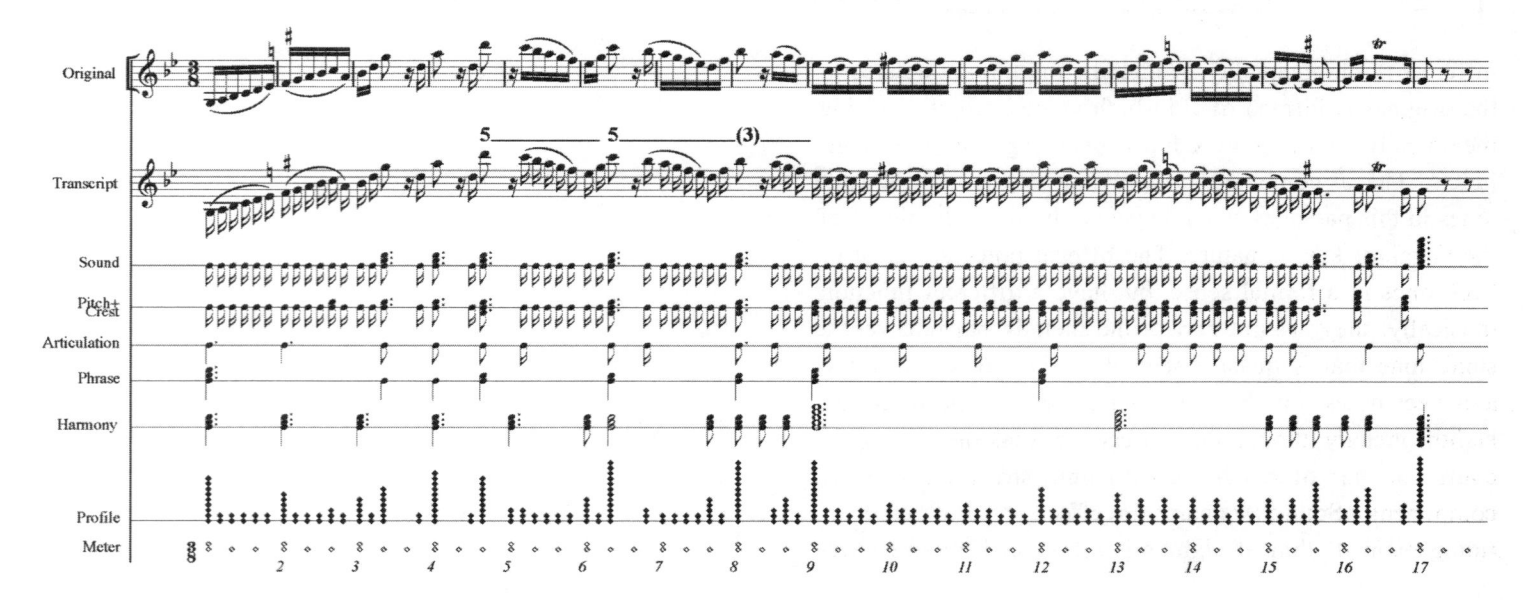

Ex. 2-120   Bach, *St. John Passion*, Aria with Chorus, No. 48, Ritornello Theme

biggest motor unrest, however, derives from five-eighths phrases that are cross-grained to the prevailing ternary meter. These five-eighths phrases (mm. 4-8) are dictated by the »Wohin?« motif, which is each time followed by an »Eilt!« element. Between the notes D6, C6 and B♭5, which are saturated with heavy rhythmic weights, there is each time a space of five eighths; after that, the rhythm finds its way back to the regularity of the 3/8 time. The five-eighths phrases are introduced by the thrice repeated »Wohin?« (with widening interval leaps), which are set so as to result in a binary dotted two-eighths rhythm (♪♪. ♪♪. ♪♪.). This formation, though, which in ternary meters often appears in hemiolic form – as it does here also at the end of the ritornello theme – enters, not on the *One* but on the *Two*, while

Ex. 2-121   Extract of the »Wohin?« Motive with Vokal Solo Part, mm. 1-65

the third dotting is at the same time the beginning of the two five-eights phrases. Since the bass part of the continuo enters exactly after three eighths and imitates the main voice (not visible in the Ex.), the basic ternary order remains present against the binary rhythms of the »Wohin?« phrases, but the five-eighths figures enter thereafter, staggered by two eighths, also by the imitating bass voice, so that the pentadic structure comes to the fore, not once, but twice.

The rhythmic profile in the rhythm score clearly depicts the sequence of three-, two- and five-eighths at the beginning, and one can trace in detail how especially the notes of the »Wohin?« motif are always charged with several components. Thus the G5 in m. 3 is weighted by its length, crest note position, articulation (staccato by means of ₇) and phrasing (inherent syllabic stress).Three of the notes (A5 in m. 4, C6 in m. 6 and B♭5 in m. 8) additionally entail harmonic changes, while D6, C6 and B♭5 are simultaneously part of the descending scaffold voice (noted below the line in the Pitch system). All additional components, such as the note repetitions and the trill at the end (noted in the system Articulation), the legato slurs (now starting on heavy beats, now on light ones) and the single cadence at the very end further differentiate the rhythmic texture, without, however, undoing the initial regular structure.

As mentioned before, the ritornello theme with its perplexing rhythm largely determines also the passages of the aria where the bass sings and the chorus interjects its queries. These »Whereto?« interjections also occur in the instrumental parts. In Ex. 2-121, the first main section of the aria is reproduced. I have included the voice of the solo bass in its entirety, of the remaining music only the »Wohin?« motif, which is defined by a short upbeat followed by an upward-leaping interval and a lenghened final note. The interval is mostly a fourth, but is also enlarged (all the way to a twelfth in the 1st violin, m. 63) and (rarely) diminished (minor third in the continuo bass, mm. 6-7).

In its vocal form the language-dictated motif occurs first in m. 49. Here it also becomes clear that the motif is anticipated by the high strings, or else that the texted »Wohin?« interjections follow the non-verbal ›calls‹ of the instruments. The »Whereto?« questions of the instruments are thus present (in the sense of a ›speaking music‹) already from m. 3 on. Bach, moreover, has arranged the three choral voices (soprano, alto, tenor) to correspond exactly to the instrument parts (1st violin, 2nd violin, viola). When the soloist urges the imaginary listeners to hurry (»Haste, ye troubled, tempted souls«), the »Whereto?« questions are as yet exclaimed wordlessly. Only once the preacher follows up with even more compelling images (»go from out your caves of torture«), the impatience of the crowd vents itself verbally, as the chorus sings its »Wohin?« fully eight times – repeating it once more, with the added emphasis of a fermata, after the magic name »Golgatha« has been uttered.

Bach uses syntactic, and thus also rhythmic, procedures to express the growing impatience of the crowd.[37] The »Wohin?« motif is partly pre-imitated already in the ritornello, specifically in the bass and violin 1 in mm. 5-8 (G3-C4 / G5-C6 and F3-B♭3 / F5-B♭5). This type of condensation recurs in mm. 23ff. and undergoes a climactic intensification in m. 51, where the »Wohin?« fourths are sounded thrice in a row at intervals of one ♪ – by low strings, high strings and chorus.

Another, so to speak purely rhythmic, means of condensation can be observed in the chorus passage in mm. 49ff. (Ex. 2-122). The eight »Wohin?« queries in mm. 49 to 57 follow each other ever faster in a downright arithmetic sequence: ♪: 5, 5, 4, 3, 2, 1) and do so quite independently of the 3/8 meter. This rhythmic structure, which exhibits an enormous inner tension, recurs twice (mm. 91ff., 159ff.). Altogether, the five-eighths phrases, which, as shown, are presented already in the ritornello theme, occur even eight times (mm. 4ff., 22ff., 51ff., 66ff., 92ff., 134ff., 160ff., 178ff.).

Ex. 2-122   mm. 49-57

Additional rhythms could be adduced in this score that all contribute to the restless, almost chaotic character of the piece. Especially the bass solo repeatedly and emphatically evades the 3/8 meter. The word »Eilt,« sung mostly in isolation (as are, later, also the words »geht« and »flieht« [»go« and »flee«]) is preferentially intoned on the *Two* or *Three* of the measure. Anticipations endow unstressed syllables with an ›unnatural‹ weight (»eilt, ihr__ ange__ focht' nen Seelen«). Only at the rare moments when the preacher adopts a consolatory tone (»des Glaubens Flügel« [»the wings of faith«], »eure Wohlfahrt blüht« [»your welfare blooms«]) do vocal and instrumental parts shift to a swaying 3/8-time rhythm.

---

[37] For comparison, see the »Wohin?« interjections in the *St. Matthew Passion* (No. 70, mm. 17f.), which occur also in the context of the Golgatha scene. The alto, having lamented the death of Jesus in a recitative (»Ach Golgatha«), in the aria following invites the believers to come »into Jesus' arms« to find mercy. However, the three-fold exchange »Kommt!« – »Wohin?« is there set in a completely serene rhythm. Embedded in 4/4-time, the »Come« sounds on the *Two*, the *Three* and again the *Two*, while the upbeat interrogative »Whereto?« – set, incidentally, as in the *St. John's Passion* – enters on *Three*, *One* and *Three*.

The Chorale »Es ist genug«

The chorale »Es ist genug« is from the Bach cantata »O Ewigkeit, du Donnerwort« (»O Eternity, thou word of thunder«) for the 24th Sunday after Trinitatis (BWV 60). It forms the conclusion to a section of antiphonal singing between two allegorical figures: »Fear« (alto) and »Hope« (tenor). The subject of the dialogue is a woman's fear of death, which her antagonist seeks to dispel by referring her to Christ's passion and promise. At the end, a bass (faith) and the chorus (congregation) join in. The bass, who is not part of the role-playing, quotes – quasi as prophet – the verse from Revelation »Blessed are the dead which die in the Lord from henceforth.« The fearful one is converted and has regained faith in the kingdom of heaven. »My bones in sleep secure from fear may rest, the spirit by a glimpse of yonder joy be blessed.« The chorale that follows, standing for the community of all believers, then grants us that glimpse of a peaceful beyond: »To Heaven's house I go, in peace I thither surely go.«

The text of the chorale is by Franz Joachim Burmeister, the melody by Johann Rudolf Ahle.[38] First published in 1662, it was taken up by Bach in 1723, when the cantata »O Ewigkeit, du Donnerwort« was composed, slightly altered and formed into a four-part cantionale setting, whose vocal parts are supported by an instrumental group (horn, oboe d'amore, strings). This chorale setting is fairly well-known today not least because Alban Berg quoted and then varied it in his Violin Concerto.

The Ex. 2-123 reproduces the chorale in its original notation. Added to it is the rhythmic profile obtained from component analysis. The complete rhythm score will be explained below. However, some conclusions can already be drawn from a comparison of the setting with the rhythmic profile. One can see, for example, that the meter of the 4/4 signature gets played across musically: the second verse (»My Jesus comes«) begins not on the *One*, like the first verse, but on the *Three*. The original melody is repositioned thereby and the rhythmically heavily weighted concluding notes of the subsequent lines slide to the middle of the measure; only the penultimate line ends, like the first one, on the *One*. The rhythmic profile shows further that Bach orients every line towards its end (the fermatas are authentic), but fills the times before the caesuras without regard to the metric dictate. The resulting phrase units, measured in ♩ (and adding in the upbeats), are of changing duration: »Es ist…«: 4+4+3 ♩; »Mein Jesus…«: 4+4+4 ♩; »Ich fahre…«: 6+6 ♩; »Es ist…«: 3+2 ♩.

The uneven phrase lengths are dictated by the meter of the text and do not depend on the isometric sequence of beats. The text is divided into four strophes and has altogether ten rhymed lines consisting of from four to nine syllables and two to four stresses:

Ex. 2-123   J. S. Bach, *Cantata »O Ewigkeit, du Donnerwort«*, BWV 60, Final Chorale

---

[38] Thomas Braatz / Aryeh Oron, »Chorale Melodies in Bach's Vocal Works: *Es ist genug, so nimm, Herr, meinen Geist*,« Internet publication under http://www.bach-cantatas.com/CM/Es-ist-genug.htm, November 2005.

Es <u>ist</u> ge<u>nung</u>;
<u>Herr</u>, <u>wenn</u> es <u>dir</u> ge<u>fällt</u>,
So <u>spanne</u> <u>mich</u> doch <u>aus</u>.

Mein Jesus <u>kömmt</u>
nun <u>gute</u> <u>Nacht</u>, o <u>Welt</u>!
Ich <u>fahr</u> ins <u>Himmelshaus</u>.

Ich <u>fahre</u> <u>sicher</u> <u>hin</u> mit <u>Frieden</u>;
Mein <u>großer</u> <u>Jammer</u> <u>bleibt</u> da<u>nie</u>den;

Es <u>ist</u> ge<u>nung</u>,
Es <u>ist</u> ge<u>nung</u>.

(It is enough; / Lord, if it pleases thee, / unyoke, unharness me! // My Jesus comes; / and so, good night, o world! / I go to Heaven's house, // in peace I thither surely go, / and all my sorrows stay below. / It is enough, / it is enough.)

The prosody of the iambic verses is largely regular. Only once a rhetorically stressed word sidesteps the metrical scheme: the word »Herr« falls on an unstressed position and thus results in an evidently intentional, emphatic upbeat of the second line. The prosodic weight relations dictated by the rhythm of the language enter the rhythm score (Ex. 2-124) as a component. Unstressed syllables are marked with one dot, stressed ones with two. The word »Herr« gets an extra point below the line, whereby the unstressed syllable becomes as strong as a stressed one.

The musical score consists of four parts, which are not, however, of equal importance. My reasons for analyzing the outer voices descant and bass in detail, while lumping the two middle voices alto and tenor, and including only the tonal entries are as follows. The bass voice is evidently shaped as an independent counterpoint. It descends to the depth in ten conjunct notes (mm. 3f.), something not exactly suitable for basses, and it changes its melodic shape despite melodically identical lines of text: »ich fahre sicher hin in Frieden« (diatonic in ♪) and »mein großer Jammer bleibt danieden« (chromatic in ♩). Compared with the shapely scaffolding of descant and bass voice, the middle voices are relatively dependent and hence to be regarded as filling voices of a lesser weight.

Individually, the component rhythms are entered into the rhythm score as follows. For the component »Sound,« the ♪ is assumed as the smallest value. The occasional ♪ appearing as transitional or auxiliary notes are reckoned in but not used for calculating durational weights. The longest values (𝅗𝅥.) therefore receive the weight 6, the shortest ones (♪ and ♪) the value 1. The fermatas are included as additional values notated below the line (in descant and bass only).

The component »Pitch« is significant in this piece in view of several note repetitions. To begin with, all pitch changes, separately for descant and bass, are registered with the weight value 1. In cases of tone repetitions, resulting in a pitch's longer durational value, the first of the repeated notes receives, in addition, the value that is notated beneath the remaining repeated notes in the component line »Sound.« To exemplify: in the descant part in m. 2, the $D_\sharp 5$ is sounded twice, first as 𝅗𝅥 with 𝄾, then as ♩. The values 6 and 2 are consequently entered under the component »Sound.« Then, in the line »Pitch,« the value 2 is added to the value 1 under the note $D_\sharp 5$, because the latter has a duration of altogether 4 ♩; the value is therefore 3 (1+2).

The component »Diastematy« has a separate system (though, as explained, only for the descant and the bass). In it, all crest and keel notes are registered (above and below the line, respectively) with the value 1, regardless of whether the note at which a change in direction occurs is preceded, or followed, by a step or a leap. In case of a repeated note, the first is regarded as initiating the directional change.

The setting for four voices is accounted for by the components »Harmony« and »Phrase.« Considering the importance of the harmonic changes in major-minor tonal music generally, and in view of this chorale in particular with its many auxiliary degrees and secondary dominants, I assign a fourfold weight to each position in the line »Harmony« (in accordance with the number of voices). One notes that the harmonic rhythm in this composition is quite diverse. The longest duration of a harmonic function is 6 ♩ (mm. 11-12), the shortest is 1 ♪ (e.g., m. 3).

Suspensions, registered with the value 1 below the line, are relatively rare. In some cases one may even wonder whether one is dealing with a genuine suspension or merely with a ›hard‹ transition. I regard the penultimate note in m. 3 ($C_\sharp$ in the bass) as a suspension pertaining to the chord-related B, but one could also read it as part of the ongoing run of eighths and consequently neglect it as a transitional note. The cadences, which have to be included as another sub-component of the »Harmony,« likewise allow some interpretive leeway regarding their weight. I distinguish between authentic cadences (with bass clause) and inauthentic (imperfect) ones (without bass clause). In the case of the authentic cadences, I further distinguish according to tonic and non-tonic. The result are three alternatives for cadences: 1 = inauthentic, 2 = authentic on a non-tonic, 3 = authentic on the tonic. These values are added onto the columns of four (harmonic changes) above the line.

The division of the chorale by phrases is very simple in this case, as the rests and fermatas indubitably signal the end and beginning of a phrase. Each beginning of a phrase has the value 1. If several phrases are combined, another value is added at the beginning of such a hyper-phrase, corresponding exactly to the division of the text into three- and two-line stanzas.

The rhythmic profile (see Ex. 2-123) confirms what every musician who is prepared to act independently of the bar lines feels instinctively. Following the language, the sentences, like large gestures, are realized as flexible units. The rhythmic components analysis thus captures an important element of this chorale setting of Bach's. It should not be forgotten, of course, that the total character of a composition depends on other musical parameters alongside the rhythm. In this instance it is above all the harmonic events that elicit our special attention. Already the twofold harmonization of the whole-tone tetrachord at the beginning of the first and second strophe transmits a density of event that cannot really be expressed by the harmonic rhythm. The critical $D\sharp$ - the tritone above the tonic – is underpinned, first, by a $G\sharp$ major fifth-sixth chord, and then by a double dominant without a fundamental.

Strongly affective in content is also the passage in mm. 15-16, in which the bass fills a whole tritone by descending chromatically from A to $D\sharp$, leading to a sequence of seventh and fifth-sixth chords, among them, rare in Bach, the seventh chord over the seventh degree of E major ($D\sharp3$-$F\sharp4$-$A4$-$C\sharp5$) in the function of a curtailed double dominant.

The two final lines, which exactly repeat the text of the beginning (»Es ist genung«) have a consolatory tenor resulting from the free inversion of the melody and transmute the whole-tone tritone tension into a tender diatonic descent (A4-B4-$C\sharp5$-$D\sharp5$ → E5-$C\sharp5$-B4-A4). This change in expression, too is not nearly realizable from the rhythmic conditions alone. Not even the deceptive-cadence turn to $F\sharp$ minor in the penultimate bar, which keeps the process open so as to allow for a last reiteration of the sentence »Es ist genung« can be captured by the rhythmic analysis, since the criterion for entering it into the rhythm score is the mere fact of harmonic change but not the quality of the harmony.

Keeping in mind such semantic and expressive qualities in music, whose relevance lies outside the parameters of our inquiry, the components theory for the first time presents a method that makes it possible to determine, down to the least detail, the mode of a composition's motion, that is, its rhythm, and therefore one of its chief characteristics, beyond any extent hitherto available. In the present case, the rhythmic weights and the texture of component rhythms accurately reproduce the flow of the chorale's language. The time signature prefixed by Bach thereby becomes irrelevant; it obeys a convention of notation, but distracts from the rhythmic sense of the composition. For the practical execution of the choral work, the results of the analysis will be useful in clarifying the compositionally inten-

Ex. 2-124　　Rhythm score

ded structural units (not to be confused with accentual marks), and, generally, in challenging the musician to attend to the differentiated inner processes of the rhythmic warp of music.

Part III: Theories of Rhythm

Preface

The present study sets forth a novel theory of musical rhythm, »components theory«, for discussion. The core of this new approach consists in disengaging the concept of duration from its bond to the individual sound and to apply it also to partial sound phenomena as well as to sound configurations. The distance between sound and sound or tone and tone is principally equated to the duration between pitch and pitch, between crest and/or keel tones, between harmony and harmony, phrase and phrase, etc. Every durational sequence deriving from significantly qualified sound signals (»components«) can function as a rhythm; the mutually coordinated rhythms (»component rhythms«) are apprehended as a temporal web comprising the rhythm of a musical concatenation.

The components theory is contiguous to other, older and newer, accentual theories. But it modifies these inasmuch as it replaces the *accent* as a discrete individual event by the *component* as a rhythm-generating phenomenon. Components are not mere additions to rhythms but necessarily and constantly occurring alterations in sound or tone setting that structure time and are consequently of rhythmic import. The conventional rhythm/accent relation thus evolves into a new rhythm/rhythm relation.

Furthermore the components theory presents a new explanatory departure for the phenomena meter and time. If the weight relations in the modern graduated accent meter can be derived from the interaction of multiple (abstract) durational sequences (see fig.), the same principle can be used to determine rhythmic weights. Component rhythms that begin at the same point in time can accumulate and thus elicit a sense of gravity. Through the control of the components rhythms, the composer is able to arrange the rhythmic stresses at equal or unequal intervals. To put it differently: the graduated accent meter is produced rhythmically, it is initially merely a guiding pattern, to which the actual composition will correspond more or less. The metrical weight relations are the result of an interplay of components rhythms, not statutory prescriptions.

In what follows I will query a number of theories of musical rhythm and meter of the past 400 years, as to whether, and to what extent, the approaches developed in the components theory are present or considered. My intention is not to present comprehensive evaluations of these theoretical edifices. To the extent that the writings contain concrete rhythm analyses, an alternative analysis will demonstrate the advantages of a components-related point of view.

General assessments of the historical contributions to the theory of rhythm and meter have to a large extent been provided already by others. Here one must cite above all the writings of Wilhelm Seidel, who not only presented his ground-breaking study *Über Rhythmustheorien der Neuzeit*,[1] but also authored diverse dictionary and handbook articles on the subject of »rhythm.«[2] Secondly, there are two great projects on the *History of Music Theory*, in whose volumes the history of rhythm theory, too, is expertly represented.[3] These surveys, however, are useful as reviews only: independent new approaches to a theory of rhythm are not offered by them.

The selection of texts and treatises to be discussed was very difficult and can certainly be questioned. The body of literature regarding matters of musical rhythm and meter is gigantic. If one includes all of the sub-disciplines of musicology, as well as the pertinent philosophical, psychological and cognitive-science literature, it will have to be admitted that no single individual can possibly survey all of it. Besides, this book had to be kept within certain bounds.

The criteria of selection are largely dictated by the questions I ask about extant rhythm theories, as determined by the method of components theory and analysis. Since I am above all concerned to understand the rhythm of concrete, written music of artistic caliber adequately and in as differentiated a manner as possible, I omit all texts that remain on a level of general and abstract discourse without adverting to actually composed music. This is not to question the value of such treatises in any way, yet their approach does not overlap with mine to a significant degree. Among 19th century discourses, therefore, the writings of Adolph Bernhard Marx, Simon Sechter and Moritz Hauptmann remain unconsidered.[4] For the same reason, the early 20th century studies of Vincent d'Indy,[5] René Dumesnil,[6]

---

[1] Wilhelm Seidel, *Über Rhythmustheorien der Neuzeit* (Berne, Munich, 1975).

[2] Wilhelm Seidel, »Rhythmus/numerus,« in *Handwörterbuch der musikalischen Terminologie*, ed. H. H. Eggebrecht (Stuttgart: Steiner, n.d.) (art. 1980); »Rhythmus, Metrik, Takt,« in MGG², subject part, vol. 8, 1998, cols. 257-317; »Rhythmus,« in *Ästhetische Grundbegriffe. Historisches Wörterbuch in sieben Bänden* (Stuttgart, Weimar: Metzler, 2003), 5:291-314.

[3] *Geschichte der Musiktheorie*, ed. Frieder Zaminer, Thomas Ertelt (since 1992), commissioned by the Institut für Musikforschung Preussischer Kulturbesitz, Berlin, 15 vols. (Darmstadt: Wissenschaftliche Buchgesellschaft, 1984ff.); *The Cambridge History of Western Music Theory*, ed. Thomas Christensen, 3rd print (Cambridge University Press, 2006).

[4] Adolph Bernhard Marx, *Die Lehre von der musikalischen Komposition*, vol. 1 (Leipzig, 1837), vol. 2 (5th ed.) (Leipzig, 1864); Simon Sechter, *Die Grundlagen der musikalischen Komposition* (Leipzig, 1853-54); Moritz Hauptmann, *Die Natur der Harmonik und Metrik. Zur Theorie der Musik* (Leipzig, 1853; reprint Hildesheim et al., 2002).

[5] Vincent d'Indy, *Cours de composition musicale* (Paris, 1903).

[6] René Dumesnil, *Le Rythme musical. Essai historique et critique* (Paris, 1921).

Edgar Willems[7] and Andres Briner[8] have been excluded. Several more recent treatises and collections that deal with fundamental questions in terms of space and time are likewise not discussed.[9]

A sizable number of writings had also to be eliminated from consideration because they address questions of rhythm and meter in thematically or historically very narrow areas,[10] or because they are interested primarily in performance practice.[11] Some approaches from the early 20th century, on the other hand, are inaccessible to a critique via the components theory because of their irrational methodology.[12]

Rhythm theories that refer exclusively, predominantly or partially to musical cultures outside the central European high culture also remain unconsidered.[13] That includes also the highly stimulating and readable book *Rhythm and Tempo. A Study in Music History* by the musicologist and polyhistorian Curt Sachs.[14] Finally, I exclude all investigations of empirical tone and music psychology and the recent cognitive science. Their mode of inquiry greatly deviates from mine, and their methodology is accessible to a historian, as which I regard myself, only to a limited degree.[15]

---

[7] Edgar Willems, *Le rythme musical. Étude psychologique* (Paris, 1954).

[8] Andres Briner, *Der Wandel der Musik als Zeit-Kunst* (Vienna, 1955).

[9] Thrasybulos Georgiades, *Nennen und Erklingen, die Zeit als Logos*, ed. posthumously by Irmgard Bengen, with a preface by Hans-Georg Gadamer (Göttingen: Vandenhoeck and Ruprecht, 1985); *Zeit in der Musik in der Zeit*, 3rd Congress for Music Theory, May 10-12, 1996, Hochschule für Musik und darstellende Kunst, Vienna, ed. Clemens Kühn (Frankfurt am Main et al.: Lang, 1997); *Zeit und Raum in Musik und Bildender Kunst*, ed. Tatjana Böhme, Klaus Mehner (Cologne, Weimar, Vienna: Böhlau, 2000); *Musik in der Zeit - Zeit in der Musik*, ed. Richard Klein, Eckehard Kiem, Wolfram Ette (Weilerswist: Velbrück 2000); *Geteilte Zeit. Zur Kritik des Rhythmus in den Künsten*, ed. Patrick Primavesi, Simone Mahrenholz (Schliengen: Argus, 2005).

[10] Hans Hirsch, *Rhythmisch-metrische Untersuchungen zur Variationstechnik by Johannes Brahms* (Hamburg, 1963); Gudrun Henneberg, *Theorien zur Rhythmik und Metrik. Möglichkeiten und Grenzen rhythmischer und metrischer Analyse, dargestellt am Beispiel der Wiener Klassik* (Tutzing, 1974); Franz Hermann Wolfgang Plyn, *Die Hemiole in der Instrumentalmusik von Johannes Brahms* (Bonn, 1984); Claudia Maurer Zenck, *Vom Takt. Untersuchungen zur Theorie und kompositorischen Praxis im ausgehenden 18. und beginnenden 19. Jahrhundert* (Vienna: Böhlau, 2001); Ido Abravaya, *On Bach's Rhythm and Tempo* (Kassel: Bärenreiter, 2006); Stephanie D. Vial, *The Art of Musical Phrasing in the Eighteenth Century. Punctuating the Classical ›Period‹* (Rochester: URP, 2008).

[11] Leopold Mozart, *Versuch einer gründlichen Violinschule* (Augsburg, 1756; reprint Frankfurt a. M., 1956); Joachim Quantz, *Versuch einer Anweisung, die Flöte traversière zu spielen* (Berlin, 1752; reprint Kassel, 1992); Marion Louise Perkins, »Changing Concepts of Rhythm in the Romantic Era. A Study of Rhythmic Structure, Theory and Performance Practice Related to Piano Literature,« Ph. D. thesis (Univ. of Southern California, 1961); *Tempo, Rhythmik, Metrik, Artikulation in der Musik des 18. Jahrhunderts*. 32nd International Scholarly Work Conference on Questions of Performance Practice and Interpretation of 18th-century Music, Michaelstein, June 16-18, 1995, ed. Bert Siegmund, Susanne Baselt (Blankenburg, 1998); Robert S. Hatten, »Musical Gesture,« Internet publication with © 2001, under http://www.chass.utoronto.ca/epc/srb/cyber/hatout.html; Klaus Miehling, *Das Tempo in der Musik von Barock und Vorklassik. Die Antwort auf ein umstrittenes Thema*, improved and greatly enlarged new ed. (Wilhelmshaven: Noetzel, 2003).

[12] Ernst Kurth, *Grundlagen des linearen Kontrapunkts. Bachs melodische Polyphonie* (Berlin ²1922); Hans Mersmann, *Angewandte Musikästhetik* (Berlin, 1926); Gustav Becking, *Der musikalische Rhythmus als Erkenntnisquelle* (Augsburg 1928); engl. ed.: *How Musical Rhythm Reveals Human Attitudes*, an annotated translation by Nigel Nettheim (Frankfurt / Main: Lang 2011).

[13] *Rhythmik und Metrik in traditionellen Musikkulturen*, ed. Oskár Elschek (Bratislava: Slovakian Academy of Sciences, 1990); Martin Pfleiderer, *Rhythmus. Psychologische, theoretische und stilanalytische Aspekte populärer Musik* (Bielefeld: transcript, 2006).

[14] Curt Sachs, *Rhythm and Tempo. A Study in Music History* (New York, 1953; reprint New York: CUP, 1988).

[15] E. g., the collection *Rhythmus. Ein interdisziplinäres Handbuch*, ed. Katharina Müller and Gisa Aschersleben (Berne et al.: Huber, 2000).

Praetorius • Terpsichore

Prior to producing his *Syntagma Musicum* in three volumes between 1614 and 1619, Michael Praetorius had already written and published a detailed preface to *Terpsichore*, a collection of several hundred French dances in 1612.[16] In this preface, he explains, inter alia, »wie diese Däntze müssen tactiret und mensuriret warden« (how these dances are to be metered and beaten in time).[17] The word »müssen« is here presumably used with the older meaning of »mögen« or »können« (may, can) and thus not intended as prescriptive, since the examples Praetorius goes on to cite would make no sense otherwise.

Looking at two dances from *Terpsichore* – a Bransle gay and a Volte[18] – Praetorius goes through several possibilities of metering melodies. He states this to be possible because the »Musici allici« had »notated [them] in such a way« that one could use them »with three kinds of time.«[19] To demonstrate this, he wrote the melodies out several times and divided them by means of shorter or longer vertical lines as Tripla, Sesquialtera or Alla breve.[20] Here, to begin with, is the melody of the Bransle gay without »Strichlin« (markings) (Ex. 3-001) but with a rhythmic profile, limited to the rhythmic weight of the tonal durations:

Ex. 3-001 Praetorius, »Bransle Gay« from *Terpsichore* No. 1

In their succession, the longer (𝅗𝅥, 𝅘𝅥.) and shorter (𝅘𝅥, 𝅘𝅥𝅮) notes of different values introduce a certain regularity into the melody that at least suggests a rhythm of 3 𝅘𝅥. This does not at first interest Praetorius, however. He presents different mensurations, without paying any attention to the actual rhythm of the melody.

Ex. 3-001a Tripla

The tripla mensuration (Ex. 3-001a, 3/2)[21] fits well into the rhythm of the melody. The repeated rhythm 𝅘𝅥𝅘𝅥𝅘𝅥 𝅗𝅥 always occurs at the same point in the mensuration.

Ex. 3-001b Sesquialtera

The sesquialtera version (Ex. 3-001b, 3/4, actually 6/4 as 3+3 𝅘𝅥) can work only if the first quarter is defined as an upbeat, something Praetorius secures by means of the two rests and the dividing line between the first two quarters.[22] By itself, the rhythm of the melody does not point to such a mensuration.

Ex. 3-001c Alla breve

The alla breve version (Ex. 3-001c, 2/2) is indicated by Praetorius by means of long lines (|) after every fourth minima (𝅘𝅥) and short lines (ᵎ) after every second. This mensuration clashes with the rhythm of the melody, as is evident, e.g., from the fact that the restart of the first phrase (after 9 𝅘𝅥) falls into the middle of the 2/2 measure, while the beginning is on the first beat.

Ex. 3-001d Alla breve (dimin.)

The final variant (Ex. 3-001d) differs from the alla breve form (Ex. 3-001c) only in being diminished at the ratio of 2:1. However, Praetorius sets his »Strichlin« here only after every fourth fusa (𝅘𝅥𝅮), that is, exactly like the bar lines in modern 2/4 time.

---

[16] Michael Praetorius, *Terpsichore, Musarum Aoniarum* […] (Wolfenbüttel, 1612). Ed. Günther Oberst as vol. 15 of the Praetorius Complete Edition (Wolfenbüttel, Berin, 1929); Praetorius, *Syntagma musicum*, vol. 1: *Musicae artis Analecta* (Wittenberg, 1614/15); vol. 2: *De Organographia* (Wolfenbüttel, 1619); vol. 3: *Termini musici* (Wolfenbüttel, 1619); reprint of the three vols. (Kassel et al.: Bärenreiter, 1958/59).

[17] *Terpsichore*, xi. In the *Syntagma Musicum*, Praetorius refers to these explanation (vol. 3, pt. 2, ch. 5, 34f.).

[18] The example of the Bransle gay occurs in the preface on pp. xif., the dance itself (No. 1) on p. 1; the example of the Volte is found in the preface on pp. xiif., the dance itself (No. 214) on p.118.

[19] Ibid., xi. Praetorius had been given the mostly single-voiced melodies by a French dancing-master for the purpose of turning them into five- or four-part settings.

[20] See also Harald Heckmann, »Der Takt in der Musiklehre des 17. Jahrhunderts,« *AfMw*, 10 (1953), 116-119; pp. 119-121; Wolf Frobenius, article »Tactus« in *Handwörterbuch der musikalischen Terminologie* (Wiesbaden, 1971), 1-11; pp. 9-11; Carl Dahlhaus, »Die Tactus- und Proportionslehre des 15. bis 17. Jahrhunderts,« in Dahlhaus et al., *Hören, Messen und Rechnen in der frühen Neuzeit* (Geschichte der Musiktheorie, vol. 6) (Darmstadt, 1987), 333-361; pp. 355-357.

[21] All of the examples are in *Terpsichore*, xi-xiii. Praetorius notates alla semibrevis, i.e., augmented at the ratio of 2:1.

[22] Ibid., xi.

Ex. 3-002 Praetorius, »Volte« from *Terpsichore* No. 214

For his second example, Praetorius cites a Volte from *Terpsichore* (No. 214), which he likewise meters according to the mensurations of tripla, sesquialtera and alla breve. I show to begin with again the unmetered melody with added rhythmic profile (Ex. 3-002). This dance tune is rhythmically more complex than the earlier one. Because of its contour, the triadic melody, faintly reminiscent of fanfares, forms an irregular, partly ternary components rhythm (C-A-F / F-C-A / A-F-C). The mensuration patterns Praetorius imposes are again unaffected by this.

Ex. 3-002a Tripla

In the tripla version (Ex. 3-002a) it comes at first as a surprise that Praetorius here construes an upbeat, emphasized not only by the rests and the small lines but by a large bar line drawn through the entire staff.[23] One may presume that in this instance he did for once attend to the rhythmic condition of the melody. In any case, this 2/2 version fits well into the mensural structure, as can be seen at the end of the first repeat period: 2 ♩, which the upbeat dovetails with organically at the repetition (omitting the rests). Such a solution would have suggested itself also in the Bransle Gay, where Praetorius did not consider an upbeat form.

Ex. 3-002b Sesquialtera

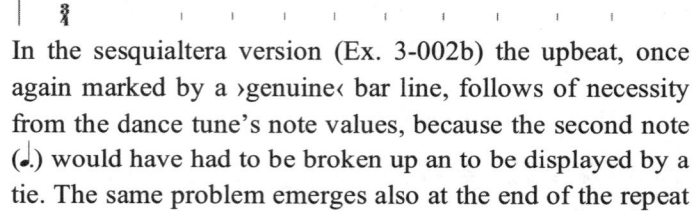

In the sesquialtera version (Ex. 3-002b) the upbeat, once again marked by a ›genuine‹ bar line, follows of necessity from the dance tune's note values, because the second note (♩.) would have had to be broken up an to be displayed by a tie. The same problem emerges also at the end of the repeat period, where Praetorius notes two semi-breves (𝅗𝅥) and places the dividing line immediately after the second. Apart from that, the sesquialtera mensuration makes for the ternary rhythm of the fanfare melody to seem well ›in time.‹

Ex. 3-002c Alla breve

Praetorius gives us the alla breve mensuration in three variants. To begin with (Ex. 3-002c), he presents an upbeat version, again signaled by an emphatic bar line, with alternating longer and shorter »Strichlin.« In the repeat, the omission of the rest creates a supernumerary 𝅗𝅥 (something Praetorius does not mention).

Ex. 3-002d Alla breve (diminished)

He then (Ex. 3-002d) transcribes this version into a ›modern‹ alla breve but omits the signal bar line after the upbeat note and dispenses with marking the half-measures by short lines.

Ex. 3-002e Alla breve (diminished and downbeat)

Finally (Ex. 3-002e), Praetorius subjoins a version without upbeat in diminished alla breve with the following commentary: »And this meter pleases me the most here and also seems the most correct, and the rest at the beginning can well be omitted and the beat begun straight from the first note: for that way it is even better.«[24] If, however, one considers the unfit conclusion resulting from the 2e variant, one must conclude that Praetorius can have approved, not of the result, but only of the form of notation: an admirer of contemporary Italian music, and especially of the modern madrigal, he here expresses a commitment to the »*note nere*,« meaning »that ¢ is no longer declared for minimae (𝅗𝅥), as hitherto, but preferentially for subminimae (♩), which are black.«[25]

Ex. 3-003 Praetorius, *Terpsichore*, Courante No. 196, Beginning

One can see from these examples alone, which Pretorius sets forth in the preface to *Terpsichore*, that the use of the »Strichlin« is neither uniform nor systematic. This is true a fortiori of the dances that follow. The majority of them are not marked at all. A relatively large number have only a single »Strichlin« behind the first note at the beginning to signal an upbeat. If an entire dance is marked with dividing

---

[23] Werner Braun first noted this under the heading »Upbeat Problems« in his study of music theory at the transition from the Middle Ages to the modern age. See his *Deutsche Musiktheorie des 15. bis 17. Jahrhunderts. Zweiter Teil: Von Calvisius bis Mattheson* (Geschichte der Musiktheorie, vol. 8 / 2) (Darmstadt, 1994), 355f.

[24] Ibid., xiii.

[25] Frobenius, op. cit. »Tactus« (see note 20), 10.

lines, they often appear only in one of the five or four voices. Only rarely are settings systematically divided into measures in every part, such as the courantes nos. 193 to 196, which are written in 6/4 time, with longer lines on the first beat and shorter ones on the fourth ♩, and mostly have ♩ upbeats. Yet it is precisely these four pieces that make it hard to agree with Harald Heckmann's view »that the tactus lines used by Praetorius have nothing in common with the modern bar lines as determinants of accent.«[26] As can be seen clearly in No. 196 (Ex. 3-003), the rhythm of each individual voice, as well as that of the entire setting, fits well into the 6/4 meter. The ambivalence of the half-measures, evident from the fact that Praetorius (M.P.C.) lets the four measures end on the weak beat (»in tempore«), whereas I (P.P.) would conclude it on the strong beat (»cum tempore«), is a well-known phenomenon, which one can still find after the modern graduated accent meter had already been widely developed.

Ex. 3-004   Praetorius, *Terpsichore* No. 201 (upper voice)

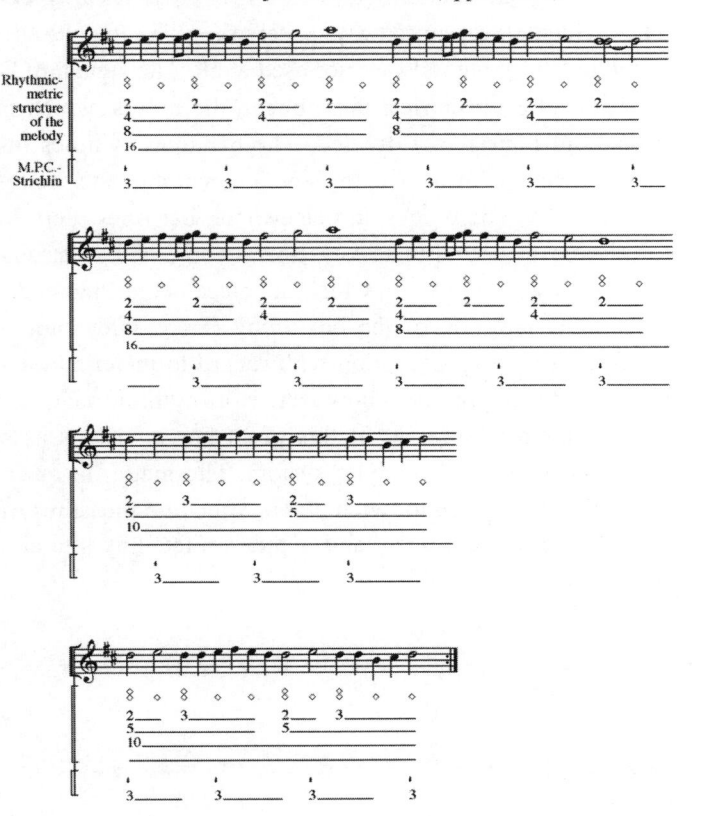

Alongside the instances proving that Praetorius, in ›metrically‹ marking the French dances, probably did have the rhythmic condition of melody and tonal setting in both view and hearing, there is at least one example that contains a mistaken metering.

The »Volte« No. 201 from *Terpsichore* is set for five voices and furnished with »Strichlin« in the tripla mensuration (3/2) in the outer parts, initially also the inner ones.[27] If one plays the piece through impartially, however, it quickly becomes clear that the dance is a kind of duplex. Whereas the first phrase (including repeat) proceeds in duple time (2/2) on the basis of several components, 2/2 and 3/2 times take turns in a second, briefer and likewise repeated phrase. Pretorius's marking wholly ignores these phenomena. Thus his 3/2 time breaks the final note of the first set of eight measures, with consequent ties in the Collected Edition. Besides the repeats each time start on a different beat. And the whole point of the piece, the alternation between duple and triple time, is lost in the 3/2 meter being barreled across the entire connection.

From the point of view of the components theory, Praetorius's reflections on mensuration and tactus are of interest for his time only insofar as there are indications that the rhythmic shape of music, that is to say, a rhythm that goes beyond the compilation and ordering of individual tonal durations, is intentionally set in relation to the metrical order. If one can affirm this with regard to Praetorius's compositional practice, it must be denied in terms of his theory. Nowhere in his writings is there a single utterance to explain why a given melody or some other musical configuration fits more or less well into one or the other mensural construct. The description, let alone analysis, of an actual musical composition was simply not within the horizon of 17th century observers and listeners. Instead, to those interested in technical questions rules were given as to how a composition was to be written down. It would be a long time yet before attempts were made to apprehend music as an aesthetic object – the precondition for being able to fathom its rhythm as well.

---

[26] Heckmann, op. cit., »Takt« (n. 20), 120.

[27] Günther Oberst, the editor of the Complete Edition, has picked up this nomenclature and transformed it into genuine bar lines going through all five staves.

Kircher • Musurgia universalis

In 1640, the native German Jesuit Athanasius Kircher published his opus magnum *Musurgia universalis sive Ars magna consoni et dissoni* in Rome.[28] The Greek word »musurgia« means roughly »actions of the Muses.« The subject of Kircher's treatise is thus the arts of drama, dance and music, with a clear emphasis on the latter, as the subtitle with the concepts »consoni« and »dissoni« already indicates.[29]

This remarkable work is of music-historical interest on account of its categorization of musical styles, and its reflections about figures and affects. Despite his openness to the music of his contemporaries – pieces by Carissimi and Monteverdi are cited – Kircher's thinking is guided predominantly by medieval conceptions. He describes phenomena not as they are but as God intended them to be. Music is conceived as a microcosm, subject to the same laws as God's »harmonious« creation. This speculative approach pervades even those passages of the *Musurgia* that deal with rhythm and meter in music. The rational values of notes and the proportions obtaining between them are welcome to Kircher above all because with the numbers won from them he can feed his penchant for combination theory and general system building. What really happens rhythmically eludes him, even in the musical examples made up by himself.

The three-part instrumental piece composed by Kircher[30] and shown in facsimile in Ex. 3-005, is an example of the church style. Not without some vanity, Kircher remarks at the end of the piece of 115 semibreves (◊): »One will find in this three-part piece everything one could wish from a perfect harmonic work of art.«[31] »Harmonic« here means »coherent,« »well-proportioned«; it thus refers to all the components of a tone setting, such as melody, harmony, rhythm and form.

Ex. 3-005   Kircher (Original)

The original notation (Ex. 3-005) is only partially exact. Accidentals are not always entered (e.g., in the alto, m. 1, 2nd note G♯); naturals are not used at all. The signature C does not refer to metrical units but to the brevis, which is throughout imperfectly divided. The bar lines at times indicate a change from 3 ◊ to 2 or 4 ◊, without this being indicated. (At line breaks and elsewhere, bar lines seem to be missing at times.) The key is A minor, with a strong tendency toward the V, on which the piece begins and ends.

My transcription of the beginning (Ex. 3-006) should be taken only as a suggestion with regard to meter and accidentals. Of importance, however, is a rhythmic fact that Kircher neither addresses at this point nor envisions as a case anywhere in his analytic system. The matter in question is the first soggetto, wich enters after five measures of introduction in the descant and is then imitated by alto and

Ex. 3-006   Kircher, Triphonium (from *Musurgia universalis* vol. 1 p. 311), Beginning

bass. This melodic sequence of falling thirds is shaped temporarily into 3/4 units (♩♩♩♩♩♩) by means of the components »Diastematy« (crest notes) and »Sound« (tonal duration). This rhythm, going athwart the 3/2 meter, has a considerable appeal, as it provides rhythmic animation and increased complexity, especially when the imitating voice (alto) follows, at an interval of one minima (♩ in the transcription), in the same rhythm (as does the bass a little later). Kircher probably included such phernomena, which he must at any rate have ›heard,‹ under such aspects as variatio or artificium; but he has no method available for ana-

---

[28] Athanasius Kircher, *Musurgia universalis*, ed., with a foreword and index, Ulf Scharlau, reprographic reprint (Hildesheim, 1970).

[29] Cf. the elucidations by Melanie Wald in her dissertation *Welterkenntnis aus Musik. Athanasius Kirchers »Musurgia universalis« und die Universalwissenschaft im 17. Jahrhundert* (Kassel, 2006), 182.

[30] Cf. M. Wald on this »triphonium« and on Kircher as composer of it, ibid. 161-170.

[31] »Habes in hoc Triphonio, quicquid in perfecto harmonico artificio desiderari potest.« *Musurgia*, 1:313.

lyzing these rhythms – and neither did any other theoretician before and long after him.

The same deficits can be detected with regard to other time-structuring and thus rhythmic phenomena. Book VII of the *Musurgia* deals, in its 3rd part, entitled »De Musicae patheticae,« with emotions that can be evoked by music. In section VI. § 5, Kircher cites an example of two contrary affects, which he titles, respectively, »Religio« and »Mundus.«

The two examples differ indeed strongly in their mode of motion (Ex. 3-007). In his preliminary commentary,[32] Kircher describes an experimental arrangement of expressing diverse affects (»diversis affectibus«) in one and the same key (»sub eodem Tono«). Even the number of bars seems to have been equalized: the »religio« phrase and the first part of the »mundus« phrase, which is to be repeated, have each six measures, and to mark this equality in number, the first chord in each case is an E major and the last an E minor.

Kircher expresses the contrary emotions through underlaid texts: for the religio setting: »Why does the world strive for empty glory, whose profit is transitory,« for the

In my transcription, I have indicated two phenomena relevant to rhythm that Kircher might have addressed if a description of the actual rhythmics had been within his purview: iso- or heterometry and harmony. The bar lines in the religio phrase mark units of 5 ♩, which are diminished to 2-♩ units with the harmonic cadence at the end. In the mundus phrase, der relational value is diminished and a dance-like 4-♩-meter is constructed, which runs through from beginning to end.

The harmonic rhythm, too, is interesting, inasmuch as it closely matches the rhythm of the other components in the religio part, while in the mundus part it progresses much more calmly than, say, the rhythms of the tonal duration. The 5-♩ measures are initially subdivided into 2+3 ♩ by the harmonic rhythm, as can be seen from the heavy harmonic weight on the third beat; in the second part, on the other hand, all regularity dissolves (note the syncopations in the 4th bar), so that the last four measures seem like an indivisible unity.

The 4/4 beats of the mundus world, by contrast, appear so dance-like because – at double tempo – the harmonic changes themselves have a leaping character (♩. ♪♩) in the first two measures) or simply follow in quick succession.

Ex. 3-007   Kircher, *Paradigma IV. »Religio« and V. »Mundus«* (from *Musurgia universalis* vol. 1 p. 618)

mundus setting: »Let us be merry together and exult by singing high-ho.«[33] On the emotional aspects of music, however, he comments only in very general terms: »seemly affects« for the religious context, »somehow rapidly flowing« music for the secular one.[34]

The merry high-hó calls alternately by the paired bass/alto and tenor/descant obtain their rhythmic pithiness from the fact that the harmonic changes always happen on the syllable –hó, with the result of clear up- and downbeat situations.

---

[32] *Musurgia*, 1: 618.

[33] »Cur mundus militat sub vana gloria cuius prosperitas est transitoria.« – »Gaudeamus unanimiter et exultemus Io cantantes« (ibid.).

[34] »affectus convenientes« – »fluxum nescio quid tumultuarium« (ibid.).

All in all, one has to conclude that Athanasius Kircher has nothing to say about the concrete rhythm in music. He recapitulates the system of note values and metrical rules, borrows some poetic meters (»pedes harmonices«) from classical prosody, and refers to the human heartbeat as frame of reference for all rhythms and meters. The fact that musical processes might include durations and durational relations other than those represented by the notes on the page lay not within his field of vision. Kircher did sense the rhythmic multiformity of single- and multivoiced music, and even demonstrated that in his own compositions, but he was unable, or unwilling, to describe it in detail.

His work, the *Musurgia universalis*, is not devalued thereby in its enormous significance for intellectual and cultural history. One may question, however, whether what Kircher aimed at can really be comprehended under the catchword »Welterkenntnis [world cognition] aus Musik,« as Melanie Wald urges in her otherwise excellent treatise about Kircher's *Musurgia*.[35] As a German Jesuit active in Rome, Kircher was really after the cognition and affirmation of the Deity from the perspective of music, not after a scientific description of reality.

Printz • Satyrical Composer

Wolfgang Caspar Printz was a novelist (in the tradition of Grimmelshausen), musicologist (with contacts to Athanasius Kircher) and composer. His *chef d'oeuvre* in music theory is the *Satyrische Componist*, whose three parts came out separately and then together in Dresden.[36] Part 3, which appeared in 1678, includes a lengthy section »of the Generibus Modulandi Rhythmicis«[37]. Without rehearsing the general doctrine of mensuration and meter,[38] Printz here describes four different »rhythmic feet« (»pedes rhythmici«) and their »joining together,« under the general aspect of rhythmic modulation. In addition, he discusses the structuration of single-voiced melodies (»Numeri Sectionales«), an area he includes explicitly under musical rhythm (»all of which have their foundation in musica rhythmica«).[39]

In describing the four most important *pedes* of his time, Printz assumes a parallelity of poetry and music: »Here it should be noted that just as speech is either bound [verse] or unbound [prose], so in music every melody is either bound or unbound.«[40] *Pedes* are found only in bound melodies, by which Printz means essentially metrical ones. One can tell this from the fact that he represents, e.g., the iamb as two equal note values, of which the first comes before the bar line, the second after.

Among the four feet Printz describes – the iamb, the trochee, the »enantius« (or »contrarius«) and the dactyl – the third is Printz's own invention, as Werner Braun has pointed out.[41] In it, as contrary to the dactyl, it is not the first beat of a ternary meter but the second that is given emphasis through lengthening: Dactyl: | ♩. ♪♩ |, Enantius (Contrarius): | ♩ ♩. ♪ |.

It is, I think, high time to subject the *pedes* doctrine, derived from classical prosody and picked up by Printz among others, to a critical and not merely descriptive scrutiny. For not only can the poetic categories of short and long not do justice to the differentiated durational dispositions in music, but the application of these rhythmic patterns also results in musical combinations appearing as if pieced together. The mechanically superimposed *pedes* sequences deprive music of its life: its character as something in flow is lost. The ambivalence of sound events within the rhythmic and metric continuum, which is part of the essence of music, can only apparently be pressed into an unequivocal frame. Feet, for example, tend to exclude the well-known iridescence between iamb and trochee, which for every musician is unproblematic and, indeed, attractive.

In chapter 16 of *Phrynis* III, Printz illustrates his argument by presenting, for each of the four *pedes*, five dance-like melodies, which he has evidently invented himself. Very systematically, though with some previously anounced licenses,[42] multi-measure »Melodiae Ligatae« in a two-part dance form (|: A :|: B :|) are constructed for every foot, whose »Numerus Sectionalis« goes from one over two, three and five to seven.[43] That means, the caesuras in these melodies are to appear always after 1, 2, 3, 5 or 7 measures.

Ex. 3-008 shows the five examples (A parts) that stand for the iamb. Since Printz points out each time that the melodies consist exclusively of iambs (»nothing but iambi«), I have tried to mark them beneath the notes (in Printz,[44] the

---

[35] See note 29.

[36] Wolfgang Caspar Printz, *Phrynis Mitilinaeus oder Satyrischer Componist*, Part I: 1676, Part II: 1677, Part III: 1678, all three parts together: Dresden/Leipzig 1696. There is to date no reprint of *Phrynis*, but the text can be found on the internet in the »Wolfenbüttel Digital Library« (http://diglib.hab.de/).

[37] Ibid., chs. 11-17, pp. 96-131.

[38] See also Wolfgang Caspar Printz, *Compendium musicae, in quo breviter ac succincte explicantur & traduntur omnia* (Guben, 1668, reprint Hildesheim, 1974); Wolfgang Caspar Printz, *Historische Beschreibung der edelen Sing- und Kling-Kunst* (Dresden, 1690; facsimile reprint ed., with new indexes, Othmar Wessely (Graz, 1964).

[39] *Phrynis*, 3:97.

[40] *Phrynis*, 3:100.

[41] Braun, *Deutsche Musiktheorie des 15. bis 17. Jahrhunderts* (see note 23), 192.

[42] *Phrynis* III: 108ff.

[43] Ibid.: 113.

[44] Ibid.: 114-116.

notes are unmarked). How the iambs are to be located is sometimes evident, but mostly unclear. Thus it is reasonable to interpret the beginning of the Binarius with its durational sequence ♩ | ♩. ♪♩. ♪ | ♩. ♪♩ as a chain of four iambs, although other ways of reading it would be possible and plausible (e.g., a dactyl in the second bar). However, to conceive the five sequential ♩ in mm. 2-4 as iambs is more problematic; moreover, the conclusion of the Binarius, where the typically dactylic rhythm ♩ ♪♪ is declared to be an iamb merely because it is upbeat, seems incomprehensible, even arbitrary.

No less contradictory is the determination of the melodic caesuras according to the »Numeri Sectionales«, especially since Printz cites no criteria for it. In the *Unitas*, e.g., a division into 1+2 bars seems preferable, since the quasi sequencing descent of the melody from A5 to G4 extends over two measures. In the *Binarius*, we are evidently dealing with a superordinate structure of 4+4 measures, which is much more effective as a structuring element than

at all costs, as one can see in the remaining chapters of the rhythm section, where now also melodies »of diverse Pedum Rhythmicorum« (chapter 17)[46] are presented, albeit limited, for lack of space, to dance tunes (minuet, courante) and to the *pedes* pair dactyl and contrario.[47] The method of analysis remains unchanged, and the insights Printz conveys to us are correspondingly meager.

The »Satyrical Composer« is garnished with numerous fictional anecdotes, which will surely have amused the educated among Printz's readers. Already the name of the composer who is the putative author of the three-volume work – Phrynidis Mytilenæus – signals a role-playing approach, in which »Wolffgang Caspar Printz / von Waldthurn / Reichs-Gräflich Promnitzischer Director Musices und Cantor der Stadt Sorau« functions ›only‹ as the editor. At times one gets the impression that even in the music-theoretical parts the fun of role-playing, e.g. that of a pernickety systematist (on the model of the »Dottore« in Commedia dell'arte), takes over.

Ex. 3-008 Printz, *Phrynis* III, 5 Examples for Iambic Melodies (J. = iamb, numbers = Numeri sectionales)

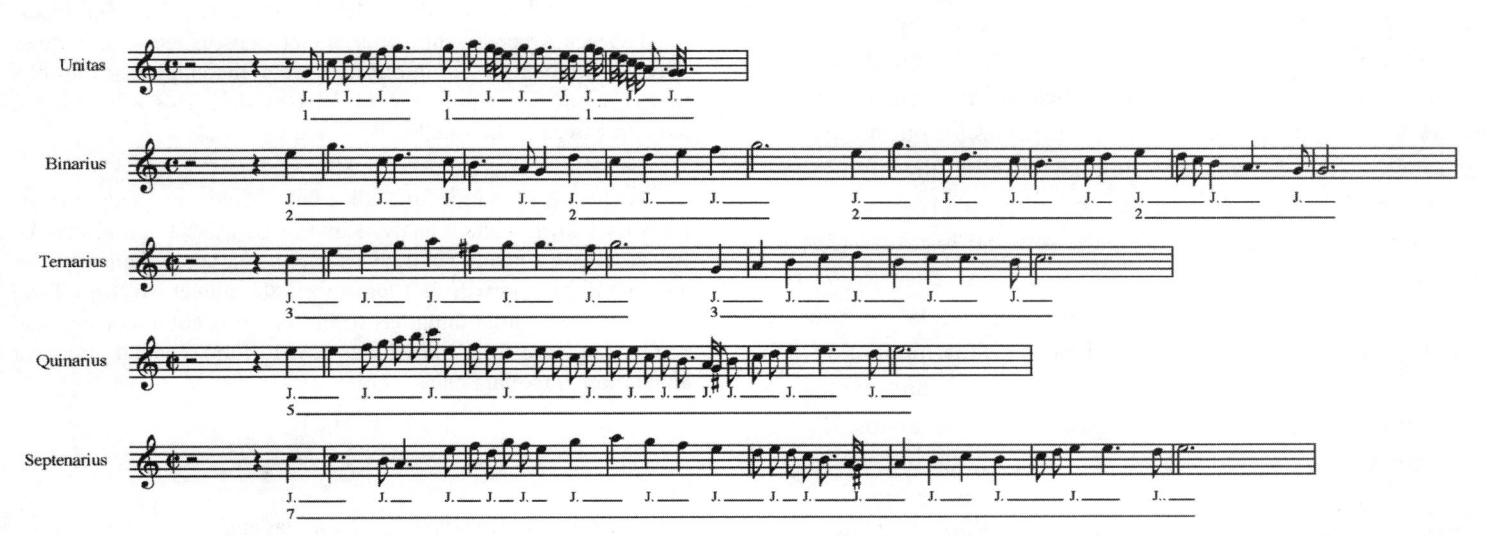

Printz's two-bar division. The *Ternarius* with its 3+3 allabreve measures is actually convincing as Printz has written it. The *Quinarius*, however, exhibits secondary caesuras that Printz lets simply go by the board (1+2+2 measures). The same is true of the Septenarius (2+3+2 measures), whose partial phrases should be noted because of their melodic drop and their inherent harmonic progression (here, as also in the Quinarius, C major → A minor → Phrygian half-close).

Printz has constructed a closed system for himself, meant to endow his expositions with a semblance of rationality and scientific rigor.[45] He applies this system stubbornly and

Printz's historical importance consist in having »effected the turn from the mensural tactus and the recognition of the modern meter (as the time-measuring quantity initially).«[48] On the other hand, one cannot say that his doctrine of *pedes* and *sectiones* conributed anything to the elucidation of the rhythmic relations in music. Rather, one cannot but admit that this explanatory pattern superimposed upon music *ab extra* more nearly obscured the actual rhythm of melodies and tone settings.

---

[45] Thomas Buchner, in his study of Printz's *Phrynis*, sees it less critically: »Prinz now pulls out all the musicological stops by calling, without any advance warning, upon the higher arithmetics of the ›ars musica.‹«; see Thomas Buchner, *Der »Satyrische Componist« von Wolfgang Caspar Printz (1641-1717) im Wirkungsgefüge des musikökonomischen und musiktheoretischen Wandels zum ausgehenden 17. Jahrhundert* (Winzer, 2007), 54.

[46] *Phrynis* III: 123.

[47] On p. 125 (*Phrynis* III), Printz proclaims what really should be done. Classified according to the two kinds of meter – duple (»vulgaris«) and triple (»proportionatus«) – he sketches the following program: »If two different *pedes* are joined together, they are either Iambi and Trochaei vulgares or Iambi vulgares und Syncopatici or Trochaei vulgares and Syncopatici, or Trochaei Proportionati and Dactyli, or Trochaei Proportionati and Contrarii, or Dactyli and Contrarii.«

[48] Heckmann, op. cit., »Tact« (see note 20), 191.

Mattheson • The Complete Capellmeister

Of the numerous writings of Johann Matthesons,[49] his theory of composition, published in Hamburg in 1739 under the title *Der vollkommene Capellmeister*, was the most important and far-reaching one. What Mattheson had to say here about rhythm and meter of vocal and instrumental music has been reviewed in detail by Wilhelm Seidel.[50] I can only give some specifications.

Mattheson defined his conception of rhythm at the beginning of chapter 6 in part II of his treatise:[51]

The meaning of the term **rhythm** is nothing other than a **number** that is, a certain measuring or counting, of syllables there, of sounds here, not only with respect to their quantity, but also in regard to their **shortness** and **length**.

The point of reference for the counting or measuring is the individual note, whose duration is a multiple of the smallest value used. By combining shorter or longer notes, rhythmic-melodic figures are formed, for which Mattheson introduced the term »Klangfüße« or „sound feet.« Seidel has rightly pointed out that the names of these sound feet which Mattheson borrows from poetics and rhetoric, do not mean that he has derived the musical rhyhms from the poetic meters. On the contrary, he realized »that the rhythms are more variable and numerous than the meters« and that one should in fact assume that »the musical formulas [...] predate the poetic ones.«[52]

The list of sound feet that Mattheson presents[53] – from the »spondee« to the »proceleusmaticus,« they number 18, the count being open at the upper end, since variants can be formed and further sound feet invented – has the status of a collection of rhythmic patterns, to which Mattheson, moreover, ascribes expressive qualities like »honorable« and »serious« (for the spondee) or »commanding« and »rousing« (for the proceleusmaticus).

One will notice here already that Mattheson loads the elementary forms with qualities that have their origin somewhere other than in the mere durational relations between the individual notes. This can be concluded directly from a series of dances he has remodeled from church hymns so as to demonstrate »the immense power of rhythmopoeia« – a pretty bold undertaking prompted by the spirit of the Enlightenment.[54] What transpires here musically (and, I think, also rhythmically) is much more differentiated than Mattheson's theory of rhythm and meter would lead one to expect. His analyses, even of his home-made (and altogether very successful) examples, fail to do justice to the actual compositional, and thus also rhythmical, facts of the case.

To document this, I will quote at some length, and then discuss, the analysis of a minuet, which Mattheson presents in the chapter »Of the Kinds of Melodies and their Distinguishing Marks« in the *Vollkommene Capellmeister*,[55] elucidating in the footnotes the not always readily intelligible terms and trains of thought.

§. 79.

It has been mentioned above that in instrumental pieces everything has to be observed that compositional art demands of vocal melodies, often even more than that.[56] This should be reemphasized here, as we move on to instrumental melodies and their genre. For here one must first consider the emotional states to be expressed by sheer sounds, without words, then the turns in the tonal speech, where again words cannot show us the way, because they are not being used; thirdly, the stress, the emphasis; fourthly, the geometric, and fifthly, the arithmetic state[57]. This will be found to be true even in the smallest of melodies.

§. 80.

As in all of nature and all created being no body can be properly known without analysis into its parts, so I will always be first to divide a melody and investigate its parts sytematically. For an experiment, we will first turn to a little minuet, so that all can see what such a little thing has within it if it is not a monster, and so one can learn from little things how to form a sound judgment about more important ones.

§. 81.

Thus
I. Le Menuet, *la Minuetta*, whether made { for playing, for singing, for dancing, } in particular

---

[49] See the complete list in Hans-Joachim Hinrichsen and Klaus Pietschmann, article „Mattheson, Johann" in MGG², Persons, vol. 11 (Kassel et al., 2004), cols. 1332-1349, index of writings by Pietschmann cols. 1337-39.

[50] Seidel, *Rhythmustheorien* (see note 1, above p. 189), 42ff.

[51] Johann Mattheson, *Der vollkommene Capellmeister* (Hamburg, 1739). Facsimile reprint ed. M. Reimann (Kassel, Basel, 1954), 160.

[52] Seidel, *Rhythmustheorien* (see note 1), 43.

[53] Perspicuously compiled by Seidel, ibid., 44-46.

[54] Mattheson, *Capellmeister*, 161-164.

[55] *Capellmeister*, 223-225. Mattheson had cited and discussed this B minor minuet already in his *Kern melodischer Wissenschaft* (*Essence of Melodic Science*) (Hamburg, 1737, reprint Hildesheim, 1990), 109f. (On the variants, see Ernst Apfel, »Ein Menuett bei Johann Mattheson«, *Die Musikforschung*, 29 (1976), 295f. In the following I quote from the *Capellmeister*.)

[56] Mattheson is here referring to Part I, chapter 10 (»Of musical Notation«), §. 65: »All playing is but an imitation and accompaniment of singing; in fact, a player who composes something for instruments must observe everything that is required for a good melody and harmony much more conscientiously than a singer or someone wo composes for voices, because in singing one has the support of very clear words, which in instrumental music is always lacking.« See for detail also chapter 12 of Part II, entitled »Of the Difference between Song and Instrumental Melodies.«

[57] What is meant by the geometric and arithmetic state is explained later.

has no other affect than that of a **moderate merriness**. If the melody of a minuet is only sixteen measures in length (for it cannot be any shorter), it will be seen to include at least a few commas, a semicolon, a couple of colons and a couple of full stops.[58] Some will find this hard to conceive, but it is so.

§. 82.

If the melody is genuine, one can also clearly register the stress,[59] not to mention the accents,[60] question marks[61] etc. that will be included. The geometric state, as well as the arithmetic [*] otherwise known as numerum sectionalem and rhythmum] are indispensable elements in animated melodies, furnishing them with the right measure and shape. We want to show an example of this in the minuet, which can serve as a model for the analysis of all others.[62]

[Emendanda[63]:]

§. 83.

Here we have now a complete melodic **paragraph** of 16 bars, which turn into 48 if one plays it through to the end.[64] This paragraph consists of two simple sentences, or periods, which, like the following sections, are expanded by one third of the whole **through the repetition;**[65] their concluding notes are marked with three dots (∴) below the note;[66] the final end, as the full stop, is marked with ⌒.[67]

§. 84.

This paragraph contains not only a **colon**,[68] but also a **Semicolon**[69], or half-colon, to be recognized by the common punctuation marks set below the notes. There are furthermore three **Commas**,[70] which turn into nine[71] and are marked with the familiar comma sign. The threefold **emphasis**, however, we have marked with three asterisks.[72] The **geometric state** here is 4, as in all good dance tunes, and therefore has 4 daggers to distinguish it.[73] The sound feet[74] of the first and second bar are used again in the fifth and sixth bar. The others, which present themselves in the ninth and tenth bar, are heard right away again in the eleventh and twelfth, which constitutes **arithmetic uniformity**.[75] That comprises the entire sub-

---

58   These structural concepts, ascending from minor to major, are taken from the realm of linguistic grammar (cf. also chapter nine of Part II: »Of the Sections and Turns of Sound Speech«). They will be explained presently by an example.

59   Meaning »emphasis« here. In II/8, §. 2, Mattheson defines the »real emphasis« as »the tone and stress of the words,« always connected with »the emotional state,« whereby the »sense or meaning of the recital« (II/8, §. 10) is made clear.

60   Accents to Mattheson means, on the one hand, manners consisting of tones added to a rising or falling melody (cf. II/3, §. 20ff.); he also calls them »Vorschlaege« (grace-notes) (II/3, §. 26). On the other hand, Mattheson also speaks of »accentus metricus« (II/8, §. 7) as signifying the weight of a syllable or analogously a lengthened melody note. See also the entire eighth chapter »Of Stress in Melody« (174ff.).

61   According to Mattheson, »question marks« can be signaled by rising final notes (genuine questions) or level or even falling ones (rhetorical questions) (II/9, §§ 61-64).

62   The melody is probably by Mattheson himself.

63   This correction is to be taken from the list of printing errors in the appendix to the book.

64   An execution according to the schema of ||:A:||:B A:|| adds up to 48 bars. Seidel errs in thinking the repetition of the middle part had inadvertently not been indicated; *Rhythmustheorien* (see note 1), 76.

65   This refers to the repetition of the first eights bars.

66   See bar 8 (twice) and bar 16.

67   See bar 8. (The mark used here only approximates the one employed by Mattheson.)

68   See the mark › : ‹ at the end of bar 4.

69   See the mark › ; ‹ at the end of bar 12.

70   See the mark › , ‹ at the end of bar 2, bar 6 and bar 10.

71   Correctly, 10 commas. The B minor period contains two commas and is played four times, while the D major period consists of one comma and is played twice: 8+2=10 commas.

72   See the asterisks beneath the G5 in bar 2 and 5 and under the E5 in m. 11 (correction by Mattheson).

73   This indicates that »geometric state« means a recurring divisional measure of four bars. The dagger (› † ‹) therefore occurs at the end of measures 4, 8, 12 and 16 (above the notes and systems).

74   On this, see the sixth chapter of Part II: »Of Length and Shortness of Sound, or of the Making of the Sound feet.« The sound feet entered above the notes by Mattheso are: | v – | = iamb (§. 6.); | – v – | = amphimacer (§. 32.); | $v\,v$ – – | = ionicus, a minori (§. 35.); | – – – | = Molossian (§. 26.).

75   We can infer from the context that »arithmetic state« or »arithmetic uniformity« signifies the regular repetition of identical rhythmic patterns. From the note cited earlier about the geometric and arithmetic state (»otherwise known as numerus sectionalis and rhythmus«) it appears that in Mattheson's view rhythmic quality results from the regular sequence of durational units (in this case the two-bar unit |♪♪♩|♩♩♩|), inasmuch as arithmetic operates with whole numbers. The division of units into sections, on the other hand, produce a geometric quality. See also Seidel, *Rhythmustheorien* (see note 1), 77f., on this.

In II/5, §. 111, Mattheson describes the two »states« as follows: »The order one observes in such application and variation of sound feet is called a geometric state: for, as the arithmetic state regards the feet on which the melody walks along, as it were, in and for themselves, the geometric state, on the other hand, indicates how they are to be combined and must signal their subdivisions properly. E. g.:

a, is a certain sound foot of three notes of different content, b is another of the same number but the same validity. Thus each has a separate arithmetic condition; c and d, on the other hand, taken together, represent the regular alternation of previous feet, making of it a whole geometric paragraph.«

division into eight parts: first, the two periods, then the colon, thirdly the semicolon, fourthly the nine commata,[76] and fifthly the emphasis; sixthly the geometric, seventh, the arithmetic state, and eighth, the final point.

Ex. 3-010   Mattheson, *Menuet*, from »Der vollkommene Capellmeister« p. 324

One can summarize Mattheson's analytic findings by entering all the references into a note diagram (Ex. 3-010). It will reveal both the schematic nature and the deficiencies of his method. One must ask, for example, why only a few rhythms are identified as sound feet, although pertinent pat-

Ex. 3-011   Rhythm Score

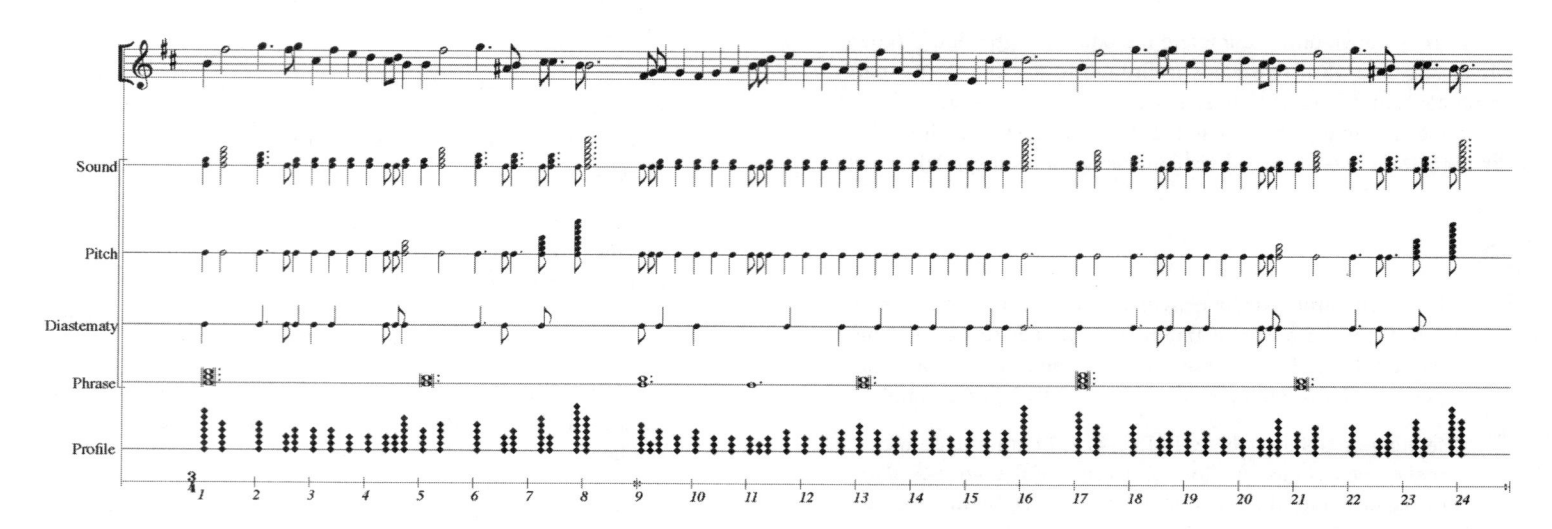

terns would be available for all measures (e.g., the molossus in m. 3, the choriambus in m. 4). Again, the ascription of the sound foot amphimacer is contradictory: if it fits m. 2, it must be out of place in m. 4, as we have a hemiolic formation there (♩. ♪♩. ♪♩. ♪), in which the third element of the amphimacer extends beyond the bar line (not notated with a tie).[77] Altogether unreasonable is also Mattheson's

selection of emphases. Altogether he assigns the asterisk standing for »stress« only three times in his musical example.[78] If at first one might still think that an upper directional change (crest note), not to mention the summit note of a phrase, might count as stressed, this is contravened by the E5 in the third measure of the middle part being marked as the only »emphatic« note, though it is followed by several tones of the same character.[79]

In no way does Mattheson do justice to the actual rhythm of his simple but pretty minuet melody. As an analyst, he is hampered by the very dogma of meter that as a composer he ignores freely and unrestrainedly. The ascription of the amphimacer to m. 6 is living proof of this. His fixation on meter may also be the reason why in the entire *Capellmeister* he nowhere discusses or even acknowledges either hemiolas or syncopations, two, after all, well-known and repeatedly theorized phenomena ever since the advent of mensural notation; these lemmas are also missing from the otherwise highly differentiated subject index.[80] Thus it

---

Translated into a modern idiom, this means that although the sound feet a and b are both tripartite, they differ in their note values. That constitutes their arithmetic state – arithmetic because all the note values are a multiple of one. The stringing together of sound feet, i.e., their spreading out in time, is called geometric; in the present case (c + d) the geometric character is constituted by the sequence of two 3/4 measures.

[76]   See note 71.

[77]   Also noted by Apfel (see footnote 55), 296.

[78]   In our Ex., the asterisk natually appears five times because of the repetitions. Note the printing error cited in footnote 65. In the 1737 version of the minuet (*Kern melodischer Wissenschaft*), the * is underneath the note.

[79]   See F♯5, E5, D5 and others.

[80]   In the index succeed the lemmas *Hemidiapente / Hemitonium / Heptachordon*.

had to escape his analysis that the main portion of his own minuet is largely hemiolic in its rhythm.

If, in my rhythm score (Ex. 3-011), one looks at the component rhythm »Sound« together with the rhythmic profile, one can instantly register the hemiolic durational relations (especially mm. 4-8). The hemiola behind the regular 3/4 structure becomes altogether obvious if one adduces yet another construct, which, while keeping the melody, uncovers the harmonic relations by means of a thorough-bass voice and fits each of two original 3/4 measures into a single 3/4 measure by diminution (Ex. 3-012) – something Mattheson would certainly have been delighted with.[81]

Ex. 3-012 (Construct)

In the middle part, the hemiolic mode seems at first to persist but is then canceled by the crest notes in favor of a ternary rhythm.[82] Altogether, the rhythm of this minuet proves to be ambiguous and oscillating between 2 𝅗𝅥. and 3 𝅗𝅥 structures. The isometric rhythm of the phrases, clearly recognizable because of the repetitions, keeps the minuet beat alive. However, the weights of the tonal durations, together with the crest and keel notes, tend more toward hemiolas. A special role is played by the note repetitions, of which there are three in the opening section (see the components line »Pitch«). The first repetition (B4-B4) reinforces the hemiolic level, the other two (C#5-C#5 and B4-B4) are conventional closing phrases, which by means of pitch anticipation lead to a blurring of the rhythmic motion.

Mattheson's theory of composition, whose significance as a step toward a »genuine musical aesthetics«[83] is undeniable, turns out to be backward-looking when it comes to rhythm. His learning spends itself in recourse to rhetoric and prosody and thereby encumbers the theory unnecessarily; it thus only gets in the way of an understanding of the objectively given rhythmic formation in the music of his time and that of his predecessors. Mattheson may have had an inkling of this. Several times he warns composers of letting themselves be bound by narrow rules. With regard to the tempo (»mouvement«) of music pieces, he writes at one point that »impulses« are active in »the heart« of musicians that cannot be explained – a concession by this rationalist that can surely be applied also to aspects other than questions of tempo:[84]

Here everyone has to reach into his bosom and see how he feels in his heart, since, depending on its state, our composing, singing and playing will receive certain degrees of an exceptional and uncommon momentum that otherwise neither the actual meter in and by itself, nor its **noticeable** retardation or acceleration, let alone the notes' own value can impart, but which only derives from an **incomprehensible** impulse. One clearly notices the effect, but does not know how it comes about.

---

[81] Cf. the bass voice added by Stefanie Vial, with which, to be sure, she wants to demonstrate exactly the persistence of the 3/4 meter vis-á-vis the hemiolas (Stephanie D. Vial, *The Art of Musical Phrasing in the Eighteenth Century. Punctuating the Classical 'Period'* (Rochester: URP, 2008), 146). In concluding her analysis, however, Vial gains the important insight that »the many rhythmical and metrical elements are all allowed to operate at their own level« (230), which could also mean that each develops its own rhythms – in other words, components rhythms.

[82] So similarly also Apfel (note 55), 297.

[83] Hinrichsen (note 49), col. 1344.

[84] *Capellmeister*, 173.

Hartung • Musicus theoretico-practicus

The *Musicus theoretico-practicus* of Philipp Christoph Hartung,[85] published in Nürnberg in 1749, consists of two parts: a *Theoria musica* and a *Clavier-Anweisung* (Piano Instruction). Included in the first part is an attempt at a theory of melody, in connection with which questions of meter and structure are also discussed. There is not a word about rhythm, however.

The intellectual orientation and aim of the treatise is made clear in the following quotation:[86]

On the basis of what we have seen from §. 309 on, we state as irrefutable: 1.) harmonies are the basis of *melodies*, 2.) *harmonies* are regular, therefore the right *melodies* are likewise *harmony*-regular. 3.) Regular *harm.* and their changes are beautiful; Regular *melodies* are therefore also beautiful. 4.) It follows that the beauty of *melodies* must be provable and errors in the *melodies* likewise provable. 5.) It must be possible to instruct a person how to make beautiful *melodies*.

Here is someone who is ›irrefutably‹ sure of himself. Arguing in a circle, he states that harmonic and melodic progressions are beautiful if they progress regularly, and if they do this, that is proof that they are beautiful.

The supposed law of regularity has been internalized by the author to such a dregree that he cites his musical examples without any indication of tonal durations, that is, only with tonal letters; evidently the reader is to assume that every note has basically the same duration. It is no wonder, therefore, that only different types of meters are discussed and the structure of melodies is identical with the structure of measures: »To properly know the ends of a short melody, it serves mainly if it is subdivided into sections of equal length, so-called bars or measures.«[87] Accents, too, are regarded as means of ordering, as »in this way, every *melody* will impress a clear order upon the ear.«[88]

In sum, we can say that this treatise makes no contribution to an understanding of what rhythm is. We must agree with Mattheson, who castigates Hartung's ›music theory‹ polemically as a know-all concatenation (*Kettenwerk*), in which »a weak link doesn't matter much.«[89]

Riepel • On Time Signatures

The Austrian composer and musicologist Joseph Riepel published a book *Anfangsgründe zur musicalischen Setzkunst* (Principles of the Art of Musical Composition) in 1752, whose first chapter is entitled »De Rhythmopoeía, or Of the Metrical Order.«[90] 24 years later he followed it up with a volume on the vocal music of his time.[91]

Riepel's *Anfangsgründe* are a whimsically written musical manual according to the motto ›composing made easy.‹ Riepel constructs a fictional teacher-pupil relationship, in which »Praeceptor« and »Discantista« discuss hundreds of small musical samples. Not unlike a course in cooking,[92] variants of mostly single-part minuets (later also symphonies and concertos) are gone through in musical examples and judged as tasty, over-seasoned or inedible. The criteria are a putative »naturalness« and »gusto«.

As the title of the first chapter already signals, rhythm means metrical order to Riepel. Beginning with the 3/4 time and the minuet as model form, time signatures are presented, and the formation of groups of measures according to the ›basic law‹ of even numbers (2, 4, 8, 16, 32) is described. Riepel writes: »For 4, 8, 16 and probably also 32 measures are the ones that are so implanted in our nature that it seems hard for us to listen to any other order (with any pleasure).«[93] We are not told how sections, periods or movements are measured, as Riepel regards that as self-evident. And indeed, examples are simple enough to let one recognize repetitions or sequencing with small variations as criteria. Groups of three, five, six, seven or nine measures are discussed as exceptions to the rule and from case to case deemed good or unusable. Rhythm in the narrower sense comes up only during the presentation of the note values. Other phenomena, like note repetitions, melodic contour, hemiolic turns or suspensions are disregarded. Riepel may well have taken them into account under aspects like ›successful‹ or ›tasteful,‹ but he does not address them explicitly.

---

[85] P. C. Humano [i.e., Philipp Christoph Hartung], *Musicus theoretico-practicus*, vol. 1: *Theoria Musica*, vol. II: *Die methodische Clavier-Anweisung* (Nuremberg, 1749); reprint ed., with a commentary, Isolde Ahlgrimm and Bernhard Billeter (Leipzig, 1977). The decryption of the pseudonym »Humano« is given in Isolde Ahlgrimm's Afterword, p. xiii.

[86] Ibid., § 327, p. 53f.

[87] Ibid., 67.

[88] Ibid., 68.

[89] Quoted by Billeter in the Afterword, ibid., i.

[90] Joseph Riepel, *Anfangsgründe zur musicalischen Setzkunst* […], vol. 1: *De Rhythmopoeía, Oder von der Tactordnung* (Regensburg, Vienna, 1752), Reprint: Joseph Riepel, *Sämtliche Schriften zur Musiktheorie* vol. 1, ed. Thomas Emmerig (Vienna, Cologne, Weimar, 1996).

[91] Joseph Riepel, *Harmonisches Syllbenmaß* (Regensburg, 1776), Reprint: Joseph Riepel, *Sämtliche Schriften zur Musiktheorie* vol. 2, ed. Thomas Emmerig (Vienna, Cologne, Weimar, 1996).

[92] The dialogues are in fact larded with similes and images from the culinary world.

[93] Riepel, *Anfangsgründe*, 23.

Ex. 3-013   Riepel: »8 Täcte« (Components Rhythms Supplied)

Here is an arbitrarily chosen example of an eight-bar group, which Riepel could imagine as an »opening tutti, as it were for a concerto «[94] (Ex. 3-013). Riepel's description of the rhythm of this minuet-like setting would be limited to noting a well-done structure of two phrases of two bars each, followed by a weakly cadenced group of four bars. If one adds some components rhythms, latent syncopations (pitch, crest notes), hemiolas in bar 6 and 7, as well as a rhythmic linking of the first two bars become evident – phenomena that are not within Riepel's visual field.

Joseph Riepel's »Rhythmopoeïa« deals exclusively with meter: rhythm is not a subject of his analyses. Thinking throughout in terms of craftsmanship and didacticism, Riepel, lacking the power of abstraction, does not break through to a »new theroretic edifice.«[95] Besides his experiential background seems to be shaped more by light entertainment and dance music than by the great musical achievements of his time. When his *Principles* came out in 1752, Bach had been dead for two years. It is questionable whether Riepel knew his music and if so, whether he would have understood it.

Scheibe • On Musical Composition

In 1773, Johann Adolph Scheibe published the first part of his planned four-volume treatise *Ueber die Musikalische Composition*.[96] The fifth and last chapter of Part One treats »Of the Nature of Meters«. Considering the plan of the treatise, including the unrealized three additional parts,[97] this chapter on meter is likely to be the only one containing any comments on the matter of musical rhythm and meter.

Scheibe initially surveys the various time signatures and then explains their accentual ordering (»accentuated and unaccentuated notes«).[98] The musical examples constructed by him include components rhythms that are registered and included in the analysis but are not reflected

---

[94] Ibid., 24.

[95] Riepel, *Anfangsgründe*, 23.

[96] Johann Adolph Scheibe, *Über die musikalische Composition* (Leipzig 1773), reprint, ed. Karsten Mackensen, with an index and list of works cited added by Dieter Haberl (Kassel 2006).

[97] On this see the introduction of the editor Karsten Mackensen, ibid., 8*. The index does not seem to be quite comprehensive; there is no entry »rhythm« or »rhythmic«, a term used bei Scheibe in the chapter about meters.

[98] Ibid., 230.

(Ex. 3-014[99]). In discussing the »internal nature of the great [strong] and small [weak] beats« of a measure, Scheibe proceeds didactically by writing series of numbers over the notes of his examples, which are designed to suggest the weights of the individual note to pupils (or choir members). Since the example concerns duple meters, it is clear that all odd numbers mean »accentuated« and all even ones »unaccentuated.« This works so long as one thinks in terms of the abstract graduated accent meter which Scheibe has earlier explained at great length.[100] Actual tonal sequences, however, contain other ›accents‹ that depend on diverse components. To mark these ›weighted‹ notes, Scheibe has added the sequence of numbers, which are to be inwardly counted out while listening to or playing the music.

Ex. 3-014
Scheibe, *Ueber die Musikalische Composition*, § 106, example 1

As long as the notes move up or down a scale, Scheibe has the listener/pupil simply count off. The positions 1, 3, 5 and 7 thus derive their weight solely from the accentual order of the (even) meters – depending on the divisional mode or level of the meter (♩, ♪, ♬). In the second bar of 1 a) the scale is abandoned and a new note value is introduced; here one is to count 1—2, rather than, as in the previous bar, 1—2—3—4. Evidently, the manner of counting here is adapted to the rhythmic events. A contradiction surfaces if one compares this measure with the second bar of 1b), where one is to count out across a syncopation with the four ♩ of the 2/2 meter, so as to make clear that the syncopated note begins on a light beat and extends into the heavy one. Now, either the syncopated bar should have been counted out by ♩ (as in 1a) or else the measure filled with ♩ in 1a) should likewise have been counted out by ♩ (as in 1b).

Example 1c), finally, furnishes proof that Scheibe was guided by a sense of components rhythms, which, however, were conscious to him neither as accents nor as inherent rhythms. In the descending ♪ scale he has us again count out from 1 to 8, while he marks the following ♪–♪ figure with the sequence 1—2—1—2—1—2—1—2. He thereby signals that the broken thirds with their crest notes produce an ›accentual sequence‹ – that is to say, a rhythm of their own, which in this case converges with the secondary

---

[99] Ibid., 234.

[100] Mackensen rightly points out in the introduction that Scheibe explains the modern graduated accent meter without recourse to the accentual system in word language (16*).

stresses of the 4/4 meter. How would Scheibe have counted if the thirds were broken in the opposite direction? Or the chains of ♪ had formed ternary groups by their contour? Since Scheibe does not explain the changes in the mode of counting in the annotations to his examples, we have to assume that listening and playing experiences had impacts on him that he nevertheless did not clearly realize.

Overall one can say that Scheibe's theory of composition does not add much to an understanding of the rhythm in the music of his contemporaries. Fixated on the metrical schemas, which he elevates to the rank of laws, his expositions are even more a hindrance than a help if one really wants to learn something about the rhythmic conditions present in compositions of the 18th century. On p. 248 Scheibe remarks: »what is rhythmic demands a separate explanation, which does not belong here.« That explanation he never got around to.

There is also little that is concrete about the rhythmic organization of melodies in an earlier work of Scheibe's, the *Critischer Musicus*, although there he makes at least a start toward distinguishing rhythm from meter.[101] In a longish footnote in the »sixty-eighth part« of the book, Scheibe writes:[102]

Meter thus orders merely the individual members, or sound feet, in music, as in poems it comprises the feet of a given line. […] So one realizes that in musical art, melodies, to appear orderly and natural to the ear, must have certain relations among each other, so that not only their ends but also the middle portions have a certain similarity regarding their extent to one another. Rhythm thus pertains not only to the beginnings and conclusions of melodies, or movements, or clauses within an entire piece […]; but it also governs the middle parts in general, even though these are aleady ordered in themselves by the meter.Thus the parts of a melody, or clause, should have a certain proportion with another melody, or clause, as should finally also the parts of all the melodies or clauses within a well-composed musical piece.

Scheibe laments that the distinction between meter and rhythm has until now been overlooked by »nearly all« »scribes« – including »Herr Mattheson in his complete Capellmeister.«[103] »The nature of the sound feets concerns the meter, but their combination and the proportion between different poetic lines or melodies that follow each other pertains to rhythm.«[104] At this point, a description of rhythm in the sense of the inner structure of sound feet, as well as of sequences of motifs, melodies and periods, could have commenced. But except for generalities, that rhythms should be »ordered and natural« because thereby »the beauty of a music« would be enhanced,[105] Scheibe is silent about the concrete means of rhythmic formation, and his conception of rhythm remains restricted to a single component: the durational sequence of individual notes.

Kirnberger • Correct Musical Setting

Between 1776 and 1779, Johann Philipp Kirnberger, since 1754 active at the court of the Princess Amalia in Berlin, published his work, *Die Kunst des reinen Satzes in der Musik* (The Art of the Perfect Setting in Music), which was highly regarded by numerous contemporaries.[106] Concerned mainly with counterpoint and harmony, Kirnberger also deals with rhythm and meter. The fourth chapter of the first section of Part Two is entitled: »Of Motion, Meter and Rhythm.«[107]

In a footnote, Kirnberger explains what he means by rhythm:[108]

The term has two meanings: at times it signifies what the Ancients called Rhythmoponie [sic!], that is, the rhythmic character of a piece; at others, it means a sentence (»Satz«) or caesura (»Einschnitt«).

Kirnberger intended to deal with rhythm in the former sense – that is, the working with note values of different durations – in a planned third part of the book that remained unwritten.[109] In Part Two of the book, however, he does talk about rhythm in the sense of structural units – in modern terms, about phrasing. Here he interprets ›rhythms‹ analogously to language, whose sentences are satisfactory only at their end, after their »sense« has added up to »a more or less complete speech.«[110] Depending on how clearly cadences were formed, »sections« (Abschnitte) or »periods« (perfect cadences) or else »caesuras« (Einschnitte) or »rhythms,« i.e., half-closes, were generated in music,[111] which were apprehensible as sense-bearing units.

---

[101] Johann Adolph Scheibe, *Critischer Musicus*. New, enlarged and improved edition (Leipzig, 1745), reprographic reprint (Hildesheim and New York, 1970).

[102] Ibid., 626.

[103] Ibid., 626f.

[104] Ibid., 627.

[105] Ibid., 626.

[106] Johann Philipp Kirnberger, *Die Kunst des reinen Satzes in der Musik*, Pt. 1 (Berlin, 1771); Pt. 2 (Berlin, Königsberg, 1776-1779); reprint (Hildesheim, 1968).

[107] Ibid., II/1: 105-154.

[108] Ibid., 137.

[109] Peter Wollny, Article »Kirnberger, Kirnberg, Kernberg, Johann Philipp,« in: *MGG*[2], personal part, vol. 10 (Kassel et al., 2003), cols. 169-176; col.174.

[110] II/1: 138. Shortly before that, Kirnberger says outright: »The rhythm of a piece of music has a lot in common with the versification of a lyrical poem: individual segments of the melody represent the verses [lines], the larger sections comprising several segments are musical strophes [stanzas]« (137).

[111] Ibid.

Here, too, Kirnberger is unmistakably thinking in terms of harmony. Thus he distinguishes between perfect cadences on secondary degrees and main degrees: the latter had to be reserved for the conclusion of a piece, lest the latter threaten to break apart.[112] Perhaps this harmonic perspective is also the reason why Kirnberger declares the length of the caesuras (»Einschnitte«) to be principally variable, even though »the best effect« in a piece would result if the measure of turns would remain as constant as the meter, which, after all, was also retained throughout an entire piece.[113] Departures from this rule, which Kirnberger cites in large numbers, are justified in terms of a desire for a special expression. Thus he adduces the example of a five-bar phrase derived from a four-bar one and continuing to count as a four-bar phrase as being »of great effect« (Ex. 3-015).[114]

Ex. 3-015

Kirnberger here (as well as elsewhere) is interested solely in the length of »rhythms« (four or five measures), but not in the effect of the change on the »rhythm« in the narrower sense of his definition above. Thus an important aspect of the original rhythm is lost through the lengthening of the first two notes in the five-bar version: the mirror symmetry of ♩♪ and ♪♩.

Kirnberger lived during a period of stylistic change between Baroque and Preclassicism. As a pupil of J. S. Bach, whose art he greatly admired all his life, he refused to brush aside the numerous forms of the older concerto and fugue practice as old-fashioned; but as a contemporary of Hasse, Graun and the Bach sons he also participated in the new thinking, which came down to a regular phrase order divisible by two or three.

In the context of discussing irregular »rhythms,« Kirnberger cites the ritornello theme of J. S. Bach's Concerto in D minor for Harpsichord and Strings (BWV 1052).[115] According to Kirnberger, this subject contains two infractions of the rules that needed to be vindicated: it has a cadence in the tonic after only six bars, and it comprises seven bars altogether (see also my Ex. 3-016). Kirnberger regards the first irregularity as amended by the fact that the harpsichord solo begins »immediately after the end of the ritornello,« thus preserving »the exactest linkage between the main parts of the piece.«[116] The early entry simultaneously corrected the second error of having 7 rather than 6 measures.[117] Beyond that, Kirnberger says nothing about the rhythmic structure of the theme, neither discussing the theme's inner structure nor noticing its truly exciting rhythms.

The theme, presented in unison, is divided – speaking in modern terms – into a brief statement, which paces the extent of the D minor triad, a three-bar spinning-out part, which begins upbeat and utilizes the upbeats by means of anticipations for subsequent syncopated effects, and a three-part epilogue, which, introduced by an ascending scale of 16ths, cadences to D minor via hinted-at secondary dominants. That the seventh bar is part of the theme is made indubitably clear by the theme's da capo at the end of

Ex. 3-016   J. S. Bach, Concerto D Minor, BWV 1052, 1st mov., Ritornello Theme

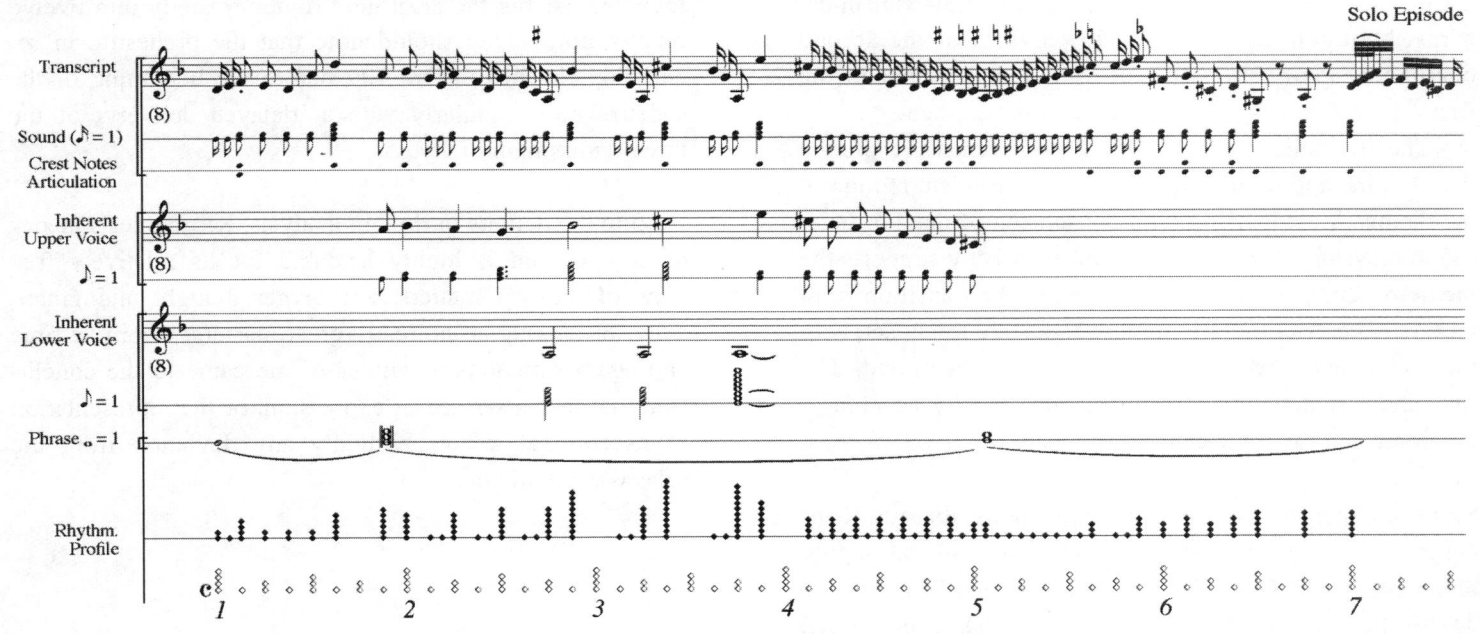

---

[112] Ibid., 139.

[113] Ibid., 142.

[114] Ibid., 145f.

[115] Ibid., 140. Contrary to Kirnberger's general meticulousness, the theme, presumably written down from memory, contains several slips of the pen.

[116] Ibid., 139.

[117] Ibid., 141.

the 189-bar movement that is constructed in the form of a developed concerto. The overlap of phrases at the beginning does not signify, therefore, that the theme is curtailed but merely that two events are heard simultaenously in m. 7: the end of the ritornello and the beginning of the solo episode.

Neither does Kirnberger address aditional details that are decisive for the rhythm of the theme. Thus it is evident that the single-voiced theme in places expands into an inherent multi-voicedness. Kirnberger himself describes this phenomenon in Part One of his *Kunst des reinen Satzes in der Musik* under the term »Brechung« (breaking or refraction).[118] In the Ex. 3-016, I have placed the inherent voices generated by the refraction into separate systems. Thus one can readily see that melodically the spinning-forth part consists essentially of a figuration of the dominant-seventh-ninth chord on A. The inherent upper voice has to be taken fully into account in the rhythmic analysis, bcause it is the one that makes the melodic progression audible.

To the finely structured original voice pertains, besides the basic component »Sound« (= tonal duration), also the component »Diastematy,« which in this case I have included in the analysis with the rhythmically relevant crest notes (second 1-line system, upper notes). For it is noteworthy that the emphatically stressed upbeat syncopations produced by anticipation, as well as other notes in the inherent upper voice, are at the same time given prominence by means of the crest notes. Since the notes of the inherent bass voice, too, enter on relatively weak beats, m. 3 contains two kinds of syncopations.

Articulation marks that Bach supplied himself (cf. the facsimile in vol. 4 of series VII of the New Bach Edition) are the staccato points over individual ♪ and the slur in the harpsichord solo m. 7 (cf. the lower lines of the second one-line system). The staccatos give added weight to the first ♪ in m.1 and especially to the ♪ in the epilogue.

The rhythmic profile yields a comprehensive picture that, I think, approximately conveys the turbulent motion of the theme. A comparison with the schema of the 4/4 meter (bottom system) shows that the meter directly supports the theme rhythmically only in m. 2 and in the transition from m. 6 to m. 7. All other rhythmic weights are freely set, with the meter being kept ›in the ear‹ in the background. The first and last notes do not fall on the *One* by accident – harmonic and rhythmic cadence are correlated.

From the perspective of the components theory, Kirnberger's remarks about rhythm and meter are thoroughly deficient. In Part One of his *Kunst des reinen Satzes in der Musik*, the chapter entitled »Of the Embellished or Colored Simple Counterpoint« deals, inter alia, with variation through diverse forms of »breaking,« but once again without considering the consequences for the rhythm. About one of his demonstrative examples Kirnberger writes: »Altogether these variations in the same harmony can furnish altered melodies, as the following example will show« (Ex. 3-017).

Ex. 3-017

Yet one cannot miss the rhythmic differences between the two variants of the broken chord, and one can assume that Kirnberger, too, did not miss them. In the first variant, the crest notes give a ♩-rhythm to the melodic contour, while in the repetition variant a syncopated ♪♩ ♪-rhythm results by pitch durations. If Kirnberger had discussed the matter at all, he would have called it simply a melodic variant and regarded the rhythm of the two variants as identical. That modifications of the melodic line would also alter the rhythm was beyond his conceptual horizon.

It is therefore also unlikely that he saw any rhythm in the cadenza-like passage of the D minor »Clavier=Concert von J. S. Bach,«[119] which he cites and certainly admired, other than a sequence of ♪ (Ex. 3-018). Yet the impression of wild commotion in this fast run results not only from the small notes, nor merely from the up-and-down undulation of the line, but from the durations between the notes where the direction changes, which yield a bizarre but evidently quite intentional rhythm (cf. the number sequence, which refers to ♪).[120] Bach does not cancel the meter (despite the fermata) but fits the crest note rhythm exactly into twelve quarter notes. One should note that the orchestra, in re-entering, finishes the m. 109 before the beginning of the cadenza quite regularly with a ›delayed delivery‹ of the three ♪ missing initially.

Despite the deficits in rhythm analysis, Kirnberger's theory of composition is highly laudable for its relatively free view of musical matters. Kirnberger thought undogmatically. In looking at the really great masters, whom he time and again summons as witnesses, he came to the conclusion that in the service of expression, or the representation of exceptional affects, virtually any deviation from the rules was justifiable.

---

[118] I/2: 205ff.

[119] II/1: 139.

[120] Cf. analogous cases in my analyses in the Bach section of this study (chapter »Chromatic Fantasy«), 161ff.

Ex. 3-018   J. S. Bach, Concerto D Minor, BWV 1052, 1st mov., mm. 109-113

Türk • Piano School

Daniel Gottlob Türk's *Klavierschule*,[121] published in 1789, is not really the place for a discussion of rhythm theory. The author occasionally notes as much himself,[122] only to then provide his pupils with some basic lessons in composition after all.

Ex. 3-019   Hasse, *I pellegrini*, final chous (as cited by Türk)

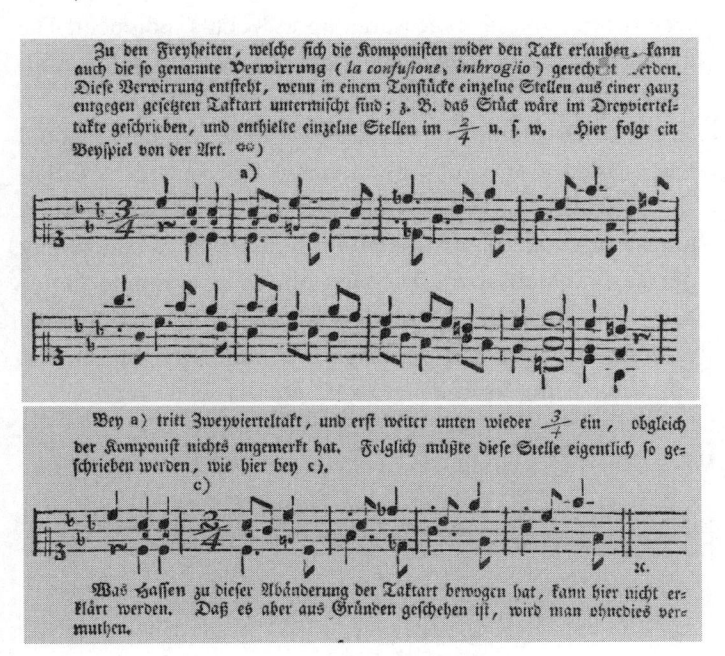

His few statements relevant to our inquiry regarding rhythmic and metric theory occur in the sections on »Meter« and »Performance«. The meters are presented in detail, and Türk explains by means of musical examples supplied with sequence of numbers how the pupil should count correctly.

Occasional rhythmic constellations that don't fit the meter are presumed to involve a change in the meter, which could also have been written differently. To illustrate, Türk cites a passage from the concluding chorus of Johann Adolf Hasse's *I pellegrini al sepolcro di Nostro Signore*, whose series of hemiolas he explains as a »so-called confusion (*la confusione, imbroglio*)« (Ex. 3-019).[123]

Unfortunately, Türk has no independent concept of rhythm at his disposal, as is evident from the section »Of Musical Interpunctuation.« There he includes the term rhythm as meaning a phrase of medium duration, in a scale of gradations from long to short modeled on linguistic syntax: period (.), rhythm (: or ;) segment (,). The relation of rhythmic phenomena to prescribed meters is thus not part of his thinking.

That the hemiolas in the Hasse excerpt initially are due to the interaction of the components »Sound« (tone durations) and »Diastematy« (crest notes) may seem evident. But Türk simply could not even describe this simple phenomenon, let alone the imitational relation between the two

Ex. 3-020

hemiolic voices (Ex. 3-020). From m. 6 on, moreover the hemiolas are realized no longer by trochees ($\quarternote. \eighthnote$), but by dactyls ($\quarternote \eighthnote\eighthnote$), which likewise have the value of a $\halfnote$. Since Türk's example, which shows a renotation into a 2/4 measure, breaks off prematurely, we cannot know whether he still regarded these bars as »confusion«. In any case, these (dactylic) hemiolas are different in their rhythms compared to the dotted ones.

Ex. 3-021

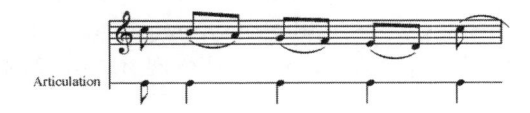

---

[121] Daniel Gottlob Türk, *Klavierschule, oder Anweisung zum Klavierspielen für Lehrer und Lernende* (Leipzig, Halle, 1789, reprint Kassel, 1962).

[122] Regarding meters, Türk writes: »This is not the place to cite and assess all the reasons one after the other; for a closer examination as to whether and why this or that meter is necessary, how it differs from others etc., belongs into a theoretical textbook.« Ibid., 89.

[123] Ibid., 93f. Türk's example starts at m. 83 of the allegro final chorus.

In the section on musical performance, Türk also addresses the phenomena interpunctuation (phrasing) and articulation. Interesting here is the instruction that the notes standing beneath the »beginning of a slur are to be »accentuated very weakly (barely noticeably).«[124] Again, however, Türk fails to address the rhythmic consequences resulting from this practice. For in an instance like the one cited by Türk, the legato play produces the effect of a components syncopation (Ex. 3-021) and thus is immediately effective rhythmically.

In summary, one can say that although some components of a given tone setting and their execution are addressed in Türk's *Klavierschule*, their significance for the rhythm of a composition remains unrecognized. As was customary with most music theoreticians and pedagogues of this and the following century, rhythm is taken to be metric order. Accents of whatever kind are mere ingredients that either coincide with the uniformity of the meter and the periods or charmingly deviate from them but do not affect the substance of the rhythmic shaping.

Koch • Instructions for Composition

Between 1782 and 1793, Heinrich Christoph Koch successively published the three volumes of his *Versuch einer Anleitung zur Composition*.[125] Viennese Classicism was in its zenith by then (Mozart died in 1791), the Storm and Stress movement was sweeping through Europe (Goethe's *Werther* appeared between 1774 and 1787), Kant was writing his main works (the *Critique of Pure Reason* was published in 1781), and in Paris the first bourgeois revolution erupted (1789). That Koch was part of these intellectual and social movements one can tell, among other things, from the fact that he knew and resorted to the concept of the »*Genie*.« Genius is the exceptional being to whom is accorded the right to expand and even negate the rules of aesthetic regulation. Accordingly, Koch asks rhetorically about the regular syntax of melodies: »Is not the genius unduly restricted or even supressed by the kinds of imitations by which a certain form is determined?« And then rejoins: »Once one has appropriated the correct way of combining the melodic parts through the imitation of correct forms, these shackles fall off by themselves,« but speedy adds the warning: »only, one should beware of overhasty steps.«[126]

Clearly Koch's intention is didactic; already on p. 3 of the Foreword, the »beginner« is directly addressed.[127] On the other hand, we read at the end of the Foreword that he will now leave »everything to the judgment of reasonable musicians.«[128] Mozart might have been able to pass such a judgment, if he had been familiar with Koch's theory of composition, something that is not documented. An indirect judgment can be abstracted from Mozart's music, whose rhythmic-metric diversity and freedom certainly leave the supposed laws of Koch's »system« far behind.

Take as an example the beginning of Mozart's Sonata in B♭ major K. 333 (315 c), which came out in Vienna in 1784 (Ex. 3-022).[129] We do not know if Koch knew this sonata, but it doesn't really matter. The sonata's opening would certainly have measured up to Koch's judgment. The question is whether the analyst can measure up to the composition.

In Koch's terms,[130] this ten-bar theme, which he would have called a »period,« divides into two sentences (»Sätze«), the first of which (mm.1-4) functions as a starting phrase (»Absatz«), the second (mm. 5-10) as a concluding phrase (»Schlußsatz«). The first phrase is a simple »four-bar« one, whose »ending formula« (»feminine ending« and position on the third) demands a continuation by another »phrase,« being itself a mere »Absatz«.

Ex. 3-022   Mozart, Piano Sonata B♭ Major K. 333, 1st mov., Main Voice (Analysis according to Koch)

---

[124] Ibid., 355.

[125] Heinrich Christoph Koch, *Versuch einer Anleitung zur Composition*, Part One (Rudolstadt, 1782); Part Two (Leipzig, 1787); Part Three (Leipzig, 1793). Reprographic reprint in three vols. (Hildesheim, 1969).

[126] Ibid., III: 11f.

[127] Ibid., I: xv.

[128] Ibid., xxiv.

[129] Cf. NMA series IX, work group 25, vol. 2, Foreword by Wolfgang Platz and Wolfgang Rehm, xiif.

[130] Cf. in Koch the sections »Of the Nature of the Melodic Parts« in II: 342ff. and »Of the Combination of the Melodic Parts, or of the Structure of Periods« in III: 3ff.

It is subdivided by a complete section (»vollkommener Einschnitt«) (m. 2) and two incomplete sections (»unvollkommene Einschnitte«) (mm. 1 and 3), down to the extent of a single bar (»melodische Interpunktion«). The second sentence (»Satz«) (mm. 5 to 10) is a »four-bar« one that has been »enlarged« or »expanded« to six by the repetition of the two opening bars (mm. 5-6 in mm. 7-8). It has an »ending formula«, with which »the whole« can be concluded, thus making it the »Schlußsatz.«

Koch calls the internal structure of such a »period« rhythmic: »The length of these parts of a melody, their proportion (»Ebenmaas«) or ratio they have in regard to their number of measures is called Rythmus [sic].«[131] The rhythmic proportion remains the same even if the phrases are »enlarged« or »pushed together,« since what counted was not the different size but »the equivalent of the norm.«[132] For the term rhythm as Koch uses it that means that its sole feature is isometry (»Ebenmaas«).

Aside from the division of the melody into »Sätze« und »Abschnitte,« Koch pays attention mainly to the »meter« (also to the »unity of key« and the »consistency of meter«). The respective chapter, entitled »Of Meter or Metric Weights,«[133] occurs at the beginning of the large section on period construction, which fills all of volume III. Curiously, the question of meter was not raised already along with the description of the »phrases« and »sections.« At the beginning of the chapter on meter, there are explanations about »feet«, which Koch (in contrast to Mattheson with his 26 »sound=feet«) reduces to four disyllabic and eight trisyllabic ones. Basically, Koch regards the transfer of prosodic feet to multivoiced music as no longer adequate. Only the classical distinction between thesis and arsis – no longer meaning length and shortness – is still used by Koch for describing and naming the »metric weight.« To Koch, every 2/4 meter filled with 2 ♩ is trochaic, and every 3/4 meter containing 3 ♩ is dactylic; the patterns are set forth accordingly (Ex. 3-023).[134]

Ex. 3-023 (Koch)

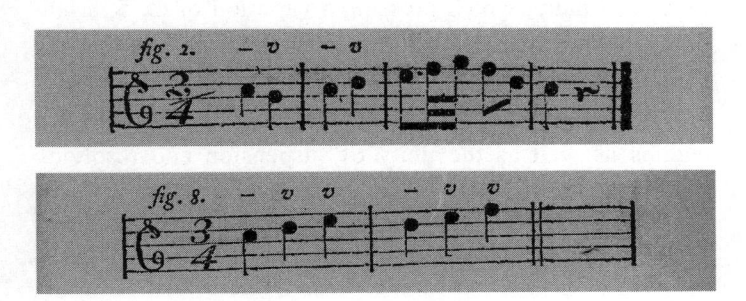

Koch writes that meter in music has »something unique not known to poetry,«[135] referring – besides the melodic embellishments – to the sprecific potentialities of multipart tonal settings, in which the meter (i.e., the »metric weight«) can be made clear any time: »If the melody of the main voice does not maintain the meter strongly enough, or departs from its motion, either the bass voice [lower voice] or a secondary voice, if present, must preserve the character of this motion.«[136]

Applied to our Mozart example, Koch would thus note that all suspensions and cadential formulas fall on strong beats, so that our »feeling [is] not offended.«[137] Notes that are extended across a strong beat and rests occurring on a strong beat (we would call both instances syncopations today) are made ›bearable‹ solely by the left hand's showing compensating entries. We must therefore fear that the start of Mozart's theme (with its delayed entry of first degree B♭4 on the second eighth of m. 1) would have been disapproved of by Koch, since metric »clarity« is evidently not assured.

Looked at in the light of day, one has to conclude from this (virtual) analysis of Koch's that he would have little to say about the specific rhythmic shape of the Mozart theme. The categories caesura, starting phrase, concluding phrase and expansion can be applied to thousands of other cases, and the analyses would in principle always yield the same result. The components theory, on the contrary, enables a mode of analysis that, while confirming the structural division that Koch has noticed, also reveals the individual rhythmic structure of the theme (see my rhythm score, Ex. 3-024).

Every rhythm analysis has to be preceded by a compositional one. In the present case this means not only that the unity of the theme extending over ten measures has to be recognized as such but that one also has to clarify the specific setting of the piece: in this case one that follows the type of melody-with-accompaniment. The voice carrying the melody must be weighted more strongly than the accompanying one, lest one mis-analyse the character of the piece. I did this inasmuch as the rhythmic weights of the component »Sound,« resulting from the multiplication of the tonal durations with the smallest occurring value, are referred to ♪ in the main voice but to ♩ in the accompaniment. Thus the weights in the melody of the right hand count twice.

---

[131] Ibid., II: 346. According to the index, this is the only example of »Rythmus.«

[132] Wilhelm Seidel: Article „Rhythmus, Metrum, Takt" in: *MGG*², Sachteil vol. 8 (1998), cols. 257-317; col. 296.

[133] Ibid., III: 13ff.

[134] Ibid., III: 16f.

[135] Ibid., III: 19.

[136] Ibid., III: 20.

[137] Ibid., III: 33.

Ex. 3-024   Mozart, Piano Sonata B♭ Major K. 333, 1st mov., Beginning (Rhythm Score)

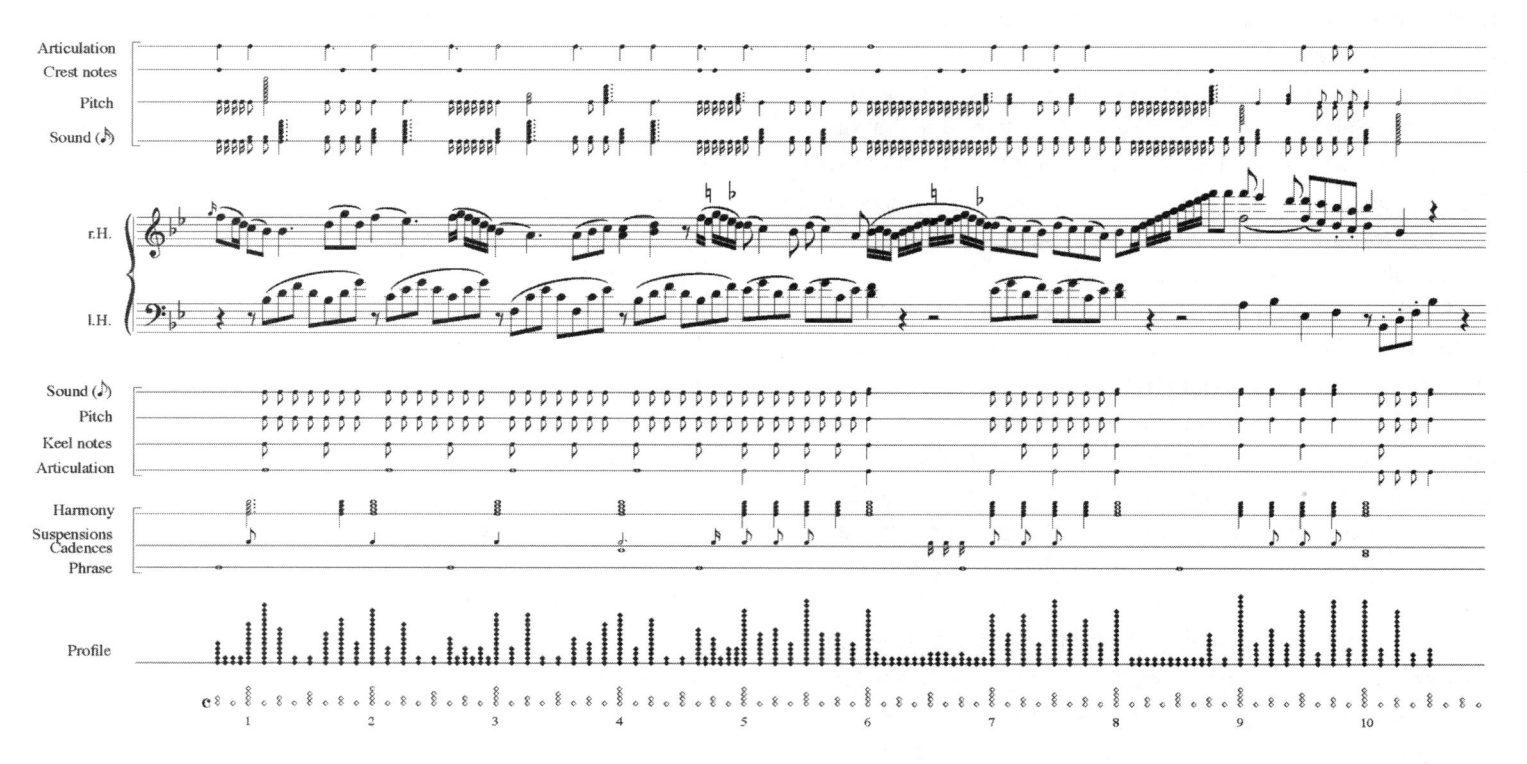

The rhythmic structure of the main voice with its four component rhythms reveals a large part of the emphases that time and again impress listeners and players alike in this theme. What accounts for its hovering effect is not only the fact that in the first bars long note values enter repeatedly on the *Two* of the 4/4 meter (later on, in diminished rhythm, on the 2nd or 6th eighth) but also that note repetitions occur more than once to anticipate the relatively long notes, which also produces a syncopated effect. This is supported by the crest notes (component »Diastematy«), which likewise occur by preference off the heavy and semi-heavy beats. Especially noteworthy and very unusual is, of course, the divergence, pleasurably disorienting to the listener, between the first heavy beat and the entry of the tonic (after the upbeat hexachord G5-F5-E♭5-D5-C5-B♭4) on the second eighth of the first measure, particularly since the lower voice, too, begins its triadic figures together with the B♭,[138] (incidentally a rhythmic gesture the accompanying voice adheres to for four measures).

Contrary to an earlier assumption, I place the beginning of the rhythm of the component »Harmony« on the *One* of m. 1. Since musical listening never attends merely to the point of the here and now but wanders back and forth reminiscing and anticipating, the tonic harmony, actually audible only from the second beat on, is instantly inferred backward and referred to the *One* of the just transpiring measure. The same applies to the suspension given here, which does not yet form a dissonance but, in hearkening back, is interpreted as a ninth's suspension. Moreover, all the harmonic function changes take place on heavy or semi-heavy beats, with the harmonic rhythm proceeding mostly in wholes in the first phrase, in the second phrase repeatedly also in quarters; the same goes for the suspensions. The two cadences (half-close in the tonic in m. 4, authentic in the tonic in m. 10) likewise mark the respective beginnings of the measure.

Nevertheless, it is mostly the syncopations that determine the total character of the theme. They are subjected to a diminution process. In the first four bars, there are only widely spanned syncopations, which result from the fact that the middle of the 4/4 measure is hardly occupied, while the second beat is multiply so.[139] Things are altogether different in m. 5: here the value of reference of the syncopation is the half-measure, which is correspondingly occupied by accumulating events: the middle of the half-measures (second and third quarter) is now rather taken back, while the second and sixth eighth are richly satiated. In m. 7, finally, which presents a variation of m. 5, a tendency toward quartering the measure emerges, in that the slurs in the right hand link two eighths each and thus support the resolution of the syncopated quarter notes into two eighths as well as the unity of suspension and resolving triad in quarter times. Thanks to the tone repetitions, however, a part of the syncopated effect remains (see the »Pitch« line above the main voice in m. 7).

---

[138] Seidel calls attention to this exceptional beginning with the felicitous remark: »Harmonic and metric ›tonic‹ step apart.« Seidel, *Rhythmustheorien* (see note 1), 101.

[139] This is especially observable in m. 3. Here only one entry of the lower voice occurs on the third beat, whereas on the second beat two note entries (left and right hand), a pitch change and a tonal lengthening can be registered. (That pitch change and note entries have to be observed separately can in this measure be explained by the pitch A, which lasts two quarters although its is sounded anew.)

In rhythmic-metrical terms, the theme is laid out for intensification and condensation. Not surprisingly, this tendency coincides with the goal-oriented design of the melody. Its ambit is initially restricted to G5 as its upper limit. It is only in m. 8 that the ambit breaks through this ceiling to reach its highest note at F6 – incidentally two eighths *before* the heavy beat of m. 9, which initiates the closing cadence.

Among the rhythmic peculiarities of the theme are the upbeats, which are varied again and again: 4 ♪ before m. 1, 3 ♪ before m. 2, 6 ♪ before m. 3, 3 ♪ (with diverging Diastematics) before m. 4, 6 ♪ (with diverging crest and keel notes) before m. 5. The ♪ run in m. 6 cannot really be interpreted in terms of upbeats. Comprehended under a single slur, it is at once downbeat and upbeat, and it would be pointless to try to determine the exact dviding line between the two functions: the measuring rod could be either the upbeat before m. 1 or that before m. 5. The ascending scale in m. 8 is similarly ambivalent: it can be taken either altogether as an upbeat gesture or as a transitional passage to a 2 ♪ upbeat (F6-F6-|F6).

Let us finally look at the rhythmic profile also as the sum of all components entering per point in time (rhythmic accumulation). As is to be expected, it reflects several of the enumerated properties and processes. Thus the rhythmic whole-measure quality of the first phrase (mm. 1-4) is recognizable from the inverted-arc contour of the profile. M. 5, on the other hand, clearly displays half-measure design, in m. 7 one can make out two quarter and one half-unit, and in the final bars the quarter times are strongly marked. The rhythmic profile thus pictures something one could call the basic gesture of the theme – always qualified by the proper soft focus, which guarantees that what is depicted are not abstract metric schemas but individually shaped rhythmic structures. No two bars are alike, though several resemble each other in their rhythmic profile.[140]

All in all, I regard Koch's theory of composition as rather unproductive, if one wants to inquire about the rhythmic-metric situation in the music of the 18th and earlier centuries. His measurements stay at the surface of the composition. They aim at the typical, which is at the same time presented as a universally valid norm. Koch's writings[141] nowhere advance toward the inner rhythmic processes. His theory is dominated by the notion of dissecting cuts (vide his concept of »Einschnitt«) made vertically through a tonal setting. Concepts like »Takterstickung, oder Taktunterdrückung«[142] (choking or suppression of meter) are typical: they reveal clearly that the idea of several processes – and thus also what I am trying to define as components rhythm – taking place and being perceived *simultaneously* was altogether alien to him.

---

[140] The results of this analysis confirm several observations by Lowinsky, who devoted a section of his study of rhythm in Mozart to this theme (cf. Edward E. Lowinsky, »On Mozart's Rhythm,« *MQ*, 42 [1956], 162-186). Lowinsky, however, determines the rhythmic qualities of Mozart's music unsystematically, as he does not have at his disposal a method for describing »that inimitable verve, that quality which sets it apart from Dittersdorf or Johann Christian Bach as much as from Stamitz and Haydn" (166). Cf. also the analysis of this theme in Gudrun Henneberg, *Theorien zur Rhythmik und Metrik. Möglichkeiten und Grenzen rhythmischer und metrischer Analyse, dargestellt am Beispiel der Wiener Klassik* (Tutzing, 1974), 170-176. and her critique of Friedrich Neumann's analytical sketch of the same theme (in: *Die Zeitgestalt. Eine Lehre vom musikalischen Rhythmus* (Vienna, 1959), 2:14. See also Wilhelm Seidel's notes on the rhythmic shape of this theme (see note 1, above p. 189), p. 100 f. My own essay on this Mozart theme and Koch's »System« (in: »Die ›Rhythmuspartitur‹: Über eine neue Methode zur rhythmisch-metrischen Analyse pulsgebundener Musik,« in: *50 Jahre Musikwissenschaftliches Institut in Hamburg. Bestandsaufnahme – aktuelle Forschung – Ausblick*, ed. P. Petersen and H. Rösing [= HJbMw 16] [Frankfurt am Main et al.: Lang 1999], 83-110) is superseded by the more detailed presentation given here.

[141] Of historical significance is above all Heinrich Christoph Koch's *Musikalisches Lexikon*, facsimile reprint of the Frankfurt/Main,1802, edition, ed. Nicole Schwindt (Kassel et al.: Bärenreiter, 2001).

[142] Thus an entry in the *Musikalisches Lexikon*, ed. cit., col. 1486.

Momigny • Theory of Music

In the first third of the 19th century, the French musicologist and composer Jérôme-Joseph de Momigny published a number of books, among them a *Comprehensive Theory of Harmony and Composition* (1803-1806)[143] and a *Theory of Music* (1821).[144] Momigny was an eminently independent thinker and at the same time a keen observer of the music of his time. Albert Palm is right in saying that Momigny's writings are not nearly known widely enough, especially since he anticipated several later approaches and theories.[145]

Unlike German music theory of the 18th and 19th century,[146] Momigny assigns a subordinate role to measure and meter. As Palm points out, »the metric factor appears as an aspect of the rhythm. The cadence is basically a qualitative (rhythmical) and only then a quantitative (metrical) value.«[147] By »cadence« Momigny means the combination of a »son antécédent« and a »son conséquent,« that is, a sequence of a first upbeat sound and a second downbeat one. Arsis (»lever«) and thesis (»frapper«), common to the beating of time and concomitant, respectively, with tension and relaxation, are thought by him to be universal phenomena of organic nature. Hence the »cadence« has to be regarded as the basic law of music, regardless of whether one is dealing with simple forms (♩ | ♩ or ♩ | ♪) or with complex combinations (half-verses, verses, periods or recapitulations).

The »cadence« principle is of far-reaching consequence for the understanding of music. Thus measure is defined by »cadence.« »Antécédent« and »conséquent« together form one measure, because together they mark a stress. Since a distinction is made between melodic and harmonic »cadences,« and, besides, the »cadences« may be disposed differently in each voice, the result is diverse metrical structures in one and the same tonal setting. In conventional meters, Momigny says explicitly, one feels like a prisoner (»prisonnière«), whereas in cadential measures one knows oneself to be in free accord with nature (»mesure naturelle«).[148]

Thanks to the »cadence« concept, Momigny's theory of phrase, too, is free and undogmatic. Based on the assumption that music is a language without words, Momigny distinguishes between a free and a bound tonal speech. »Le rythme peut être régulier ou symétrique, ou irrégulier et non composé de pieds qui se correspondent.«[149] For the isometric rhythms, in which the »cadences« are placed at identical intervals, he borrows the concepts foot, verse, half-verse, strophe or stanza or period from prosody. As Palm summarizes:[150]

Momigny transfers the shape of the cadence [...] to the larger forms but leaves all metrical schemas on the side, establishing no groups of two, four or eight cadences. What determines the combination of smaller forms into larger units is always their meaningful relations. Since he does not refer the combination and delimitation of the significant parts to a ›metrical‹ base – duration and intensity are factors of rhythm for him – he also does not recognize any reinterpretations. He distinguishes solely between a symmetrical and a free rhythm. If metrical schemata freely conform to the sense structure, they are acknowledged as fully as the smallest significant part, the cadence.

The question, now, is how Momigny applies these theoretical principles analytically. It is worth noting to begin with that Momigny generally analyzes contemporary music, including instrumental works by Haydn and Mozart, masters ecstatically praised by him.[151]

His analysis of the opening movement of Mozart's String Quartet in D minor K. 421 has gained a certain notoriety. A look at the brief excerpt from the first violin part quoted in Ex. 3-025 will show in detail how Momigny proceeds. He marks the violin 1 part, which he has written out separately, only with ordinal numbers indicating the »cadences« and the »vers.«[152] How the melodic »cadences«

---

[143] Jérôme-Joseph de Momigny, *Cours complet d'harmonie et de composition, d'après une théorie neuve et générale de la musique*, 3 vols. (Paris 1803/1806).

[144] Jérôme-Joseph de Momigny, *La seule vraie théorie de la musique ou Moyen le plus court pour devenir mélodiste, harmoniste, contrepointiste et compositeur* (Paris 1821); reprographic reprint (Geneva, 1980).

[145] Albert Palm, *Jérôme-Joseph Momigny. Leben und Werk. Ein Beitrag zur Geschichte der Musiktheorie im 19. Jahrhundert* (Cologne, 1969). Already in 1957, Palm had submitted a thesis on the life and work of Momigny in Tübingen.

[146] Carl Dahlhaus put it concisely: »From the middle of the 18th to the early 20th century, the theory of rhythm was [...] a theory of metric rhythm.« Carl Dahlhaus, *Die Musiktheorie im 18. und 19. Jahrhundert, 2. Teil: Deutschland*, ed. Ruth E. Müller (Geschichte der Musiktheorie, vol. 11) (Darmstadt, 1989), 157.

[147] Palm (1969), 171.

[148] Quoted from op. cit., 158.

[149] Quoted from ibid., 177.

[150] Ibid., 325.

[151] Palm (1969) discusses the detailed analyses in the chapter »Die musikalische Analyse«, p. 213. His discussion of Momigny's analysis of Mozart's great Symphony in G Minor had appeared already in 1968: Albert Palm, »Mozart im Spiegel der Encyclopedie Methodique,« *Mozart-Jahrbuch 1967* (Salzburg 1968), 314-325. Evidently, the brief examples Momigny inserts in the main text of his theoretical writings, include, along with schematic melodies designed by himself, also themes by other composers, for example one from Haydn's String Quartet op. 76 no. 1 in the *Cours complet* (p. 143). These quotations from the works of others for the most part did not include an author and evidently have not yet all been identified.

[152] Cf. the facsimile included in Hermann Danusers »Vers- oder Prosaprinzip? Mozarts Streichquartett in d-Moll (KV 421) in der Deutung Jérôme-Joseph de Momignys und Arnold Schönbergs,« *Musiktheorie* 7 (1992), 245-263; pp. 252f.

are individually positioned has to be inferred. Momigny generally marks the »cadences« with Arabic numerals, 1 for antécédent and 2 for conséquent.[153] I have simplified the marking system in Ex. 3-025, so as to readily distinguish also incomplete (elliptical) from normal and feminine »cadences«:

a   antécédent
c   conséquent
a-   antécédent with rest or tie-over instead of conséquent
c+ conséquent with feminine ending
-c conséquent without antécédent

Ex. 3-025
Mozart, String Quartet D Minor, 1st mov., K. 421, mm. 15-18 (Momigny)

Momigny's ›cadencing‹ of the violin part is not exactly plausible. Hermann Danuser has justly pointed out that the first two three-note motifs, whose parallelism readily catches the eye (and ear), are cadenced differently by Momigny and on top of that are equated with the following half-verse (hemistich).[154] Problematic are also the syncopations regarded as divided in m. 17, each of which is supposed to add up to a cadence, as well as the 16ths figures in m. 18, in which, supposedly, one elliptical »cadence« follows the other.

As interesting as the approach in his analysis is of inquiring into the rhythmic weights of even the smallest melodic motions, in practice Momigny gets entangled in his own predetermined system. He never asks why a note has a specific weight but assumes that of two successive notes the first has to be *levé*, the second *frappé*. Components analysis, on the other hand, makes it possible to explain why the weight of one note is greater than that of another.

In Ex. 3-026, three component rhythms relevant to this four-bar melody are represented and interrelated. The valuation of the durations between the tonal entries (»Sound«) is based on ♪ = 1. In case of repeated notes (»Pitch«), the rhythmic weight of the repeated notes is added to the first note that introduces the new pitch, while the repetitions themselves are disregarded. As for the melodic contour (»Diastematy«), I have confined myself to the upper directional changes (»crest notes«), of which there are only two in this excerpt. The »Articulation« rhythm is based on two

Ex. 3-026 mm. 15-18, Violino 1, Rhythm Score

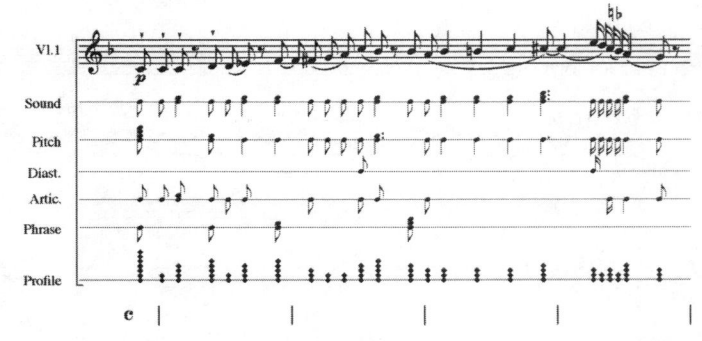

marks: the staccato wedge (stemmed upward) and the legato slur (stemmed downward), with the eighths rests having to be regarded, and also reckoned separately, as additional shortening marks. Finally, rhythm and weight of the »Phrases« were likewise included.

The rhythmic profile resulting from the accumulation of all of the components-rhythmic weights gives prominence above all to the accentuated upbeats of the phrases. There is an agreement here with one of Momigny's axioms, who – contrary to Hugo Riemann – assumes accentuated upbeats in all »cadences,« since the first action (»antécédent«) is supposedly always attended by tension, the second (»conséquent«) by relaxation.[155] Apart from that, however, the rhythmic profile coincides in no way with Momigny's cadencing schema. Rather, melodic gestures, which are noticeable to every listener and player, come about in that between the beginning and the end weights of the phrases the profile values are flat. Half-, whole and double measures thereby become recognizable as rhythmic units that the composer, in his predominantly syncopated mode of writing, evidently wished to create.

If one extends the excerpt from the Mozart movement to include the transitional passage from m. 15 to m. 24 as well as the other voices of the quartet, including the harmonic progressions and accents, one finds Mozart's intention confirmed of modeling the transition to the second theme in F major as an intensification. The essay by Hermann Danuser already cited refers to exactly these ten bars, as he contrasts Momigny's way of reading with that of Arnold Schoenberg. If one spoke of »verses«, the other heard »prose«.[156]

---

[153] If there are more than two notes in the formation of a melodic »cadence,« e.g. with feminine endings or ternary forms, the conséquent may also be represented by a 3 or even a 4.

[154] Danuser (see note 152), 256. In individual cases, I interpret Momigny's numbering somewhat differently from Danuser.

[155] See the pertinent statements of Momigny's in Palm (1969), 425f. (under no. 13).

[156] Danuser (1992), see note 152. Schoenberg's annotations are found in his famous text »Brahms the Progressive«, in: Arnold Schoenberg, *Style and Idea*, ed. Dika Newlin (New York 1950), 52-101, esp. 72f.

Ex. 3-027　　mm. 15-24, phrasings by Petersen, Momigny and Schoenberg

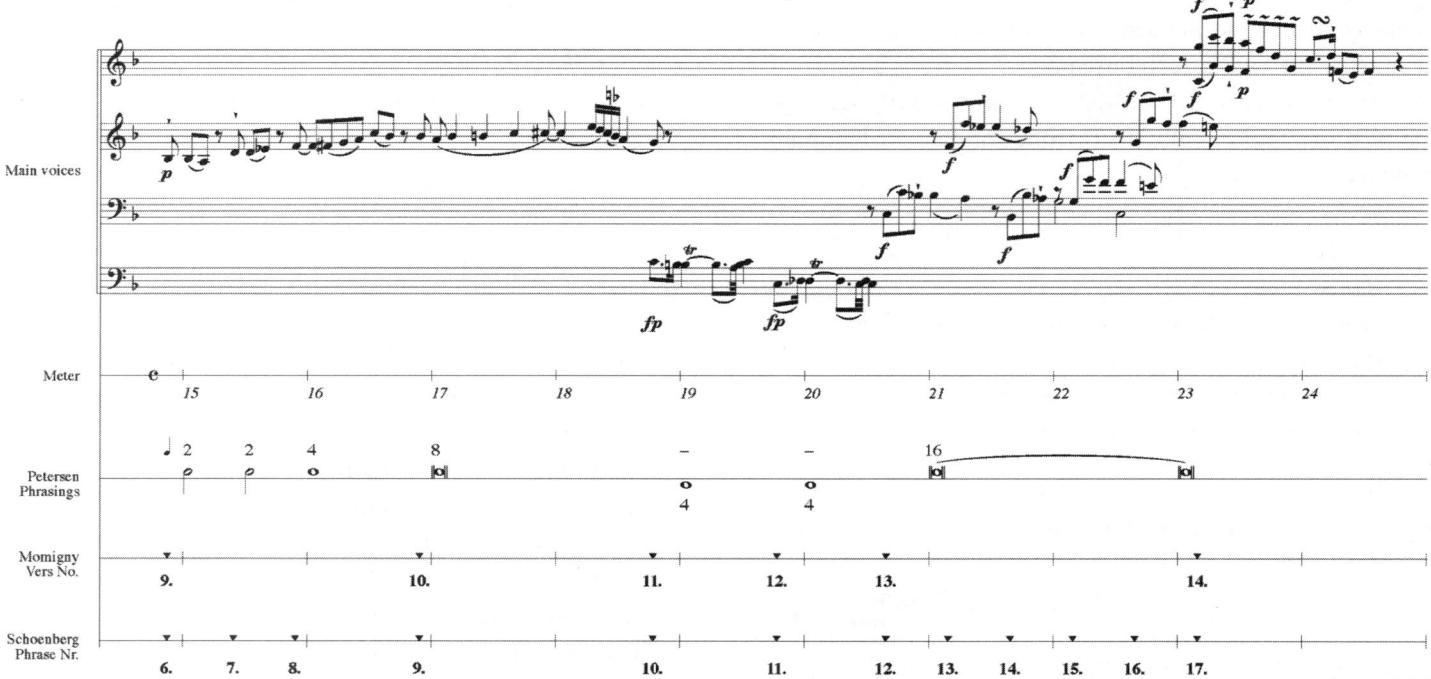

In reality, the views of the two analysts are not far apart. Both, however, failed to ask in which part the principal voice is to be found at any one time. Yet questions about phrasing are best considered by looking at leading voices. Thus, for example, there are good reasons for locating the main voice at the beginning (upbeat to m. 15) in the second rather than the first violin (cf. Ex. 3-027). Then, too, the voices that usher in the upbeat 3-♪ motif seem to me to have equal rights between them, so that they cannot be simply brushed »aside« as »imitations,« as Schoenberg thought.[157]

The excerpt of principal voices, finally, also clarifies the special role of the trill figures in cello and viola, which serve a retarding, episodic function. Looked at without prejudice, the construction of these ten bars is really clear and simple: 2+2+4+8+16 ♩ structure the movement, interrupted only by the two extraterritorial measures 19 and 20, in which the V of F major is stabilized as a secondary dominant. The expansion of the phrases is accompanied by an expansion of the upbeats, as the first upbeats are 1 ♪ in length, those before mm. 19 and 20 have the value of 2 ♪,

the beginning, a drop to small C3 in the middle, and just before the end the climactic note of C6.

This phrasal structuration is largely confirmed by both Momigny and Schoenberg, without, however, their addressing the formal idea of the number of parts increasing in geometric progression or the special role of the trill motif. At the end, both authors sequester two bars as a separate phrase or verse. I do not regard this as justified – at least from the perspective of the principal-voice action. The upbeat motifs, overlapping in ascending octaves and always articulated in the same way, extend beyond the beginning of m. 23. If at all, one could, starting with the *(subito)* **p**, assume a flourish-like final phrase, except that it would thereby receive too much weight within the overall architecture. In any case, this has nothing to do with »prose,« and the »cadence« principle, too, does not really contribute to the elucidation of the phrasal rhythms.

The phrasing of a leading voice is one thing, the analysis and representation of the rhythm of a complex four-part composition something altogether different. I have therefore submitted the 10-bar transition to a components-rhyth-

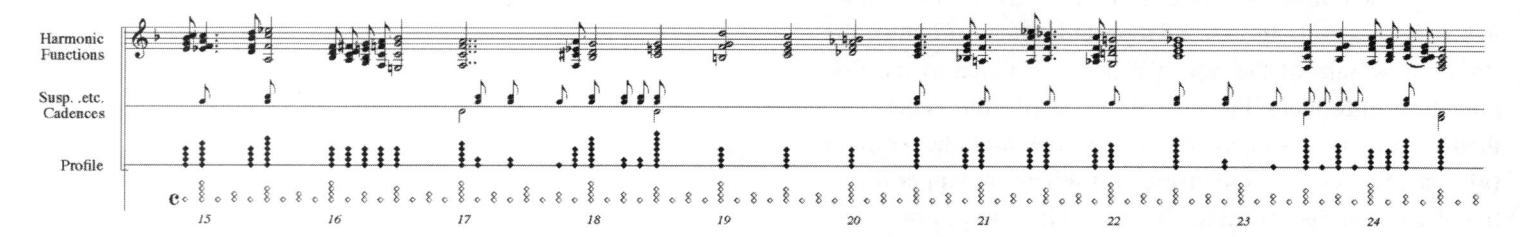

Ex. 3-028　　mm. 15-24, Harmony

while the four-bar final phrase is based on a motif with 3 ♪ upbeat. To this correspond the longer suspensions from m. 4 on (♩–♪, earlier ♪–♪). To be added is the expressive ambit planning of the main voices: the one-line octave at

mic analysis – in continuation, so to speak, of the analysis of violin 1. To save space, I have presented only the rhythmic profiles, not the individual components rhythms from which the profiles are derived (Ex. 3-029). New is the harmonic rhythm (Ex. 3-028). It is based on the change of harmonic functions, without differentiating between the inversions of the chords (uppermost system). To be added

---

[157] Schoenberg, »Brahms« (note 156), 50.

Ex. 3-029   mm. 15-24, Rhythmic Profiles

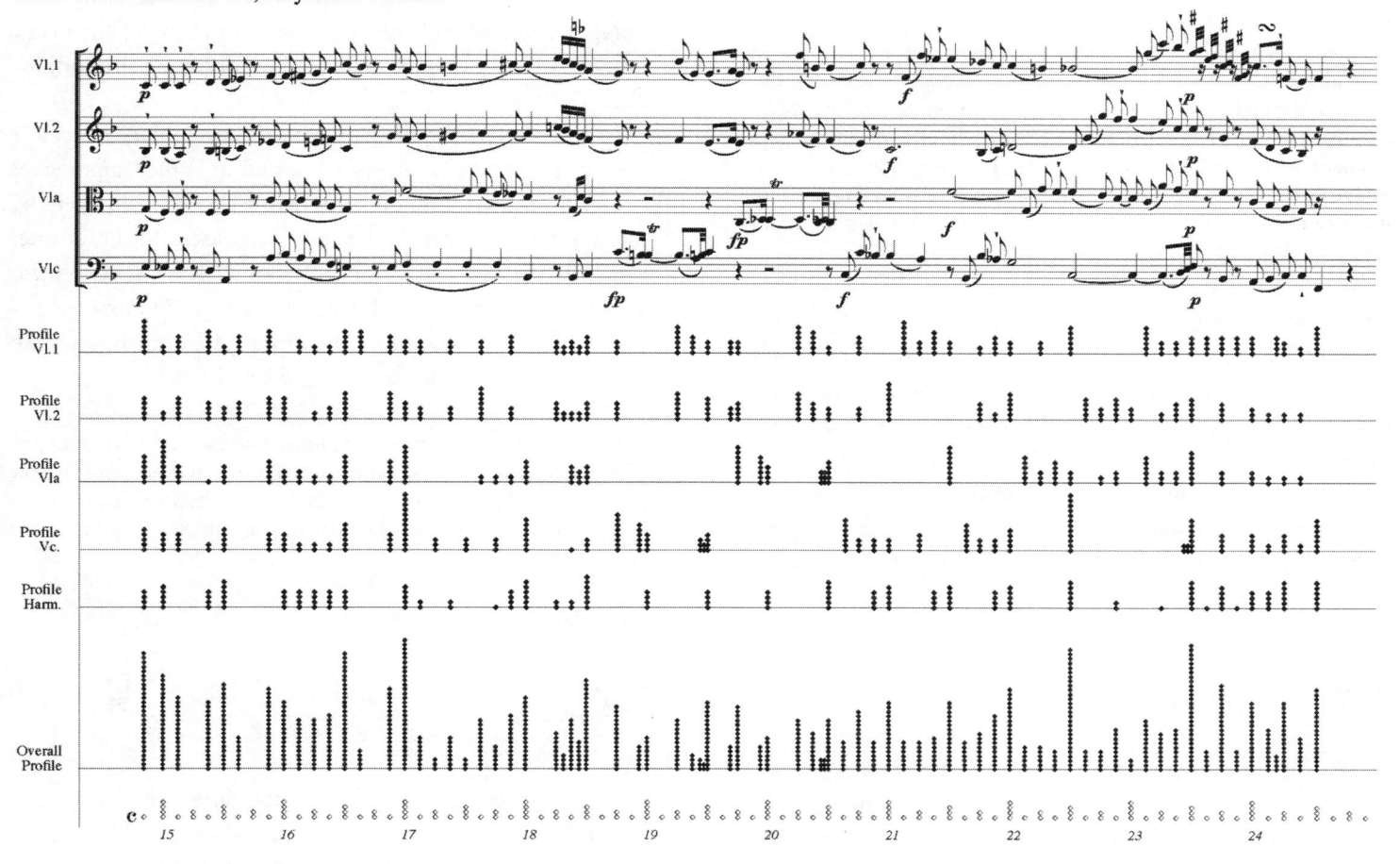

are all non-chord tones (stemmed upward) and the (harmonic) cadences (two weak tonic cadences, one imperfect cadence on the V and an authentic cadence in F major). In the profile of the harmonic rhythm, function changes are reflected by four points each, non-chord tones by one point, and the cadences by one or two points. I regard the augmented chord in m. 17 (F-E♭-A-C♯) as a harmony all its own with double dominant function.

A comparison between the harmonic-rhythmic profile and the metric one reveals, not unexpectedly, the very large coincidence between changes of harmonic function and strong beats. Both at the beginning and at the end, the harmonic rhythm is small-scale. In the middle, at the resting-place where cello and viola suround the C with trill figures (mm. 18-20), the rhythmic activity of the harmonies is at its lowest.

In Ex, 3-029, the rhythmic profiles of the four voices and the profile of the harmonic rhythm have been juxtaposed and combined into a total profile. The upshot may be a confusing degree of complexity, beneath which, e.g., the really perfectly clear phrase structure seems to disappear. Yet the result is not altogether uninstructive.

That the four voices here are taken as of equal weight may be a matter of opinion. One will agree, however, that Mozart has indeed shaped them highly individually, as one can see, among other things, from the articulation – e.g., at the beginning, the 2nd violin as against viola and cello.[158]

The four climactic measures toward the end, too, seem to me to speak clearly in favor of an equivalence of the four voices.

The comprehensive rhythmic profile is telling above all with regard to the relation between rhythm and meter. The strong beats *One* and *Three* of the 4/4 meter, for example, are by no means always accentuated *rhythmically*. Things clear up only in the middle of m. 22, where a shifted 4/4 meter establishes itself: four ♩ C^7 and four ♩ cadencing down to the tonic of F major, which is reached at *Three*. This finding coincides with the intensifying design of the passage and thus with its transitional function within the sonata form exposition.

Momigny's new and really fascinating approach of letting the meter emerge from the rhythm promises more than it is able to deliver. In the final analysis, the principle of the »cadence« remains too general to cast much light onto the actual rhythmic relations of a concrete tonal setting. Yet Momigny paved the way to the eventual overcoming of the »squaring of compositional construction« (R. Wagner).

An apropriate assessment of Momigny's theory is provided by Wolfgang Ruf, who also concerned himself with the Frenchman's analysis of Mozart's quartet movement. Ruf writes:[159]

---

[158] See the references to other subtle compositional means like this in Wilhelm Seidel, »Pathetische Gesten. Über Mozarts Streichquartett in d-Moll, KV 421,« *Mozart Studien*, ed. M. H. Schmid, vol. 8 (Tutzing, 1998), 53-74; e.g., p. 58.

[159] Wolfgang Ruf, »Mozart in der Musiktheorie des frühen 19. Jahrhunderts,« in: *Mozart. Aspekte des 19. Jahrhunderts*, ed. Hermann Jung (Mannheim, 1995), 44-58; p. 48.

Momigny's analysis is meticulous and comprehensive, but does not exhaust the substance of Mozart's composition. […] the conducting and layering of the four voices and their changing roles, as well as the relationship of the unfolding motivic shapes, their derivation from the intervallic and rhythmic configurations of the beginning: […] The full extent of the conception of *unité* and *variété* is thus not sounded, and the reason is plain: for Momigny it is a primarily aesthetic maxim and not a compositional / technical one; it concerns the style and the content but not the containing structure.

The same has to be said also of Momigny's rhythmic analyses. Even so, he did indicate ways by which one might attain to a freer and more comprehensive rhythmic analysis. It is not until the end of the 19th century that Hugo Riemann, who – *after* having established his own theory – came to recognize an important forerunner in Momigny and expressly drew attention to him,[160] would take further steps – only to get lost in cul-de-sacs of his own.

Weber • Rhythm and Meter

In 1832, Gottfried Weber published his *Versuch einer geordneten Theorie der Tonsetzkunst* (Essay on an Ordered Theory of Composition) in a »third, newly revised edition«; its first volume includes a »Forechapter« entitled variously »Rhythmics. – Meter« and, more simply, »Rhythm and Meter.« [161]

Rhythm without meter is unthinkable for Weber. Congregatonal singing, recitatives, acceleration or retardation and *senza battuta* passages are »unrhythmical« for him, whence he concludes that rhythm does not of necessity belong to the »being« of music, though it may »greatly heighten its appeal.«[162] Interestingly, Weber also regards »five-part, seven-part and similar groupings« as »unrhythmical« because not »symmetrical.«[163]

The terms rhythm and meter are not used altogether synonymously by Weber but are closely linked: »The theory of rhythm is called rhythmics, or rhythmopoesis, or also metrics.«[164] But whereas »metrical division« offered »really only dry mechanics, that is, only the measure of rhythmic figures, but in no way the figure itself,«[165] the combination of tonal or phrasal durations (»rhythmic figure«[166]) was multiform. Inasmuch as the diverse rhythmic durations and weights always »stand in ratios of the prime numbers 2 or 3 to each other,« the »rhythmic proportion« remained constant.[167]

From the perspective of components theory, Weber's theory reveals the same deficits as all the other approaches before him. Rhythmic diversity is measured exclusively by the duration of individual notes or phrases. In the chapter »Sounds Viewed in Rhythm,« Weber analyzes several measurs from the Andante of Mozart's Jupiter Symphony[168] – which I have likewise described in the chapter about hemiolas above. Weber writes (see also Ex. 3-030):

[At ex. 31] each of the diverse figures even ends on a different part of the measure. The first starts with the measure and ends on the second beat; the second starts with the third beat and ends on the first of the following bar; the third begins on the second beat and ends on the third.

Ex. 3-030 (Example by Weber)

Not within Weber's purview are the durations that extend beyond the motivic (or phrasal) beginnings, which yet in this case are all rendered more than distinct by several components (crest notes C6, *f-p* alternations, harmonic degrees and melodic triads). The structure is a hemiolic one, which overlays the 3/4 meter, so that one hears a succession of ♩ simultaneously with the continuing metrical puls (♩.). Since Weber can comprehend music only in terms of meter, he misses the essence of Mozartian rhythm, which not infrequently aims at seriously questioning or modifying the metrical order from time to time.

By the same template Weber also describes special rhythmic cases like upbeats, shifts and syncopations. The concept of the hemiola he does not employ at all, even though he cites an example from Johann Gottlieb Graun, which documents the hemiola even in the old sense of a temporary change of mensuration.[169] Accents, that is to say, whatever their kind, are considered solely in terms of their position in the measure, not according to whether they form rhythmic situations of their own.

---

[160] Hugo Riemann, »Ein Kapitel vom Rhythmus,« *Die Musik*, 3 (1903-04), 155-162. Cf. also Palm (1969), 11.

[161] Weber, Gottfried, *Versuch einer geordneten Theorie der Tonsetzkunst*, third ed. newly revised, in four vols. (Mainz, Paris, Antwerp, 1830-1832), 1:80-141.

[162] Ibid., 80 f.

[163] Ibid., 123 ff.

[164] Ibid., 81.

[165] Ibid., 129.

[166] Ibid.

[167] Ibid., 130.

[168] Ibid., 132 and musical inset.

[169] Ibid., 141 and musical example 50.

Westphal · Musical Rhythmics

Rudolf Westphal was a classical philologist, much respected in the 19th century, who had specialized in rhythm and meter. From the perspective of Greek »mousiké« Westphal found an approach also to the music of modern times. His *Allgemeine Theorie der musikalischen Rhythmik* (Universal Theory of the Musical Rhythmics)[170] appeared in Leipzig in 1880. It represents yet another attempt to utilize ancient prosody for an analysis also of the rhythm of modern music.

In the Foreword to his book, Westphal announces the aim of his study:

The principal task of this book is to rouse and animate the professional musician's awareness of rhythmic structure according to cola, periods and systems, and that therein lies the sum total of rhythm, and to show him how to give expression to this structure.[171]

In the first part, Westphal deals with the »rhythmical divisions in poetry,« in the second with the »musical verse feet and measures« and in the third with the »musical cola.« In determining the verse feet and measures, he takes off from Aristoxenes' concept of the »chronos protos« (»the short as the measuring unit of all rhythmic quantities«),[172] stating that while the chronos protos had lost its validity in music since Bach, it lived on in the nomenclature of the metrical kinds.[173] Westphal nevertheless applies the chronos protos also to rhythmic situations. Thus he can identify a chain of 4 ♪ as a dactylic rhythm, because a dactyl in Greek verse consists of four chronoi protoi (2+1+1). In the chapter about the »caesuras« within cola, he reflects that in a four-beat dactylic verse foot (♪♪♪♪) the caesura could come after any of the four notes, but that the variant ♪♪♪♪| should be avoided because the Greeks, too, had »purposely avoided it in the hexameter.«[174] This detail basically reveals the problem in Westphal's approach: he frankly thinks and writes normatively, and he projects what he has experienced as beautiful in Greek art onto his beloved music[175]:

We are all certain that the way in which Greek artists execute or design something […] always hits the essence of the beautiful. So it is also with the caesuras in the Greek meters. And accordingly, the art of the ancients should be a model for the modern. The caesura no. 4 [♪♪♪♪|] is strictly excluded by the ancient poets, […] it is anxiously avoided as if it were something evil.

Westphal applies his method of setting caesuras above all to examples from Bach's fugues and Beethoven's sonatas. I will restrict myself to the beginning of his analysis of the D major fugue from the *Well-Tempered Clavier* vol. 1 (Ex. 3-031). »System« to Westphal is tantamount to strophe. The entire exposition thus consists of two strophes, each of them formed of a »stollen« and a »counterstollen,« which, in turn, each contain two »cola.« All of these eight cola begin after the first beat and are exactly two bars in length, corresponding to the subject of the fugue.

Ex. 3-031 (Westphal's analysis)

Ex. 3-032   Bach, WTC I, Fugue B Major, Theme

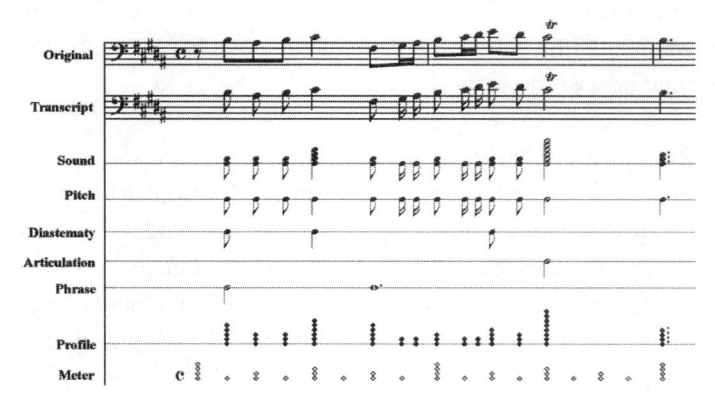

A closer look at the rhythmic structure of the theme (Ex. 3-032), however, shows that Bach specifically did *not* want to emphasize the caesura suggested by the bar line but to play across it. This is indicated both by the run-through of the complete seventh chord from F♯3 to E4 and by the striking hold on the fourth note of the theme (♩ C♯4). The theme is one of the more heterometric fugal subjects of the *Well-*

---

[170] Rudolf Westphal, *Allgemeine Theorie der musikalischen Rhythmik seit J. S. Bach, auf Grundlage der antiken und unter Bezugnahme auf ihren historischen Anschluss an die mittelalterliche, mit besonderer Berücksichtigung von Bach's Fugen und Beethovens Sonaten* (Leipzig, 1880, reprint Wiesbaden, 1968).

[171] Ibid., xxxviiif.

[172] Ibid., 34.

[173] Ibid., 40f.

[174] Ibid., 110.

[175] Ibid.

Ex. 3-033 Bach, WTC I, Fugue B Major, Exposition

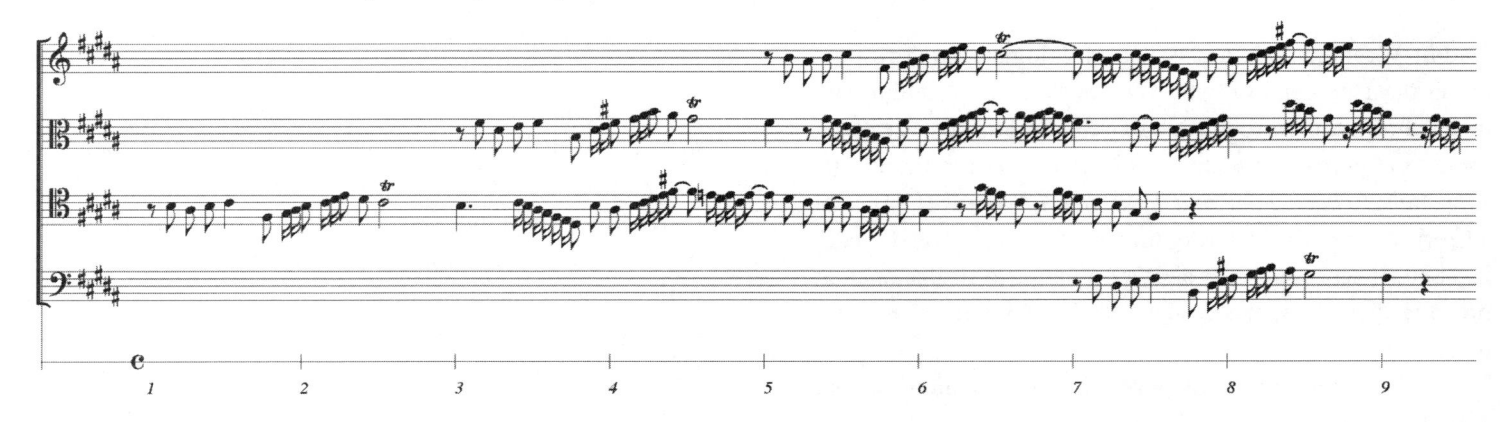

Tempered Clavier, something not typical of this collection.[176] In the »Profile« line of my components-rhythmical analysis of the theme, the irregularities can be ascertained from the heavy weights on weak beats, as well as from the distances between the high-peaking rhombus towers.

The same results from an analysis of the eight-bar fugal exposition (Ex. 3-033). Westphal's division into cola, verses (here stollen) and strophes (systems) imposes a regularity that may be possible for dances and marches but is wholly incongruous in the case of this four-part fugue. The unique melodic and rhythmic life of the various voices is simply ignored by Westphal. For instance, it is noteworthy that the tenor stops in the middle of m. 7 and thus does not take part in the cadence to $F_\sharp$ major at the end of the exposition. The alto does participate in the cadence in m. 9 but, by a small upbeat motif ($D_\sharp 5$-$C_\sharp 5$-$B4$-$A_\sharp 4$ and $G_\sharp 4$-$F_\sharp 4$-$E4$-$D_\sharp 4$), minimizes the effect of the caesura – at least in this voice. Similar peculiarities can be observed in the tenor in mm. 4-6. Here the voice pursues a superordinate stepwise descent ($F_\sharp 4$—$E4$–$D_\sharp 4$–$C_\sharp 4$–$B3$–$A_\sharp 3$-$G_\sharp 3$) played over the theme entry in the soprano.

To do justice to the polyphonic character of this composition, Westphal should have placed his caesuras separately for each voice. Only thus would it be possible to weight individual dividing points against each other and to ferret out that Bach has composed only *one* caesura in which all the voices actually come together, namely the final beat of the entire fugue!

Rudolf Westphal's *Allgemeine Theorie der musikalischen Rhythmik* does not deserve the name it bears. It trims »the musical actuality rigorously to a theoretical model,« as Seidel justly criticizes.[177] Instead of founding a genuine theory of musical rhythm, Westphal has restituted an obsolete theory of meter, making it look scientific by dressing it up in a highfalutin terminology foreign to the subject.

Lussy • The Musical Rhythm

In 1883, the Swiss musicologist and pianist Mathis Lussy, who mostly worked in Paris, published his chef d'œuvre, *Le Rythme musical*, which in 1874 had been preceded by a treatise on *L'expression musicale*.[178] Both works went through several editions, and the one on musical expression was translated into several other languages, including German.[179] A detailed and careful assessment of Lussy's theory can be found in Seidel.[180]

According to Lussy, the term rhythm means that sounds (*sons*) are arranged »alternately strong and weak« in such a way that »one note conveys to the ear the feeling of a rest, a hold, a more or less complete end,« at intervals that can be regular or irregular. »The notes between two halting points [...] form a rhythm the Greeks called colon or member of a rhythmic form [*construction rythmique*].«[181] Rhythm, for Lussy, is therefore a concrete sound shape, not a sequence of abstract durational values.

The weights of notes or sounds seem more important to Lussy than their durations. The alternation of »fort et faible« governs the expressive content of a musical combination, as well as expressive playing. Lussy also calls the halting-points between which rhythms unfold »ictus« (stresses). If a note is strong (*fort*), and if it comes either at the beginning or at the end of a rhythm, it is said to have the quality of an ictus, as distinguished from a regular thesis.[182] As a vault rests on its pillars, so the »rythmes, véritables arceaux musicaux« rest on the rhythmic ictus.[183]

---

[176] Cf. The first chapter in Part II of the present study.

[177] Seidel, *Rhythmustheorien* (see note 1, above p. 189), 214.

[178] Mathis Lussy, *Le rythme musical. Son origine, sa fonction et son accentuation* (Paris, 1883), deuxième édition, revue et corrigée (Paris, 1884); Mathis Lussy, *Traité de l'expression musicale* (Paris, 1874).

[179] Mathis Lussy, *Die Kunst des musikalischen Vortrags. Anleitung zur ausdrucksvollen Betonung und Tempoführung in der Vocal- und Instrumentalmusik*, transl. and ed., by authorization of the author, by Felix Vogt (Leipzig, 1886).

[180] Seidel, *Rhythmustheorien* (note 1, above p. 189), 206-214.

[181] Lussy, *Rythme* (1884), 1f.

[182] Ibid., 5.

[183] Ibid.

But how does Lussy recognize the heavy or light weight of a note or sound? He refers to »le temps fort« (the strong beat), linking the concept of rhythm to that of meter. »...la note de l'arrêt, du repos final, doit [must] tomber sur le temps fort, c'est-à-dire au commencement de la mesure.«[184] The desire for measure, regularity, order and symmetry is said to be innate to man (»naît«). Lussy even derives this need explicitly from human physiology (»le principe physiologique«[185]) and deems it as absolutely necessary as breathing in and out is for life:[186]

Breathing, in reality, consists of two physiological moments, two movements: *inhaling* and *exhaling*. Inhaling personifies action, while exhaling represents repose, the time of rest. Exhalation is symbolized by the *strong beat* of the measure, the *thesis* (strong syllables), the *downbeat*; inhalation corresponds to the measure's *weak beat*, the *arsis* (weak syllables, mutes), the *upbeat*.

Apart from this natural meter with its earmarks of proportion and weight, Lussy recognizes other means of emphasizing notes and sounds. In his *L'Expression musicale*, he devotes an entire chapter each to three kinds of accent: metric, rhythmic and pathetic. The metric accent refers to the meter; and is recognizable »in performance by the stronger accent [...] on the note coinciding with the first beat of the measure«.[187] The rhythmic accent results from understanding the »parts of a musical phrase,« that is – in Lussy's terminology – of the individual »rhythms«, whose »beginning and end notes« always had to be »given special emphasis.«[188] To mark these rhythms or partial phrases graphically, Lussy introduces the slur, which identifies the ictus on the first and last note. He complains that composers used these phrasing arcs carelessly or erroneously. The lengths of the rhythms, and thus the temporal intervals between the ictus, could be both »regular and irregular.«[189] There were five ways of forming irregular rhythms: contraction, expansion, repetition, melodic progression and echo.

At the start of the chapter on the third, or »pathetic,« accent, Lussy begins by summarizing once more the nature of the metric and rhythmic accents:

We have hitherto moved in the sphere of *instinct* and *intelligence*. It thus should come as no surprise that machines have been built that fairly exactly reproduce both *metric* and *rhythmic* accents, which, as we have seen, recur at regular intervals and are separated by unaccented notes.[190]

With the pathetic accent, we enter »the realm of *feeling*.« Lussy writes:[191]

To be felt and reproduced, the *pathetic accent* requires a soul; it is therefore also the highest artistic trait. One could rightly call it the *poetic accent*, as it is the one that impresses a particularly expressive character upon certain compositions. The more the pathetic elements, i.e., departures from any and all rules, the more repetitions, the more lower or upper adjacent peak notes, the more exceptional syncopations, the more chromatic intervals, harmonic suspensions or anticipations, dissonances etc. a work contains, the more poetic, more expressive it is.

As much as the means of accentuation Lussy enumerates here may remind of the list of rhythmically relevant components, as little do they actually have to do with them. Lussy nowhere says anything to the effect that secondary durations, and thus independent rhythms, occur between accentuated notes. He describes the pathetic accents rather as isolated attacks on the metric and rhythmic uniformity.

Apart from the (rather naive) psychological explanation for the pathetic accent – namely that a special effort was required to make a change of metric, rhythmic or tonal relations plausible to the listener who expected the continuation of what is always the same – there is no clarification as to why individual sound phenomena should be accentuated one way and not another. Instead of the »exact analysis down to the smallest detail« that Lussy promises,[192] we find nothing but directions how to play ›correctly.‹

When all is said and done, the directions and markings Lussy attaches to his numerous musical examples are merely the precipitations of a subjective feelings or of a certain period taste. Consider Lussy's rule that triplets that have not previously occurred in a piece should at their first appearance all be individually accentuated;[193] or that, in a context of rhythmic diversity (mixture of small and large note values), measures of unexpectedly uniform values should be accentuated if the motion is ascending, but recited »flexibly« if the motion is one of descent.[194] Equally arbitrary seems the norm Lussy proclaims at the end: »In pieces of lively tempo, the pathetic accent is to be avoided at all cost.«[195]

I am unable to agree with Wilhelm Seidel's benevolent judgment that the strength of Lussy's theory was to have uncovered the »temporal layering« of the music of his time.[196] Lussy was sensitive to the tensions that can build up between bars and phrases on the one side and accents on the other. But he was unable to apprehend these phenomena theoretically. He described music like a listener who con-

---

[184] Ibid., 2.

[185] Ibid., 3.

[186] Ibid., original emphasis.

[187] Lussy, *Kunst des ... Vortrags* (1886), 21.

[188] Ibid., 56.

[189] Ibid., 60.

[190] Ibid., 141.

[191] Ibid.

[192] Ibid., 143.

[193] Ibid., 150.

[194] Ibid., 148f.

[195] Ibid., 178.

[196] Seidel, *Rhythmustheorien* (see note 1, above p. 189), 213.

centrates on a single mode of motion and, in ›digging‹ it, zestfully suffers the manifold attacks on the steady »fort et faible.« I miss precisely the aspects that illuminate the conflictual relations of layered processes, not to mention the diverse simultaneous rhythms within a single voice.

Riemann • Musical Metrics and Rhythmics

Prior to publishing his *System der musikalischen Rhythmik und Metrik* (System of the Musical Rhythmics and Metrics) in 1903, Hugo Riemann had already, in 1884, brought out his *Musikalische Dynamik und Agogik* (Musical Dynamics and Agogics), which bears the following telling subtitle: »Textbook on Musical Phrasing on the Basis of a Revision of the Doctrine of Metrics and Rhythmics«.[197] Both works deal with the same problem complex. The author wishes to explain how rhythmic and metric aspects of musical compositions – sequences of tonal durations and sequences of stresses – are related to each other. Riemann's main cognitive interest is ultimately dictated by the wish to contribute to an improvement in artistic practice, He wants to show by his analyses how a musician can phrase correctly and generally perform music intelligently. His gauge of ›right‹ and ›wrong‹ is ultimately his own feeling. Wilhelm Seidel hits the nail on the head when he summarizes Riemann's teachings by writing: »What is behind Riemann's analyses is frequently nothing more than the formative impulse of a listening culture typical of its period but nevertheless subjective.«[198]

This is not the place to delineate and critically assess Riemann's theory yet once more: it has been done several times already by other authors.[199] I query his texts only as to whether they contain any references to the rhythmic relevance of components, and whether his conception of metric weight has anything in common with the aspect of rhythmic weight developed by me.

In the section »The Melodic Motifs« of chapter 8 of his *Musikalische Dynamik und Agogik*,[200] Riemann presents a

Ex. 3-034   Riemann, *Dynamik und Agogik*, p. 173

self-made example of a melodic sequence consisting entirely of ♩, whose melodic turns (Diastematy) are said to result in a quadruple time (NB 3-034). After citing the sequence of notes once nakedly and once with small markers (so-called »reading marks«[201]), Riemann puts the melody into diverse meters, including four times into the 4/4 and once into the 3/4 beat (NB 3-035).

Ex. 3-035   Riemann, *Dynamik und Agogik*, p. 174

He remarks:[202]

The dynamics of the motifs is determined once the meter and the first strong note have been given to us; that is to say, the motifs delimited by the motion of the melody may still come to mean different things depending on the meter in which they appear.

Riemann's experiment here is on shaky grounds, inasmuch as by his own terms there cannot be any motif without an inner dynamics.[203] The tonal groups that, in the unmetered version of the melody, he divides by »reading marks« (without, incidentally, explaining why in this and not another way) do not in fact have the quality of motifs, since they lack that »peculiar vitality« inherent in a true »motif (element of motion).« They are mere »concatenations [...] of indifferent particles.«[204]

We are therefore dealing with a motif only once it has been embedded in a metric system, as shown by Riemann in Ex. 3-035. Here one can readily see that all the dynamics ascribed to the diverse variants by the crescendo and decrescendo forks comes from outside of the melody. The main stress of the motif is always the *One* of the measure, what changes is only the upbeat crescendos and downbeat feminine endings – both of varying lengths. The most complicated case is that in which the melody is embedded in a 3/4 meter, for which Riemann provides the ›dynamic‹ resolution in an extra follow-up (Ex. 3-036).

---

[197] Hugo Riemann, *Musikalische Dynamik und Agogik. Lehrbuch der musikalischen Phrasierung auf Grund einer Revision der Lehre von der musikalischen Metrik und Rhythmik* (Hamburg, St. Petersburg, Leipzig, 1884); Hugo Riemann, *System der musikalischen Rhythmik und Metrik* (Leipzig, 1903).

[198] Wilhelm Seidel, article »Rhythmus, Metrum, Takt,« in: *MGG²*, subject part, vol. 8 (1998), cols. 257-317; col. 304.

[199] Ernst Apfel and Carl Dahlhaus, *Studien zur Theorie und Geschichte der musikalischen Rhythmik und Metrik*, vol. 1 (Munich, 1974), »Zur Kritik des Riemannschen Systems,« pp. 184-203; Wilhelm Seidel, *Über Rhythmustheorien der Neuzeit* (Berne, Munich, 1975), 157-199; Carl Dahlhaus, *Die Musiktheorie im 18. und 19. Jahrhundert*, Part II: *Deutschland*, ed. Ruth E. Müller (Geschichte der Musiktheorie Bd. 11) (Darmstadt, 1989), 157-204.

[200] Riemann, *Dynamik*, 173.

[201] Ibid., 9.

[202] Ibid., 174.

[203] Ibid., 10f.

[204] Ibid., 11.

Ex. 3-036 Riemann, *Dynamik und Agogik*, p. 175

To clarify the metric weights, Riemann in this case has added whole-measure harmonies, to which individual notes are in a dissonant relation, mostly in the form of suspensions, which regularly fall on strong beats. The first 3/4 variant starts with a single ♩ (as an incomplete motif), after which two upbeat ♩ lead twice to a masculine and once to a feminine ending. In the second variant, we have to begin with the feminine ending of an incomplete motif and then three identically positioned motifs with feminine endings. What role the melody's own divisional points, with which the experiment started, play in the new metric environment is not explained.

Ex. 3-037
Deviation of Diastematic Rhythms and Meter

If we free ourselves of the compulsion of having to determine a motif around each and every metrical stress, we gain the freedom to hear the rhythm of the melodic sequence as an event independent of the meter, or the beats of the measure, in which the melody is embedded (Ex. 3-037). That means that one participates in a tensional relation of greater or lesser discrepancy. After all, the 4 ♩ rhythm of the melody deriving from the latter's diastematy (crest and/or keel notes) remains in effect even if a changing metric milieu is constructed. Riemann never attained to the insight, either here or elsewhere, that even single-voiced melodies embody different rhythms at one and the same time, and that these may diverge from each other. Thus the melody given by Riemann contains simultaneously the rhythm of the tonal entries (19 ♩), the rhyhm of the crest notes (4 ○ = upper slurs) and the rhythm of the keel notes (4 ○ = lower slurs).

For the most part, Riemann determines and delimits motifs and phrases in ›living objects,‹ that is to say, in actually composed music. In his *Rhythmik und Metrik* of 1903, he discusses melodic lines from scherzo movements of three Beethoven symphonies, of which one theme is without upbeat and two with (Ex. 3-038).[205]

Ex. 3-038 Riemann, *Rhythmik und Metrik*, p. 31

The marks added to the music are Riemann's. They include single and double »reading marks« to delimit the smallest motivic units and square brackets or parentheses to identify motifs of a higher order or phrases. New are the dotted bar lines, which occasionally replace the original ones and serve to mark secondary stresses in expanded measures, which Riemann takes to be intended by Beethoven (quasi 6/4 meter). The bar numbers added in parentheses likewise refer to these joint measures; they reveal that Riemann ascribes an upbeat function to some of the original measures in relation to the enlarged ones (A major Symphony: 3 ♩ upbeat, *Pastorale*: 4 ♩ upbeat.).

In his commentaries to these examples, which are detailed, Riemann sticks to the definitions of the terms »motif« and »phrase« set down elsewhere:[206]

A musical motif [...] is the musical content of what to our sense is a comfortably medium time [...], that is to say, in no way merely a rhythmic formation but a musical concretum determined on every side, in which melody, harmony, rhythm, even dynamics, timbre, etc. all have a part.

---

[205] Riemann, *Rhythmik*, p. 31.
[206] Ibid., 13 / 14.

Important for an understanding of Riemann's analyses is his fixation on the notion that a single motif can have only one main stress, while the number of notes preceding or following that stress will vary. It follows that if there are two or more main stresses, we have to do with chains of motifs, for which Riemann uses the term »phrase« (or else »sentence« or »period«):[207]

The enormously wavering terminology for the metric-rhythmic dimensions ordinarily calls groups of measures constituting a higher unit *rhythm* – one speaks of two-, three-, or four-bar rhythms (ritmo di due, tre, quattro battute); [...] In more recent times, it has become customary to denominate the higher unit into which single-measure motifs combine *phrases*, which does away with the ambiguity of the term rhythm.

Riemann does consider another possibility of linking motifs without thereby necessarily creating a phrase. This »expansion of the term motif to the size of two basic time units«[208] constitutes a »motif formation of a higher order,«[209] which for the most part obtains when the meter chosen by the composer has to be ›adjusted,‹ as Riemann fairly frequently presumes (see the remarks on the ancillary bar lines above).

The Scherzo theme from Beethoven's 7th Symphony constitutes an example of this (Ex. 3-038 a). In commenting on his quoted example, Riemann says explicitly that his »brackets above the notes [...] mark off two-bar motifs (four bars in the original notation)«. How is one to understand that? Since his premise is that a motif can have only *one* main stress, Riemann here seems to posit doubly composite measures, i.e., not just a 6/4 meter but even a 12/4 one. I have reconstructed in Ex. 3-039 how he may have felt.

Ex. 3-039

The ›gesture‹ of the theme seems to have been actually captured. Riemann did not hesitate to circumscribe the nature of the »thematic motif« also metaphorically: »...comparable to an individual mimic gesture, a negating shake or an affirming nod of the head, a smile, a frown, a beckonig or dismissing wave of the hand, a stamping with the foot, etc.«[210] What Riemann has sensed by way of self-observation may in this case be even confirmed by a more objective method that does not encroach upon Beethoven's notation (Ex. 3-040).

Ex. 3-040 Beethoven, 7th Symphony, 3rd mov., mm. 3-10 (Rhythm Score)

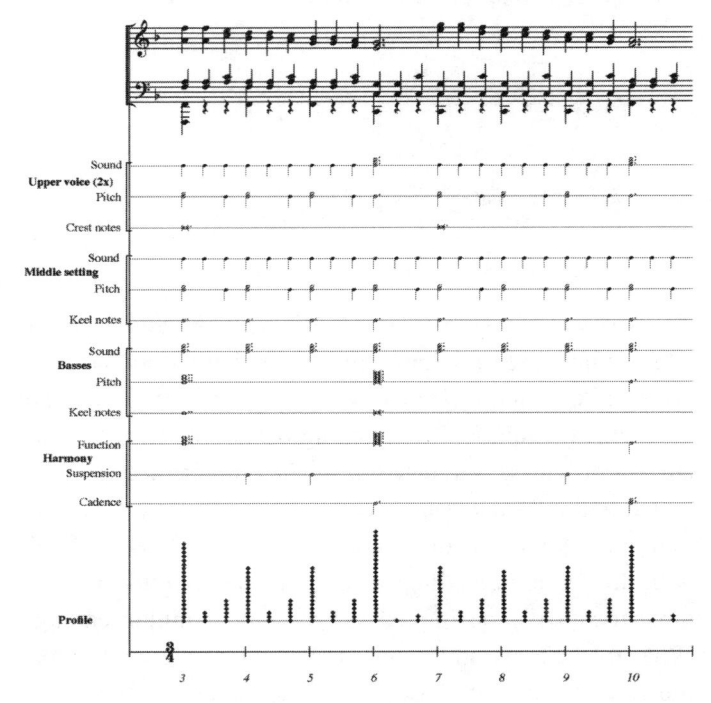

The rhythmic situation in this theme is so simple that to describe it one hardly needs the elaborate procedure of a rhythm score. If I have resorted to it anyway, it is to precisely name those details that are responsible for the greatest rhythmic weight falling on the fourth (m. 6) and eighth (m. 10) bar. Thus the main voice in these measures has the only long note values. Moreover, the change from tonic to dominant likewise enters in m. 6, and the F major recurs only after another four bars. These occurrences are given support by the bass voice, which for three bars repeats the note F and thereafter the C for another four bars. Note repetitions play a role also in the main voice and in the middle voices, inasmuch as they result in a pitch rhythm that gives an additional weight to the *One* of every measure (♩ ♩ ♩ ♩ ♩ ♩). To be added are also the suspensions in mm. 4, 5 and 9.

The problem with Riemann's analysis is that he feels forced by his predetermined system to ferret out and justify not only the secondary motifs (twice four measures) but also the »subdividing motifs« (down to the value of a single ♩). As the »reading marks« in his notation (Ex. 3-038) indicate, the *One* of every (original) measure is the end of a subdividing motif, including the very first note, which is called an incomplete motif. He does observe that the main voice actually embodies the rhythm of ♩ ♩ ♩ ♩ ♩ ♩.[211] Unable, however, to see in this the proof for the copresence of two rhythms within a single melody, he never explains why with this trochaic rhythm there should be a motif limit after the first quarter of the measure. Here as elsewhere Riemann is a victim of his self-imposed dogma that there cannot be any full-measure motif beginnings, so that in all cases where a piece or a phrase commences without upbeat, one had to assume incomplete motifs, whose ends could be

---

[207] Riemann, *Dynamik*, 243.

[208] Riemann, *Rhythmik*, 22.

[209] Ibid., 23.

[210] Ibid., 14.

[211] Ibid., 31.

heard but whose beginnings had to be supplied mentally. As numerous critics have noted before me, this dogma burdened Riemann's entire theory and earned it a good deal of ridicule. Instead of listening into the music without prejudice and picking up every signal that might be significant for the structure of phrases and periods, Riemann labored under the illusory notion of a natural law of musical motion according to the model of light→heavy.

inforce the tendency of the latter toward binary structures, as the slurs begin only two ♩ before the *One* beat. Musical phrases, besides, are recognizable not only from the slurs added by the composer but also from repetitions within the melody. Thus the section of mm. 207-210 is heard twice, and the third beginning of the repetition (m. 215) continues on, now at an interval of two double measures (mm. 217, 219).

Ex. 3-041 Beethoven, 3rd Symphony, 3rd mov., Trio, mm. 207-226

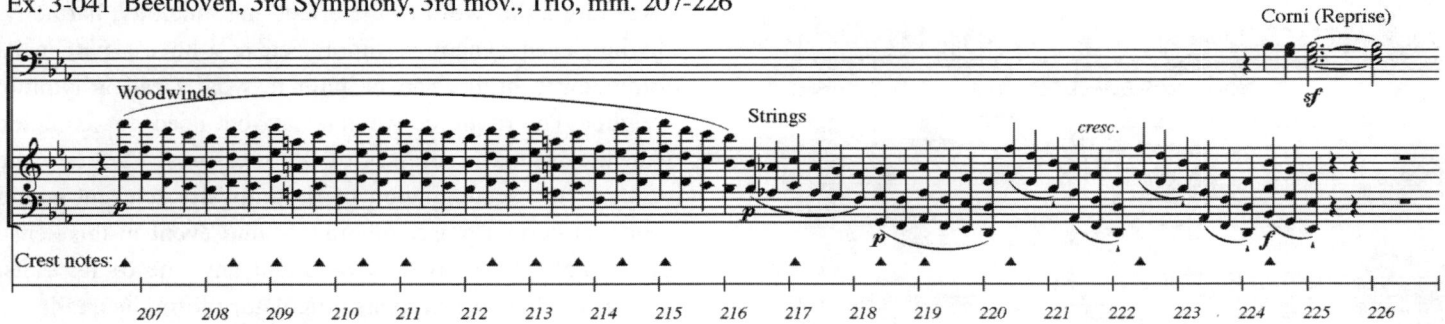

Let us also look at the example from Beethoven's *Eroica*. I juxtapose Riemann's analysis of the transitional passage from the Trio in the Scherzo (cf. Ex. 3-038 b) with Beethoven's unretouched notation (Ex. 3-041).[212] In this unisono passage, the following components are rhythmically relevant: »Sound«, »Diastematy«, »Articulation«, »Dynamics«, »Phrase« and »Timbre«. The tonal durations are limited to a single value (♩). In such monochronic processes, the other components come strongly to the fore, because only they can add rhythmic animation to the music. From the line »crest notes« (of the component »Diastematy«) one can see that Beethoven arranged several binary rhythms (distance of the crest notes: 2 ♩) within the sequence of quarter notes. A listener (or performer), who hears (or plays) the passage strictly from the perspective of the ternary meter may entirely miss this rhythmic layer.[213]

The components »Articulation« and »Dynamics« come into their own only in the second part of the passage. The staccato wedges after m. 221 mark the rhythm ♩. ♩. ♩. ♩. (♩.), supported by the slurs that here (mm. 220ff.) probably indicate a legato. There are virtually no changes in dynamics; only in the final bar before the recapitulation an *f* is called for, which is prepared for by a *crescendo* and produces a stressed double upbeat.

The phrasing arcs are applied with deliberation by Beethoven, so as to support by diminution the compression to be observed elsewhere in this passage. An initial value of 28 ♩ under a single slur, which is hardly graspable as a single durational unit, is followed by phrasing slurs at the rhythm of two double measures and five single ones, which, however, are shifted off the basic meter. They are set parallel to the component »Diastematy« and thus re-

That leaves the component »Timbre« to be commented on, which in this instance is doubly relevant: as instrumental color and as octave register. After some nine measures, the timbre changes from woodwinds to strings. The duration of the woodwind timbre is identical with that of the 28 ♩ long phrasing slur and thus rhythmically insignificant. The turning-point at m. 216 is all the more striking, especially since the change in timbre now commences two ♩ before the *One*, whereas at the beginning of the passage it started with one ♩ upbeat. From m. 216 on, clear rhythms are formed by means of different octave registers: single and double octave unisonos alternate in a rhythm of 6+6+3+3+3+6 ♩.

In sum, one can say about the rhythm of this transitional passage that after eight bars of clearly ternary structure, which precede our passage (not described here), the rhythmic situation from m. 207 on at first ranges from the amorphous to the ambivalent, but that thereafter binary rhythms come increasingly to the fore, which exhibit a tendency toward a 3/2 meter (with two quasi upbeat ♩). Just before the onset of the recapitulation, these double measures are diminished to likewise diminished single ones. Only a few staccato wedges announce the ›real‹ *One*, which then also actually establishes itself (*sf*) with the reentering horn theme.

Riemann's analysis of the »Grave« theme in Beethoven's *Pathétique* (op. 13), too, will show that the all-too narrow conception of the motif does not greatly help an understanding of rhythmic, and, indeed, generally musical realities, but more nearly hinders it (Ex. 3-042). Riemann first discussed the slow introduction to the Allegro movement in his *Dynamik und Agogik* of 1884.[214] It reappeared, substantially modified and supplemented by harmonic annota-

---

[212] My transcription is only for clarification. It reproduces the sound intended by Beethoven.

[213] Se, e.g., Seidel, *Rhythmustheorien* (see note 1), 174.

[214] Riemann, *Dynamik*, 245-248, which include Ex. 3-042.

tions, in 1918 in Riemann's three-volume study of Beethoven's complete piano sonatas.[215]

Ex. 3-042 (Riemann's analysis)

The facsimile (Ex. 3-042) reproduces the »Grave« theme with Riemann's markings. With the exception of the last bar, all the motif stresses fall on the *One* or *Three* of the 4/4 meter. If there is a rest before the *One*, the following stressed note gets a dividing line,[216] so that the next, now complete, motif can have an upbeat. The results, however, are

Ex. 3-043

---

[215] Hugo Riemann, *L. van Beethovens sämtliche Klavier-Solosonaten. Ästhetische und formal-technische Analyse mit historischen Notizen*, 3 parts (Berlin, 1918), 2: 1-5. The main change in 1918 vis-á-vis the analysis of 1884 is an intervention of Riemann's in Beethoven's notation: Beethoven is said to have »rendered the rhythm of the last bar of the Grave not quite correctly«: »2/4 of a measure was lost beause of the notation with too-short notes« (p. 3). Riemann therefore enlarges the note values of the last half-measure before the Allegro so that two quarter notes are added. Since Riemann also regards Beethoven's 4/4 meter as inappropriate and therefore notates the theme in 2/4 meter (which he did not yet dare to do in 1884), the entire Grave now consists of 21 ›new‹ 2/4 bars instead of the ten original 4/4 ones.

[216] The line was evidently forgotten in the last bar, after the C6.

discrepancies that illuminate the dilemma Riemann's upbeat dogma puts him into. For example, the main motif at the C minor beginning is made to seem composite, while its E♭ major variant starting in m. 5 is undivided (no dividing line after the first note). Yet the two variants are rhythmically undifferentiated, except for the diminished beginning notes and th suspensions – even the number of notes struck in the main voice is the same (Ex. 3-043).

If one takes up Riemann's idea of the motif stress and takes him at his word to the effect that »melody, harmony, rhythm, even dynamics, timbre, etc.«[217] have a part in its formation, a bridge can be built to what I call »rhythmic weight.« The rhythmic weights can, but need not, coincide with the isometric stresses of the measures. They are the result of the accumulation of rhythmically relevant sound events at certain points of time. Sound event in this sense means both the individual note and any one of its traits, e.g., its pitch, its volume, its articulatory form, its quality as a melodic turning-point. These traits, with which composition is done and which I therefore call components, form, as we have seen, rhythms of their own, which, taken together, accumulate into rhythmic weights.

Ex. 3-044 Beethoven, Sonata op. 13 *(Pathétique)*, Beginning

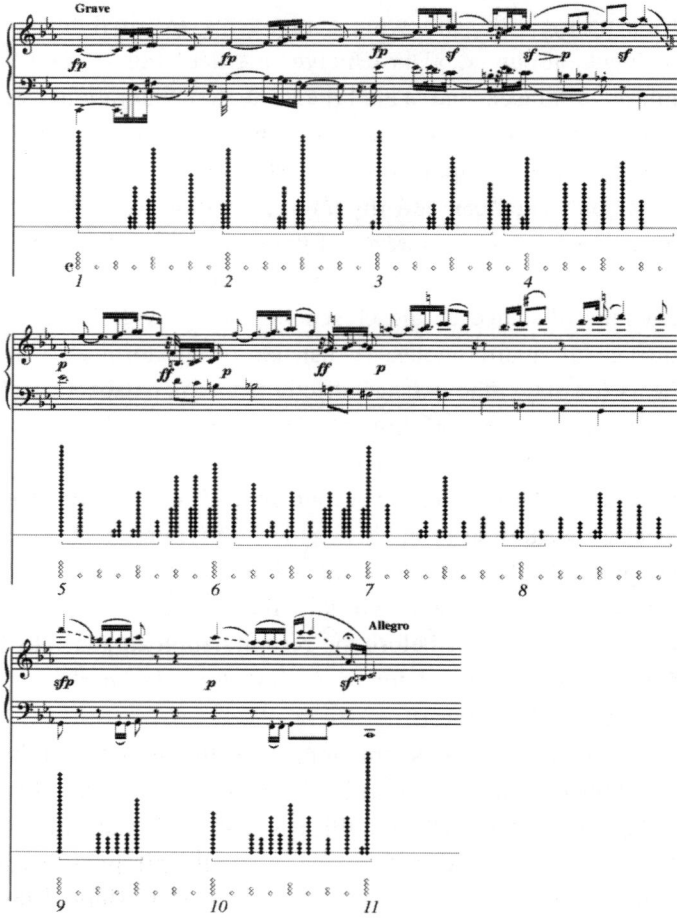

Ex. 3-044 conveys the result of my components-rhythmic analysis of the Grave introduction (rhythmic profile). To save space I dispense with a reproduction of the complete rhythm score. I executed it according to the criteria I have described in the first part of the present book.

---

[217] For the quotation, see footnote 206.

With its highest peaks, the rhythmic profile reveals an isometric weight distribution that for the most part yields the same 2/4 distances that Riemann also regarded as typical for this Grave. At the beginnning of the E♭ major part (mm. 5 and 6), the repeatedly subdivided 4/4 meter emerges faintly. Once the melody rises chromatically to the sixth octave, the rhythmic profile becomes more level: owing to the standing harmony of the partly foreshortened, partly complete dominant ninth chord, there are no weights to be added for changes in harmonic function.

A look at the profile from the perspective of the thematic motifs and phrases, which I have bracketed below the profile line, shows that most of these sense-bearing units have *two* main stresses. This finding can be regarded as largely objective. It thus refutes Riemann's view that a motif can have only one main accent and that there can be no motif without an upbeat.

While Hugo Riemann has probably listened more discriminatingly into the rhythmic-metric processes of compositions than any theoretician before him, he did not in the end arrive at an analytic instrumentarium that would have permitted him to let meter be meter and to recognize, through a real rhythm analysis, meter as the result of the act of composing.

Wiehmayer • Rhythmics and Metrics

In 1917, the theoretician Theodor Wiehmayer, who mostly taught at the Stuttgart Conservatory, published his study *Musikalische Rhythmik und Metrik* (Musical Rhythmics and Metrics)[218] in Magdeburg, and until 1926 followed it up with several essays on the same general subject.[219] Though writing in answer to Riemann's *System der musikalischen Rhythmik und Metrik*, which had appeared in 1903, Wiehmayer did not succeed in formulating a convincing new approach of his own (beyond some just critical observations). According to Wiehmayer, Riemann's theory not only brought confusion to the subject but presented an actual danger to the musical heritage.[220] Wiehmayer fell back on the »old accent theory« as a basis on which to erect »a new edifice of musical metrics,«[221] and summoned Mattheson, Koch, Hauptmann and Westphal as witnesses to a correct and sensible conception of musical meter. Wilhelm Seidel, who has presented an exhaustive critical account of Wiehmayer's theory, reaches the conclusion that the author proceeded in an entirely »eclectic manner« and had presented »nothing really new.«[222]

Assuming the human heartbeat as the basic standard, Wiehmayer distinguishes rhythm and meter as follows:[223]

> The division [of the standard measure] into smaller time values belongs in the realm of *rhythmics* as the doctrine of the different tonal durations. The combination [of the standard measure] into groups, on the other hand, takes us into the area of *metrics,* the doctrine of symmetries, of the comparison of similar sections. The basic rhythmic standard is thus the crucial watershed between the two areas.

An unusual aspect is Wiehmayer's distinction of the kinds of accentuation, of which in his opinion there are three: rhythmic stress at the end of a tonal group, metric stress at the beginning of a primary or secondary beat in the measure, and declamatory stress depending on the ups and downs of a melody.[224] In the schema below a) exhibits the metric, b) the rhythmic and c) the declamatory accentuation (Ex. 3-045).[225]

Ex. 3-045   Wiehmayers schema of accentual kinds

Wiehmayer accepts the weight relations as historically given. That rhythmic figures should on principle be oriented toward the end, on the other hand, is something Wiehmayer posits, while crescendo and diminuendo forks (declamation) are said to elude all regulation, opening the doors to an artistically free interpretation with an eye solely to musical content. As Wiehmayer has it:

> There is no part of a phrase or a sound foot that could not receive a content-dictated stress, regardless of whether it is a matter of a climax reached by gradual crescendo or a suddenly irrupting *sforzato* or some other accent mark.[226]

---

[218] Theodor Wiehmayer, *Musikalische Rhythmik und Metrik* (Magdeburg: Heinrichshofen, 1917).

[219] Theodor Wiehmayer, *Die Auswirkung der Theorie Hugo Riemanns. Zwei Aufsätze über wichtige Grund- und Streitfragen der musikalischen Metrik*; (1) »Die Auswirkung der Theorie Hugo Riemanns,« pp. 3-18; (2) »Hugo Riemanns metrisches Betonungsschema,« pp. 19-32 (Magdeburg, 1925); T. Wiehmayer, »Über die Grundfragen der musikalischen Rhythmik und Metrik,« in: *Bericht über den I. Musikwissenschaftlichen Kongreß der Deutschen Musikgesellschaft in Leipzig 1925* (Leipzig, 1926), 445-459.

[220] At the conclusion of the essay »Die Auswirkung [Effect] der Theorie Hugo Riemanns,« we read: »And more than ever it is imperative today to preserve this priceless possession from irreverent interference, to smooth the way, by any means possible, toward a complete understanding of the master works, and ruthlessly to combat every obstructing error.« (p. 32)

[221] Wiehmayer (1917), viii.

[222] Seidel, *Rhythmustheorien* (see note 1, above 189), 215.

[223] Wiehmayer (1917), 28.

[224] Wiehmayer (1926) (see note 219), 447f.

[225] Ibid., 448.

[226] Wiehmayer (1917), 101.

The numerous musical examples Wiehmayer attaches to this statement all contain forks of the one or the other sort, though no criteria are given as to why a crescendo or diminuendo should be executed just the way it is written. At the moment when a rhythmic microanalysis should commence, we are referred to the musician's »stylistic instinct.«[227]

In the chapter »Upbeat and Accent Determination,« Wiehmayer cites a piano piece by Robert Schumann (»Erster Verlust«), in his analysis he undertakes two appraisals (without saying so): principal voice and harmony (Ex. 3-046). Of the piece constructed in *lied* form (8+8 ||:4+4+8:||) Wiehmayer starts by writing out the first eight bars (a), which function as the first phrase of a 16-bar repeat period with half-close in the dominant and then authentic cadence in the tonic of E minor. He takes over the phrasing and articulation slurs from Schumann but passes over the latter's *fp* beneath the first note. Instead, he inserts a dividing mark in the fourth measure to indicate the second half of the first phrase.

Ex. 3-046
Schumann, Piano Piece op. 68 No. 16 (Wiehmayer)

[a]

[b]

[c]

»At first glance,« Wiehmayer writes,[228] the opening 5 ♪ could be regarded as an upbeat to a hyper-measure beginning with m. 2. But if one includes the harmony (b), it becomes clear that such a reading is out of the question, because of the two-bar dominant at the end of the first phrase (mm. 7 and 8).[229] Thereupon Wiehmayer writes the whole first phrase out once more (c), accompanying the putative upbeat notes (F♯5-E5-D♯5-E5) with the harmonic sound of the tonic, whereby the F♯ and D♯ become defined as non-chord tones. The »correctness of this stress determination,« Wiehmayer says, is confirmed by the final measures of the piece.[230]

One can follow this argumentation, but it leads to an unequivocalness that Schumann precisely did not want. The initial motif occurs eight times in the course of the piece. Of these, the first four appearances (mm. 1, 9, 17, 19) are monophonic, i.e., not harmonized, while of the remaining four instances two (mm. 21 and 23) are in the subdominant, one (m. 22) in the dominant, and the last (m. 25) in the tonic. I do not doubt that the unaccompanied motif appearances can be heard as Wiehmayer does, but is such a fixation really in Schumann's interest? The harmonic openness is incidentally accompanied by a metric one: as a single-voiced melodic turn of phrase the motif bears its upbeat character within, even if its ambiguity is lost later on.

Aspects other than melody and harmony are left out of account in Wiehmayer's analysis. Yet Schumann composed this miniature with great attention to detail – down to the few sharply and loudly accentuated chords in mm. 29 and 30, which within this childlike piano world are perhaps meant to represent the shock of a »first loss.«[231]

In order to determine the rhythmic weights as the composition itself (rather than some supposed law) conveys them, I have constructed a partial rhythm score of the two eight-bar phrases concluding in E minor (second phrases). Like Wiehmayer, I analyse the upper voice including harmonic givens (Ex. 3-047).

The result is not spectacular. Except for the stressed upbeat at the start of the two phrases – brought about by the crests notes, the legato slurs drawn in front of the measure[232] and the *fp* before m. 9, or the suspension chord before m. 25 (now *without* dynamic accent) – are hardly any ›assaults‹ on the 2/4 meter. Even so, one notices a higher rhythmic complexity toward the end, which is due above all to the smaller-scale harmonic rhythm. At the ›shock‹ point, moreover, the dynamic and articulatory accents in the rhythmic profile, including the eighth rest in m. 29, draw our attention.

---

[227] Ibid., 107.

[228] Ibid., 110.

[229] Ibid.. Wiehmayer writes that a »pre-measure« in the sense of a large upbeat »goes strongly against the grain of our harmonic instinct.«

[230] Ibid.

[231] The piece is from the first section of the *Album für die Jugend*, which is designed »für Kleinere« (for younger ones).

[232] To clearly distinguish the legato slurs from the ties, I have adopted the notation form of the tie beam developed by Hans Werner Henze for the latter.

Ex. 3-047   Schumann, Piano piece op. 68 No. 16, mm. 9-16 and 25-32

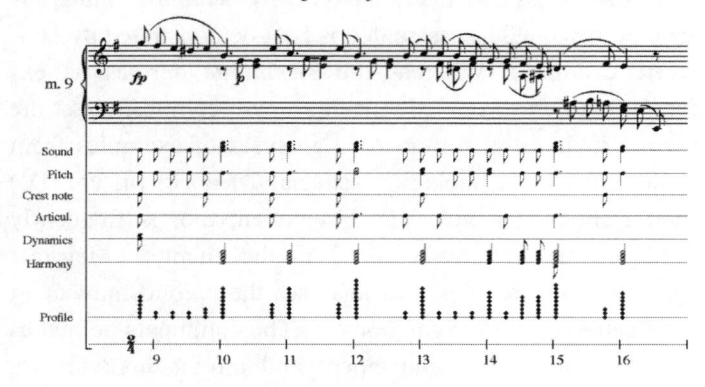

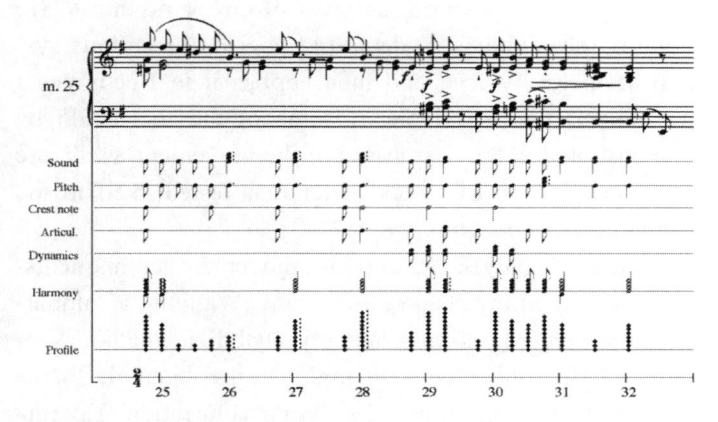

Striking is also the double measure at the start of the last phrase (mm. 25/26), which comes about because, thanks to the moved-up tonic harmony of m. 25, all is harmonically quiet on the *One* of the next bar. The comparable point in m. 10, on the contrary, is precisely the moment where a chord appears for the first time, so that the weight on the *One* there is pretty hefty.

This components analysis, as I said, is incomplete, because the rhythmic conditions of the accompaniment have been left out of account. With its individual component rhythms and the rhythmic profile, it nevertheless provides a fairly differentiated picture, not only of the composition's rhythmic situation but also of the metric one. Yet no chief stress and no ›natural‹ rhythmic accent (how ever to be ascertained), let alone a »declamatory« accent, have been conjured. The sole basis is the ›data‹ the composition itself has at the ready. Hardly a single one of the 2/4 measures is identical in its weight relations with any other, and yet the isometry of the metric order is recognizable (nearly) everywhere. In other words, no auxiliary means, like »sound feet« or the »graduated accent meter,« are needed to recognize that the meter of the piece is the result of free composing – with components rhythms.

Messiaen • Rhythm

In 1944, Olivier Messiaen published his two-volume work *Technique de mon Langage Musical*, which 12 years later also appeared in English.[233] He continued to write this book, if you will, all his life, prompted largely by his work with his composition students, for whom he opened paths to an understanding of music of all eras, as well as of distant regions. The result was his seven-volume opus magnum *Traité de Rythme, de Couleur, et d'Ornithologie*, on which Messiaen continued to work until his death in 1992 – though he was no longer able to undertake the final revision. Alain Louvier, in close cooperation with Messiaen's widow, Yvonne Loriod, prepared the printed, posthumous version.[234]

At the end of his Foreword to the *Traité,* Louvier quotes a sentence ascribed to Messiaen: »In the beginning was the rhythm«.[235] Applied to music – of whatever tradition or culture – that means that each and every musical phenomenon can have a rhythmic significance. What Messiaen meant by that appears from an enumeration he jots down, under the heading »Ordres rythmiques,« in chapter 2 of vol. I, which deals with the concept of »rhythm.« After introductory remarks, in which he explains that he prefers the expression »rhythmic language« (»l
angage rythmique«) to »rhythmic order« (»ordre rythmique«) because the former term is »richer« (»terme plus riche«), he lists the following »rhythmic languages,« all of which can occur in a piece of music (»peuvent coexister dans une même musique«):[236]

1) *the rhythmic language of durations* (long and short durations – quantitative order) –
2) *the rhythmic language of intensities* (loud and soft notes – crescendo and decrescendo – dynamic order) –
3) *the rhythmic language of density* (thickness – number of simultaneous notes – also belonging to the dynamic order) –
4) *the rhythmic language of pitch* (high, low – changes of register) –
5) *the rhythmic language of timbre* (phonetic order) –
6) *the rhythmic language of sound entries* (tied, slurring, all forms of staccato, sforzando, etc., also coming under the phonetic order) –
7) *the rhythmic language of rhythmic motion* (arsis, thesis – accent – kinetic order) –
8) *the rhythmic language of the tempi* (rallentando and accelerando – differences in tempo – also coming under the kinetic order – [...]) –

---

[233] Olivier Messiaen, *Technique de mon Langage Musical*, 2 vols. (Paris, 1944); English: *The Technique of my Musical Language*, transl. John Satterfield (Paris, 1956).

[234] Olivier Messiaen, *Traité de Rythme, de Couleur, et d' Ornithologie* (1949-1992), 7 vols. (Paris: Leduc, 1994).

[235] Ibid. t. I, p. viii (»au Commencement était le Rythme«).

[236] This and the following quoatations, ibid. p. 46f.; emphases are Messiaen's.

9) *the rhythmic language of durational inversion* (all possible permutations and inversions, retrograde movement, middle between extremes, extreme in the middle, and hundreds of millions of others ...) –
10) *the polyrhythmic language* –
11) *the rhythmic language resulting from polyrhythmics* –
12) *the rhythmic language of harmony* (rhythms can be formed of chords [...], nowadays there might be special and very complex rhythms of chords that are independent of pitch rhythms and very short rhythms: thus there could be harmonic rhythms, melodic rhythms and rhythmical rhythms, if you will permit the pleonasm ...) –
13) *the rhythmic language of the tonal systems* (system [lieu] = modality, tonality, polymodality, polytonality, atonality, twelve-tone series, all other kinds of series, etc. Contrast or mixture of these diverse systems, to each of which a special duration is assigned) –
14) *the rhythmic language of silence* –

Messiaen here lists pretty much all of the compositional means at his disposal; in my terminology, he describes the »components« with which he composes. What is less clear is the exact meaning of the expression »rhythmic language.« If, to speak with Justin London,[237] one starts from musical »whats and whens,« one can say that some of the phenomena cited by Messiaen refer to sound objects and their properties (intensity, density, pitch, timbre, articulation, motion, harmony, tonal system), while others belong to the category of time designation (tonal duration, tempo, retrogression, polyrhythm). In its mixture of »what« and »when« phenomena, derived from the intuitional modes of space and time, the list really represents »musical language« generally rather than »rhythmic language« in particular. To differentiate the specifically rhythmical from the generally musical requires a specific analytical perspective or problem formulation. If one does not assume this perspective, one winds up dealing with music *in toto* rather than with the partial aspect of rhythm.

Rhythmic perspective and problem-setting must focus on the concept of duration. Light and dark, sharp or soft, bowed, blown or sung tones, that is, the »whats,« are, after all, not intrinsically rhythmical. It is only when time intervals are formed between several light or dark, sharp or soft, etc. notes that rhythms, that is the »whens,« come into play. The expression formulated under no. 1, »rhythmic language of durations,« is thus an involuntary tautology. Messiaen apologizes under no. 12 for having constructed a pleonasm with the expression »rhythmical rhythms.« But the turn of phrase under no. 1 is just as pleonastic. Since there are no durations without sound objects to mark the time, Messiaen's formulation »the rhythmic language of durations« can only mean that there are »long and short durations« between the sound entries. He should have written ›the rhythmic lanugage of sound entries,‹ rather than ›the durational language of durations.‹[238]

How Messiaen deals analytically with the numerous components he has assembled is best demonstrated by concrete examples. Whereas the *Technique* derives its examples solely from Messiaen's own compositions, the *Traité* includes also numerous analyses of examples from other composers, including especially Mozart (in vol. IV) and Debussy (in vol. VI). Beethoven, too, is frequently adduced, as already in vol. I in the chapter »Métrique grecque,« where Messiaen analyses the second movement of Beethoven's 7th Symphony.[239] The comments he makes on the form of the movement and on its three themes pursue the basic idea of »survival of Greek rhythms«. He initially recapitulates, in detail (42 pages), the antique system of meter by feet, and then applies it to Beethoven's movement: the »survival« of some of the feet could be demonstrated in the first theme of the movement, while the free modification of Greek meter manifested itself in the cantabile second theme.

Since I analyzed the same movement components-rhythmically in my chapter »Rhythmic Weight«, a comparison between Messiaen's and my analytical method suggests itself. I will here limit myelf to the cantabile theme and begin by presenting Messiaen's conception. He furnishes the note text of the second theme's main voice with some annotations (Ex. 3-048).[240]

Ex. 3-048   Beethoven, 7th Symphony, Allegretto, 2nd theme, Messiaen's analysis

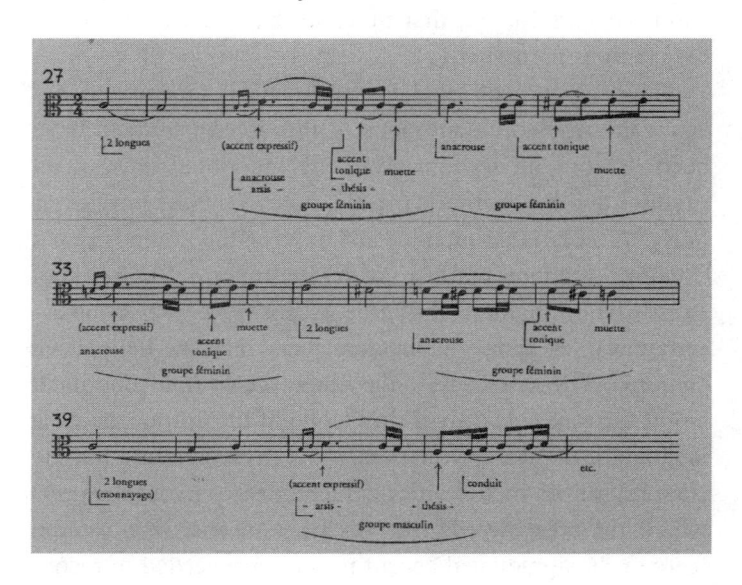

To understand Messiaen's annotations, one must have recourse to his conception of accent. Vol. IV includes a chapter entitled »Mozart and Accentuation,« at whose end is a »Glossaire« that includes the following definiton of the term »Accent«:[241]

---

[237] See the London chapter, below.

[238] It is possible that Messiaen here means the succession of rhythmic-melodic figures he calls »rythmes.«

[239] *Traité* t. I, p. 117-119.

[240] Facsimile after Messiaen, *Traité* t. I, p. 117f.

[241] *Traité* t. IV, p. 200.

Accent: Strong and long sound, preceded by a note or group of notes that prepares it (upbeat) and followed by a weaker note (mute) or group of notes (ending). The tonal accent [›l'accent tonique‹] is of great rhythmic and melodic importance. The expressive accent [›l'accent expressif‹] (which belongs to the dramatic order) can surpass the tonal accent, but only the tonal accent gives the melody its rhythmic equilibrium.

The same glossary defines masculine and feminine rhythms as follows:

The masculine rhythm goes straight ahead and ends on the dot, without accent. The feminine rhythm ends on an accent followed by a weak tone [›muette‹] (or an ending [›désinence‹]).

To return to the Beethoven example: Messiaen identifies altogether four accents (»accents toniques«): mm. 30, 32, 34 and 38, always on the *One*, all with feminine ending and having long upbeats (»anacrusis«), and thus forming two-bar rhythmic units (»groupe féminin«). The final two bars of the excerpt (mm. 41-42₁) are defined as masculine: they end without accent (see above) on the *One* and have no upbeat. In Messiaen's view, there are, in addition, three expressive accents (»accents expressifs«): mm. 29, 33 and 41, also each time on the *One*. Twice Messiaen ascribes, besides, the metric quality »arsis – thésis«, once to a feminine rhythm (mm. 29-30) and once to a masculine one (mm.41-42). The half-notes with which the theme or its partial phrases begin (mm. 27, 35 and 39), are left out of account as exceptions; Messiaen simply denotes them by their values (»2 longues«), once with the addition »monnayage«, which is perhaps to take note of the rhythmic »stamp« (»coinage«) of the second half by means of two quarters in mm. 39/40 (♩ ♩♩).

The entries below the note text are not commented on by Messiaen, their interpretation thus not justified. It is questionable, for instance, why m. 29 is to be regarded as an upbeat (to m. 30), whereas the (identical) m. 41 is not. It is likewise inexplicable why Messiaen calls all of the feminine endings »muette,« even though they are, after all, all groups of notes, that is, »désinences« that follow the »accent tonique.« Finally, one would have liked an explanation as to why the opening long notes supposedly have no relation to the rhyhmic-melodic process. The melodic nexus with what follows is surely evident, if one considers that the core of the melodic motion follows very common patterns (beginning: C–B–D–C; middle: E–D♯–D♮–C♯).

In actuality, these annotations of Messiaen's are not so much an analysis as a protocol of a very musical person who tries to phrase Beethoven's theme sensibly and – quite subjectively – listens into himself without considering any possible alternatives. From the vantage point of the components theory, moreover, one has to note that Messiaen rarely if ever points out really rhythmic, that is, time-defining, matters.

In the very brief commentary on his musical example, several »rhythmic figures« are named, including the two »longues« (♩ ♩), the diminution of the (thematic) dactyl (♪♫), the dotted quarter note (♩.) and the inversion of the first theme's dactylic rhythm (♩♪♪ → ♪♪♩).[242] Of component rhythms Messiaen does not address even the most common, for example the isometric phrase structure at the rate of four 2/4 measures, which is in a characteristic tension with the harmonic rhythm. The tone repetitions, beginning in this case mostly before the strong beats, would likewise be interesting and important.[243]

With regard to rhythm, Messiaen's analyses of Debussy don't differ much from his Beethoven and Mozart commentaries. Here is his reading of the beginning of the *Prélude à l' après-midi d'un faune* (Ex. 3-049).[244] ›The‹ rhythm is (as elsewhere) simply abstracted from the note values. Add to that his conception of phrase: as a performer, he seems to ›feel‹ that the first two bars function like long upbeats, the second upbeat including also a large part of the third measure. The first accent (»accent tonique«), in Messiaen's view, does not occur until the B in m. 3, which is then followed by three notes of »désinence« in the sense of a feminine ending.

Ex. 3-049 Debussy, *Prélude à l'après-midi d'un faune*, Messiaen's analysis

Since here, too, a more thoroughgoing rhythm analysis is missing, I will juxtapose Messiaen's description of the Debussy theme with a components analysis of my own, applied both to the monophonic (mm. 1ff.) and to the harmonized form (mm. 11ff.) of the theme (Ex. 3-050).

Messiaen's rhythm of tonal entries is found under the component »Sound« – here furnished, however, with the weight of long and short notes (scale ♪ = 1). Beneath that, the crest and keel notes are entered (component »Diastematy«). Their initial rhythm of ♩. ♩. ♩. ♩., which goes well together with the 9/8 meter, moves into syncopated position at the end of the phrase (G♯5, G♯4 and C♯5). The third component (»Phrase«) yields a far-flung rhythm of 1+1+2 measures, which in this case is marked explicitly with slurs by the composer. These components (of the monophonic version) are accumulated in the rhythmic »profile,« so that the rhythmic weight per point in time can be depicted.

---

[242] Ibid. p. 118.

[243] Cf. my components analysis of the »cantabile theme« above, p. 67ff.

[244] *Traité* t. VI, p. 30.

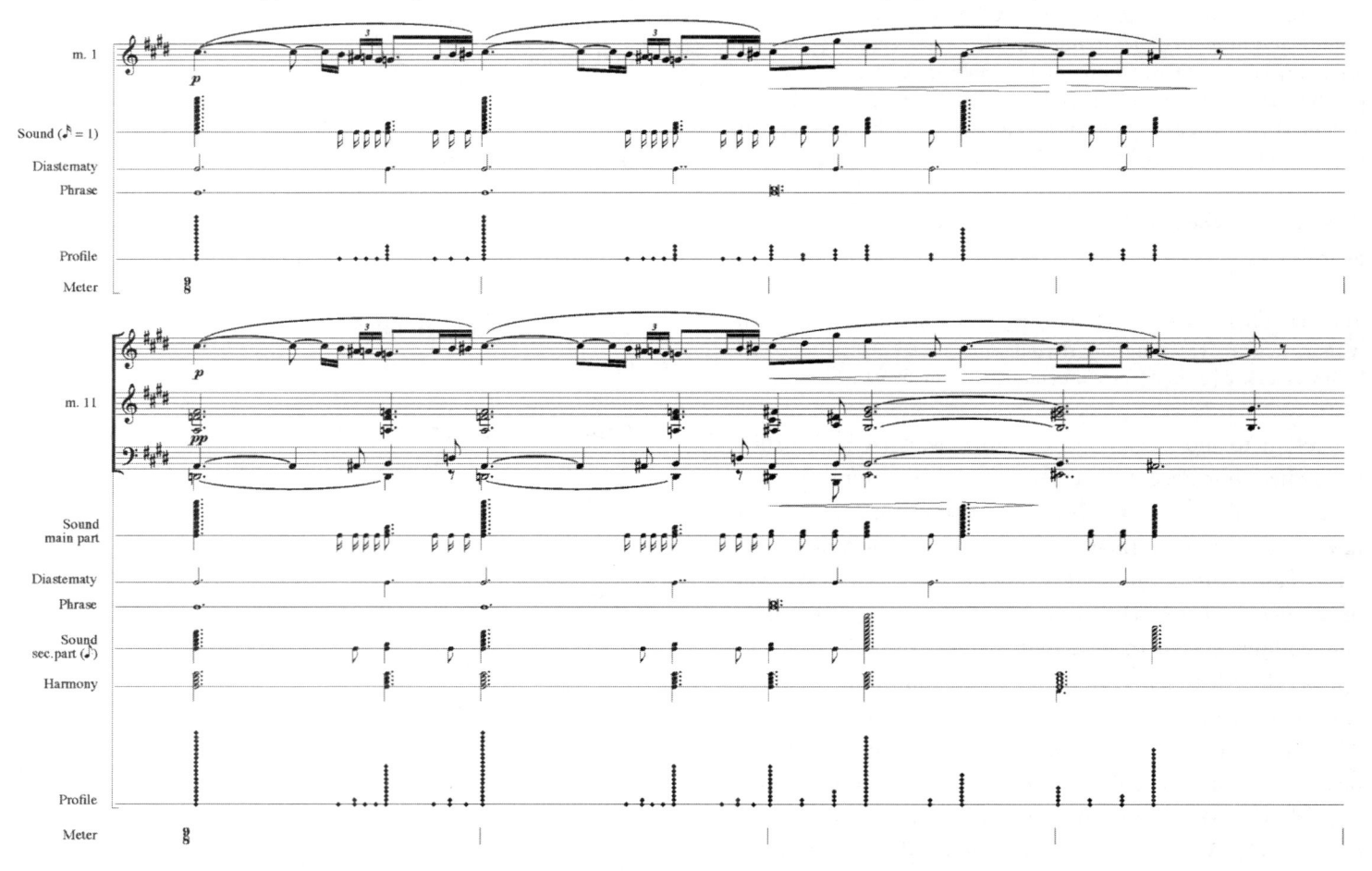

Ex. 3-050   Debussy, *Prélude à l'Après-Midi d'un Faune*, mm. 1-4 and mm. 11-14 (Rhythm Scores)

One sees what one also hears: in the first two measures, the melody forms a trochee (𝅗𝅥. 𝅘𝅥.), while thereafter the weights are distributed more freely, though still in such a way that relatively high values fall on the strong beats of the 9/8 meter (whose metric »accents« were *not* considered here).

In the polyphonic form of the theme (from m. 11), the components rhythms and weights of the main voice recur unchanged. Added to that is a secondary voice in the cellos, whose durations and weights I weigh less heavily than those of the main voice, so as to acknowledge the ranking of primary and secondary voice (scale ♩ = 1). The remaining voices of the accompaniment are neglected as »voices« but show up indirectly in the harmonic rhythm (component »Harmony«). The changes of harmonic function (of which one can still speak in the case of this E-major piece) have been entered uniformly with the weight value of 4. The leading criterion here is the fact that certain four-note chords (e.g. the dominant seventh chord) have for a long time (at the latest since the 18th century) counted among the standard chords in triadic harmonics. Though the resultant harmonic rhythm is very simple, it exhibits one peculiarity: the second and third bar are quasi hemiolically combined (3 𝅗𝅥. : 2 𝅝.), with the second 𝅗𝅥. being split into two 𝅘𝅥.. As a result, and because of the accompaniment as a whole, the rhythmic profile of the many-part version of the theme differs markedly from that of the single-voiced version. If in the two first measures, the accompaniment merely produces greater rhythmic weights, the third and fourth measure bring about a shift in the disposition of heavy accents. Owing to the turn to the tonic E major in m. 13_4, together with the long-held note B in the secondary voice (vc.), most of the weight falls on the note E5 in the flute, which was barely weighted in the single-voiced variant. As a result, the ensuing rhythmic weights are overshadowed until the final note of $A_\sharp 4$.

I think the reader will agree that this rhythm analysis, incorporating the components rhythms, produces more differentiated and more objective results than Messiaen's merely intuitive observations. Though as a composer Messiaen was a great rhythmic innovator, he remained on the whole rather conventional as an analyst of rhythmic structures.

Messiaen's rhythmic innovations were important for part of the post-war avant-garde – one need only think of the series of durational values, the rhythms with added values, or the incorporation of ancient Indian rhythms in his compositions. Among his predilections were also symmetric structures, both within and outside of music. He called symmetric rhythms »non-retrogradable rhythms,« since a retrograde reading, as in a palindrome, produces the same result as a forward one.

Ex. 3-051 Messiaen, *Quatuor Pour la Fin du Temps*, 6th mov., mm. 26-39 (schematic)

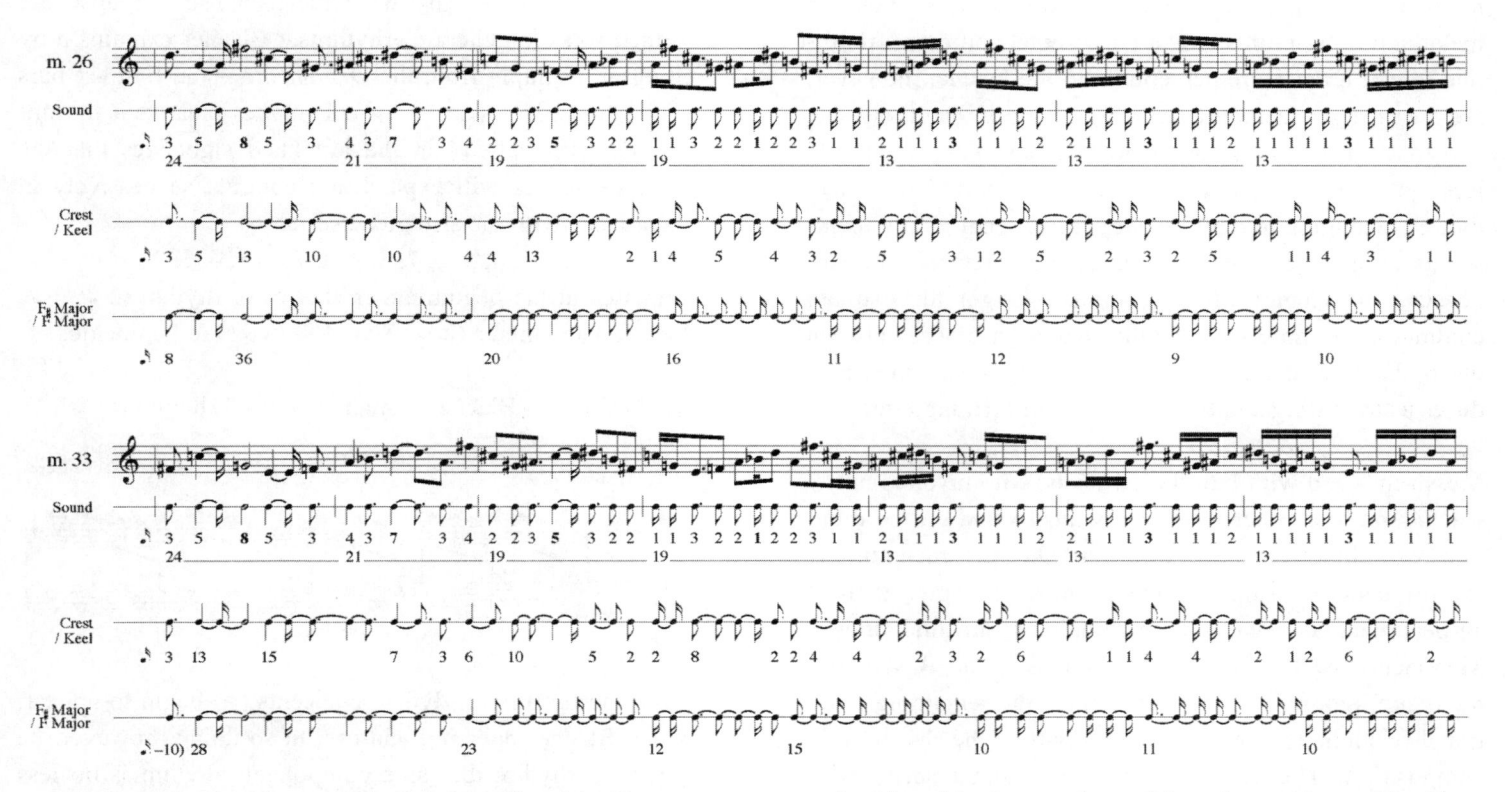

One of Messiaen's examples is taken from his *Quatuor pour la fin du temps* (1941-42).[245] In the extensive unison of all four instruments (violin, clarinet, violoncello, piano) entitled »Danse de la fureur, pour les sept trompettes,« a *subito p*, accompanied by the performance mark »lointain«, occurs in m. 26. This section of twice seven bars of unequal length is based on groups of symmetric rhythms (Ex. 3-051), which, separated by bar lines, result from note values, i.e., derive exclusively from the component »Sound.«

Here is a list of the rhythms executed in two series:[246]

mm. 26 / 33	♪	3 5 8 5 3	(24)
mm. 27 / 34	♪	4 3 7 3 4	(21)
mm. 28 / 35	♪	2 2 3 5 3 2 2	(19)
mm. 29 / 36	♪	1 1 3 2 2 1 2 2 3 1 1	(19)
mm. 30 / 37	♪	2 1 1 1 3 1 1 1 2	(13)
mm. 31 / 38	♪	2 1 1 1 3 1 1 1 2	(13)
mm. 32 / 39	♪	1 1 1 1 1 3 1 1 1 1 1	(13)

The rhythms[247] are superimposed on an ostinato note repetition (Ex. 3-052), whose number of notes (8+8) does not coincide with the number of impulses. About this divergence between melodic ostinato (quasi Color) and symmetric rhythm (quasi Talea), Messiaen remarks: »The melodic motion [...] repeats and thereby undergoes considerable rhythmic variants.«[248] He probably meant that the individual notes of the melody appear endowed with different note values. For example, the first note of the series, a D5 with the value 3 ♪, acquires the value of 2 ♪ in the second run-through, later also 3, 1 or 7 ♪.

Ex. 3-052
Recurrent set of notes (twice 8 notes)

One should not erroneously assume that this covers the rhyhmic structure of the passage completely. There are at least two additional rhythms that play a role in the unisono piece, even though Messiaen did not describe, and perhaps not even think, of them. These component rhythms result from the position of the crest and keel notes (»Diastematy«), as well as from the alternation of the two keys used, ›F♯ major‹ and ›F major‹ – more accurately, 6♯ diatonic and 1♭ diatonic (»Harmony«).[249] The contour of the eight-plus-

---

[245] *Technique* t. I, p. 12f., t. II, examples 33 and 34.

[246] On the recurrence of these rhythms in other works of Messiaen, see Aloyse Michaely, *Die Musik Olivier Messiaens. Untersuchungen zum Gesamtschaffen* (Hamburg: Wagner, 1987), 51f. Michaely's statement, with reference to Messiaen's *Visions de l'Amen* for two pianos, that the quoted and canonically worked rhythm appears in the 6th movement (mm. 24ff.) in only two parts is incorrect: of the four voices, three are set in canon.

[247] In aesthetically justifying retrogression in music, Messiaen referred to Gaston Bachelard's *La dialectique de la durée* (Paris, 1950; new ed. Paris, 1989), which describes music as a constant recalling of what has already been sounded, wherefore musical retrogression was no problem, since in listening to it it would be remembered as what it is: a symbol of temporal inversion. See the Bachelard quote in Messiaen, *Traité* t. I, p. 45.

[248] Messiaen, *Technique* t. I, p. 12f.

[249] An additional component that might have to be considered is the placment of phrasing slurs, which is executed individually despite the unison of the four parts.

eight tonal line, strictly fitted into the frame of a major ninth, is constant and, above all, expressive, so that the melodic turning-points emit a clear signal and thus a rhythmic effect. Even more perceptible to the listener, however, are the changes in timbre, which go hand in hand with the half-tone shift from F♯ major to F major. This is initially less noticeable, because the notes D5 and A4, which, though belonging to the F major sphere, seem to ally themselves to the F♯5 that follows, obscure, rather than emphasize, the change of key. But the longer the ostinato continues, the more strongly the change in timbre between the 6♯ diatonic and the 1♭ diatonic emerges and thus produces a structuring and thereby a rhythm-forming effect.

Messiaen – and with him the serialists, who invoked him – was bound to a conception of rhythm fixated on the durations of individual notes. For all that, he was uncommonly inventive and developed a unique musical language. But I suspect that, as regards their serial, or punctual, music, Messiaen as well as Boulez, Stockhausen and B. A. Zimmermann, ignored, i.e., left to chance, the remaining durational relations that are objectively part of the rhythm of a composition. The construction of durational series with note values from 1 ♪ to 12 ♪ is in any case tied to the individual note. I know of no durational series with reference to crest and keel notes, dynamic accents, harmonic changes, etc. In reality the rhythm of serial compositions is thus inevitably even more complex than their compositional technique already signals.

Blacher • Variable Meters

In 1950, the composer Boris Blacher published a brief article entitled »Über variable Metrik.«[250] A year before, his cycle *Ornamente. Sieben Studien über variable Metren für Klavier* had appeared,[251] with an introductory note that partly coincides with the article but also explains the principle of the metric construction of each of the seven piano pieces.

By meter Blacher means the pervasive pulse, »quasi the heartbeat of music.«[252] Rhythms or measures were the result of group formation. »If according to some principle one combines metric units into groups, the result is rhythm. […] Music has from ancient times used meter as a regulative support for rhythm. Meter and rhythm can be identical, but need not be.«[253]

The question is, by what means these »groups« are formed so as to generate »rhythms.« Blacher explains it by citing an example from the *Ornamente* – the first six bars of the first piece (Ex. 3-053). It makes clear that the unvarying fifth F♯3-C♯4 in the left hand signalizes that the tonal sequences will expand and contract successively in accordance with the arithmetic series

2, 3, 4, 5, 6, 7, 8, **9**, 8, 7, 6, 5, 4, 3, 2

intimated at the beginning. In this case, rhythm (2 ♪, 3 ♪, 4 ♪, etc.) and meter (2/8-, 3/8-, 4/8-meter etc.) coincide.

Ex. 3-053   Blacher, Ornamente No. 1, beginning

From the fourth bar, dynamic accents (>) begin to appear, which Blacher does not address. In so doing, however, he ignores a rhythm that as a components rhythm is no less concrete and effective than the empty fifths at the beginning of each phrase. Evidently, the rhythm of the dynamic accents is supposed to inject some interference with the serializing process otherwise running like an automatic apparatus. The durations between the dynamic accents (down to m. 12, not included in the Ex.) are 5+7+7+4+3+3+3+4+4+3+4+3+3+2+3 ♪.

Of some interest is Blacher's remark that it was possible for »musical and metric phrases to overlap«[254] and that a novel »reciprocal action of form – rhythm«[255] was observable. What he means by this can be ascertained from the *Ornament* No. 2. If one surveys the entire main voice of the 26-bar piece and juxtaposes the schema of the metrical series (Ex. 3-054), it becomes clear that the sections of the main voice do not coincide with the rise and fall of the arithmetic sequence.

Ex. 3-054   Blacher, *Ornaments* for Piano, No. 2, Main part

---

[250] Boris Blacher, »Über variable Metrik,« *ÖMZ*, 6 (1951), 219-222.

[251] (Berlin / Wiesbaden: Bote & Bock, 1949).

[252] *ÖMZ*, 219.

[253] Ibid., 219f.

[254] Ibid., 222. Cf. also the preliminary note to the score.

[255] Ibid., 221.

Ex. 3-055 Blacher, *Ornaments* for Piano, No. 2, mm. 1-6

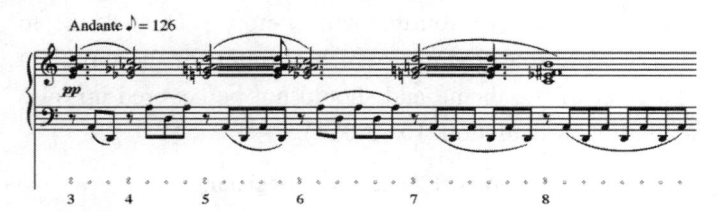

The three sections of the largely diatonic, descending melody commence with a 3/8, a 7/8 and a 8/8 measure, and the renewed beginning of the arithmetic expansion and contraction process falls into the midst of the second line of the melody. Formal and metrical structure, that is, are organized independently of each other.

The opening measures of this *Ornament* include additional components that also do not coincide with the structure of the »variable meters« (Ex. 3-055). I refer to the eighths pendulums in the left hand, which generate binary rhythms by their diastematy. While the fifths figures lengthen in accordance with the expanding measures, the rhythmic form of the eighths pendulums does constitute a steady element that makes for a binary subdivision of the 3/8, 4/8, 5/8, 6/8, 7/8 and 8/8 meters.

In sum, Blacher's »variable meters« rests primarily on the procedure of changing time signatures, as the author himself indicates.[256] The rhythmic means leading to the variable series are not attended to. Thus Blacher also does not envision those other component rhythms with which he composes without grasping them conceptually.

Keller • Phrasing and Articulation

In 1955, the organist and musicologist Hermann Keller published his book *Phrasierung und Artikulation. Ein Beitrag zu einer Sprachlehre der Musik* (Phrasing and Articulation. Toward a Linguistics of Music).[257] It deals with the

Ex. 3-057 Mozart, *Gigue in G* for Piano, K. 574, mm. 17-28 (Transcript)

components »Phrase« and »Articulation« as applied to the music of the 18th and 19th century, with emphasis on Bach, Mozart and Beethoven. Conceived mainly as a handbook for performers (instrumentalists, conductors), the slender volume is yet well informed historically. Especially the numerous musical examples are a treasure trove for special forms of phrasing and articulation. The author does not, however, investigate the significance of the two components dealt with for the rhythm of a composition. Keller distinguishes them as follows:[258]

Phrasing is tantamount to creating a meaningful structure. Its function is to order and differentiate ideal contents (phrases); its task is the same as that of punctuation in language. […] The task of articulation, on the other hand, is the linking or division of notes; it leaves the ideational content of a melodic line untouched, but determines its expression.

If Keller ever talks about the connection between articulation, phrasing and rhyhm, it is only under the aspect of suitedness to character. Thus an »even rhythm« would fit with a legato, an »abrupt, jerky« one with the staccato.[259] Behind that lurks a rhythmic concept defined by a single component, »Sound,« and its duration.

Once, in connection with an example from Mozart, Keller makes a remark that suggests that he has sensed the rhythmic potential of the components »Articulation« and »Phrase,« though without fully recognizing these components as actually generative of rhythm. The work in question is Mozart's late piano piece »Gigue in G« (K. 574), of which Keller quotes an excerpt (Ex. 3-056). Here he remarks that »the Articulation temporarily threatens to abolish the 6/8 meter.«[260]

Ex. 3-056
Mozart, *Gigue in G* for Piano, K. 574, mm. 20-24 (after Keller)

If one pursues this correct observation and ascertains the actual component rhythm »Articulation«, the largely quaternary structure of the voices comes clearly to the fore (Ex. 3-057). A 4 ♪ figure (e.g., m. 20: $F\#4$-$E\#4$-$A4$-$G\#4$), which characterizes the piece as a whole, is always articulated alike: the first two ♪ are linked by a legato slur, the other two are furnished with staccato wedges. If this figure appears several times in succession, as it does from m. 20, a rhythm of ♩ emerges, measured by the sequence of legato slurs.

---

[256] Ibid., S. 220.

[257] Hermann Keller, *Phrasierung und Artikulation. Ein Beitrag zu einer Sprachlehre der Musik* (Kassel, Basel: Bärenreiter, 1955).

[258] Ibid., 12.

[259] Ibid., 36.

[260] Ibid., 76.

As can be seen from the metric schema (bottom line in Ex. 3-057), the 4-♪ figure comes in mostly before the secondary accent of the 6/8 meter, as at the start of the second part of the *Gigue*, with which our example begins. Alternately in the left and right hand, the legato mark of the four-note motif appears initially every six ♪, so that a kind of phrase accent is created on the third ♪ of every measure. In m. 20, too, the motif, or soggetto,[261] enters on the third ♪, but then is reiterated uninterruptedly and, in both hands, parallel in both articulation and intervals (thirds). Whereas therefore the 6/8 meter is initially jolted only slightly by a secondary accent, from m. 20 on it appears altogether canceled by five articulatory halves (♩).

Ex. 3-058 Mozart, *Gigue*, mm. 33-38

It is interesting to compare this with the end of the *Gigue* (Ex. 3-058), as there the rhythm derived from the legato slurs becomes consistently ternary, in such a way that the legato accents always come one ♪ before the main accents of the 6/8 meter. The beats are thereby syncopated, because two isometric rhythms – the articulatory and the metric one – are both coordinated with a fixed temporal interval.

In this example by Mozart, the articulation is meticulously marked.[262] That was not always the case in older music. Keller therefore includes a separate chapter on »The Articulation of Bach's Unmarked Piano and Organ Music« in his book. The criterion by which Keller makes his recommendations for these cases is said to be style. »To interpret unmarked works in the proper style«[263] is said to be the challenge to the performer.

A differentiated rhythm analysis might be helpful in determining appropriate and reasoned articulations. Thus I would object to Keller's proposal to either tie the theme of the A major fugue of *Well-Tempered Clavier* I throughout or to articulate it like a Siciliana »by accenting the strong beats«[264] by saying that the rhythm in this case precisely does not support the triply ternary meter (9/8). Decisive here are chains of fourths with ♪-notes. They result in binary crest-note rhythms, which account for the turbulent character of the theme and should not be covered up by a smoothing articulation (Ex. 3-059).

Ex. 3-059 Bach, WTC I, Fugue in A, Beginning

Keller's notion of a swaying Siciliana articulation is probably based on the 9/8 time signature, whose contemporary descriptions did not envision a formation like the present one. But it would be adverse to the idea of the work to impose putative stylistic norms belatedly upon so individual and exceptional a theme. As I have shown in my comparative analysis of two 9/8-pieces from the *WTC*,[265] totally contrary character pieces can be composed in the same meter. Especially in the case of J. S. Bach, one should always be prepared to encounter compositions that depart from the style of the time and have their greatness and truth within themselves.

Jan LaRue • Harmonic Rhythm

In 1957, the American musicologist Jan LaRue published a path-breaking essay on »Harmonic Rhythm in the Beethoven Symphonies«.[266] In it he called attention to the fact that changes in harmonic function occurred more or less quickly, and he demonstrated by numerous examples that Beethoven used these »harmonic rhythms« among other things to add significantly to the shaping of phrases and even entire movements.

LaRue calls the harmonic rhythm explicitly one of numerous »components,« but he is skeptical about any attempt to include several components simultaneously in any rhythmic analysis. »Doubtless all of these variables could be handled by some monster cybernetical calculator. But each of the basic standards for the calculations would be a subjective judgment, too shaky a foundation for such weighty apparatus.«[267] Well, this was written half a century ago, before there were any computers. All the same, LaRue's speculation that a machine could carry out the components analysis would not have been fulfilled.

---

[261] The concept soggetto, at home in Baroque music, is appropriate here, because the entire piece is composed in the style of a Bachian fugato invention. It points clearly to Mozart's reception of the music of J. S. Bach and G. F. Handel.

[262] Keller incidentally replaced the staccato wedges by dots and added additonal dots and a legato slur at the end of his excerpt (Ex. 3-056).

[263] Ibid., 68.

[264] Ibid., 70.

[265] Cf. the chapter »Two 6/4 and Two 9/8 Pieces from the *Well-Tempered* Clavier« in Part II of this study.

[266] Jan LaRue, »Harmonic Rhythm in the Beethoven Symphonies,« *The Music Review*, 18 (1957), 8-20.

[267] Ibid., 10.

Ex. 3-060   Beethoven, 7th Symphony, 1st mov., Introduction (Harmonic Rhythm)

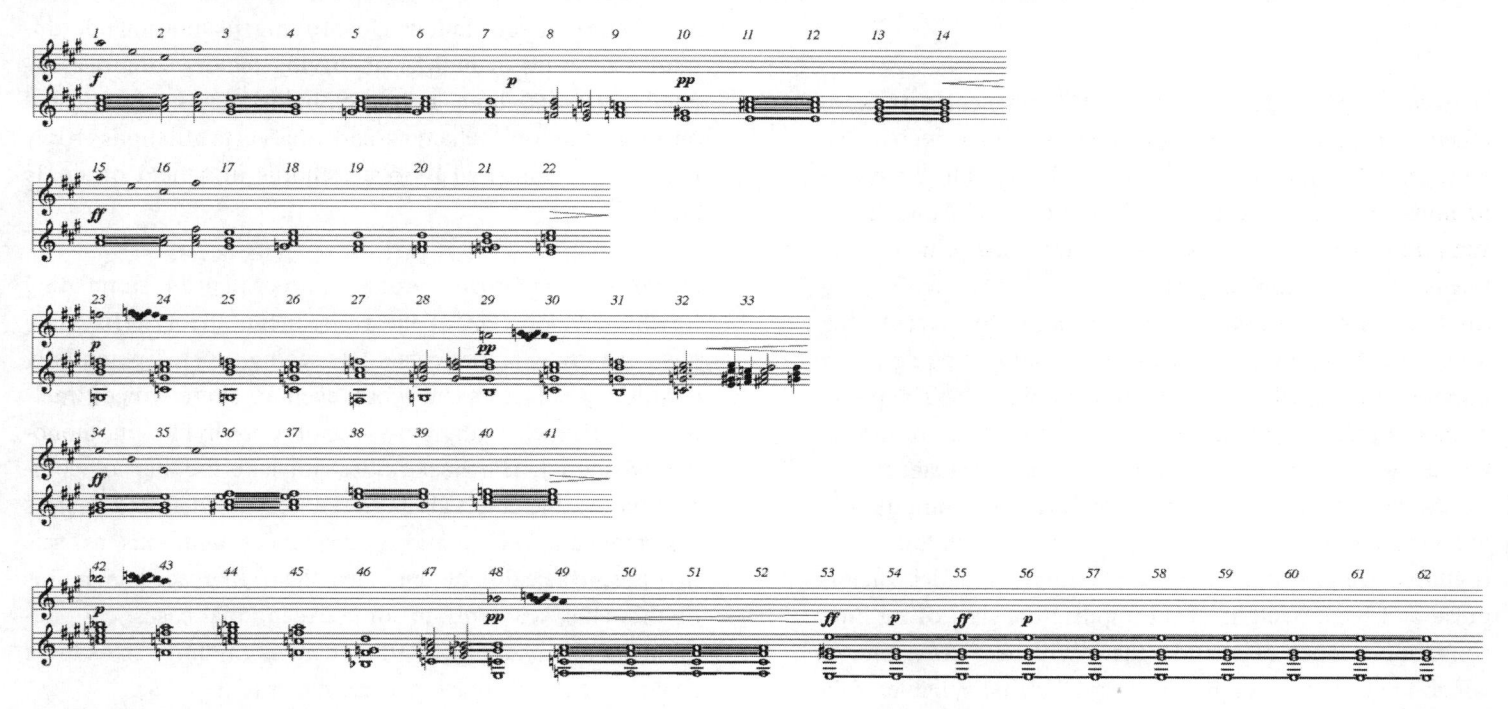

It takes indeed numerous »judgments« to assess the individual components in line with the style of the time, and to include them commensurately in the analysis, but why must these be »subjective«? Our discipline, so far as it deals with the analysis and interpretation of music, constantly involves historically contextualized judgments that can be substantiated and are therefore to a certain degree objective. Yet even though LaRue, for practical reasons, confines himself to the »analysis of harmonic rhythm« because it reduces »the factors which need be considered at any one time,«[268] his findings are convincing and hardly questionable.

In one portion of his essay, LaRue describes the slow Introduction of Beethoven's A major Symphony. Looking at individual sections, he discusses their harmonic rhythms and then subjoins a 60-bar notation of the complete harmonic rhythm on a single staff line without clef.[269]

In Ex. 3-060, I have chosen a somewhat different mode of presentation, in which the durations of the respective functions are represented by an extraction of the harmonies. Unlike LaRue, I see the structure of the Introduction not as tripartite (mm. 1, 15, 34) but as consisting of five parts (mm. 1, 15, 23, 34, 42).

In particular, LaRue points out the following peculiarities in the harmonic rhythm of the Introduction: harmonic acceleration in the reprise of the opening phrase (mm. 15ff.), whose function is to modulate to C major; syncopation by means of changing harmonic functions in mm. 32 and 33, which lends additional dynamics to the crescendo from *pp* to *ff*; and – by contrast – the harmonic stasis at the final crescendo (mm. 49ff.), where the F major chord is held for four bars before being resolved to E major. One might add two harmonic anticipations (mm. 28 and 47) rendering the onset of the turn theme in *pp* – once in G^7, once in C^7 – even more inconspicuous than it already is.

At the start of the essay, LaRue introduces three classes of harmonic change: »ornamental changes«, »root changes« and »sustained harmonies«.[270] The last of these are chords that are animated, e.g., by transitions or changes in position. The »root changes« refer to harmonic progressions with function changes. Of the third group (»ornamental changes«) LaRue says himself that they are »elusive« and one should not ask for additional subcategories. These are fleeting harmonic changes of the most diverse kind (e.g., I-V-I). In his subsequent investigation, LaRue confines himself to the »root changes.«

Unhappily, LaRue's method of including the harmonic change as a separate rhythmic level in analyses has elicited scant attention. Critics may speak of harmonic accents and their relation to time signatures, but not about genuine rhythms produced by the component »Harmonics.« I myself regard the harmonic rhythms as crucial features in the total rhyhmic make-up of a composition.

---

[268] Ibid.

[269] Ibid., 15-17, Ex. 19, 20, 21, 22 and 23.

[270] Ibid., 11.

Hławiczka • Rhythm and Meter

Between 1958 and 1971, the Polish musicologist Karol Hławiczka published three essays in German, which may be regarded as making essential contributions to the theory of musical rhyhm and meter.[271] He proceeds from the assumption that musical rhythm contains two principal elements: the rhythmic and the metric.[272] The rhythmic in rhythm can be grasped as a collaboration of diverse »factors,« which Hławiczka divides into quantitative (e.g., tonal durations) and qualitative (e.g., tone volume).[273] The metric element of rhythm is said to be manifest in a uniform pulse borne into the sound event by the performer or listener.[274]

Additional key terms for Hławiczka are »impulse«[275] and »profilation«.[276] Both terms have to do with the idea of rhythmic weight. Each and every simple sound is an impulse and has a weight. If an impulse consists of multiple consecutive tones or sounds, there will be a core note on which the impulse weight falls (e.g., the first syllable of the dactyl ♩♩♩). In the graduated accent meter, Hławiczka calls the impulses centers of gravity (Schwerpunkte) and declares them to be the result of simultaneously occurring pulse sequences (in the abstract 4/4 meter, for example, the pulse sequences 𝅝, 𝅗𝅥, ♩♩♩♩, ♪♪♪♪♪♪♪♪ all meet on the *One*, thereby making that position heavy).[277]

The term profilation refers to the succession of lighter or heavier impulses or beats. It is interesting that Hławiczka assumes, and also describes, profilations also in the area of elementary rhythms.[278] In metrically bound music, of course, they could be described more precisely, that is through numbers, whereby metric and rhythmic profiles appear in their relation to each other – either converging or diverging (in Hławiczka's terms, they are »equal-beating« or »counter-beating«).[279]

Kind and degree of profilation depend on the means and factors of profilation. Quantifying factors include durations of notes or motifs, qualifying factors comprise dynamic stresses, high notes, embellishments or repeated phrases, harmonic changes and »baryc profilations« (low notes, notes followed by rests, chords in a field of single notes.)[280]

Hławiczka's approach proved extraordinarily stimulating for the development of the components theory. His »factors« are my »components«. His seeing several, potentially conflicting, »factors« at work even in single-voiced melodies coincides with my view of polyrhythm in monophony, though Hławiczka does not take the step of comprehending the intervals between certain qualified factors systematically as durational sequences and thus as true rhythms. Basically he includes them like accents in his rhythm analyses. Only in some exceptional cases, e.g., hemiolic patterns, does he define them as rhythms, so as to be able to cite the proportion to the meter (e.g., 2 : 3).

Hławiczka retains the antithesis of rhythm and meter, therein adhering to traditional ›rhythm-and-meter-theories.‹ Though he regards the metric and the rhythmic as equally inherent in musical rhythm, the »delimitation of rhythm and meter«[281] is nonetheless important to him. A components-based rhythm analysis can show, however, that meters, i.e., measures and beats, can be rhythmically produced in concrete music while being kept variable in the detail.

Hławiczka is especially interested in two phenomena: that of »rhythmic exchange« (*Verwechslung*) and that of »rhythmic displacement« (*Verschiebung*). An exchange obtains when an isometric sequence of durations (e.g., ♩♩♩) is replaed by another isometric sequence whose values do not divide into the original one (e.g., 𝅗𝅥 𝅗𝅥).[282] The result is proportions like 2 : 3, 3 : 4, 4 : 5 etc., for each of which Hławiczka cites conclusive examples.[283] He speaks of a displacement, on the other hand, when two durational sequences have metric values of the same family (e.g., ♩♩♩ and ♩♩♩), but these are shifted against each other (e.g., | ♩♩♩♩♩♩𝄾 | against| 𝄾♩♩♩♩♩|𝄾).[284] It is his declared intent to define these two rhythmic characters that are so wide-spread in musical history and thereby to counter the fuzzy terms »conflict rhythm«, »syncopation« and »hemiola« with more precise characterizations.

---

[271] Karl Hlawiczka [sic], »Die rhythmische Verwechslung,« *Die Musikforschung*, 11 (1958), 33-49; Karol Hławiczka, »Zur Chopinschen Walzerrhythmik,« in: *Chopin-Jahrbuch* (Vienna, 1963), 43ff.; Karol Hławiczka, »Musikalischer Rhythmus und Metrum,« *Die Musikforschung*, 24 (1971), 385-406.

[272] Hławiczka (1971), 385.

[273] Ibid., 393.

[274] Ibid., 391. At the beginning of the paragraph introducing the discussion of the metric in Hławiczka's essay »Musikalischer Rhythmus und Metrum,« a regrettable slip of the pen was allowed to remain: instead of »das Elementarrhythmische« it should, of course, read »das Elementarmetrische« (390, 6th line from the bottom).

[275] Hławiczka (1958), 33.

[276] Ibid., 35.

[277] Hławiczka (1971), 391f.

[278] Ibid., 387-390.

[279] Ibid., 394.

[280] Hławiczka (1958), 36-38.

[281] Ibid., 33.

[282] Hławiczka does not formulate this definition explicitly, but it can be inferred from the examples he cites. In particular, he fails to point out that the rhythms (or meters) have to be isometric on both sides of the proportion – perhaps because he understood it as a matter of course.

[283] See the essay of 1958, which is devoted to the »rhythmische Verwechslung.«

[284] »Rhythmic Displacement« is central to the essay of 1971.

Ex. 3-061   Mozart, Symphony in C Major K. 551, 2nd mov., mm. 23-27 (extract)

The collection of examples of rhythmic exchanges and displacements that Hławiczka offers is impressive and almost always plausible. His example of a rhythmic exchange by means of harmonic profilation is from the slow movement of Mozart's Jupiter Symphony (Ex. 3-061). He says about these five measures: »The harmonic profilation is reinforced by stresses, low bass notes and repetition of figures. A displacement occurs besides in the figures of the melody.«[285] But if one looks at the harmonic rhythm by itself (Ex. 3-061, »Suspensions/Harmony«), it is clear that while initially supporting the hemiolas, in mm. 25, 26 and 27 its ›harmonic trochees‹ coincide exactly with the beat of the 3/4-meter. I assume here that the E5 in m. 25_1 is a suspension before the F5, just as the D♭5 in m. 23_3 and the E♭5 in m. 24_2 are suspensions (or hard transitions) before D5 and E5 respectively.

Even so, the hemiolic structure of these measures is beyond doubt.[286] At least three additional component rhythms realize the ratio of 2 : 3 typical of hemiolas, here the rhythmic durations (♩♩♩) against the metric ones (♩. ♩.): the phrasing slurs in the melody-carrying first violins, the *fp*-accents in all parts of the orchestra, and the tonal durations of the horns, which realize the ♩-rhythm pure and simple. Of special interest is the resolution of the hemiola from the third quarter note of m. 25 on. The phrasing slur in violins I now brackets 4 ♩ and thus can still be taken as a continuation of the hemiolic ♩-rhythm, before it reaches the trochaic rhythm (♩♩) in m. 27. The horns simply stop out, the basses play at m. 26 ♩ ♩, what the harmonic rhythm has constituted already from m. 25 on.

Hławiczka derives many highly interesting examples from the pianistic œuvre of Chopin.[287] Since he was a great expert in this area, it is really presumptious to want to add to, let alone correct, his remarks. The Chopin Etude op. 25/2 is interesting because of its interpretive ambiguity, wherefore I want to address it briefly. Here, to begin with, is the example as Hławiczka cites it (Ex. 3-062):[288]

Ex. 3-062

Hławiczka comments on this example only with the following brief note: »Application of values of equal length in the *gegenschlägige* sense.«[289] He looks only at the figures in the left hand, where the triplet ♩ stands in a ratio of 3 : 2 to the duplet ♩ of the meter: the triplet eighths in the right are not mentioned. Yet by their diastematy they likewise form specific rhythms, whose relation to the bass figuration is sometimes »gleichschlägig« and sometimes »gegenschlägig.« At the beginning, there are clues suggesting that the melodic figures of the right hand (r. h.) are adjusted to the 6/4 meter of the left hand (l. h.) (Ex. 3-063).

Ex. 3-063   mm. 1-3

---

[285] Hławiczka (1958), 37.

[286] See also my own analysis of this passage in the chapter on »Hemiolas,« above, p. 120.

[287] Hławiczka (1958), 36, 37, 38, 39, 41, 42, 45, 47; Hławiczka (1963), passim; Hławiczka (1971), 396, 398, 402, 404.

[288] Hławiczka (1958), 36.

[289] Ibd.

Ex. 3-064   mm. 4-6

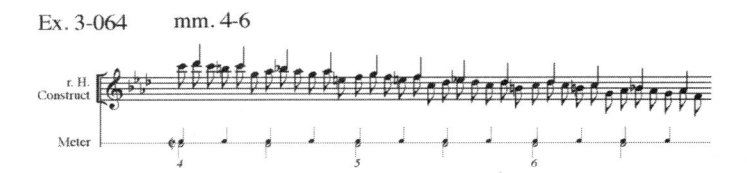

All the six-eighths groups have a similar shape. One note (e. g., the C5 at the beginning) is encircled by its upper and lower auxiliary note, while the remaining two eighths are placed freely. These six-note figures thereby resemble a turn executed on a (triplet) ♩ (see the line »construct« in Ex. 3-063). The rhythm thus heard fits into the 6/4 meter of the left hand, which in turn stands in a triplet relation to the alla breve of the time signature.[290]

Things are different several bars later. Though it is possible here, too, to read in terms of a turn, the superordinate descent of the sequence (from D♭6 down to F4) brings an isometric conjunct motion to the fore that is made directly audible in its crest notes (Ex. 3-064). One can see that the crest notes by themselves have the durations of alla breve ♩, but lag behind the latter by a triplet ♪. Since these off phenomena are constant, the crest notes actually support the time signature.

Ex. 3-065   Chopin, Etude F Minor op. 25 No. 2, Beginning (schematic)

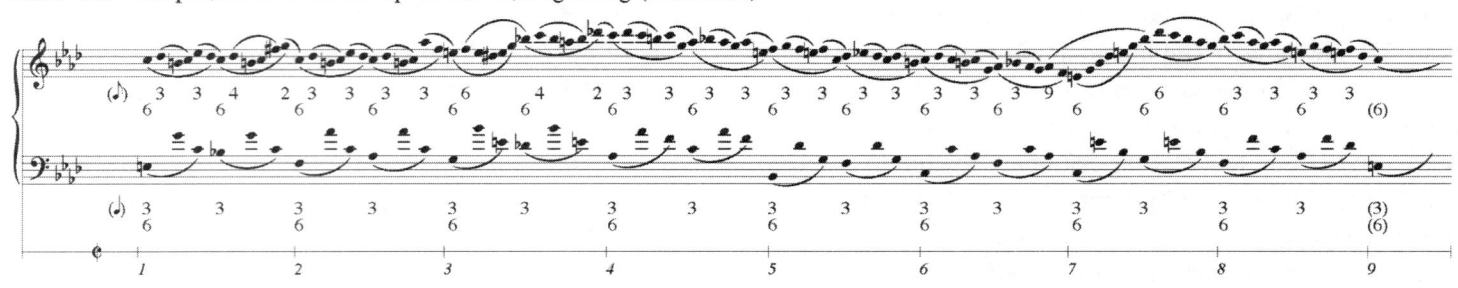

The Etude, which comprises a total of 169 bars, has, rhythmically speaking, an ambiguous character. What predominates is certainly the 6/4 meter marked by the left hand, which incidentally is clearly bipartite (legato slurs) and has a more strongly »profiled« *One* (lower bass notes). The presto eighths (MM ♪ = 672) tend partly toward the triplet quarters of the left hand (at groupings of six), partly toward the duplet quarter notes of the alla breve meter (at groupings of three[291]). Ex. 3-065 attempts to synthesize the results of this rhythmic micro-analysis.

Neumann • »Zeitgestalt«

In 1959, the composition teacher from Salzburg Friedrich Neumann, who last taught in Vienna, published his study *Die Zeitgestalt* (The Time Shape), whose subtitle »A Theory of Musical Rhythm« promises an analysis of rhythmic structures.[292] Declaring, to begin with, for Goethe's morphology, and invoking »gestalt psychology and the newer holistic philosophy,«[293] Newman develops something of an essential vision of musical form, which (naturally) can unfold only in time that is, in »Zeitgestalt.«

The point of departure is the »Ganzheit« (totality) of a musical shape, graspable »finally only *intuitively* and immediately.«[294] By way of »Ausgliederung« (exclusion), one gets »from totality and unity to the diversity of the parts.«[295] In embarking upon this road from the general to the particular, Neumann invents a language that only infrequently touches upon musicological terminology. Always impelled by an inner, participatory experience of music, which he describes, Neumann uses a free vocabulary, which does not shy away from occasional neologisms. If one slogs through this eccentric terminology, learning to decipher also the non-verbal marks (e. g., the notational sign meaning a 24-fold whole), one soon discovers that Neumann's descriptions of »Zeitgestalt« are really amount to a theory of phrasing. Beginning with the »rhythmic pair« whose two halves are connected to the psychic actions of »expectation« and »recollection,« the presentation advances to larger-scale forms. Only rudimentarily does Neumann come to speak of this rhythmic micro-structuration, which, after all, constitutes the real rhythmic life – as in identifying short and long upbeats, or in detecting metric accelerandos or ritardandos.[296]

A concrete example may demonstrate how Neumann interprets »Zeitgestalten«, and what musical phenomena, on the other hand, he misses because he will not venture on any rhythmic microanalysis. In the sub-chapter »Concluding and initial *Widerspruchsakzent*,« (contradictory accent), he adverts to the second movement of Beethoven's Sonata in A♭ Major op. 110, from whose Trio section he copies out several bars (Ex. 3-066 = Ex. 110 in Neumann).[297]

---

[290] The original has an Alla breve signature; Hławiczka writes 4/4.

[291] The crest note rhythm consists mostly of 3+3, but occasionally of 4+2 ♪.

[292] Friedrich Neumann, *Die Zeitgestalt. Eine Lehre vom musikalischen Rhythmus*, two vols. (Vienna, 1959).

[293] Ibid., 9.

[294] Ibid., 29. Emphasis original.

[295] Ibid.

[296] Ibid., 56ff.; 63ff.

[297] Ibid., vol. of examples, 21.

Neumann's arrow and bracket marks (replacing Beethoven's phrasing slurs) mean – in the order of their appearance – »initial contradictory accent« (anticipated F6), »rhythmic equilibrium« (bracket over the first four bars) and »concluding contradictory accent« (bracket and arrow over the F4).

Ex. 3-066

In his rather terse commentary,[298] Neumann merely refers to the anticipating syncopation at the start. He does not explain why the first four bars are in »rhythmic equilibrium« but not the following ones, which continue the sequence. One also misses a discussion of the question whether the eight measures that determine the beginning of the Trio start at the bar indicated by Neumann and not rather one bar earlier, that is, at the final note F of the Scherzo part.[299]

Ex. 3-067
Beethoven, Sonata op. 110, 2nd mov., Trio (2/4)

The $f\!f$ cadences in D♭ major (m. 48), G♭ major (mm. 56 and 64) and E♭ minor (m. 72) certainly favor that.

In the musical examples below I have represented the Trio part in its entirety, at first (Ex. 3-067) in the original notation, except that the beams are not drawn in groups of four (as in Beethoven), but in accordance with the sequenced three-note motif (ascending third, falling second), so as to indicate the diastematic rhythm of 3+3+2 ♪ in the right hand. Linked to these diastematic rhythms (r. h.) are syncopated ♩, rendered staccato by means of rests (l. h.). The two voices cross over, further underscoring thereby the unity of eight bars each. This (Ex. 3-068) is followed both by a reduction of the core voice (r. h.) and by the reconstruction of the harmonic rhythm.

With its large, clear gestures, the Trio reminds of corresponding movements in Beethoven's last string quartets. In a manner not unlike that of an etude, Beethoven works with models: at the level of rhythm, with sequences that produce the above-mentioned rhythm (3+3+2) and the chains of syncopations; at the level of form, with eight-bar phrases of the simplest harmonic setting (D♭ | D♭→ | G♭ | G♭→ | e♭ / A♭^{7} | D♭ | D♭ ||). Unusual, and yet also typical for Beethoven's latest works, is the surprisingly brief return to the recapitulation (mm. 72-74). It is probably no accident that the three transitional measures, which disturb the »squaring of

Ex. 3-068   Harmonics and Core Melody

---

[298] Ibid., text vol., 56.

[299] The movement is marked allegro molto by Beethoven, yet is formed like a scherzo: F minor || D♭ major || F minor da capo || Coda ||.

compositional construction« (R. Wagner) with their odd number, are complemented by a five-bar epilogue (which prolongs the departure of the main voice) to make for another set of eight bars. Thus the total number of measures

(56) is divisible by 8, while the phrase structure is only partially isometric.

These details escaped Friedrich Neumann, because he did not really engage with the composition. At the same time, by imposing a preconceived perceptual model from organic morphology, he also missed the ›essence‹ of the piece. With its quasi-mechanical manner of structuring, the Trio stands rather for a crisis in composition than for an ideal evenness and pure harmony.

As a final point I would like to draw attention to the enlarged syncopations in the coda of this Scherzo.[300] Whereas in the Trio (l. h.) the syncopated notes are halves, their value in the coda is that of wholes (Ex. 3-069 and 3-070). Beethoven thus obtains in a subtle manner the mixture of materials from the scherzo and trio parts usual for the codas of his da capo movements. The key of F minor represents the Scherzo, while the syncopes stand for the Trio.

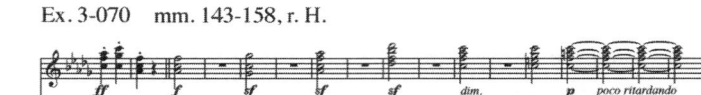

Ex. 3-069   mm. 40-48, l. H.

Ex. 3-070   mm. 143-158, r. H.

Cooper & Meyer • Rhythmic Structure

In 1960, the American musicologists Grosvenor W. Cooper and Leonard B. Meyer published a book entitled *The Rhythmic Structure of Music*, which earned a good deal of attention in the U. S.[301] Starting from a conception of rhythm as universal (»To study rhythm is to study all of music«[302]), the authors hope to have excluded all »easy ›rules of thumb‹ and pat, simplistic answers.«[303] Unfortunately they do not keep their promise, since what the two authors spread out here is not exactly distinguished by subtlety of approach and analytic method.

Their point of departure consists of two basic ideas: the alteration between heavy and light and the enlargement of temporal dimensions.

As is evident from Ex. 3-071 (in Cooper & Meyer, Ex. 53),[304] the authors apply the trochee in several different orders of magnitude (»architectonic levels«): Schubert's *Wanderer-Fantasy* (a) and Bach's little *Preludio* (BWV 926) (b) thus become assimilated to each other. That this seems to work is due to the fact that both excerpts are notated in 3/4 time, whose accentual conditions are regarded as the sole criterion.

Ex. 3-071 (analysis from Cooper&Meyer)

In the first bar of the Schubert piece, one might accept a trochee on the basis of the articulation (legato ♩, staccato ♪), but not a definition of the first four ♪ as likewise trochaic, nor that the identical measures should be taken as heavy/light instead of light/heavy or else as heavy/heavy or light/light. It is also anyone's guess why in the third and fourth of Schubert's measures the dactyl is not considered as »sound foot« in Mattheson's sense and the trochee is chosen instead.

By the simplistic principle of heavy or light, and with a restriction to five patterns (iamb, anapaest, trochee, dactyl and amphibrach), we are marched through musical history from Purcell to Bartók. Rhythmic differentiations, which are objectively given, are equalized. The iambic proportion of 1:2, for example, can appear in Cooper & Meyer also as 1:3, 1:4 etc., or as 2:3 or 3:4 etc., or else also as 1:1. The criterion for the correlation to one or another sound foot remains unspoken. Neither is any distinction made according to voices or registers, let alone component rhythms, in a composition.

If the authors had entitled their book ›The Metric Structure of Music,‹ they would have hewn a little closer to what they wanted to show – while nevertheless missing their objective, music. For to stretch temporal dimensions simply to infinity, so that in the end an entire symphonic exposition is equated with one syllable of an anapaest, means to reify a musical event and to leave psychological principles out of account.[305] Altogether, Cooper & Meyer's analytic method leads to a flattening of all rhythmic and metric perception. Whoever plays or listens to music on Cooper and Meyer's terms experiences the musical proceedings as through an acoustic filter that causes the most precious part of a composition, its protean rhythmic variety, to disappear.

---

[300] This has been observed by Carl Schachter, who remarks moreover that Beethoven, in a sketch of the coda, writes syncopations like hypermeasures. See Carl Schachter, *Unfoldings. Essays in Schenkerian Theory and Analysis*, Ed. Joseph N. Straus (New York / Oxford: OUP 1999), 55f.

[301] Grosvenor W. Cooper and Leonard B. Meyer, *The Rhythmic Structure of Music* (Chicago and London, 1960).

[302] Ibid., 1.

[303] Ibid.

[304] Ibid., 42.

[305] Ibid., 203. Here the first movement of Beethoven's Eighth Symphony is ›analyzed‹ as consisting of two shorts (exposition and its repetition) and one long (development with recapitulation and coda).

Stockhausen • Unity of Musical Time

The composer Karlheinz Stockhausen reflected all his life about the metier of composing, not only with reference to his own creations, but also in principled reference to the nature and history of music. His writings about musical rhythm and meter originated in the 1950s and 60s, beginning with his examination paper on Bartók's *Sonata for two Pianos and Percussion*, whose problems I have discussed elsewhere,[306] down to the essay »Die Einheit der musikalischen Zeit« (The Unity of Musical Time) of 1963.[307]

In the latter essay, Stockhausen had written the program for himself by which he would thereafter compose: every single sound would have to be assembled for a specific work so as to »let a general law operate for all areas of time.«[308]

Thus his 1974 piece *INORI* with the subtitle »Adorations for 1 or 2 Soloists and Orchestra,« for example, is based on an »urgestalt (›formula‹)« ca. 60 seconds in length, whose subdivision into five »parts« (12+15+6+9+18 ♪) predetermines the form of the entire work in advance (»projection«). This is to be guaranteed by magnifying the units of the »urgestalt« by a factor of 60; the total length thus becomes ca. 60 min. whose five sections have a length of 12+15+6+9+18 min. That the number 60, which, of course, derives from the (non-musical) subdivision of hours into minutes and seconds, is structurally significant in *INORI* also in other ways appears from the fact that Stockhausen operates with a »volume scale« of 60 degrees for the »composition« of the individual sounds.[309]

Stockhausen held the belief that the »law for all areas of time« also extended to the ratios among acoustic cycles of pitches and sounds.[310] He was convinced that the predilection, in »traditional occidental music,« for »periodic time intervals (also called measures)« and tonal durations divisible by whole numbers resulted from the restriction of the material to distinct pitches (thus excluding noises), because their harmonic sound spectra were also based on the whole-number division of basic cycles.[311] He dealt with that subject in detail in his text about Mozart, which I will now take a closer look at.[312]

After some introductory passages about conceptions of rhythm among some of his contemporaries (including Messiaen, Stravinsky), Stockhausen comes to the point: »In what follows I would like to use the terms cadential metrics and cadential rhythmics in analogy to tonal cadential harmonics and cadential melodics.«[313] By the cadential principle he means quite generally processes dictated by the alternation of tension and relaxation, with tension being generated by the combination of simple with complex conditions, relaxation, conversely, by complex conditions being followed by simple ones.

Stockhausen thinks he recognizes a first analogy between cadential harmony and cadential rhythm in the circumstance that the ratio of 2:3 in the fifth interval turns up also in the durational ratio, e.g., of duplet ♪ and triplet ♪. As an example, he cites the Trio from the Minuet of Mozart's Quartet in A major K. 464.[314] The Trio is in E major, its middle part in B major. While the main section consists of ♩ and ♪, the shift to the dominant suddenly brings in ♪³: the tonic-dominant relation (2:3) is reflected in the duplet-triplet relation (2:3). The tension built up by the middle section is therefore doubly produced: harmonically and rhythmically. The recapitulation returns us to the tonic and thus brings about a resolution.

Now it so happens that Mozart has triplet eighths gamboling about also in the recapitulation (in mm. 29-30 triplet eighths play against duplet eighths and sixteenths), so that instead of a resolving cadential rhythm we get a heightened rhythmic tension at the end of the Trio such as occurs not even in the middle portion. Stockhausen does not advert to this state of affairs. Besides, he really should have explained why the key relation of a fifth between Minuet and Trio (A major / E major) was not also reflected in rhythm and meter (both parts are in 3/4 time). It would likewise have been appropriate to remark that his example was an isolated instance. In the cycle of the six quartets dedicated to Haydn, which includes altogether twelve minuets or trios with middle portions shifting to the dominant, there is no second case of a switch from duplets to triplets besides the one adduced by Stockhausen.

Selective perception is a danger to which we are all regularly exposed. The scholar tries to counter that hazard by recognizing the problem and building suitable controls

---

[306] Karlheinz Stockhausen, »Die Sonate für 2 Klaviere und Schlagzeug von Béla Bartók,« State examination paper at the Music Academy Cologne, 1951 (typescr.). And see Peter Petersen, »Rhythmik und Metrik in Bartóks *Sonate für zwei Klaviere und Schlagzeug* und die Kritik des jungen Stockhausen an Bartók,« *Musiktheorie*, 9:1 (1994), 39-48.

[307] Karlheinz Stockhausen, »Die Einheit der musikalischen Zeit,« in: *Texte zur elektronischen und instrumentalen Musik*, vol 1: Aufsätze 1952-1962 zur Theorie des Komponierens (Cologne: DuMont, 1963), 211-221.

[308] Ibid., 221.

[309] Karlheinz Stockhausen, »INORI. Anbetungen for 1 or 2 Soloists and Orchestra (1973-74), in: *Texte zur Musik. Band IV. 1970-1977* (Cologne: Du Mont, 1978), 214ff.

[310] Cf., i. a., Stockhausen's Texte »Struktur und Erlebniszeit,« in: *Texte zur elektronischen und instrumentalen Musik* (see note 306), 1: 86-98, and »...wie die Zeit vergeht...,« ibid., 99-139.

[311] »Die Einheit der musikalischen Zeit« (see note 306), 220f.

[312] Karlheinz Stockhausen, »Kadenzrhythmik im Werk Mozarts,« in: op.cit. (*Texte*), vol. 2: Aufsätze 1952-1962 zur musikalischen Praxis (Cologne: DuMont, 1964), 170-206.

[313] Ibid., 172.

[314] Ibid., 173.

into his procedural method. Controls like that Stockhausen seems to have neither applied nor even searched for.

That is true also of the numerous examples by which he seeks to document the analogy between cadential descending pitch and certain elementary rhythmic phenomena. Starting from identical periodic tone sequences, which he equates with the tension-free status of a tonic sound (e. g., ♩♩♩♩♩ ...), he designates every rhythmic deviation from this evenness as tension-building and calls the departures »syncopes.«[315] Stockhausen distinguishes four different kinds of syncopations: post-beat (*nachschlagend*) (e.g.. ♩.♪), pre-beat (*vorschlagend*) (e.g., ♪♩.), tied (e.g., ♩_♪♪ or ♪♪_♪♪) and rest-produced (e.g., ♩,♪ or ♪♪,♪).[316] The succession of regular and syncopated rhythms is again to be regarded as akin to tonic-dominant changes on account of the identical proportions involved ($c\,g = 2{:}3$, ♩♩. = 2:3).

To be sure, according to Stockhausen, the changes from relaxed→tense (cadence-opening) or tense→relaxed (cadence-closing) in Mozart are by no means always simultaneous; on the contrary, harmonic-melodic and metric-rhythmic events occur in every conceivable combination, as he shows schematically (Ex. 3-072):[317]

Ex. 3-072 Cadence-openings and Cadence-closings (after Stockhausen)

In the end, it seems to be Stockhausen's wish to be able to describe the interplay between the various areas of a Mozartian tonal setting. In this, of course, details and their appropriate assessment are crucial.

Here is an example of a metrical analysis of Stockhausen's (Ex. 3-073).[318]

A third example from the »Jagdquartett« K 458 shall demonstrate again different modes of execution of independent and simultaneous rhythmic cadences.
The upper part is cadence opening with a rest syncopation:

the middle part is cadence closing with a rest syncopation and a tie syncopation:

and the bass is cadence opening with a rest syncopation and a tie [?]:

Together the three parts – two of them opening and one closing, thus opening being the dominant factor here – look like this.

---

[315] Ibid., 174.

[316] Stockhausen's eccentric use of the term syncope derives from his basic assumption that any departure from periodic uniformity is a syncopation. However, one may question this regarding certain tie-overs and rests that are simply matters of writing convention, or else articulations, as different rhythms, when in truth they are for all practical purposes identical, e.g., ♩.♪ and ♩_♪♪ or ♩.♪ and ♩,♪.

[317] Ibid., 178.

[318] Ibid., 192.

Ex. 3-073 Mozart, String Quartet B♭ Major (after Stockhausen)

Ex. 3-074
Mozart, String Quartet B♭ Major K. 458, 4th mov., mm. 97-102

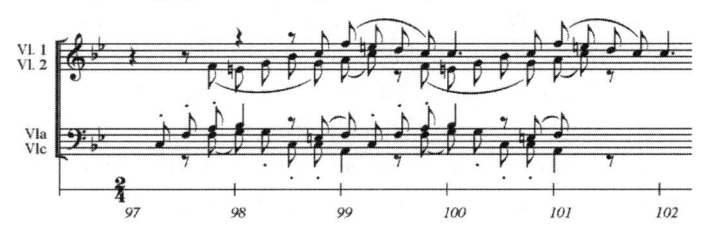

At issue are mm. 98 and 99 from the 4th movement of Mozart's B♭ major Quartet K. 458. Stockhausen excerpted them as with a cookie-cutter exactly at the bar lines. In this case, however, that is problematic, as sense-bearing motifs or melodic turns thereby become unrecognizable, with repercussions also in the rhythmics of the passage. In Ex. 3-074, I show these measures with upbeats and overlappings. As one can see, Mozart starts the legato slur in Vl. II before the bar line (mm. 97/98), whereas Stockhausen starts it with the E4 in m. 98. The F4 in m. 99_4 is isolated thereby, and the rhythm can appear as a bar-filling syncopation (♪♪,♪), which is clearly not intended. The same goes for the viola and cello voices, whose staccatoed three-eighths upbeats (in staggered imitation) as well as, again, the legato upbeats before the bar line are lost in Stockhausen's analysis. The voice of Vl. I is not even included by Stockhausen, because he would then have to retract his assertion that the dominant m. 98 and the tonic m. 99, which form a closing cadence, are opposed, on the rhythmic level, by predominantly cadence-opening structures.[319]

Similar flaws also mark the concluding analysis of Stockhausen's Mozart essay, in which – quasi as a summary – he wants to show once more, in an eight-bar phrase, »how Mozart, in applying the devices of ambiguous opening, alternating syncopes of various kinds and twofold resolution, utilizes the rhythmic-metric and melodic-harmonic cadencing for composing richly associative periods.«[320] Stockhausen again cuts out, and comments on, isolated measures along the bar lines and then, at the end, presents the whole period in excerpts (Ex. 3-075).

---

[319] Ibid.

[320] Ibid., 202. On the second quarter note of m. 5 in Stockhausen's Ex., A♭-G has been mistakenly notated instead of G-F.

Ex. 3-075 (from Stockhausen's essay)

The theme is from the Allegretto finale of Mozart's Piano Concerto in C minor K. 491. This movement, shaped as a variation rondo, has two episodes, one in A♭ major, the other in C major. The transition from the C minor refrains to the episodes and back occurs without modulation.

The formal model of the theme is a 16-bar period, whose phrases are repeated with variations: p1: 8 – p1': 8 – p2: 8 – p2': 8. Stockhausen presents the varied first phrase (p1', mm. 104-111), which modulates from A♭ major to E♭ major and half-closes with an authentic cadence. The same path is traced by the first phrase (mm. 96-103), but the cadencing after the modulation has a different rhythm, so that the first half-close appears weaker than the second. The following second phrase, which leads from E♭ major back to A♭ major (mm.113-128, not analyzed here), likewise plays out in two variants, of which again the second, which is dominated by the piano, appears to have a stronger close than the first.

Ex. 3-076   Mozart, Piano Concerto C Minor K. 491, 3rd mov., Couplet Theme I, mm. 96-103 (extract)

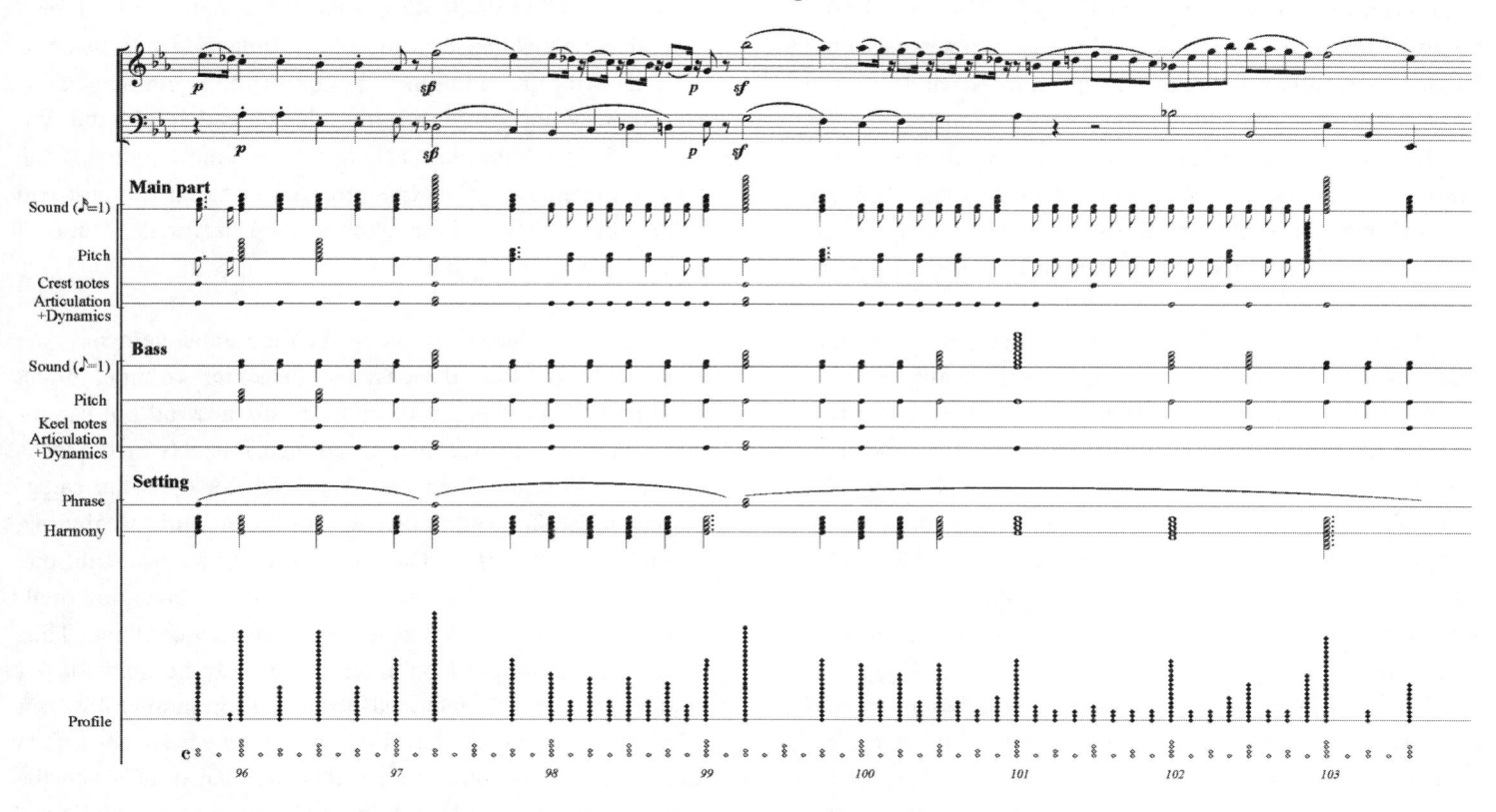

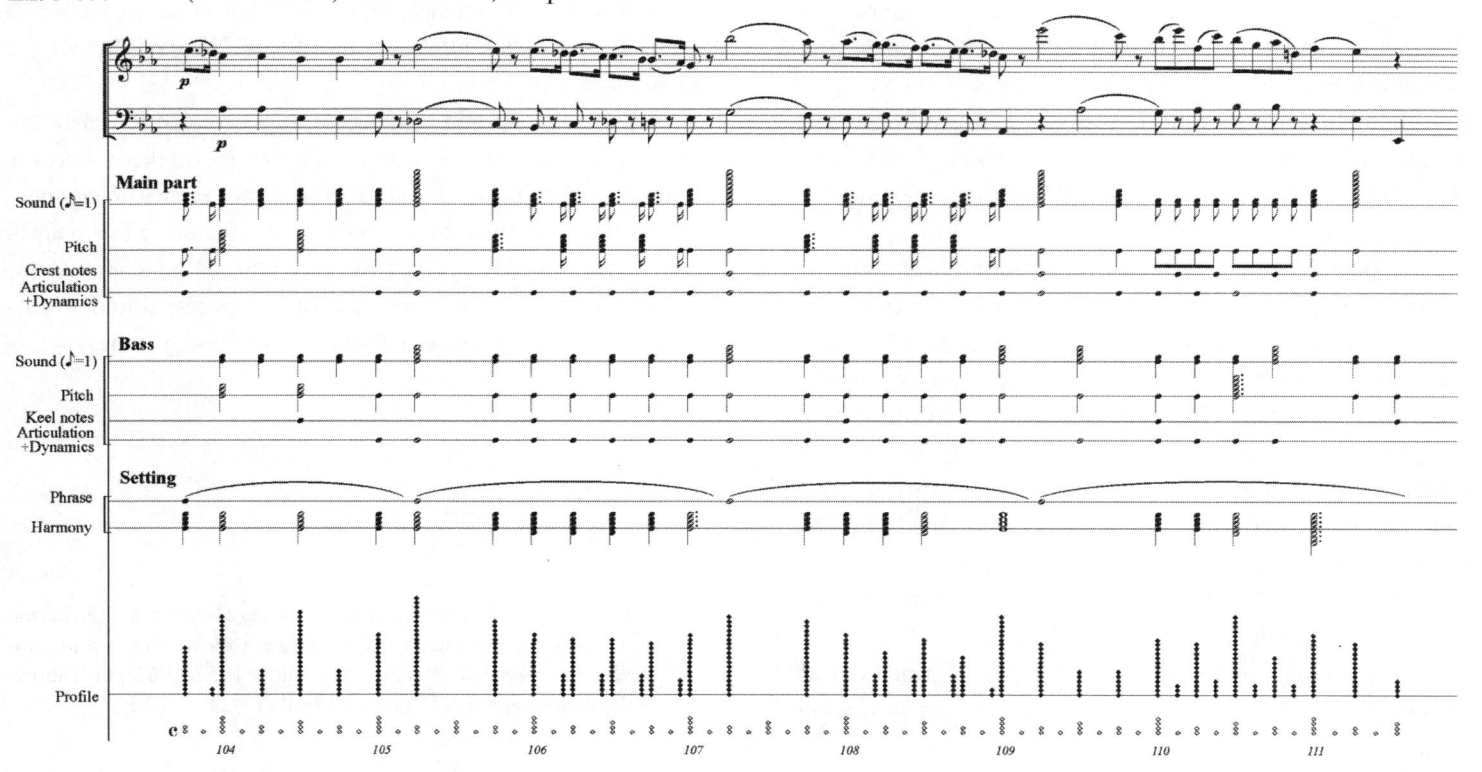

Ex. 3-077   (Continuation) mm. 104-111, Couplet Theme I$^{var.}$

As an alternative analysis, I have constructed rhythm scores of the two variants of the first phrase of the A♭ major theme, which can demonstrate that by means of component rhythms Mozart actually brings about a lowering that converges with the harmonic cadence (Ex. 3-076 and 3-077).

To hold down on the data and keep from overloading the picture, I have (like Stockhausen) confined myself to the analysis of the outer voices (the scaffolding) plus the harmony. Owing to its greater significance, the upper voice is given twice as much weight in its component rhythms »Sound« and »Pitch« as the lower voice (♪=1 vs. ♪=1). The components »Diastematy« (»crest notes« in the upper voice, »keel notes« in the lower) and »Articulation« (including ‿), along with »Dynamics« and »Phrase,« get one point each (except for the four-bar phrase of mm. 99-103, to which I have given two points because of its exceptional length). Harmonic function changes are each weighted fourfold, suspensions singly and cadences doubly.

The component »Pitch« is relevant to this theme because of the many note repetitions. In mm. 96 and 104, the pitches move in ♩ in both upper and lower voice, which earns them additional weight. To be added are the figures in mm. 98 and 100 and – characteristically altered – in mm. 106 and 108, where the note repetitions keep the seemingly weak, post-beat notes from being lost rhythmically.

At the beginning, the rhythmic profiles of the two variants are virtually identical, but they diverge noticeably toward the end. In the course of the modulations to the dominant key – from the 6th bar in the first phrase, in the second not until the 7th – the profile clearly exhibits the 4/4 meter (mm. 101-103) or marks the individual quarter notes and thus gives additional emphasis to the cadential process (mm. 109-111).

Since rhythmic profiles accumulate the beginnings of the durations of all pertinent component rhythms per point of time, one should attend not only to the high peaks but also to the absence of peaks. In the present case, the syncopes with values of ♩ that are at the same time marked as crest, legato and sforzato notes are certainly the most prominent events of the two eight-bar passages. They result in high rhombus towers on the *Two* of the measures. But since the succeeding *Ones* are noticeably reduced in weight (mm. 98, 100, 106, 108), the upshot is something like double measures.

Of special interest is the rhythmic-metric situation in the variation phrase, where there are three ♩ syncopes instead of a mere two. In m. 109, where the third syncope is heard, the *One* is suddenly weighted more strongly than the *Two*. This is because the lower voice here does not join in the syncopated accent but plays relatively long durations on *One* (♩.) and *Three* (♩). Besides, the entire measure is filled with the tonic harmony. As already mentioned, the A♭ major in the second phrase actually prevails for a full six bars (mm. 104-109); only thereafter the modulation to the dominant key occurs in a few marked steps.

The principal rhythmic process can be summarized as follows: both phrases begin with simple patterns of motion that are oriented on the model of metrical hierarchy. The heavily weighted syncopes on the *Two* of the 4/4 measures add dynamism to the process and at the same time tense it into double measures. In the closing phases, the initial isometry returns, sedately in units of 4 ♩ in the initial first phrase (m. 100), vitally, with stress on every single ♩ step, in the subsequent one (m. 110). Here, at the end, the harmonic-melodic cadence and the rhythmic-metric one are in conformity with each other.

There is no trace in the rhythmic sphere, to be sure, of Stockhausen's 2:3 ratio between the tonic as starting point and the dominant as the goal. The raising and lowering of rhythmic tension functions independently of such merely speculative suppositions. Instead of searching for 2:3 and 3:2 ratios in tonic-dominant and tonic-subdominant progressions, Stockhausen would have done better to listen to and describe the harmonic rhythm at the beginning of his example. What is rhythmically relevant is that with the syncopated F5 a harmonic step from the tonic parallel to the subdominant is performed – not that between F minor and D♭ major there is an interval of a major third with a ratio of 4:5 between the key notes.

In 1952, Stockhausen wrote: »The individual element is the tone with its four dimensions: duration, volume, pitch, timbre.«[321] What is problematic in this now all but canonical-sounding quartet of tone »dimensions« (which Stockhausen and others later called »parameters«) is the categorical equation of »durations« with the qualities »volume«, »pitch« and »timbre.« The *duration* of a process is not one of its *qualities*. Tones with their constant or changing qualities can be interrogated as to how long they continue. Thus a note *C*, reproduced on a cello in *f*, may be held for 4 ♩ before changing to piano and sounding for another 4 ♩. But that does not make the durations of twice 4 ♩ one of its qualities. Rather, one can say that the quality »C« and the quality »string sound« last altogether 8 ♩ and the qualities *f* and *p* 4 ♩ each. Metaphorically expressed: a man's white hair is one of his qualities, but not the years in which he had black hair.

The wide-spread and age-old misconception that the duration of a tone or sound is one of its qualities became consolidated in the middle of the 20th century in connection with the idea of a »pointillist music.« Stockhausen seems to have recognized the problem, as he searched for terms to denominate the durations between sound events that don't signify just the beginning and end of tones.

---

[321] Karlheinz Stockhausen, »Situation des Handwerks. (Kriterien der punktuellen Musik),« in: *Texte zur elektronischen und instrumentalen Musik*, vol. 1: Aufsätze 1952-1962 zur Theorie des Komponierens (Cologne 1963), 17-23; p. 19.

In his analysis of Webern's *Concerto for 9 Instruments* of 1953, he speaks of »entry distances,«[322] later also of »time intervals«[323] and »phases.«[324] The term duration Stockhausen generally reserved for the actual length of a tone or sound, although he occasionally applied it also to other temporal phenomena (e.g., »durations of phase groups«[325] or »in the area of durations« including »meters«[326]).

The fact that Stockhausen was unable to see his way through to the emancipation of the concept of duration from its being tied to the individual note is surely connected to the above-mentioned misconception of duration as a tonal quality. Yet there can be no real objection to an understanding of the term »duration« to mean simply elapsing time and to using it to denote any time intervals between beginning and end, or else beginning and beginning of sounds or sound configurations. A concept of duration disconnected from the individual note or sound is the necessary precondition for being able to describe all temporal measures and structures of the rhythmic dimension uniformly, that is, to recognize and analyze components rhythms.

Actually, Stockhausen was aiming at something similar, as the following statement makes clear: »Yet in fact a musical composition is nothing other than a temporal order of acoustic events.«[327] But tied as he was to the »parameters« of »timbre, pitch, volume and duration,« which he thought he had to absolutize,[328] he was unable to call rhythm what in reality *is* rhythm. Referring to dynamic accents in works by Mozart (>, *sf* etc.), whose »time intervals« he was certainly aware of, he wrote expressly:[329]

I could add one more category, namely that of accent syncopation, whereby regular rhythms are made irregular without any change in duration [...]. But that category is a pseudo-rhythmic one; it belongs into the area of an investigation dealing with the function of Dynamics in relation to the other parameters.

Benary • Rhythm and Meter

In 1967, the Swiss musicologist and composer Peter Benary published »a practical guide« to *Rhythm and Meter*.[330] Conceived as a manual for the practicing musician, the slender book nevertheless contains a number of fundamental reflections that warrant its inclusion here.

Rhythm and meter are two sides of the same coin for Benary, one being unthinkable without the other, at least for the music from 1750 to ca. 1900. Rhythm is defined as »the theory of musical durational relations,« meter as »the theory of musical weight relations.«[331] Rhythm, however, is seconded by an additional »ordering principle,« whose earmark is said to be the »accents.«[332] Rhythmic accents have something in common with metric weights, but must be strictly distinguished from the latter. Whereas one can actually hear an accent (or a stress) – for example, when a tone is increased in length or volume – a metric weight can only be »felt.«[333]

This view of the relation between rhythm and meter is widely accepted. However, there is a logical difficulty, in that while in rhythm the durational organization is said to be decisive, accents nevertheless play a role. Yet duration and accent belong to different modes of perception. An accent changes the quality of the tone, whereas duration, as we have said, is not a quality – any more than one would regard a person's life span as one of his or her qualities. Tones or sounds can be distinguished by diverse characteristics, which are mutable. *When* a sound stops or changes is an entirely different question. Like everywhere else, time and space interlock. Since questions of rhythm and meter have to do with the temporal category, the concept of duration is central. Accents, therefore, have to be interrogated as to the intervals at wich they follow each other – what durations exist between them. Only then do they become rhythmically relevant, and even generate rhythms of their own – components rhythms, as I call them – perceptible concurrently with the primary rhythm of the tonal durations.

Benary does not take this step. Although he says toward the end of his book, »The position [!] of the accents is the rhythmic ordering principle,«[334] he never describes sequences of accents as real rhythms. Instead, he takes off from meter and queries the position of accents in the metric structure so as to determine their convergence with or divergences from metric weights.

---

[322] Karlheinz Stockhausen, »Weberns Konzert für 9 Instrumente op. 24. Analyse des ersten Satzes,« in: *Texte* (see note 320), 24-31; p. 30f.

[323] »Struktur und Erlebniszeit« (see note 308), 88.

[324] »...wie die Zeit vergeht...« (see note 308), 99.

[325] Ibid.

[326] »Die Einheit der musikalischen Zeit« (see note 306), 220.

[327] Ibid., 213.

[328] Ibid., 211.

[329] »Kadenzrhythmik im Werk Mozarts« (see note 311), 193.

[330] Peter Benary, *Rhythmik und Metrik. Eine praktische Anleitung*, 2nd ed. (Cologne: Gerig, 1973).

[331] Ibid., 9.

[332] Ibid.

[333] Ibid., 10.

[334] Ibid., 89.

Ex. 3-078   Schubert, Piano Trio E♭ Major op. 100 (Deutsch 929), 2nd mov., Beginning

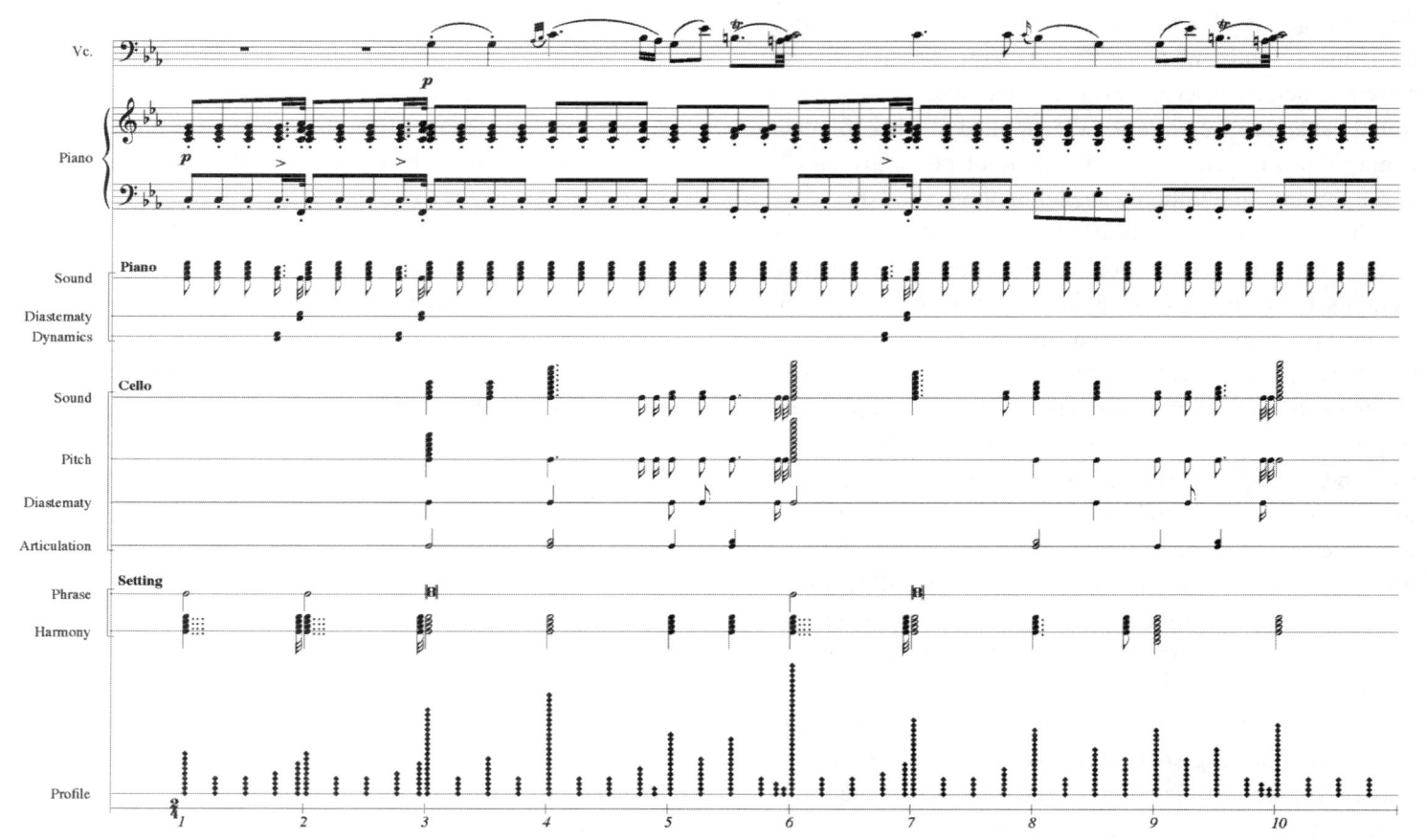

From the examples he cites in great numbers one can clearly tell that the make-up of metric weights is the starting point of his analyses and in his opinion also decisive for the interpreter. Speaking about the beginning of the slow movement of Schubert's Trio in E♭ major (Ex. 3-078), he remarks about the first two bars:[335]

> The first two measures are identical. A differentiation in the performance would thus already come under the shaping of bar groups. Let us therefore limit ourselves to the first bar. The articulation of the measure is uniform: staccato on every note. The character prohibits agogical modifications. The smallest rhythmic value is the measure's last one. There can thus also be no question of increasing tension by lengthening the lightest of the light. Characteristic and ›irregular‹ is the accent on the fourth eighth. To raise it to a sharp syncopation would run counter to the character of the movement, to simply ignore it, to its later motivic importance. […]. So everything suggests minimizing the distinction between heavy and light. The 2/4 meter has to be made clear to begin with, mainly by not letting the 3rd eighth become equal to the first. Analogously, one also expects the 4th eighth to be lighter than the 2nd, so that the unexpected accent can be realized all the more easily. One can add a slight shading of the staccato, since uniformity is always most suitable for letting other kinds of difference come to the fore, such as here the heavy-light succession from the first to the second half of the measure.

The question is whether the weights of a measure have to be brought into the notation if there are no compositional indications to do so. If, therefore, one starts from the actually sounding components, rather than from an inwardly felt meter, one discovers that the composer has produced a metric structure that, while it does not run counter to the dictates of the 2/4 meter, nevertheless modifies nearly every bar by means of rhythmic weights (cf. the line »Profile« in Ex. 3-078). Thus, in the first measure, the first eighth differs from the two following ones in that it introduces the tonic, which is held for more than three ♪, and that with the first note a phrase commences. The second and third eighth, on the other hand, are absolutely identical. The last note of the measure, again, is relatively heavy, because it initiates a harmonic function change. At the tempo of a 32nd, a change to the subdominant occurs shortly before the tonic, which, in terms of rhythm, gives ›importance‹ to this smallest temporal value. (It is for this reason that in the piano part I have chosen the 32nd as the unit for measuring the durational weights of the notes, while 16ths are basic for the cello: the 32nds here are trill terminations and, like the slides and short grace-notes, can be regarded as irrational values).

Contrary to Benary, who wants to make the alternation of heavy and light quarters dictated by the time signature felt in every single bar, I think that in the two piano measures preceding the cello cantilena, the composer deliberately at first composed in whole measures, realizing the light weights of the 2/4 meter only after the entry of the melody. Thus m. 3 (in the rhythmic profile) presents a fairly exact picture of the heavy first and semi-heavy second beat with light eighths floating in between. After that, there are sometimes whole-, sometimes half- or sometimes also quarter-measure fillings. The rhyhmic profile also shows that there is a greater rhythmic density in the second half of the period. The enlargeded metric weights as a result of bar groups presumed by Benary, on the other hand, are not confirmed.

---

[335] Ibid., 39f.

Ex. 3-079　　　　Beethoven, *Grande Sonate Pathétique* op. 13, 2nd mov., Beginning

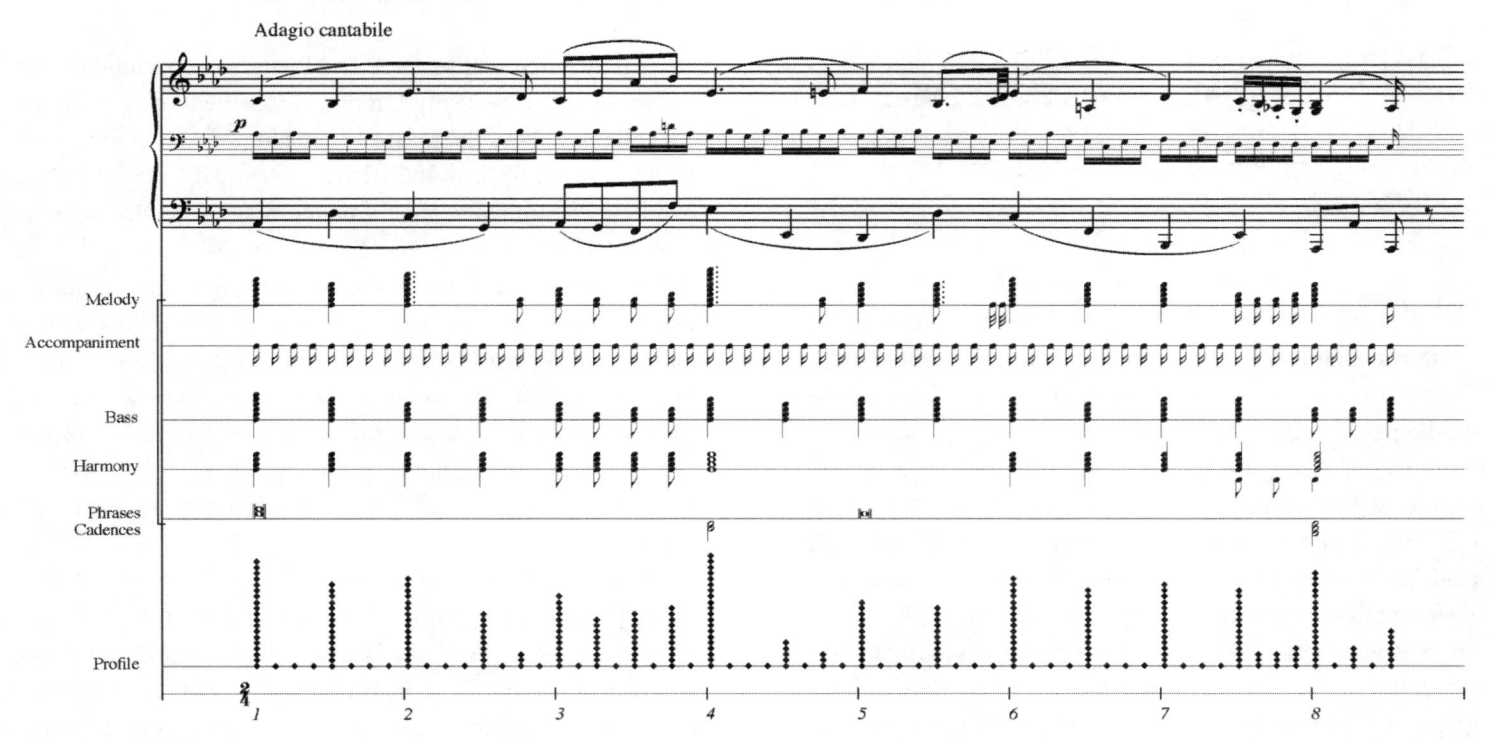

A second example to show that Benary's view of meter as »the superordinate element of temporal order and tension in music«[336] should be questioned is the beginning of the slow movement of Beethoven's sonata *Pathétique* op. 13 (Ex. 3-079). Fairly apodictically, Benary says about this case:[337] »These normal-structured eight bars are mostly played wrongly metrically, i. e, with the weight on the 2nd, 4th, 6th and 8th measure instead of the 1st, 3rd, 5th and 7th one.«

So long as one goes by the ›felt‹ weight of the one or the other measure, one will dispute forever the ›correct‹ or ›false‹ solution. It is more productive to ask whether the composer has really adopted the alleged law that tension and relaxation have to alternate regularly, that is, at equal intervals, or if that is an assumption made by theoreticians, who like to look for regular laws where actually the goal is rhythmic-metric variability (Mattheson, Riepel, Koch etc.).

A certain reification is attained when all the rhythmically relevant components are included in the analysis. Which components are »relevant« in the individual case can be determined only on the basis of a compositional analysis. In the case of the »Adagio cantabile« (Ex. 3-079), it is probably beyond question that the outer parts constitute the principal event and that the 16ths figurations are a kind of filler. For the two melody-carrying voices descant and bass I have therefore included (and weighted) three components each, for the inner setting only one. Besides the melody's tones, which are weighted acording to their length (component »Sound«), the crest and keel tones (component »Diastematy«) and the phrasing slurs are taken account of in the outer voices. To that we must add the harmonic function changes (plus three suspensions in mm. 7 and 8), the two halves of the period and the imperfect and perfect cadences.

The compilation of all the rhythmic weights shows that the 2/4 meter is faintly noticeable, the controversial bar group metric not at all. The rhythmic weights on all the ♩ are relatively large. That may be a reason why the eight-bar theme seems so coherent. The bridging of the main caesura after the 4th bar contributes to that effect: here Beethoven, in both voices, draws the phrasing slur across the bar line. He also stretches the harmonic function of the dominant all the way into the 5th measure, though he there lets the basic position of the dominant triad (m. 4) shift into the secondary position of the dominant ninth chord. Finally, the pitch disposition of the upper voice causes a grouping of 3+5 bars to be in effect along with the division of the period into 4+4 bars, inasmuch as the top tone of B♭4, from which it goes down steadily in waves, is reached already shortly before the 4th bar. In this connection, it may be of some significance that the highest peak in the rhythmic profile occurs exactly on the *One* of m. 4 (instead of m. 5).

One of the distinctions of Peter Benary's book is that it contains many interesting examples from a wide spread repertory. I want to look at two more of these, because they represent special cases, which Benary recognized and describes as such.

---

[336] Ibid., 14.

[337] Ibid., 42.

Ex. 3-080 Chopin, Nocturne op. 15 No. 2, Middle Section (Beginning)

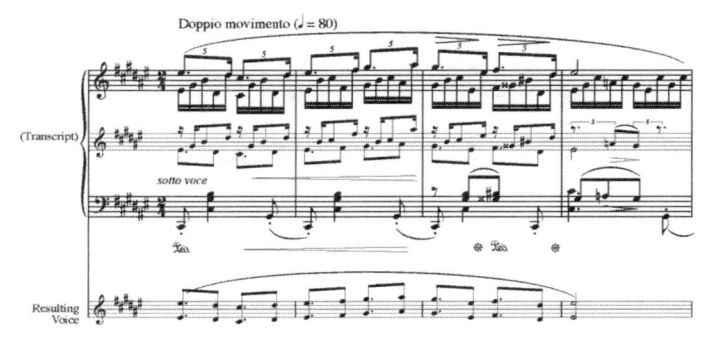

In his chapter »Two and Three,« Benary talks about the Nocturne op. 15 no. 2 in F♯ major of Chopin[338], in whose middle part ♪-quintuplets are set against a binary accompanying pattern (Ex. 3-080). Benary regards it as undecidable, whether the quintuplet groups should be taken as 2+3 or as 3+2. But if one sorts out the inherent voices of the right hand, marked by beams by Chopin, and notates them in a separate system, it becomes plain that the lower of the two inherent voices (E♯-D♯-C♯, etc.) moves in consecutive octaves to the main voice, with the octaves alternately coincident and *nachschlagend*. What is intended, however, and also heard, is one main voice in octaves and in a (heterometric) rhythm of 3+2 ♪.

Ex. 3-081 Bartók, *Mikrokosmos* No. 100, Beginning (Transcript)

The second, likewise very interesting example derives from Bartók's *Mikrokosmos*.[339] The piece No. 100 (vol. 4), entitled »Népdalféle – Folksong-like« (Ex. 3-081), is essentially in two voices and is written in 5/8 and 3/8 meter. The bar lines are drawn solidly through both systems, which, as Benary noticed, is not in keeping with the sounding reality. Benary presents a transcription with bar lines staggered in the two staves, in order to indicate that the beginning constitutes »a ›meter canon‹ at a distance of three eighths.« Benary's finding can hardly be questioned. I would perhaps go one step further in the transcription to emphasize that the lower voice, which has longer notes, also shares the 3+2 subdivision of the 5/8 measures.

Dahlhaus • What is Musical Rhythm?

All his academic life, Carl Dahlhaus was occupied with questions of musical rhythm and meter, beginning with his Ph.D. thesis about the masses of Josquin[340] and ending with the chapter on »Meter and Rhythm: Ancient Categories and Modern Phenomena« in his posthumously published volume *Die Musiktheorie im 18. und 19. Jahrhundert*.[341] He did not present an original theory of rhythm. He did, however, discuss some basic questions in his 1967 essay, »Was ist musikalischer Rhythmus?«,[342] as well as in two chapters he contributed to the volume *Studien zur Theorie und Geschichte der musikalischen Rhythmik und Metrik*.[343] Further remarks are found in the text »Polemisches zur Theorie der Ryhthmik und Metrik,«[344] as well as in other, thematically narrower essays.[345]

In the phenomenology chapter of his *Esthetics of Music*, Dahlhaus champions the idea (against Roman Ingarden) that rhythm in music is not a single- but a multi-layered phenomenon.[346] A heavy metrical beat, for instance, could be represented by several »qualities,« such as dura-

---

[338] Ibid., 25.

[339] Ibid., 109.

[340] Carl Dahlhaus, *Studien zu den Messen Josquins des Prés*, Diss. Univ. Göttingen, 1952, (typescr.); PDF file in vol. 10 of the Collected Writings of Carl Dahlhaus (Laaber 2006).

[341] Carl Dahlhaus, *Die Musiktheorie im 18. und 19. Jahrhundert*, Pt. 2: *Deutschland*, ed. Ruth E. Müller (= Geschichte der Musiktheorie, vol. 11) (Darmstadt,1989), 157-203. See also his »Die Tactus- und Proportionslehre des 15. bis 17. Jahrhunderts,« in: Geschichte der Musiktheorie, vol. 6) (Darmstadt, 1987), 333-361.

[342] Carl Dahlhaus, »Was ist musikalischer Rhythmus?« In: *Probleme des musiktheoretischen Unterrichts* (= Veröffentlichungen des Instituts für neue Musik und Musikerziehung Darmstadt, vol. 7) (Berlin, 1967), 16-22.

[343] Ernst Apfel / Carl Dahlhaus, *Studien zur Theorie und Geschichte der musikalischen Rhythmik und Metrik*, vol. 1 (Munich, 1974), »Zur Kritik des Riemannschen Systems,« 184-203, and »Zur Rhythmik und Metrik um 1600,« 273-290.

[344] Carl Dahlhaus, »Polemisches zur Theorie der Rhythmik und Metrik,« in: *Mf*, 29:2 (1976), 183-186.

[345] Carl Dahlhaus, »Über Symmetrie und Asymmetrie in Mozarts Instrumentalwerken,« in: *NZfM*, 124 (1963), 208-214; »Musikalische Prosa,« in: *NZfM*, 125 (1964), 176-182; »Rhythmus im Großen,« in: *Melos / NZfM*, 1 (1975), 439-441; »Probleme des Rhythmus in der neuen Musik,« in: *Terminologie der neuen Musik* (= Veröffentlichungen des Instituts für neue Musik und Musikerziehung Darmstadt, vol. 5) (Berlin, 1965), 25-37; »Rhythmische Strukturen in Weberns Orchesterstücken Opus 6,« in: *Beiträge '72/'73. Webern-Kongreß* (Kassel, 1974), 73-80; »Zur Rhythmik in Beethovens Diabelli-Variationen,« in: *Neue Wege der musikalischen Analyse* (= Veröffentlichungen des Instituts für neue Musik und Musikerziehung Darmstadt, vol. 6) (Berlin, 1976), 18-22.; »Zum Taktbegriff der Wiener Klassik,« in: *AfMw*, 45:1 (1988), 1-15.

[346] Carl Dahlhaus, *Esthetics of Music*, transl. William W. Austin (Cambridge & New York: CUP, 1982), 83: »Musical rhythm, contrary to Ingarden's argument, is ›many-levelled‹.«

Ex. 3-082   Wagner, *Parsifal*, Introduction mm. 1-19, »Last Supper«-Theme

tion or intensity. Like other theoreticians before and after him, Dahlhaus relates the term duration primarily to the individual tone or sound: if individual tones or sounds combine into groups, they produce durations that co-determine the rhythmic events of a composition in the form of measures, phrases, figures, etc.

Dahlhaus' main interest was in the relation between rhythm and meter. His view of rhythmic structures included phenomena that seem to negate metric relations: »A grouping of tonal durations can constitute a rhythm without being related to any beat consisting of heavy and light stresses.«[347] Dahlhaus even admits that tonal duration could appear as a »secondary characteristic« in cases where »the distances between [...] accents« are decisive.[348] Such accents could be represented by high or lengthened notes, *sf*, harmonic functions, bar lines or beginnings of phrases.

As an example of the predominance of rhythm over the time signature, Dahlhaus, in his essay »What is Musical Rhythm?« refers to the beginning of the Prelude to *Parsifal*. In this at first monophonically played melody, »the notated time scheme [4/4] [is] overlaid and invalidated by the disposition of the time values,« making the time signature »musically irrelevant.«[349]

Let us take a closer look at the situation (Ex. 3-082). Aside from the fact that the first phrase of this beginning known as the »Last Supper« theme does not end at m. 6 but echoes for two additional measures before the theme is repeated, the rhythm of the monophonic melody can be referred back to a basic form I have reconstructed, in which the relation to the 4/4 meter becomes less enigmatic. A comparison of the indvidual rhythmic values of model and original makes clear that while the longs and shorts are modified, their difference does not disappear altogether:

A♭3	4 ♪	→	6 ♪
C4	4 ♪	→	4 ♪
E♭4	4 ♪	→	5 ♪
F4	8 ♪	→	7 ♪
G4	4 ♪	→	4 ♪
A♭4	4 ♪	→	2 ♪
G4	4 ♪	→	4 ♪
C4	2 ♪	→	3 ♪
D4	2 ♪	→	1 ♪
E♭4	10 ♪	→	10 ♪

[347] Dahlhaus (1967) (see note 342), 18.

[348] Ibid.

[349] Ibid., 16.

It is true that the 4/4 time is not inferrable at first: instead, the listener perceives an agogical gesture of the melody (»very expressive«), which is, so to speak, composed into the piece, but the melody remains subliminally tied to the unwavering ur-form. One should also consider that already from the third bar onward we observe a half-measure structure, recognizable from the greatly lengthened notes on the *Three* or the *One*. Moreover, the eight-bar theme is immediately repeated in a metrically stabilized version – now expanded to 13 bars by a filled-in fermata – whereby the listener can retrospectively reinterpret his impression of the first six, monophonic, bars in the manner of a 4/4 beat that seems to sway agogically.

The harmonized restatement of the theme (which Dahlhaus does not discuss) acquires a metric point of reference from a counter-voice sounding in triads and rhythmicized mainly in ♩, though it continues to deviate ›agogically‹ from that reference (Ex. 3-083).

The harmonic progressions, too, advance mostly in ♩ (see especially mm. 12-15 with their regular cadence F minor – D♭ major – b♭[7]minor – E♭[7] major – A♭ major). But Wagner evades the squaring of the period system by shaping the harmonic rhythm in such a way that the turn from I to III takes place in *three* measures (mm. 9-11), the return to the tonic via VI, IV, II and V is done in two (mm. 12-13), while the tonic is held fermata-like for *six* bars (mm. 14-19, visible only in part in the Ex.).

To the main rhythmic events, determined by the ›agogically‹ free thematic voice, the metrically stable counter-voice and the changing harmonic degrees, is added an accompaniment with its own rhythmic microstructure (Ex. 3-084). It serves to create a phantasmagoria, with which the composer wants to evoke the idea of a sacred rite bathed in iridescent light. What is shown is the transition from the first to the second presentation of the theme (mm. 6-11).

In m. 6, along with the counter-voice commencing already here, the strings and wind instruments come in, whose overall ascending pitches enact a rise from relative darkness to luminous brightness. The strings play undulating 32nds arpeggios in the (prescribed) 4/4 meter, while the winds simultaneously repeat triadic chords in (likewise prescribed) 6/4 meter – the chord repetitions themselves being further rhythmed by alternating triplet and duplet eighths. The result is a set of complex proportions, which, while rationally comprehensible, are thoroughly irrational in their effect.

Ex. 3-083 Wagner, *Parsifal*, Introduction mm. 9-15 (Melody, Counterpoint, Harmonies)

The irrationality is further reinforced in that the upper-voice melody of the chords and arpeggios (upward-stemmed notes) executes its pitch changes in ascending triads *off-beat*: on the fourth 32nd in the 4/4 time layer, on the second triplet eighth in the 6/4 time layer. What is striking and powerfully effective is that when the winds reach the top note of G6, the stress is suddenly on the *One* after all: the tone, that is, enters not off- but down-beat, so that the moment at which the entire period reaches the *f* and that mysterious-sounding C minor chord is heard, receives additional point from the rhythmic quarter.

rhythmic in nature.[350] It springs from the composer's desire to evoke, here at the beginning of his »consecrational stage festival play,« a sense of unfathomable temporal relations and religious contemplation.

In his article »On Rhythm and Meter about 1600,« Dahlhaus addresses the significance of the lyrics for the rhythm of vocal music. With reference to the seconda prattica of the Monteverdi period, he operates with the term »›oratorical‹ rhythm«,[351] which means that at the time when the graduated accent meter was only just emerging, the free

Ex. 3-084 Wagner, *Parsifal*, Introduction mm. 6-11 (Melody, Counterpoint, Accompaniment)

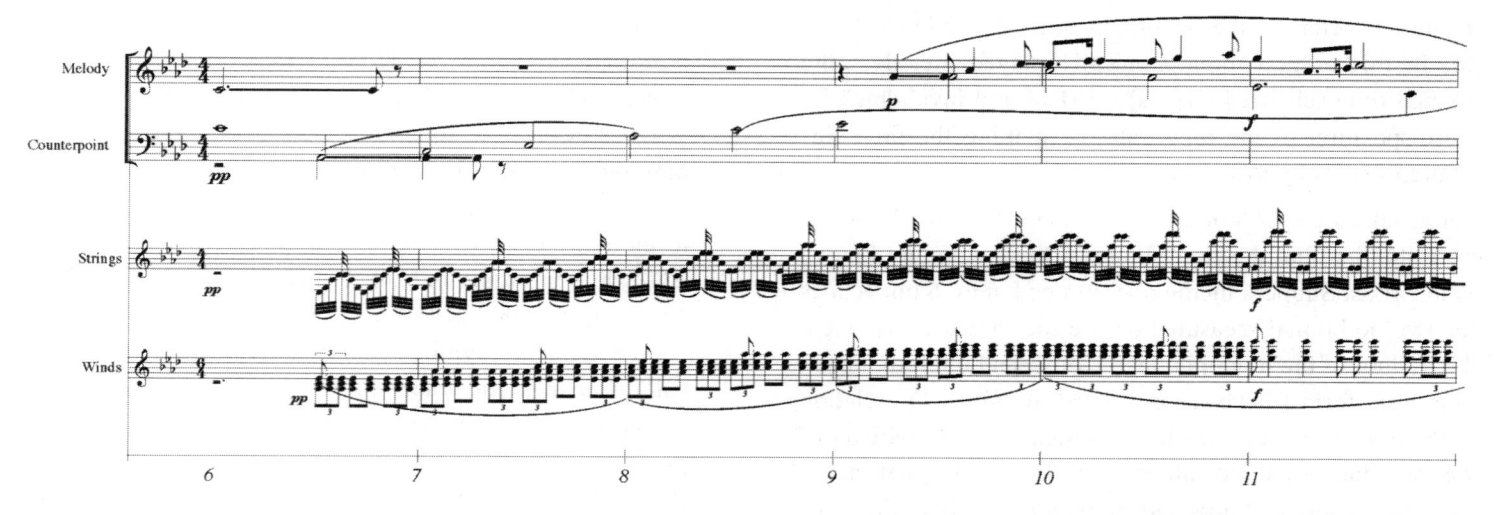

A final element in the sum of rhythmic-metric phenomena is the phrasal overlapping by which the two thematic melody lines are bracketed together (Ex. 3-085). While the formal model for the »Last Supper« theme is the free, eight-bar period, whose repetition is expanded simply by holding the final note and chord, the tonal enchantment of the accompaniment enters simultaneously with the final note, spanning a unit of 14 measures. Beginning in m. 6 and ending only after the theme is already completed, the accompaniment occludes the caesura between mm. 8 and 9 and thus blurs the eight-bar pattern. This device, too, is

flow of sung speech could be decisive for the shaping of phrases and stresses. As an example he cites the beginning of the *Lamento d'Ariana* of Claudio Monteverdi in its monodic version (Ex. 3-086). Impressed by the effect produced even today by its »paradigmatic line« (»Lasciatemi morire«), Dahlhaus confesses to having difficulties coming up with an analysis »that goes beyond mere negation – beyond the determination of what does not happen.«[352]

[350] Others may call it metric or formal, an opinion I could not contradict.

[351] Dahlhaus (1974) (see note 343), 273.

[352] Ibid.

Ex. 3-085 *Parsifal*, Introduction mm. 1-19 (Overlapping of Phrases)

Ex. 3-086   Monteverdi, *Lamento d'Ariana* (Monodic Version), Beginning

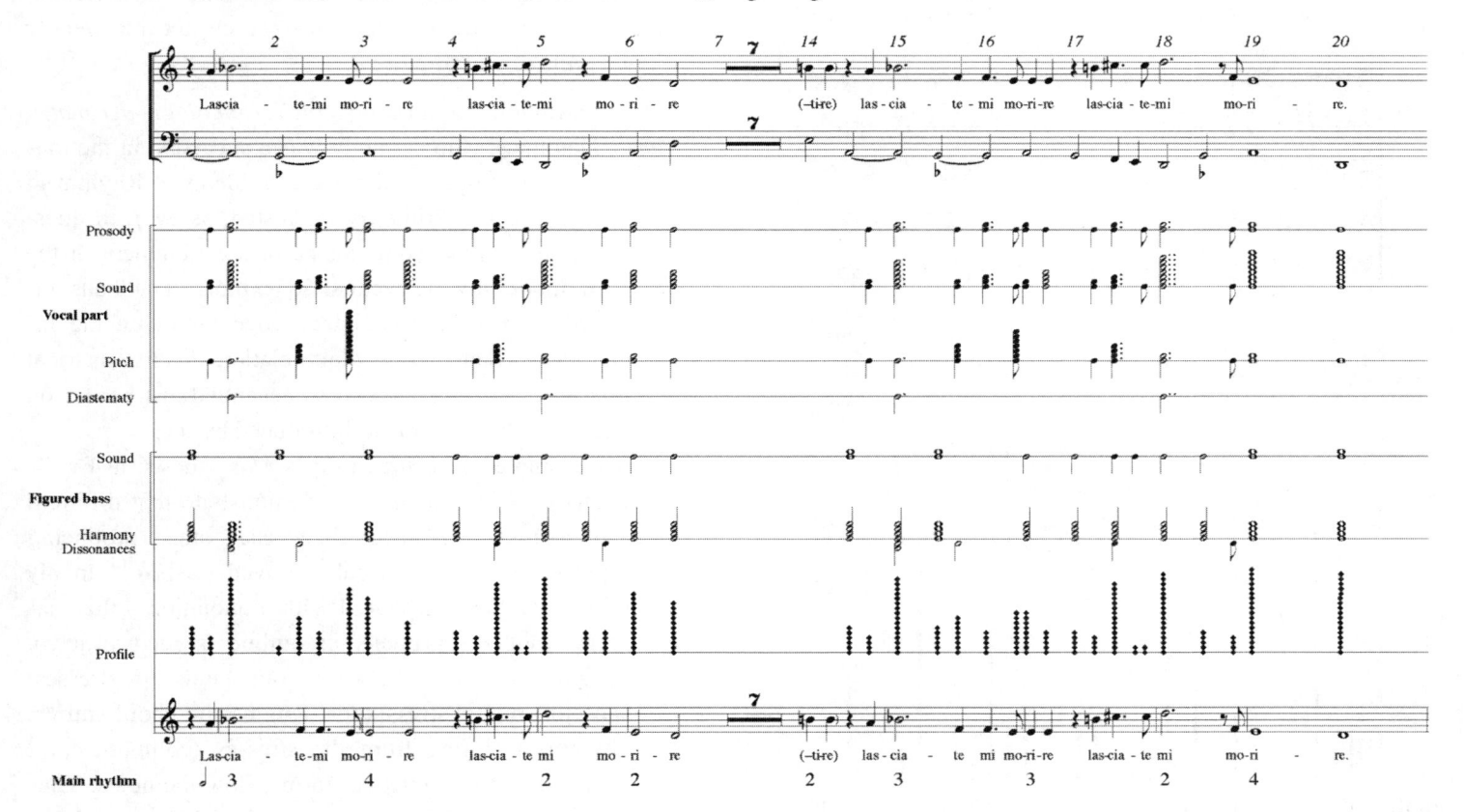

He hesitates to use the term measure, only then to point out that (according to the Malipiero edition) the first three measures recur at the end of the first section shifted by one 𝅗𝅥,[353] so that either one of the two notations had to be wrong or the division into measures was metrically meaningless. In the observations that follow, however, about the handling of dissonances, »of which one expects insight into the ›metric quality‹, the weight gradation of the measure's parts (the half notes),«[354] Dahlhaus does not refer to either of the two alternatives (wrong or else meaningless bar division). Thus he misses the chance to read the first 𝅗𝅥 of the piece as an upbeat to the second 𝅗𝅥.

If one does so – and thereby accepts that the time signature C here (as elsewhere) means solely that brevises and semibrevises are to be divided imperfectly – the dissonant suspension A2/B♭4 is unproblematic. At the end of the day, Dahlhaus sees it very similarly, as he sums up by saying: »The underlying priniciple of Monteverdi's ›oratorical‹ rhythm is the idea of a side-by-side of the parts of the measure (which thus are not ›part-measures‹, strictly speaking), not one of subordination, as that rules in modern ›meter-rhythmics‹ (Taktrhythmik).«[355]

If one analyzes the piece according to the components theory, it becomes possible to obtain a picture of the rhythmic weights in place of the supposed metric ones rightly rejected by Dahlhaus. They firmly preclude the notion, which Dahlhaus likewise negates,[356] that the example is one of »unstructured, rhythmically amorphous, exclusively ›affective‹ declamation.« The rhythmic profile, instead, sets forth a kind of dominant rhythm, which combines three, four or two 𝅗𝅥 into units that, directed by the syllabic weights, resemble changing meters, though they do not involve any figuring in of metric weights (Ex. 3-086, bottom line: »Main rhythm«).

In the voice part, I posited ♪ = 1 for the weight apportionment to the tonal durations, but 𝅗𝅥 = 1 for the general bass. The ♪ value has to be regarded as a substantial magnitude in this case, when one considers how carefully Monteverdi varies, say, the upbeat syllable of »mo-rire« (cf., i.a., mm. 6 and 18). In the reiterated notes (»Pitch«), several emphatic anticipations stand out, which support the »mo-rire« now on the first, and now on the second syllable. Another notable feature is the generous design of the vocal part's range, as there is only one upper turning-point each in the »Lasciatemi« phrases. It is used by Monteverdi to emphasize the line differently: at first the weight is all on the »Lasciate,« then on the »mi.« Whether the harmonic functions should be weighted with 4 points, as I have done, or with 3, as is also conceivable, is a judgement call, as is the differentiation of the dissonances into minor seconds (relatively hard) and minor sevenths (relatively soft). These variants would make little difference to the result, however.

It is interesting and instructive to juxtapose the monodic form of the *Lamento d'Ariana* with the madrigal version. Already the attention to a mere three components rhythms (»Sound«, »Harmony« and »Prosody«) reveals a

---

[353] Ibid.
[354] Ibid.
[355] Ibid., 274.
[356] Ibid.

Ex. 3-087

Monteverdi, *Lamento d'Ariana* (Madrigalic Version), Beginning

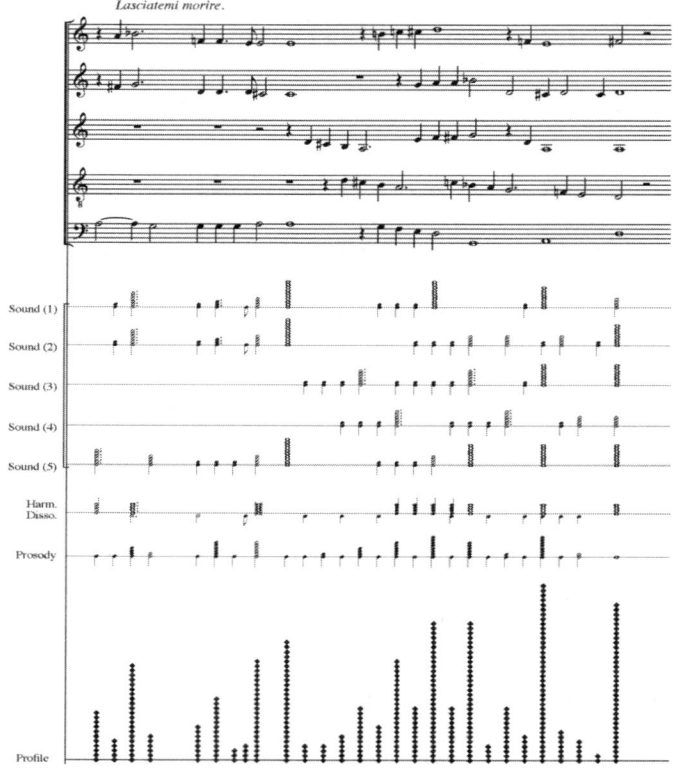

totally different rhythmic structure (Ex. 3-087). The descant of the five-part madrigal is nearly identical with the solo voice of the Ariana-Madrigal. Three times half notes are enlarged to wholes, and the melody is occasionally chromaticized (C5–C#5 as well as the final F#4). The harmonic-cadential sequence, too, remains unchanged (V–IV–V–I–IV–V–I). The imitationally conducted lower voices, which only gradually reach the full five-part setting, then cause an accumulation of durational weights (second textual line on »mi«), among which, in turn, the top note D5 stands out in the descant because of its exceptional length and weight (10). The harmonic rhythm, too, is denser than in the monodic version, as can be seen in the fully harmonized chromatic steps of the melody. Since all five voices declaim syllabically, the prosodic accents likewise multiply. Light syllables are again entered with 1 point, heavy syllables with 2; the top value is 8, because (here at the beginning) never more than four voices sing a heavy syllable simultaneously.[357]

Additional component rhythms could be included, among which the time intervals between the imitating voices (»Texture«) would claim considerable weight. But even without these additional rhythms, the rhythmic profile shows that in the madrigal variant of the *Lamento* Monteverdi was intent on dynamization and intensification. What the vocal performer of the monodic version has to master solely by expressive singing is given from the start, and brought to inevitable effect, by the setting in the choral version and the rhythm active in it. As a (rhythmically induced) metric quality, only the 𝅗𝅥 stands out, which – exactly as in the monodic version – can cluster into weakly formed units of two or more 𝅗𝅥.

In his contribution to the collection *Terminologie der neuen Musik*, Dahlhaus, who certainly was a specialist in the music of the 20th century, addressed »Problems of Rhythm in the New Music.«[358] Primarily interested, as ever, in questions of meter, whose continuance or abandonment in the music of modernity he wanted to explore, Dahlhaus incorporated diverse kinds of stress, depending on the individual case,[359] and tested their relation to the »metrical rhythmics«.[360] Stresses as well as accentuations border on the concept of the component introduced by me.

The example from Stravinsky's *Mass* shown in Ex. 3-088 is analysed by Dahlhaus to demonstrate that different forms of »stress« can »neutralize« each other, producing the impression of an »internally moved stasis.«[361] In my example – Dahlhaus dispensed with a quotation – the analysis that Dahlhaus presents in outline is reconstructed. Dahlhaus distinguishes between four kinds of stresses: word accents, metric stress, tonal lengths and chord entries. The rhythms resulting from the stresses (components) I have summarized in numerical form below the notes. Thus the several changes of meter appear as a rhythm of 3+2+4+4+3+4+4+4 ♪, as do the other entry intervals (heavy syllables: 2+2+3+3+2+3+2+2+4+2+2 ♪; tones lengthened to quarters: 3+5+3+4+3+5+2 ♪; chord repetitions: 2+3+3+2+3+2+2+3+3+2+3 ♪). Dahlhaus does not refer to these accentual sequences as rhythms. He rather proceeds from the sung text, coordinating the accents as individual events to its syllables. He writes: »An analysis of the ›Laudamus te‹ shows that Stravinsky realizes in every textual syllable at least one possibility of emphasis and in no syllable more than two.« Thus is produced the seeming »arrest of time […] that Stravinsky has in mind.«[362]

I think this reading is exaggerated. If one regards the time intervals between the emphases as durations and these as rhythms, additional phenomena become recognizable.

---

[357] In the seconda parte, Monteverdi has the words »Teseo mio, si« declaimed once in five homophonic parts (m. 11), so that the three heavy syllables here acquire the weight value of 10.

[358] Dahlhaus (1965) (see footnote 345).

[359] Ibid., 31.

[360] Dahlhaus, in this essay, speaks consistently (and frequently elsewhere) of »metrical rhythmics«, which meets my own approach in part. I regard the basic principle of meter, its isometry, as a rhythmic phenomenon. As repeatedly set forth in this treatise, isometric structures can be recognized by observing components rhythms, so that the time signature is the result of (and not just prescription for) the composition.

[361] Ibid.

[362] Ibid.

Ex. 3-088   Stravinsky, *Mass*, »Laudamus Te«, Beginning (Transcript)

For one thing all four of the textual lines are teleological orientated: each time the »Te« forms a caesura, since it is isolated, there being no musical activity under the second half of the ♩. It is also noteworthy that the chord sung to the »Te« by the chorus is the same each time, regardless of what harmonies precede it. There is thus unmistakable phrasing within this first passage of the »Laudamus«, which I have marked by broken vertical lines in Ex. 3-088. The length of these phrases is always 1 or 2 ♪ longer than the sentence has syllables (4+1 ♪; 6+2 ♪; 5+2 ♪; 6+2 ♪).

The component rhythm »Chord« (winds) makes clear that in this layer of the setting Stravinsky forms heterometric measures. If one listens to the wind chords as a separate layer and ignores the conventional notation with ties across the bar lines (see my transcription),[363] one can hear the heterometric 5–, 8–, 7– and 8–eighths measures. The ratio of the last of these irregular ›beats‹ to the last choral chord – the »Te« sound – is the same each time.

It is interesting that this principle of recurrence in subsequent bars, which Dahlhaus did not consider in his analysis, continues. Though the text changes, the compositional construction does not. There is even a kind of rondello that forms itself (see Ex. 3-090): the melody of the line »Benedicimus Te«, which the line with the text »Glorificamus Te« repeats exactly, also underlies the lines »Agimus Tibi« und »Gloriam tuam«. In the Ex. this is represented by the descant voice, but the identity is present in all the voices of the chorus and the brasses.

In order to be able maintain the initially installed rhythm of the voices, Stravinsky, from m. 9 on, inserts melismas, even if the pitch has to remain unchanged (»Gratias«). Unlike what happens at the beginning, the music in this second part of the section thus clearly dominates over the text. The altogether 16 bars of this section of the »Laudamus Te« (fig. 13 and 14) are thus structured by four mu-

sically identical 8/8 phrases, which alternate with shorter phrases of changing durations. The passage thereby acquires a downright metrical regularity, in contrast to the impression of a rhythmic neutrality felt by Dahlhaus. One can perhaps sum up by saying about this passage from Stravinsky's *Mass* that what was in the mind of the composer was less an »arrest of time« than the severity of a ritualistic ceremonial. The rhythm is clearly and audibly structured by the repetitions and lacks any subjective element such as is certainly possible in mass settings of other composers.

Ex. 3-090   Stravinsky, *Mass*, »Laudamus Te«, Discanti

Dahlhaus' reflections on rhyhm and meter in diverse eras of ›occidental‹ music are manifold, stimulating and in the detail also enlightening. If he did not break through to a genuinely new conception of rhythm, it is, in my view, because he did not take the step of interpreting metric order strictly rhythmically. That is possible only if all of a musical work's components relevant to an epochal style are recognized as rhythm-building and the respective rhythms are related to each other. Hand in hand with that would go the retirement of the concept of accent, to be replaced by the more neutral concepts of »component,« meaning sound event or change, and »rhythmic weight.« Whatever happens in sound can have consequences for the rhythm, irrespective of whether it is stressed or unstressed.

---

[363] In the original, the first B♭ trumpet is notated thus:

NB 3-089

Ex. 3-091   Mozart, Piano Sonata F Major K. 533, 2nd mov., Beginning

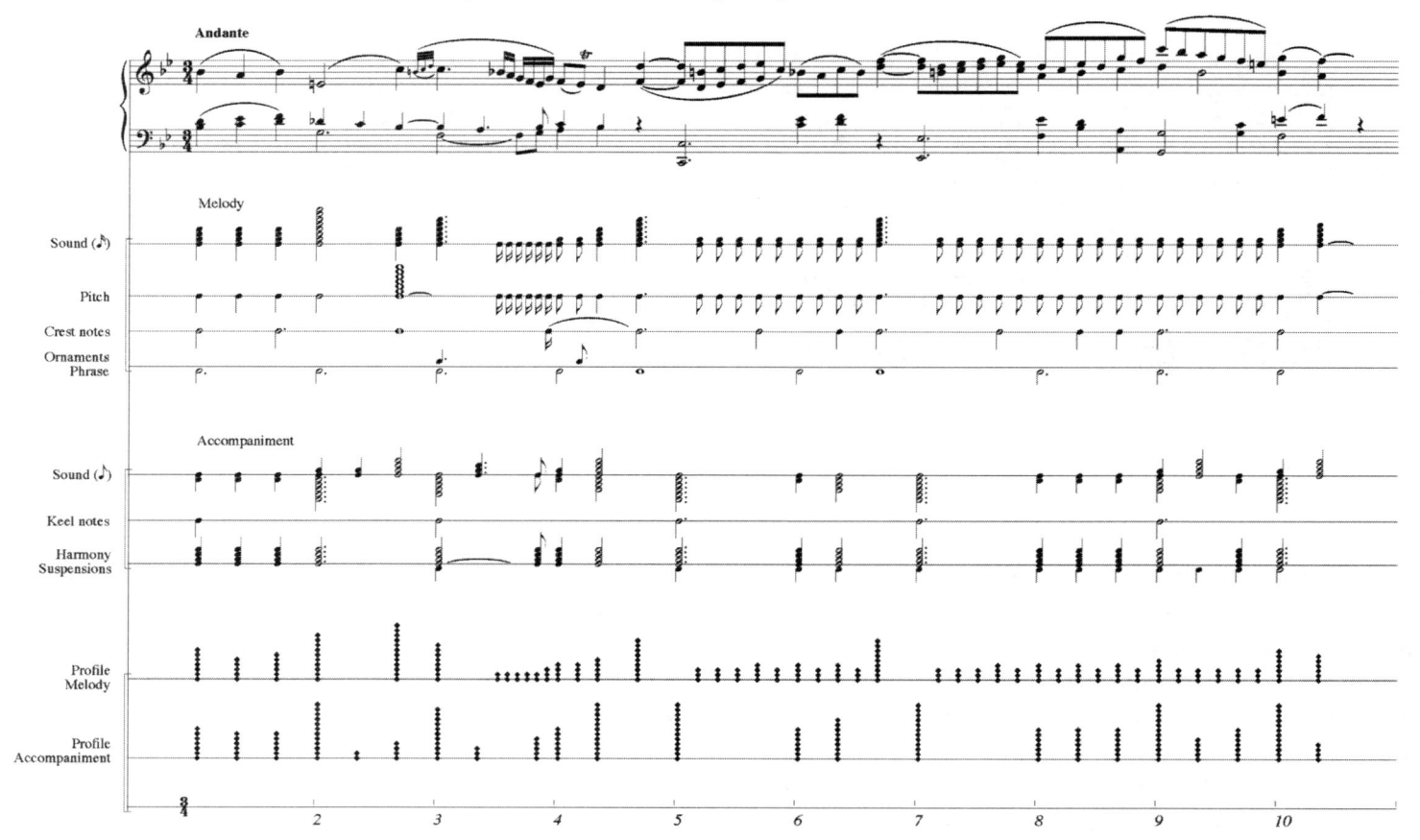

Erpf • Form and Structure in Music

Hermann Erpf's *Form and Structure in Music*, his ambitious attempt to set forth »laws« of musical formation independent of history and cultural region, also incorporates the area of rhythm and meter.[364] The starting-point of his reflections is the individual »musical note,« said to be determined »unequivocally« by its four »properties or qualities« »pitch, volume, duration and timbre.«[365] In line with these qualities, Erpf distinguishes formative categories, understood as the establishment of relations between notes: melodic, dynamic, rhythmic and timbre relations.[366] Already on the most elementary level of musical formation »additional properties« accrue, »which do not pertain materially to them,« that is, »the harmonic and the metric quality«.[367] The latter Erpf traces back to physiological (pulse) and psychological (expectations) conditions, regarding the metric »Betonung« (stress), coming »from the area of tonal volume,« as the historically given »normal case.«[368]

Rhythm and meter are entirely different domains for Erpf. He spells out the following terminological principle:

For the purpose of our inquiry, the expression »rhythmics« is to designate only the tonal durations and durational conditions that pertain to *every* tone and are »objectively« measurable. »Metrics,« on the other hand, is to mean those weight relations that are only »subjectively« given in musical life and can be produced or else avoided by the suitable arrangement of the tonal material.[369]

The principal problem in Erpf's approach is his tying the aspect of duration to the individual note. Only the written note value is to be accepted as an »objective« duration and thus the sole basis for the formation of rhythms. Referring to a theme in Mozart's piano sonata K. 533, Erpf writes about a »differentiated rhythmic shape,« which, however, because »the accompanying voices still proceed in mostly simple subdivisions,« would still be »understood within the timing of the meter.«[370] That is true enough, but one will hardly be able to gauge the theme's actual degree of complexity with a conception of rhythm as narrow as this of Erpf's is.

The subject of the slow movement of Mozart's late F-major sonata (Ex. 3-091) is one of truly classical beauty and ex-

---

[364] Hermann Erpf, *Form und Struktur in der Musik* (Mainz, 1967). In his introduction, Erpf writes: »This ›general theory of form‹ does not ask: ›What forms of musical works are there?‹, but rather ›How is form in music possible?‹, or ›Can general formal laws be found for music, and how do more specific forms derive from them?‹« (9f.).

[365] Ibid., 174f. Erpf admits that »in the context, additional qualities« could be identified (ibid.).

[366] Ibid., 176.

[367] Ibid., 180.

[368] Ibid., S. 182.

[369] Ibid., 184.

[370] Ibid., 183, also 181, the no. 5 in the example.

pressiveness. The first ten bars reproduced here form the first phrase of a 22-bar repeat period, without the 12-bar consequent actually fulfilling the expectation generated (the 1st phrase diverges into the dominant, the consequent modulates all the way to the secondary dominant). Modeled on the pattern of main voice and accompaniment, the right and left hand work together to produce a steady ascent to a high point in the penultimate measure (see C6). The rhythmic weights, which I have ascertained by components analysis and represented separately (profile Melody and profile Accompaniment), coincide at the beginning and again at the end. They here mark the first beats of mm. 1, 2 and 10, with large profile peaks in both parts. In mm. 2 to 9, on the other hand, the main weights of the right and left hand diverge. Remarkably, not only the melody-carrying voice exhibits large weights on light beats, but the secondary voices, too, twice place heavy weights on light beats (mm. 4 and 6), owing to harmonic changes and tonal lengthenings.

As for the degree of differentiation of the main voice, one has to consider no fewer than five components to obtain an adequate picture of its rhythmic structure. Erpf documents the »more differentiated rhythmic shape« of the main voice solely by copying the succession of note values (Ex. 3-092).[371]

Ex. 3-092 (Erpf)

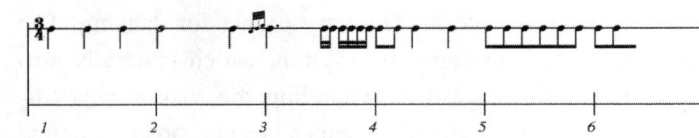

It may be symptomatic of his fixation on the notation that he overlooks the tie-over from m. 4 to m. 5 and thus misses one of the syncopations that are so characteristic of this melody. Since two thirds of the theme consist mainly of eighths runs in the right hand, the rhythm purely of the tonal durations, if Erpf had continued to write it out, would have been pretty monotonous. In reality, it is different components that provide rhythmic diversity here, above all the component »Diastematy,« which, with its crest notes, forms a quiet rhythm of ♩., ♩ und ♩ from m. 4₃ on.

Mozart counters the quasi-syncopated crest tone rhythm with isometric sequences of ♩. (phrasing slurs, component »Phrase«). Only in the above-mentioned anticipations in mm. 4 and 6 do the phrasing slurs, too, begin before the measure does. At any rate, however, this finding can demonstrate that the tension supposedly existing only between free rhythmic flowing and lawfully retained meter actually builds up already between the different component rhyhms of the monophonic melody.

With one exception, there are no repetitions in this theme. The exception occurs in the transition from m. 2 to m. 3. If one grants that the slide-like embellishment on the

One of m.3 does not cancel the pitch of the main note C5, the durational value of this pitch amounts to 10 ♪, starting from the 3rd quarter of m. 2. This lengthening of the pitch proves to be a phenomenon related to the already discussed tonal anticipations in mm. 4 and 6, as it likewise leads to a weight shift to before the One.

The accompanying voices progress »in simple subdivisions«, as Erpf correctly notes.[372] The unit for determining their weight is the ♪, whereas for the main voice the ♪ was chosen (Ex. 3-091). Even so, the weight peaks in the profile of the accompaniment are still considerable, largely due to the harmonic function changes. The sum of eleven suspensions (downward-stemmed) helps additionally to bring out the metric beats, and isometric sequences generally, in the accompanying voices.

Of rhythmic significance are also the few long and low notes (C - E♭ - G mm. 5ff.) in the left hand. They occur at a distance of six ♩ from each other, thus structuring the second half of the theme by double bars. This goes along with the briefly touched-on sequence in the main voice, which starts from the repeatedly mentioned syncopated anticipations and is likewise divided into double measures.

The component rhythms thus demonstrated in the main and accompanying voices are no less »objectively« present than the tonal durations in the main voice that Erpf accepts as the sole rhythm. His basically correct remark that »the leading melody is still understood within the timing of the meter«[373] can be extended to the rhythm of the theme in its entirety, which while following the isometric pattern of the 3/4 time, nevertheless elaborates it variationally and, in fact, *produces* it rhythmically.

Pierce • Rhythm in Tonal Music

Anne Alexandra Pierce's 1968 Ph.D. dissertation *The Analysis of Rhythm in Tonal Music*[374] picks up Heinrich Schenker's *Ursatz* theory.[375] Pierce wants to supplement theoretically and analytically what Schenker's reductive method rather loses sight of: meter and rhythm.

The work starts out by sounding as though the author intended to outline a components theory. Beginning with a simple melody with ♩ and ♪, whose succession lets the 3/4 meter appear like a matter of course, she states:

---

[371] Ibid., 181.

[372] Ibid., 183.

[373] Ibid.

[374] Anne Alexandra Pierce, *The Analysis of Rhythm in Tonal Music*, Ph.D. diss., Brandeis University (MA), 1968.

[375] See Oswald Jonas: *Introduction to the theory of Heinrich Schenker: The nature of the musical work of art*, transl. John Rothgeb (New York and London 1983). For additional sources, see David Carson Berry, *A Topical Guide to Schenkerian Literature: An Annotated Bibliography with Indices* (Hillsdale, NY, 2004).

However, these elements most obviously thought of as articulating the ›Flow‹ of the composition […] are not the only means by which the compositional flow is divided into parts. A change in any of the musical elements – pitch, timbre, dynamics, register, texture – creates a division of the time span.[376]

»Division of time span,« however, means rhythm for A. Pierce; that is, any suitable sound event, and any change in tonal quality, can result in rhythms. She documents this with two self-constructed examples (Ex. 3-093 and 3-094) transformed by her into a rhythm score.

Ex. 3-093

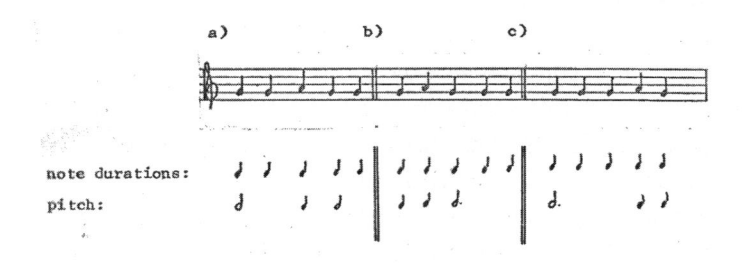

Ex. 3-094

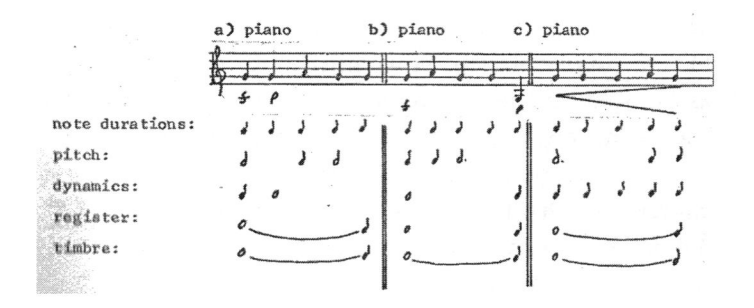

The first example (Ex. 3-093) comprises two simultaneously perceived rhythms: the durations of the sounded notes and the durations of the pitch changes. In the second example (Ex. 3-094) Pierce even identifies five different rhythms within a monophonic tonal sequence, derived from tones, pitches, volume marks, octave registers and timbre. Unfortunately, Pierce drops this approach to a rhythm analysis, the reason being her evident commitment to the Schenker method. If she had pursued what she sketched out in her »Introduction,« she might have come up with a kind of components theory.

As a prime example for her subsequent discussion, the author selects a piano piece by Franz Schubert (Ex. 3-095).[377] It has a simple bipartite periodic dance form, whose two eight-bar units are repeated. The first period begins and ends in the tonic of B♭ major; the half-close in the 4th measure remains likewise in the tonic but cannot provide closure because of the melody's caesura on the fifth and the continuing waltz accompaniment. The second period briefly diverges to E♭ major via a secondary dominant, but then, after a mere four bars, already forms an authentic cadence in B♭ major by means of a long-held suspension six-four chord (mm. 13-15).

The homophonic, purely chordal piano composition is modeled on the pattern of melody and accompaniment. The melody in the right hand, which is harmonized throughout in three voices, begins upbeat, while the left hand, with its accompanying pattern of a low bass note on the *One* and off-beat quarter notes on the *Two* and *Three* are throughout downbeat (note the quarter rests at the start of mm. 1 and 9). It may be asumed that the few dynamic accents (> and *fp*) are to be realized by the right hand; only the *f* in the upbeat to m. 9 and the decrescendo in m. 12 are probably executed by the left hand as well.

Four components pertain to the rhythm of the right hand: »Sound,« »Pitch,« »Diastematy,« (here restricted to the crest notes) and »Dynamics.« Taken by itself, the basic rhythm consisting of the durations of the notes struck already lets the triple meter emerge clearly, supported throughout by the dynamic accents (and of course by the accompaniment). Even the crest notes fall on the heavy beats. The rhythm is enlivened mainly by the note repetitions, which frequently introduce a new pitch ahead of the main beats (rhythmic anticipation).

In the accompaniment, too, a mildly syncopated pitch rhythm (| ♩ ♩ |) results from the nearly consistent tone repetitions on the *Two* and *Three*. In addition, the keel notes in the left hand provide the isometry proper for dancing. The same goes for the harmonic rhythm, which generally emphasizes double measures (including the suspensions [directly below the line] and cadences [second position below the line]). Of note here is the anticipated secondary dominant before m. 9 (B♭^{7}), which for once underscores the upbeat of melody and phrase.

If one now compares Pierce's representation of the rhythm of this Schubert piece (Ex. 3-096),[378] it can be seen that even on the level of detailed analysis (»foreground«) most of the components relevant to the rhythm are left out. The only component included is the pitch rhythm, whose anticipatory effects Pierce highlights with slurs. But why just this component, since generally it is the durations between sounded notes that are regarded as the most important basic rhythm? The reason is probably again the model of the Schenker analyses, which seek to determine the nexus of a composition primarily via the disposition of pitches. Since according to the »Ursatz« model every melodic line exhibits a natural slope toward the tonic, all intervening notes are »prolonging« ones, that is, notes directed toward the concluding resolution in a graded importance: first the notes of the triad, then the transitions, and finally the changing notes.

---

[376] Pierce, 3.

[377] Ibid., 24 and passim.

[378] Ibid., 31.

Ex. 3-095 Schubert, Deutscher Tanz op. 33 No. 7

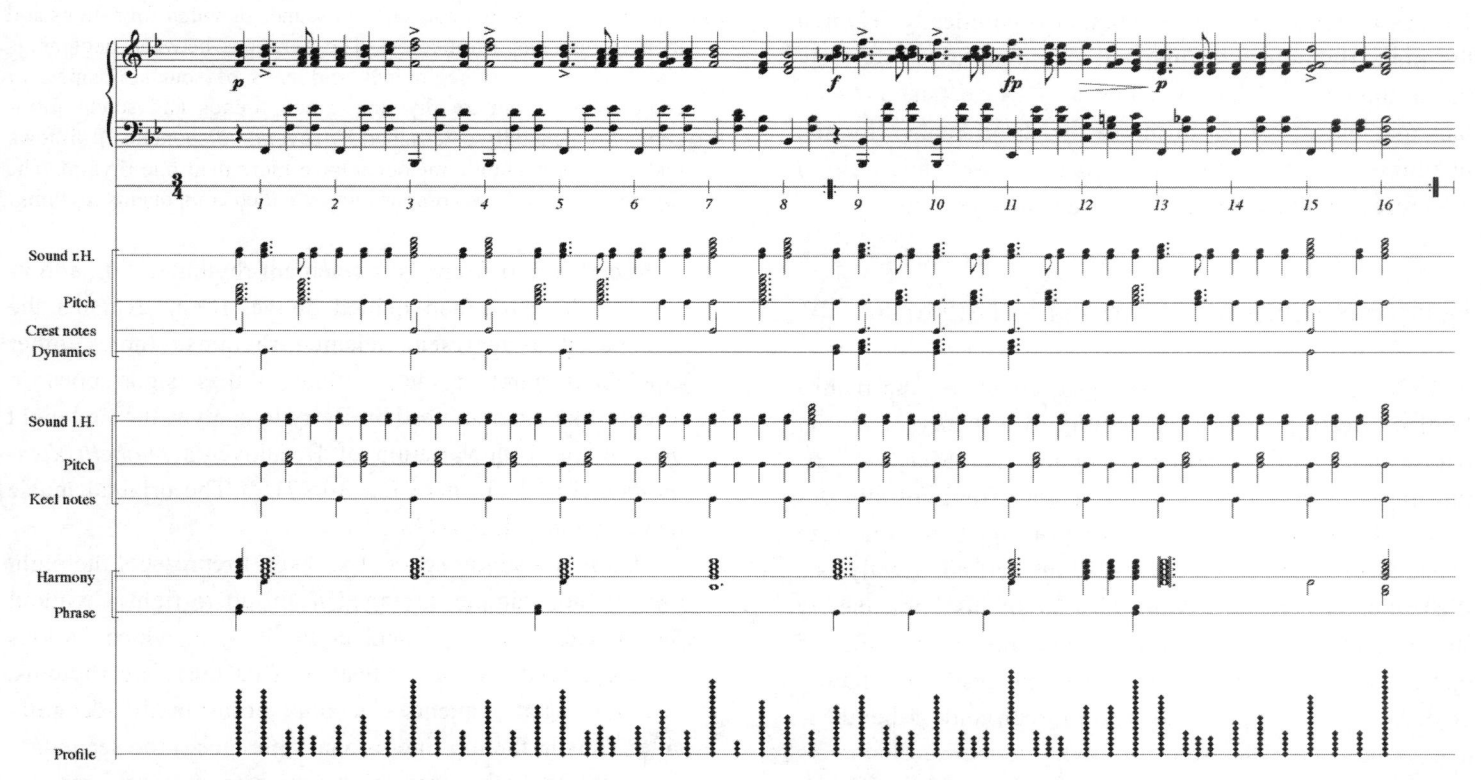

As a comparison of the three »levels« foreground, middleground and background will show at a glance, the melody tones F5–E♭5–D5–C5–B♭4 are the ones that are effective even in the background. The problem in Pierce's application of the Schenkerian model to rhythm analysis resides in the fact that she regards the notes qualified by »structural accents« as the most important also for the rhythmic design of the voice.

In contrast to the rhythms Pierce comes up with by reduction according to the »Ursatz« – fully aware, naturally, of the increasing levels of abstraction – the rhythmic profile I have put together to include all of the component rhythms embodies the original rhythmic complexity of this admittedly simple, yet subtly swaying composition. The problem is not that Pierce operates at all with reductions, but that she applies a tonally oriented method of reduction 1:1 to the description of the principal rhythmic-metric process. A sensible reduction from a rhythmic perspective would start out from the bipartite 16-bar dance form, identify its main caesura in m. 9 and secondary caesuras in m. 4 and – more faintly formed – m. 13, and then move on to motifs and individual rhythms and finally to the (differentiated) pattern of upbeats. Arrived in the ›foreground,‹ one would then take a comprehensive look at the entire rhythmic structure.

Ex. 3-096 Schubert, Deutscher Tanz op. 33 No. 7 (Pierce)

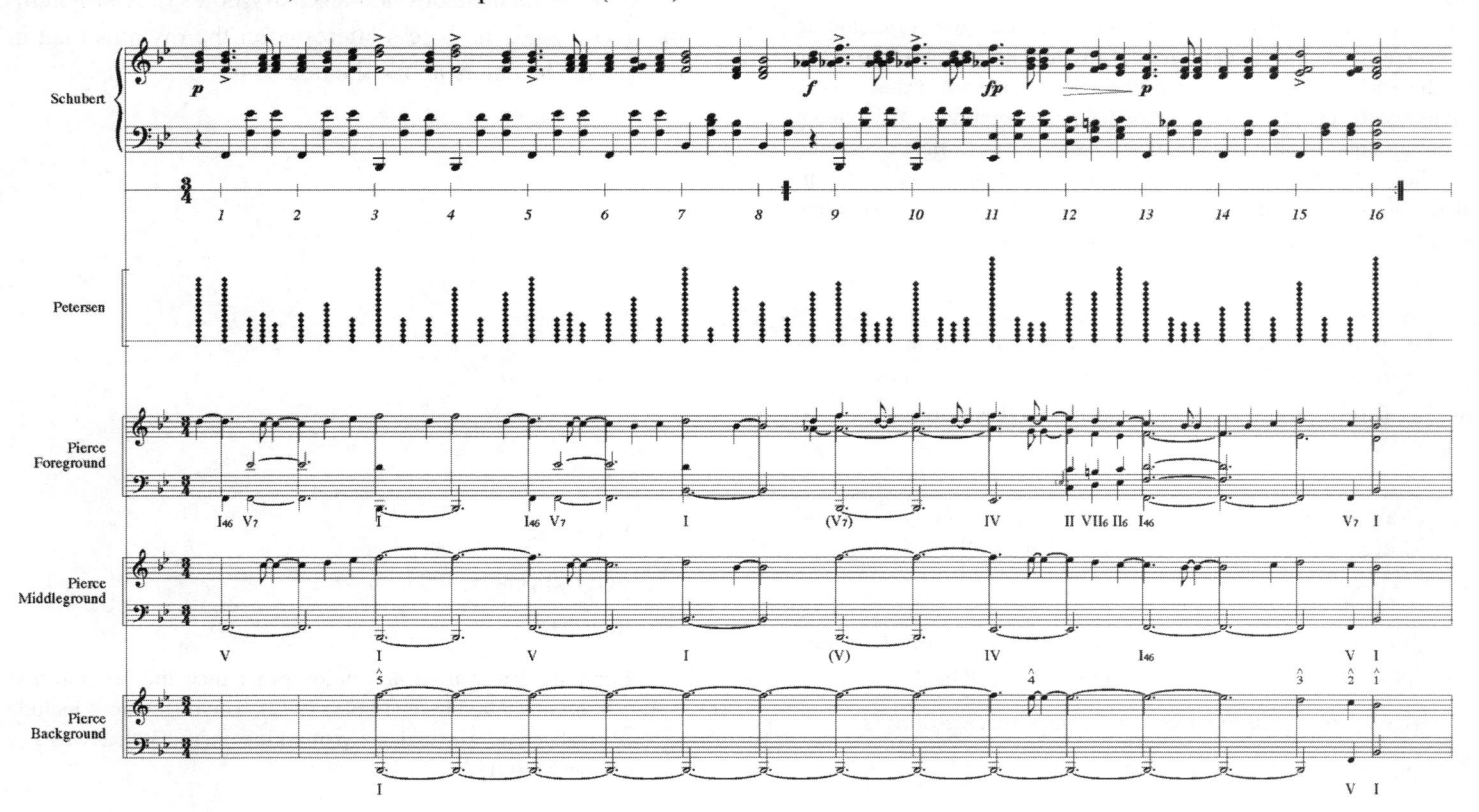

That would also include the observation that of the piece's 16 measures none resembles another rhythmically. Though the main rhythmic weights (tall rhombus towers) clearly reveal the ternary beat – whether as 3/4 or 6/4 meter – the fact that the measures differ in the detail makes for the liveliness of the composition, which is observable only in the »foreground« and not at all in the »background.«

Berry • Structural Functions in Music

In 1976, the American musicologist, composer and pianist Wallace Berry published something of a theory of music, whose third part is entitled »Rhythm and Meter.«[379] Its illustrative background is music history from Josquin des Prez to Pierre Boulez. In contrast to many U.S. American music theoreticians, Berry regarded himself not exactly as a ›Schenkerian,‹ as the rhythm chapter of his book clearly shows. Here he states explicitly that the dependence of metric structures on tonal background processes »is sharply denied«.[380] It was the events in the foreground of the music that to him were decisive for rhythmic-metric characters and processes.

Berry adopted a statement of Cooper and Meyer's, who wrote in 1960: »To study rhythm is to study all of music. Rhythm both organizes, and is itself organized by, all the elements which create and shape musical processes.«[381] However, he did not then follow the finally heavily simplifying approach of his two older colleagues, but endeavored to do full justice to the diversity and complexity of rhythmic and metric relations in art music. Under the rubric »The rhythms of element successions,« Berry posits some principles:[382]

… the important principle that *every structural element is, in its distributions and qualities of events, expressive of rhythm*. There is thus a rhythm of pitch-line (rhythm seen of course as including meter), a harmonic rhythm, a tonal rhythm, and a rhythm of each of the other elements and parameters of musical events. These rhythms are preeminently: (1) of pacing or tempo – the rate of event articulation and change; (2) of pattern, as manifest in varying durational combinations; (3) of proportions, comparative durational relations among units, or groups of events; and (4) of relative qualities of events and event-successions – degrees (distances) of change, of accent.

If one equates components with elements, these maxims correspond roughly to my first thesis on components theory, as formulated in the introduction to this book:[383]

Musical rhythms are dependent on sounds or sound formations and their components (properties). The durations between beginnings and beginnings, or beginnings and ends of sounds, shapes, or components constitute rhythms. Since sounds and sound formations are generally determined by several components, it follows that even monophonic melodies have more than one rhythm. The rhythms derived from components are called components rhythms.

A crucial term of Berry's is »element-rhythm«.[384] In a footnote to the paragraph quoted above, Berry explains the signs used to represent »element-rhythms« (notes, other graphemes, numbers, etc.).[385] Some of these signs appear in a score-like diagram uesd by Berry to analyze the first eight bars of the 14th variation of Beethoven's *Diabelli-Variationen* (Ex. 3-6b, here Ex. 3-097).[386] The original music text is given in Ex. 3-098.[387]

Berry's analytic score (Ex. 3-097) represents the eight bars of the example, arranged from left to right – without the upbeat in m. 1 – and eight lines, in which various »element-rhythms« are indicated. That these are rhythms, i.e., durational sequences, is only occasionally recognizable. Thus in the top line (»tonal reference«) the secondary dominants, which announce a new reference key, are entered with their position in the 4/4 meter, but not the distances (durations) between these tonal »events.« The legend then speaks about »a strong event,« which makes clear that Berry really means accents, though he is talking about rhythms.

In the line »Harmony,« Berry enters function changes, but not (or only partly) the durations resulting from the length of a certain function. For example, the duration of the initial tonic (7 ♩) is no more recorded than the duration of the D^7 (8 ♩). At the end, admittedly, Berry has noted the harmonic-rhythmic processes very preccisely on two levels: harmonic function changes (downward-stemmed) and anticipations or suspensions and auxiliary notes (upward-stemmed). But again he is less interested in the rhythms than in the accents he enters above the notes.

---

[379] Wallace Berry, *Structural Functions in Music* (Englewood Cliffs, 1976). Ch. 3: »Rhythm and Meter,« 301-424.

[380] Ibid., 321.

[381] Grosvenor W. Cooper and Leonard B. Meyer, *The Rhythmic Structure of Music* (Chicago and London, 1960), 1.

[382] Berry, *Structural Functions*, 313; emphases are Berry's.

[383] Introduction, 7, above.

[384] Berry, 313.

[385] Berry, appendix, 420 n.

[386] Ibid., 315.

[387] Berry evidently used an edition other than the original text edition consulted here (Henle, 1972). The differences include several legato slurs and a *p* marking in m. 3 that was not known to Berry.

Ex. 3-097 (Berry, p. 315)

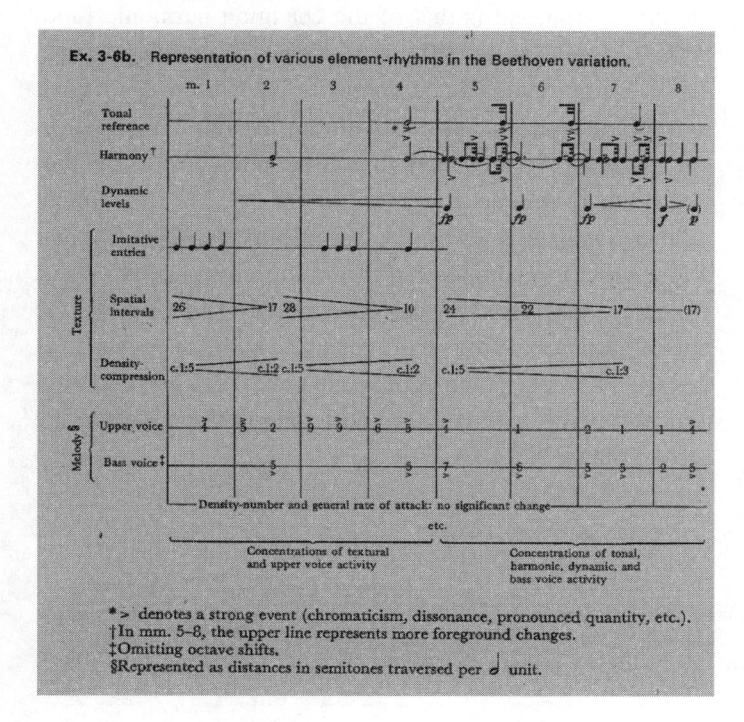

Ex. 3-6b. Representation of various element-rhythms in the Beethoven variation.

* > denotes a strong event (chromaticism, dissonance, pronounced quantity, etc.).
† In mm. 5–8, the upper line represents more foreground changes.
‡ Omitting octave shifts.
§ Represented as distances in semitones traversed per 𝅗𝅥 unit.

Ex. 3-098 Beethoven, *Diabelli Variations* No. XIV, Beginning

Overall, Berry's analytic references are rather few and not very precise. The harmonic rhythms, for example, can be traced very exactly by means of a harmonic extraction (Ex. 3-099). The same goes for the core melody of the main voice, whose overall structure Berry indicates only vaguely under the aspect of »Spacial intervals« (l. 5, Ex. 3-097; and cf. again Ex. 3-099). Moreover, the rhythm of the distances between entries of imitating voices should be ascertained. (Berry, for example, does not address the motif in the bass in m. 2 or the sixth-chord version of that motif in m. 4.) I do not understand Berry's numerical analysis of the »Upper voice.« The interval notations for the lower voice (»Bass voice«), too, are questionable, since the alternation between

Ex. 3-099 Core melody and extraction of harmonies

fourth (5) and fifth (7) do not follow any recognizable criteria and the only chromatic step (A–A♯ in m. 7) goes unnoted and uncommented. Especially infelicitous I find the incoherent manner of representing the ›rhythms‹: it hampers the recognition of the interaction between the »element-rhythms« that is Berry's chief concern.

A components-rhythmic analysis offers several advantages here. Its method of representation is that of the »rhythm score,« in which the individual component rhythms are coordinated with the actual music text as in a regular score, so that one can quickly see which rhythms coincide at any given point in time and which don't.

In this Beethoven variation (No. XIV), the homophonic composition is based from beginning to end on a rhythm characterized by double dots. In the first part, the short values, which in the left hand appear as 32nds, are split into 64ths in the upper and middle voices. The constantly recurring figure created thereby has hardly any motivic quality: its function is basically that of a modifying presentation of the core melody, whose notes mostly pace in quarters among the notes of the triad. The second part (from m. 4₄) dispenses with the animating 64ths. The thematic rhythm now appears in pure form, with simple, undotted quarters occurring in regular intervals. To compensate for the simplified rhythm, the now steadily rising core melody repeatedly touches on chromatic auxiliary notes, owing to a modulatory process that unexpectedly cadences, not in the dominant of C major, as the theme of the variation would suggest, but in its parallel key of E minor.

Ex. 3-100 mm. 5–8, Sound Rhythm

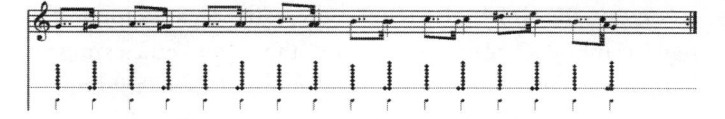

The essential feature of this character varation is thus its uniform mode of motion. The 64ths have no intrinsic value but modify the 32nds like appogiaturas and should therefore also be included as such in the rhythm analysis. That is to say, while they do not constitute the smallest value for determining the durational weights, they do, on the other hand, add a weight grade above the 32nds in the component rhythms »Articulation« and/or »Ornament«. The principal rhythm abstracted from the tonal or chordal entries has a purely isometric shape (♩) in the second phrase of the period (Ex. 3-100).

In addition to the tonal entries, tone repetitions play an important role, because they lead to a shift in pitch. Looking only at the upper voice and again at mm. 5–8, one can

Ex. 3-101 mm. 5-8, Sound Rhythm plus Pitch Rhythm

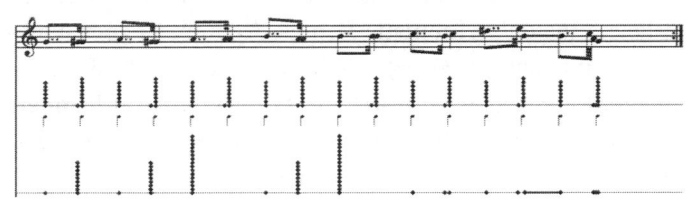

see that the individual pitch changes come sometimes before the beat and sometimes with it. Alternately with the prime rhythm of the tonal entries, the resulting bizarre pitch rhythm (Ex. 3-101) leads to an accentuation of the 32nds, which thereby gain a special pitch weight. The long durations of the notes A4 and B4 (16 32nds each) likewise impact the total rhythm.

Of the remaining components relevant to this example, the most important is that of the changing harmonic functions (see also Ex. 3-099). Some dissonant auxiliary sounds are also important. The component »Dynamics« is difficult to treat, inasmuch as swelling eludes rhythmic analysis. In our example, we thus have to confine ourselves to Beethoven's actual volume markings (*p fp f*). The component »Phrase« can in this case be based only on sense-bearing units, since the composer did not add any phrasing slurs. Going by the reconstructed core melody (Ex. 3-099), the phrase structure of this eight-bar unit can be ascertained as 2+2+1+1+2 bars (each time with upbeat). Very odd (but typical for Beethoven) is the shortening of the upbeat to the second phrase (F5 ♩ → ♪).

Ex. 3-102   mm. 1-4, Secundary Components Rhythms (upper voice)

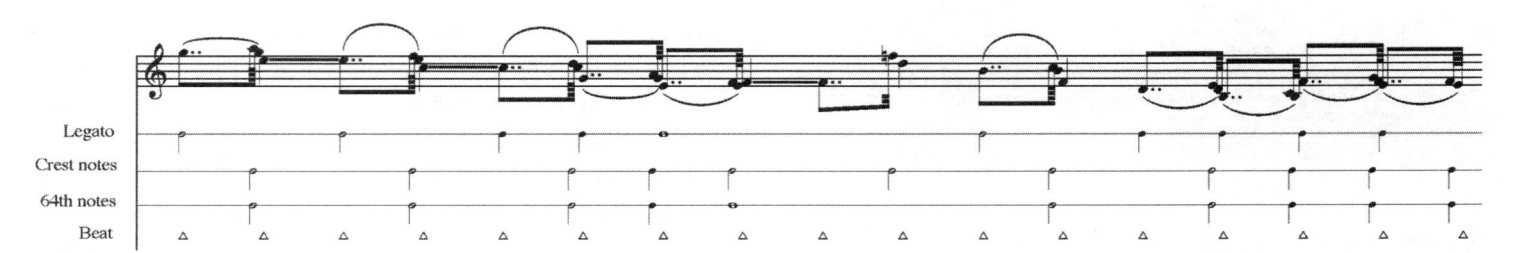

The rhythms of the components »Diastematy« (melodic contour), »Ornament« (here 64ths) and »Articulation« (here legato slurs) can be elucidated by looking at the first four bars of the upper voice (Ex. 3-102). One can see that Beethoven uses the »crest notes« to support the 32nds. Their time intervals are four or eight 32nds in length, albeit in anticipatory position vis-à-vis the beats. The same is true of the 64ths, which all sound on the 32nds of the principal rhythm. The slurs, on the other hand, mark the quarter positions of the 4/4 meter. Since the ratio of anticipating to regular impulses remains constant, the 32nd values support, in the concentus, the isometric structure of this variation.

In Ex. 3-103 I have placed the rhythmic profile beneath the musical text and chosen a strictly proportional form of representation. This gives ›objective‹ visibility to the rhythmic movements, impulses and weights the composition carries. On this basis a performer could then play freely, paying attention only to his artistic sense of feeling.

Ex. 3-103 mm. 1-8, Rhythmic Development Within a Period of 8 Measures

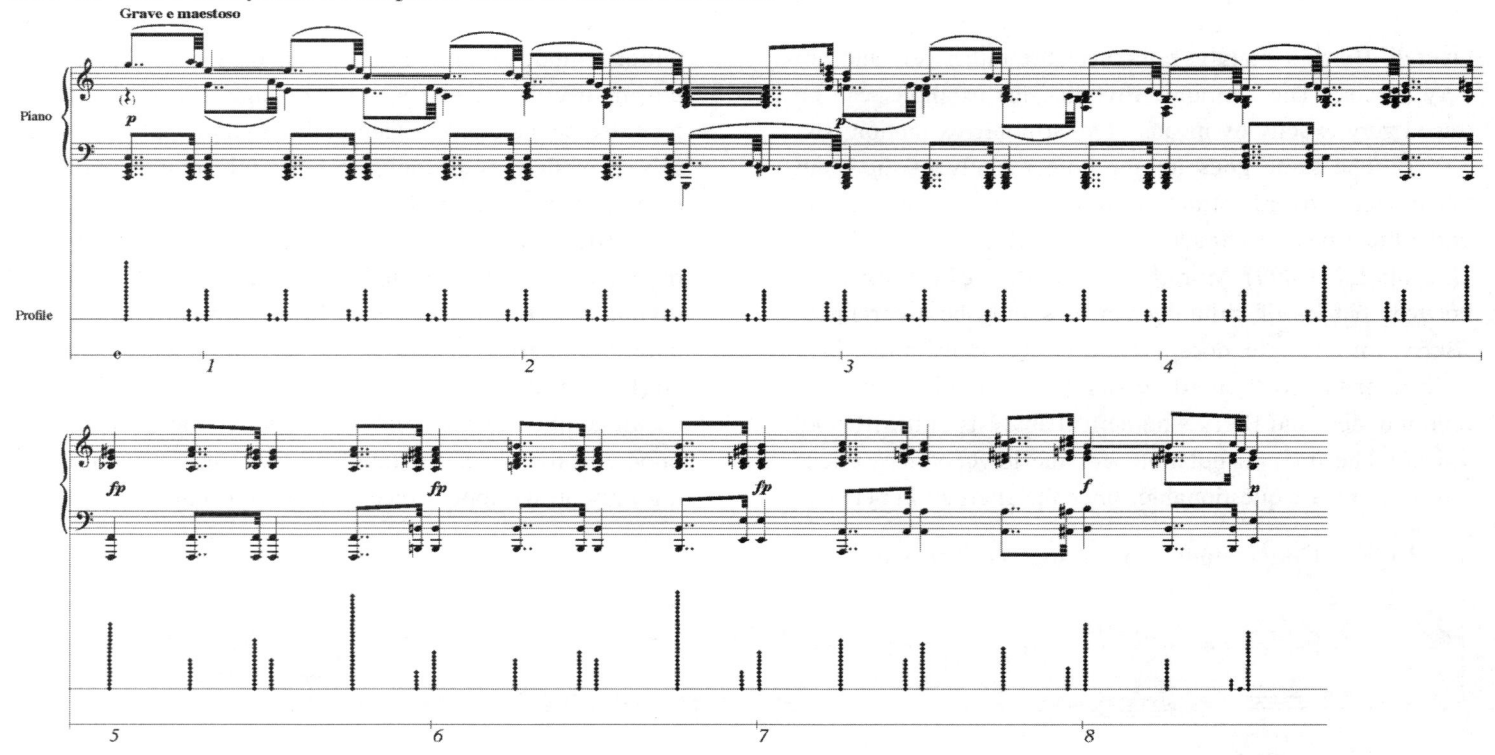

The different types of movement in the two halves of the period can be made out at a glance: nearly uniform steps at quarter intervals in the first phrase, major weight differences in the second, with the 32nds upbeats in the second phrase being accented much more heavily than those in the first. The fact that the quarter upbeat in m. 1 has a relatively large weight should not puzzle anyone, since it introduces the tonic harmony, there is a legato slur, and a phrase commences. A correspondingly large weight does not recur until seven quarter notes later: in the middle of m. 2, when the D^7 sets in, combined with a slur twice as long (left hand). From m. 4 on, however, similarly large weights appear at narrowing intervals in the profile. This phrase feels more vital rhythmically than the first, something to which certainly the top weights on the fourth beat (mm. 5, 6) and the richly sated upbeat 32nds (mm. 4→5, m. 5_2→5_3) make a contribution.

The two highest weight peaks in mm. 5 and 6 reflect the long pitch (A4 and B4), which each time begins like a syncopation before the measure and continues across the bar line. A ›normal‹ 4/4 beat is suggested only once in the rhythmic profile: in the final measure with its long fourth-sixth chord suspension. Though the quarter positions are well marked in the first phrase, the graded accent order of the measures is leveled. In the second phrase, everything is more restless and irregular. The weight on the *One* is frequently exceeded by that on the *Two*, *Three* or *Four*. While the listener is not in danger of ›losing the beat,‹ he will rather orient himself on the quarter steps and trace the main rhythm with its double dots than enact the schema of the four-part metric hierarchy mechanically within himself.

Wallace Berry will have noticed, and certainly heard, all of these findings. He writes: »The rhythms of element-actions to which the above analysis calls attention *are functionally and complementarily accelerative in the second half of the variation excerpt.*«[388] In my opinion, however, he did not succeed in developing a suitable analytic method commensurate with his listening experience. »Strong events« or »strong accents« are terms that are too vague. Thus he did not, in the end, contribute anything really new to the refinement of rhythm theory and analysis.

Yeston • Stratification of Musical Rhythm

The noted musical composer Maury Yeston capped his initial academic career with a 1974 Ph.D. dissertation on music theory: *The Stratification of Musical Rhythm*.[389] In using the concept of »Stratification,« Yeston applies aspects of the Schenkerian analytic method to the area of rhyhm and meter. His approach is innovative insofar as he assumes that in principle – that is to say, also in monophonic compositions – diverse event sequences happen simultaneously in musical processes and are also perceived at the same time. Yeston holds that the »gross rhythmic structure is in fact the resultant of all its constituent rhythmic patterns«.[390] »Rhythmic patterns« and »sub-patterns« are derived from sounds that »may vary in quality of attack, dynamic level, timbre, pitch class, pitch function, register, density, and duration.«[391] The result is an »interaction of strata»[392] and thus makes possible the generation, or derivation, of rhythmic structures.

Ex. 3-104   Mahler, 1st Symphony, 2nd mov., Beginning (Bass)

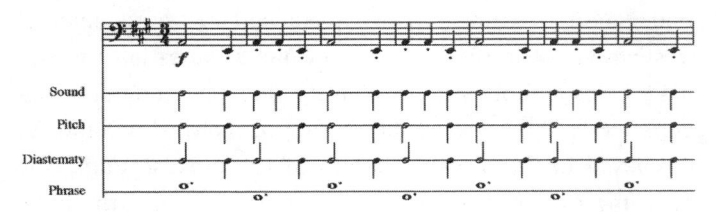

At one point, Yeston describes his manner of proceeding by looking at a very simple example taken from the beginning of the second movement of Gustav Mahler's First Symphony (Ex. 3-104). The component rhythms I have added correspond essentially to the »strata« Yeston refers to. Here is his analysis of the bass voice:[393]

1. The first two bars contain a pattern of varied durational values [Sound] linked to the pitch contour [Diastematy]. This is repeated by the next two bars. [Phrase above]
2. The attack-point rhythm [Sound] of the first bar, linked to pitch contour [Diastematy], is a sub-pattern of the second bar. By this criterion, the second bar is a recurrence of the first; i.e. foreground rhythm is different, but the attack and contour pattern of the first bar is included within it.
3. The odd-numbered bars create a stratum of motion by the recurrence of the durational pattern of the first bar [Pitch].
4. The even-numbered bars create a chain of patterns whose beginning is displaced with respect to the chain formed by the odd-numbered bars [Phrase below].

---

[388] Ibid., 315 (emphasis is Berry's).

[389] Maury Yeston, *The Stratification of Musical Rhythm* (New Haven & London: Yale University Press, 1976).

[390] Ibid., 37.

[391] Ibid., 38.

[392] Ibid., 77ff.

[393] Ibid., 51f.

I regard Yeston's approach as a preliminary stage of the components theory. What constitutes the proximity to the latter is not only that Yeston observes the properties of sounds (pitch, contour, phrasing, etc.) in isolation – they have always been included under the rubrics of accentuation and stress – but that he newly registers the durations between recurring qualities and describes their effect as a separate rhythmic level. Though he does not speak directly of contour rhythms or the like, he represents the facts in such a way as though they were rhythms (see the musical example included in his text in which the rhythm ♩ ♪♪ ♩ is represented numerically as 2 1 2 1).

I am also intrigued by Yeston's explanation of the metric hierarchy as the result of an interaction between different rhythmic levels: in a 2/4 meter, isometric pulses of ♩ work together with pulses of ♩. Beat is said to be »an outgrowth of the interaction of two levels – two differently rated strata, the faster of which provides the elements and the slower of which groups them.«[394] Oddly enough, Yeston does not advance to metric and rhythmic weights at this point. Since the two isometric »strata« of the (abstractly understood) 2/4 time – ♩♩♩♩♩ etc. and ♩♩♩ etc. – interact in such way that after every two ♩ one ♩ comes in, it would have been a short step to identify this accumulating concurrence as the cause of the feeling of metrical weight. As discussed in the second chapter of the present study, the principle of accumulation can be applied to all »rhythmic strata« – alias component rhythms – so that the weight gradations of meter can be represented as the result of interacting rhythms.

Schoenberg prefaced his brief analysis with the remark that the Mozart theme was an »enigma – not for the performer, but for the analyst interested in the grammar, the syntax, the linguistics of music.«[396] Schoenberg did not try to solve the enigma: instead, he juxtaposed several different readings of the phrasing, including two re-meterings, without deciding which one was the ›right‹ one. His primary criterion is the dynamic markings in the right hand of the piano part. What »complicated« that matter for him was the fact that five ♩ elapsed between the *sf* markings, even though the reigning meter was 4/4. Secondly, there was the shape of the melody, whose top notes F5, G5 and F5 again imposed pentadic units. Besides, the accents fell on relatively light beats (*Three* and *Four*). Schoenberg does not overlook the divergent accentuation in the cello in mm. 63 and 64, which result in a structure of four ♩. Finally he presented three variants of structuring the main voice, of which one retains the original meter, while the other two introduce a metric change (Ex. 3-106).[397]

Ex. 3-106 (Schoenberg)

Ex. 3-105   Mozart, Piano Quartet G Minor K. 478, 1st mov., Second Theme (Exposition) mm. 57-65

In the 1950 version of his famous essay, »Brahms the Progressive«, Arnold Schoenberg drew attention to an interesting passage in Mozart's Piano Quartet in G Minor, which he wanted to be understood as proof of Mozart's penchant for irregular phrase formation.[395] Schoenberg's interpretation has been repeatedly commented on since then, and Yeston, too, devotes several pages of his dissertation to it. Look at the Mozart theme in its original form (Ex. 3-105).

Yeston, too, discusses several structural variants, while distinguishing, after Heinrich Schenker, between primary and secondary notes of the »middleground motions.«[398] Of the three top notes F5, G5 and F5, the fifth (interval) is supposedly more important than the sixth, making the F5 the crucial dividing point. But since in m. 57 the first phase in the left hand of the piano began on *One*, and, besides, the quarter rests in mm. 57 and 60 corresponded to each other, the main voice commenced »not with F5 but rather with D4.«[399] In short, the structure of the theme's first phrase

---

[394] Ibid., 66.

[395] Arnold Schoenberg, »Brahms the Progressive« (see footnote 156 above), p. 95f.

[396] Ibid., 67.

[397] Ibid.

[398] Yeston, *Stratification*, 130ff.

[399] Ibid., 132 n.

presents itself like this to Yeston: mm. 57_1 to 61_2 (14+4 ♩) constituted the main stratum, mm. 57_3 to 61_2 (10+6 ♩) being a »sub-pattern«.[400]

More interesting than this rather aberrant interpretation are Yeston's remarks about the pentadic structures in the main voice already observed by Schoenberg. Starting from the three meter-related strata (♪, ♩, ♩), installed by real sound events (the ♪ in the left hand, their grouping into ♩ by octave alternations, the entry of the main voice after 1 ♩), Yeston regards the melody-carrying voice as a further stratum, based on even larger values than the ♩ and not divisible by two: the 5-♩ intervals between F5, G5 and F5. This »slower rate,«[401] however, comes about only if one executes the Schenkerian reduction, i.e., leaves out all the quarter and eighth notes between the main ones. Yet it is questionable whether this reduction, which may make sense in the analysis of cadential turns, will contribute anything to rhythm analysis. The respective notes marking the 5-♩ intervals are qualitatively defined in three ways, by length, by their crest-tone position and by the *sf* (mm. 57 and 58), or else the articulating rest (m. 60). They thus clearly stand out from the flow of the melody and can form their own components rhythms, perceived simultaneously with the basic rhythm of the tonal entries. Whereas with a reduction of the composition in terms of middle- and background, less and less rhythm remains recognizable, the components analysis leads to more and more rhythm, depending on how many components of the composition are included. I am firmly convinced that the rhythmic qualities of a composition are best ascertained from the surface happening with all details taken into account.

---

[400] Ibid. As far as the position of the theme in the metric context is concerned, Cone is right in seeing clearly that the eight-bar period is shifted by half a measure at the beginning, to be straightened out again at the end by the phrasal overlap (3-106a):

Apart from that, however. Cone does everything to efface the rhythmic peculiarities of this theme (Edward T. Cone, Communication [with respect to Peter Westergaard, »Some Problems in Rhythmic Theory and Analysis,« in: *Perspectives of New Music* 1 (Fall, 1962), 180-191] in: *Perspectives of New Music* 1 (Spring, 1963) 206-210). Joel Lester argues that »the metric hierarchy has been firmly established for many measures before the appearance of this theme« (Joel Lester, *The Rhythms of Tonal Music* (Carbondale, 1986), 81). A very different approach is taken by Claudia Maurer Zenck. She presumes that Mozart really had a theme in 3/4 meter in mind, which she construes and puts up for discussion. This assumption seems rather remote to me. See Claudia Maurer Zenck, »Gegenprobe: Das Überleben traditionellen Formdenkens bei Schoenberg,« in: *Jahrbuch des Staatlichen Instituts für Musikforschung, Preußischer Kulturbesitz 1998* (Stuttgart & Weimar: Metzler, 1998), 245-267, esp. 251-253.

[401] Yeston, *Stratification*, 133.

In the examples 3-107 and 3-109, I offer a components-rhythmic analysis of the theme for discussion. I include the version of the theme in the recapitulation, which hitherto has been considered neither by Schoenberg nor by any other analyst. This G minor variant is interesting because here a new counter-voice appears in the violin, which is also heterometrically structured but does not converge with the pentadic division of the upper, piano voice.

Let us first turn to the B♭ major version of the theme (Ex. 3-107). The rhythm analysis will be conducted separately for three areas: upper voice, lower voice(s) – in mm. 61-64 two different bass voices are to be noted – and setting. The component rhythms of the three areas are then combined in the rhythmic profile.

Because of the greater significance of the melody-carrying upper voice, I weight the durations of the basic rhythm (»Sound«) twice as heavily as the lower voice (the rate for the upper voice is ♪ = 1, that of the lower voice, ♩ = 1). For the dynamics, *p* is valued as 1, *sf* as three. The harmonic rhythm, which refers to function change irrespective of functional quality, is generally assigned the weight degree of 4.

The components »Harmony« and »Phrase,« in this case, are given some interpretive leeway. The first bar of both first and second phrase exhibits a harmonically incomplete tonal setting. Over the pedal point we hear only the melody, which is colored with lower thirds. Nevertheless, cadential motions, audible independently of the pedal point, are to be presumed. The lower voice constructed by me in Ex. 3-108 indicates these progressions: B♭ - B♭$^{5<}$ - E♭ - F - B♭$_3$ - g - E♭^{6} - F$^{6-5}$ in the first phrase and B♭ - B♭$^{5<}$ - E♭ - F - B♭$_3$ - F$^{6-5}$ - B♭ in the second (minuscules: minor).

While this harmonic interpretation will be generally agreed to, the phrasal division is more disputable. What is certain is that the slurs drawn by Mozart are legato slurs here, not phrasing slurs. In my view, which does not claim to be the only possible one, both of the falling fifths (G-C and F-B♭) are crucial for the structuration (Ex. 3-108).

Ex. 3-108 mm. 57-65 (Virtual Bass)

Now the G in m. 58_4 is notated as a tied-over ♩ in the original, the F in m. 60_1 as a ♩ followed by a rest. The tie, however, is owing to notational convention and not necessarily of rhythmic significance, while the rest at this point can be taken as an articulating one, which would be tantamount to a staccatoed ♩. Rests always have to be queried as to whether they mean a caesura between phrases or the articulation of a note. In m. 57, 𝄽 functions evidently as a caesura, while in m. 60, an articulatory rest was probably meant because the phrase ends only in m. 61.

264 Rhythm Theories

Ex. 3-107   mm. 57-65, Rhythm Score

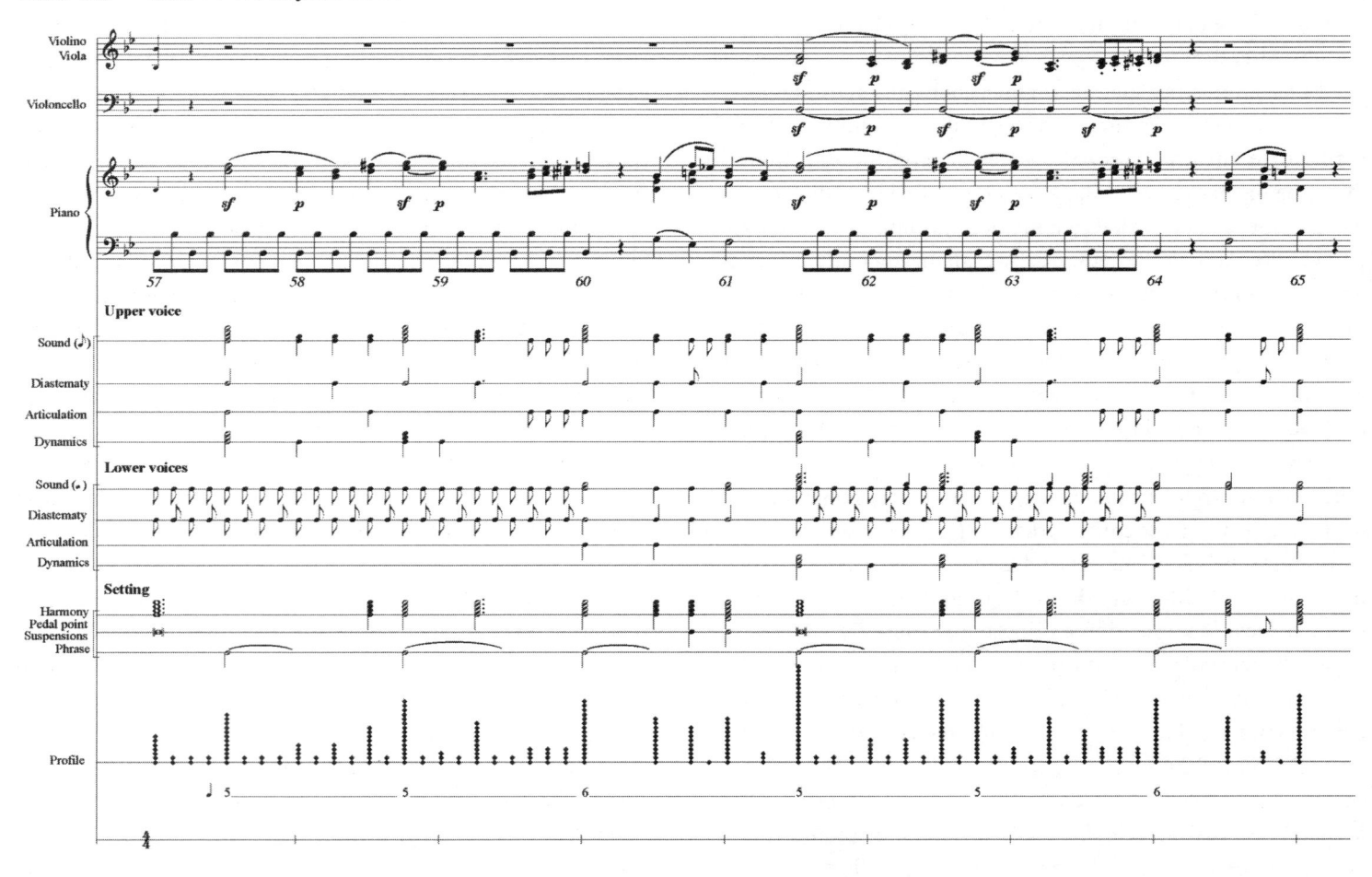

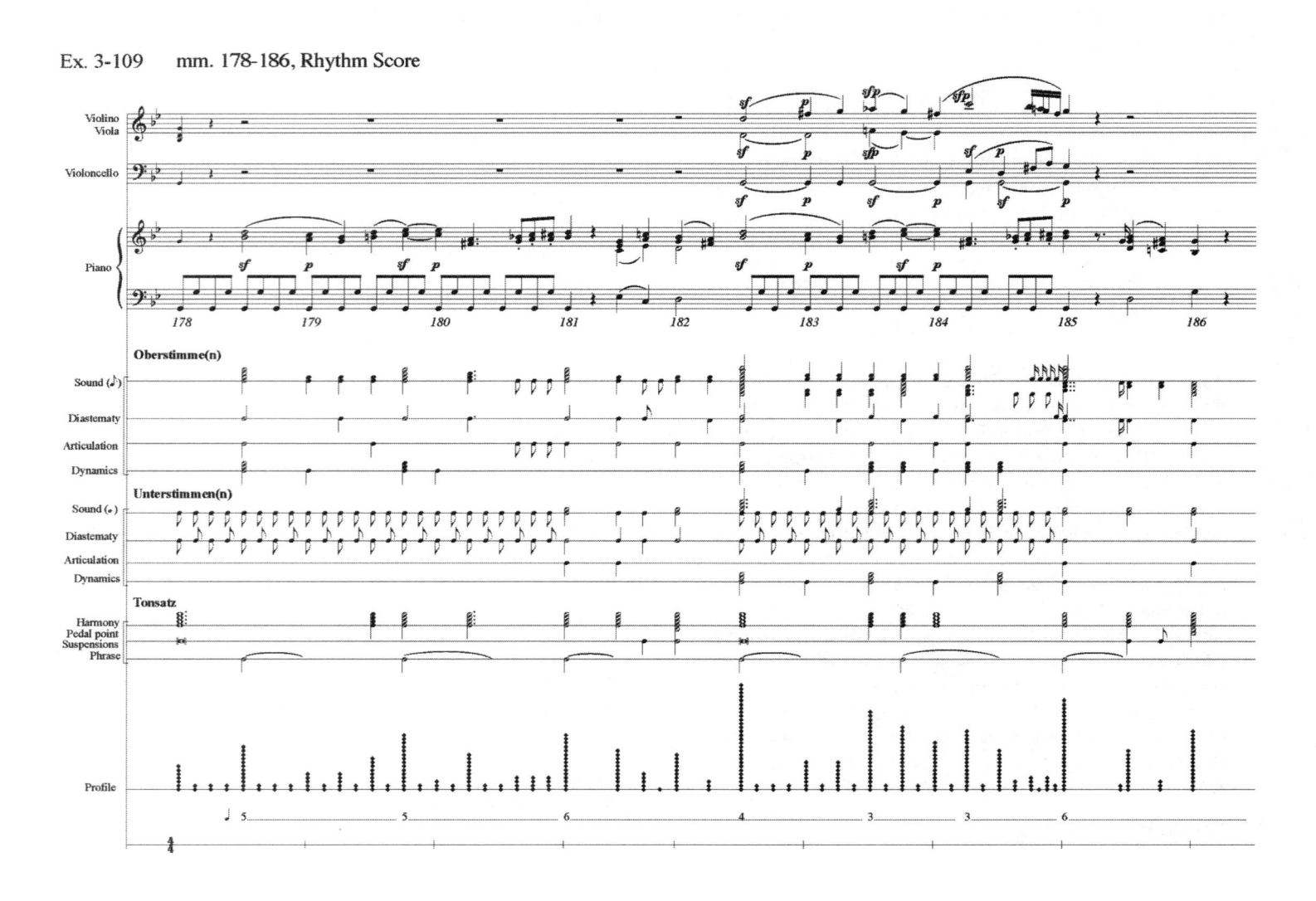

Ex. 3-109   mm. 178-186, Rhythm Score

The rhythmic profile (Ex. 3-107), which registers all the component rhythms and, if need be, also their weight profile, makes the division of the eight bars into a first and second phrase of four bars each clearly stand out. The beginning of the theme is presumed to occur on the 3rd beat of m. 57. Because of the cadences in m. 61 (open) and m. 65 (final), no other reading is possible. The ♪ coming in early in the left hand of the piano do not mark the beginning of the phrase but a lead-in, whose function lies in the connection of the first (mm. 45-57) and second (mm. 57-65) part of the B♭-major complex, which is then followed by yet a third part (mm. 65-88) prior to the concluding group.

The intriguing point is that the profile reveals the heterometric inner division of the theme's first and second phrase, and thus essentially confirms Schönberg's hypothesis. The towering thirds columns marking the accumulation of rhythmic events per point in time are at distances of 5+5+6 ♩ from each other. This is even more evident in the first phrase than in the second. There the individually formed cello voice with its durational and dynamic accents results in a high weight on the *Three* of m. 62, which slightly relativizes the accent of the main voice on the *Four* of the measure.

All in all, this – as one will have to admit – fairly objective analysis furnishes the picture of an eight-bar period shifted by half a measure within the 4/4 system, whose two phrases are heterometrically formed.

Let us now take a look also at the G minor version of the theme in the recapitulation (Ex. 3-109). In the first phrase, all the component rhythms, and thus also the rhythmic profile, are identical with those of the theme in the exposition, with the sole exception of the harmonies in m. 181. In the second phrase, however, as noted, Mozart enriches the texture with an additional voice in the violin, which, moreover, ushers in a likewise independent voice in the viola in its wake. The most striking innovation is the position of the *sfp* mark, which deviates from that in the piano. Furthermore, there are new tonal durations, new crest and keel notes, and differently drawn slurs.

Ex. 3-110   mm. 178-186 (Virtual Bass)

m. 184 (∗) makes for the entire measure's having a dominant function.

The different rhythm of the main voices and, not to forget, the cello voice, which in the second phrase appears in a regular 4/4 beat, is experienced as a rhythmic interaction by the listener. If one combines all the rhythmic events, as is done in the profile, the structuration of the new contrapuntal voices comes through. The highest rhombus towers reveal distances of 4+3+3(+6) ♩ from each other.

The last part of the phrase enclosed in parentheses (6) is to point to a fact that I have not yet addressed. The second phrases of the theme are in both instances characterized by the entry of the strings, which, however, do not then join in the conclusion. Strictly speaking, therefore, the components »Timbre« and »Texture« should be supplementally added to the rhythm score. The result would be that the first eleven ♩ of each of the two second phrases would together obtain a heavier weight, and that the point at which the texture alters – changing from solo to quartet setting and back – would be marked. I dispensed with that because it would not make much of a difference in the final result. Admittedly, however, this caesura in m. 185 of the G minor version makes itself strongly felt, thanks to the contribution of the violin and the viola. Even so, the principal proceedings seem to be dominated by the piano here as well, so that the phrase division of 5+5+6 ♩ remains valid.

In conclusion, it should be recognized that Yeston provided important impulses for the development of a components theory with his idea of a »stratification of musical rhythm« and the observation that the »strata« do not simply merge into a »main rhythm« but enter into reciprocity with each other. In the diagram of a rhythm score both aspects can be clearly recognized: the interaction of rhythms and their accumulation into rhythmically generated weights.

As Ex. 3-110 shows, not only are the two main voices structured differently (piano: 5+5+6 ♩, violin: 4+3+3[+6] ♪), but so is the harmonic rhythm. The F♯5 on the *One* of

Lester • The Rhythms of Tonal Music

In 1986, Joel Lester published a study tellingly entitled *The Rhythms of Tonal Music*.[402] The choice of the plural »Rhythms« in the title is crucial, since Lester starts out from the assumption that all rhythmic process in tonal music is determined by a multiplicity of factors, all of which »give rise to accent«[403] and thus are potentially conducive also to rhythms.

Already in his Foreword, Lester announces »a new approach to the treatment of accent,«[404] and an expanded theory of accent seems indeed to form the core of the entire book. Lester defines accent as follows:[405]

An accent is a point of emphasis. In order for a point in musical time to be accented, something must occur to mark that point. It is the beginning of a musical event that marks off accented points in time. Accents are, therefore, *points of initiation*.

The entry of a sound event, whether altogether new or based on a modification of previous events, is important to Lester because he regards everything in music as a consequence of, and related to, preceding events. The schema of metric accent, too, represented as a pyramid by others, is arranged by him as oriented toward the starting point of a measure (see fig.).[406] Since Lester also assumes that simultaneously occurring accents can reinforce each other (»accumulation of accents«[407]), he has the explanation for accentual gradation in modern meter: 5 weight degrees on the *One*, 1 degree on the second ♪, 2 degrees on the second ♩, etc. Yet what applies to metric accents must also apply to rhythmic ones: these, too, can accumulate at certain points in time, so that both single and multiple accentuations can result. This, to my mind, logical step, however, Lester oddly enough does not take with the same consistency he applied to metric hierarchy. Though he describes the interaction between accents (in monophonic melodies), he neither marks the intervals between accents as durations and thereafter as rhythms, nor does he assign precise weights to coinciding accents.

NB 3-111 (Lester, p. 23)

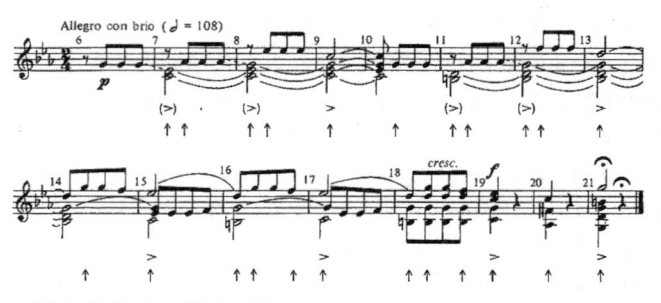

To illustrate his point, Lester cites a passage from the beginning of Beethoven's Fifth Symphony (Ex. 3-111).[408] Values larger than an eighth are given the mark, pitch changes in the upper voice (a kind of composite main voice) receive the mark ↑. If one counts the number of eighths between these ↑, genuine accentual rhythms – I would say component rhythms – can be determined – which Lester, however, does not name as such and, in any case, does not make explicit.

Ex. 3-112 Beethoven, 5th Symphony, Beginning, Pitch Rhythm (schematic)

Lester limits himself to two kinds of accent: lengthened notes and changes in pitch. We can test the procedure by looking at the example of the pitch changes (marked by Lester with the sign ↑) (Ex. 2-112). I notate the ›accentual sequence‹ as rhythm and trace it through 62 bars. The main voice is simplified (without stems or flags), whereas the rhythm resulting from the pitch durations is in regular

---

[402] Joel Lester, *The Rhythms of Tonal Music* (Carbondale & Edwardsville: Southern Illinois University Press, 1986).

[403] Ibid., ch. 2, sect. 2: »Factors That Give Rise to Accent«, 18 ff.

[404] Ibid., vii.

[405] Ibid., 16, emphasis is Lester's.

[406] Ibid., 17.

[407] Ibid., 20.

[408] Ibid., 23.

notation. The difference to Lester consists, to begin with, in my recording the duration of a pitch (in the case of note repetitions), while Lester marks only the beginning of a new pitch. Lester leaves the first G in m. 6 unmarked, because he does not think in terms of durations but in terms of accents.

If one conceives of the sequence of pitches independent of the ♪ attacks as rhythm, the entire process within the main and the transitional period can be described precisely in terms of an increasing condensation. From m. 14, the initial pattern of the three-note upbeat (|♩ ♩. |♩) is replaced by a syncopated variant (|♩ ♩♩|♩). Entire chains of syncopations follow later (from m. 37), and at the climax (mm. 48-51) there even occurs a disorienting shift of the rhythmic stresses vis-à-vis the 2/4 meter (Ex. 3-113).

Ex. 3-113 mm. 48-52

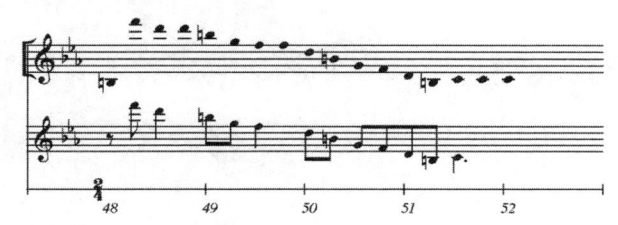

That this final complication is an intentional one on Beethoven's part is evident from the fact that the dominant seventh chord, which is held by the winds and basses and traversed by the melody-carrying strings, issues into the tonic C minor exactly on the terminal note of the downward motion, the C4 in m. 51$_2$. A harmonic anticipation thus corresponds to the rhyhmic and metric one.

Lester's study is distinguished by the fact that numerous »factors« (which he occasionally calls »components«[409]) are isolated and described in it. Since these accent-generating factors form strata between which the rhythmic process unfolds (»interaction«[410]), there are points of contact with the components theory developed by me. Lester's factors largely tally with my concept of the »component«: »new events« (»Sound«), »pitch changes« (»Pitch«), »harmonic change« (»Harmony«), »textural change« (»Texture«), »contour change« (»Diastematy«), »dynamics« (»Dynamics«), »articulation« (»Articulation«), »pattern (motif) beginning« (»Phrase«).

Whereas thus »factors« and »components« mean more or less the same, Lester's concept of accent must be regarded as problematic, because it is not clearly distinguishable from the concept of the »factor.« Since »accents,« according to Lester, can be both louder and softer, and both denser and looser in their texture than their surroundings, the terms »accent« and »factor« mean practically the same thing. Lester writes: »textural change accents can be caused by changes to both a denser or thinner texture, and to both a larger or smaller registral scope.«[411] On the other hand, Lester determines the nature of accents in terms of the emphasis that emanates from them.[412] But how does an emphasis come about, if the accents are nothing but signals[413] marking a change of whatever kind?

NB 3-114 (Lester)

To elaborate, let us take Lester's example from the first movement of Beethoven's Seventh Symphony (Ex. 3-114).[414] Lester writes about it:

Because of the accumulation of accents, rhythmic patterns with successive durational accents provide quite emphatic accentuations on the final duration, especially if the final duration is longer than the total of any preceding activity.[415]

Now the accents Lester has written beneath the notes all look alike. Very likely, however, Lester felt in reading along that the »emphatic accentuation« increases because of the enlarged values – e. g., in m. 66 (♪ → ♩ → ♩.). Would it not be better to assign larger weights to the larger values, according to the multiple of the smallest (relevant) note? Here is my suggestion (Ex. 3-115).

Ex. 3-115

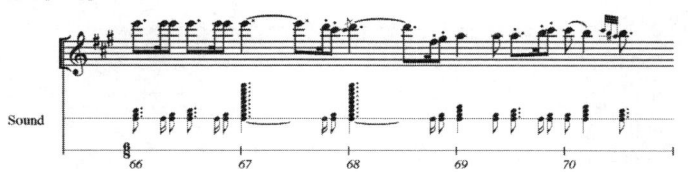

To discuss »metric hierarchy« (Ex. 3-116), Lester adduces Mozart's piano sonata in C major K. 545.[416] He believes he found in its beginning a typical example of a 4/4 meter composed in full detail. He identifies all the note values between 𝅝 and ♪ and maintains that the first ♪ of every pair of ♪ is accentuated in relation to the second, every first ♩ in relation to the second, etc., with the metric relation between the strata in this Mozart passage being »the same from beginning to end.«[417]

---

[409] Ibid., 30.

[410] Ibid., 20 and passim.

[411] Ibid., 29.

[412] See above, note 404.

[413] On p. 87, Lester employs the word »signal« in the sense of »accent«. Perhaps the term signal would even have been the more appropriate for what Lester wanted to present.

[414] Ibid., 20.

[415] Ibid.

[416] Ibid., 49.

[417] Ibid., 48f.

Ex. 3-116 (Lester)

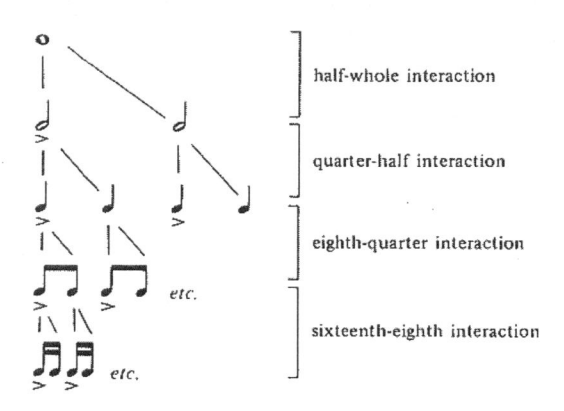

half-whole interaction

quarter-half interaction

eighth-quarter interaction

sixteenth-eighth interaction

3–5. Mozart, *Piano Sonata*, K. 545, first movement

Ex. 3-117 Mozart, Piano Sonata C Major K. 545, 1st mov., mm. 1-12

1.[418] The »Phrases« I have weighted according to their length in the right hand, but not in the left (gradation between main voice and accompaniment). The changes in harmonic function (»Harmony«) are weighted fourfold throughout.[419]

The component rhythms are all very simple, and the interaction between them mostly follows isometric patterns. What is striking is the etude-like regularity with which crest and keel notes are set in mm. 5-9, while their shifted position at the end provides a slight contrast. Very characteristic is the harmonic rhythm with its three phases: half-measured at the beginning, whole-measured in the middle and in quarter or eighth motion at the end.

The picture of the rhythmic profile, which unites all the rhythmic activities, is similar. The large weights (rhombus towers) highlight the even meter, at first according to the schema of the 4/4 meter, from m. 5 on in whole measures, toward the end in condensed small scale after the manner of a 2/4 meter. Importantly, however, no bar is like another, with the exception of the four bars of scales, whose rhythmic profiles are identical.

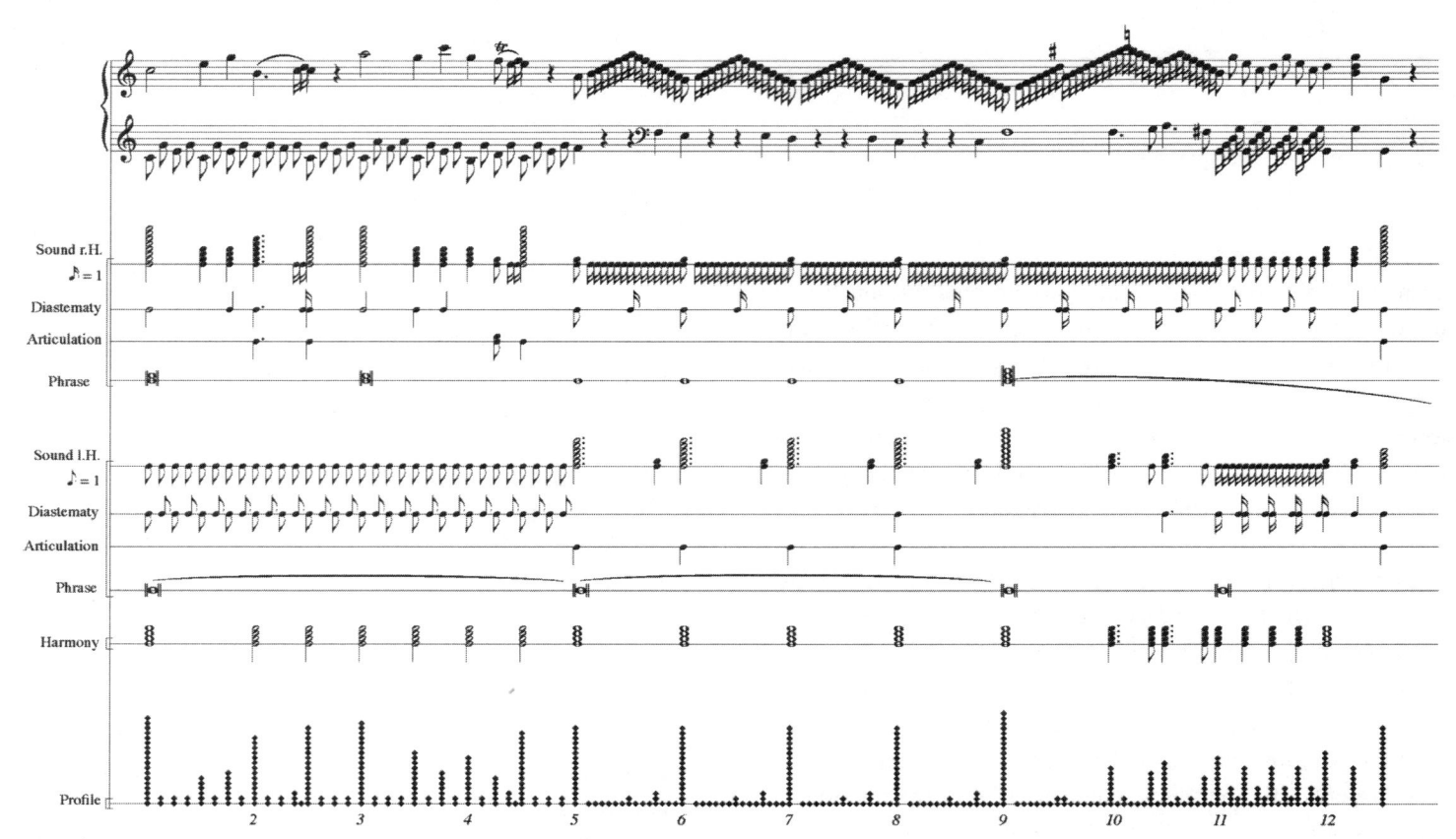

A rhythm score can show, on the contrary, that the meter is by no means firm and unchanging, but is subject to deviations caused by the working with components (Ex. 3-117). The method I have used to establish the rhythmic profile (bottom line) basically corresponds to the accumulation by which Lester weights the metric »levels« per point in time. In this case, only rhythmic components (»factors«) have been considered. The durational values of the main voice (Sound r. h.) are reckoned as multiples of ♪, while those of the accompaniment (Sound l.h.) are figured as multiples of ♪, so that the order of importance of the two ›sound factors‹ will be reflected in the total picture. The crest and keel notes of the component »Diastematy,« as well as the notes especially articulated by legato slurs, trills or rests (»Articulation«) are entered with a weight point of

[418] The doubled value in m. 4 of the right hand is due to the fact that it features both a legato slur and a trill.

[419] One can perhaps quarrel about mm. 9-10, where one might assume that the subdominant extends across the bar line together with the fifth rather than the sixth. But I refer to the discrepancy of C♯ and C, which I think suggests that the sixth chord of D minor is meant first followed by the basic chord of F major.

This is not the place to review all of Joel Lester's book, which extends the radius of its subject all the way to considerations of form and style. From the perspective of the components theory, however, it must be said in summary that – despite the nuancing of the analytic aspects – the promise made by the title of the book, namely to extract, not the *rhythm* but the *rhythms* of a composition is not kept. Accents just aren't rhythms. It is only by systematically analyzing the durations *between* accents/components that one arrives at those rhythmic derivations that, while not *notated* as note values by the composer, have nevertheless been *composed*. As a second deficit in Lester's study I deem the fact that he did not really explore the weight relations in *rhythmic* processes the way he did with respect to the *metric* dimension.

Kramer • The Time of Music

When the American composer and musicologist Jonathan D. Kramer, in 1988, became professor at New York's Columbia University, he wrote two books, of which the first, *Listen to the Music*,[420] is mainly introductory in nature, while the other, *The Time of Music*,[421] advances claims to theory. In our connection, it is primarily the *Time* book that is interesting, more particularly the 4th chapter (of a total of 12), entitled »Meter and Rhythm.«[422]

Kramer takes up from the discussion of rhythm and meter in the music theory and musicology of the past thirty years, albeit only referring to publications in English.[423] He is of the opinion that scholars have hitherto worked only with a rather narrow conception of meter. He refers to all those approaches that regard »meter as somehow apart from music, as an abstract temporal grid against which rhythm operates,« as »the static frame of reference against which we understand musical motion«.[424] Kramer wants to show that – especially in »sophisticated music« – »meter can nonetheless be supple and artistic«.[425]

Interesting is also Kramer's hypothesis that the widespread notion that motion in music can best be perceived in metrical processes is based on an illusion. Against that mistaken view, he asserts:[426]

It is the music itself, not its beats and hence not its meter, that moves through time. Failure to appreciate this important but subtle distinction has led several theorists into unfortunate confusions.

If I understand Kramer correctly, he is trying to show that meter and rhythm are shaped and not merely obeyed by the composer. Following Lerdahl & Jackendoff, he assumes three different types of accent: stress accent, rhythmic accent und metric accent. According to Kramer,[427] such accents can be brought about by »factors« like tonal length, melodic contour, tonal weight, etc. On the other hand, Kramer defines metric accent by saying it could come only at the beginning (»a metric accent […] must be a point of initiation«)[428]. In view of this unambiguous assertion, the question arises, however, whether metric accent – analogously to the other accent types – can be influenced at all by »factors.« Kramer does not discuss this problem on the level of metric hierarchy, though he does so on that of bar groups (»hypermeasures«). By the stretching, compressing or overlapping of phrases, Kramer writes, »hypermetric irregularities« can be brought about.[429] Of the beginning of Haydn's »Andante« from his Sonata Hob. XVI, 51, for example, he offers the following »hypermetric analysis« (Ex. 3-118)[430]:

Ex. 3-118 (Kramer)

```
e |                                      |
d |              |              |         |
c |        |     |     |     |     |     |
b |   |    |  |  |  |  |  |  |  |  |  |  |
a | | | | | | | | | | | | | | | | | | | |
  1       5          11       15       20
```

The irregularity of 4+6+4+5 bars suggested here, though, results only if one ignores the internal division of the phrases (cf. Ex. 3-119). In the present case, we can see that the first theme (1st period) of this »Andante« movement is formed on the model of the 8-bar repeat period, whose first phrase (mm. 1-4) ends with a half-close in the dominant and whose (expanded) second phrase (mm. 5, 6, 10, 11) conducts to an authentic cadence in the tonic via a dominant six-four chord. After m. 6, Haydn interjects a three-bar internal expansion (mm. 7, 8, 9) making use of motivic material from mm. 3 and 4. The theme is thus 11 bars long, something not changed by the phrasal overlap of the second theme (2nd period) setting in in m. 11.

Now Kramer simply disregards the theme's internal structure. He neither describes the model of the two phrases à four bars, nor does he accept the fact that m. 11 is part of the subject. In his view, the theme simply transpires in »hypermeasures« of two bars' duration each.

---

[420] Jonathan Kramer, *Listening to Music, the Essential Guide to the Classical Repertoire* (London, 1991; originally in 1988 with the title *Listening to the Music*).

[421] Jonathan Kramer, *The Time of Music. New Meanings, New Teporalities, New Listening Strategies* (New York: Schirmer, 1988).

[422] Ibid., 81-122.

[423] Ibid., 81.

[424] Ibid., 82.

[425] Ibid.

[426] Ibid., 94.

[427] Ibid., 86.

[428] Ibid.

[429] Ibid., 102ff.

[430] Ibid., 102; see also the commentary on the preceding pages.

Ex. 3-119 Haydn, Piano Sonata D major, Hob. XVI, 51, 1, »Andante,« mm. 1-21 (analytically simplified notation)

The second theme (2nd period), too, is constructed on the model of the 4-bar first phrase (mm. 11-14) with half-close in the dominant plus four-bar second phrase (mm. 17-20) with an authentic cadence in the tonic. Again there is an internal expansion, located this time at the beginning of the second phrase (mm. 15, 16) and identical with the opening of the theme, which makes it hard to recognize it as such. But if one registers the temporary modulation to the subdominant in the consequent and the strong cadencing via the six-four chord suspension in m. 19, there can be no doubt that the actual second phrase only begins in m. 17, mm. 15 and 16 thus having the function of an internal expansion. The last (tonic) measure again is part of the theme, even though a third period – still in the basic key of D major – commences at the same time.

Kramer, who cites the example in order to point out metrical irregularities, overlookes the actual internal irregularities in both subjects, because, to begin with, he proceeded from the false assumption of pervasive double measures and, secondly, did not properly appreciate the phrasal overlaps. Although he knows that in overlappings the respective measures have a double function, he does not include them in their double aspect. Both the beginnings and the ends (mm. 11/12 and 20/21) should have been marked in his graph (Ex. 3-118). Only if the overlap bars are recorded twice can both the metrics of the preceding theme and, *at the same time*, the succeeding thematic form be registered correctly. There is more complexity, not less. Already H. C. Koch erred when he spoke of »metric choking« in such cases, though it is actually a matter of metric multiplication.

At the end of the section »Rhythmic Groups and Rhythmic Accents,« Kramer makes the remarkable concession that to date no one had succeeded in finding a method whereby rhythmic-metric processes of contrary voices or compositional levels could be described. He writes:

One of the pitfalls in the analysis of rhythmic groups […] is that no one has yet devised a viable method for studying simultaneously sounding groups that conflict. Yet much music is polyphonic. Although polymeter is not particularly common […] polyrhythms (by which I mean simply the simultaneous existence of different rhythmic groups in different voices) are pervasive in music.[431]

Referring to his metrical analysis of the beginning of the Allegro finale of Beethoven's ›Pathétique,‹ Kramer confesses self-critically that he really looked only at the right hand, »even though the left hand sometimes implies different groupings.«[432]

One of the most important maxims of musical listening and analyzing, however, is that of the simultaneity of the diverse. As I have expounded in Part One of the present book, it does not even take polyphony for simultaneous rhythmic processes (»components rhythms«) to crop up. Perhaps Kramer (who sadly passed away in 2004) would have agreed with me that the components theory, in which all sound phenomena of a composition are united under the master concept of rhythm, provides just the method he longed for.

Ex. 3-120 (Kramer)

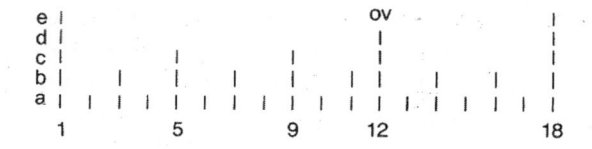

Ex. 3-121
Beethoven, *Grande Sonate Pathétique* op. 13, 3rd mov., Rondo Theme

---

[431] Ibid., 112.

[432] Ibid.

Ex. 3-122 Beethoven, *Grande Sonate Pathétique* op. 13, 3rd mov., Beginning

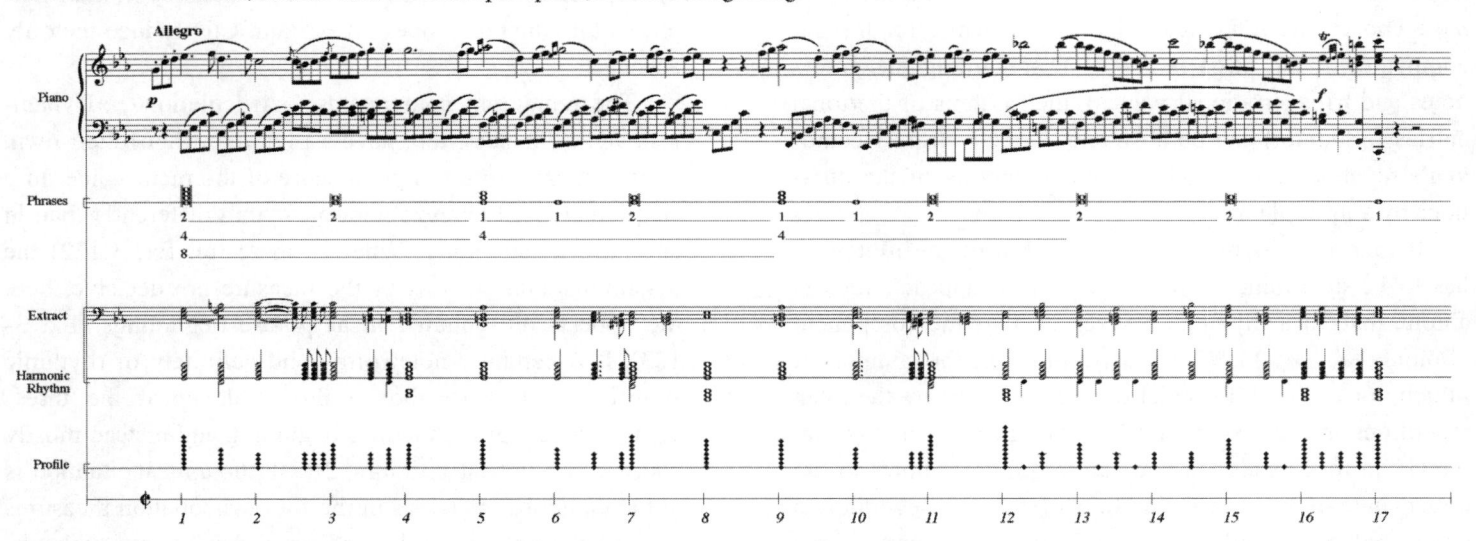

A closer look at the Beethoven theme, which Kramer analyzes for its phrasal metrics, will elicit several objections. Kramer's result is seen in Ex. 3-120,[433] an alternate reading in Ex. 3-121. Kramer assumes a phrasal overlap in m. 12 (»ov«), through which the 4-bar pattern is suppposedly altered to 4+4+3+6 meaures. I believe, however, that the 17-bar theme involves rather an increasing phrasal foreshortening, accompanied by a reiterated concluding affirmation terminating in C (Ex. 3-121). Instead of proceeding from the assumption of disrupted »hypermeasures,« it is more plausible to assume a foreshortening phrasal rhythm, i.e., 8+4+ 2+2+1 bars. This phrasal rhythm, which, of course, includes sub-rhythms, e.g., 8 = 4 (2+2) + 4 (1+1+2), can be brought into relation with the harmonic rhythm (change of harmonic function).

If one now weights the phrases and sub-phrases according to their duration, and assigns the weight of 4 to each harmonic function change plus suspensions and imperfect or perfect cadences, a rhythmic profile can be constructed by accumulating the weights per point in time that comes close to the accentual schema of the 2/2 meter, although it was erected on the basis of component rhythms.

The goal of the analysis, however, should be to represent and interpret the total rhythmic-metric structure of the theme. To do that, we will have to analyze the main voice (r. h.) and the accompaniment (l. h.) separately, so that then they can be added to the component rhythms »Phrase« (referring to the entire period) and »Harmony« (see Ex. 3-122). To treat main voice and accompaniment on a par with each other would be inadequate.

Ex. 3-123 Right Hand, Rhythm Score

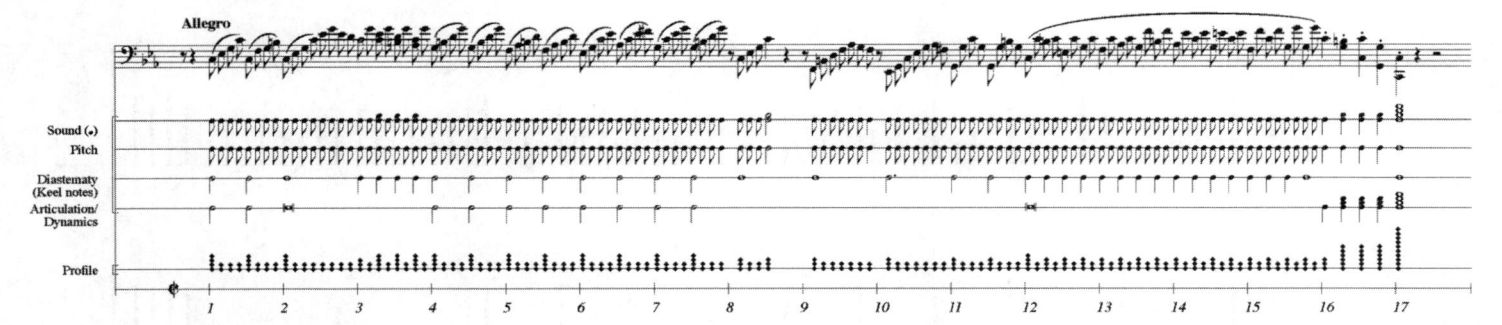

Ex. 3-124 Left Hand, Rhythm Score

[433] Ibid., 107.

In the analysis of the main voice (Ex. 3-123) I therefore have chosen the reference value ♪ = 1, while for the accompaniment the basis is ♩ = 1. Disregarding the gracenotes and trills (irrational values), the rhythms of the tonal entries (»Sound«) can be abstracted directly from Beethoven's notation. To be added is the weighting of the durations by a multiple of ♪ = 1.

If tone repetitions occur, the rhythm of the »Pitches« has to be determined separately. Thus it appears, for example, that, in a rhythmic respect, m. 1 of the component »Sound« (♩. ♪♩. ♪) is identical with m. 7 of the component »Pitch« (♩. ♪♩. ♪). Of special rhythmic weight are the pitch repetitions in mm. 3-4 and 12. Although one can say that the G5 in m. 3 leads via two staccato quarter notes to the dotted half of m. 4, the duration of the G5 nevertheless begins before the end of the first group of four bars. In the syncopes toward the end of the theme, too, the rhythmic relevance of the component »Pitch« manifests itself. In the first instance (m. 12), the syncopated note (B♭5) is weighted more heavily because it is repeated. In the second instance (m. 14, C6) its effect is weaker because the pitch duration is not any longer than that of the sound.

The directional changes of the melodic line (»Diastematy«), taken by themselves, produce a sometimes bizarre, sometimes also simple rhythm. The rhythmic effect the crest and keel notes can have can be read at both syncopated points. The absence of a directional change after the syncopated notes (downward scale) makes the motion flatter, so that the crest tones on B♭5 and C6 produce the only accents.

The remaining components (»Articulation«, »Dynamics« and »Phrase«), too, have a rhythmic life of their own, which enters into the rhythm score of the main voice. In a single melody, I analyze phrasal rhythm differently than in an entire tonal setting. Whereas there (cf. Ex. 3-122) the beginnings and stresses of the measure are decisive, here the upbeats are counted in as phrase beginnings (Ex. 3-123). It is certainly noteworthy and definitely of rhythmic significance that Beethoven does not repeat the three-eighths upbeat of the theme's beginning and instead mostly chooses two upbeat ♪. In mm. 2 to 4, the upbeat situation is not unequivocal, whereas in the four syncopation measures (12-16) the only possible reading is that of long upbeats, each comprising seven ♩ (from B♭5 down to C5 and from C6 down to C5).

The »rhythmic profile« of the main voice generated by the accumulation of all the component rhythms confirms toward the end the double-bar character (mm. 12/13 and 14/15) and thus the presumption of long upbeats. Apart from that, the profile mostly reveals isolated alla-breve times. A striking exception occurs in m. 3 with its high weight peak owing to the long-continuing pitch of G5. Mm. 6-7 and 10-11, according to their profile, are shaped like hyper-measures – a tendency, however, that is not confir-

Ex. 3-125   Synopsis of Profiles

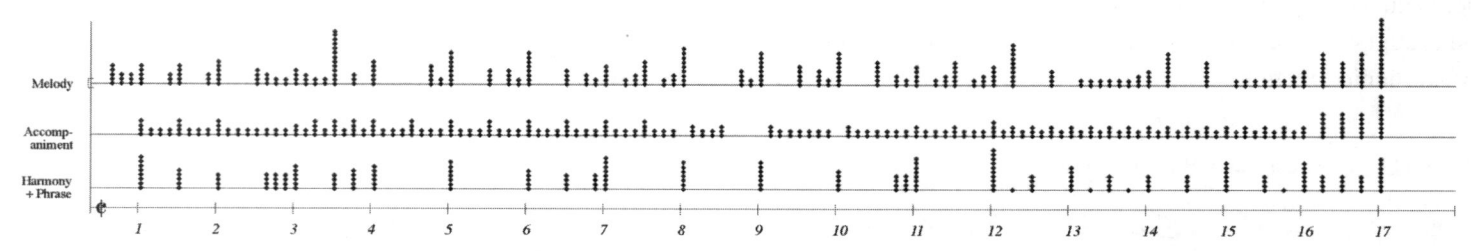

NB 3-126   Integral Profile (>0, >5, >10)

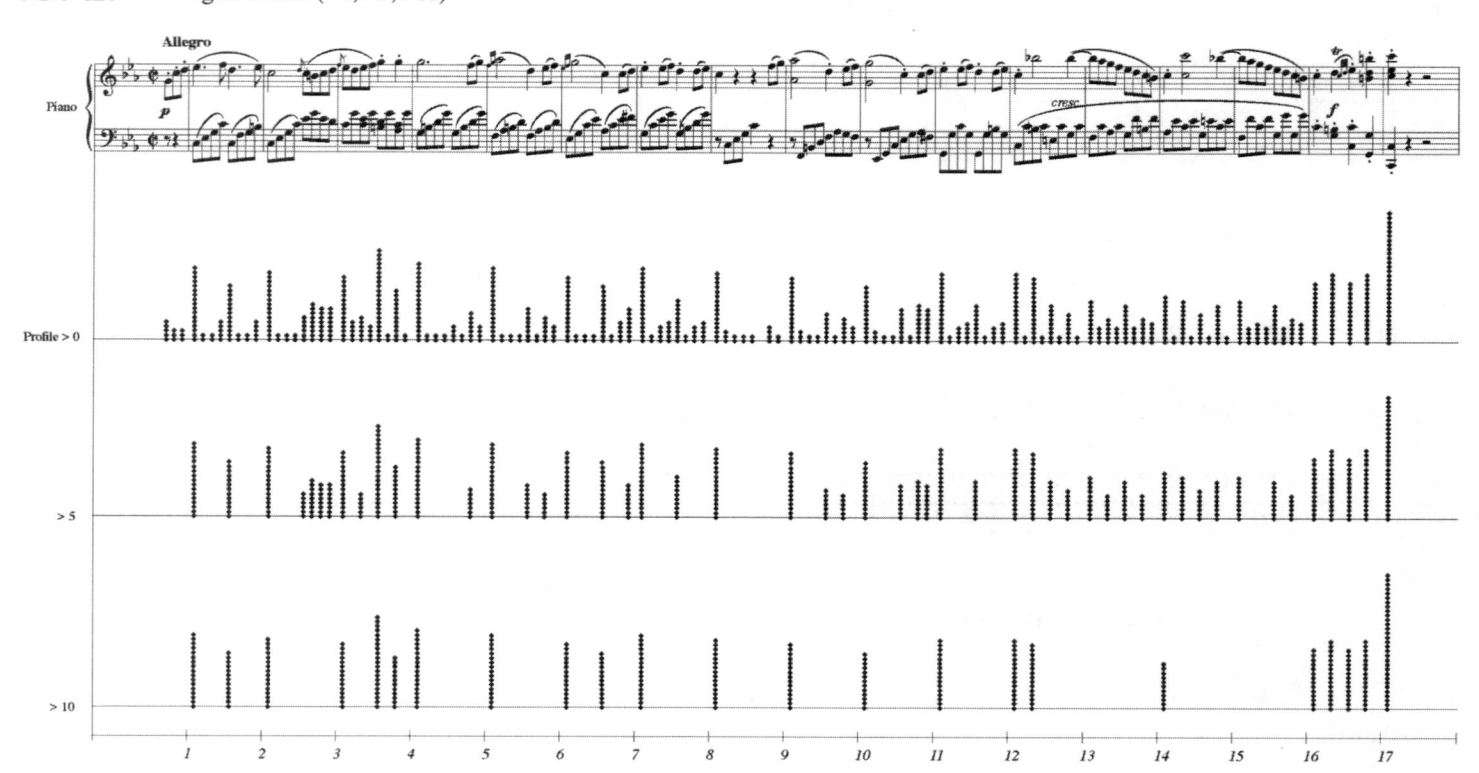

med by the inclusion of the accompaniment, let alone with regard to the components that pertain to the entire setting (»Harmony« and »Phrase«).

The accompaniment in the left hand has a very simple rhythmic structure (Ex. 3-124). It lays down a quiet, hardly contoured basis, above which the melody of the right hand can unfold. Almost entirely set for ♪, the components »Diastematy« (in which in this case I have counted only keel notes) and »Articulation« (legato slurs) infuse simple isometric rhythms (mostly ♩) into the accompanying voice.

Looking at the »rhythmic profile« of the accompaniment, one can say that the meter of the theme is realized fairly purely. Here, too, however, we are dealing with a rhythmically produced meter and not with the abstract schema of a metric hierarchy. One can tell because the *One* and the *Two* of the alla breve time are not differentiated. In mm. 13 to 15, the meter seems to be completely equalized, being absorbed into the quick pulse of ♩ and ♪.

To take up Kramer's observation that »the left hand [in comparison with the main voice] sometimes implies diffe–rent groupings,«[434] I arrange the three hitherto ascertained rhythmic profiles without further commentary beneath each other (Ex. 3-125). More telling, though, is the complete rhythmic profile of the theme, reproduced in Ex. 3-126. In the top line, it is complete (> 0). Beneath that, the lighter rhythmic weights are masked (> 5), while the third line presents an even more filtered profile of the highest peaks (> 10).

The appearance of double measures toward the end of the theme is evident from the fact that in the most severely reduced profile the *One* of mm. 13 and 15 is unoccupied. The lesser reduction, and the complete profile, of the final six bars exhibit the shape of a suspension bridge bearing the two double measures within itself.

The rhythmic unity of mm. 12 to 17 corresponds exactly to the last six bars of Kramer's graph (see above). But it has been arrived at in another way and is also accounted for differently. The cause is not the putative »overlap« in m. 12, but the rhythmic weight ratios created by the composer, which here at the end, by the device of phrasal foreshortening, lead to a prolongation of the actual final measure (m. 12) by several long upbeats.

In addition, one should stress that the rhyhmic profile clearly reflects the metric relations on all levels of reduction (> 0, > 5, > 10). It proves that one does not need the assumptions of metric hierarchy in order to arrive at the metric situation. One can likewise dispense with the problematic accent theory, since the components analysis makes it possible to depict both rhythmic *and* metric weights equally well and with the appropriate differentiation.

J. D. Kramer's enormously stimulating book *The Time of Music* – which, as noted, also, and even predominantly, raises other questions besides those of rhythm and meter in music – is likely to break up quite a few dogmas of older theories. But the problem the author set himself, of showing that »meter can [...] be subtle and artistic«[435], is not solved within the frame of the study. What Kramer wanted to show can be demonstrated better and more adequately by the components theory, which, as a pure rhythm theory, includes metrics as well.

Rothstein • Phrase Rhythm in Tonal Music

In 1989, the American musicologist William Rothstein, who uses the (slightly modified) Schenker method, published his book *Phrase Rhythm in Tonal Music*.[436] Part one of the study explains, to begin with, what is meant by a phrase, then how »phrase rhythms« are formed from regular or irregular combinations of phrases, and finally the processes of expansion that in the end lead to large forms. In part two of the book, entitled »Phrase Rhythm and Style,« Rothstein presents four case studies, in which works by Haydn, Mendelssohn, Chopin and Wagner are analyzed.

By phrase Rothstein means a unit of musical meaning ending with a cadence that conveys the feeling of a satisfying conclusion.[437] The coherence of the individual sections of a phrase, some of which can also be partial or subphrases, is guaranteed primarily by the tonal conjunct progression (following Schenker). Metric ocurrencies such as measures and hyper-measures, can play a role in this but often demonstrate independence from the phrasal structure.[438] Rhythmic microstructures are not included in Rothstein's reflections. On the contrary, the rhythm of melodies and settings is lost sight of in proportion as the reductionism typical of Schenkerian analyses proceeds.

One can gather this clearly from the example Rothstein cites in the very first chapter: Johann Strauss Jr,'s *Blue Danube* waltz. At the beginning of the analysis, the first 32 bars of the waltz are presented in every detail (except for the instrumentation) in the form of a piano accolade.[439] Then follows the reduction in four steps. In the first step, called »Reduction (foreground),«[440] most detailed rhythms drop out, including all of the ♩ upbeats, most articulation marks, isolated notes of the main voice and the basic rhythm of the accompaniment. Maintaining the metric conditions, the main steps of the cadencial progression are

---

[434] Ibid., 112.

[435] Ibid., 82.

[436] William Rothstein, *Phrase Rhythm in Tonal Music* (New York: Schirmer, 1989).

[437] Ibid., 3ff.

[438] Ibid., 9.

[439] Ibid., 4f.

[440] Ibid., 6.

given and the cadences are marked.[441] In a further reduction, we get a diminishing transcription of the central happening, at a proportion of 3:1, from a 3/4 time to a 4/4 time notated with triplets. This is followed by a yet more extreme diminution of values, so that one 4/4 measure takes the place of 16 3/4 measures. Rothstein further presents a non-rythmical and non-metrical version of the phrase »in Schenkerian notation.«[442]

voice (»Pitch«), which does not coincide with the IOI rhythm (»Sound«), inasmuch as the durational value of certain pitches is prolonged by the note repetitions, which increases their weight. Thus the pitch A4 in mm. 1 and 2 each has a duration of 3 ♩, of which the first ♩ is placed before the bar line, which endows the upbeat with the weight given in the »Sound« rhythm by the ♩ on the *One*. Both at the beginning and in the following measures, one hears

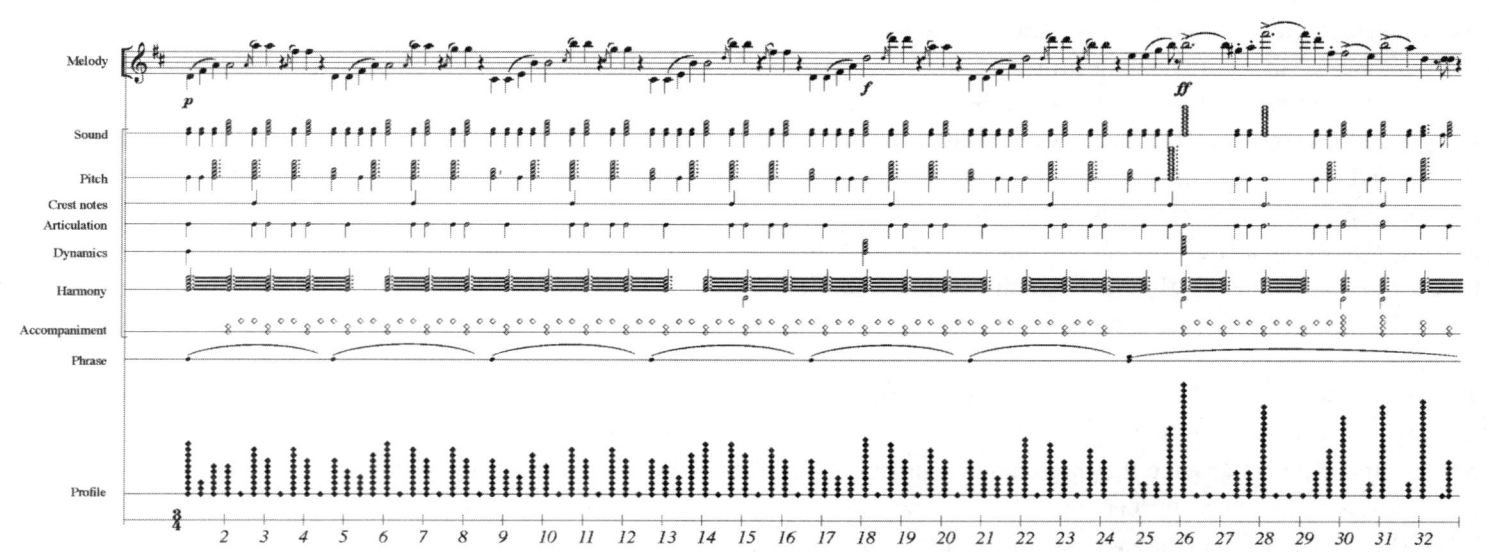

Ex. 3-127   Johann Strauss jr., Blue Danube *Waltz*, Beginning (Rhythm Score)

The insights Rothstein extracts from the various reductive steps are largely persuasive. Thus the entire phrase of 32 bars is shown to cohere above all by its harmonic progression. Besides, the ambitus planning of the main voice, beginning and ending with D4 or D5 respectively reaching a top note of F#6 toward the end, is identified as the means of an »overarching motion.«[443] Rothstein could have gone on to adduce *rhythmic* occurrencies as in turn establishing coherence, but he does not do so. To supplement his tonal phrase analysis, I will therefore conduct a rhythmic one (Ex. 3-127).

For perspicuity's sake, I have limited myself to reproducing the main voice in simplified form, though with all the details that are rhythmically relevant. The waltz accompaniment is indicated schematically. It is interrupted twice: in m. 24, where the »patterns« briefly pause, and in mm. 30 and 31, where they change into whole-measure note values (line »Accompaniment«). The harmonic expanses are notated as durations (line »Harmony«), whose tendency toward foreshortening is evident at first sight (15+ 24+24+12+6+3+ 3+6 ♩).

The rhythmic character of the waltz is formed primarily by the patterns in the accompaniment, combined with the inter-onset-intervals (IOI) of the main voice. The ›Viennese‹ hallmark of this waltz, however, is due to other component rhythms, above all the pitch rhythm of the main

time and again those stressed upbeats that first make the waltz really swing. The effect is all the more powerful when from m. 18 on several pitches are *not* anticipated (D5, later F#6), as thereby a rhythmic cadence is initiated by firm steps that moves hand in hand with the harmonic one.

The upbeats, already underscored by the pitch rhythm, are further marked by crest notes, while the articulations, (legato slurs, short grace notes, staccato and accent markings, notes cut short by rests) fall sometimes on the *One*, sometimes before it. If we think of the piece in terms of hypermeasures (quasi 12/4), we get large (𝅗𝅥.) rhythmic upbeats along with the small (♩) ones, e.g., at the very beginning, where m. 1 is upbeat to mm. 2-5. The partial phrases thus anticipate the hypermeasures in exactly the same way as the pitches do the regular ones. The ›upbeat measures‹ can therefore be regarded as stressed. This is true especially of the beginning, because the tonic harmony is in force already in m. 1, although the accompaniment, and with it the first actual D major chord, come in only in m. 2 – that is, on the *One* of the first hypermeasure.

The eight component rhythms considered by me for this Strauss waltz (»Sound,« »Pitch,« »Diastematy« [crest notes], »Articulation,« »Dynamics,« »Harmony,« »Accompaniment« and »Phrase«) coincide at several points of time, strengthening the signal rhythmic effect at those points. Such accumulation results in rhythmic weights, which, presented as a comprehensive rhythmic weight profile, reveal additional factors that highlight the unity of the 32 waltz measures.

---

[441]   Rothstein reads the tonic harmony under the top note of the theme, the F#6, as the closure of a first, albeit weaker, cadence. I regard that as problematic.

[442]   Ibid., 9. See also the other reductions before and afterward.

[443]   Ibid.

Thus we notice that from m. 18 the height of the profile peaks gradually increases so as to issue into the strongly profiled eight concluding measures. The point most heavily weighted, the *One* of m. 26, is identified as the climax not only by its *ff* but also because here a long note, a crest tone, a dynamic accent, a harmonic function change and a harmonic suspension are all heard simultanously.

Corresponding to the gradual increase of the rhythmic weights and its heightening effect is a change in the rhythmic motion proceeding in three steps. During the first phase, comprising 13 measues, the typical, rather small-scale waltz rhythm with its regularly stressed ♩ upbeats is installed. From m. 14, where the high weight peaks on *One* beats start to increase, we see, or hear, groups of four bars, which after a strong initial impulse regularly lose weight as the group progresses. In this second phase, phrase durations of twelve ♩ thus assert themselves, as measured by the profile columns in mm. 14, 18 and 22. The duodecimal rhythm is finally compressed in the following, concluding phase (from m. 26). The large distances between the prominent columns on the *Ones* of mm. 26, 28, 30, 31 and 32 are now 6+6+3+3 ♩.

Rothstein's book about »phrase rhythms« oddly enough neglects precisely »the rhythms within phrases«. The shape and delimitation of phrases, however, depend not only on tonal but also on rhythmic conditions.

Epstein • Shaping Time

David Epstein, conductor, composer and professor at the Massachusetts Institute of Technology, is one of those reflective musicians who are at home not only on concert stages but also in research laboratories and panel discussions. This was evident already from his 1979 book about basic questions of musical formation. Even more ambitious was his treatise of 1995, *Shaping Time. Music, the Brain, and Performance.*[444]

A survey of the five parts of his »Time« book[445] makes clear that Epstein is fascinated above all by questions of tempo; his thoughts on rhythm and meter, on the other hand, are somewhat meager, as well as less independent. Starting from a distinction between »chronometric time« and »integral time«[446], Epstein concentrates on the more comprehensive phenomena, so that »motion« seems more important to him than rhythmic details, »accents« more interesting than the means of their production. With reference to the ideas of Cooper & Meyer,[447] he magnifies the dualistic relation of meter/rhythm from the smallest to the largest units of musical time: »Beat and Pulse«[448], »Measure and Motive«[449], »Hypermeasure and Phrase«[450] etc.

Epstein explains the difference between »beat« (metric) and »pulse« (rhythmic) by referring to three familiar examples – albeit only in outline. Thus the military march *Stars and Stripes Forever* is marked by the fact that pulse and beat coincide so extensively »that they seem as one.«[451] The processional march in Act II of *Aida,* on the other hand, is said to be an instance where »beat and pulse are not always fully in phase«.[452] In the funeral march in Beethoven's *Eroica*, again, the pulse is »often discrepant from metric frame«, due, inter alia, to the slides preceding the *One* in the basses.[453] These observations are all true enough, but they are not supported by detailed analyses.

Ex. 3-128   Haydn, Symphony No. 101, 3rd movement, Trio, middle section (mm. 122-127), Epstein's analysis (there Ex. 3.4., p. 70)

The examples Epstein adduces reveal an experienced musician with an extensive knowledge of the repertoire. In the Trio of the Minuet of Haydn's Symphony No. 101 in D major, for example, Epstein discovered pentadic groupings that enter into a »mélange of articulations«[454] with metric and other accents (NB 3-128). The representation of his analysis of the five bars relies on graphic symbols like » < « for dynamic, metric and pitch accents, dotted brackets to mark the pentadic units, and arrows pointing up or down to signalize upbeat and downbeat tendencies. Apart from the fact that the score used by Epstein does not correspond completely to the ur-text (the *f* comes one bar early, the slurs diverge), the accents are not really interpreted rhythmically, but only in relation to the 3/4 meter.

---

[444] David Epstein, *Shaping Time. Music, the Brain, and Performance*. (New York: Schirmer, 1995). The older book: David Epstein, *Beyond Orpheus. Studies in musical structure*. (Cambridge Mass., 1979).

[445] *Shaping Time*: I: Introduction; II: Rhythm, Meter, and Motion (ca. 70 pages); III: Tempo (ca. 260 pages); IV: Flexible Tempo (ca. 80 pages); V: Epilogue.

[446] Ibid., 23.

[447] Ibid., 24.

[448] Ibid., 29.

[449] Ibid., 30.

[450] Ibid., 32.

[451] Ibid., 29.

[452] Ibid., 30.

[453] Ibid.

[454] Ibid., 72.

Ex. 3-129 Haydn, Symphony No. 101, 3rd mov., Trio, Middle Section (mm. 122-137), Upper Voice

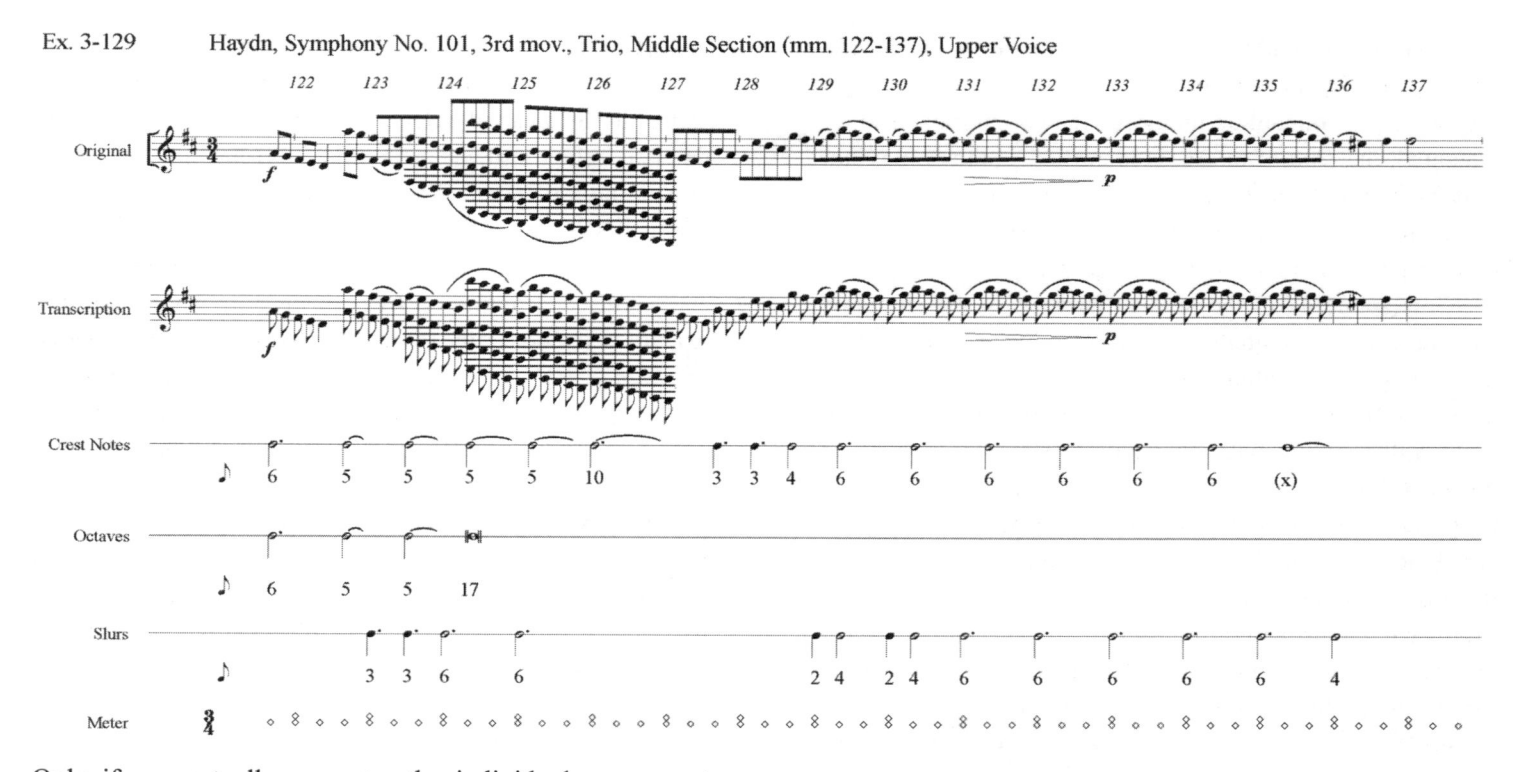

Only if one actually separates the individual component rhythms, as is done in Ex. 3-129, will one obtain a solid basis for describing the degree to which Haydn has tried here to, in fact, all but annul the 3/4 meter. What especially contributes to this is the formation of octaves at intervals of 5 ♪, which reinforces the equally pentadic crest tone rhythm. The crest notes, initially supported by slurs, additionally sound out units of 3-♪ (mm. 123, 127, 128), which begin sometimes on the first eighth, sometimes on the second and thus also go counter to the meter. On the other hand, however, the slurs tend to confirm the complete bars as units (mm. 124 ff., 131 ff.).

If one looks at the three component rhythms represented together, one will have to admit that the five- and three-♪ rhythms at times tend to obliterate the regular meter. This was evidently intentional on the part of the composer and should be allowed to stand as a structural fact. Epstein's analysis, however, tends to describe accentual occurrencies only from the perspective of the time signature. We see once again that the concept of accent if anything gets in the way of an actual determination of rhythmic conditions.

David Epstein's book deals only marginally with musical rhythm. Prompted by the concerns of the practicing musician, Epstein thinks less analytically than integrally. What interests him is above all questions of agogics and, here in particular, of tempo fluctuations (»Nonlinear Tempos«[455]). These guarantee a lasting value to the book.

Agmon • Musical Durations

The music theoretician Eytan Agmon – one of the founders of ESCOM (European Society for the Cognitive Sciences of Music) – published an essay in 1997 entitled »Musical Durations as Mathematical Intervals: Some Implications for the Theory and Analysis of Rhythm,« in which he problematizes the concept of »duration« and offers suggestions how to deal with it meaningfully.[456]

Agmon's approach is »mathematical« insofar as he adduces definitions of »point«, »line« and »interval« to enable him to speak about musical phenomena like »moment« and »duration« with greater precision. The end result, however, is not a mathematical theory of duration but a musical one. Intervals mathematically defined are delimited by points that lie on a (straight) line and are of four types: closed [a,b], open (a,b), half open on the right [a,b) and half open on the left (a,b]. What makes the difference in each case is whether or not the points of demarcation are included in the interval (see the different brackets). Since a mathematical point has no extension, it would make no difference from an empirical perspective whether it is included in the segment or not. But this is not true in the abstract world of mathematics. Whether an interval is closed, open or half-open depends on whether or not the end points are part of the segment.

---

[455] Ibid., 367 ff.

[456] Eytan Agmon, »Musical Durations as Mathematical Intervals: Some Implications for the Theory and Analysis of Rhythm,« *Music Analysis* 16:1 (1997) 45-75.

In music, too, one can think in this abstract manner, especially when one is working solely with written notes. The equivalent of the point would then be the moment, and that of the interval would be the duration. Agmon, in fact, plays this situation through by postulating four abstract types of duration in analogy to the four types of mathematical intervals:[457]

a) The closed duration

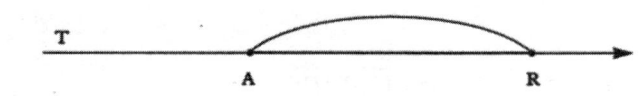

b) The open duration

c) The metrical duration

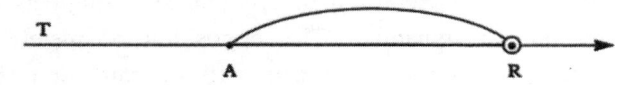

d) The anti-metrical duration

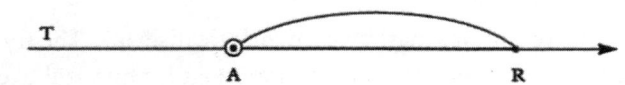

Located on a straight line T (time, always forward-pointing temporal axis) are the beats (moments in the sense of points in time) A (attack, entry of a note or chord) and R (release, ceasing of a note or chord). Between the beats A and R extends a duration, defined as »continuum of all beats between two distinct beats.«[458]

Analogous to the demarcating points of a mathematical interval, the beats »may or may not be associated with« the duration. If A and R are part of the duration, the latter is a »closed duration.« Agmon later exemplifies this by durations that are bordered by an overlapping of phrases or turns of a melodic line.

If neither A nor R are connected with the duration, the latter is an »open duration.« But something that can be imagined mathematically – a segment of a straight line without boundary points – is problematic in the musical world. Agmon thinks that this case can happen only when there are rests, but then promptly restricts that again, rests being merely »pseudo-durations.«[459] He therefore in the end excludes the possibility of an »open duration« altogether.[460]

The variants of the half-open duration – left- or right-closed – Agmon calls, respectively, »metrical« and »anti-metrical durations.« »Metrical« here means simply »measured.« As prototypes of such »metrical durations,« one can adduce familiar note values like 𝅗𝅥, 𝅘𝅥, 𝅘𝅥𝅮 etc. They have an unequivocal beginning, the »attack,« but an open end, which, while it cannot really be demarcated by a rest,[461] as a rule can be determined by subsequent notes. For the reverse case, where A is open and R is closed, Agmon thinks of examples that begin with a notated rest (see his analysis of the transition to the Finale in Beethoven's Fifth Symphony[462]).

Altogether one can conclude from Agmon's presentation that musical time intervals are constituted by the succession of sound events. The end of *individual* notes, sound figures, or even entire music pieces, results not from actual sound but from a determination *ab extra*. Decisive for rhythmics is therefore the sequence of durations, not the individual note value.

In the course of discussing »phrase overlaps,« Agmon observes that at the moment where two phrases overlap, two things happen simultaneously: the end of a past phrase and the beginning of a new one. By thereupon generalizing the principle of the simultaneity of the different, he takes a step that could have led to the formulation of a components theory:

It appears that any musical event capable [...] of being conceived simultaneously as an end and a beginning can give rise to a duration that contains its release.[463]

If one takes »musical events« to mean also »musical components«, then the durations derived from sound events correspond to the durations determined by components. Agmon does not, however, take the relatively obvious step of specifying the (secondary) durations thus identified by the note-value signs that are readily available. Instead, he employs graphic symbols such as circles, arrows, parentheses and square brackets to mark durations and their overlappings (Ex. 3-130).

NB 3-130 Chopin, Etude Op. 10 No. 1, Beginning: Analysis of Eytan Agmon[464]

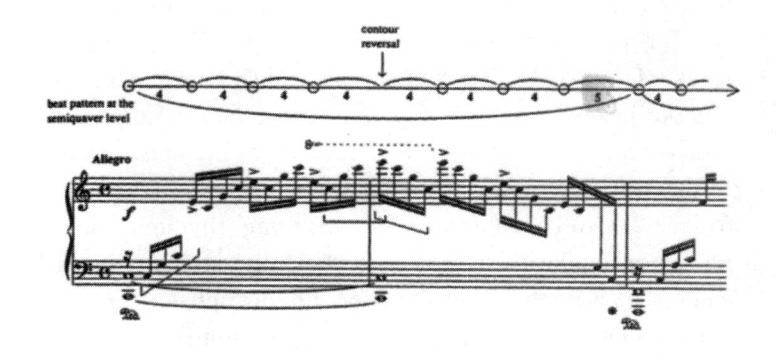

---

[457] Ibid. 53.

[458] Ibid. 51.

[459] Ibid. 55.

[460] Ibid.

[461] See his intriguing reflections on the exact end of the first movement of Beethoven's Fifth Symphony, for which four (!) alternatives are discussed, all of which are in fact valid possibilities (ibid. 49 ff.).

[462] Ibid. 62 ff.

[463] Ibid. 62.

[464] Ibid. 67.

In his analysis of the beginning of Chopin's C major Etude from Op. 10, Agmon marks the moment of the overlap by a downward-pointing arrow (»contour reversal«) and two overlapping square brackets beneath the notes. In his view, the duration of the arpeggio motif (C6-G6-C7- | E7) here overlaps with that of the overriding crest tones at an interval of two bars (E7-E7). Since, Agmon continues, the »large-scale contour reversal«[465] results in the broken-chord pattern's appearing no longer anti-metrically (with ♪-rest), but metrically (on the *One*), the upshot at the transition from m. 2 to m. 3 is a supernumerary ♪ – and therefore a pentadic unit (see the numbering in the line »beat pattern at the semiquaver level«[466]).

As persuasive as the questions and the approach of Agmon's analysis are, as definitely do the details need to be problematized. For example, I think the notion that the arpeggio motif of m. 2 is to be regarded as down-beat is quite arbitrary. Since the dynamic accents (>), which occur regularly on the quarter positions of the alla breve meter, signal an unchanging goal tone for the three ›upbeat‹ ♪, the arpeggio motif can continue to be heard and played with an ›upbeat‹ even after the great direction change (C7-G6-C6- | E6).

Ex. 3-131 Chopin, Etude No. 1 from Op.10, Beginning, Schema and Rhythm Score

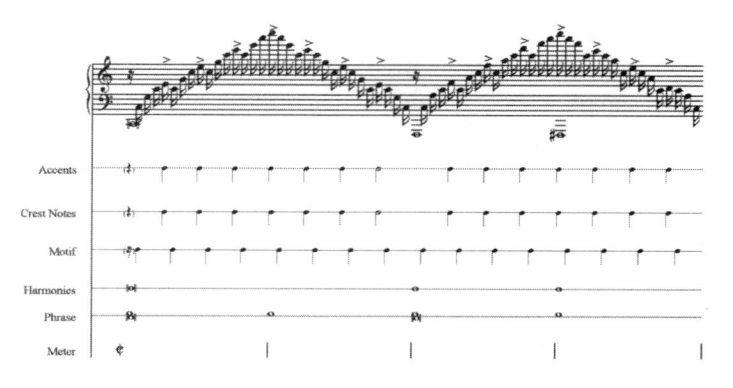

What crucially matters in such analyses is that the components are sharply separated to begin with so that they can then be related meaningfully to each other. This can be seen in my alternative analysis of the same Chopin measures. (Ex. 3-131). Beneath the ♪, which I have notated without beams, the following five component rhythms are indicated: those of the dynamic accents, of the crest notes, of the arpeggio motif, of the harmonic changes and of the (divided) two-bar phrases. The resulting rhythmic field reveals a regularity such as is to be fully expected in an etude. The isometry is thus, in fact, not disrupted by any 5-♪ units. On the contrary, the arpeggio motifs regularly entering in the Off confirm the periodic motion of the passage by their unvaryingly *nachschlagende* position relative to the accentual durations (♩).

With his essay on musical durations, Eytan Agmon has contributed substantially to the clarification of a fundamental concept in rhythmics and metrics. What is musically relevant is not the duration of the individual note but the durations/rhythms resulting from the sequence of tones, chords and tonal configurations. By also including the concept of simultaneity in his reflections, he comes close to Thesis 1 of the components theory, according to which even monophonic melodies have more than one rhythm.[467]

Hasty • Meter as Rhythm

Christopher F. Hasty's book *Meter as Rhythm* appeared in 1997.[468] The author proposes to abolish the supposed conflict betweeen meter and rhythm by interpreting meter, so to speak, rhythmically. Instead of regarding it as a rigid temporal grid, meter is to be recognized through its forward-pointing dynamics. The opposition of meter and rhythm »disappears if we can shift our attention from objects or products to process and from static being to dynamic becoming.«[469]

Hasty entitles part two of his treatise »A Theory of Meter as Process«. Even more important for him is the term »projection«, so that he also speaks of »meter as projection« or of a »theory of projection.« Projection »as a ›throwing forth‹« is, to begin with, understood as a mental activity on the part of the listeners or players, who in a sequence of musical events take the duration of a sound »event« as the model of the duration of a subsequent sound event. Hasty calls the duration of such an event »projected«, its potential of dictating the duration of the next sound event »projective«.[470] Whether or not the expectation thus built up from event to event is fulfilled, it at all events determines the musical listening, which is thus always forward-directed. If the music is »mensurally determinate,« meter and the expectation of subsequent durations are one and the same thing. As Hasty sums it up:[471]

… two immediately successive events begun with sound will necessarily result in projection if the first event is mensurally determinate and the duration of the second sound ist not greater than that of the first event. If the duration of the second sound ist greater than that of the first event, projection may nevertheless occur, but I will not claim that this is a necessary outcome. More broadly […] I will claim that projection is nothing other than meter – that projection and meter are one.

---

[465] Ibid., 65.

[466] Ibid.

[467] Cf. the Introduction to this book, p. 7, above.

[468] Christopher F. Hasty, *Meter as Rhythm* (New York, Oxford: Oxford University Press, 1997).

[469] Ibid., Preface, viif.

[470] Ibid., 84.

[471] Ibid., 91.

When Hasty deals abstractly with certain phenomena like accent, division, hierarchy, upbeat, pulse and duple or triple time, he employs only notes without concrete pitches or other characteristics of sound. In the chapter »Metrical Particularity,« he then turns to the metric-rhythmic analysis of specific music. His observations here depart most clearly from older theories about mensuration and meter. Hasty states, in a nutshell, that to his mind rhythm is not the antipode of meter, but that meter can realize itself only within rhythmic processes, and hence every measure or metric unit can be unique and special, even where there is a general time signature. Rhythmic conditions thus change the meter, they neither supersede nor are in opposition to it. As Hasty says in the introduction to the tenth chapter:[472]

If any measure is reducible to an instance of a type and thus to a typical organization of equal beats, and if meter is equated with this ›underlying‹ organization, the uniqueness or particularity of any actual measure will be viewed as a product of rhythm and not meter.

This line of reasoning tallies with my deductions from the components theory to the effect that meter is not just something prescribed but is produced by rhythm. Measures have a structure that is variable in the detail and in that respect is shaped meter. From the perspective of components theory, however, the question arises to what exactly the term duration refers for Hasty and what he means by a musical »event.«

For the analyses Hasty presents show that, against expectation, he proceeds, after all, from metric schemata. This can be gathered from his description of two of J. S. Bach's Courantes for violoncello solo. The following of Hasty's examples (Ex. 3-132 and 3-133) include marks for the beginning of a metric unit (|), for the upbeat (/) or no upbeat (\ ) function and for projections (arc).[473]

Ex. 3-132 (Hasty, p. 158)

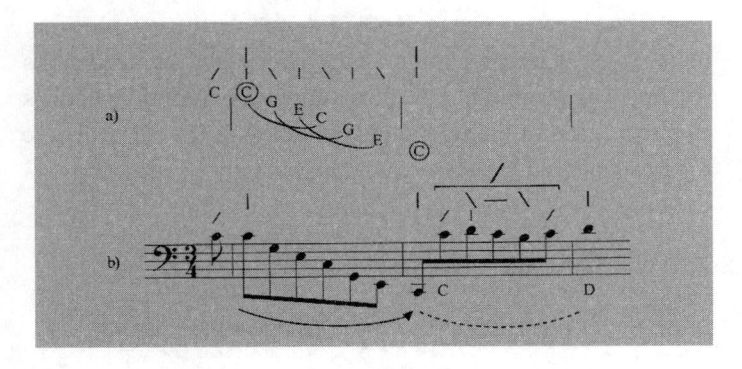

About the C major Courante (Ex. 3-132) Hasty remarks that the beats, that is, the paired eighths, are »not very sharply articulated.« As the only structural element in this uninterrupted arpeggio gesture he cites the recurring pitch classes, e.g., C4 – C3 – C2. The distance between these notes equals 3 ♪. As can be gathered from the accentual diagram drawn by him above the note letters, the pitch class C falls sometimes on a metrical stress and sometimes not. Hasty does not consider the possibility that Bach wanted to offer an allusion to a 6/8 meter (3+3 ♪) here at the beginning. He thinks in terms of the given time signature.

The second bar, too, is interpreted conventionally by him. He reads the duble-beat figure of 5 ♪ after the change of register (C2 - C4) as a long upbeat, which makes good sense. But the accents within the five eighths are placed by him on the model of the 3/4 meter: light weights (\ ) on the *Two* and *Three*, upbeat eighths (/) toward the *Two* of the second bar and the *One* of the third, respectively. The step from C4 to B3, incidentally, is not accepted as a (small) upbeat, which is not quite consistent.[474]

Things are similar in the analysis of the E♭ major Courante (Ex. 3-133). The accentual relations are entered on the upermost line (under a)). Then follows the metric microstructuring, with light eighths following the main beats. In the third place, Hasty brings an authentically rhythmic component into play, i.e., the harmony (see the function markings below the notes of a)). The brackets indicate that the harmonic rhythm here proceeds in quarters. Since the composition is monophonic, one has to expect variants, which Hasty describes under b). As convincing as the analysis is – it boils down to making it possible for the expanded variant with its subdominant having the value of 3 ♪ (F-A♭-C-E♭) to coexist with the quarter motion of the harmonic functions – it is regrettable that Hasty does not really pursue the aspect of the harmonic rhythm. As Jan LaRue has already suggested,[475] Hasty could have noted – and notated – the harmonic functions as actual rhythms.

Ex. 3-133 (Hasty, p. 163)

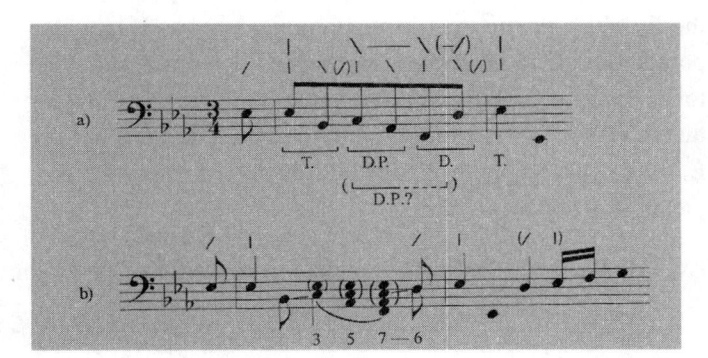

I believe that Hasty would have been better able to realize his intention of describing »Meter *as* Rhythm« if in his analyses he had initially disregarded the given time signatures and derived the rhythmic process from the individual

---

[472] Ibid., 148.

[473] The courantes in question are those from J. S. Bach's Suites for Violoncello Solo BWV 1009 (C major) and BWV 1010 (E♭ major). The examples are cited on pp. 158 and 163 in Hasty's book.

[474] Later in the analysis of the C major courante, Hasty also offers a series of »recompositions« (variants constructed by him), which, however, I will not discuss here (see Hasty, 160f.).

[475] LaRue, »Harmonic Rhythm« (see note 266, above).

Ex. 3-134   J. S. Bach, Courante from the Suite for Violoncello Solo BWV 1009 (Beginning)

components of the composition. As an alternative example I offer, in what follows, a comparative components-rhythmic analysis of the two Bach themes (Ex. 3-134 and 135).

With respect to the component »Sound«, the two soggetti differ insofar as in the C major theme a single note value reigns (♪), whereas the E♭ major theme contains several values (♩, ♪, ♪³, ♪). The resulting component profile »Sound« is completely level in the C major subject (except for the final note), whereas the E♭ major theme exhibits clear peaks (the calculatory basis is ♪ = 1, ♪ and ♪³ = 2, ♩ = 4). These peaks of the component »Sound« in the E♭ major theme are reinforced by other component rhythms, whereas in the C major theme these components provide the only contributions to the development of a rhythmic profile.

The component »Pitch« (pitch change) is relevant especially at the beginning of both subjects, since it causes the ♪ upbeats to appear somewhat accentuated, the pitch being placed before the bar line. In the remaining note repetitions in the E♭ major theme (mm. 5 and 6), on the other hand, a syncopated effect appears, though it is only faintly developed.

The component »Contour«, too, is more prominent in the E♭ major theme than in the C major one, as Hasty also points out, though without including the crest and keel tones systematically as rhythm-generating. If the C major theme consists of a simple, undivided melodic gesture, the E♭ major subject, with its ups and downs of interval steps, yields an irregular rhythm.

The component »Articulation« here refers only to those sound »events« that are actually notated by Bach. Aware that there was a considerable interpretive leeway, we may not figure in the other conceivable but not assessable articulatory forms. For all that, Bach's placement, in the C major theme, of the legato slurs is rhythmically significant, because these slurs begin three times on the second eighth, though, as part of the cadence to the tonic, also once on the first eighth.

To incorporate the component »Harmony« is, as previously mentioned, problematic in monophonic pieces. Bach evidently composed following a definite cadential plan, but the points at which a harmonic function changes are ambiguous. In the present cases, the changes occur in m. 6 in the C major theme (I regard all of this measure as being in the dominant, though a slipped-in subdominant on the *One* of the measure is conceivable), whereas in the E♭ major theme, they come in mm. 1 and 3 (an instance of the ambiguity described in detail by Hasty). Apart from these ambiguities, the harmonic rhythms of these two subjects differ enormously: mostly double-measure values in the C major theme, mostly quarter motions in the E♭ major one.

The component »Phrase« always permits some interpretative leeway. Since Bach did not draw any phrasing arcs, it takes interpretation to determine the intended units of musical meaning. The most important criterion here is the repetition of melodic units, whether on the same degree or in sequential processes, whether exactly or only approximately. The C major theme, I believe, exhibits a structure

Ex. 3-135   J. S. Bach, Courante from the Suite for Violoncello Solo BWV 1010 (Beginning)

of 2+2+4 bars, with the two two-bar units being again subdivisible into 1+1 because of the new starts in mm. 2 and 4. In the E♭ major subjects, I presume at first 2-bar phrases, because the initial melody with its feminine ending (E♭3-E♭2 and B♭3-B♭2) in each case heavily occupies the second respective measure. Owing to the sequence in mm. 5 to 8, on the other hand, these bars are clearly phrased into 1+1+2. The longer a phrase lasts, the more weight it has; the points assigned by me are matters of estimation, but my solution is not arbitrary.

An accumulation of the points in time at which component rhythms are active – that is, have an entry – results in a rhythmic profile. A first comparative glance at the profiles of the C major and E♭ major subject will already reveal the difference in rhythmic character of the two 3/4 themes. The profile of the C major theme is whole- or double-measured and throughout quite level, while that of the E♭ major subject is initially based on quarter notes and throughout brings about higher peaks. Since these profiles were constructed without the assumptions of metric hierarchy, they constitute purely rhythmic ones. But as one can see, they nevertheless clearly exhibit the structure of the 3/4 meter. At the same time, no measure is like another. To use Hasty's words: »the uniqueness or particularity of any actual measure [is] a product of rhythm and not meter.«[476]

The method of analyzing according to the components theory makes it possible fully to extract the rhythm, and through it also the meter, of a composition. The same cannot be said of the analyses offered by Hasty. By using the schema of the graduated accent meter as the court of final appeal, he undermines his own objective of explaining meter rhythmically.

Schachter • Rhythm à la Schenker

Carl Schachter is regarded as one of the foremost representatives of ›Schenkerism‹ in the Anglo-American world. As an indirect pupil of Heinrich Schenker – mediated by Felix Salzer, who prior to his flight to the U.S. had been an actual student of Schenker in Vienna – Schachter to this day feels committed to the Schenkerian theory of the »Ursatz« and the »Urlinie.« Since Schenker had rather neglected questions of rhythm and meter, Schachter took up these subjects in the 1970s, discussing them in a series of three essays under the general heading of »Rhythm and Linear Analysis.« In 1999, these essays were republished without substantial changes, in a volume entitled *Unfoldings. Essays in Schenkerian Theory and Analysis*.[477]

Already in the first essay (»A Preliminary Study«), Schachter introduces the terms that are crucial for his entire conception of rhythm: »tonal rhythm« and »durational rhythm«. In order to be able to determine the difference between tone-dependent and duration-dependent rhythms precisely, he adduces examples that are either monochronous but diastematically lively (for »tonal rhythm«) or monotone but diverse in rhythm (for »durational rhythm«).[478] His example for »tonal rhythm,« the »scales in spirals« by Ferruccio Busoni (Ex. 3-136 a), makes clear that »duration« to Schachter means simply »note value.« In the Busoni example, Schachter says, the durations remain constant (there are only ♪), and consequently there is no »durational rhythm.« On the other hand, there are »tonal rhythms« resulting from the recurring pitch C5 and from the expanding melodic contour (C5- D5 - B4 - E5 - A4 - F5 - G4 etc.).

As persuasive as these observations are, the terminology applied to the phenomena discussed is wholly unconvincing. Since Schachter reserves the term »duration« for the temporal value of the individual notes, he has no word to designate the distances between the cited ›signals‹ of the ascending and descending scale melody. Since the term »tonal rhythm« indicates only the derivation of the rhythm from the tonal givens, it does not say anything about the time intervals of which such a »tonal rhythm« is composed. Schachter's descriptions are thus accordingly vague: »The contrast between the stable referential tones [C5, crest/keel notes] and the transitional ones produces an impression of patterned movement, in other words, an impression of rhythm.«[479]

---

[476] See note 447, above.

[477] Carl Schachter, *Unfoldings. Essays in Schenkerian Theory and Analysis*, ed. Joseph N. Straus (New York & Oxford: OUP 1999). Includes: »Rhythm and Linear Analysis« I: »A Preliminary Study« (1976), pp. 17-53; II: »Durational Reduction« (1980), pp. 54-78; III: »Aspects of Meter« (1987), pp. 79-117. The three essays appeared originally in the journal *Music Forum*.

[478] Ibid., 37.

[479] Ibid.

Ex. 3-136   Busoni, ›Scales in Spirals‹
a)   Example 1.10 in Schachter (p. 37)

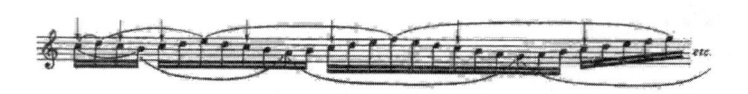

b)   Analysis according to components rhythms ($\flat = 1$)

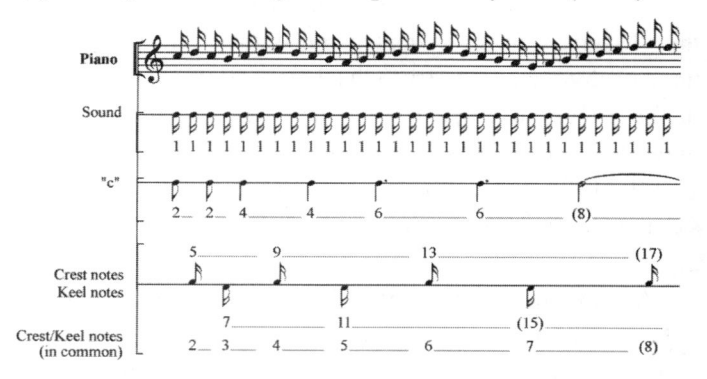

If one takes the time spans between the signal tones (which Schachter marks with arrows or slurs) as what in fact they are, namely secondary durations, and treats them on a level with the primary durations, i.e., the ♪ notated by Busoni, one can determine not only all the individual time values exactly but can also describe the primary and secondary rhythms composed of the durations (Ex. 3-136 b). Accordingly, three »tonal rhythms« – »component rhythms« in my terminology – are here interwoven as in a fabric, whereby the successive enlargement of the secondary durations (C5: 2, 4, 6 etc. ♪; crest notes: 5, 9, 13 etc. ♪; keel notes: 7, 11, 15 etc. ♪; crest and keel notes combined: 2, 3, 4, 5, 6, 7 etc. ♪) contrasts with the invariably short primary durations (♪).

The expression »durational rhythm« – Schachter's second basic concept – likewise entails problems, which the author himself names but does not resolve. With reference to three examples selected by him from Handel and Beethoven, in which rhythmicized note repetitions occur, Schachter writes: »I would like to emphasize again that duration is not the only component of what I call, for the sake of convenience, durational rhythm.«[480] Now the expression »durational rhythm« seems to me infelicitously chosen to begin with, because rhythms always consist of durations, so that ›durational rhythm‹ is all but a pleonasm. Add to that that for Schachter the term »durational rhythm« also subsumes »stresses.« In his view, though stress is properly part of metric, it could for the sake of »convenience« also be treated under the »durational rhythms.« What is behind this is an endeavor to define meter and metrical accents as phenomena largely independent of tonal givens (»tonal rhythms«). Schachter writes:

The composers of our three excerpts [the examples from Handel and Beethoven] certainly had in mind a pattern of stresses as well as of durations. Stress and duration together give rise to clearly expressed pulse and meter […] and to subtler aspects of rhythm as well.[481]

Here, too, Schachter's linking the term duration to the concept of note value proves a disadvantage, because he now has to find other expressions to denote metrical structures. In his essay »Aspects of Meter,« he speaks of »equal divisions of time« that alone make meter possible – here understood literally as what is ›measured.‹ While the means for producing isometry are said to be many and diverse, Schachter does not allow that the resulting equal »time spans« are basically also »durations«:

Some of these time spans arise directly out of the pacing of sounds; others – most obviously the larger ones – must be inferred by the listener out of patterns of long and short, of loud and soft, of repetition and change, of voice leading and harmony, of all of these elements and others, singly and in any imaginable combination.[482]

To illustrate his arguments, Schachter analyzes the ›Scherzo‹ from Beethoven's Piano Sonata op. 27 No. 1, addressing specifically the question of division into hypermeasures.[483] The results of the analysis are all apt in my view. They boil down to the conclusion that the first three 3/4 measures should be read as an upbeat and that only the fourth bar should be accorded the quality of a *One* in what is to be taken as a 12/4 time. Schachter argues as one would in a components-rhythmic analysis: if harmonic changes, motif beginnings, melodic progressions etc. coincide, the result is strong weights (he says »strong beats«), which in the end reveal a certain hypermetric structure. But such detailed observations are missing from the layered diagram (cum note-value diminution at a ratio of 3:1 [»durational reduction«]) with which Schachter represents the four levels of the »middle ground.« It is evidently made to depict not the rhythm but the tonality, that is to say, the intermediate steps on the road from the surface of the individual composition to the deeps of the »Ursatz« (fundamental structure). It is, finally, in these »tonal structures« that the real cognitive interest of Schachter lies, who here, too, proves to be a decided ›Schenkerian.‹ He once touches on the deficiencies of his rhythmic analyses himself: »the smaller details of rhythm, those at the most immediate level of foreground, do not show up at all in these reductions«[484] – something that, Schachter thinks, must be accepted as an »unavoidable drawback.«[485]

---

[480]   Ibid., 38.

[481]   Ebd.

[482]   Ebd., S. 80.

[483]   Ebd., S. 83-86.

[484]   Ibid., 76.

[485]   Ibid.

Ex. 3-137 Beethoven, Sonata op. 27 no. 1, ›Scherzo‹, mm. 1-16, Rhythm Score

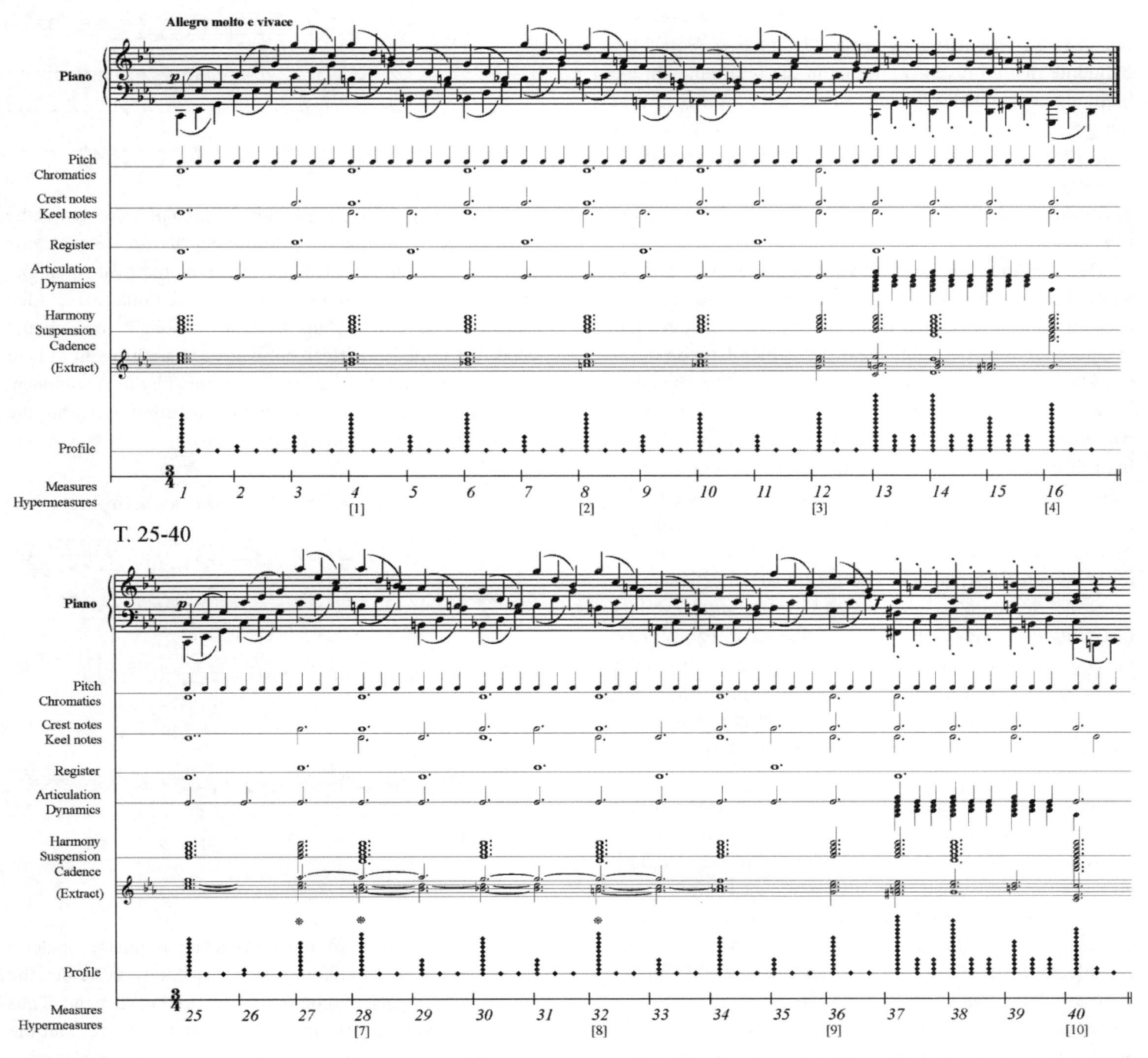

In the method of components-rhythmical analysis, however, we now have an instrument that makes it possible to advance into the ›depths‹ of rhythmic structures, as the Schenkerian analyses seek to plumb the ›deeps‹ of the tonal connections. I have therefore analyzed the very same Beethoven passages scrutinized by Schachter and have reduced them to a rhythm score that makes it possible not only to replicate Schachter's observations but also to substantiate his conclusions on the basis of more rigorous data (Ex. 3-137).

The example is arranged in such a way that exposition (mm. 1-16) and recapitulation (mm. 25-40) line up one beneath the other note for note and bar for bar (the middle section is not represented). Thus it is possible to view both the agreements and the occasional divergences (∗) at a glance. In his commentary – though not in his diagram – Schachter has pointed out certain rhythmically relevant subtleties, e.g., certain suspensions that occur only in the Scherzo's recapitulation (mm. 28 and 32). They are said to be the reason for the late emergence of the four-bar structure.[486] By comparing the rhythmic weight profiles of the two 16-bar passages one can see that the heavy weights (rhombus towers) of measures 4, 6, 8, 10 and 12 are all equal, while mm. 28 and 32 of the recapitulation have an additional weight unit each. The cause of this weight gain is solely two suspensions (A♭5 before G5 and G5 before F5). Since the duration between these two suspensions equals 12 ♩, a unit of four bars is thereby constituted.

A further modification occurs in m. 27, where the upper voice leaps up to A♭5, whereas the exposition does not rise beyond the fifth to G5. Here, too, nearly all component rhythms are unaltered: the pitches in ♩-rhythm, the chromaticism inherent in the bass in triple or double bars, the

---

[486] Ibid., 84.

crest and keel notes of the upper and lower voice respectively at intervals of 𝅗𝅥 or 𝅝., the changes in octave register in 𝅝, and the articulation by means of slurs in 𝅗𝅥.. Solely the harmonic rhythm diverges, in that in the recapitulation the harmony does not shift from the tonic after three measures but goes to the VI already after two bars (m. 27) and thus makes for an increase in the respective rhythmic weight[487] – though the weight under the first A♭5 is still less than that under the second in m. 28 ([7]), as that marks the beginning of a »hypermeasure.«

The rhythmic profile portrays metrical weight relations without taking the familiar metrical hierarchies into the account. Thus one can tell immediately that Beethoven has composed mostly in double measures, which later on occasionally coalesce into quadruple-bar units. The rhythmic weights are therefore determined solely on the basis of component rhythms, which accumulate to higher or less high rhombus towers. The fact that in the process the metrical or else hypermetrical structure manifests itself as the result of the compositional act may confirm the thesis that time signatures are not simply pre-established but are the result of artistic strategies. The accentual order emerging from the rhythmic weight relations, to be sure, exhibits flexibility throughout. That can be gathered as readily from the emphatic upbeat just described (m. 27→28) as from the end of the two 16-bar passages, where the inner life of the two cadencing hypermeasures [3] and [9] is relatively irregular, at least by comparison with the preceding bars.

It is one of the characteristics of Schenkerian analyses that the so-called »surface« or »foreground« of a composition receives less attention than the layers of the »middle ground«, through which the analyst proceeds by various degrees of reduction to the »depth« of the »Ursatz.« If one adheres to this method also in rhythm analyses, the inevitable result is less and less differentiation and finally, upon reaching the »Ursatz,« a state of rhythmlessness. Schenker himself thought the Ursatz was arrythmic.[488] Schachter rejects this notion (and thereby proves even more ›Schenkerian‹ than the master himself), but his analyses tend to confirm it, as can be gathered, among other things, from the fact that exact note durations are rare in his middle-ground diagrams.

Against this reduction method, which may make sense for large-scale tonal and formal relations, I would like to posit an ›exfoliation‹ method suitable for bringing to light the rhythmic ramifications embedded in compositions. The »surface« of a piece of music contains more rhythm than

Ex. 3-138   Schubert, Sonata in G Major op. 78, Beginning (Descant)

meets the eye. When Schachter, for example, says about the beginning of Schubert's G-Major Sonata op. 78 that only the second bar revealed the rhythmic-metrical situation, because here both the beat level of dotted quarters and the subdivisions into eighths became audible,[489] one should add that in m. 2 metrical ambivalences are brought to hear as well, as the rhythm ♪♪♩ ♩ 𝅗𝅥, formed by the component »Pitch,« is equivalent to a hemiolic distribution within the fourfold ternary 12/8-time (Ex. 3-138).

Ex. 3-139
J. S. Bach, Bourrée from the Suite BWV 996, Crest Note Rhythms (Descant)

Suchlike secondary rhythms Schachter regularly neglects elsewhere as well, although he occasionally describes the phenomena themselves on which the rhythms depend. Thus he notes about the Busoni scales, as stated above, that the melodic contour with its turning-points produces a rhythm of its own (»tonal rhythm«). Why then does he not pick up the aspect he observes in Busoni's Scales in Spirals also in his detailed discussion of the opening bars of one of Bach's Bourrées?[490] As my comparison of three phases in the Bourrée (BWV 996) shows (Ex. 3-139), it is precisely the diastematic rhythms that enable one to differentiate the superficially evenly rhythmicized melodies in their specific rhythmic structure.

In the line »Sound« one can see the primary rhythm, which is abstracted directly from the duration of the individual notes (♪♪♩ ♪♪♩), and which embodies the typical (courtly) bourrée gesture. In the »crest note«-lines,

---

[487] On the fourfold weighting of harmonic changes, see the »Introduction« (p. 10) and the chapter »Rhythmic Weight« (p. 71) in this study.

[488] Cf. Schachter in his »Preliminary Study«: »Is the Ursatz arrhythmic, as Schenker maintained? My answer to this question is a qualified no. I believe that progressions in the Fundamental Structure embody tonal, but not durational, rhythm.« See Unfoldings (cf. footnote 473), 38f.

[489] Ibid., 87f. : »In measure 2 of the Schubert Sonata [...] both the dotted quarter note beats and their eighth-note subdivisions become fully evident.«

[490] Cf. ibid., 43ff.

those rhythms are reproduced whose durations are determined by the upper turning-points of the melodies. These rhythms, which are fairly irregular, are related quasi contrapuntally to the bourrée rhythm. They also document that the rhythmic density of the dance piece, which is divided into 8+8+8 bars, increases from phrase to phrase.

NB 3-140 J. S. Bach, *Bourrée*, Kieltonrhythmen (Bass)

The same situation can be observed in the bass voice (Ex. 3-140). While there are few lower turning-points (»keel notes«) at first, there are noticeably more in the second and third part. They are also adapted to the meter in the first eight-bar segment (strong and semi-strong beats), whereas later they are set post-beat (second quarter) or as anticipations (third quarter).

Ex. 3-141 mm. 21-24, Descant and Bass (Components »Sound« and »Contour«)

The rhythmically most complex measures are the last four (Ex. 3-141), where the bass voice picks up the bourrée rhythmic pattern but in an off-set manner, so that for seven quarters an uninterrupted sequence of eighth notes results. Interestingly, Bach has smoothed out the diastematic rhythms again in this final phase of the bourrée, so that the attention of listeners and musicians is focused entirely on the imitational interplay of the two voices.

The inclusion of additional component rhythms in the analysis would further confirm the trend toward increased rhythmic density at the end of the piece. Thus the harmonic rhythm proves to be liveliest in the third part, and the micro-structuration of the phrases is more tightly framed at the end than at the beginning. The question to be put to Carl Schachter would be whether such processes of rhythmic tension and relaxation correlate with the overriding tonal motion. His analyses, which reveal a high degree of musical intelligence and certainly make for profitable reading, could gain even more if rhythm were not regarded as subordinate to the tonal motions, but were recognized as a powerful ›second chamber‹ of the compositional ›polity.‹ It is a matter of categorical alternatives, of the »Whats« and »Whens.« What and when questions in music concern areas that are interrelated. But before beginning to view the dimensions of sound and time conjointly, one should scrutinize them separately so as to recognize their distinct functions.

Krebs • Metrical Dissonance

Harald Krebs – a musicologist at the University of Victoria – is, since 2010, president of the »Society for Music Theory.« In 1999, he published his book *Fantasy Pieces. Metrical Dissonance in the Music of Robert Schumann*, in which he summarized his researches, pursued since the 1980's, in rhythmics and metrics.[491]

Krebs calls his expression »metrical dissonance« a »metaphor.«[492] Analogously to the realm of pitches and chords – the proper home of the terms »consonance« and »dissonance« – the superimposition of rhythmic-metrical »layers,« he says, can produce the impression of ›sounding asunder‹ if the »layers« deviate from each other, either because of different modes of division (Type A: »grouping dissonance«) or due to displacements of congruent rhythms (Type B: »displacement dissonance«).[493]

What exactly is meant by the expression »layer« can be inferred from Krebs' analyses: an actual definition is not given. In most cases, the term refers to individual voices, but also to specific components of a composition, such as left and right hand in a piano piece, harmony, accompaniment, etc. However, Krebs includes a »layer« in his analysis only if it possesses the specific feature of being structured periodically. If a first layer contains, say, nothing but ♪, a second one only ♩ and a third one nothing but ♩ values, the »layers« are said to »consonate«; if, on the other hand, ♪, ♩. and ♩. stand against each other in the layers, the layers »dissonate.«

Meter Krebs defines as follows: »I define the meter of a work as the union of all layers of motion (i.e., series of regularly recurring pulses) active within it.«[494] A relatively fast basic pulse is said to be »interpreted« by slower pulse sequences (»2-layers«, »3-layers«, »4-layers« etc.), whereas pulse sequences that are faster than the basic pulse are mere ornamental additions and are metrically irrelevant.[495]

[491] Harald Krebs, *Fantasy Pieces. Metrical Dissonance in the Music of Robert Schumann*. (New York/Oxford: OUP, 1999). Note an early article of H. Krebs: »Some Extensions of the Concept of Metrical Consonance and Dissonance,« *Journal of Music Theory* 31 (1987), 99-120.

[492] *Fantasy Pieces* 13, 16.

[493] Ibd., 31, 33.

[494] Ibd., 23.

[495] Ibd.

Krebs' conception differs from earlier definitions inasmuch as, in his view, a meter can be erected also independently of the dictate of the time signature. Krebs thus has recourse to the original meaning of the Greek word *metrón* = measure, according to which the mere fact that an extent of time is measured at all constitutes a meter.

Ex. 3-142 Schumann, Intermezzi op. 4 No. 4 (after Krebs p. 24)

If we now look at Krebs' approach from the perspective of components rhythmics, we find numerous points of contact. What Krebs denominates and analyses as the metrical quality of a »layer« corresponds in principle to the secondary rhythms deriving from components. Take the very first example in Krebs' Chapter 2, with which the investigation properly commences (Ex. 3-142). The illustration in question is a segment from the middle part of the 4th intermezzo in Robert Schumann's op. 4.

In his commentary[496] on this example, Krebs analyzes the two 6-♪ meters, which he has noted in numerical form beneath Schumann's music text. The six-note sequence beginning on the *One* of the 12/8 measure is said to result from the »durational accents« of the main voice in the right hand and, in addition, to be supported by the »harmonic rhythm.« The second six-note sequence, on the other hand, leading to a »displacement dissonance,« is said to derive from the dynamics (>, »dynamic accents«) and the contour of the voice in the left hand (»registral accents«).

If one subjects the example to a rhythmic components analysis, the result is similar to Krebs', but one also comes up with some divergences or additional findings relevant both rhythmically and metrically (Ex. 3-143). Thus the 6-♪ rhythm commencing on the *One* registers amplitudes in the component »Sound« (thematic voice, r. h.) that are larger than two, thus agreeing with Krebs' »layer.« But already pitch rhythm and weight – because of the repetition (the upper voice in this measure has only two, drawn-out pitches, E5 and D♯5) – result in a different subdivision of the 12/8

Ex. 3-143 Schumann, Intermezzi op. 4 No. 4, m. 8

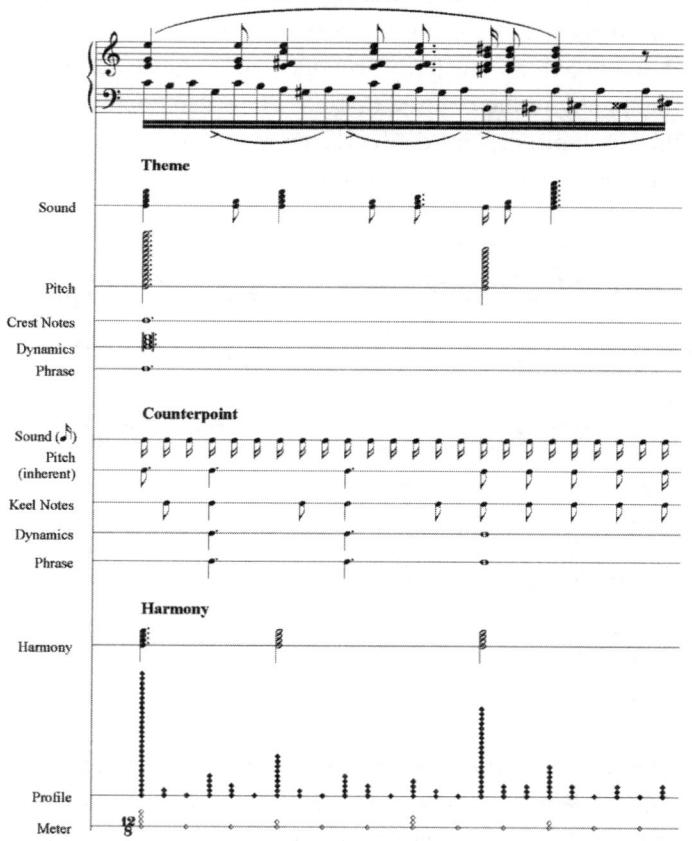

bar, namely 15 + 9 ♪. Since, additionally, a change in harmonic function takes place at this point (together with the pitch change of the descant voice from E5 and D♯5), an additional weight results. Interestingly enough, one of he time points of the second sequence of six notes, which Krebs analyzes with regard to the contrapuntal voice in the left hand, likewise coincides with the change in pitch and harmony on the 16th ♪. Five different component rhythms (»Sound,« »Pitch,« »Crest notes,« »Dynamics« and »Phrase«) are involved in marking the »displacement 6-layers« of the figural voice, the inherent pitches (2nd system under »counterpoint«) being C-G-E-B-B♯-C♯-C𝄪-D♯-(E). What with the chief weights falling on the 1st, 7th and 16th ♪, the rhythmic profile, combining the separate analyses of theme, counterpoint and harmonics, reveals a main rhythm based on the time intervals 6+9+9 ♪.

Ex. 3-144 Schumann, Intermezzi op. 4 No. 4, mm. 7-10, Rhythm Profile

[496] Ibd. 23 f.

Extension to additional measures of the segment – which are linked, among other things, by a sequence of major thirds (mm. 7–10: A♭–C–E–A♭) (Ex. 3-144) – yields a recurrent pattern of 6+9+9 ♪ that ›dissonates metrically‹ with the 12/8 of the time signature, though not as Krebs represents it (he evidently missed the delayed harmonic change from $a^{5-6\sharp}$ to B^7, or he weighted it differently). Involved are not suspensions but regular harmonic progressions on very weak beats, resulting in temporal intervals of 9 ♪, which ›dissonate‹ with the primary rhythm of the right hand.

Ex. 3-145 Schumann, Piano Sonata op. 11, Finale, Beginning (Krebs' analysis, p. 125)

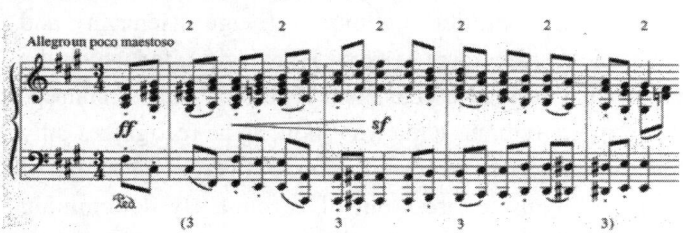

In another example cited by Krebs, too, his results can be partly confirmed, but partly also made more specific by a components-rhythmic analysis. Krebs adduces the theme of the Finale in Schumann's Sonata in F♯ minor (Ex. 3-145) as proof that a compositionally produced meter – in this case a »2-♩-layer« – can completely obliterate the nominal meter. For this reason the primary »3-♩-layer« appears in brackets, while the actually sounding binary meter is indicated above the notes accentuated by slurs (2 2 2 2 2 2 = ♩♩♩♩♩♩).

The resultant 3/2 meter (»larger triple grouping«[497]) is marked by the staccato and legato articulation – something that seems so obvious to Krebs that he does not even specify it. There are, of course, additional components that generate rhythms and rhythmic weights of their own and thus materially alter the total rhythmic-metrical structure of the theme.

In my rhythm score of mm. 1–4 (Ex. 3-146), the piano setting is notated in simplified and purely rhythmic form (no beams, all flags pointing in the same direction, no bar lines). In weighting the scaffolding voices (descant and bass), I have accorded the main voice twice as many values

Ex. 3-146 Schumann, Sonata op. 11, 4th mov., Beginning, Schema, Rhythm Score

under the component »Sound« as I did the lower part (1 = ♪ to 1 = ♩). The changes in harmonic function are weighted fourfold, dynamic and phrase rhythms are slightly gradated in their durational weights.

Of decisive importance (but not addressed by Krebs) are the components-dependent syncopations resulting from tonal repetitions, on the one hand, and from the durations of harmonic functions, on the other.

Ex. 3-147

In Ex. 3-147, I have paired the original with two constructed variants, which are to make clear how strongly the component »Articulation« is ›beset‹ by the component »Harmony.«

Ex. 3-148 Schumann, Sonata op. 11, 4th mov., Beginning, Rhythmic and Metric Profiles

[497] Ibid. 125.

In Construct a, the harmonic durations are notated as ♩ (instead of ♪♪), so that a progression in quarters with an ♪ upbeat results, while in Construct b the harmonies are shifted, so that the notes of the melody appear as a chain of dissonant anticipations (instead of scale-specific notes). However, the entire theme has neither suspension nor anticipation dissonances. Instead, the harmonies in this strictly chordal setting change in a ♩ tempo, with these ♩ being ›displaced‹ by 1 ♪ against the notated meter. Altogether it becomes clear that behind the anapaestic groupings in 4-♪ units, which Krebs describes quite correctly, there is simultaneously a syncopated »layer« of ›displaced quarter notes,‹ which results in a metrical dissonance. As Ex. 3-148 shows, this syncopated pattern resolves itself only with the cadence at the end.

In the first piece of the piano cycle *Carnaval*, at the point of transition from the *Animato* to the *Presto* (Stretto, from m. 114) (Ex. 3-149), the durations ♩. = 3 and ♩ = 2 can be readily attributed to compositional facts: a long bass note and a dynamically accentuated high note before the double bar line, polka rhythms and ♩ durations after it. If one leaves it at that, however, the real sensations, which give to the concluding part of this *Préambule* its special character, remain unrecognized.

Ex. 3-149 Schumann, *Carnaval* op. 9, Préambule, mm. 112-116 (Krebs' analysis, p. 87)

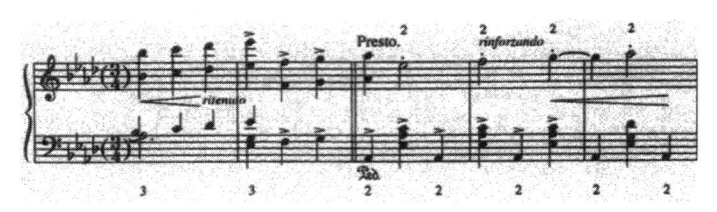

As can be discerned in Ex. 3-150, where the entire concluding section is represented, Schumann has built certain irregularities into the Stretto, which cause little shocks in the listener, because he must think that something has gone haywire here. I have marked the spots in question with an ! In the meter line at the bottom, the exclamation marks signal an *unmarked* change of meter: twice Schumann alters

with a kind of duble-beat figure (E♭-D-E♭-G-F-D♭-C) into the third of A♭ major. The seven quarter notes conform neither to the »2-layer« nor to the notated »3-layer« (1 = ♩). Besides, they effect a shift of the entire phrase, so that the repetition of the theme is in a different metrical relation to the accompaniment from that of the first time. The accompaniment, which in the example is notated in simplified form (♩ ♩ → ♩), seems wholly unaffected by this ›irregularity.‹ It persists in its rhythm, regardless of metrical changes or melodic shifts. Equally constant is the harmonic rhythm (6+6+6+6+6+6+6+8 ♪), which conforms to the 3/2 and 4/2-rhythm of the polka accompaniment.

Harald Krebs' book impresses by its numerous striking examples of »conflict rhythmics« (Hugo Riemann) and »rhythmic displacement« (Karol Hławiczka), for which the author has designed a consistent typology. Krebs' conception of meter remains somewhat odd, as he recognizes only equal time intervals as his criterion, but leaves questions of metric or rhythmic stress out of account. By determining the temporal structure of the »layers« according to compositional characteristics, he hits upon secondary durations. If one applies the simplest of all definitions of rhythm as a ›sequence of durations‹, Krebs' meters would simply be special rhythms, that is to say, rhythms with equal durations.

I regard this conception as correct and have justified it in the components theory. The second major characteristic of meter, its weight or accent structure (not treated by Krebs) is incorporated by me in terms of the new aspect of »rhythmic weight«, whose gradations are determined by lengths (as multiples of short durations) or accumulations of components durations.

By this means the subtlest of transitions from hetero- to isometric structures can be described – that is, all that used to be occluded by the supposed opposition of rhythmics and metrics. If one wanted to name a weakness in Krebs' wonderful and also very charming book, it would be the failure to set metrical *and* rhythmic facts – whether dissonant or consonant – in relation to each other. That would surely also have delighted Florestan and Eusebius.[498]

Ex. 3-150   Schumann, *Carnaval* op. 9, Préambule, Coda (Presto), Scheme

the meter by simply placing four quarters (| ♩♩♩♩ |) instead of three (| ♩♩♩ |) between two bar lines. Linked to this irregularity are two groups of seven notes in the right hand. The melody, which marches up and down the A♭ major scale, proceeds at first in (staggered) halves, before it leads

[498] Krebs titles his book *Fantasy Pieces* in allusion to Schumann's *Phantasiestücke* op. 88. He continues the play with romanticisms by including fictive dialogues between Schumann's well-known fictional disputants Florestan and Eusebius in his theoretical arguments.

Lerdahl • Tonal Pitch Space

In 2001, the American musicologist and composer Fred Lerdahl published a study of tonal pitch space.[499] Almost 20 years earlier, he had brought out a generative theory of tonal music jointly with the linguist and cognitive scientist Ray Jackendoff.[500] The more recent book recapitulates and modifies the older theory, in order to then build upon it.

Though fundamentally different in approach and objective, Lerdahl's theory nevertheless borders on the components theory insofar as he operates with centers of musical attraction that are significant not only for tonal but also for rhythmic-metric listening. By means of reductionist analysis, in which note values are reduced fourfold and rhythms are simplified thereby, phrasal structures (»metrical and hypermetrical grids«[501]) can be illustrated and combined with tree diagrams. On the final level of reduction, all that generally remains are V-I-V sequences, which remind of Heinrich Schenker's background formula.[502]

Lerdahl's method can be clearly exemplified in his reduction analysis of Chopin's Prelude in E minor op. 28 No. 4. The author begins by reproducing the original piano score (Ex. 3-151) and then presents a diagram of the various levels of reduction (Ex. 3-152), isolating two different operations: »time-span reduction« (TSR) and »prolongational reduction« (PR). The »time-span« analysis is focused on the rhythmics and metrics of a composition, as Lerdahl states explicitly. What is needed are

> two analytic graphs for a piece, one for the rhythmic analysis and the time-span reduction, the other for the prolongational analysis […] which is of greater musical and psychological interest. At the same time, it would be a mistake to eliminate the time-span component altogether. Because it evaluates events as heard in the rhythmic structure, this kind of reduction contains essential information for the prolongational analysis, which requires rhythmic as well as pitch values to establish its tensing and relaxing patterns.[503]

Ex. 3-151 Chopin, *Prélude* op. 28 No. 4, E minor (Lerdahl)

NB 3-152 Lerdahl, Analysis of Chopin's Prelude[504]

---

[499] Fred Lerdahl, *Tonal Pitch Space* (Oxford: OUP, 2001).

[500] Fred Lerdahl and Ray Jackendoff, *A Generative Theory of Tonal Music* (Cambridge (Mass.) and London: MIT Press, 1983).

[501] Lerdahl (2001), 89.

[502] Ibid., 106/107.

[503] Ibid., 14.

[504] Ibid., 106/107.

In both procedures, the aim of the reduction is to get to the heart of the matter, which, on the one hand, fuses a motif, a phrase, a period etc. into a rhythmic-metric unit, and, on the other, makes the melodic and harmonic events to be experienced as a tonal unity.

In the first stage of reduction (TSR f), the notes are minimized at the ratio of 4:1. In addition, Lerdahl introduces beams and structuring lines that make the original alla breve meter appear like individual beats of a 4/4 meter. In the melody, notes that in the analyst's opinion are not part of the main event are omitted (e.g., the anticipation of the B4 prior to m. 1, the notes B4, D5 and E4 in m. 9, the suspensions and triplet eighths in m. 12), while in the accompaniment, the rhythmics of the individual voices is smoothed out along with dispensing with the eighths repetitions (e.g., the anticipation of the G♯ in the inner voice of m. 4 disappears, along with several suspensions). The criterion for the reduction is evidently the meter.

The second reduction stage (TSR e) deals with a detail of mm. 15-19 and can be omitted here. The third stage (TSR d) gets down to the rate of two measures (1 ♩ = 2 bars), whose content in each case is condensed in a single main event. It is left to the reader to decide whether the first or else the second measure is the decisive one, as no explanantion is given. In the origial first four-bar phrase, for example, the tonic E minor chord stems from m. 1_1 and the secondary dominant E^7 from m. 4_1. In the second four-bar phrase, Lerdahl selects the chords C^{56} and $G♯^{dim}$ without attending to the fact that in the first chord the notes E and G are suspensions to D♯ and F♯.

Apart from such arbitrarinesses, one has to ask what is still »rhythmic« or »metric« in these extracts. The actual rhythms and meters, after all, are de facto step by step eliminated. Yet I regard it as rhythmically and metrically essential, for example, that the transformation of the E minor tonic into an E major secondary dominant is organized in such a way that the dominant of A minor is reached only in the fourth measure rather than in the third, as the reduction level TSR d suggests. Besides, there are, between these relatively stable harmonies, several unstable, ambiguous or sometimes wide-spanned ones (e.g. in m. 3). They cause the four initial largo measures to melt into a unified whole, something perceptible only so long as one does not overlook – or rather overhear – a single note, suspension or rhythmic detail.

In contrast to the reductionist method, in which the rhythm is reduced step by step, the rhythmic components analysis aims at making rhythm *more* visible step by step. Beginning with the basic component of the tonal durations, the picture that listeners and performers obtain of the rhythmic process becomes increasingly differentiated as additional component rhythms are detected. Combined into a rhythm score, we see in the end a texture of mutually coordinated rhythms, which operate simultaneously and can reveal something about the degree of rhythmic complexity of a given composition.

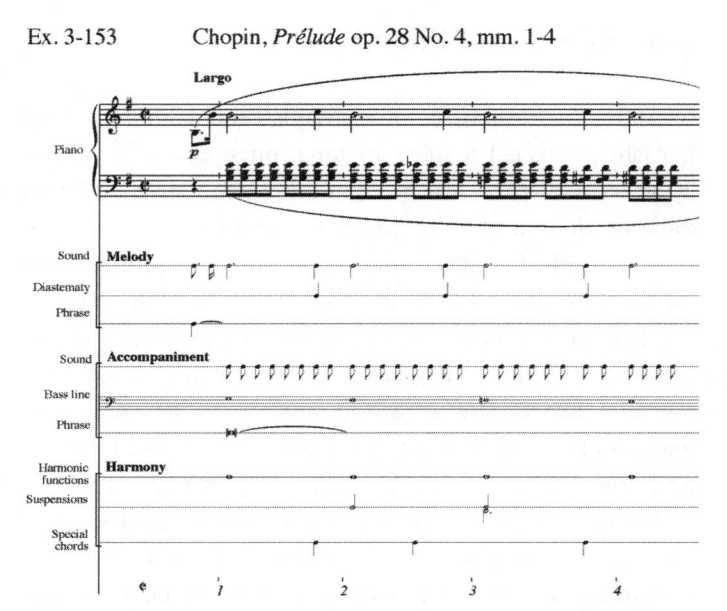

Ex. 3-153   Chopin, *Prélude* op. 28 No. 4, mm. 1-4

I therefore want to try to show, in an alternative analysis of the Chopin piece, that in matters of rhythm (and as well as meter), it is not reduction but accumulation that reveals the gist of the phenomenon. The first four bars of the Prelude will suffice initially to explain my procedure (Ex. 3-153). Given the simplicity of design of this cantilena with accompaniment, the component rhythms should be determined separately for the areas of main voice, accompaniment and harmonics. In the principal part, we should note the tonal entries (»Sound«), the crest notes (»Diastematics«) and the phrase mark drawn from the upbeat. What is remarkable here is that the crest notes (C5) are regularly placed so as to give some support to the upbeats (4th quarter); the first phrase of the cantilena correspondingly also sets in before the start of the measure. The steady pulse of ♪ (»Sound«) in the left hand adds a motoric element that seems, as it were, to bear up the long tones of the main part. Besides, this typically pianistic repetition technique can create the illusion of chords held at an undiminished volume. More important, however, is the bass line that emerges as an inherent voice from the reiterated chords (G-F♯-F♮-E). Its conjunct descent characterizes also the subsequent measures, so that one has to assume a regular counter-voice to the melody-bearing cantilena of the right hand. The rhythm of the bass line in the first four bars is as simple as can be (𝅝), though that changes later on. The rhythm of the harmonics likewise consists of several subcomponents. The chief one is the change of harmonic functions, which at the beginning of the piece takes place quite regularly (𝅝). In tonal music, suspensions, too, are significant, since they traditionally point forward to metrically strong beats. In m. 2, a seventh suspension sounds in the alto (E4-E♭4), where the E♭ can at first be heard as a D♯. There are two suspensions in m. 3: E4 before D4 as ♩ and A3 before G♯3 as ♩. (the G♯ can at the same time be regarded as an anticipation of the G♯ in m. 4). To the suspensions we must add, as a third sub-component, some special harmonic events – events that largely produce the melancholic character of this »Largo« Prelude, but that also emit strong rhythmic signals. Among them we may reckon the auxiliary note C along with simultaneously held

Ex. 3-154 Chopin, *Prélude* op. 28 No. 4, Rhythmic Profile

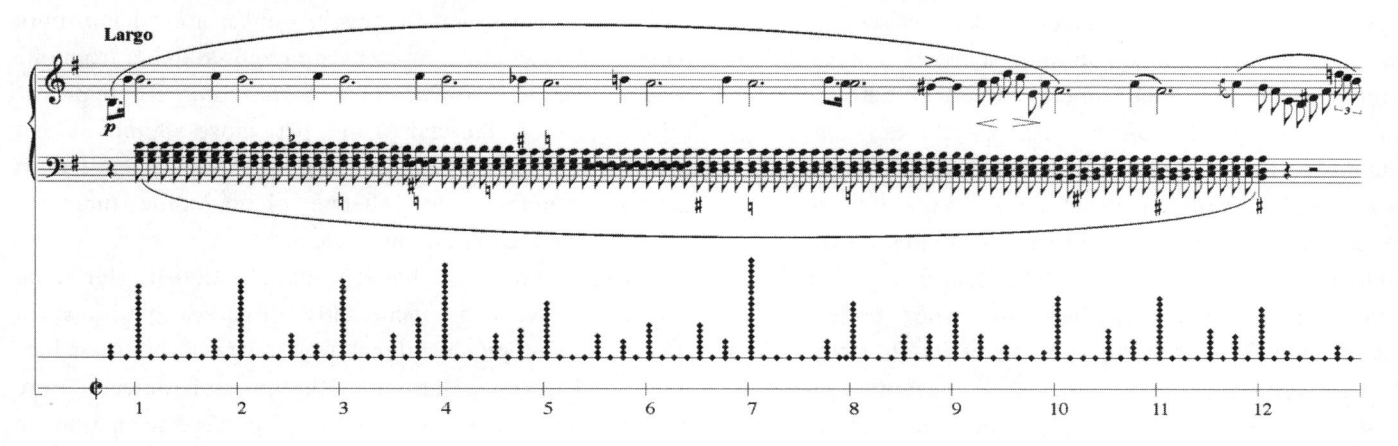

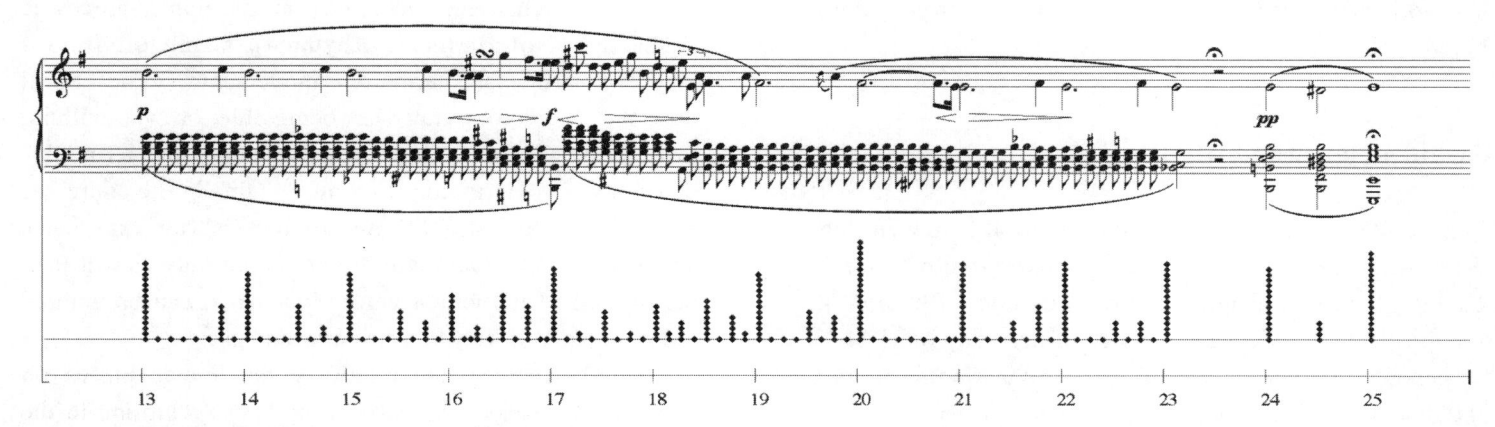

B (m. 1), the ambiguous chord F#3-A3-E♭4-B4 (m. 2₃) and the F3-G#3-D4-C5 immediately before the E⁷ chord (mm. 3 to 4). Altogether, the first four bars are unexciting rhythmically. Even so, one cannot say that they simply represent the alla breve meter: there is a tendency toward stressed upbeats and a slight increase in suspensions and special chords.

A glance at the rhythmic profile of the entire prelude (Ex. 3-154) will make clear that the isometry of the main heavy beats remains in effect throughout, but that the rhythmic filler between the tallest weight columns varies greatly. Occasionally there are suggestions of rhythmic groups of two (mm. 5-6, 17-18) or three bars (mm. 7-9). The highest degree of rhythmic density coincides with the dynamic climax of the piece around m. 17.

In any case, the phrase structure Lerdahl proposes and that makes the basis of his tree diagram – groups of four bars from beginning to end plus a supernumerary final measure –, does not do justice to the actual situation in this piece formed as a widely spanned repeat period (12+13 bars). One only has to compare the inherent lower voice of the first phrase with that of the second one to realize that the two parts are heterometric within themselves and are differently structured in comparison with one another (Ex. 3-155).

Most conspicuous is the relation of the time spans between the G at the beginning of the two parts and the target note B, which represents the function of the dominant and stays on as a half-close at the end of the first phrase, while at the end of the second it leads into the tonic via an enharmonically changed second chord (B♭-C-E-G = A#-C-E-G). To reach this target takes nine bars for the first phrase, but only four for the second. A corresponding proportion obtains in the striking B-C pendulum, which comprises three bars the first time (mm. 10-12), but six the second time (mm. 17-22).

Rhythmically noteworthy are also the two four-bar groups at the beginning of both first and second phrase. The chromatic tetrachord G-F#-F♮-E, which at first is traversed at a pace of four whole notes, appears compressed in the second phrase. In consequence, the secondary dominant chord of E⁷ is reached sooner and, besides, is declared a transitional step on the way to the dominant. One can see from this that a phrasal unit of four bars expresses very little by itself, since the two sections of mm. 1-4 and 13-16 are wholly different in the structure of their harmonic rhythm. The same is true of the entire rhythmics of the piece, as a comparison of the rhythmic profile of the two period halves (mm. 1-12 and 13-25) proves. The »squaring of compositional construction« (Richard Wagner) is suspended in this Chopin prelude: Lerdahl forces it back on.

Ex. 3-155 (Inherent Bass Line)

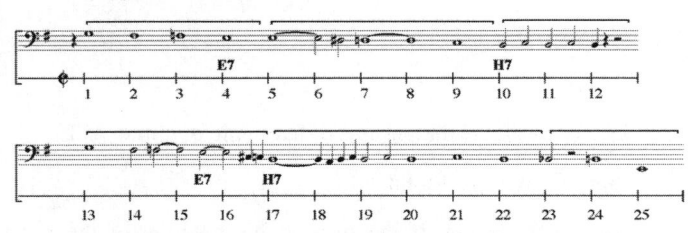

Fred Lerdahl's theory is aimed primarily at exploring the laws governing tonal relations (pitches, pitch classes). In my view, it casts little light on rhythm analysis. The reduction method does not seem to me to agree well with the nature of musical rhythm. Unless one makes the time signature the measure of all things, it is indispensable to begin by ascertaining, by detailed analysis, the *rhythmically* produced meter, which is quite unschematic, even though metric periodicity can be discerned in it. It keeps alive the memory of all the component rhythms, from whose collaboration it resulted. That is what gives meter its elasticity, while it grants the composer the freedom – speaking generally – of integrating unwritten changes in meter, heterometric excursions, even well organized scenes of chaos, in his work and thereby keeping the audience from getting bored.

Swain • Harmonic Rhythm

In 2002, the American musicologist Joseph P. Swain published *Harmonic Rhythm. Analysis and Interpretation.*[505] Taking off from a chapter entitled »Harmonic Rhythm« in Walter Piston's widely read theory of harmony of 1944,[506] he laments the lack of a solid theory of harmonic rhythm and then adds: »This book presents such a theory.«[507]

Indeed, there had been no attempt to analyze the rhythmic structures of the component »Harmony« in as much detail as Swain provides in the 200 pages of his book. In the first part, »Analysis of Harmonic Rhythm,« he describes six approaches to the subject. His point of departure is the totality of all durations of a composition as the condition for harmonic rhythm (»The Rhythm of the Texture«[508]). Since harmonies are always linked to pitches, any change in pitch would automatically lead to alterations in chordal structure and these in turn to durations, whose sequence Swain calls »Phenomenal Harmonic Rhythm.«[509] Since the bass in a composition plays a traditionally significant role in harmonic configurations, the rhythm of the bass part, according to Swain, has to be included in rhythmic analyses as a separate layer (»Bass Pitch Harmonic Rhythm«).[510] Where triads are the basis of rhythmic movements, the sequence of changing triads can form rhythms of its own, which do not have to be identical with the changes in functions (»Root/Quality Harmonic Rhythm«).[511] Changes from one triad to another involve tonal movements within the voices, which, Swain thinks, are all the more tension-charged the more steps are required to get from one triad to the other (»Densities of Harmonic Rhythm«).[512] Swain leaves to the end of this part those alterations that most analysts treat as the sole defining quantities of harmonic rhythms: the change of harmonic functions (»Rhythm of Harmonic Functions«).[513]

In part two of the book, »Interpretation of Harmonic Rhythm,« Swain preponderantly discusses questions of music psychology, in which even relations between harmony and meter (»Harmonic Rhythm and Meter«[514]) are regarded more nearly as a matter of perception than as an object of objective analysis. Swain discusses in detail the question of changing velocities in harmonic processes (»The Speed of Harmonic Rhythm«), taking off from a kind of principal harmonic movement (»The Focal Stream«[515]), without, however, being able, or even willing, to describe that movement exactly. Under the term »Independence in Harmonic Rhythm,«[516] finally, he addresses also what both listeners and performers can experience anytime, i.e., that harmonic rhythm is not only slower than the rhythm of individual voices but that it can be applied independently of its rhythmic environment.

Included among the relatively few music pieces on which Swain bases his analyses (he keeps returning to the same pieces from different perspectives throughout the book) is the Adagio from Arcangelo Corelli's »Christmas Concerto« (Op. 6 No. 8), of which the author claims that it exhibits »all« aspects of harmonic rhythm.[517] Ex. 3-156 displays the rhythm score of the first five bars of the Concerto Grosso movement in the form in which Swain designed it.[518] The first line beneath the score bracket marks the rhythm resulting from the sum of all the sounds (»Texture Phenomenal«). This rhythm (notated in note values without lines) serves as frame of reference for the harmonic movements and thus is not by itself a »harmonic rhythm,« Beneath that appears the rhythm of the bass part (»Bass pitch«), which, strictly speaking, is not »harmonic« either but represents simply the rhythm of one voice.[519]

---

[505] Joseph P. Swain, Harmonic Rhythm. Analysis and Interpretation (Oxford University Press, 2002).

[506] Walter Piston, Harmony (New York, 1944), 41-55.

[507] Swain, v.

[508] Ibid., 15ff.

[509] Ibid., 22ff.

[510] Ibid., 29ff.

[511] Ibid., 40ff.

[512] Ibid., 58ff.

[513] Ibid., 68ff. Toward the end of the book, Swain also addresses music not composed according to the rules of functional harmony, e. g. medieval music or compositions by Claude Debussy (»Rhythms of Non-Functional Harmony«, pp. 129ff.).

[514] Ibid., 91ff.

[515] Ibid., 101ff.

[516] Ibid., 116ff.

[517] »...shows all the dimensions of harmonic rhythm«, p. 85.

[518] Ibid., Ex. 8-1, pp. 86-88.

[519] Swain's inclusion of the rests in his notation of the pitch rhythm (»bass pitch«) seems inconsistent to me, since rests do not affect the duration of the pitch but result in a brief sound, i.e., modify the form of the note.

In third place, Swain records the rhythm of changing basic triads (»Root«), interrogating the respective note inventories but negating certain tonal functions (e.g.. the suspensions 9-8 and 7-8 in the A♭-major sixth chord on the *One* of m. 2. The voice movements between the triads (»Density«) are notated in fourth place on a specially designed system: vertical beams on a staff of multiple lines (here five, but at other points it may be fewer or else more) touch as many lines as voices have moved. The bottom line of the rhythm score, finally, records the harmonic functions and the durations between them. As Swain points out in the chapter, he distinguishes between different dimensions.[520] For example, he interprets the second half of m. 2 in two different ways: once, rough-grained, as a simple dominant (𝅗𝅥), the other time, in fine grain, as a dominant-tonic-dominant alternation (♩♩♩).

Of all of Swain's observations, that of the rhythm of the function changes seems to me the most telling, with the level of the fine-grained durations revealing more than the more abstract, rough-grained one does. Piston, to represent harmonic rhythms, had merely written degree designations beneath the musical notation, without registering the exact durational values of the respective functions. Swain, in criticizing[521] and correcting this, might have referred to LaRue,[522] who in his Beethoven analyses indicates the harmonic rhythm exactly as Swain does, by means of note symbols.

Ex. 3-156   Corelli, Concerto op. 6 No. 8 (Swain)

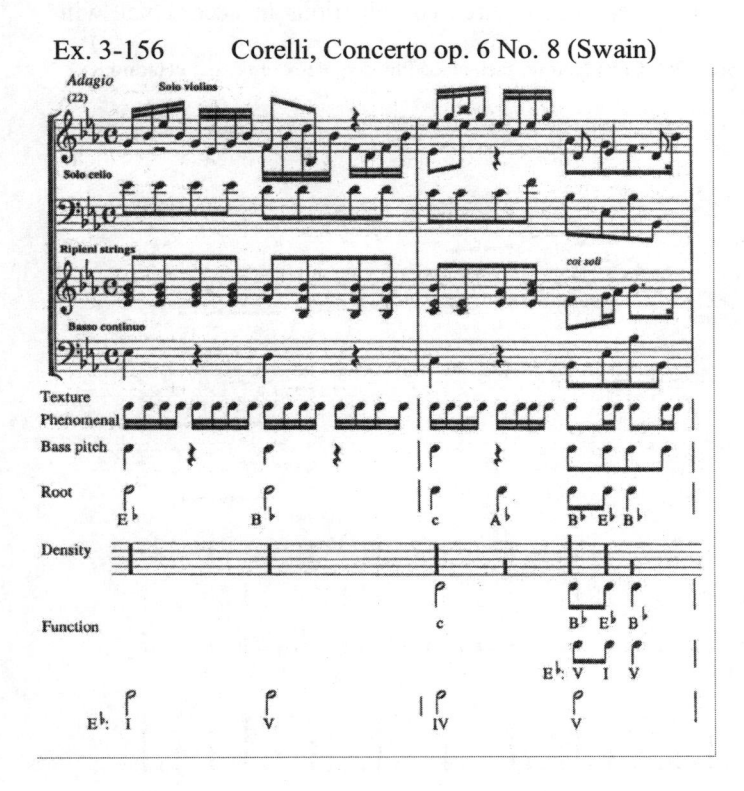

I think it is odd that Swain accepts only three principal harmonic functions, tonic, dominant, and subdominant, without naming their substitutes (VI of I, II of IV and III of V) as such. He likewise disregards suspensions and anticipations, although these have a long tradition as special harmonic phenomena and besides supply the link between harmonic rhythm and overall metrics (suspensions on strong beats, anticipations on weak ones). He also does not address cadences, which likewise have a long tradition and, at least in the form of imperfect and authentic cadence, extend into the area of metrics and phrasing.

Since the levels »root« and »function« in most cases differ little from one another, they could in my judgment be combined. On the other hand, however, cadences and suspensions should definitely be included. Besides, I regard the aspect of »density« as superfluous and would prefer an overall higher valuation of function-harmonic steps in

---

[520] Ibid., 72ff.

[521] Ibid., 69.

[522] Cf. Jan LaRue, »Harmonic Rhythm in the Beethoven Symphonies,« Music Review, 18 (1957), 8-20.

Ex. 3-157   Corelli, Concerto op. 6 No. 8, Adagio, Beginning, Harmonic Rhythm

rhythm analyses (four values per step in the 18th century, because chords of four tones, such as D^7 oder S^6_5, were already standard at the time; see Ex. 3-157).

The harmonic rhythm of Corelli's five adagio measures proves to be extremely simple. The fact that the two perfect cadences (on the tonic in m. 3, on the dominant in m. 5) fall once on the *One* and once on the *Three* of the 4/4 meter means only that in Corelli's time the graduated accent meter (*Akzentstufentakt*) was not yet fully developed. For the same reason it appears unproblematic that the suspension dissonances in mm. 3 and 4 fall on seemingly very weak beats. If one regards the 4/4 time as composed of two 2/4 measures, and also considers the slow tempo, the quarter positions on *Two* and *Four* no longer appear as merely weak but as relatively strong in relation to the intervening eighths, and thus capable of suspension.

To determine the component rhythm »Harmony« really makes sense only if it is seen in relation to the rhythm of the composition as a whole. Swain largely dispenses with that. The rhythms extracted by him from the sum of all the notes of every voice (line »Texture Phenomenal«) are not very telling, since they cannot register the actual rhythmic texture of a composition. Besides, the relation of harmonic rhythm to meter remains indeterminate. Swain lacks the necessary analytical apparatus (whence also his addressing this question, not in the part on »Analysis«, but in the part on »Interpretation«). In a components-analytical method, such as I have developed in this book, the harmonic rhythm can be set in relation to both the rhythm and the phrasal structure of the individual voices, as well as to the meter of the entire composition, and described with complete exactness.

The Ex. 3-158 is set up in such a way that, to begin with, the rhythms of the solo voices are determined and represented with their rhythmic weights (♪ =1, crest notes = 1). Then follow three combinations in accordance with

Ex. 3-158   Corelli, Concerto op. 6 No. 8, Adagio, Beginning, Rhythmic Profiles (»Sound«, »Crest Notes«, then also »Phrase«, »Texture« and »Harmony«)

the principle of rhythmic accumulation: first the profile of the concertino as the sum of the three solo voices, then the ripieno profile, less-weighted ($\eighth = 1$, no crest notes) and enriched with phrasal and textural rhythms, and finally the profile values of the harmonic rhythm (taken over from Ex. 3-157). In view of the diverse profiles, the effect contributed by the component »Harmony« can now be measured exactly. For example, the first beats of mm. 2 and 3 emerge clearly only upon the inclusion of the harmonic rhythm. If the post-beat eighths (2nd, 4th, 6th and 8th eighth) in mm. 3 and 4, down to the ripieno profile have an eminently high rhythmic weight, the harmonic rhythm largely levels these quasi syncopated peaks again.

Ex. 3-159 Debussy, Prélude I/1 (following Swain[523])

Let us take a look also at Swain's analysis of a piano piece by Debussy: »Danseuses de Delphes« from vol. 1 of the *Préludes*. It occurs in Part One of his book, in the chapter »Density of Harmonic Rhythm« and continues in Part Two (in the recapitulation).[524] Swain chose this example in order to test his method of determining harmonic rhythms also in the border region between function-harmonic and free harmonic technique.

The first bar (Ex. 3-159) already makes clear how Swain proceeds. Decisive for him is the bass voice, whose notes B♭, A and F seem to point to the tonic (once) and to the dominant (twice). The second chord is therefore interpreted such that the B natural is regarded as a chord-alien note[525] and therefore passed over, while the notes C and E♭ are seen as complementing the diminished triad (»a-«). The G in the descant is disregarded, because Swain ›allows‹ only triads of thirds under the rubric of »Root.«[526] The upshot of this, however, is that from the point of view of harmonic function a sarabande-like rhythm comes to the fore ($\quarter \quarter$), whereas in the line »Root« even quarters appear.

But is it really Debussy's intention to relate the whole-tone chord on the *Two* of the first bar, A2-G3-B3-E♭4-G4, in a conventional way to a function chord, rather than let it stand in its own value – analogously to the directly following augmented triad F-A-C♯? In the parallel passage a few bars later (m. 6), at any rate, a post-beat chord in multiple octaves (G3-B3-E♭4-G4-B4-E♭5-G5), appears, which, in the (inside) main voice, seems to confer an emphatic weight of its own on the B in question.

Swain concedes that other interpretations are also possible and justified[527] but nevertheless derives far-reaching conclusions for the entire composition from his assumptions. He calls the Prélude »a grand experiment in the denaturing of traditional harmonic functions,« a process that begins already in measure 1, takes a »drastical« step forward in the repetition of the first phrase, exhibits symptoms of disintegration in the major triads that are displaced by thirds (mm. 21-24), and ends with B♭ major chords that in terms of function harmony are extremely tenuous.[528]

[523] Ibid., 167 and 169. Unfortunately there are some errors in Swain's example, among which the A4 in m. 4 and m. 9 (2nd notes r.h.) is serious. Correctly, the first three notes are G4-B♭4-F4 – a pentatonic pattern, which is picked up again at the end of the B part (mm. 18/19: D5-f5-C5).

[524] Cf. ibid., 58ff. and 167ff.

[525] Ibid., 58.

[526] Swain addresses this problem in note 1 of his 6th chapter p. 192).

[527] Ibid., 60.

[528] Ibid., 171f. The »plagal effect in the bass« cited by Swain is actually not there.

Ex. 3-160   Debussy, Préludes I/1, Beginning, Rhythm Score (»Sound«, »Harmony«)

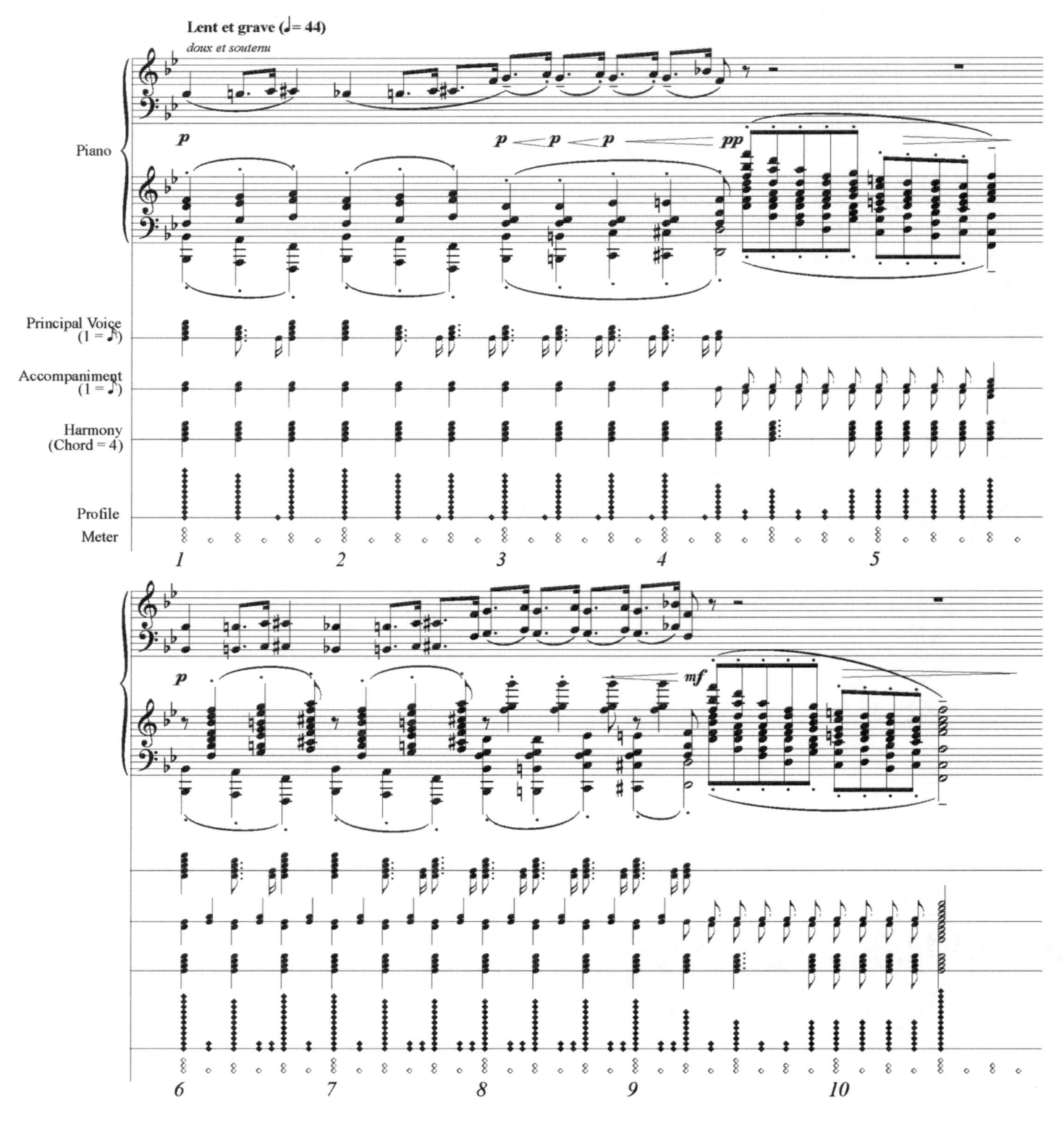

It may be because of his subject's narrow definition that the author occasionally tends to over-interpret. Dispassionate observation, at any rate, will not be able to verify the supposedly »drastic« changes in the harmony of mm. 1-5 and 6-10 (Ex. 3-160). The intensification and animation of this varied repetition of the theme is due to the saturated timbre of the post-beat chords. The use of octaves in the main voice and the raised dynamic level may also contribute to the impression of heightening, but definitely not the harmony, which is unchanged.

It is generally regrettable that the author did not pay greater attention to the *context* of the harmonic rhythm.

Harmony, after all, is only one of the numerous components of a composition. All the voices, and sometimes the piece as a whole, develop component rhythms of their own, which stand in a particular relation to the harmonic rhythm. The aim of an analysis should be to grasp the rhythmic structure of a piece of music as a whole; in the present case, this would mean to describe the contribution the harmonic rhythm makes to the total rhythmic disposition.

Debussy's Prélude suggests, moreover, that harmony and harmonic rhythm should not be analyzed merely in terms of chords. The sequence of tonal systems, too, can have rhythmic effects. Thus the change from a D-Mi-pentatonic scale to a G-Mi-pentatonic one in the main voice in mm. 11-14 produces clear six-fourths units, which correlate with the textural features of the accompaniment: parallel chords in a diatonic-heptatonic scale. In the main parts, chromaticism plays a dominant role, as can be seen from the head motif (B♭-B-C-C♯), which in m. 3 wanders into the bass (B♭-B-C-C♯-D). In the recapitulation, which at the same time has the marks of a coda, the chromaticism is pushed to the extreme, in that the head motif is now sounded in sevenfold parallel, and of the four notes B♭-B-C-C♯ the last three are stacked with augmented triads, so that there is a total of 12 chromatic steps. Besides, the voice-leading here at the end can be interpreted by saying that the head motif still lives on as C♯4 in the post-beat chords in mm. 27 and 28, leading to the D4 of the upper voice of the concluding tonic chords – thus corresponding to the continuation as in m. 4 (bass: C♯-D). For the overall rhythmic structure of the Prélude, we get the following durations per tone system:

m. 1	A	11 ♩ chromatic
		5 ♩ diatonic
m. 6	A'	11 ♩ chromatic
		5 ♩ diatonic
m. 11	B	12 ♩ Mi-pentatonic, simultaneously:
		12 ♩ diatonic
m. 15		19 ♩ diatonic-chromatic mixture
m. 21	(return)	12 ♩ diatonic-chromatic mixture
m. 25	A"	12 ♩ chromatic
–31		8 ♩ diatonic

Overall, I regard Joseph P. Swain's book as an essential contribution to musical rhythm theory. Of fundamental significance seems to me that Swain perceives the temporal distances between harmonic events (changes of basic triads, changes in harmonic function) as genuine durations and consequently reproduces them like rhythms in notation. He is one of the few who do not speak merely of accents but describe changes in the composition under the aspect of secondary durations. But since he does not extend this way of seeing from the area of harmony to the other components of a piece of music, he does not, in the end, reach the point of adequately analyzing the relation of harmonic rhythm to the remaining rhythms and the metrics of a given composition.

London • Hearing in Time

Justin London's treatise *Hearing in Time* appeared in 2004.[529] It was preceded by numerous publications on matters of rhythm and meter, including his Ph.D dissertation, directed by Leonard B. Meyer,[530] and his »Rhythm« article in the *New Grove Dictionary of Music and Musicians* 2000.[531]

London sets out from a broad conception of rhythm: »as all music involves duration(s), all music necessarily has some manner of rhythm.«[532] The crucial question from the perspective of components theory – and I want to discuss London's great theoretical edifice only from that perspective – is to what exactly the »durations« that conduct to »rhythm« refer. I will therefore begin by discussing the table in London's *New Grove* article on »Rhythm», in which he juxtaposes characteristics of meter and rhythm.[533]

Metre	**Rhythm**
A series of articulations of time-points which form measures.	A series of durations or time-spans which form groups.
Musical ›whens‹ – metre functions as a means of locating durations of time.	Musical ›whats‹ – objects formed by the concatenation of phenomena that have duration.
Usually regular, requiring isochronous spacing of beats and/or downbeats in a measure.	Usually not regular, as groups typically are comprised of varying durations within a group.
Metric accent stems from the listener's active engagement with the music, the fall-out from counting/foot-tapping behaviour.	Rhythmic accent stems from phenomenal aspects of the musical surface such as differences in loudness, duration, contour etc.
Metric accent is always the first event in a measure.	Rhythmic accent may occur anywhere within a rhythmic group.
Measures are continuous: no gaps or breaks within a metric unit.	Rhythmic groups are continuous: no gaps within a group.
Measures are contiguous: no	Rhythmic groups are not nec-

---

[529] Justin London, *Hearing in Time. Psychological Aspects of Musical Meter* (Oxford: Univ. Press, 2004).

[530] Justin London, *The Interaction between Meter and Phrase Beginnings and Endings in the Mature Instrumental Music of Haydn and Mozart*, Ph.D. diss. (University of Pennsylvania, 1990).

[531] Justin London, Article »Rhythm,« in: *The New Grove Dictionnary of Music and Musicians*, 2nd ed., vol. 21 (London, New York, 2000), 277-309.

[532] Ibid., 277.

[533] Ibid., 278.

gaps between successive measures.	essarily contiguous: often there are gaps between successive groups.
Strongly predictive: metric patterns usually remain constant and are thus a reliable basis for anticipating when subsequent events will occur.	Weakly predictive: though durational patterns may be repeated, often they are not, and rhythm is not a reliable basis for anticipating subsequent events.

London attaches the term rhythm to concrete sound phenomena, whereas he conceives meter as something subsisting in the head of the listener: »Metric accent stems from the listener's active engagement with the music,« whereas »Rhythmic accent stems from phenomenal aspects of the musical surface.« It can be concluded from this that meter does not really involve »durations« as does rhythm, but only imagined temporal patterns in the sense of regular pulses or beats.

If this distinction will be immediately plausible (especially since it has always played a role in the history of rhythm theory), doubts arise when it comes to pigeonholing »musical ›Whens‹« and »musical ›Whats‹« in the polar grid of meter and rhythm. What and when questions aim at the fundamental modes of perception of space and time, or, in the words of Aristoxenos, at the rhythmed and the rhythming.[534] It therefore will not do to reserve one for rhythm and the other for meter.

Regardless of whether or not a specific meter underlies a piece of music, durations and time intervals depend on ›when‹ a sound or sound figure begins, ends or is replaced. The same goes for meter, whose ›whats‹ – e.g., metrical accents – are events merely imagined by the listener. At the end, London himself says that isochronous events enable one to foresee »when [!] subsequent events will occur.«

It may have to do with this fuzziness that London also does not express himself with precision about rhythmic accents. In the fourth box of the table he suggests something like an open-ended list of rhythmic accents (»loudness, duration, contour etc.«), but he does not say whether or not the intervals between accents result in rhythms. »Rhythmic accent may occur anywhere within a rhythmic group« suggests that while accents are added to rhythms they do not generate any by themselves.

Referring to researches in listener psychology, London points out that »we are able to pick out some sounds in our environment and hear them as connected and coherent, whether they are a single voice in a crowded room or a single part in a complex musical texture.«[535] He even adduces an example to the effect that in monophonic melodies one can hear several rhythms at once, though the case in question involves a phenomenon of inherent polyphony: »we are able to hear compound melodies, and hence perceive a series of different durations within a musical surface consisting of even articulations, as in ex. 2«[536] (cf. Ex. 3-161).

Ex. 3-161 (Justin London)

What has here been separated out into two voices, to be sure, has nothing to do with ›accent‹ rhythms but rather involves a reconstruction of a latently two-part setting, whose voices, thus obtained, are analyzed according to their tonal durations in the conventional manner. Even so, London admits that the rhythms of the two voices do not obliterate the basic rhythm of the eighths, but that the deduced rhythms are heard simultaneously »within a musical surface.«

In 2004, Justin London published an analysis of the first movement of Beethoven's Fifth Symphony under the aspect of »Metric Flux in Beethoven's Fifth.«[537] In it, the time signature of 2/4 is taken as a single beat, and London observes that the process can nearly throughout be divided into double and quadruple measures. Only in the development (Ex. 3-162) the metric is said to get out of step, so that there one could speak of a »metric crisis.«[538] This ›crisis‹ is seen as particularly evident in the passage consisting solely of chord changes and half notes with which the return to the recapitulation begins.

Ex. 3-162

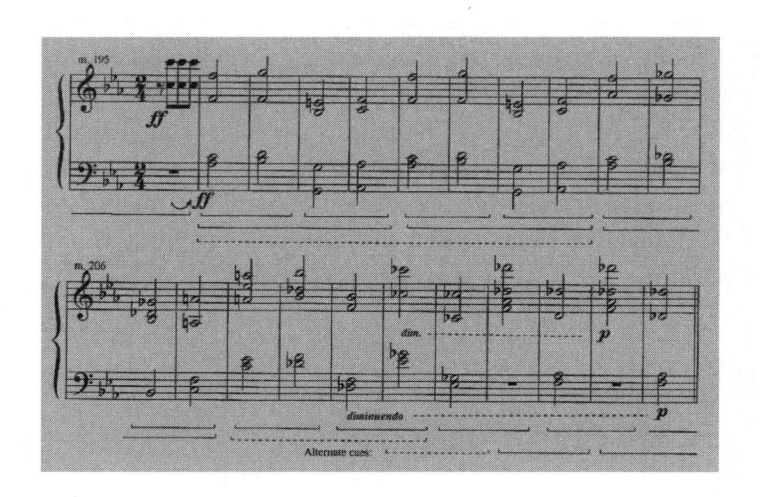

---

[534] Cf. also the section »Definition of Terms« in the Components chapter in this book, 19f.

[535] London, »Rhythm« article, 279.

[536] Ibid..

[537] London, *Hearing in Time* (see note 458), 89-99; the example appears on p. 95.

[538] Ibid. 94f.

Ex. 3-163   Beethoven, 5th Symphony, 1st mov., mm. 195-232

London correctly recognizes that m. 195, with its rhythmically pithy head motif, should be perceived as an upbeat, making m. 196 heavy. There follows a sequence of double and quadruple measures. At the beginning of the diminuendo in m. 210, however, due to the change in register from bar to bar, the metrical reading becomes ambiguous (»alternate cues«), something London marks by means of staggered brackets. At m. 216, his analysis breaks off – too soon, as we shall presently see.

What London has sensed here can nevertheless be described in a more precise, detailed and adequate manner by a rhythmic components analysis (cf. Ex. 3-163). The analysis covers mm. 195 to 232. Except for the upbeat eighths, the tonal entries here are exclusively ♩ which makes for the special appeal of the passage. The volume is reduced (*ff* — *p* – *pp*), until in m. 228 suddenly *ff* recurs. The constant alternation between winds and strings, combined with changes of octave register and harmonic progressions, provides for some rhythmic mobility in this otherwise monochronous episode.

Of crucial significance in these 33 bars, which modulate from F minor to G major (as the V of C minor), is the harmonic rhythm, as it grows gradually from halves over whole notes up to a dotted brevis (6 ♩) and finally a longa (8 ♩). These very large harmonic durations drop down to the piano and pianissimo sphere, which, however, does not lessen their rhythmic weight. A special tension arises from the enharmonic change that manifests itself in m. 215 in the hybrid notation of an F♯/G♭ minor triad (F♯-A-D♭).[539] Introduced as G♭ minor with a preceding D♭ major, the harmony changes to F♯ minor in the strings and then – upon the appearance of the *pp* – to D major (sixth chord).

But these progressions become rhythmically relevant only in relation to the remaining component rhythms. »Timbre« (winds / strings) and »Octave Register« (1st and 2nd octave) form rhythms of four or two, resulting from the constant alternation. At the beginning, the register brevises are staggered in relation to the wholes of the harmonic rhythm. The units of four halves that result, in m. 196, from the changes in timbre and octave register are metrically heavy, being defined as metrical *Ones* by the always upbeat head motif. But then, around m. 208, the whole-measure harmonic progressions assert themselves as metric stresses. The rhythm of the register changes adapts itself – *vide* the dotted whole note (2+1 ♩) in m. 208 (Register line) – and thereafter moves in step with the harmonic rhythm.

The »metric crisis« that London observed quite correctly thus takes place within 19 measures – an odd number! – in which the harmonic durations gain the upper hand. It is one of the finesses of Beethoven's compositional style – and once more attests to the high aesthetic quality of his music – that this transformative process takes place in combination with a decrescendo from *ff* to *pp* (mm. 195-221), which renders it fairly inconspicuous. Aside from this, we can see here a reason why Beethoven wrote the movement in 2/4 time: with an alla breve notation, which would otherwise suggest itself, he would have had to announce a change of meter at m. 208 at the latest. The case proves once more that the metric situation is the result of composing with component rhythms and not prescription or a priori law.[540]

In a lecture, whose written version is available on the internet, London occupied himself again with the phenomenon of metric ambiguity, this time with the aid, *inter alia*, of an example from Stravinsky.[541] Under the title »Stravinsky's Hiccups,« he analyzes the beginning of the second tableau from *Les Noces*. Confining himself to the main voice, London cites the following example (Ex. 3-164):[542]

Ex. 3-164 (Justin London)

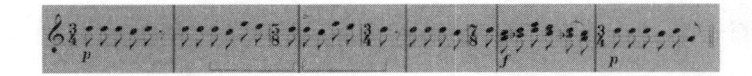

---

[539] A reading error at this point caused London to overlook the change from D♭ major to G♭ minor and thus to break off the analysis prematurely. Besides, the D♭ is current since m. 197.

[540] Cf. Claudia Maurer Zenck, *Vom Takt. Untersuchungen zur Theorie und kompositorischen Praxis im ausgehenden 18. und beginnenden 19. Jahrhundert* (Vienna: Böhlau, 2001), 126: »…this shows Beethoven's intention not to regard the chosen meter constituting the basic tempo as an irrevocable quantity.« Maurer Zenck, incidentally, describes the situation exactly as I do, though without the assumption of divergent and converging rhythms.

[541] Justin London, Cognitive and Aesthetic Aspects of Metrical Ambiguity, Colloquium talk given at The University of Alberta and The University of Pennsylvania, Fall 2008, online under:http://www.people.carleton.edu/~jlondon/Metric Ambiguity.pdf. (15. Nov. 2009)

[542] Ibid., p. 3.

London assumes that the opening figure (D-D-D-C-D) with its extended duration at the end (inter-onset-interval) seems to set up a 3/4 time, but that the 3-♩ measure was disrupted by the varied repetitions of this micro-phrase regularly marked by a drum roll. London's subtle analysis of the (sung) upper voice leads to a persuasive structural suggestion: (♪) | 6 | 6+1 | 6 | 6–1 | 6 | 6 |. The question remains unanswered, however, why Stravinsky chose his meters as he did and not otherwise.

Ex. 3-165
Stravinsky, *Les Noces*, 2me Tableau (fig. 27), Beginning

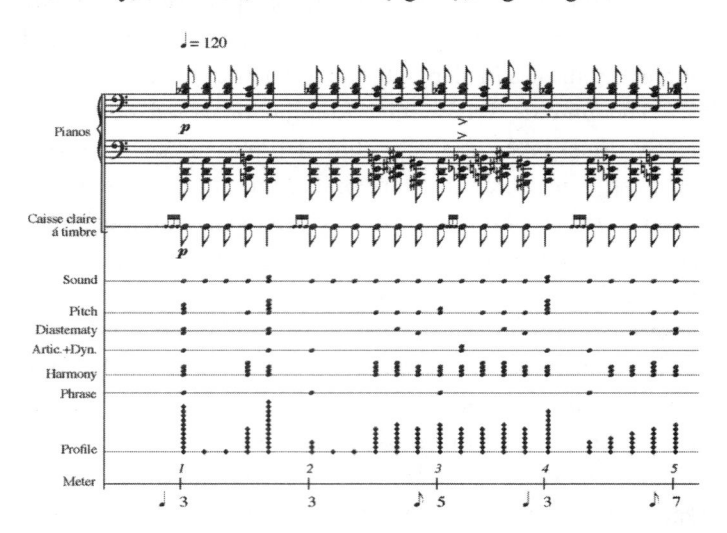

Let us see whether a components-rhythmical analysis might yield additional insights (Ex. 3-165). I limit myself to the first four bars but consider the full instrumentation of two pianos and snare drum (the male chorus goes colla parte). The entry durations (»Sound«) are weighted on the scale of ♪ = 1. The pitch changes (»Pitch«) form a rhythm of their own, with each of the held pitches additionally receiving the value of the repeated notes. The contours (»Diastematics«) of the high and low voices set in contrary motion (tonal or real mixtures) are registered as crest (upper region) or as keel notes (lower region). »Articulation« (staccatos,[543] drum roll) and »Dynamics« (>) are combined into a single rhythm system and are weighted with 1 point each (at one point dynamic accent and drum roll coincide, resulting in a weight of 2). The chords (»Harmonics«) in this excerpt consist of either three or four notes and are throughout dissonant: they enter the rhythm score weighted according to the number of notes in them. The repeat sections (»Phrase«) are entered with their respective first note and the value 1. The exact beginning of the third phrase is debatable or ambiguous: to my mind, m. 2 is repeated in abbreviated and varied form in m. 3 (only two *d* instead of three), whereas London has the third phrase begin with the accentuated second ♪.

What emerges, and is depicted by the rhythmic profile, is a sound action of high »variability« and low »predictability«. Of Stravinsky's measures, none resemble each other. The tall weight columns frequently stand on the *One* but in m. 3 also on the *Three*. Mm. 2 and 3 (3/4 and 5/8 time) are (except for a weak beginning – no changes in pitch) shaped like a coherent double measure. The fourth bar is noteworthy in that, after a ›strong‹ *One* (10 points), the subsequent weights rise evenly like a set of stairs (3, 4, 5, 6, 7 points).

Overall, my analysis confirms the »metrical ambiguity« that interests London. Why Stravinsky prescribes 5/8 in the third bar I cannot explain either. The fact that the beginning of the measure tallies with my view of the phrasing does not suffice as an explanation, as a look at the heterometric meters occurring later (next to 5/8 also 7/8) does not reveal any practice apt to become a rule. On the other hand, the rhythmic profile also does not point to any »metric patterns« by which all other instances could be assessed in terms of ›deviations.‹ Justin London, too, sees it that way in the end when he writes: »The background meter here (and elsewhere) is not robust enough to be maintained by the listener while these putative displacements take place.«[544]

Of course it does not take examples from Stravinsky or Reich to ferret out ambiguities of this sort. As the numerous components-rhythmic analyses in the present book have shown, metric variability and ambiguity are characteristic of nearly all more fully developed music. Since, according to the central theses of the components theory, metric forms are the emanation of rhythmics and not the other way round, such ambiguities merge into the multifariousness of rhythmic processes.

---

[543] In the part of the chorus the staccato quarters are notated with ꜞ- pauses (see Ex. 3-139).

[544] London (2008/2009), 6.

Appendix

Music Examples (continuing)

Introduction

0-001	Haydn	Symph. No. 94, 2nd mov. m. 1
0-002	Haydn	Symph. No. 94, 2nd mov. m. 1
0-003	Haydn	Symph. No. 94, 2nd mov. m. 1
0-004	Haydn	Symph. No. 94, 2nd mov. mm. 1, 75, 107
0-005	Haydn	Symph. No. 94, 2nd mov. m. 115
0-006	Haydn	Symph. No. 94, 2nd mov. mm. 1-16

Part One: Theory of Components
Rhythms and Components
Sound

1-001	Beethoven	Symph. No. 5, 3rd mov. mm. 324 ff.
1-002	Beethoven	Symph. No. 5, 3rd mov. mm. 1, 236 ff.
1-003	Berg	Wozzeck II/2 mm. 310 ff.
1-004	Berg	Lulu I/3 mm. 833 ff.
1-005	Berg	Wozzeck III/2-3 mm. 109 ff.

Pitch

1-006	Beethoven	Symph. No. 1, 3rd mov. Beginning
1-007	Anon.	Lamento di Tristano
1-008	Beethoven	Symph. No. 9, Finale Beginning
1-009	Vivaldi	La Primavera mm. 47 ff.
1-010	Chopin	Etude op. 25 No. 12, Beginning
1-011	Brahms	String Quartet op. 51/2, 4th mov. mm. 13

Diastematics

1-012	Beethoven	Symph. No. 2, 2nd mov. mm. 66-73
1-013	Monteverdi	Vesperae beatae Mariae Virginis, Psalm 109
1-014	Bach, J. S.	Präludium BWV 926, mm. 1, 21, 45
1-015	Bauldeweyn	Missa »Da pacem«, Credo
1-016	Beethoven	Symph. No. 5, 3rd mov. mm. 1 ff.
1-017	Beethoven	Symph. No. 5, 3rd mov. mm. 350 ff.
1-018	Brahms	Kl.Konzert No. 2, 1st mov. mm. 260
1-019	Brahms	Kl.Konzert No. 2, 1st mov. mm. 256-61
1-020	Ligeti	Continuum

Articulation

1-021	Beethoven	Symph. No. 4, 3rd mov. Beginning
1-022	Beethoven	Symph. No. 6, 2nd mov. Beginning
1-023	Beethoven	Symph. No. 6, 2nd mov. Beginning
1-024	B. de Bononia	Vince con lena (section)
1-025	Corelli	Concerto op. 6 No. 8, Pastorale
1-026	Corelli	Concerto op. 6 No. 9, Allemande
1-027	Schumann	Davidsbündler No. 12, Beginning
1-028	Mahler	Symph. No. 9, 2nd mov. mm. 18 ff.
1-029	Webern	Konzert op. 24, 1st mov., Beginning
1-030	Bartók	String Quartet No. 4, 3rd mov., Beginning

Dynamics

1-031	Beethoven	Symph. No. 2, 1st mov. mm. 112-127
1-032	Monteverdi	Vesperae beatae Mariae Virginis, »Audi« mm. 23 ff.
1-033	Corelli	Concerto op. 6 No. 6, Vivace
1-034	Haydn	String Quartet D major Hob. III, 42, 3rd mov.
1-035	Mozart	String Quartet K. 387, 2nd mov. mm. 65
1-036	Schumann	Davidsbündler No. 13, Beginning
1-037	Strauss, R.	Elektra near fig. 64
1-038	Stravinsky	Sacre du printemps, near fig. 13
1-039	Ligeti	Études, »Désordre«, Beginning
1-040a	Ligeti	Études, »Désordre« r.H.
1-040b	Ligeti	Études, »Désordre« l.H.

Timbre

1-041	Beethoven	Symph. No. 3, 3rd mov. mm. 127-133
1-042	Beethoven	Symph. No. 1, 4th mov. mm. 238
1-043	Schütz	»Geistliche Chormusik« 16, Beginning
1-044	Mozart	String Quintett K. 516, 3rd mov. mm. 5-9
1-045	Brahms	Variations op. 9 No. 5, mm. 12-23
1-046	Wagner	Tristan Introduction, mm. 1-17
1-047	Bruckner	Symph. No. 4, 3rd mov. mm. 93-112
1-048	Schönberg	Piece for Orchestra op. 16 No. 3
1-049	Henze	Antifone, Beginning

Harmony

1-050	Beethoven	Symph. No. 7, 2nd mov., Beginning
1-051	Mozart	Symph. K. 551, 4th mov., Transition
1-052	Mozart	Symph. K. 551, 4th mov. mm. 166 ff.
1-053	Mozart	Symph. K. 551, 4th mov. mm. 172-207
1-054	Gesualdo	Madrigals 4th book, »Invan dunque«
1-055	Liszt	Sonata B minor, mm. 105-120
1-056	Debussy	Préludes Bd. I No. 10, mm. 1-28
1-057	Debussy	Préludes Bd. I No. 10, mm. 28-32
1-058	Ligeti	String Quartet No. 2, 2nd mov., Beginning
1-059	Ligeti	String Quartet No. 2, 2nd mov. mm. 1-12

Texture

1-060	Beethoven	Symph. No. 8, 1st mov. mm. 104-127
1-061	Vivaldi	Concerto op. 3 No. 3, 2nd mov., Beginning
1-062	Anon.	Alleluja from the Christmas Mass
1-063	Fux, J. J.	Missa di San Carlo, Benedictus
1-064	Haydn	String Quartet Hob. III, 37, 2nd mov. mm. 13-21
1-065	Brahms	String Sextet op. 36, 3rd mov., 3rd Var.
1-066	Berg	Wozzeck III/3-4, mm. 211-218

Phrase

1-067	Beethoven	Symph. No. 6, 5th mov. (theme)
1-068	Beethoven	Symph. No. 6, 5th mov. (construct)

Music Examples (continuing)

1-069	Mozart	Symph. K. 543, 1st mov. (main theme)
1-070	Anon.	Gregorian cantilation for St. Mary
1-071	Machaut	Motet No. 20, Tenor
1-072	Machaut	Motet No. 1, Color
1-073	Machaut	Motet No. 1, Talea
1-074	Machaut	Motet No. 1, Tenor
1-075	Schumann	»Album für die Jugend« op. 68 No. 39
1-076	Chopin	Nocturne op. 15 No. 3
1-077	Liszt	Faust-Symphonie, Beginning
1-078	Brahms	String Quartet op. 51 No. 2, 1st mov. mm. 46-61
1-079	Brahms	String Quartet op. 51 No. 2, 4th mov.
1-080	Ravel	Piano Trio, 1st mov., Beginning
1-081	Bartók	Music for string instruments…, 1st und 4th mov.
1-082	Henze	Symph. No. 10, 4th mov. mm. 84-90

Prosody

1-083	Beethoven	Symph. No. 9, 4th mov. mm. 216-248
1-084	Beethoven	Symph. No. 9, 4th mov., Song of Joy, var.
1-085	Wagner	Siegfried
1-086	Strauss, R.	Elektra, before fig. 37
1-087	Berg	Wozzeck I/4, mm. 488, 577
1-088	Zimmermann	Die Soldaten III/5, after fig. e
1-089	Monteverdi	Messa a 4 voci, »Osanna«
1-090	Bach, J. S.	Missa B minor, »Osanna«
1-091	Mozart	Missa K. 317, »Hosanna«
1-092	Bruckner	Missa F minor, »Hosanna«
1-093	Stravinsky	Mass, »Hosanna«
1-094	Schoenberg	Moses and Aaron II/3, mm. 380-384

Rhythmic Weight (Beethoven's Seventh, 2nd mov.)
Weight of Components and Durations

1-095	Beethoven	mm. 3 ff., Vla
1-096	Beethoven	mm. 27 ff., Vla
1-097	Beethoven	mm. 102 ff., Klar.
1-098	Beethoven	mm. 183 ff., Vl. I+II
1-099	Beethoven	mm. 75
1-100	Beethoven	mm. 150
1-101	Beethoven	mm. 3 ff., Viola
1-102	Beethoven	mm. 27 ff. (Profile)
1-103	Beethoven	mm. 103 ff. (Profile)
1-104	Beethoven	mm. 27 ff. (Profile)
1-105	Beethoven	mm. 3 ff. (Phrase)
1-106	Beethoven	mm. 27 ff. (Phrase)
1-107	Beethoven	mm. 102 ff. (phrases)
1-108	Beethoven	mm. 144
1-109	Beethoven	mm. 255
1-110	Beethoven	Harmony 1st+2nd Th
1-111	Beethoven	Harmony 3. Th
1-112	Beethoven	mm. 183-212
1-113	Beethoven	mm. 27 (Accompaniment)
1-114	Beethoven	mm. 51 (Accompaniment)

Accumulation of Rhythmic Weights

1-115	Beethoven	mm. 3 (Accumulation 1)
1-116	Beethoven	mm. 3 (Accumulation 2)
1-117	Beethoven	mm. 3 (Accumulation 3)
1-118	Beethoven	mm. 27 (Accumulation 1)
1-119	Beethoven	mm. 27 (Accumulation 2)
1-120	Beethoven	mm. 27 (Accumulation 3)
1-121	Beethoven	1st + 2nd Theme
1-122	Beethoven	3rd Theme
1-123	Beethoven	mm. 75 ff. (Accumulation)

Rhythmic and Metric Weight

1-124	Beethoven	mm. 3 ff. (Meter)
1-125	Beethoven	mm. 17 ff. (Meter)
1-126	Beethoven	mm. 101 ff. (Meter)
1-127	Beethoven	mm. 75 ff. (Meter)

Aspects of Rhythm
Rhythmic Proportions

1-128	Bauldeweyn	Missa »Da pacem«, Credo, »confiteor«
1-129	Bauldeweyn	Missa »Da pacem«, Credo, »expecto«
1-130	Bauldeweyn	Missa »Da pacem«, Credo, »expecto«
1-131	Schütz	Motet »So fahr ich hin«
1-132	Stravinsky	Sacre du Printemps, fig. 13/14
1-133	Sweelinck	Fantasia chromatica
1-134	Anon.	Dies irae (gregorian)
1-135	Zimmermann	Die Soldaten, Preludio (Section)
1-136	Zimmermann	Die Soldaten, Preludio (Section)
1-137	Anon.	White Mensural Notation (Scheme)
1-138	Ockeghem	Missa prolationum, Kyrie I
1-139	Ockeghem	Missa prolationum, Kyrie I (Plamenac)
1-140	Brahms	Symph. No. 2, 1st mov. mm. 1 and mm. 298
1-141	Brahms	Symph. No. 2, 1st mov. mm. 1-43
1-142	Brahms	Symph. No. 2, 1st mov., motivic variations
1-143	Brahms	Symph. No. 2, 3rd mov., motivic variations

Rhythmic Iso-, Hetero- and Symmetry

1-144	Machaut	Motet No. 20, Beginning
1-145	Machaut	Motet No. 20, Profile
1-146	Machaut	Motet No. 20, Modus
1-147	Josquin	Missa »De Beata Virgine«, Gloria
1-148	Josquin	Missa »De Beata Virgine«, Amen
1-149	Bach, J. S.	WTC I, Prelude D minor
1-150	Beethoven	String Quartet op. 135, 2nd mov.
1-151	Berg	Wozzeck II/2, mm. 273 ff.
1-152	Berg	Wozzeck II/2, mm. 313 ff.
1-153	Tchaikovsky	Symph. No. 5, 3rd mov., Beginning
1-154	Tchaikovsky	Symph. No. 6, 2nd mov., Beginning
1-155	Tchaikovsky	Valse (construct)
1-156	Ligeti / Bartók	»Désordre« / Mikrokosmos No. 150
1-157	Bartók	Sonata for 2 Pianos…, 1st mov. mm. 32 ff.
1-158	Bartók	Sonata for 2 Pianos…, 1st mov. mm. 27 ff.
1-159	Bartók	Sonata for 2 Pianos…, 1st mov. mm. 84 ff.
1-160	Bartók	Sonata for 2 Pianos…, 1st mov. mm. 105 ff.
1-161	Bartók	Sonata for 2 Pianos…, 1st mov. Introduction theme
1-162	Bartók	Sonata for 2 Pianos…, 1st mov. Introduction theme
1-163	Bartók	Sonata for 2 Pianos…, 1st mov. Introduction theme

1-164	Bartók	Sonata for 2 Pianos…, 1st mov. mm. 195 ff.	1-206	Beethoven	Symph. No. 3, 1st mov. 23-37
1-165	Bartók	Sonata for 2 Pianos…, 1st mov. mm. 266 ff.	1-207	Beethoven	Symph. No. 3, 1st mov. 266-284
1-166	Bartók	Sonata for 2 Pianos…, 1st mov. mm. 239	1-208	Anon.	Hemiola Coloration
1-167	Machaut	Rondeau »Ma fin est …«	1-209	Purcell	Anthem »O sing…«, Halleluja I
1-168	Josquin	Missa »L'homme armé« II, Agnus III	1-210	Purcell	Anthem »O sing…«, Detail
1-169	Bach, J. S.	The Musical Offering, Canon I	1-211	Händel	Sonata for Recorder HWV 365
1-170	Bach, J. S.	The Musical Offering, Canon I, Detail	1-212	Händel	Sonata for Recorder, Detail
1-171	Schoenberg	Pierrot lunaire No. 18, mm. 8-12	1-213	Mozart	Symph. K. 551, 2nd mov. mm. 19-27
1-172	Berg	»Kammerkonzert«, 2nd mov. mm. 117-124	1-214	Mozart	Symph. K. 551, 2nd mov. mm. 19-20
1-173	Berg	Lulu II/1-2, mm. 658-716	1-215	Mozart/Brahms	Hemiolas (Comparison)
			1-216	Mozart	Symph. K. 550, 3rd mov. mm. 28-36

Rhythmic Characters
Upbeat

1-174	Beethoven	Symph. No. 8, 3rd mov., Beginning	1-217	Brahms	String Quartet op. 51 No. 2, 4th mov. mm. 13 ff.
1-175	Anon.	Lamento di Tristano	1-218	Brahms	String Quartet op. 51 No. 2, 4th mov. mm. 334 ff.
1-176	Schubert	»Winterreise« No. 1, Beginning	1-219	Brahms	Piano Concerto No. 2, 3rd mov. mm. 92-96
1-177	Schubert	»Winterreise« No. 1, Voice	1-220	Brahms	Piano Concerto No. 2, 3rd mov. mm. 92nd94
1-178	Brahms	Symph. No. 2, 1st mov. mm. 54-60	1-221	Brahms	Piano Concerto No. 2, 3rd mov. mm. 92-93
1-179	Brahms	Symph. No. 2, 1st mov. mm. 54-60, Detail	1-222	Brahms	Piano Concerto No. 2, 3rd mov. mm. 92-95
1-180	Strauss, R.	Elektra, near fig. 144a	1-223	Brahms	Piano Concerto No. 2, 3rd mov. mm. 41
1-181	Mahler	Symph. No. 9, Adagio, mm. 70-74	1-224	Berg	Violin Concerto, 1st Part 2nd mov., Beginning
1-182	Mahler	Symph. No. 9, Adagio, Detail	1-225	Berg	Violin Concerto, Main Rhythm
1-183	Beethoven	Symph. No. 1, Finale, Introduction	1-226	Berg	Violin Concerto, 2nd Part 3rd mov. mm. 125-136
1-184	Beethoven	Symph. No. 1, Finale, mm. 238 ff.	1-227	Henze	Tristan, Epilogue, p. 150, 4th bracket
1-185	Beethoven	Symph. No. 1, 3rd mov. Trio, Beginning	1-228	Henze	Tristan, Epilog, Detail
1-186	Weill	Mahagonny, No. 18, fig. 15			
1-187	Liszt	Piano Concerto No. 2, mm. 64			

2nd Part: Rhythm in the Music of J. S. Bach
Introduction

1-188	Beethoven	Symph. No. 6, 3rd mov. mm. 87 ff.	2-001	Bach, J. S.	Brandenburg Concerto No. 3, Beginning (Botelho)
1-189	Beethoven	Symph. No. 6, 3rd mov. mm. 87 ff. (Detail)	2-002	Bach, J. S.	Brandenburg Concerto No. 3, Beginning
1-190	Schumann	»Kinderszenen« No. 7			
1-191	Henze	Requiem, »Agnus Dei«, Beginning			

48 Fugue Themes of the Well-Tempered Clavier
Part I

Syncopation

1-192	Beethoven	Symph. No. 5, Finale mm. 13-26	2-003	Bach, J. S.	WTC I, Fuga C major
1-193	Beethoven	Symph. No. 5, Finale mm. 22, 80, 363	2-004	Bach, J. S.	WTC I, Fuga C minor
			2-005	Bach, J. S.	WTC I, Fuga C♯ major
1-193a	Beethoven	Symph. No. 5, Finale mm. 363	2-006	Bach, J. S.	WTC I, Fuga C♯ minor
1-194	Anon.	Motet »Benche partito«	2-007	Bach, J. S.	WTC I, Fuga D major
1-195	Anon.	Motet »Benche partito« (Facsimile)	2-008	Bach, J. S.	WTC I, Fuga D minor
			2-009	Bach, J. S.	WTC I, Fuga E♭ major
1-196	Bach, J. S.	St Matthew Passion, »Erbarme dich«	2-010	Bach, J. S.	WTC I, Fuga D♯ minor
1-197	Bach, J. S.	St Matthew Passion (Detail)	2-011	Bach, J. S.	WTC I, Fuga E major
1-198	Bach, J. S.	St Matthew Passion (Detail)	2-012	Bach, J. S.	WTC I, Fuga E minor
1-199	Wagner	Siegfried Motif (Model)	2-013	Bach, J. S.	WTC I, Fuga F major
1-200	Wagner	Siegfried Motif (Varianten)	2-014	Bach, J. S.	WTC I, Fuga F minor
1-201	Wagner	Siegfried Motif (Schema)	2-015	Bach, J. S.	WTC I, Fuga F♯ major
1-202	Bartók	Dance Suite, 2nd mov., Beginning	2-016	Bach, J. S.	WTC I, Fuga F♯ minor
			2-017	Bach, J. S.	WTC I, Fuga G major
			2-018	Bach, J. S.	WTC I, Fuga G minor

Hemiola

			2-019	Bach, J. S.	WTC I, Fuga A♭ major
1-203	Beethoven	Symph. No. 3, 1st mov. mm. 103 ff.	2-020	Bach, J. S.	WTC I, Fuga G♯ minor
			2-021	Bach, J. S.	WTC I, Fuga A major
1-204	Beethoven	Symph. No. 3, 1st mov. 338 ff.	2-022	Bach, J. S.	WTC I, Fuga A major, Detail
1-205	Beethoven	Symph. No. 3, 1st mov. 118-132	2-023	Bach, J. S.	WTC I, Fuga A minor
			2-024	Bach, J. S.	WTC I, Fuga B♭ major

Music Examples (continuing)

2-025	Bach, J. S.	WTC I, Fuga B♭ minor		2-078	Bach, J. S.	Brand. Conc. No. 1, 1st mov., m. 14
2-026	Bach, J. S.	WTC I, Fuga B♭ minor, Detail				
2-027	Bach, J. S.	WTC I, Fuga B major		2-079	Bach, J. S.	Brand. Conc. No. 1, 2nd mov., Synopsis
2-028	Bach, J. S.	WTC I, Fuga B minor		2-080	Bach, J. S.	Brand. Conc. No. 1, 2nd mov., m. 14

Part II

2-029	Bach, J. S.	WTC II, Fuga C major		2-081	Bach, J. S.	Brand. Conc. No. 1, 3rd mov., Beginning
2-030	Bach, J. S.	WTC II, Fuga C minor				
2-031	Bach, J. S.	WTC II, Fuga C♯ major, Beginning		2-082	Bach, J. S.	Brand. Conc. No. 1, 3rd mov., mm. 12 f.
2-032	Bach, J. S.	WTC II, Fuga C♯ major		2-083	Bach, J. S.	Brand. Conc. No. 1, 4th mov., Menuet
2-033	Bach, J. S.	WTC II, Fuga C♯ minor				
2-034	Bach, J. S.	WTC II, Fuga D major		2-084	Bach, J. S.	Brand. Conc. No. 1, 4th mov., Detail
2-035	Bach, J. S.	WTC II, Fuga D minor				
2-036	Bach, J. S.	WTC II, Fuga E♭ major				
2-037	Bach, J. S.	WTC II, Fuga D♯ minor				**Concerto II**
2-038	Bach, J. S.	WTC II, Fuga D♯ minor, Construct		2-085	Bach, J. S.	Brand. Conc. No. 2, 1st mov., Beginning
2-039	Bach, J. S.	WTC II, Fuga E major				
2-040	Bach, J. S.	WTC II, Fuga E minor		2-086	Bach, J. S.	Brand. Conc. No. 2, 2nd mov., Beginning
2-041	Bach, J. S.	WTC II, Fuga F major				
2-042	Bach, J. S.	WTC II, Fuga F minor		2-087	Bach, J. S.	Brand. Conc. No. 2, 2nd/3rd mov., Beginnings
2-043	Bach, J. S.	WTC II, Fuga F♯ major				
2-044	Bach, J. S.	WTC II, Fuga F♯ minor				
2-045	Bach, J. S.	WTC II, Fuga G major				**Concerto III**
2-046	Bach, J. S.	WTC II, Fuga G minor		2-088	Bach, J. S.	Brand. Conc. No. 3, 1st mov., Beginning
2-047	Bach, J. S.	WTC II, Fuga A♭ major				
2-048	Bach, J. S.	WTC II, Fuga G♯ minor		2-089	Bach, J. S.	Brand. Conc. No. 3, 1st mov. mm. 51 ff.
2-049	Bach, J. S.	WTC II, Fuga A major				
2-050	Bach, J. S.	WTC II, Fuga A major, Construct		2-090	Bach, J. S.	Brand. Conc. No. 3, 1st mov. mm. 132 f.
2-051	Bach, J. S.	WTC II, Fuga A minor				
2-052	Bach, J. S.	WTC II, Fuga B♭ major		2-091	Bach, J. S.	Brand. Conc. No. 3, 1st mov. mm. 78 ff.
2-053	Bach, J. S.	WTC II, Fuga B♭ major, Construct				
2-054	Bach, J. S.	WTC II, Fuga B minor		2-092	Bach, J. S.	Brand. Conc. No. 3, 3rd mov., Beginning
2-055	Bach, J. S.	WTC II, Fuga B major				
2-056	Bach, J. S.	WTC II, Fuga B minor				

Two 6/4 and two 9/8 Pieces
from the Well-Tempered Clavier

Concerto IV

				2-093	Bach, J. S.	Brand. Conc. No. 4, 1st mov., Beginning
2-057	Bach, J. S.	WTC I, Prelude C♯ minor				
2-058	Bach, J. S.	WTC I, Prelude C♯ minor, Profile		2-094	Bach, J. S.	Brand. Conc. No. 4, 1st mov. mm. 13 ff.
2-059	Bach, J. S.	WTC I, Fuga F♯ minor		2-095	Bach, J. S.	Brand. Conc. No. 4, 1st mov. mm. 202 ff.
2-060	Bach, J. S.	WTC I, Fuga F♯ minor, Profile				
2-061	Bach, J. S.	WTC I, Fuga F♯ minor, Detail		2-096	Bach, J. S.	Brand. Conc. No. 4, 1st mov. mm. 79 f.
2-062	Bach, J. S.	WTC I, Prelude A minor				
2-063	Bach, J. S.	WTC I, Prelude A minor, Profile		2-097	Bach, J. S.	Brand. Conc. No. 4, 2nd mov., Beginning
2-064	Bach, J. S.	WTC I, Prelude A minor, Detail				
2-065	Bach, J. S.	WTC I, Fuga A major		2-098	Bach, J. S.	Brand. Conc. No. 4, 2nd mov., End
2-066	Bach, J. S.	WTC I, Fuga A major, Profile				
2-067	Bach, J. S.	WTC I, Fuga A major, Profiles		2-099	Bach, J. S.	Brand. Conc. No. 4, 3rd mov., Beginning

Chromatic Fantasia

				2-100	Bach, J. S.	Brand. Conc. No. 4, 3rd mov., mm. 229 ff.
2-068	Bach, J. S.	Chrom. Fant., Beginning				
2-069	Bach, J. S.	Chrom. Fant., mm. 17 ff.		2-101	Bach, J. S.	Brand. Conc. No. 4, 3rd mov., mm. 106 ff.
2-070	Bach, J. S.	Chrom. Fant., mm. 21 ff.				
2-071	Bach, J. S.	Chrom. Fant., mm. 63 ff.				
2-072	Bach, J. S.	Chrom. Fant., mm. 63, Detail				**Concerto V**
				2-102	Bach, J. S.	Brand. Conc. No. 5, 1st mov., Beginning

From the Brandenburg Concertos
Concerto I

				2-103	Bach, J. S.	Brand. Conc. No. 5, 1st mov. mm. 9 ff.
2-073	Bach, J. S.	Brand. Conc. No. 1, 1st mov., Beginning				
				2-104	Bach, J. S.	Brand. Conc. No. 5, 1st mov., Solo Theme
2-074	Bach, J. S.	Brand. Conc. No. 1, 1st mov., Motif a				
				2-105	Bach, J. S.	Brand. Conc. No. 5, 1st mov. mm. 152 ff.
2-075	Bach, J. S.	Brand. Conc. No. 1, 1st mov. m. 6				
2-076	Bach, J. S.	Brand. Conc. No. 1, 1st mov., m. 10		2-106	Bach, J. S.	Brand. Conc. No. 5, 1st mov. m. 195
				2-107	Bach, J. S.	Brand. Conc. No. 5, 1st mov. 201
2-077	Bach, J. S.	Brand. Conc. No. 1, 1st mov., m. 20		2-108	Bach, J. S.	Brand. Conc. No. 5, 2nd mov., Themes

2-109	Bach, J. S.	Brand. Conc. No. 5, 3rd mov., Beginning
2-110	Bach, J. S.	Brand. Conc. No. 5, 3rd mov. mm. 257 ff.
2-111	Bach, J. S.	Brand. Conc. No. 5, 3rd mov. mm. 79 ff.

Concerto VI

2-112	Bach, J. S.	Brand. Conc. No. 6, 1st mov., Beginning
2-113	Bach, J. S.	Brand. Conc. No. 6, 1st mov. mm. 17 ff.
2-114	Bach, J. S.	Brand. Conc. No. 6, 2nd mov., Beginning
2-115	Bach, J. S.	Brand. Conc. No. 6, 3rd mov., Beginning
2-116	Bach, J. S.	Brand. Conc. No. 6, 3rd mov., Detail
2-117	Bach, J. S.	Brand. Conc. No. 6, 3rd mov., mm. 9 ff.
2-118	Bach, J. S.	Brand. Conc. No. 6, 3rd mov., mm. 46 f.

The »Eilt!–Wohin?« Aria with Chorus

2-119	Bach, J. S.	St. John Passion, Aria with Chorus, No. 48, Motives
2-120	Bach, J. S.	St. John Passion, Aria with Chorus, No. 48, Ritornello
2-121	Bach, J. S.	St. John Passion, Aria with Chorus, No. 48, Extract
2-122	Bach, J. S.	St. John Passion, Aria with Chorus, No. 48, Chorus

The Chorale »Es ist genug«

2-123	Bach, J. S.	Chorale »Es ist genug!«
2-124	Bach, J. S.	Chorale »Es ist genug!«, Rhythm Score

Part Three: Theories of Rhythm

1612 Praetorius

3-001	Praetorius	Terpsichore No. 1
3-001a	Praetorius	Terpsichore No. 1, Tripla
3-001b	Praetorius	Terpsichore No. 1, Sesquialtera
3-001c	Praetorius	Terpsichore No. 1, Alla breve
3-001d	Praetorius	Terpsichore No. 1, dimin.
3-002	Praetorius	Terpsichore No. 214
3-002a	Praetorius	Terpsichore No. 214, Tripla
3-002b	Praetorius	Terpsichore No. 214, Sesquialtera
3-002c	Praetorius	Terpsichore No. 214, Alla breve
3-002d	Praetorius	Terpsichore No. 214, dimin.
3-002e	Praetorius	Terpsichore No. 214, downbeat
3-003	Praetorius	Terpsichore No. 196, Courante
3-004	Praetorius	Terpsichore No. 201

1650 Kircher

3-005	Kircher	Triphonium (Facsimile)
3-006	Kircher	Triphonium (Transcription)
3-007	Kircher	»Religio« and »Mundus«

1678 Printz

3-008	Printz	Phrynis vol. 3, p. 108

1739 Mattheson

3-009	Mattheson	Menuet (Facsimile)
3-010	Mattheson	Menuet (Transcription)
3-011	Mattheson	Menuet (Rhythm Score)
3-012	Mattheson	Menuet (Construct)

1752 Riepel

3-013	Riepel	Menuet, Beginning

1773 Scheibe

3-014	Scheibe	Construct

1779 Kirnberger

3-015	Kirnberger	Construct (Facsimile)
3-016	Bach, J. S.	Concerto BWV 1052, 1st mov., Beginning
3-017	Kirnberger	Construct (Facsimile)
3-018	Bach, J. S.	Concerto BWV 1052, 1st mov., Detail

1789 Türk

3-019	Hasse	I pellegrini, Final Chorus
3-020	Hasse	I pellegrini, Final Chorus, Analysis
3-021	Türk	Construct

1739 Koch

3-022	Mozart	Sonata K. 333, 1st mov., Beginning (quasi Koch)
3-023	Koch	Construct
3-024	Mozart	Sonata K. 333, 1st mov., Beginning

1821 Momigny

3-025	Mozart	String Quartet K. 421, 1st mov. (Momigny)
3-026	Mozart	String Quartet K. 421, 1st mov.
3-027	Mozart	String Quartet K. 421, 1st mov. mm. 15-24
3-028	Mozart	String Quartet K. 421, 1st mov., Harmony
3-029	Mozart	String Quartet K. 421, 1st mov., Profile

1832 Weber

3-030	Mozart	Symph. K. 551, 2nd mov. mm. 31-33

1880 Westphal

3-031	Bach, J. S.	WTC I, Fuga B major, Beginning (Westphal)
3-032	Bach, J. S.	WTC I, Fuga B major, Beginning
3-033	Bach, J. S.	WTC I, Fuga B major, Beginning, Parts

1884 Riemann

3-034	Riemann	Construct (PP)
3-035	Riemann	Construct (HR)
3-036	Riemann	Construct (HR)
3-037	Riemann	Construct (PP)
3-038	Beethoven	Symph. No. 7, 3, 6, Scherzi
3-039	Beethoven	Symph. No. 7, Scherzo
3-040	Beethoven	Symph. No. 7, Scherzo, Rhythm Score
3-041	Beethoven	Symph. No. 3, 3rd mov. mm. 207-226
3-042	Beethoven	Sonata op. 13, Beginning (Riemann)
3-043	Beethoven	Sonata op. 13, first Motif
3-044	Beethoven	Sonata op. 13, Beginning

1917 Wiehmayer

3-045	Wiehmayer	Construct
3-046	Schumann	»Album für die Jugend« No. 16

3-047	Schumann	»Album für die Jugend« No. 16 (Rhythm Score)

1944 Messiaen

3-048	Beethoven	Symph. No. 7, 2nd mov. mm. 27
3-049	Debussy	Prélude à l'aprés-midi … (Messiaen)
3-050	Debussy	Prélude à l'aprés-midi …
3-051	Messiaen	Quatuor pour la fin… No. 6, mm. 26-39
3-052	Messiaen	Quatuor pour la fin… No. 6, Scheme

1951 Blacher

3-053	Blacher	Ornaments No. 1, Beginning
3-054	Blacher	Ornaments No. 2
3-055	Blacher	Ornaments No. 2 (Detail)

1955 Keller

3-056	Mozart	Gigue K. 574 mm. 20-24
3-057	Mozart	Gigue K. 574 mm. 17-28
3-058	Mozart	Gigue K. 574 mm. 33-38
3-059	Bach, J. S.	WTC I, Fuga A major, Beginning

1957 LaRue

3-060	Beethoven	Symph. No. 7, Introduction

1958 Hławiczka

3-061	Mozart	Symph. K. 551, 2nd mov. mm. 23-27
3-062	Chopin	Étude op. 25 No. 2
3-063	Chopin	Étude op. 25 No. 2 mm. 1-3
3-064	Chopin	Étude op. 25 No. 2 mm. 4-6
3-065	Chopin	Étude op. 25 No. 2 mm. 1-9

1959 Neumann

3-066	Beethoven	Sonata op. 110, 2nd mov., Trio (Neunann)
3-067	Beethoven	Sonata op. 110, 2nd mov., Trio
3-068	Beethoven	Sonata op. 110, 2nd mov., Trio
3-069	Beethoven	Sonata op. 110, 2nd mov., Trio
3-070	Beethoven	Sonata op. 110, 2nd mov., Trio

1960 Cooper & Meyer

3-071a	Schubert	»Wanderer« Fantasia (Section)
3-071b	Bach, J. S.	Prelude BWV 926, Beginning

1963 Stockhausen

3-072	Stockhausen	Construct
3-073	Mozart	String Quartet K. 458, 4th mov. mm. 98 f.
3-074	Mozart	String Quartet K. 458, 4th mov. mm. 97 f.
3-075	Mozart	Piano Concerto K. 491, 3rd mov. mm. 96 ff.
3-076	Mozart	Piano Concerto K. 491, 3rd mov. mm. 96 ff.
3-077	Mozart	Piano Concerto K. 491, 3rd mov. mm. 104 ff.

1967 Benary

3-078	Schubert	Piano Trio op. 100, 2nd mov., Beginning
3-079	Beethoven	Sonata op. 13, 2nd mov., Beginning
3-080	Chopin	Nocturne op. 15 No. 2, Middle Section
3-081	Bartók	Mikrokosmos No. 100, Beginning

1967 Dahlhaus

3-082	Wagner	Parsifal, Introduction, Beginning
3-083	Wagner	Parsifal, Introduction, mm. 9-15
3-084	Wagner	Parsifal, Introduction, mm. 6-11
3-085	Wagner	Parsifal, Introduction, mm. 1-19
3-086	Monteverdi	Lamento d'Ariana (Monody)
3-087	Monteverdi	Lamento d'Ariana (Madrigal)
3-088	Stravinsky	Mass, Laudamus Te
3-089	Stravinsky	Mass, Laudamus Te, Detail
3-090	Stravinsky	Mass, Laudamus Te, Detail

1967 Erpf

3-091	Mozart	Sonata K. 533, 2nd mov.
3-092	Mozart	Sonata K. 533, 2nd mov., Detail

1968 Pierce

3-093	Pierce	Construct
3-094	Pierce	Construct
3-095	Schubert	»Deutscher Tanz« op. 33 No. 7
3-096	Schubert	»Deutscher Tanz« op. 33 No. 7

1976 Berry

3-097	Beethoven	Diabelli Variations No. 14, Diagram
3-098	Beethoven	Diabelli Variations No. 14, Beginning
3-099	Beethoven	Diabelli Variations No. 14, Section
3-100	Beethoven	Diabelli Variations No. 14, mm. 5-8 (1)
3-101	Beethoven	Diabelli Variations No. 14, mm. 5-8 (2)
3-102	Beethoven	Diabelli Variations No. 14, mm. 1-4
3-103	Beethoven	Diabelli Variations No. 14, mm. 1-8

1976 Yeston

3-104	Mahler	Symph. No. 1, 2nd mov. Beginning
3-105	Mozart	Piano Quartet K. 478, 1st mov. mm. 57-64
3-106	Mozart	Piano Quartet K. 478, 1st mov., Extract
3-107	Mozart	Piano Quartet K. 478, 1st mov. mm. 57-64
3-108	Mozart	Piano Quartet K. 478, 1st mov., Detail
3-109	Mozart	Piano Quartet K. 478, 1st mov. mm. 178 ff.
3-110	Mozart	Piano Quartet K. 478, 1st mov., Detail

1986 Lester

3-111	Beethoven	Symph. No. 5, 1st mov. mm. 1-21 (Lester)
3-112	Beethoven	Symph. No. 5, 1st mov. mm. 1-62
3-113	Beethoven	Symph. No. 5, 1st mov. mm. 48-52, Detail
3-114	Beethoven	Symph. No. 7, 1st mov. mm. 66-71 (Lester)
3-115	Beethoven	Symph. No. 7, 1st mov. mm. 66-71
3-116	Mozart	Sonata K. 545, 1st mov. Beginning (Lester)
3-117	Mozart	Sonata K. 545, 1st mov. Beginning

1988 Kramer
3-118	Haydn	Sonata Hob. XVI, 51, 1st mov. (Kramer)
3-119	Haydn	Sonata Hob. XVI, 51, 1st mov.
3-120	Beethoven	Sonata op. 13, 3rd mov. (Kramer)
3-121	Beethoven	Sonata op. 13, 3rd mov.
3-122	Beethoven	Sonata op. 13, 3rd mov. mm. 1-17 (Harmony)
3-123	Beethoven	Sonata op. 13, 3rd mov. mm. 1-17 (Phrasing)
3-124	Beethoven	Sonata op. 13, 3rd mov. mm. 1-17 (Accompaniment)
3-125	Beethoven	Sonata op. 13, 3rd mov. (Profiles)
3-126	Beethoven	Sonata op. 13, 3rd mov. (Profile)

1989 Rothstein
3-127	Strauss, J. jun.	Blue Danube Waltz, Beginning

1995 Epstein
3-128	Haydn	Symph. No. 101, 3rd mov., Trio
3-129	Haydn	Symph. No. 101, 3rd mov., Trio

1997 Agmon
3-130	Chopin	Etude op. 10 No. 1, Beginning
3-131	Chopin	Etude op. 10 No. 1, Beginning

1997 Hasty
3-132	Bach, J. S.	Cello Suite BWV 1009, Courante
3-133	Bach, J. S.	Cello Suite BWV 1010, Courante
3-134	Bach, J. S.	Cello Suite BWV 1009
3-135	Bach, J. S.	Cello Suite BWV 1010

1999 Schachter
3-136	Busoni	Scales in Spirals
3-137	Beethoven	Sonata op. 27 No. 1, Scherzo
3-138	Schubert	Sonata op. 78, Beginning
3-139	Bach, J. S.	Bourrée from BWV 996, Descant
3-140	Bach, J. S.	Bourrée from BWV 996, Bass
3-141	Bach, J. s.	Bourrée from BWV 996, Ending

1999 Krebs
3-142	Schumann	Intermezzo op. 4 No. 4, m. 8 (HK)
3-143	Schumann	Intermezzo op. 4 No. 4, m. 8
3-144	Schumann	Intermezzo op. 4 Nro 4, mm. 7-10
3-145	Schumann	Sonata op. 11, Finale, Beginning
3-146	Schumann	Sonata op. 11, Finale, mm. 1-4
3-147	Schumann	Sonata op. 11, Finale (Konstructs)
3-148	Schumann	Sonata op. 11, Finale, mm. 1-8
3-149	Schumann	Carnaval op. 9, Préambule, mm. 112-116
3-150	Schumann	Carnaval op. 9, Préambule, mm. 114-139

2001 Lerdahl
3-151	Chopin	Prélude op. 28 No. 4
3-152	Chopin	Prélude op. 28 No. 4 (Lerdahl)
3-153	Chopin	Prélude op. 28 No. 4 mm. 1-4
3-154	Chopin	Prélude op. 28 No. 4
3-155	Chopin	Prélude op. 28 No. 4, Detail

2002 Swain
3-156	Corelli	Concerto op. 6 No. 1 (Swain)
3-157	Corelli	Concerto op. 6 No. 1 (Harm.)
3-158	Corelli	Concerto op. 6 No. 1 (Rhy.)
3-159	Debussy	Préludes Bd. I No. 1 (Swain)
3-160	Debussy	Préludes Bd. I No. 1 (PP)

2004 London
3-161	London	Construct
3-162	Beethoven	Symph. No. 5, 1st mov. mm. 195 ff. (London)
3-163	Beethoven	Symph. No. 5, 1st mov. mm. 195-232
3-164	Stravinsky	Les Noces, fig. 27 (London)
3-165	Stravinsky	Les Noces, fig. 27

Music Examples (by Composers)

Anon., Alleluja from the Christmas Mass *50*
Anon., Dies irae (gregorian) *83*
Anon., Gregorian cantilation for St. Mary *53*
Anon., Lamento di Tristano *23 102*
Anon., Motet »Benche partito« *112*

Bach, J. S., WTC, 48 Fugue Themes *134-150*
Bach, J. S., WTC I, Fuga A major *140f. 158-160*
Bach, J. S., WTC I, Fuga B major *217f.*
Bach, J. S., WTC I, Fuga F♯ minor *139 154-156*
Bach, J. S., WTC I, Prelude A minor *156f.*
Bach, J. S., WTC I, Prelude C♯ minor *151-153*
Bach, J. S., WTC I, Prelude D minor *90*
Bach, J. S., Chromatic Fantasia BWV 903 *161-163*
Bach, J. S., Prelude BWV 926, *26*
Bach, J. S., Lauten-Suite BWV 996 *284f.*
Bach, J. S., Cello Suites BWV 1009 + 1010 *279f.*
Bach, J. S., The Musical Offering, Canon I *98*
Bach, J. S., Brandenburg Concerto No. 1 *164-167*
Bach, J. S., Brandenburg Concerto No. 2 *168f.*
Bach, J. S., Brandenburg Concerto No. 3 *170f.*
Bach, J. S., Brandenburg Concerto No. 4 *172-174*
Bach, J. S., Brandenburg Concerto No. 5 *174-177*
Bach, J. S., Brandenburg Concerto No. 6 *177-179*
Bach, J. S., Harpsichord Concerto BWV 1052 *205 207*
Bach, J. S., Chorale »Es ist genug!« *183-186*
Bach, J. S., St. John Passion, Aria with Chorus, No. 48 *180-182*
Bach, J. S., St Matthew Passion, »Erbarme dich«, No. 39 *113*
Bach, J. S., Missa B minor, »Osanna« *62*

Bartók, Mikrokosmos No. 100, Beginning *248*
Bartók, Mikrokosmos No. 150, Beginning *94*
Bartók, Sonata für 2 Pianos an Percussion *94-97*
Bartók, String Quartet No. 4, 3rd mov., Beginning *33*
Bartók, Music for String Instruments… 1st mov. *57*
Bartók, Dance Suite, 2nd mov., Beginning *116*

Bauldeweyn, Missa »Da pacem«, Credo *26 81f.*

Beethoven, Diabelli Variation No. 14 *259f.*
Beethoven, Sonata op. 13, 1st mov. *224*
Beethoven, Sonata op. 13, 2nd mov. *247*
Beethoven, Sonata op. 13, 3rd mov. *270-273*
Beethoven, Sonata op. 27 No. 1, 3rd mov. *283*
Beethoven, Sonata op. 110, 2nd mov., Trio *239f.*
Beethoven, String Quartet op. 135, 2nd mov. *91*
Beethoven, Symphony No. 1, 3rd mov. *22 106*
Beethoven, Symphony No. 1, 4th mov. *106*
Beethoven, Symphony No. 2, 1st mov. *33*
Beethoven, Symphony No. 2, 2nd mov. *25*
Beethoven, Symphony No. 3, 1st mov. *117f.*
Beethoven, Symphony No. 3, 3rd mov. *39 221 223*
Beethoven, Symphony No. 4, 1st mov. *39*
Beethoven, Symphony No. 4, 3rd mov. *31*
Beethoven, Symphony No. 5, 1st mov. *266f. 293*
Beethoven, Symphony No. 5, 3rd mov. *20 27f.*
Beethoven, Symphony No. 5, 4th mov. *111*
Beethoven, Symphony No. 6, 2nd mov. *31*
Beethoven, Symphony No. 6, 3rd mov. *108 221*
Beethoven, Symphony No. 6, 5th mov. *52*
Beethoven, Symphony No. 7, 1st mov. *235 267*
Beethoven, Symphony No. 7, 2nd mov. *45 64-80 228*
Beethoven, Symphony No. 7, 3rd mov. *221f.*
Beethoven, Symphony No. 8, 1st mov. *49*
Beethoven, Symphony No. 8, 3rd mov. *101*
Beethoven, Symphony No. 9, 4th mov., Beginning *23*
Beethoven, Symphony No. 9, 4th mov., Freudenmelodie var. *59*

Berg, Chamber Concerto, 2nd mov. *100*
Berg, Violin Concerto *123f.*
Berg, Wozzeck I/4 *61*
Berg, Wozzeck II/2 *20 92*
Berg, Wozzeck III/2-3 *22*
Berg, Wozzeck III/3-4 *52*
Berg, Lulu I/3 *21*
Berg, Lulu II/1-2 *100*

Blacher, Ornaments for Piano *232f.*

Bononia, B. de, Vince con lena *31*

Brahms, Variations for Piano op. 9 No. 5 *40*
Brahms, String Quartet op. 51 No. 2, 1st mov. *56*
Brahms, String Quartet op. 51 No. 2, 4th mov. *25 56 121*
Brahms, String Sextet op. 36, 3rd mov. *51*
Brahms, Symphony No. 2 *86f. 103*
Brahms, Piano Concerto No. 2, 1st mov. *28*
Brahms, Piano Concerto No. 2, 3rd mov. *122f.*

Bruckner, Symphony No. 4, 3rd mov. *42*
Bruckner, Missa F minor, »Hosanna« *62*

Busoni, Scales in Spirals *282*

Chopin, Étude op. 10 No. 1 *277f.*
Chopin, Étude op. 25 No. 12 *24*
Chopin, Étude op. 25 No. 2 *237f.*
Chopin, Nocturne op. 15 No. 2 *248*
Chopin, Nocturne op. 15 No. 3 *55*
Chopin, Prélude op. 28 No. 4 *289-291*

Corelli, Concerto op. 6 No. 6 *34*
Corelli, Concerto op. 6 No. 8 *32 293f.*
Corelli, Concerto op. 6 No. 9 *32*

Debussy, Préludes for Piano vol. I No. 1 *295f.*
Debussy, Préludes for Piano vol. I No. 10 *47*
Debussy, Prélude à l'après-midi d'un faune *229f.*

Fux, J. J., Missa di San Carlo, Benedictus *50*

Gesualdo, Madrigals 4th Book, »Invan dunque« *46*

Handel, Sonata for Recorder HWV 365 *120*

Hasse, I pellegrini, Final Chorus *207*

Haydn, Sonata Hob. XVI, 51, 1st mov. *269f.*
Haydn, String Quartet Hob. III, 37, 2nd mov. *51*
Haydn, String Quartet Hob. III, 42, 3rd mov. *34*
Haydn, Symphony No. 94, 2nd mov. *8-11*
Haydn, Symphony No. 101, 3rd Mov. *275f.*

Henze, Antifone, Beginning *43*
Henze, Requiem, »Agnus Dei«, Beginning *110*
Henze, Symphony No. 10, 4th mov. *58*
Henze, Tristan, Epilog *125*

Josquin, Missa »De Beata Virgine«, Gloria *90*
Josquin, Missa »L'homme armé« II, Agnus III *97*

Kircher, »Religio« and »Mundus« *195*

Kircher, Triphonium *194*
Ligeti, Continuum for Harpsichord *29f.*
Ligeti, Études for Piano, »Désordre« *37f. 94*
Ligeti, String Quartet No. 2, 2nd mov. *48f.*

Liszt, Sonata B minor, T. 105-120 *47*
Liszt, Faust-Symphony, Beginning *56*
Liszt, Piano Concerto No. 2, T. 64 *107*

Machaut, Motet No. 1 *54*
Machaut, Motet No. 20 *54 89*
Machaut, Rondeau »Ma fin est mon commencement« *97*

Mahler, Symphony No. 1, 2nd mov. *261*
Mahler, Symphony No. 9, 2nd mov. *32*
Mahler, Symphony No. 9, 4th mov. *105*

Mattheson, Menuett *199f.*

Messiaen, Quatuor pour la fin du temps No. 6 *231*

Monteverdi, Lamento d'Ariana *251f.*
Monteverdi, Missa a 4 voci, »Osanna« *62*
Monteverdi, Vesperae beatae Mariae Virginis, »Audi« *33*
Monteverdi, Vesperae beatae Mariae Virginis, Psalm 109 *26*

Mozart, Gigue for Piano K. 574 *233f.*
Mozart, Sonata K. 333, 1st mov. *208*
Mozart, Sonata K. 533, 2nd mov. *254*
Mozart, Sonata K. 545, 1st mov. *268*
Mozart, String Quartet K. 387, 2nd mov. *34*
Mozart, String Quartet K. 421, 1st mov. *213-215*
Mozart, String Quartet K. 458, 4th mov. *242*
Mozart, Piano Quartet K. 478, 1st mov. *262-265*
Mozart, String Quintett K. 516, 3, mov. *40*
Mozart, Symphony K. 543, 1st mov. *53*
Mozart, Symphony K. 550, 3rd mov. *121*
Mozart, Symphony K. 551, 2nd mov. *120 216 237*
Mozart, Symphony K. 551, 4th mov. *45f.*
Mozart, Piano Concerto K. 491, 3rd mov. *243*
Mozart, Missa K. 317, »Hosanna« *62*

Ockeghem, Missa prolationum, Kyrie I *85*

Praetorius, from »Terpsichore« *191-193*

Printz, Jambic Melodies *197*

Purcell, Anthem »O sing…« *119*

Ravel, Piano Trio, 1st mov. *57*

Riepel, Menuet *203*

Schoenberg, Pierrot lunaire No. 18 *98*
Schoenberg, Piece for Orchestra op. 16 No. 3 *42*
Schoenberg, Moses and Aaron II/3 *63*

Schubert, German Dance op. 33 No. 7 *257*
Schubert, Sonata op. 78, Beginning *284*
Schubert, Piano Trio op. 100, 2nd mov. *246f.*
Schubert, »Winterreise« No. 1 *103*

Schumann, »Album für die Jugend« No. 16 *226f.*
Schumann, »Album für die Jugend« No. 39 *55*
Schumann, »Carnaval« op. 9, Préambule *288*
Schumann, »Davidsbündler« No. 12 *32*

Schumann, »Davidsbündler« No. 13 *34*
Schumann, Intermezzo op. 4 No. 4 *286*
Schumann, »Kinderszenen« No. 7 *109*
Schumann, Sonata op. 11, Finale, Beginning *287*

Schütz, »Geistliche Chormusik« No. 16 *40*
Schütz, Motet »So fahr ich hin« *82*

Strauss, J. jun., Blue Danube Waltz, Beginning *274*

Strauss, R., Elektra *61 35 104*

Stravinsky, Les Noces, fig. 27 *294*
Stravinsky, Mass, »Hosanna« *63*
Stravinsky, Mass, »Laudamus Te« *253*
Stravinsky, Sacre du Printemps, near fig. 13 *36 82*

Sweelinck, Fantasia chromatica *83*

Tchaikovsky, Symphony No. 5, 3rd mov. *93*
Tchaikovsky, Symphony No. 6, 2nd mov. *93*

Vivaldi, Concerto op. 3 No. 3 (RV 310), 2nd mov. *50*
Vivaldi, Concerto »La Primavera« (RV 269) *24*

Wagner, Parsifal, Introduction *249f.*
Wagner, Siegfried III/1 T. 295 *60*
Wagner, Siegfried Motives *114f.*
Wagner, Tristan, Introduction *41*

Webern, Concerto op. 24, 1st mov. *32*

Weill, Mahagonny, No. 18 *107*

Zimmermann, »Die Soldaten«, Preludio *83f.*
Zimmermann, »Die Soldaten«, III/5 *61f. 87*

Index of Names

Abravaya, Ido *130 190*
Agmon, Eytan *20 24 276-278*
Ahle, Johann Rudolf *183*
Ahlgrimm, Isolde *202*
Apel, Willi *32 82 84 112*
Apfel, Ernst *198 200f. 220 248*
Aristoxenos *14 217 292*
Aschersleben, Gisa *190*
Austin, William W. *248*

Bach, Johann Christian *211*
Bach, Johann Sebastian *12 14 20 26 62 90 98 113 124-125 127-186 190 205-207 217f. 234 240 279f. 284f.*
Bachelard, Gaston *231*
Bartholomeus de Bononia *31*
Bartók, Béla *14 33 37 57 94-97 115f. 241 248*
Baselt, Susanne *190*
Bauldeweyn *14 26f. 81f. 89*
Becking, Gustav *190*
Beethoven, Ludwig van *11 20 22f. 25 27 31 33 39 45 49 51-53 58-60 64-80 91 101f. 106 108f. 111f. 117f. 217 221-225 228f. 234f. 238-240 247 259-261 266f. 270-273 277 282-284 298f.*
Benary, Peter *245-248*
Bengen, Irmgard *190*
Berg, Alban *19-22 51 61 92 99f. 123-125*
Berry, David Carson *255*
Berry, Wallace *258-261*
Bert, Siegmund *190*
Besseler, Heinrich *77*
Billeter, Bernhard *202*
Blacher, Boris *232f.*
Böhme, Tatjana *190*
Botelho, Mauro *130-132 171*
Boulez, Pierre *37 99 232 258*
Bouliane, Denys *36f.*
Braatz, Thomas *183*
Brahms, Johannes *14 25 27f. 40f. 51 56f. 85f. 98 103f. 121-123 125 190*
Braun, Werner *192 196*
Breslauer, Peter *130*
Briner, Andres *190*
Brinkmann, Reinhold *86f.*
Brittany, Thomas of *125*
Bruckner, Anton *42 62*
Buchner, Thomas *197*
Burmeister, Franz Joachim *183*
Busoni, Ferruccio *281f.*

Carissimi, Giacomo
Chopin, Frédéric *24 55-57 125 236-238 248 273 277f. 289-291*
Christensen, Thomas *12 189*
Clarke, Samuel *19*
Cone, Edward T. *263*
Cooper, Grosvenor W. *107 240 258*
Corelli, Arcangelo *32 34f. 293f.*

Dahlhaus, Carl *191 212 220 248-253*
Danuser, Hermann *212f.*
Debussy, Claude *47f. 228-230 292 295f.*
Del Mar, Jonathan *59*
Dittersdorf, Ditters von *211*
Donington, Robert *130*
Dumesnil, René *189*
Dvořák, Antonín *14*

Eggebrecht, Hans Heinrich *189*
Elschek, Oskár *190*
Emmerig, Thomas *202*
Epstein, David *275f.*
Erpf, Hermann *254f.*
Ertelt, Thomas *12 189*
Ette, Wolfram *190*

Floros, Constantin *36 51 124*
Franklin, Don O. *130*
Fricke, Harald *64*
Frobenius, Wolf *191f.*
Fuß, Hans-Ulrich *51*
Fux, Johann Joseph *50*

Gadamer, Hans-Georg *190*
Geiger, Friedrich *27*
Georgiades, Thrasybulos *190*
Gesualdo, Carlo *46*
Glass, Phil *92*
Goethe, Johann Wolfgang *110 238*
Gottschewski, Hermann *130*
Graun, Johann Gottlieb *205*
Grimmelshausen, Johann Jakob Christoffel von *196*
Gropius, Manon *122*
Gulda, Friedrich *160*

Haberl, Dieter *203*
Handel, Georg Friedrich *120 234 282*
Harnoncourt, Nikolaus *130*
Hartung, Philipp Christoph *202*
Hasse, Johann Adolf *207*
Hasty, Christopher F. *278-281*
Hatten, Robert S. *190*
Hauptmann, Moritz *189 225*
Haydn, Joseph *8-11 20 34 50 64 98 212 269f. 275f. 297*
Heckmann, Harald *191 193 197*
Henneberg, Gudrun *190 211*
Henze, Hans Werner *43f. 58 110 125 129 226*
Hinrichsen, Hans-Joachim *130 198 201*
Hirsch, Hans *190*
Hławiczka, Karel *161f. 236-238*

Indy, Vincent d' *189*
Jackendoff, Ray *131 269 289*
Jacobs, Kai *13*
Jander, Owen *130*
Jonas, Oswald *255*
Josquin de Prez *14 26f. 89f. 97 258*

Kant, Immanuel *208*
Keller, Hermannn *233f.*
Kiem, Eckehard *190*
Kilgore, Edna *130*
Kinzler, Hartmuth *36f.*
Kircher, Athanasius *194-196*
Kirnberger, Johann Philipp *204-206*
Klein, Richard *190*
Koch, Heinrich Christoph *208-211 225*
Kramer, Jonathan *131 269-273*
Krebs, Harald *285-288*
Kühn, Clemens *190*
Kurth, Ernst *129 162 190*

LaRue, Jan *45 234f. 279 293*
Leibniz, Gottfried Wilhelm *19*
Leichtentritt, Hugo *55*
Leisinger, Ulrich *130*

Lenz, Jakob Michael Reinhold *62 84*
Lerdahl, Fred *131 269 289-292*
Lester, Joel *263 266-269*
Lichtenfeld, Monika *37*
Ligeti, György *13f. 24 28f. 36f. 48f. 94*
Liszt, Franz *46f. 56 107*
London, Justin *20 130 228 297-300*
Loriod, Yvonne *227*
Louvier, Alain *227*
Lowinsky, Edward E. *211*
Ludwig, Friedrich *54*
Lussy, Mathis *218-220*

Machaut, Guillaume de *54 89 97*
Mackensen, Karsten *203*
Mahler, Gustav *32 58 104f. 261*
Mahrenholz, Simone *190*
Malipiero, Gian Francesco *251*
Marx, Adolph Bernhard *189*
Mattheson, Johann *198-201 202 204 240*
Maurer Zenck, Claudia *190 263 299*
Mehner, Klaus *190*
Mendelssohn Bartholdy, Felix *273*
Mersmann, Hans *190*
Messiaen, Olivier *227-232 241*
Meyer, Leonard B. *107 240 258*
Michaely, Aloyse *231*
Miehling, Klaus *130 190*
Momigny, Jérôme-Joseph de *212-216*
Monteverdi, Claudio *25f. 33 40 62 251f.*
Mozart, Leopold *190*
Mozart, Wolfgang Amadé *14 34 45f. 53 62 98 120f. 208-212 216 228 233f. 237 241-245 254f. 262-265 268 273 297*
Müller, Katharina *190*
Müller, Ruth E. *220 248*
Müller, Wilhelm *103*

Nettheim, Nigel *190*
Neumann, Friedrich *211 238-240*

Oberst, Günther *191 193*
Ockeghem, Johannes *85*
Oron, Aryeh *183*

Palm, Albert *212*
Perkins, Marion Louise *190*
Perotinus *82*
Pfleiderer, Martin *190*
Pierce, Anne Alexandra *255-258*
Pietschmann, Klaus *198*
Piston, Walter *292*
Plamenac, Dragan *85*
Platz, Wolfgang *208*
Plyn, Franz Hermann Wolfgang *190*
Praetorius, Michael *191-193*
Primavesi, Patrick *190*
Printz, Wolfgang Caspar *196f.*
Purcell, Henry *119*

Quantz, Joachim *190*

Rampe, Siegbert *130*
Ravel, Maurice *57*
Rehm, Wolfgang *208*
Reich, Steve *92*
Reichert, Georg *54*
Riemann, Hugo *12 45 117 129 216 220-225*
Riepel, Joseph *202f.*

Rösing, Helmut *211*
Rothgeb, John *255*
Rothkamm, Jörg *36*
Rothstein, William *131 273-275*
Ruf, Wolfgang *215*

Sachs, Kurt *190*
Sackmann, Dominik *130*
Satterfield, John *227*
Scarlatti, Domenico *24*
Schachter, Carl *240 281-285*
Scharlau, Ulf *194*
Scheibe, Johann Adolph *203f.*
Schenker, Heinrich *240 255 273 281-285 289*
Schiller, Friedrich *59*
Schindler, Anton *108*
Schneider, Albrecht *14*
Schneider, Frank *99*
Schneider, Marius *23*
Schoenberg, Arnold *42f. 48 63 98f. 212-214 262f.*
Schubert, Franz *102f. 240 246 256f. 284*
Schumann, Robert *32 34f. 40 55f. 109f. 226f. 285-288*
Schütz, Hannes *36*
Schütz, Heinrich *40 82 84*
Schweitzer, Albert *132*
Schwindt, Nicole *211*
Sechter, Simon *189*
Seidel, Wilhelm *12 130 189 198 209-211 215 218-220 223 225*
Siegele, Ulrich *130*
Stamitz, Johann *211*
Steinitz, Richard *36 61*
Stockhausen, Karlheinz *14 232 241-245*
Straus, Joseph N. *240 281*
Strauss, Johann jr. *273f.*
Strauss, Richard *35 104 123*
Stravinsky, Igor *36 62f. 82 119 129 241 252f. 299f.*
Struck, Michael *27*
Swain, Joseph P. *292-297*
Sweelinck, Jan Pieterszoon *82 84*

Toch, Ernst *86*
Tchaikovsky, Pyotr Ilyich *57 93f.*
Türk, Daniel Gottlob *207f.*

Vial, Stephanie D. *190 201*
Vivaldi, Antonio *24 49f.*
Vogt, Felix *218*

Wagner, Richard *14 41 60 114f. 125 239 249f. 273 291*
Wald, Melanie *194 196*
Weber, Gottfried *216*
Weber, Horst *98*
Webern, Anton *32f. 99 245*
Weill, Kurt *107*
Wessely, Othmar *196*
Westergard, Peter *263*
Westphal, Rudolf *129 217f. 225*
Wiehmayer, Theodor *225-227*
Willems, Edgar *190*
Winter, Hans-Gerd *84*
Wollny, Peter *204*

Yeston, Maury *261-265*

Zaminer, Frieder *12 189*
Zimmermann, Bernd Alois *61 83f. 232*